THE PERSONAL WORLD

HAROLD GRIER McCURDY

UNIVERSITY OF NORTH CAROLINA

THE PERSONAL WORLD

AN INTRODUCTION TO THE STUDY OF PERSONALITY

UNDER THE GENERAL EDITORSHIP OF

CLAUDE E. BUXTON, YALE UNIVERSITY

HARCOURT, BRACE & WORLD, INC.

NEW YORK / BURLINGAME

TO MARY

21316

EDITOR'S FOREWORD

This is not an ordinary book about personality—not in style, intentions, or content. The style of writing is polished and provocative rather than pedestrian. The intentions of the author are to open wide any possible window through which we may look into the realm of personality, and thus the orientation is also provocative and even disturbing at times. (At least, the orientation may be disturbing to those who hold to a narrow or provincial view of personality, or to methods of studying personality, although it will be regarded as refreshingly different by many others.) The content reflects these intentions in the range of topics covered, the use of materials from other eras of psychology, from other languages, from other cultures, from other disciplines.

While Professor McCurdy has the contemporary psychologist's respect for the power of theory, he is much taken, in a field so unevenly matured as personality, with the importance of open-mindedness in the search for any kind of pertinent fact. Facts eventually get ordered by means of theories, but in the initial explorations of any aspect of personality, facts may appear to be disorderly, in need of most critical assessment. Only a thoughtful person will begin to find the order, and even he must curb the natural tendency to reach for conclusions where none are as yet justifiable. The reader of this book, then, is expected to read it with an open mind, a questioning attitude, and a willingness to reserve judgment until old facts are reexamined for their significance and new facts are put in their proper place.

In a field such as personality, which is only gradually taking shape and contains much unassimilated material, the author faces a tactical decision at the outset. He may survey the entire field so that the reader knows what is in it, at the risk of less than thorough treatment of many topics; or he may select portions of it which are reasonably representative or most significant, then discuss them in sufficient detail so that the reader knows, in these more limited areas, not only the background and status of current knowledge but also the methodological problems, the knotty controversies, and, not least, how his own predilections relate to his evaluation of the material he reads. Professor McCurdy has chosen the second alternative and has written with such care and clarity that a thorough understanding becomes possible.

The author invites the reader into the workshop where a science of personality is gradually being created. The venture will prove stimulating and rewarding, and if the reader finally does not agree with everything he reads but has been challenged enough by the text to arrive at his own conclusions, no one will be more pleased than Professor McCurdy.

CLAUDE E. BUXTON

Yale University
New Haven, Connecticut
June 1961

PREFACE

Twenty-three years ago I began my teaching career in psychology at a small college in the mountains of Tennessee. I found that the modest educational background of my students at Milligan did not prevent them from dealing intelligently with fundamental questions, provided that their interest was aroused; and that the best guarantee of their interest was my own. I have written this book on those principles. I have pursued questions which interested me and have not spared the reader difficulties if they arose naturally in the development of the argument. Whether the result is a book which can be widely employed as a text in college classes at the second level will have to be decided in the academic marketplace. My own experience with it has been encouraging. I lectured from the manuscript to such a class at the University of North Carolina this spring, and was gratified with the results; in fact, I cannot recall ever having had more attentive undergraduates. At the same time, I judge that the book may have some appeal for graduate students, containing as it does facts, theories, problems, and lines of reasoning with which they may not be familiar; and it may be a useful supplement to such typical graduate reading matter as Hall and Lindzey's *Theories of Personality* and the latest *Annual Review of Psychology.*

For the benefit of instructors, let me point out that the order of chapters in the book is not random; the later chapters presuppose the earlier ones. Doubtless it is Chapter 6, "Consciousness and the Conscious Self," which is the most crucial. Here I deal with the core of personality, the center without which there can be no personal world. Some readers may find this chapter either radically reactionary or radically progressive. For me, it is neither. Yet I admit that laying stress on consciousness does involve us in problems of scientific method, since it runs counter to that behavioristic trend which has appropriated as exclusively its own such terms as "objective," "measurable," "testable," and "scientific." I argue that the behavioristic approach is limited, not that it is absolutely wrong; and that in studying personality we must employ methods of a nonbehavioristic kind which bring the conscious subject into clear focus. Once we do this, of course, a personal world is revealed which is characterized not only by the fact that three-dimensional objects have an arrangement in it governed by the *here* and *now* of the "I," but also by the fact that it contains values and intimations and relations and ultimates which cannot be touched or seen. In the last chapters I glance, rather tremblingly, at facts of experience which fall within this latter category, considering man in his duplicity and mysteriousness and in attitudes of love and worship which place him little lower than the angels.

There is a stylistic feature of the book which may seem a bit unconventional. I have frequently used the first person singular in expressing my opinions. I have done so to avoid circumlocutions and the false appearance of Olympian detachment, but likewise for the sake of my theme; for I thought that it would be incongruous to insist on the reality of the "I" in others and simultaneously, by my manner, to deny it in myself.

Furthermore, one cannot enter into "I-thou" relations without admitting the "I." At this point, for example, I could not express my gratitude to other people except on that condition, and I could not be realistic about the book without thus indicating that I am aware of the continual interdependence which unites us all. I can only hint at the complex network of these personal relationships by referring to the numerous authors I have cited (and the still more numerous ones whom I have not) and naming a few particular names. Among those who have helped me by their reactions to my manuscript, I here thank: the consulting editor for Harcourt, Brace & World's psychology series, Claude Buxton; my colleagues, John Thibaut and Eugene Long; graduate and undergraduate students Jean Harmon Thrasher, Zenomena Pluzek, Michael Merbaum, Bob Costello, John McCurdy; my assistant for a year through the courtesy of the Institute for Research in Social Science, Ronald Fox; and, above all, my wife, Mary Derrickson McCurdy, who more than anyone else has lived this book with me. I must also mention the courteous staff of the Louis Round Wilson Library, and the fact that a leave of absence, 1959-60, from my teaching duties at the University enabled me to complete the manuscript at approximately the promised time. Finally, I wish to acknowledge my long indebtedness to my teachers, William McDougall, Helge Lundholm, William Stern, Donald Adams, and Karl Zener.

HAROLD GRIER MC CURDY

Chapel Hill, N.C.
June 10, 1961

CONTENTS

Part three: Methods of describing personality

Part four: Problems

I
GROWTH AND
LEARNING

1

ON SCIENCE AND
THE ORIENTATION
OF THIS BOOK

Perhaps the author of a textbook on personality will be excused for admitting at the outset that some of the peculiarities of his book originate in himself. Two of the peculiarities to which I want to draw attention in the opening pages are these: (1) my rather simple conception of the business of science; and (2) my concern with the development of the student as a thinker. I separate these peculiarities here for the sake of calling attention to them, but they will be found to be intimately blended in the discussion which follows because they are intimately blended in my own mind.

Scope of the enterprise

The range of facts about human nature is very great. One way of trying to embrace them is to formulate a theory of personality. Some theories stretch until they crack in the vain effort to embrace them all, others contract narrowly around a few congenial ones and try to ignore the rest. Neither strategy is satisfactory in the end. We all have our preferences, however, and mine is for the former alternative: I should rather be inconvenienced by the facts than ignore them.

Our problem is not only that the facts are numerous and varied, but that they are often astonishing. Jean Charcot (1825-93), the eminent neurologist at the Salpêtrière, the Paris mental hospital, where strange things happened every day, warned his students that they should be astonished at nothing. He put it in a Latin phrase: *nil admirari*. His student Pierre Janet (1859-1947) carried out the injunction to a point of coolness which was in itself astonishing. He reports the most extraordinary sufferings and actions in his patients, and then muffles the facts by shoving these very real human beings into some convenient psychiatric pigeonhole, usually "hysteria," and writing off the drama lightly as a comedy. Sigmund Freud (1856-1939), on the other hand, also a student of Charcot's, seemed to have retained his capacity for astonishment; and it may be to this cause that we owe his valuable insights. At any rate, the facts of human nature are often so bizarre and so powerful in their emotional impact on the observer that one must either be astonished or erect the deliberate defense of *nil admirari*. When the refusal to be astonished is combined with a refusal to look at the facts which might astonish, the result, in my opinion, is to preclude the development of an adequate personality theory.

I do not wish to cast aspersions. Specialization has its virtues. Science often calls for sharp focus on some particular thing, and it is highly convenient at those times to exclude everything else from consideration. Trouble begins, however, when this tactical maneuver becomes a constrictive doctrine, as has more than once happened in American psychology. One sees the beginnings in that broadest of American psychologists, William James. James (1842-1910) remained all his life receptive to every kind of fact, and he continued to struggle, in public too, with the most difficult and embarrassing questions; but in defending his famous *Principles of Psychology* against the criticisms of Ladd he stated a number of arbitrary limitations as requirements for the construction of psychological science, and in this regard he has been followed with increasing rigor by later methodologists who have wanted to set even narrower limits than he. In "A Plea for Psychology as a 'Natural Science,'" under date of 1892, James has this to say:

What is a natural science, to begin with? It is a mere fragment of truth broken out from the whole mass of it for the sake of practical effectiveness exclusively. *Divide et impera.* Every special science, in order to get at its own particulars at all, must make a number of convenient assumptions and decline to be responsible for questions which the human mind will continue to ask about them. . . . If, therefore, psychology is ever to conform to the type of the other natural sciences, it must also renounce certain ultimate solutions, and place itself on the usual common-sense basis by uncritically begging such data as the existence of the physical world, of states of mind, and of the fact that these latter take cognizance of other things.[1]

Psychology in these words parts company with the questions of philosophy, and especially of theology. James then proceeds to define the subject matter of psychology as an independent natural science and adds a little sales talk on its practicality:

Now if there is any natural science in possession of a subject-matter well set off and contrasted with all others, it is psychology. However much our self-consciousness, our freedom, our ability to conceive universals, or what not, may ally us with the Infinite and Absolute, there is yet an aspect of our being, even of our mental being, which falls wholly within the sphere of natural history. As constituting the inner life of individual persons who are born and die, our conscious states are temporal *events* arising in the ordinary course of nature,—events, moreover, the conditions of whose happening or non-happening from one moment to another, lie certainly in large part in the physical world. Not only this; they are events of such tremendous practical moment to us that the control of these conditions on a large scale would be an achievement compared with which the control of the rest of physical nature would appear comparatively insignificant. All natural sciences aim at practical prediction and control, and in none of them is this more the case than in psychology to-day. We live surrounded by an enormous body of persons who are most definitely interested in the control of states of mind, and incessantly craving for a sort of psychological science which will teach them how to *act.* What every educator, every jail-warden, every doctor, every clergyman, every asylum-superintendent, asks of psychology is practical rules. Such men care little or nothing about the ultimate philosophic grounds of mental phenomena, but they do care immensely about improving the ideas, dispositions, and conduct of the particular individuals in their charge.[2]

[1] James (1920), pp. 317 f. Used by permission of Longmans, Green & Co., Inc.
[2] *Ibid.,* pp. 318 f.

James goes on to justify the main thesis of his book, namely, that mental events depend on states of the brain, still emphasizing the practical values held by all those persons in the schools and the jails and the asylums who stand so eagerly ready to control us. He admits that our knowledge of the brain is at the best schematic and not really equal to the task of explaining the mental events, but he pins his hopes on it nevertheless.

In the years since 1892, various other constrictions have been attempted; some methodologists have tried to empty psychology of the Jamesian mental events, and others (or the same ones) have thrown out the brain—either for the sake of tidying up psychology as a natural science or for the sake of greater practicality or both. It is interesting how the practical aim has grown more and more dominant. Some would now be willing to surrender the older ambition to make psychology a pure natural science in order to make it a pure technology.[3] I believe it is correct to say that the interest in personality in this country is in part an expansive reaction against the tendencies just noted. This seems to be eminently true of such landmarks as Allport's *Personality* in 1937 and Murray's *Explorations in Personality* in 1938. Constrictive tendencies also affect personality study, however, as could be abundantly proved by the nature of the criticisms directed against Allport and Murray.

Those who want psychology to be a natural science like physics or a technology like engineering often state that psychology aims to predict and control. The suggestion that there is an element of freedom in human beings naturally comes as an unwelcome thought in the midst of such a program. If I am not mistaken, there is a corresponding distaste for untrammeled facts. Three degrees of receptivity to facts may, I think, be distinguished, corresponding to three degrees of commitment to the desire to predict and control. (1) If prediction and control are taken as the primary marks of science, and one wishes to be a scientist, then only those facts will be tolerated with good grace which fall into the prediction-control formula; the more disorderly facts will be dismissed as of no interest to science. (2) If one lays great but not exclusive emphasis on prediction and control, one may accept a number of disorderly facts on the supposition that eventually the march of science will bring them under strict discipline. This was about the position of James. He was actually tolerant of a wide range of

[3] See Rychlak (1959).

facts, most of which could not be shown to have any distinct basis in the structure and function of the brain; but he was inclined to believe (at least, when he was arguing with Ladd) that in the course of time brain physiology would mend this deficiency. (3) There are, finally, those who do not care whether a particular scheme of explanation and prediction holds now or ever will hold, but who do value facts. The predicting-controlling ardor seems to be at a minimum in this class of investigators: it gets in the way of trying to see the facts, and they are often willing to settle for something a good deal less ambitious than prediction-control formulas, preferring instead a sort of understanding or appreciation, nearly aesthetic, of the total picture as far as they can make it out. They believe that there is order in the total picture, that in essence it is intelligible, but they also believe that we have a smoky view of it because of theories and methods which interfere with inspecting the canvas, and a necessarily limited view because of the enormous extent of the canvas and the infinite detail in every part. This attitude, sometimes condemned by stricter theorists as lacking in rigor, happens to be mine, and it has much to do with the writing of this book.

I must confess another motive besides simple curiosity about facts. It is a pedagogical or therapeutic one. I have tried to communicate some of my thoughts as if I were carrying on a dialogue with the reader; I have wanted both of us to be involved in the discussion, as partners in a common enterprise of puzzling things out and deepening our awareness of human existence. Even alone in my room I have often felt what Rogers has described:

> I launch myself into the therapeutic relationship having a hypothesis, or a faith, that my liking, my confidence, and my understanding of the other person's inner world, will lead to a significant process of becoming. I enter the relationship not as a scientist, not as a physician who can actually diagnose and cure, but as a person, entering into a personal relationship. . . . I risk myself, because if, as the relationship deepens, what develops is a failure, a regression, a repudiation of me and the relationship by the client, then I sense that I will lose myself, or a part of myself. At times this risk is very real, and is very keenly experienced.[4]

I should not like to think, however, that personal involvement in the charms and dangers of free communication has entirely blinded

[4] Rogers (1955), p. 267.

me to the elementary problems of science, some of which will be considered now.

Facts and explanations

From one point of view, science is just a human effort to wrest ourselves free from human deceitfulness. All earnest scientists contend steadily against error and falsification and bias. Yet these enemies are always creeping in—sometimes as deliberate fraud, as in the case of Piltdown man, more often in smaller and subtler ways. Various defensive measures have been proposed. Legal or quasi-legal accreditation of individual scientists is one; general reputation is another; the constant checking and cross-checking of observations and experiments is the best of all. Much reliance is often placed on "scientific method" itself, i.e., on certain rules of procedure in conducting experiments, reporting results, and so on; and no doubt the passion for predicting and controlling (against which I have complained) is partially motivated by the desire to have repeatable, and therefore thoroughly testable, results. There is no scheme known, however, for preventing absolutely even gross dishonesty, much less those unfortunate errors and twists of bias to which the most honest sometimes fall prey. For example, it would be entirely possible, if one were so disposed, to fabricate psychological data and present them in polished, acceptable form, replete with minute descriptions of apparatus, statistical tests, and all the rest. Against this ever-present *possibility* (in fact, such events are rare in the scientific community) what guarantee can we have? As I have said, our best, but imperfect, guarantee against error and falsification is the constant checking and cross-checking which occupies the scientific community—and which, for example, eventually caught up with the fraud of Piltdown man. But this is a slow process, and it may as well be admitted that scientists, like other human beings, depend to a great extent on their general impressions of the honesty and competence of other scientists in the preliminary stages of evaluating their reports. One even makes self-evaluations of this sort: all of us think that we are better equipped to observe and report on some things than on others.

Suppose that we are satisfied with the trustworthiness of a report or our own observation of a happening. Another problem then arises: we seek an explanation. Sometimes, in our eagerness, we may go far beyond the available facts. So quick are we with the question "Why?" that sometimes the question "What?" has not been fully answered before we are off on our speculative quest. It takes a good deal of scientific discipline, or a naturally meek spirit, to make us pause a long time over the mere "What?"

A case in illustration is the quarrel which broke out over the discovery by Torricelli (1608-1647) that when the open end of a glass tube full of mercury was set down in a bowl of mercury, the column of mercury in the tube fell a certain distance and left a space (the "Torricellian vacuum") in the closed upper end of the tube. Torricelli had inferred that the height of the mercury column depended on the weight of the air pressing down on the mercury in the bowl, but he died before producing convincing evidence for this hypothesis, which was opposed by Aristotelians maintaining the old doctrine that "nature abhors a vacuum," previously used for explaining the action of suction pumps. Those who maintained this proposition were not only countering Torricelli's hypothesis about atmospheric pressure but denying that the empty space at the top of the tube was truly a vacuum. The realistic scientist Pascal (1623-1662), however, concentrating on the observable phenomena, repeated Torricelli's experiment in a hundred new versions, found that at a constant altitude the mercury column remained at the same height under a variety of conditions and concluded, in agreement with Torricelli, that the mercury column was held up by atmospheric pressure. He then checked on this conclusion by having the apparatus carried up a mountain peak, the Puy-de-Dôme, so that the height of the mercury column could be measured at different altitudes—an experiment which confirmed the Torricellian hypothesis and led Pascal on to further experiments on the general relations between liquids and gases. It was the primacy of observed fact in Pascal's mind which made his approach to the question fruitful.[5]

But let us turn to more psychological examples. A famous incident occurred at the Greenwich observatory in 1796. The Astronomer Royal Maskelyne fired his assistant, Kinnebrook, because he and Kinnebrook differed by eight-tenths of a second in their observation of stellar transits. There was no doubt about the fact that they differed; but Maskelyne's presumable explanation—that his assistant had deliberately or from sheer incompetence developed an incorrect method of observation—was overhasty. Such an explanation

[5] See Mortimer (1959).

assumes, in the first place, that an experienced and competent observer, like Maskelyne, is capable of making an absolutely accurate observation of a stellar transit (i.e., the moment at which a star passes a line in the telescopic field), and thus can judge the accuracy of another observer to a very fine degree. Some years later another eminent astronomer, Bessel, began to suspect that even very skilled observers might not be able to agree absolutely in making such observations. He accumulated and compared observations made by himself and several other highly competent astronomers and was able to show not only that different observers differed by as much as a second (which is a large difference in astronomical work) but that each observer differed with himself from time to time. Bessel's discovery of individual differences and variability in reaction-time provided a more favorable explanation of Kinnebrook's behavior than his employer presumably had; but its importance extends far beyond that—into the whole question of variability and individual differences, which has been a major field of investigation in psychology ever since.[6]

The search for explanation in science, as in detective stories, leads to the facts behind the facts, not simply to speculation. Speculation is a half-way house, and one in which the detective may be slugged over the head by a preconceived idea. I should like to be able to illustrate this point, but I am afraid that adequate illustration would require a whole book; I shall therefore offer two examples that barely graze the surface. Perhaps they will serve. I have in mind some experiments on human conditioning and animal problem-solving. (1) It has sometimes been assumed that a conditioned reflex is a true reflex, i.e., an involuntary, "automatic" reaction to a stimulus. The assumption is at times a part of the air which is breathed in psychology classrooms. But some experimenters have varied the conditions for establishing conditioned eyeblink reflexes in human subjects by asking them to resist or to yield consciously to the conditioned stimulus. The results are striking. Human subjects can raise or lower the rate of conditioned responding very markedly indeed by conscious effort. Under these circumstances we cannot hold to the view that such a conditioned reflex is a strict reflex at all. It has some of the characteristics of a purposeful defensive action. We cannot apply this particular variation to conditioning experiments with animals because animals cannot be instructed or requested to cooperate in

[6] See Boring (1950).

so simple a fashion, but it is possible that the conditioned reflex is no more automatic and ungovernable in animals than in human beings. Now, the assumption of automaticity of the conditioned reflex might have prevented or at least delayed the experimental variation described. That would be a case of a preconceived idea slugging the detective scientist into stupidity. (2) It has sometimes been assumed that an animal solves problems in order to receive a food reward or something else directly involving the viscera. Most problem-solving experiments are based on the model of the animal as a consumer of real goods, a sort of "economic man" in the maze or the locked box. Rarely does an experimenter ask himself, "What would happen if I left the food reward out of the design of my experiment?" In fact, however, the question has been asked at times, and the experimenter has been rewarded by finding that the animals did not become entirely random in their behavior. Rats will probably run mazes successfully when all they get at the end is a pat on the head by an affectionate experimenter. Some animals will disregard food and other supposedly primary needs while they fiddle with mechanical puzzles. These animals, such as monkeys and apes, act as if they had a good deal of curiosity about how the world is put together and were satisfied by getting answers to their questions. Is this being too anthropomorphic? At any rate, animals are not simply hunger-driven. But suppose that all our experiments were designed as if they were. Suppose that every time we tested a monkey's ability to open a latched box we were careful to put a bit of food reward inside. In that case, we should never be able to discover that the food reward was not necessary. It would be another case of the detective scientist being slugged in the head, this time by an assumption.[7]

A more delicate problem still is posed by research into the occult. The medium Eusapia Palladino was reputed to be able to raise objects into the air by spiritual power. Very good observers indeed, like Madame Curie, attested the levitation of tables in her presence. The medium, however, was often accused of fraud and a few times caught in suspicious acts. A resolute committee of three apparently well-qualified men, who knew a lot about conjuring tricks, undertook a thorough investigation. They were able to study Eusapia and her marvelous phenomena at close range under exceptionally favorable conditions. They professed to be

[7] Cf. Hilgard and Marquis (1940), and Harlow (1953).

skeptical at the outset: but they were strongly persuaded in the end that the phenomena were not due to trickery by the medium. Their long report, taken at face value, is impressive. But there is a flaw in it which is closely allied to its major virtue. Repeatedly the observers themselves were put in the position of being so close to the event in question—the levitation of a table or a piece of rope, or a tambourine apparently crawling up the side of a curtain— that they themselves might have been suspected of the trickery they were looking for and they also could have been charged with collusion. In detective stories, too, suspicion may fall on the detective. That is to say, in some investigations the observer has to create conditions—special knowledge, closeness to the observed event, etc.—which would make it *possible* for him to cause the event. If the event is very strange, the shadow of doubt begins to fall on the observer himself. We find it difficult to accept as honestly reported what cannot be accounted for in customary terms.[8]

A part of the strategy of science is to keep the descriptions pure and not rush in with explanations too soon. Suppose that a friend says, "I saw a flying saucer." The description is more than likely impure. His experience might have been more accurately worded: "I saw a circular light moving north-north-east at high speed for about a second." To add that it was a flying saucer is to provide an explanation, and a very dubious one at that. Other possible explanations might have been "a meteor," "a firefly," "a physiological disturbance in my retina." But while scientists aim at purity of description, absolute purity unmixed with any explanatory element whatsoever is difficult or impossible to achieve. Take these statements: (1) "He moved his hand," (2) "His hand moved." Neither is quite pure. The first may be held to imply the operation of a person with free will, and to some scientists this assumption is unattractive. The second statement, however, contains an even weirder suggestion, namely, that the hand has power of movement in itself. Of course, the defender of this kind of statement

---

[8] See Feilding, Baggally, and Carrington (1909). A recent allegation of fraud as the true explanation of paranormal phenomena was that of G. R. Price in his article, "Science and the supernatural," in *Science,* August 26, 1955. The January 6, 1956, issue of *Science* carried an editorial by Dael Wolfle and articles by S. G. Soal, J. B. Rhine, P. E. Meehl and Michael Scriven, P. W. Bridgman, and G. R. Price, in further discussion of the case. Price's explicit charge of fraud against the parapsychologists was based on theory, not on observation.

may retort: "That's silly. All that I was saying was that a change took place in my field of observation consisting in the displacement of an object 'hand' from point X to point Y." Most descriptions in science do not reach this high degree of purity. We are usually content with something a good deal cruder. In fact, we may at times positively object to pure description.

Usually we do not mind a little explanation mixed in with our descriptions. To return to the example of Eusapia Palladino: If it could have been reported that the table moved upward whenever Eusapia nudged it with her knee, we might be happier than with the bare statement that the table moved upward, cause unknown. It is exactly the purity of the description in this case which troubles us. We accordingly look around for an explanation (i.e., some linked facts either real or presumed), and think we have found it or at least the possibility of it in the conditions of observation; we hint at fraud in the observers themselves, although this may be completely unjust and is certainly at variance with their announced intention to catch Eusapia in fraud. Why not simply suspend judgment, accepting the phenomena as described, and wait for another opportunity to test out the necessary conditions for their occurrence? Well, as already remarked, we love explanations. Things just happening do not quite satisfy us. From early childhood we have been in the business of linking one thing to another to make some sort of intelligible unity. Furthermore, we not only like to have things explained, but we like to have them explained in familiar terms which are congenial with our general theory of the nature of the world. At this period of history, the majority of educated people shrink from an explanation of the Palladino phenomena in terms of mischievous or evil spirits and prefer to believe in fraud. We are all painfully aware of the possibility of deceit.

Science is an effort to wrest ourselves free from human deceitfulness. But it is not just a set of rules for being cautious and suspicious. There is another side to it, the adventurous side. Science has to face the unfamiliar, the hitherto unbelieved, even the theoretically unbelievable. That is the way discoveries are made. One goes into the unknown at the risk of respectability and even one's life. Textbooks of science, I think, ought to share in this risk a little, and not always be trying to keep up with the dignified rear of the march. After all, there are no absolute rules for being right.

The freshness of the old

One of the riskiest things I have done in this book is to make generous excerpts from the psychological literature of the past, sometimes of the far past. This is partly for the sake of reminding the student that psychology has a history. It is also because some kinds of highly interesting material are more plentiful in older sources than in more recent ones. Full accounts of experiments and lively descriptions of behavior are, I think, more characteristic of the older literature. Partly this is due to editorial pressure toward brevity of report in our crowded journals; partly, to the constrictive movement in psychological science already noted, combined with an almost obsessive preoccupation with methodological details. Of course, it is also true that modern sophistication makes some of the older work appear excessively naïve and anecdotal; but I suspect that this is more appearance than reality.

Let me illustrate the situation with the topic of hypnosis, which in any event needs to be taken up historically in order to understand the thinking of Freud.

There is a recent book on the subject by Weitzenhoffer for which I have great respect.[9] It summarizes a vast amount of experimental work and goes keenly into the theories. But there is not a single fully described hypnotic session in it, much less a whole series with any one particular person; and it is my guess that, because of the lack of this concrete material, Weitzenhoffer's book could not possibly persuade a student new to the subject that there is anything especially noteworthy about a deep hypnotic trance. One gets a very different impression from reading the older book of J. Milne Bramwell.[10] Here the spectacular features of hypnotic phenomena stand out so as to challenge thought. Now, one could argue that hypnotism is not as spectacular as Bramwell makes it out to be. I doubt, however, that he has overdone it. He has used some remarkable cases, certainly; but we need to know of these extreme cases. As Weitzenhoffer remarks, much of the recent experimental work has not touched the depths of trance explored by earlier investigators and cannot therefore be accepted as crucial evidence regarding the properties of deep trance states. Furthermore, many of the modern investigators have been graduate students making a few observations for the sake of a thesis and then dropping the subject, while Bramwell devoted many of

[9] Weitzenhoffer (1953).   [10] Bramwell (1930).

his best years to it and dealt personally with hundreds of cases. Hull's book on hypnosis and suggestibility,[11] often cited as a model of experimental procedure, has many attractive features, but it is based largely on essentially amateur graduate student work and refers mainly to light states of trance induced by a few minutes with the experimenter or even by a phonograph record. This contrasts signally with Charles Richet's report of his hypnotic sessions with Léonie which yielded, according to him, supernormal clairvoyant or clairvoyant-like phenomena.[12] Richet, one of the most distinguished of French physiologists, not only sat up whole nights with his subject in order to extract a few card guesses from her, but found it necessary to hypnotize her repeatedly for long periods to obtain the results which interested him; he mentions two and a half months of hypnotizing before beginning one of his card-guessing experiments. Such passionate thoroughness could scarcely be expected of Hull's experimenters and in fact in most academic settings would not be tolerated, because of the fear of scandal.

Weitzenhoffer has some kind words to say about the early work in hypnosis, even the very early work of Franz Anton Mesmer (1734-1815) and the Marquis de Puységur (1751-1825). He states:

Much of the investigational work performed in those days fails to meet the criteria of the scientific method. Yet, in view of the fact that science was then still in its infancy and that the scientific method had not been yet clearly formulated, much of this work has earned the right to be called scientific. By 1825 the supporters of animal magnetism had uncovered all the well-known major hypnotic phenomena, such as negative and positive hallucinations, hypnotic analgesia and anesthesia, catalepsy, lethargy, and posthypnotic phenomena.[13]

The work up to 1825 seems to have been fruitful in spite of the regrettable lack of method. Incidentally, Weitzenhoffer does not expand on what he means by "scientific method," and so it is not clear what he is objecting to in the earlier workers; but it is a little harsh to exclude from this particular fold all those who came before, let us say, 1933, the date of Hull's book, which seems to be approximately Weitzenhoffer's reference point. Thus he comments, after drawing up a long list of posthypnotic phenomena:

[11] Hull (1933).
[13] Weitzenhoffer (1953), p. 5.

[12] Richet (1889).

This list is far from exhaustive, and certainly does not represent the only way in which hypnotic phenomena may be classified. It should also be kept in mind that, although Milne Bramwell declared that all of the above have been obtained, and although there is no question but that he was writing in good faith, he was doing this in a period when the exactitude of modern science was at best to be found only in the physical sciences.[14]

He then states that one of the major aims of his own book is to examine the validity of Bramwell's claims. It is comforting to learn that Bramwell comes through the fire of the recent literature virtually unscathed.

It is not by the date of a publication but by its content and by the competence of its author that it should be judged. Furthermore, an awareness of our predecessors may help us to judge the value of recent work, especially where they have approached things with different ideas and different methods from those which are currently favored. Finally, there are some kinds of information of high interest which we cannot get at all unless we turn to old sources. It might even be suggested that one of the easiest ways to make discoveries in psychology is to read books which have become dusty.

Laws and theories

As must be apparent by now, the raggedest fact appeals to my empiricist mind more than any number of highly polished theories. Yet we need theory, too. That is to say, it is a normal craving to wish to put our facts together into some kind of intelligible order. Perhaps the simplest such ordering is the statement that facts A and B go together. This is the nature of scientific *law*.

Much scientific work is concerned merely with the constancy of certain relationships, with the question whether A and B can be counted on to go together. We have all become sophisticated enough to know that in most cases we have to speak of some degree of association rather than 100 per cent invariability. The value of repeating observations is partly that we thus form an estimate of the frequency with which A goes along with B. We also learn something about the attendant conditions. Take the commonplace matter of striking a match. We know that ordinarily the sequence A (striking) and B (bursting into flame) occurs, but we know

[14] *Ibid.*, p. 19.

also that the sequence presupposes certain other things. We have to strike hard enough, not just strike. The match must not be wet. If it is a safety match, it must be struck against a specially prepared surface. We have to assume certain conditions before we can be satisfied with our little law about the relation between A and B. In general, we find that a statement about a connection between some A and some B involves us in statements about other things X, Y, and Z. Even the striking of a match is analytically complex. We do not have a science until we can state some lawful connections. At the same time, it is true that no such statements can be considered final because we cannot be sure that the analysis is complete. Our laws are only relatively true.

Now, it does not seem to me that our interest in establishing scientific laws should reduce our interest in rare phenomena and unstable connections. The words of Richet (who was a competent enough scientist to be the Nobel prize winner in physiology in 1913) are very sensible, even though they were written with regard to a type of subject matter which many psychologists today find repulsive, namely, clairvoyance or "lucidity"—these words:

> In the experimental sciences, one thing is necessary, viz., to be able to control the conditions of the experiment. If a chemist were to find a new substance and were to declare himself unable to say how he found it or to produce it again, nobody would listen to him, and that would perhaps be reasonable. In the same way, I have obtained some phenomena of lucidity, but I frankly declare myself unable to tell how I obtained them or why I succeeded sometimes and sometimes failed, and I cannot undertake to produce them again. This is empiricism, not science. I cannot, however, draw from this any discouraging conclusion. On the contrary, we have here a whole series of absolutely new phenomena immersed in deep shadow, like every science in its infancy. The problem then must be attacked resolutely but methodically, as in experimental science.[15]

The facts always have richer possibilities than any theory is able to accommodate. Moreover, some uncertainty attaches to the simplest A and B connections. As I have been trying to make clear, it is my opinion that the proper way to meet this situation is to acknowledge it, not to hide from it. Beginning students, I think, ought to be exposed to the disorderly facts and the uncertainty of science. If, instead, they are drilled in neat paradigms of laws

[15] Richet (1889), p. 83.

and a single triumphant system in which there is no untidiness, they are in danger of developing a model of science which is unrealistic and idolatrous. Therefore in this book I set forth a number of facts which are so untidy as to be downright indecorous. The purpose is to encourage thoughtfulness not gullibility.

Even when we are dealing with some of the less elusive phenomena of psychology, we learn that quite reputable connections do not always hold up under examination. For instance, if we survey the literature on a given experimental question, we find both denials and affirmations of certain results. We cannot resolve the problem by merely counting the yeses and noes. It is necessary to analyze. The failure of two sets of experimental results to agree does not mean that nature is lawless, but that something important has been overlooked. A beautiful illustration is found in a paper by Schmidt, in which he was able to show that a dispute between two previous investigators about the behavior of earthworms in a T-maze arose from the fact that they used two different species of earthworms; it was the *species* difference which had been ignored.[16] In line with these reflections, I have chosen in this book to examine a few studies in detail rather than attempt to summarize all the available literature. I think that this kind of thing is more useful to students than brief abstracting. My analyses, however, are not to be taken as authoritative no matter how strongly worded they may be, but simply as one fallible mortal's attempt to understand another's piece of work and assess its value. The student should be able at least to benefit from my mistakes.

So much for laws. As for theories, I regard them as ways of looking at facts and laws from some distant vantage point. A theory in this sense is not the final word on anything, but an orientation which may supply general meanings and suggest further investigations. It is full of hypotheses, some definitely stated, more only implied. There are numerous theories about personality. I do not pretend to sample them all. I do not even pretend to give the one right theory, though in the concluding chapter I state one of my own.

Theories, as I said earlier, are ways of trying to embrace the facts; they are doing their part well if they keep reminding us of the facts, and doing it ill if they make us forget. Every student should try to be his own theorist. As Blake rather fiercely put it,

[16] Schmidt (1955).

"I must Create a System or be enslav'd by another Man's." Yet even so we must beware of enslavement—by ourselves.

A brief outline of the book

It would be premature to introduce a definition of personality at this point. The whole book is a fragment of a definition. Yet, of course, everyone comes to a book such as this with some half-formed definition in mind. Furthermore, one can always turn to a dictionary and get an array of definitions which will serve very well in a pinch, e.g., "all the constitutional, mental, emotional, social, etc., characteristics of an individual," "existence as a self-conscious being," "the essential character of a person as distinguished from a thing." There is no more harm in these definitions than in that for "universe"—"the totality of existing or created things, including the earth (with all on or in it), the heavenly bodies, and all else throughout space." There is not much help in them, either.

This book goes at our complex subject from several angles. The first section, *Growth and Learning,* is concerned with personality as a biological organism genetically determined, following the life course of the species, and modified by learning. The principal idea here is that learning is a very important, but still secondary, factor in development—in the sense that it works upon an organism which has an inherited forward thrust of its own with characteristics both common to the species and unique to itself. Since the human being, from this angle, is one biological organism among others, there is value in utilizing animal and even plant studies for the light they throw on the developmental processes.

The second section, *Psychodynamics,* considers personality from the inside; that is to say, the mental processes, both conscious and unconscious, which we can observe individually in ourselves and infer in other persons. We here deal with a kind of knowledge which would be impossible if it were not for the sovereign fact that we are self-conscious. The concept of the unconscious, for instance, which has played such a large role in modern psychology, would itself be impossible but for the fact of self-consciousness. This section naturally deals extensively with Freud.

The third section, *Methods of Describing Personality,* takes up personality testing methods, both projective and objective, and some current typologies. It also has something to say about the assessment and understanding of others in direct, face-to-face situations, and the implications for personality theory. The view is stressed that such direct engagement with others points to a different kind of psychology from that which has occupied us hitherto.

The fourth section, *Problems*, ventures into some of the obscurer regions of psychology where it verges on metaphysics. The facts and speculations of this section will, I hope, stimulate the reader to reflect boldly on the meaning of human life without becoming either superstitious or antiscientific. Psychosomatics, perception, and values are familiar enough words, but they lead us into profound questions which tax our scientific resourcefulness to the limit; and yet these questions, many of which are very old, become sharper as science advances and seem to occupy a perfectly natural place in the sphere of personality study.

A very brief concluding chapter sketches a theory of personality which I should be the first to admit is inadequate. But by the time the reader comes to that, he should be fortified enough by his own thoughts on the subject to resist any enslavement by a formula of mine.

References for chapter 1

Allport, G. W. (1937) *Personality: a psychological interpretation*. New York: Holt.

Boring, E. G. (1950) *A history of experimental psychology*. New York: Appleton-Century-Crofts.

Bramwell, J. M. (1930) *Hypnotism, its history, practice and theory*. 4th ed. Philadelphia: Lippincott.

Feilding, E., Baggally, W. W., and Carrington, H. (1909) Report on a series of sittings with Eusapia Palladino. *Proceedings of the Society for Psychical Research*, 23, 309-569.

Harlow, H. F. (1953) Mice, monkeys, men, and motives. *Psychological Review*, 60, 23-32.

Hilgard, E. R., and Marquis, D. G. (1940) *Conditioning and learning*. New York: Appleton-Century.

Hull, C. L. (1933) *Hypnosis and suggestibility: an experimental approach*. New York: Appleton-Century.

James, W. (1920) *Collected essays and reviews*. New York: Longmans, Green.

Mortimer, E. (1959) *Blaise Pascal; the life and work of a realist*. New York: Harper.

Murray, H. A. *et al.* (1938) *Explorations in personality*. New York: Oxford Univ. Press.

Richet, C. (1889) Further experiments in hypnotic lucidity or clairvoyance. *Proceedings of the Society for Psychical Research*, 6, 66-83.

Rogers, C. R. (1955) Persons or science? a philosophical question. *American Psychologist*, 10, 267-78.

Rychlak, J. F. (1959) Clinical psychology and the nature of evidence. *American Psychologist*, 14, 642-48.

Schmidt, H., Jr. (1955) Behavior of two species of worms in the same maze. *Science*, 121, 341-42.

Weitzenhoffer, A. M. (1953) *Hypnotism: an objective study of suggestibility*. New York: Wiley.

2

THE POWER
OF HEREDITY

Preview   *In a perfectly uniform environment people would not be all alike. Hereditary factors would produce variety. The power of heredity is often doubted, however, because of the modifying effects of differing environments. Yet studies of human beings under varied environmental conditions are in harmony with studies on other biological organisms under controlled conditions: genetic factors operate in a lawful fashion and guide development.*

The study of personality includes much more than the study of individual differences. It is primarily concerned with the individual as an organized psychological system. Nevertheless, one convenient point of entry into the study of personality is found in the obvious fact that people do differ. If we ask why they differ, we are immediately caught up in the nature-nurture controversy, which remains alive in spite of efforts to throttle it.

So pervasive is the fact of individuality that a biochemist, much against his original inclination, has recently asserted that there is no such thing as a standard, average human being.[1] According to his analysis, if you select a person with an average reaction to a particular chemical dosage, you will probably not find him to be average in the next trait you happen to measure; and as the number of measured traits increases, the more likely it is that your specimen will depart from the average values. To put it in a slightly different way, it is fairly easy to match quite a number of people with respect to a single trait, like height; but it is hard or impossible to find even two who are alike in a dozen or so different traits.

Now, the whole solid science of genetics, which originated in the precise experiments of Mendel, is based on the proposition that unit characters are transmitted unchanged from generation to generation (except for such interesting accidents as mutations), and this would seem to mean that heredity makes for similarity rather than variety; but it is also based on the companion proposition that these unit-characters do not necessarily stick together, which provides for the opposite result. The Mendelian laws predict both similarity and difference, without being either self-contradictory or ambiguous.[2] Without deserting these laws, however, we may say that kinship makes for similarity and lack of kinship for difference, and at the same time admit that the closest kinship does not eliminate difference altogether. We can admit this last statement because we realize that the biochemical units, the genes, which correspond to the Mendelian unit-characters, are dynamic; that is to say, they respond to environmental conditions plastically, adaptively, without losing their basic determining tendencies.

How much variety there may be when kinship is as close as possible is shown by some studies initiated by Werner Wolff.[3] If a straight-on photograph of a human face and a reverse print thereof are split down the middle, the parts can be reassembled so that the new artificial faces are constructed of two right and two left halves. Figure 1 shows a pair of these synthetic faces along with the original. It is apparent that the two sides of the same face are different; and this amounts to saying that the same genetic material may express itself in different ways even where

[1] Williams (1957).
[2] For a readable exposition, see Goldschmidt (1952).
[3] Wolff (1933, 1944).

1 *Faces are asymmetrical. Compare the original portrait above with the two below it which were composed by uniting a half of the face with its mirror image.*

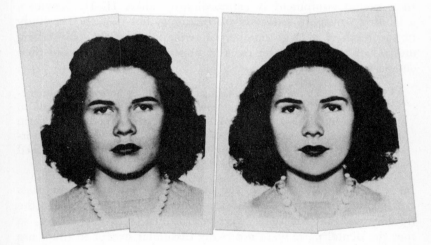

it might be expected to yield identical results.

It might be noticed here that the difference between the two halves of the face is not simply a difference of physical proportions. As Wolff has stated, there is also a difference of expression. One half of a face may look comparatively lively, the other half comparatively dead. The concentration of expressiveness on one side leads to the result that the whole face, dominated by that expression, may resemble one of the half-faces more than the other. Wolff thought at first that the dominant expression was always borne by the right side. Later studies point to a less absolute rule: it is usually the right side, but not infrequently the left. It is rare to find the expression distributed equally over the whole face.[4]

How similar are twins?

If, as we have seen, there are differences between the two sides of one face, we should not be surprised that twins originating in a single fertilized egg are not perfect duplicates. In spite of that, such twins are called "identical." Their genetic identity is partially disguised by unequal development. Nevertheless, the resemblance of monozygotic (one-egg) twins is often remarkable.

Everybody knows examples of extreme twin similarity. It is not quite so well known that monozygotic twins are always and necessarily of the same sex. Their blood type is always the same. Even their dental equipment is extraordinarily alike. H. H. Newman, a leading American authority on twinning, has described a study of the teeth of a large number of twin pairs by the painstaking method of molding plaster casts of upper and lower jaw and then comparing these minutely:

> One of the most remarkable findings was that in many pairs of one-egg twins the plaster cast of the lower jaw of twin A, when fitted to that of the upper jaw of twin B, showed nearly as perfect occlusion with the latter as with the cast of his own upper jaw. All dental irregularities, including overlapping teeth protruding outward or turned sidewise, were alike in both twins of such pairs.[5]

In several pairs, to be sure, the fit of the upper and lower casts crossed over in this way was extremely poor. In these cases, the trouble was that the twins were mirror-images of each other, so that the dental parts were not really dissimilar except in the sense that they were reversed. Such mirror reversal is fairly common in twinning and may affect the placement of the heart and other internal organs. It occurs early in prenatal development because of the interaction between the two halves of the dividing egg—on the same principle as that governing the development of a left and a right side in a single body, where mirror-imaging of feet and hands is a regular phenomenon.

[4] McCurdy (1949); Lindzey, Prince, and Wright (1952).
[5] Newman (1940), pp. 129 f.

The similarity between monozygotic twins may be great, but it is never perfect. Prenatal environmental influences have to be taken into account. Twins are unavoidably in competition in the uterus. Frequently one develops at the expense of the other. Sometimes this goes so far that only one survives, and only a shriveled remnant of the other remains at birth. More frequently both twins develop to full-term babies, but one is born bigger, stronger, healthier than the other. Often, of course, the difference in physique is slight. The prenatal period is hazardous for all twins, but especially for monozygotic twins because they share the same placenta and their blood vessels may become fused, with the result that one twin robs the other of its blood supply. Birth injuries are also more common for twins than for singletons. For these reasons a considerable inequality between the members of a twin pair may exist at the time of birth in spite of their hereditary equality. Such are some of the facts which must be remembered when it is stated, truly enough, that on the average monozygotic twins are much more alike than ordinary brothers and sisters.

We are half inclined to expect similar behavior in people who look alike, and in the case of monozygotic twins the expectation is not unrealistic. Their effect on each other after birth, however, just as before birth, may work toward difference rather than similarity. For example, Burlingham has reported prolonged bullying by one of a pair during infancy.[6] Later the roles were reversed, after the previously dominant child had been weakened by illness. It is unsafe to assume that twins growing up together are under equal environmental influences. Just as a tree may fail to grow symmetrically because another one close by cuts out the sunlight, so twins living together may actually interfere with equality of development. In addition, twins like other individuals may attend to different aspects of the same environment. Siamese twins, though more confined to the same environment than ordinary monozygotic twins, are not more alike in consequence. Newman, in fact, says that they are less alike.

On theoretical grounds, one would predict that the genetic equality of a pair of monozygotic twins would be fully expressed only if they were separated at birth and brought up in *duplicate* environments. Such an experiment has not been performed with human beings, and practically speaking, is impossible. But twins

[6] Burlingham (1952).

have, of course, been separated shortly after birth and brought up in *different* environments without the resemblance, either physical or behavioral, being obliterated.

Let us consider Kallmann's story of the identical twin girls Kaete and Lisa, who, although reared apart from infancy, developed schizophrenia at nearly the same time.[7] The uncles who adopted them lived in different cities and were on such bad terms with each other that the girls met only rarely and briefly during childhood. Later, when they were able to meet more often, they proved to be inharmonious. They were difficult children, stubborn, callous, intractable, reducing their foster parents to despair by their refractory conduct, and yet intellectually capable of advancing to the upper grades in their different schools. Kaete had a light case of measles at ten; otherwise, the girls were healthy, maturing at the same rate and becoming quite pretty. They began to menstruate in the same month in their twelfth year. At the end of their school careers they went to work, Kaete in a factory, Lisa as a domestic servant. At fifteen Kaete was seduced by another worker at the factory and before she was sixteen bore an illegitimate child. A few days after the birth she went into a catatonic stupor, was committed to a mental hospital, and remained there for more than a year. She returned home for a short time but soon began to manifest renewed symptoms and had to be committed again. Lisa, in the meantime, though living in a separate environment and undisturbed by a precocious sexual experience, also developed schizophrenia. Her first definite symptoms appeared at the time Kaete was entering her second phase. She had to be committed to the hospital in the same month that Kaete returned to it. At this time, their mental condition was similar, though Kaete's psychosis was severer.

Kallmann interprets the facts of this history as supporting his view that schizophrenia depends heavily on hereditary determinants. He points out, nevertheless, that particular environmental stresses may speed up the diseased behavior or render it more serious, and he might have added, as others would do, that the full expression of such hereditary tendencies may be restrained by environments of the right kind. Still, he emphasizes that people are disposed to exaggerate the importance of single events, such as Kaete's pregnancy. Here there is a control check on that line of reasoning: Kaete's twin did not undergo the trauma which seemed

[7] Kallmann (1938).

to precipitate Kaete's illness, and yet she too fell prey to schizophrenia.

Those who are unfavorable to Kallmann's views (which are supported by massive statistical evidence) like to think that the girls were brought up by people who might have exposed them to the same kind of bad training in childhood. This criticism cannot be directly refuted by the Kallman data. In fact, it is extraordinarily difficult to get the kind of data which would be decisive. Theories which stress the importance of early childhood experiences typically deal in subtleties of parent-child relations which are extremely elusive. These theories nevertheless deserve to be seriously weighed, and they will be taken up in due course. The mere unfashionableness of Kallmann's views should not be allowed to hide them, however; and it must be admitted that not only his statistics, but also general genetic theory, argues in his favor.

Twins reared together and apart

The most comprehensive study of twins from a behavioral point of view is that of Newman, Freeman, and Holzinger published in 1937. Their aim was to shed light on the question of the interaction of heredity and environment by comparing (1) monozygotic and dizygotic (two-egg) twins reared together, and (2) monozygotic twins reared apart. Their measures and comparisons bore upon the physique, the intelligence, and the personality of the twins. They concluded that hereditary control was tightest for physique, looser for intelligence, and loosest of all for personality. There are reasons for thinking that hereditary control is not quite so lax for intelligence and personality as they would like to persuade us. If by "heredity" we mean the baby's condition at birth (and this is approximately where the line is drawn in their study, for all practical purposes), then "environment" in the sense of postnatal environment seems to have had less to do with the differences between twins than they estimate from the data.

Let us first consider the logic of the study. Monozygotic twins are genetically the same. Dizygotic twins are no more alike genetically than ordinary brothers and sisters. We therefore expect greater differences between dizygotic than between monozygotic twins. By the same token we should expect no greater resemblance between dizygotic twins than between any two ordinary brothers and sisters, if environment could be left out of the reckoning. But nearly everyone argues that the environment of two children of the same age growing up together, as is normally the case with twins, is bound to be more alike for them than for two children of different ages, and it is presumed that such equality of environment will lessen the native differences between dizygotic twins, with the result that they will wind up more alike than ordinary siblings. Oddly enough, the Newman, Freeman, and Holzinger study does not support this argument. They compared parallel series of 52 like-sexed pairs of dizygotic twins and 52 like-sexed pairs of ordinary siblings, and found that the average differences between these pairs in height, weight, and IQ points were almost identical. The prediction based on genetics is sustained in this case. But it still might be supposed that the environmental pressures would tend to equalize monozygotic twins more than dizygotic, simply because of their initial resemblance which might invite more equal treatment from their parents and others. Separation into different environments would at least eliminate this possible source of equality. In addition, we should expect two different homes to provide more differentiating experience for a pair of twins than would a single home. If the genetic factor is not very important, then, we should expect separated monozygotic twins to become much more unlike than such twins reared together in the same home. This is the hypothesis which Newman, Freeman, and Holzinger endeavored to test with their painfully gathered data on 19 pairs of monozygotic twins who had been separated at an early age and reared in different homes.

A judicious appraisal of these and some other data has been published by Woodworth.[8] He concludes that the monozygotic twins reared apart were not very different from those reared together. We must examine the evidence in detail, however, before we can appreciate the force of this conclusion.

INTELLIGENCE AND PHYSIQUE   Newman, Freeman, and Holzinger did, of course, find differences of IQ between the separated pairs. For example, the monozygotic twin sisters Gladys and Helen had IQ's of 92 and 116. This difference of 24 points was the largest found. It happened to correspond also with the largest educational difference found in their sample, for Gladys had attended school only through the third grade whereas Helen had acquired a college degree. Furthermore, the correlation between intrapair IQ

[8] Woodworth (1941).

differences and estimated educational differences for the whole sample (.79) indicates some connection between amount of education and amount of IQ. But a correlation does not tell you which is the dependent and which is the independent variable. Newman, Freeman, and Holzinger argue that the educational differences caused the IQ differences. It might be, on the contrary, that the IQ differences accounted for the educational differences. One cannot actually tell from the data. There is one interesting fact, however: Newman, Freeman, and Holzinger make no attempt to explain the intrapair IQ differences between the *unseparated* monozygotic twins on the basis of educational differences, and yet the range of differences for them is about the same as for the separated twins (i.e., 2 to 17 points for the 50 unseparated pairs, 1 to 24 points for the 19 separated pairs). An explanation which might very well apply to both sets of twins without any strain on the argument would be that the intrapair IQ differences simply reflect the differences already present in them at birth. We shall return to this suggestion in a moment.

Woodworth has briefly summarized the essential facts regarding physique and intelligence in twins in the accompanying table. As the table shows, the tendency to differ is somewhat greater for the monozygotic twins reared apart than for those reared together, but the increase of diversity supposedly due to environmental influence is not overwhelmingly impressive. If environmental differences were very powerful and genetic factors negligible we might expect the monozygotic twins reared apart to differ more within

Table 1
Differences and correlations between twins

		dizygotic twins	*monozygotic twins*	
			REARED TOGETHER	REARED APART
AVERAGE	stature	4.4 cm	1.7 cm	1.8 cm
INTRAPAIR	weight	10.0 lb	4.1 lb	9.9 lb
DIFFERENCES	Binet IQ	9.9 points	5.9 points	8.2 points
	stature	.645	.932	.969
CORRELATIONS	weight	.631	.917	.886
	Binet IQ	.631	.881	.767

Adapted from Woodworth (1941), p. 19.

pairs than the dizygotic twins reared together and the correlations to be less than for the dizygotic twins. This is clearly not the case.

Our question is not whether environment influences development. Everyone admits this, and it is in harmony with genetic theory. The question is rather whether genetic factors can be ignored. It not only appears that they cannot be, but that the New-man, Freeman, and Holzinger interpretation of data is too favorable to environment. Woodworth was able to combine their results with those for three other cases of separated monozygotic twins, and, referring to the whole set of 22 cases, he comes to the following conclusion:

> Taken without regard to sign, the average IQ difference between separated identicals is 7.6 points. Correction for chance errors of observation would bring this difference down to 6 points net, a figure to be compared with the estimated net difference of 3 points between identicals reared together, and of 15 points or more between children paired at random from the same community. It is probable, then, that environment did make these separated twins differ in tested intelligence, though not to any such extent as obtains among the children of a community.[9]

As the reader probably realizes, IQ measures cannot be accepted as completely reliable. Successive test results on the same individual vary on the average about 5 IQ points. Because of this "error of measurement," which in reality depends on the variability of individual performance from time to time, a person who is a few points superior to another on one occasion may very well be a few points inferior on the next. Larger differences are not so likely to be reversed, although it is not impossible. This fact must be kept in mind when studying the figures in Table 1. The average intrapair difference for monozygotic twins reared together, for instance, is about the size of the error of measurement.

Without forgetting this fact, we may still raise the question whether some of the IQ differences reflect organic disparities present in early infancy. The information on this point is not adequate, and, in view of the measurement unreliability already referred to, no final judgment can be made, but the facts, such as they are, support the hypothesis that prenatally determined differences within a pair contributed to the IQ differences discovered later. Let us

[9] *Ibid.*, p. 25.

examine the evidence. Of the 19 separated pairs, there were 5 for whom some difference of physical condition at birth or in early childhood was noted. Ruth weighed 3½ pounds at birth, her sister Mildred, 6; their respective IQ's were 77 and 92. Alice was much weaker than Olive; their IQ's were 85 and 97. Paul C. was sickly, Paul O. was stronger; IQ's, 99 and 101. Gladys was delicate, Helen was healthy; IQ's, 92 and 116. Reece differed from James in having a deformed left arm; IQ's, 77 and 96. In each of these five cases the IQ difference is in favor of the child who was healthier or more physically sound at birth. The average IQ difference for these 5 pairs is 14.4 points. For the other 14 pairs, where no physical difference was noted, the average IQ difference is only 6 points. The difference between these average differences is 8.4, and the *t*-test reveals that we may accept the hypothesis that an organic factor is somehow involved at better than the 1% level of confidence. In less technical words we have evidence that some of the inequality between members of the twin pairs with respect to measured intelligence should be traced back to biological inequality originating before birth. Certainly we must agree with Woodworth that in a perfectly satisfactory piece of research on nature and nurture in twins, "the medical history of each child, including prenatal and natal conditions, would be essential."[10] This is especially needful where small samples are being used to test large and important generalizations.

PERSONALITY   At the time the Newman, Freeman, and Holzinger study was made—1937—it was customary to refer to personality as something apart from intelligence. Today personality is usually taken in a more inclusive sense, intelligence being one of its aspects. It is easy to understand, however, that these scientists were aiming at something besides intelligence when they used several of the personality tests then popular—the Downey Will-Temperament, the Pressey X-O, the Kent-Rosanoff, the Woodworth-Mathews Personal Data Schedule, and a handwriting test. Perhaps the cleanest-cut instrument of this collection (all of which are now largely out of fashion) was the Woodworth-Mathews, a questionnaire about traits of mood and behavior designed to measure neurotic tendencies. No attempt will be made here to assess its value beyond noting that it is the ancestor of a number of tests now enjoying wide clinical use. It

[10] *Ibid.*, p. 87.

is perhaps not unfair to say that the results from this test were probably the most significant which Newman, Freeman, and Holzinger obtained in the personality area.

An average, normal score on the Woodworth-Mathews is around 15. (The higher the score, the more neurotic the person is supposed to be.) All the twins averaged at about this level. The average for the separated monozygotic twins was 15.7; for the monozygotic twins reared together, 14.7; and for the dizygotic twins reared together, 14.9. The average intrapair differences for both sets of monozygotic twins were virtually the same—5.0 for the separated, 5.3 for the nonseparated; for the dizygotic twins reared together it was 6.7, slightly larger. There is nothing here to indicate that rearing twins in different environments produces personality differences; in fact, the Woodworth-Mathews score was apparently less affected by environment than the IQ.

It must be admitted that the correlation between the monozygotic twins on this test is not high, whether separated or nonseparated, though it is higher than for dizygotic twins reared together. For the monozygotic twins the coefficients are only .58 and .56. The test was less reliable than the IQ test, and this would tend to lower the correlations. But even if we take the correlations at face value, we do not have any clear indication of the source of the differences between the twins. The fact that the correlation is not significantly lower for the separated twins as compared with the nonseparated rather argues *against* environmental effects and points to prenatal factors. In short, while this study indicates greater temperamental differences between twins than intellectual ones, it is very far from showing that these differences rest on postnatal environmental factors.

Siblings who are not twins

Even twins differ. Monozygotic twins differ, but the power of heredity tends to hold these differences within narrow limits. Dizygotic twins differ more, largely because they bear different assortments of genes. And, of course, ordinary siblings differ, being derived from different assortments of genes just as the dizygotic twins are. They do not, however, differ from each other as much as do individuals picked at random from a large population, because some restriction is placed upon the variety of gene combinations possible for their two parents to pass on; and whatever similarity is introduced by being carried in the same uterus and reared in the same family would theoretically still further limit the variability.

One study which every student who is interested in this matter should know was published by Karl Pearson, one of the greatest of statisticians, more than fifty years ago. He wanted to estimate how much resemblance there was between brothers and sisters both physically and psychologically, and to decide whether the facts pointed to hereditary influence on psychological traits.

Pearson started with the acceptable assumption that certain physical characteristics, for example, eye color, are inherited. He then proceeded to argue that

> if fraternal resemblance for the moral and mental characters be less than, equal to, or greater than fraternal resemblance for the physical characters, we may surely argue that parental inheritance for the former set of characters is less than, equal to, or greater than that for the latter set of characters.[11]

On the surface this argument has much to commend it, though perhaps some reader may detect a flaw in it; but it ran counter to some biases in Pearson's own day, and still does. Pearson met the objections head-on, in the following words:

> A majority of the community would probably also admit today that the physical characters of man are inherited with practically the same intensity as the like characters in cattle and horses. But few, however, of the majority who accept this inheritance of physique in man, apply the results which flow from such acceptance to their own conduct of life—still less do they appreciate the all important bearing of these results upon national life and social habits. Nor is the reason for this—or better, one out of the several reasons for this—hard to find. The majority of mankind are more or less conscious that man has not gained his preeminence by physique alone. They justly attribute much of his dominance in the animal kingdom to those mental and moral characters, which have rendered him capable of combining with his neighbors to form stable societies with highly differentiated tasks and circumscribed duties for their individual members. Within such communities we see the moral characters developing not only under home training, but under the guidance of private and public teachers, the whole contributing to form a complex system of national education. To use technical terms, we expect correlation between home influence and moral qualities, and between education and mental power, and

[11] Pearson (1904), p. 133.

the bulk of men too rashly, perhaps, conclude that the home and the school are the chief sources of those qualities on which social stability so largely depends. We are too apt to overlook the possibility that the home standard is itself a product of parental stock, and that the relative gain from education depends to a surprising degree on the raw material presented to the educator.[12]

The basic data employed by Pearson in analyzing sibling resemblance were ratings of various characteristics which were supplied by numerous teachers in England for pairs of siblings well known to them. The characteristics in question were carefully defined by Pearson for the guidance of the raters, and he gave detailed instructions as to how their judgments should be registered. For example, the teachers were asked to rate intellectual ability on a scale of six degrees running from "Quick Intelligent" to "Very Dull"—as in Table 2. If they were undecided as between two categories, they were to mark the rating chart on the dividing line; it is because of this that fractional values appear in this table.

INTELLIGENCE   At the time of Pearson's study, intelligence tests as we know them today did not exist. It is extremely interesting, therefore, that the grading of intelligence into six broad categories yielded results for him comparable to those we get by refined

Table 2
Intellectual ability: pairs of brothers (N = 1868)

first of pair	second of pair						
	quick intelli- gent	intelli- gent	slow intelli- gent	slow	slow dull	very dull	TOTALS
quick intelligent	88	62.25	42.25	11	2	2	207.5
intelligent	62.25	313.5	183.75	72.5	9.5	1	642.5
slow intelligent	42.25	183.75	255.5	73	22.5	8	585
slow	11	72.5	73	97.5	39	4	297
slow dull	2	9.5	22.5	39	28	7	108
very dull	2	1	8	4	7	6	28
TOTALS	207.5	642.5	585	297	108	28	1868

Adapted from Pearson (1904), p. 189.

[12] *Ibid.*, pp. 131f.

modern tests. In particular, the sibling correlations are very similar. Thus, Pearson by his rating method in 1904 obtained a correlation of .46 between brothers. Later, as Pearson himself noted in 1919, Kate Gordon using the Stanford-Binet test found a correlation of .51 between 91 pairs of siblings in California orphanages.[13] And we read in the 1949 text of Anastasi and Foley this summing-up of various independent investigations:

> That the sibling correlation on most intelligence tests is in the neighborhood of .50 has been repeatedly confirmed. The correlation between 384 pairs of siblings tested during the standardization of the revised Stanford-Binet Scale was found to be .53. The same correlation (.534) was obtained with about 650 pairs of siblings tested in Scotland.[14]

The Pearson results based on teachers' ratings are thus amply confirmed by various later studies employing standardized tests.

OTHER TRAITS When it is a question of traits other than intelligence, however, Anastasi and Foley object to Pearson's rating method as inherently faulty. They insist that raters have a tendency to see more resemblance between related children than actually exists, and that the rating method thus produces results which inflate the correlation coefficient. How odd this reasoning sounds! For why should the rating method break down when applied to nonintellectual traits like general health or temper after succeeding so well with intelligence, which would seem to be harder to estimate? Perhaps the problem with which Anastasi and Foley are wrestling lies in this fact—that whereas later test methods yield very much the same correlational result that Pearson got for intelligence, they yield much lower correlations for nonintellectual personality variables. They judge Pearson's results correct where they agree with the results of modern standardized tests; they judge them incorrect where they fail to agree, charging the difference up to a "halo effect" in the ratings.

But to pass judgment in this way is to disregard both the logical puzzle as to why the rating method should break down at the point that it allegedly does and the nature of the modern tests. For it is essential that we note, in regard to the tests, that the Stanford-Binet intelligence test on the one hand and the so-called

[13] Pearson (1919).
[14] Anastasi and Foley (1949), p. 320. Used by permission of The Macmillan Company.

Table 3

Temper: pairs of brothers (N = 1846)

first of pair	second of pair			
	quick	good-natured	sullen	TOTALS
quick	138.5	152.25	39.75	330.5
good-natured	152.25	1026.5	106.25	1285
sullen	39.75	106.25	84.5	230.5
TOTALS	330.5	1285	230.5	1846

Adapted from Pearson (1904), p. 188.

personality tests on the other have a different basis. The Stanford-Binet (and its derivatives) should agree pretty well with experienced teachers' ratings, because it was founded by Binet on school performance and teachers' estimates of intelligence. In a roundabout way, the modern intelligence tester is still relying on teachers' ratings. The so-called personality tests have no such origin: they are assemblies of items drawn from psychiatric files, theories of adjustment, and elsewhere, and they have not been systematically checked against teachers' ratings as the original Binet was. The discrepancy between certain results obtained by Pearson and results based on these personality tests must be admitted; but we need not therefore discount Pearson's results. It seems more proper to conclude that Pearson's raters and these tests disagree because they are not concerned with exactly the same things.

GENERAL RESULTS   Whatever one may think about the solution to the problem just discussed, the general outcome of Pearson's massive study is clear: The degree of resemblance between siblings is virtually the same for every trait considered, whether physical or psychological, whether impressionistically rated or measured with calipers.

Tables 2 and 3 are examples of the form in which Pearson cast the data for each of the traits. These are in effect correlation tables, and it is possible to calculate correlation coefficients from them by a method invented by Pearson himself. Table 2 compares the intellectual ability of one member of a pair of brothers with the other member. It happens at times that a quick-intelligent boy has a brother who is very dull; but more often, if one brother is quick-intelligent, so is the other. Likewise, in Table 3 we observe that there is a tendency for degrees of temper to go together in a pair of brothers, though the possession of a quick temper by one is by no means a guarantee that the same will be true of the other, for he may be good-natured or even sullen. Similar trends can be seen in the numerous other tables constructed by Pearson, comparing brother with brother, sister with sister, and brother with sister, on these and many other traits. Incidentally, it is worth noticing the large numbers of individuals represented in these tables.

Table 4 sums up the Pearson results. The correlation coefficient for trait after trait is in the neighborhood of .50. The physical traits are no more closely related than are psychic ones. And this, to Pearson's mind, was of tremendous significance; for, according to the logic of his argument quoted a few pages back, it means that

Table 4
Correlations between siblings in physical and psychical traits

	brothers	N (pairs)	sisters	N (pairs)	brother and sister	N (pairs)
health	.52	1918	.51	2037	.57	893
eye color	.54	2000	.52	2102	.53	832
hair color	.62	1984	.57	2134	.55	829
hair curliness	.50	2034	.52	1908	.52	659
cephalic index	.49	1982	.54	1936	.43	732
head length	.50	2114	.43	2002	.46	795
head breadth	.59	2120	.62	1880	.54	759
head height	.55	2114	.52	1846	.49	764
MEAN OF PHYSICAL TRAITS	.54		.53		.51	
vivacity	.47	1852	.43	2104	.49	752
assertiveness	.53	1572	.44	1700	.52	573
introspection	.59	1640	.47	1754	.63	657
popularity	.50	1626	.57	1674	.49	554
conscientiousness	.59	1690	.64	1752	.63	686
temper	.51	1846	.49	2152	.51	704
ability	.46	1868	.47	2014	.44	860
handwriting	.53	1862	.56	1566	.48	728
MEAN OF PSYCHICAL TRAITS	.52		.51		.52	

Adapted from Pearson (1904), pp. 154 f. and pp. 166-90.

psychological traits are as truly inherited, and as strongly inherited, as the physical traits. The reader may want to ponder over Table 4 and Pearson's argument a long time.

Light on nature-nurture from plant studies

Human passions get aroused by the nature-nurture controversy when the Mendelian laws or other genetic principles begin to be suspected of threatening our freedom to do just as we please educationally. For some purposes it is best to examine the problem where it does not seem to touch us so closely. Since plants are pleasantly remote from us but share in many of the same life processes, and since it was in plants that the Mendelian laws were first discovered and are still extensively investigated, we may be able to gain a useful perspective on the nature-nurture question by confining our attention to them for a few pages.

The power of the environment to modify inherited tendencies is not entirely a matter of learning, even in the case of the human being. There are many and extremely important immediate effects which are not usually brought under that head. For example, a change of atmospheric pressure or of the oxygen content of the air can influence mood and behavior radically. In this aeronautical and space age, this is a commonplace, and much scientific research time has been devoted to studying these effects precisely because air-pilots and space-men cannot ignore them. Doubtless we have hardly begun to understand our complex relations with the environment in this sense. We do not know, for instance, what may be the significance for human behavior of the fact that there is a regular daily rhythm of cosmic radiation and the electrical conductivity of the air, as well as the alternation of day and night, though careful investigators of bee behavior have thought it worth their while to take such variables into account.[15] Preoccupation with learning has somewhat blinded psychologists to the vital give-and-take between organism and environment which is continually going on in ways like those alluded to here. I particularly stress this point as we turn to consider the behavior of plants because there the situation is just the reverse: plant physiologists have closely examined the direct linkage between organism and environment while ignoring the question whether plants learn. The very idea of plants learning may seem absurd to them. One reason for this is

[15] Renner (1959).

that the definition of learning is often confounded with the notion that learning is a function of a highly developed nervous system —which is simply an example of that hasty confusion of explanation with fact, of the "Why?" with the "What?," discussed in the first chapter. If we define learning as a change in behavior altering an organism's previous relations with the environment, we can at least raise the question about plants as well as about earthworms and human beings. As in so many instances, our definition controls our question.

GROWTH AND SURVIVAL   What happens if plants of uniform heredity are raised in a uniform environment? They grow at a closely similar rate, develop the same form, attain the same height, and exhibit the same periodic changes. What else should we expect? Under the complete temperature and light control possible in such botanical laboratories as those at the California Institute of Technology, the variability of plants from the same genetic stock can be reduced almost to zero.[16] On the other hand, by varying the environment in certain ways the experimenter can cause plants of the same stock to vary over a wide range in morphology, behavior, and chemical constitution. This capacity of the plant to vary in the face of varying environmental conditions is a demonstration of the dynamic quality of hereditary factors, not a denial of them. Heredity sets limits to the kinds of environment which a plant can tolerate, and it sets a limit also to the range of reactions which it will exhibit under varying conditions. For each kind of plant there is an optimum combination of environmental factors, a combination permitting the fullest expression of the hereditary potential. Different kinds of plants have different optima. Went, who directs the California Institute of Technology plant laboratory writes:

> Actually the optima of some plants are so different that they cannot be grown together at all. The optimal temperatures for the African Violet are so high that the English Daisy dies in them, whereas the African Violet dies under the optimal growing conditions for the English Daisy.[17]

Seeds of the same stock planted in different natural environments react in widely different ways. In some environments they die; in others, they sprout but fail to develop properly. Within that range

[16] Went (1956).   [17] *Ibid.*, p. 387.

of environments in which the plants grow and flower and fruit, noticeable differences may still occur in size and form and in the time of flowering and fruiting, depending on the local conditions. On the other hand, plants of different stocks flourish in different degrees in any one environment. Everyone knows these facts.

An important consequence of these familiar facts is that under natural conditions of competition plants which are well suited to the environment by their genetic make-up reproduce at a greater rate than those which are not so well suited. To use Darwin's phrase, natural selection favors one variety over the others, and the result is that some varieties may disappear from a locality because of the competition even though they might be able to grow there well enough if cultivated alone. A contemporary American student of evolution, Stebbins, describes a field experiment which proves the reality and power of this process. The experiment was performed by Harlan and Martini and reported by them in 1938. Says Stebbins:

> In this experiment a mixture containing equal quantities of seed of eleven different commercial varieties of cultivated barley (*Hordeum vulgare*) was planted in each of ten different experiment stations located in various parts of the United States. The seeds were sown on field plots prepared under as nearly uniform cultural conditions as possible. At the end of each growing season, the mixed crop was harvested in bulk, the seeds were thoroughly mixed, random samples of 500 seeds each were extracted, sorted into varieties, and the number of seeds of each variety was counted. The remainder of the mixture was saved for planting in the following spring at the same rate as that of the preceding season. The length of the experiment varied from four to twelve years, depending on the locality.[18]

Table 5 gives a portion of the results. As it shows, at every experiment station one variety of barley came to dominate that locality.

LEARNING? Plants do not merely grow. Their growth, to be sure, is itself a form of behavior. It even has a goal-seeking character, as can be seen in the marked tendency of flowering plants to grow toward the light. But, besides that, there are various kinds of special adjustments which plants make to the daily variations in their environment. The leaflets of clover fold together every night and open up again every morning. Many blossoms open and close in reaction to changes of light and temperature and adjust their

[18] Stebbins (1950), pp. 109 f. Used by permission of the Columbia University Press.

Table 5

Survival of competing varieties of barley at different experiment stations

varieties	number of seeds per 500 after several years					
	ARLINGTON, VA. (4 YRS.)	ITHACA, N. Y. (12 YRS.)	ST. PAUL, MINN. (10 YRS.)	MOCCASIN, MONT. (12 YRS.)	MORO, ORE. (12 YRS.)	DAVIS, CALIF. (4 YRS.)
Coast and Trebi	446	57	83	87	6	362
Hannchen	4	34	305	19	4	34
White Smyrna	4	0	4	241	489	65
Manchuria	1	343	2	21	0	0
Gatami	13	9	15	58	0	1
Meloy	4	0	0	4	0	27

Adapted from Stebbins (1950), p. 110.

position to the position of the sun. The specialized leaves of the Venus's-flytrap snap shut on the luckless insects which come to rest on them and then digest their victims. Many other reactions to the environment could be cited.

Under natural conditions, plant movements appear to be appropriately tuned to the environment. So close is the harmony that one might suppose that the environmental control was absolute. As a matter of fact, periodic movements like the "sleep-movements" of leaves and blossoms are partially independent of environmental conditions, as can be experimentally shown. When the normal environmental rhythms of day and night and so on are artificially interrupted or changed, the plant does not necessarily alter its behavior at once. For example, in the case of the common dandelion, periodic floral movements which are normally correlated with temperature changes in the natural environment will go on regularly for several days after the plant has been put in an environment of unchanging temperature.[19] This might be likened either to inertia or to memory. Some of these persisting plant rhythms can be experimentally altered, but only within certain limits characteristic of the plant species. In such phenomena we have a marvelous opportunity to study the interaction of heredity and environment.

Some plants (like the Venus's-flytrap mentioned above) react swiftly and conspicuously to environmental stimuli, and some are quite selective as well as sensitive. The tendrils of *Passiflora gracilis* are extremely sensitive. Darwin tells us that they will react to "a

[19] Goldsmith and Hafenrichter (1932).

loop of soft thread weighing ⅟₃₂nd of a grain (2.02 mg.) placed most gently on the tip" by beginning within a few seconds to curl around it. And yet these same tendrils will fail to react in this way to other kinds of stimulation which are far stronger. Darwin reports that he

> placed several plants . . . so close together that their tendrils were repeatedly dragged over each other; but no curvature ensued. I likewise repeatedly flirted small drops of water from a brush on many tendrils, and syringed others so violently that the whole tendril was dashed about, but they never became curved. . . . Hence it is clear, that the tendrils either have become habituated to the touch of other tendrils and drops of rain, or that they were from the first rendered sensitive only to prolonged though excessively slight pressure of solid objects, with the exclusion of that from other tendrils.[20]

We do not know whether the first alternative proposed by Darwin, namely, that the plant becomes habituated (develops a habit by learning), is possible for plants. On the other hand, the more probable second alternative, i.e., that the plant's differential sensitivity is inherited, raises the interesting question whether the same type of explanation might not be applicable to certain human performances which psychologists are prone to ascribe to learning.

PLANTS AND HUMAN BEINGS   We have barely glanced at the fascinating topic of plant behavior, but perhaps enough to give meaning to some generalizations. The growth and movements of plants are characteristics based upon hereditary nature, and this includes the plant's ways of selecting and responding to environmental stimuli. No plant is infinitely adaptable. If its inherited characteristics of form and performance are very much out of harmony with its environment, or if it comes into competition with other plants better fitted to that environment, it does not flourish; it deals with its environment in its own variable but limited way, adapting to certain changes (perhaps even "learning") and resisting others, and if it fails to meet the conditions imposed, it perishes. The individual members of a species act somewhat alike, to the extent that environmental conditions can be found which no member of that species can endure, although the members of some other species may welcome them; but within the species limits there is always, of course, individual variety permitting some to survive while others of the same species droop and die.

[20] Darwin (1897), p. 156.

Biologically speaking, the rules seem to be very much the same for the human species. Neither any single human being nor the species entire is infinitely adaptable. Limits are set upon us genetically. For example, it is probable that some human individuals respond very poorly to a bringing-up which most other members of the species would be able to tolerate or even enjoy. This is all that one need imply when stressing the importance of heredity. To acknowledge so much is to acknowledge a good deal. One may go further, however. There is the possibility that various kinds of personal qualities and patterns of behavior characterizing the individual are primarily rooted in the genes.

It was Sir Francis Galton who, more than seventy-five years ago, began serious inquiries into human inheritance by the method of studying monozygotic twins. His results seemed to him to demand the conclusion that heredity is enormously powerful, whether it is a question of the likenesses or the differences between people. He summed up his position in the following words:

> There is no escape from the conclusion that nature prevails enormously over nurture when the differences of nurture do not exceed what is commonly to be found among persons of the same rank of society in the same country. My only fear is that my evidence seems to prove too much, and may be discredited on that account, as it seems contrary to all expectation that nurture should go for so little. But experience is often fallacious in ascribing great effects to trifling circumstances. Many a person has amused himself by throwing bits of stick into a tiny brook and watching their progress; how they are arrested, first by one chance obstacle, then by another; and again, how their onward course is facilitated by a combination of circumstances. He might ascribe much importance to each of these events, and think how largely the destiny of the stick has been governed by a series of trifling accidents. Nevertheless all the sticks succeed in passing down the current, and they travel, in the long run, at nearly the same rate. So it is with life, in respect to the several accidents which seem to have had a great effect upon our careers. The one element, which varies in different individuals, but is constant for each of them, is the natural tendency; it corresponds to the current in the stream, and inevitably asserts itself.[21]

These are strong words, and they run counter to a considerable flood of opinion and well-meant propaganda (and propaganda not so well-meant), but they are based upon a careful study of the

[21] Quoted in Pearson (1914), p. 8.

evidence available to a man who was, above everything else, an inquisitive, factually oriented scientist.

It is time that we cease regarding the nature-nurture problem as either a dead issue or a nuisance. It is not dead. A recent text in educational psychology by Cronbach cites with approval Shuttleworth's 1935 analysis of the relative contributions of nature and nurture to intelligence in these words: "One summary, with which most others agree fairly closely, is that the variation in tested intelligence among school children is accounted for

> 75 per cent by heredity
> 21 per cent by environment
> 4 per cent by accidental factors

Environment has an effect, but not so great as to wipe out hereditary advantages and disadvantages."[22] More recently still, a manuscript which refers to the nature-nurture controversy as one which is fast dying away states that as a practical measure it would be wise for a psychologist testing the intelligence of a preschool child to shade his estimate of its future intellectual standing in the direction of the general family level.[23] As long as the effects of heredity are acknowledged, the issue may be called dying; but it is not dead. Neither is it in that case a nuisance. In fact, the very fruitful work of the ethologists (students of the natural patterns of animal behavior) in recent years suggests that keeping nature in mind as we study nurture is one of the smartest things scientists can do.

Races

In the broad sense of the word, all men are brothers. That is to say, all human beings are related by ties of blood, all have a common ancestry. But there are degrees of kinship.

Resemblance tends to decrease the more distant the biological relationship. Two degrees of likeness occur in the children of one set of parents, and these two degrees are based on the simple biological factor of reproductive origin: (1) Twins originating in a single egg tend to correlate both physically and psychologically at around .90; (2) ordinary siblings and twins originating in separate eggs tend to correlate at around .50. If kinship is disregarded and individuals are drawn from a large population and paired off at random, the correlation drops toward zero.

[22] Cronbach (1954), p. 210.   [23] Bradway and Robinson (1961).

Put the matter another way. A community composed entirely of one's own brothers and sisters would appear much more uniform than is usually true of a town; and it would be still more uniform if all the individuals in it had been derived from a single fertilized egg, as would be possible by an extension of the assembly-line system of reproduction imagined by Aldous Huxley in *Brave New World.* Yet, in comparison with the human variety present in the world at large, even a great city is relatively homogeneous. The explanation lies to a considerable extent in the fact that the inhabitants of a city are biologically more akin than the total population of the globe. The homogeneity is further increased in appearance, of course, by the imposition of common styles of clothing and behavior by fashions and by learning, but this is an additional factor and not the fundamental one.

So we come to the subject of race. A city which was closed off from the rest of the world and remained so for generations would, in the course of time, by inbreeding and selection produce a distinctive class of human beings. If, in the meantime, catastrophes had destroyed the closest of their kindred in the external world, their distinctiveness would be even more marked and they might deserve to be called a race. The actual human races do not seem to have originated in quite this way, but isolation, inbreeding, and selective forces have evidently been involved in their formation, beginning at a time long before recorded history.

When we talk about races, the emphasis has to be on *group* characteristics rather than on the distinctiveness of every individual of the line. Since there is always wide variation within a race, some of its members may be enough like some of the members of other racial groups to slip unnoticed across the boundary.

Consider two groups differentiated chiefly by height. In both groups there would be a variety of individual heights around the group average, and a tall individual from the shorter group might slip over into the taller group as one of its short members; but as long as the groups remained apart, occupying different regions, they could be significantly described as the tall and the short groups. Such is the case with two African groups, the Pygmies of the Congo and the Dinkas of the White Nile. There are other differences between these two groups, but the height difference is conspicuous. In the samples diagramed in Figure 2 there is not any overlap at all between the tallest Pygmies and the shortest Dinkas. Preservation of such a difference depends upon the continued isola-

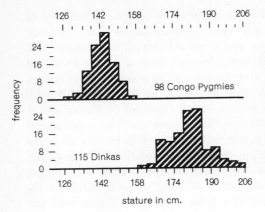

2 *Human groups living in similar environments may differ markedly and may maintain their differences by inbreeding. The graph shows the distribution of heights in samples of Congo Pygmies and White Nile Dinkas. (After Morant, 1939)*

tion of the two groups as breeding units. If they should intermarry extensively, the result would be a new sort of group having an intermediate average height, and the two original groups would simply disappear into the new blended group. This does not mean that the genetic factors responsible for height would disappear; they would still remain, but in new combinations.

THE ADAPTIVENESS OF RACE   The term "race" as used by biologists and anthropologists is applied to units of population larger than a single tribe and involves more than a lone differentiating trait such as height. Distinguishing between individual members of different races is often difficult in practice, partly because group rather than individual characteristics must be kept in mind, and partly because the comparison of races has been troubled by fierce emotions. From a scientific viewpoint, racial characteristics are simply genetic variations on one common human pattern—variations which have been useful in enabling mankind to penetrate into different environments and to survive. There is nothing in being white or black or yellow or brown which forthwith stamps the individual as either superior or inferior to the rest of the species. On the other hand, the possession by large numbers of people of such distinguishing traits is presumptive evidence that the traits have some positive value. It is this point which the present discussion is meant to emphasize.

Just as certain stocks of plants are better fitted to a given environment than are other stocks, so the races of men appear to be especially well fitted to their native habitats and often less well fitted to others. To be sure, the application of science may enable individuals and groups to overcome natural barriers, but all this is very recent in the long history of the species; and it needs to be added that scientific development itself puts a strain on many people and may become an important factor in the evolution of man. Already it is evident that atomic radiation is a cause of genetic mutation and may become a powerful selective force. But until the brief historical era of science, the creative ingenuity of man intervened between him and his natural environment only to a relatively minor degree. During this immeasurable length of time, the environment exerted a direct selective effect on whatever variations happened to appear. Any characteristic which promoted survival was an advantage likely to be preserved—not by human choice, but by environmental necessities. Such a characteristic is skin color.

The dark skin of the Negro is an advantage in the tropics where ultraviolet radiation is intense and where temperatures are high. If the whole earth had a tropical climate and there were no special man-made devices for warding off excess ultraviolet radiation, then in the course of time we should expect, on the principle of natural selection explained by Darwin, that those variants of the human species who possessed dark skins would survive and the others would perish or become distinctly subordinate in numbers and influence. The earth, however, provides climatic conditions of great variety, so that the advantages do not all run one way. Coon, Garn, and Birdsell comment:

> Dark skins obviously absorb more visible radiation than do lighter ones. If albino skin is rated as 1, then nearly 100 times as much radiation in the visible spectrum is absorbed, under strong light, by that of a blue-black Senegalese. But the invisible heat rays of the spectrum, the infrared, are absorbed equally by Blacks and Whites alike. On the other hand, the lack of pigment in the epidermal layers of the albino's skin or the very slight desposit in that of the fish-belly White allows the equally invisible ultraviolet rays, from the opposite end of the spectrum, to penetrate deeply. The pigmented layer in the Negro, however, acts as a filter, absorbing and degrading the ultraviolet so that far less of it gets through to the dermis and its vascular system. When it does penetrate, it severely damages the dermal papillae and inhibits subsequent regeneration of epidermis, thus leading to ulceration. Enough penetrates, however, to be used in the production of vitamin D. In the reduced light of our northern cities, the greater susceptibility of Negro children to rickets than in the case of Whites, may be more

than a dietary deficiency; physicians working on a clinical hunch feel that it may be due to the absorption of the insufficient (for the Negroes) amount of ultraviolet before it can irradiate the precursor of the vitamin in the epidermal layers. They think that what is good for Timbuktu is bad for Boston.[24]

In short, the dark skin of the Negro is positively adapted for the tropics, but negatively adapted for northern regions of reduced sunlight.

Just as there are racial adaptations to light and heat, there are racial adaptations to extreme cold. One of the coldest regions in the world is eastern Siberia. A temperature of 96 degrees below zero Fahrenheit has been recorded in this territory, and for long periods of the year the climatic conditions are intolerable for the white man. Here live the Tungus, members of the Mongoloid race. As explained by Coon, Garn, and Birdsell, there is reason to believe that their Mongoloid features developed under the selective pressure of the last Ice Age when their ancestors were cut off by glaciers from warmer regions and compelled to endure winters with temperatures of 80 to 90 degrees below zero. Presumably the rigors of such a climate eliminated those whose bodies were not adapted to prolonged intense cold, and gradually built up a population with special characteristics. Among these characteristics were thick-set bodies, flat faces, slitty eyes, coarse straight black hair, and scanty beards. Every one of these traits is an advantage in a cold climate. The thick-set bodies preserve heat because they present a minimum of skin surface in proportion to volume, the flat fat-padded faces ward off the cold which would quickly strike through to the bone of a sharper face such as one finds in Arabia, the heavy eyelids with their narrow openings protect the eyeballs from freezing, the coarse head hair collects ice less readily than fine or kinky hair would do, the scanty beards can be shaved or plucked with little inconvenience and offer no entangled web as heavy beards do for the congelation of breath moisture into a freezing ice pack.

If an engineer were to sit down with pencil and paper and try to figure out how to make over the face of an undifferentiated human being to meet the world's greatest cold, he could only end up with a blue-print of existing Mongoloid features. Three principles are in-

[24] Coon, Garn, and Birdsell (1950), pp. 51 f. Courtesy of Charles C. Thomas, Publisher, Springfield, Illinois.

3 *The face of this Mongoloid girl illustrates evolutionary adaptation to an extremely cold climate.*

Pictorial Press, Ltd.

volved: (1) reducing the surface area to a minimum, by flattening out as much as possible all protuberances; (2) padding the surface with fat, to prevent loss of body heat, just as in the case of the whale; and, (3) banking up the nasal passages to provide the maximum heat for the air on its way to the lungs.[25]

Such a well-engineered face is shown in Figure 3.

The differences between races are an expression of the same tendency to vary that accounts for individual differences. The human species is not absolutely homogeneous, absolutely uniform; and though we may ignore the differences for certain purposes, the recognition of both individual and racial differences is simple realism when it is a question of dealing with all the facts. These individual and racial differences are intimately bound up with adaptation to the environment. They are based upon genetic laws. They make possible—in fact, they make almost inevitable—the

[25] *Ibid.,* p. 71.

wide geographical dispersion, the division of labor and the complex relations between man and man which are features of human life on the earth.

The significance of heredity in the study of personality

The present chapter has dealt with heredity as a source of important human traits, both physical and psychological. It has tried to impress the reader not only with the reality of genetic factors but also with their dynamic quality, i.e., their capacity for interacting with the environment. Difficult as it may be, we must try to keep in mind a dual fact: that the genetic factors provide for the general direction and levels of development and at the same time provide for the organism's flexibility in a changing environment. To revert to Galton's analogy, the hereditary current has power and direction but it also shapes itself to the contours of the world around and changes those contours, as is true of the brook flowing in its channel.

Without being able to state what the precise limits are which a given genetic endowment places upon the development of an individual, we are able to state that there are limits, or certainly restraints. These limits or restraints affect both interests and abilities, both the direction of striving and the level of attainment. A few psychologists have tried to sketch out some features of the genetic ground plan for the human species. These efforts have not always been welcome. McDougall's attempt to list the major human instincts or native propensities and build a personality theory on this basis has not been popular in America. Yet instincts, or drives, or unconditioned reflexes, or other comparable terms, keep cropping up in various psychological theories to remind us that the notion of some kind of genetic patterning of behavior is a vital one. Personally, I am also dissatisfied with these lists; but I believe that we must recognize in some form the shaping power of the genetic factors for behavior as well as for morphological traits like the two-leggedness and one-headedness of the normal human body. One way of approaching this problem is to try to define the ordinary course of individual human life, the stages of development from conception to death. It is true that knowledge of the life cycle of a species does not cleanly separate the genetic contribution from the environmental contribution, but it does at least give us hints, and it helps us to assess the relative importance of the learning process as a modifier of behavior. It seems fairly clear that we can never have an adequate educational theory or an adequate learning theory unless our experiments take into account much more than they have in the past the logic of development within a given species, and also the fact of species differences. It matters profoundly, for instance, exactly *when* in the course of a human life a particular experience occurs. All educators seem to recognize this now when they talk about such things as "reading readiness."

In harmony with this line of thought, then, the next chapter will be devoted to a study of the human life cycle, as a continuation of our reflections on genetics, and as preparation for the two chapters on learning which follow.

References for chapter 2

Anastasi, A., and Foley, J. P., Jr. (1949) *Differential psychology.* New York: Macmillan.

Bradway, K. P., and Robinson, N. M. (1961) Significant I.Q. changes in twenty-five years. *Journal of Educational Psychology.* In press.

Burlingham, D. (1952) *Twins: a study of three pairs of identical twins.* New York: International Universities Press.

Coon, C. S., Garn, S. M., and Birdsell, J. B. (1950) *Races: a study of the problems of race formation in man.* Springfield, Ill.: Thomas.

Cronbach, L. J. (1954) *Educational psychology.* New York: Harcourt, Brace & World.

Darwin, C. (1897) *The movements and habits of climbing plants.* New York: Appleton.

Goldschmidt, R. B. (1952) *Understanding heredity: an introduction to genetics.* New York: Wiley.

Goldsmith, G. W., and Hafenrichter, A. L. (1932) *Anthokinetics: the physiology and ecology of floral movements.* Washington: The Carnegie Institution.

Kallmann, F. J. (1938) *The genetics of schizophrenia.* New York: Augustin.

Lindzey, G., Prince, B., and Wright, H. K. (1952) A study of facial asymmetry. *Journal of Personality,* 21, 68-84.

McCurdy, H. G. (1949) Experimental notes on the asymmetry of the human face. *Journal of Abnormal and Social Psychology,* 44, 42-46.

Morant, G. M. (1939) The use of statistical methods in the investigation of problems of classification in anthropology. *Biometrika,* 31, 72-98.

Newman, H. H. (1940) *Multiple human births.* New York: Doubleday, Doran.

————, Freeman, F. N., and Holzinger, K. J. (1937) *Twins: a study of heredity and environment*. Chicago: Univ. of Chicago Press.

Pearson, K. (1904) On the laws of inheritance in man. II. On the inheritance of the mental and moral characters in man, and its comparison with the inheritance of the physical characters. *Biometrika*, 3, 131-90.

———— (1914) *The life, letters and labours of Francis Galton*. Cambridge, Eng.: Cambridge Univ. Press. Vol. 1.

———— (1919) Inheritance of psychical characters. *Biometrika*, 12, 367-72.

Renner, M. (1959) The clock of the bees. *Natural History*, 68, 434-40.

Stebbins, C. L. (1950) *Variation and evolution in plants*. New York: Columbia Univ. Press.

Went, F. W. (1956) The role of environment in plant growth. *American Scientist*, 44, 378-98.

Williams, R. J. (1957) Standard human beings versus standard values. *Science*, 126, 453-54.

Wolff, W. (1933) The experimental study of forms of expression. *Character and Personality*, 2, 168-76.

———— (1943) *The expression of personality*. New York: Harper.

Woodworth, R. S. (1941) *Heredity and environment: a critical survey of recently published material on twins and foster children*. New York: Social Science Research Council.

3

THE LIFE CYCLE

Preview   *Like other living organisms, the human individual passes through a series of changes typical of the species. The life story which begins with the union of sperm and egg goes forward in a broadly predictable fashion until death. Though the human organism is constantly under the influence of the environment which sustains it, it is self-directed in its growth, both anatomically and behaviorally. Central trends in the species make possible such outlines of development as those of Gesell, Binet, Freud, Bühler, and others.*

The idea of the life cycle is a commonplace in biology. Individual plants and animals go through a succession of stages characteristic of the species. For some, these stages grade gently into the next; for others, the stages come and pass so abruptly that the plant or animal seems to change into a distinctly different individual. If you were not acquainted with the typical story of the butterfly, you would naturally regard the winged form and the caterpillar form as unrelated creatures. Yet these are simply stages in a series of events repeated over and over, generation after generation. Egg, caterpillar, hard-shelled pupa in a cocoon, the winged form that mates with another winged form, and the egg again—this is the life story of the butterfly as it has been unfolded millions upon millions of times since the origin of butterflies long ago in the Oligocene period. Rather, this is the naked outline. Most butterfly eggs do not live long enough to get past the beginning of the script; those that do are bound to the plot as long as they live, but with countless variations of detail in their roles which are left out of the generalized scenario. Each individual life is unique. Even if every individual followed exactly the same course as all others of the species, its life from its own point of view would be full of novelty.

The idea of a species-determined life cycle fits the human being as surely as it does the butterfly, the dandelion, the mushroom, the spirochete. An individual life is a short segment of the long spiral through time which constitutes the history of the species. Starting out (in many species) as a fertilized egg, the individual organism reaches a stage of maturity where it joins with another to produce another fertilized egg. (The sexual union which perpetuates the cycle may be passed by, of course; but this is usually by accident rather than by choice.) Immediately after this union or somewhat later, depending on species and sex, it completes its individual journey along a path tangential to that which it has initiated in the act of reproduction. Individual after individual lives a short while and dies; the species goes on for ages, until it too may cease to exist because the rate of reproduction has not kept ahead of the cataclysms and gradual processes which eliminate individuals. The terminus of death is implicit in the egg, and there is no escaping it.

"That's all the facts when you come to brass tacks," chants Sweeney to Doris, as he outlines to her the unadorned realities in T. S. Eliot's *Sweeney Agonistes*. In outline, the story that Sweeney tells is not only bare but depressing. Richer in detail but scarcely more reassuring is a passage from Shakespeare which has been so often quoted that the bright edge of it has been worn dull. It is the melancholy Jaques of *As You Like It* who speaks:

> All the world's a stage,
> And all the men and women merely players:
> They have their exits and their entrances;
> And one man in his time plays many parts,
> His acts being seven ages. At first the infant,
> Mewling and puking in the nurse's arms.
> And then the whining school-boy, with his satchel
> And shining morning face, creeping like snail
> Unwillingly to school. And then the lover,
> Sighing like furnace, with a woeful ballad
> Made to his mistress' eyebrow. Then a soldier,
> Full of strange oaths and bearded like the pard,
> Jealous in honor, sudden and quick in quarrel,
> Seeking the bubble reputation
> Even in the cannon's mouth. And then the justice,
> In fair round belly with good capon lined,
> With eyes severe and beard of formal cut,
> Full of wise saws and modern instances;
> And so he plays his part. The sixth age shifts
> Into the lean and slipper'd pantaloon,
> With spectacles on nose and pouch on side,
> His youthful hose, well saved, a world too wide
> For his shrunk shank; and his big manly voice,
> Turning again toward childish treble, pipes
> And whistles in his sound. Last scene of all,
> That ends this strange eventful history,
> Is second childishness and mere oblivion,
> Sans teeth, sans eyes, sans taste, sans everything.

Many a change has been rung upon this theme of the life cycle. It interests poets because they are involved in it along with all other men and women. It interests scientists because it expresses a natural law of organic development.

The prenatal period

Shakespeare's Jaques began his account of the human story at a very late point in time biologically speaking. The period before birth is full of significance. Heredity, represented by the genes, combines with the uterine environment to give an impetus and direction to the developing individual which will not die away till death itself intervenes.

THE EMBRYO   The drama of individual human existence begins with the union of an egg the size of a dot just barely visible to the naked eye and of a sperm so much smaller that it can only be seen with the aid of a microscope. The diameter of the spherical egg is about forty times greater than the head of the sperm at its widest. The sperm which unites with it is one among some 200,000,000 released in the fertilizing ejaculation. Its union with the egg shuts out all the others.

This fateful union normally takes place at the upper end of the Fallopian tube leading from the ovary into the uterus. The zygote, as the combined egg and sperm are called, immediately begins the processes of cell division. For several days it moves down the Fallopian tube on its journey to the uterus, developing as it travels. By the time it arrives at the uterine cavity it has become a cluster of numerous cells packed closely together within a pellucid outer covering, like a tiny mulberry encased in a globe of clear plastic. For several days more it lingers on the surface of the uterus, unattached as yet, its cells grouping themselves as well as dividing, until the embryo has become a hollow sphere of cells lined up along the bounding outer zone of clear gelatinous material. In one spot the cells are more numerous than elsewhere, forming a clump which is destined to be the organizing center of the complex body to come.

At about the tenth day from fertilization, implantation begins: the sphere of the embryo begins burrowing into the tissues of the uterine wall, which has been thickened and enriched by glandular secretions. Before this time the little living globe has probably been nourished by liquids poured out on the surface of the uterus; afterwards, soon after implantation has begun, it is completely embedded in the uterine tissue and sends out numerous branching cells, or villi, to penetrate this tissue as the roots of a plant penetrate the soil, and to absorb from it, as roots do, the nutriment required for further development. Before long the surface of the invading embryo and the mother's tissue surrounding it have formed a completely united special organ which eventually adheres to a large area of the uterus. This is the placenta. Through it oxygen and nourishment are received from the mother, and carbon dioxide and other wastes are excreted by the embryo, as long as the two are united.

A series of marvelous adjustments within the woman's body

prepare the uterus for the embedding of a fertilized egg. This preparation occurs every menstrual cycle even though the egg is unfertilized; once the egg is fertilized and finds a suitable place in the uterus to embed itself, the menstrual cycle is suspended. This timing is only a single instance out of millions of such arrangements in nature—some within organisms, some between them and their environments. Thus, at a certain moment of the year the blossoms of a certain plant will open to receive the visit of a particular kind of insect (the yucca flower and the yucca moth, for example).

Within another ten days or so of implantation the development of the embryo has proceeded so far that its minute primordial heart is beating and blood is circulating in the beginning arteries and veins. This early circulatory system is one example of the fact that from the start of its existence the organism is independent in the sense that it has its own boundaries and internal mechanisms and self-regulated rhythms. At the same time, it is dependent—in the sense that only within a suitable environment can it survive and flourish. The implanted embryo feeds on the maternal tissues, in particular on the maternal blood; but no particle of this blood enters the embryo. The blood of the mother transports to the boundaries of the embryo the necessary chemicals, and from this nourishing river the blood of the embryo takes what it needs and turns back through it the waste products of its metabolism.

There is reason to believe that with the very first cell-division after fertilization the general organization of the body has begun, the ground plan has been sketched in, determining the location of head and tail, right and left, front and back. This happens well before any bodily part can actually be distinguished. At two weeks what is called the "primitive streak" clearly marks out the axes of development, but the embryo at this stage is still without a definite head, or arms or legs, or internal organs; it is the shape of a tear —a very small tear, 1.5 mm. long. By the end of the third week or thereabouts when the first bit of a heart is beating, there is evidence of a brain, of eyes, of ears, of a lower jaw, and of a tail. Later, about the fifth week, the rudimentary buds of arms and legs begin to show. By the seventh week, when the length of the embryo from crown of the bowed head to incurved rump is some 17 mm., fingers and thumbs protrude slightly from each disc of a hand, and the discs of the feet are shaping up; the eyes and the ears and the mouth are distinctly sculptured; and, internally, the major organ systems have been roughed out. In a week or two more the sex of the embryo can be clearly determined.

It takes about two months, therefore, from the time of fertilization for the spherical egg with its diameter of .15 mm. to become a recognizable human body of definite sex, a miniature body measuring about 35 mm. (not quite an inch and a half) from crown to heel. During the remainder of the gestation period the increase of height averages about 1.5 mm. per day. If this rate of growth were maintained, the ten-year-old child would be twenty feet tall. But, rapid as it is, this rate of expansion is immensely slower than the rate during the first two months after conception. In spite of deceleration, weight increases six billion times from egg to full-term fetus. According to Patten, who is the chief source of the preceding summary, "Arey has made the arresting calculation that if the body weight continued to increase postnatally at the rate which prevailed *in utero,* 'the weight of the adult would be two millions of millions times that of the earth.' "[1] Nothing remotely like this happens, of course. The curve of growth for most people asymptotes, as the mathematicians like to say, somewhere between five and six-and-a-half feet or so and one and two hundred pounds or so.

SPEED OF DEVELOPMENT AND SELF-REGULATION   Two generalizations are worth making here. (1) In the first place, the embryo's speed of development in both size and complexity is enormous. Within a very short time, the original single cell becomes an organized collection of millions on millions of cells, each one of them the result of inherited chromosomal material brought together from egg and sperm and redivided countless times. Some go to make up the brain, some the teeth, some the bones, some the liver, and so on; and this immense diversification of structure is going on in preliminary fashion from the very beginning.

One of the really impressive discoveries of experimental embryology is that long before a region of a developing organism is formed into a definite organ, the cells of that region are assigned to their function. For example, if they are grafted into a different region, they continue to develop as they started out to do, so that, for example, an eye may be caused to grow in some inappropriate place like the back. If an injury occurs near the organizing primitive

[1] Patten (1947), p. 189.

streak of the tear-drop embryo (two weeks in the human), it will not remain harmlessly at that point as a skin injury in an adult would do, but will be displaced to that part of the body for which the injured region is destined and hence show up as a gross defect in the developed brain or eye or whatever it may be. In other words, what might be called a silent organization in the very young embryo becomes outspoken as the various organs emerge and develop over the succeeding months and years.

(2) The second generalization is that the developing organism is self-regulating, in the sense that it moves toward an adult form of limited size and with proportions typical of the species. The rapid expansion of the early period decelerates and a nearly steady state is reached at adulthood. The proliferation of various organs, also, is controlled; after a certain number and kind have been roughed out, further development consists largely in refining these.

So widespread and so impressive is this self-regulation of the growing organism that many thinkers, from Aristotle to the contemporary German biologist-philosopher Hans Driesch (famous for his work in experimental embryology), have concluded that each organism contains within itself its own patterns and its own goals. "Entelechy" is the word which Aristotle used and which Driesch revived to stand for this idea.[2] Broadly speaking, everybody admits this. It is as certain as anything can be that a human zygote will become a human adult, if allowed to develop, and not a giraffe; and this it does without obvious external guidance. Every organism stubbornly insists on being itself. As Walter de la Mare has remarked,

> It's a very odd thing—
> As odd as can be—
> That whatever Miss T. eats
> Turns into Miss T.[*]

FAILURES AND CRITICAL POINTS   The steady development from zygote to healthy newborn infant, is, of course, the ideal or optimum. Multitudes of eggs never become zygotes, multitudes of zygotes never become implanted in the uterus, multitudes of embryos are aborted long before their time of birth, and various monstrous or imperfect children are born, some of whom survive into adulthood and reproduce. It is estimated that 80 pregnancies in 100 end in the

[2] Driesch (1908).
[*] From Walter de la Mare, *Peacock Pie*, (New York: Holt, n.d.). Used by permission of the Literary Trustees of Walter de la Mare and The Society of Authors.

birth of normal babies. Of the 20 other conceptions, 7 are aborted; 1 is a full-term monster, and 12 have defects which tend toward monstrous development. Some of the viable monsters are known to be following their own peculiar inherited pattern. An example is the condition in which hands and feet are lacking at birth, the arms and the legs tapering into narrow stumps. In such cases, the genes themselves are at fault. Other monsters are due to some accident occurring at a critical point of development.

We shall return frequently to this important idea of critical points of development. Here we may take note of a special theory advanced by the American experimental biologist C. R. Stockard to explain faulty embryonic development.[3] His experimental animal was a small fish of the genus *Fundulus*. He discovered that it was not the *nature* of the disturbance from the environment but the *time* of its occurrence which was important in causing defects. Patten sums up:

> The effect which all the disturbing agents seemed to have in common was the power of slowing or stopping growth. Any effective treatment —whether it was a drop in temperature, a lowering of oxygen supply, or a deleterious alteration of the balance of the salts in the sea water— would exert this retarding action most strongly on whatever developmental process happened to be in a rapidly changing phase at the moment the treatment was applied. . . . According to Stockard's conception, the inhibiting action does not need to last long, for the center of accelerated activity shifts from one organ to another as development progresses, and if an organ fails to "take its tide at the full" and differentiate at the time of its transient metabolic dominance, it never can carry out fully the critical changes which should then have culminated.[4]

Patten regards this as a brilliant conception, but warns us that it cannot explain every case of developmental defect.

Birth

When the infant emerges at birth into his air-breathing existence he leaves behind a whole organic apparatus designed for life in the uterus and now quite useless. Up until birth the infant was enclosed in a fluid-filled sac which grew from the outer layer of cells of the embryo when it embedded itself, as a hollow sphere,

[3] Stockard (1921).
[4] Patten (1947), p. 231.

in the uterine tissues. At first the sphere was covered all over with a woolly tangle of villi; later the villi became concentrated on one side, and on this side the placenta developed as an extensive living disc clasping the uterine wall, while the remainder of the globe's surface expanded and became smooth and thin—to form the membranous sac within which the baby floated, anchored to the placenta by the life-giving umbilical cord. The baby's head bursts through this thin membrane as it passes out of the uterus and through the vagina into his new world of air and light. The umbilical cord is then severed, and after a few days only the curious whorl of the navel remains to mark his old mode of existence. His lifeline to the sustaining environment till birth was anatomical. It is now behavioral. He must breathe for oxygen, he must cry and suck and swallow for food.

Yet the newborn is not unprepared or even unpracticed in these activities. Some while before birth he was exercising spasmodically inside the uterus, with total body movements which the mother could easily feel and also with unobservable movements of the eyes, the mouth, and other limited segments. We know about these latter movements through the study of premature infants.

Arnold Gesell (1880-1961), on whose work these pages are based, gives a useful account of these matters. According to him, behavior develops by lawful, inner-determined sequences quite as much as anatomy does. He writes: "Environmental factors support, inflect, and modify; they do not generate the progressions of development, nor do they create detached entities of behavior. Every behavior form has its origin in a unitary total action system and is configured by the intrinsic dynamics of the organism as a whole."[5] Gesell has had his critics. They think that he carries the principle of the entelechy too far, and they question his research methods. Perhaps his strongest evidence relates to the prematurely born.

PREMATURE INFANTS Gesell states that the premature infant does not differ much from the full-term baby in its development, in spite of its early contact with the extra-uterine environment. A baby of seven lunar months (28 weeks) can survive out of the uterus if the environment behaves like a uterus by providing steady temperature, freedom from excessive light and sound, and protection from violent jarring, and if the difficult task of swallowing food is carefully assisted. Such an infant is only seven-tenths of the

[5] Gesell and Amatruda (1945), p. 105.

way through the ordinary course of prenatal life, can be held in the palm of one hand, is flaccid of body and wizened of face because of imperfect muscular development and lack of adipose; yet this infant, though so weak, can already perform the basic movements of breathing and swallowing and even crying (though the cry may be soundless) which are expected, in higher perfection, in the full-term baby. If kept in an incubator and fed by nose spoon and *gavage*, the premature infant gains strength as the days pass, and the rhythms of his movements and his waking and sleeping become more definite. By about eight lunar months he may show traces of satisfaction and annoyance, though without reference to the people around him.

By normal birth time—forty weeks—this incubator baby has the bodily and behavioral equipment of the full-term neonate. For a while he may even seem superior in these respects. But Gesell thinks we should make allowance for the shock of birth experienced by the normal neonate. As he sees it, we are comparing an infant who has been treated gently for two or three months with one who has just been squeezed through the birth canal, has perhaps suffered partial asphyxiation in the process, and has been anaesthetized by the drugs used to relieve the birth pains of the mother. A week later the initial adjustments have been made and the recent traumatic effects reduced enough to make the comparison more legitimate. At that time, when one has been in the world one week and the other two or three months, the more worldly-wise premature infant does not appear much in advance. Gesell admits a slight advantage for the prematurely born, here called "the fetal-infant." He writes:

The mature fetal-infant tends to function somewhat more smoothly. His homeostasis is more equable. Breathing is more regular, regurgitation less frequent, sucking more efficient. He is better adapted to his postnatal environments, internal and external. Visual and attentional behavior are also a little more advanced; he displays a passive sort of inspection, and evinces at times a vague, diffuse interest in visual impressions. He gives some heed to the human face. He seems a little more finished, more composed, more expert, and more efficacious than the neonate, who is only in the transitional stage to the same degree of competence. The neonate is by contrast less well organized, more unpredictable, more irritable, a little less responsive than the fetal-infant.[6]

[6] *Ibid.,* pp. 141 f.

In Gesell's opinion, very little of this apparent superiority can be attributed to the educational influence of the environment. He sees no real advantage in being born before term.

> Any behavioral differences which favor the mature fetal-infant are temporary and superficial. . . . The sequences of the growth cycle are not readily dislocated. The premature infant simply gives a slightly earlier prefigurement of what both infants will be when they reach the coequal age of 4 weeks.[7]

In short, the same principle of organic self-determination holds for the infant of prenatal age whether it remains inside the uterus shut away from the world or comes forth prematurely into an environment which is, theoretically, more stimulating. In either case, the infant requires oxygen and food, it must not be disturbed, and it proceeds to develop new behavior without needing or profiting much from training or encouragement.

Postnatal infancy and childhood

Study of the prenatal phase of the life cycle is mostly confined to anatomical matters. Relatively little can be said about behavior, not only because so much of it is beyond direct observation, but also because the behavior itself (aside from growth) is so tentative, nascent, half asleep. We might fancy that the prematurely born would display more of note, since it is exposed to all the goings-on of the external world. Apparently this is not the case. Whether inside or outside the uterus, the infant of prenatal age is far more vegetative than active; it is busy growing, it has little concern with environmental changes outside the incubator. As for experience, who can say? The embryo or fetus does not report its thoughts and feelings, if any; and the memories of existence within the womb which have been reported by a few adults have doubtful value. In general, the prenatal infant's reactions to definite stimulation—by stroking, flash of light, sound—appear to be mainly avoidant, a twitch or a wriggle tending to remove the infant from the source of annoyance. It behaves like a sleeper who resists being awakened. In fact, the infant is usually somnolent, with short spasms of activity quickly fading into torpor. This early behavior has little obvious pattern; in comparison with the anatomic picture, it is vague.

[7] *Ibid.,* p. 142.

ANATOMICAL DEVELOPMENT   Once the child is born, the study of behavior can begin in earnest. Partly this is because the vital relations with the environment are now behavioral; partly, because the behavior is more open to observation. It is not that behavior abruptly begins at birth. Even the zygote "behaves." To the behavior of the newborn the prenatal development leads by gradual steps. But it is true that when we speak of human behavior we usually have in mind what happens after birth.

Yet as we turn our attention more to behavior, we should not forget anatomy. Behavior is intricately involved with anatomy. Anatomical features are, in fact, somewhat predictive of future behavior, the male and female sex organs, for example. Even the ratio of shoulder width to hip width is related to the probability of an individual's becoming an athlete. And no doubt if we set ourselves to it, we might find many anatomical indicators of future personality in the newborn child.

Growth curves are familiar anatomical evidence that the course of human development is lawful. Height and weight tables constitute a time schedule which is reliable within a not unreasonable margin of error. Patten asserts that it is possible to estimate the age of embryos with considerable accuracy from tables and graphs constructed on the basis of a sample of measurements from embryos of known age. Figure 4 is an example.

Growth curves for the postnatal period are equally useful. Their usefulness is increased when certain differentiating factors such as sex and somatotype—bodily build (see Chapter 10)—are taken into account. Such graphs tell us that a general trend is present in the species which is sufficiently close to individual trends to furnish some knowledge of the individual case. To be sure, the graphs miss the actual individual at various points and in various ways, but this is partly because of faults in averaging the data. Thus it is known that there is a spurt of growth at puberty; this spurt will not show up in a graph which does not allow for the fact that puberty does not occur at the same chronological age for everyone. The time schedule is not so fixed that individual variation cannot occur. Every individual has his own, slightly different, schedule. But knowledge of variation could be worked into such graphs so that the general species schedule would more and more resemble the individual one. One of the facts which would have to be worked into the ideal growth curve would be the seasonal changes. The organism, for all its self-determination, is always in contact

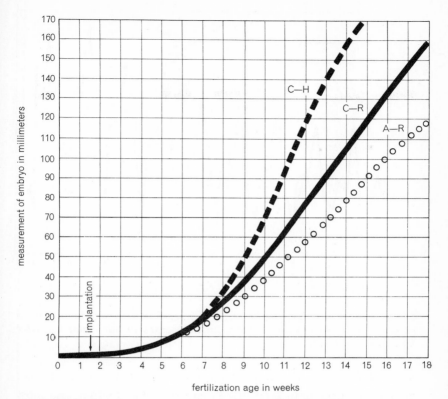

4 *Individual embryonic growth can be predicted with fair accuracy from average growth curves like these. The three lines represent three length measurements: crown to heel (C-H), crown to rump (C-R), and axilla to rump (A-R). (From B. M. Patten,* Human Embryology, *copyright 1947 by McGraw-Hill Book Co., Inc. Redrawn with permission of the publisher.)*

with the environment and responding to it in some manner. Figure 5, which is a graph showing the seasonal wave of increase in weight, illustrates a lawful periodicity based upon organism-environment relations of a type we are prone to overlook.

GENERAL BEHAVIORAL DEVELOPMENT   The systematic study of regularly emerging patterns of behavior has been somewhat neglected in comparison with other lines of behavioral research. This neglect is partly due to the strong environmentalist bias of modern psychology. But it is also due to the fact that adequate knowledge of behavioral sequences calls for continuous records

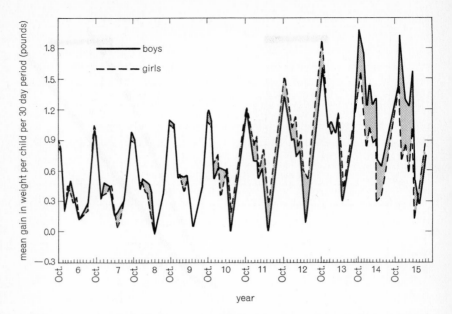

5 *Growth in childhood varies with the seasons. Increase in weight is greatest in October, least in May, for both sexes in our country. (After Shuttleworth, 1949)*

extending over long periods of time. Few psychologists have even gone to the trouble to keep diaries on their own children, and most of these diaries do not extend beyond the first several years. Dennis and Dennis, however, have summarized forty such records for the first year.[8]

The ideal method would be to follow a large number of individuals from birth to death. No single observer is capable of doing this. An elaborate organization would be required, perpetuated by careful recruitment and guided by great foresight. An intimation of the possibilities is furnished by the notable research of Terman and his associates on gifted children. After identifying and describing over 1500 children with very superior intelligence, the Terman group made periodic checks on their progress, and, in particular, two major reports on their status as adults twenty-five and thirty-five years later.[9] We might note, in passing, that Terman found good reason for concluding that the promise of childhood is

[8] Dennis and Dennis (1937).
[9] Terman and Oden (1947, 1959).

in general fulfilled in maturity. Important as this piece of research is, it falls short of the ideal of day-by-day or even year-by-year observation of development through entire lifetimes. Besides, it was designed more for the purpose of studying the persistency of intellectual gifts and their association with other personal qualities than for the purpose of tracing stages of development.

Longitudinal studies thus are rare. As a substitute we have cross-sectional studies—studies made of different sets of individuals at different ages—in which the results are combined by averaging and then treated as if they represented the course of events for a single average individual. To some extent, these cross-sectional results are supplemented by scattered longitudinal studies of one or a few individuals observed for some length of time. Even height and weight tables are constructed from cross-sectional data. Under the circumstances, any picture of the behavioral development of children must be regarded as a rough preliminary sketch. Nevertheless, we do know something—enough to lend credibility to the proposition that behavior unfolds according to an inherent plan. It must be granted, of course, that the existence of a behavioral plan does not tell us that development proceeds without reference to the environment. It may very well be that certain steady factors in the environment are exceedingly important, and that their experimental removal or alteration would have radical results. A later chapter will focus on this question. For the present, our theme is the usual course of development in more or less normal environments.

Maturation is the term usually applied to that aspect of development which is supposed to be independent of learning. Gesell, as already mentioned, thought of maturation as extending throughout life, though with diminishing power as age increased. The following outline covering the first five years is in Gesell's own words:

In the *first quarter* (4-16 weeks) of the first year the infant gains control of his twelve oculomotor muscles. In the *second quarter* (16-28 weeks) he comes into command of the muscles which support his head and move his arms. He reaches out for things. In the *third quarter* (28-40 weeks) he gains command of his trunk and hands. He sits. He grasps, transfers, and manipulates objects. In the *fourth quarter* (40-52 weeks) he extends command to his legs and feet; to his forefinger and thumb. He pokes and plucks. He stands upright. In the *second year* he walks and runs; articulates words and phrases; acquires bowel and bladder control; attains a rudimentary sense of personal identity and of personal possession. In the *third year* he speaks in sentences, using words as tools of thought. He shows a positive propensity to understand his environment and to comply with cultural commands. He is no longer a "mere" infant. In the *fourth year* he asks innumerable questions, perceives analogies, displays an active tendency to conceptualize and generalize. He is nearly self-dependent in routines of home life. At *five* he is well matured in motor control. He hops and skips. He talks without infantile articulation. He can narrate a long tale. He prefers associative play; he feels socialized pride in clothes and accomplishment. He is a self-assured, conforming citizen in his small world.[10]

Here is a crude scenario of development as it is acted out by child after child in our own and in foreign cultures. The rate is that of the average American child in the Gesell samples. It may be faster or slower in individual cases, but the logic of it, the sequence of the activities, is rather faithfully maintained.

The maturational view gains in importance when the observations of a number of independent workers agree, especially when the observations are scattered over thirty years of changing ideas as to proper baby care. Table 6, which is taken from Shirley's *The First Two Years*, compares certain items of behavior observed in a group of children and published by Shirley in 1931 with observations made on single babies and published by Shinn in 1899, Myers in 1922, and Fenton in 1925. This table shows how the sequence tends to run and what sort of variation may occur in individual cases. Shirley comments:

> In progress toward creeping and walking long-skirted Baby Shinn of the nineties traveled the same route at the same speed as did be-romped young Fenton of 1922, and as did the sun-suit clad babies of 1928. This is an interesting comment since Miss Shinn attributed the little girl's early awkwardness to her encumbering petticoats.[11]

Miss Shirley's comparison warns the doting parent that what may seem peculiar to the individual child or the circumstances of the moment may, in fact, represent a species trend.

An important longitudinal study covering the first fourteen months is that of Dennis who reared fraternal twins under conditions of minimal stimulation.[12] Although these children were not encouraged by their caretakers to practice various skills and were given an environment bare of everything but the necessities, their

[10] Gesell (1954), p. 339.   [11] Shirley (1931), pp. 182 f.
[12] Dennis (1941).

Table 6
Motor behavior of babies as recorded by different observers

age in weeks at first appearance of behavior

SHINN (1899)		MYERS (1922)		FENTON (1925)		SHIRLEY (1931) (MEDIAN OF 25 SUBJECTS)	
16	sit propped on lounge	16	sit on lap	14	sit propped on pillow	18.5	sit on lap
19	sprawl and wriggle	25	pivot on shoulders	21	make vigorous crawling movements	25	swim
26	roll	25	roll off blanket			29	roll
26	sit alone on floor	30	sit alone	17	sit alone	31	sit alone on floor 1 min.
32	get on hands and knees	32	get on hands and toes			38.5	"suspension bridge"
33	draw forward on stomach to reach toy; half-sprawl, half-creep			31	crawl 1 foot for toy	35	rock or pivot on stomach; some progress
35	creep backward by pushing with hands	41	creep backward	42	creep; as likely to go backward as forward	39.5	scoot backward pushing with hands
36	real creeping	42	creep forward well	43	scuttle ahead rapidly	44.5	creep
38	pull to stand	44	pull to stand in carriage	39	pull to stand in play-pen	45	pull to stand
41	lower self carefully from standing position	46	sit down easily when standing by person			47	sit from stand
45	stand alone	53	stand and squat			62	stand alone
50	walk alone	54	walk 15 feet	56	walk across room	64	walk alone

Adapted from Shirley (1931), pp. 184 f.

development proceeded through the familiar stages at a normal rate during the first nine months. There was some falling off later from the normal in such activities as standing, talking, and discriminating objects, where we might expect adult encouragement to be important or vital, but even some of this retardation might have been due to the infants' hereditary potential. One of them, it turned out, had received a cortical injury at birth; but even this had not disturbed the early phases of development. At four years of age, the injured twin had an IQ of 70; the other, an IQ of 107.

We must not forget that the motor sequences which we have been examining are accompanied by much else in the child's experience. Emotion, sometimes violent, is always present, but there is some evidence that maturation holds sway here, too. Differentiation of emotional capacity appears to follow a developmental scheme, as illustrated in the familiar diagram shown in Figure 7 on a later page. Furthermore, the child's emotional reaction to a given situation does not remain the same even though nothing startling has happened in connection with the situation. Gesell describes an experiment in which a child was placed in a small ventilated, illuminated, open-ended enclosure at different ages. Summing up the results with a number of children in terms of an average child, Gesell writes:

> At ten weeks he may accept the situation with complete complaisance; at twenty weeks he may betray a mild intolerance, a dissatisfaction, persistent head-turning and social seeking, which we may safely characterize as mild apprehension; at thirty weeks his tolerance to the same situation may be so vigorously expressed by crying that we describe the reaction as fear or fright. Here then are three gradations of response: First, no disquietude; second, mild disquietude; third, robust disquietude. Is not this a genetic gradation of fear behavior which is based upon maturational sequence rather than upon an historical sequence of extrinsic conditioning factors?[13]

Gesell's answer to his question may not be conclusive, but the question is well asked.

Let us turn now to two other aspects of child development which have received a good deal of psychological attention and which appear to have a maturational quality—intelligence and sex.

INTELLIGENCE   It was probably not the intention of Binet (1857-1911) to construct a developmental scale when he set out at the

[13] Gesell (1930), p. 290.

request of the French government to devise a convenient method for separating the dull children from the bright in the public school system. Nevertheless, this is what he wound up with.

We know that Binet wanted to grasp intelligence in its essence, and that the words in which he spoke of it did not imply that it was something which grew or was added to with the passage of time. In one place he said:

> There is in intelligence, it appears to us, a fundamental organ, any defect or alteration in which is of the greatest consequence to the practical life. This basic factor in intelligence is judgment, otherwise spoken of as good sense, practical judgment, initiative, the ability to adapt oneself. To judge well, to comprehend well, to reason well, these are the essentials of intelligence.[14]

By 1911, however, Binet had arrived at a test of intelligence not exactly conforming to this definition, a sort of inventory of performances arranged according to the age at which the normal child (or 75 per cent of normal children) could be expected to show them. The 1911 scale began operation with the third year and had five test items at each yearly level; but Binet had also experimented with items running back to the third month, where the single item was "shows visual coordination."[15] Binet's instrument, therefore, can be regarded as a sketchy developmental scale adjusted to the attainments of the average child. Many of its items seem to have nothing to do directly with judgment, either practical or abstract. All, however, may be brought under the rubric of the child's adaptation to his environment.

Now, Binet's scale was written in the French language and contains some strictly French details, but in translation and with some minor revisions it proved useful in the United States, where it appeared under Terman's auspices in 1916 as the "Stanford-Binet," and has continued (with revisions) to do service ever since as the dominant standard intelligence test. It has likewise penetrated many other countries. The logical deduction from these facts would seem to be that Binet discovered a fundamental behavioral sequence, largely maturational, applicable to all children in the broad framework of Western culture, and perhaps beyond. Obviously, the test is not free of the effects of learning. To count in *sous* or pennies it is necessary to become acquainted with them in the environment. On the other hand, it appears that the operation of counting (apart

[14] Quoted in Peterson (1925), pp. 170 f.   [15] *Ibid.*, esp. pp. 234 f.

from *what* is counted) is something which takes time to develop and which develops at about the same rate for children of many different nationalities using different coinage.

There are certain tribes of people who do not count very high even as adults. Is this a limitation imposed by the culture or does it reveal innate capacity? (Curiously enough, there are several species of birds which are able to solve problems involving a rudimentary number concept going up higher than these human tribes can count.[16]) Debate rages over such questions. Still, despite the difficulties of making cross-cultural comparisons, it seems clear that a Hottentot Binet could work out a scale that would apply within the boundaries of his own culture, and maybe beyond.

Binet's scale and its relatives are not always thought of as maturational outlines. They are thought of, rather, as precise measuring instruments, yielding an estimate of IQ. Many people are touchy about the IQ. A few are so equalitarian in their philosophy that they would like to change the tests so that they would no longer reveal IQ differences between socioeconomic strata. Certainly the IQ *stands* for an important value, whether it adequately represents it or not. It stands for power of thought. Aristotle was perhaps not speaking just for Aristotle when he said that a man is not truly a man unless he thinks. Insofar as IQ's do represent thinking power, we have a right to be concerned about them. But the relationship between IQ and power of thought is at best indirect. What the Binet type of scale *directly* shows is the path and rate of travel usually followed by a child growing toward maturity, in terms of certain performances which have a strong intellectual ingredient.

PSYCHOSEXUAL DEVELOPMENT   An organism is constantly changing. The changes often have a time order which seems typical of the species. These species trends are worth knowing, whether or not they are strictly genetic in origin, and they are of many varieties. One investigator, for instance, studies the rate of ossification of the human wrist bone and finds that it can be expressed in a pleasing curve. Another studies the increasing ability of children to spell the word "transfer" as they go up through the grades and works out an equally pleasing curve for that—one resembling the curve for ossification of the wrist bone, as you can see in Figure 6, A and B. Another, tackling a question which cannot be answered in quite the

[16] Thorpe (1956), pp. 340-49.

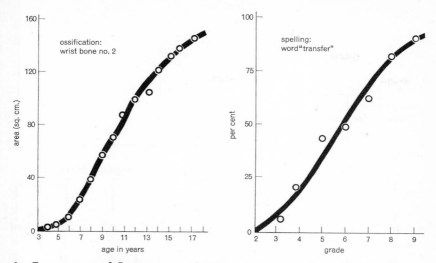

6 *Processes as different as ossification of the wrist bone and learning to spell "transfer" follow a sigmoid growth curve. (After McGraw, 1946)*

same terms, finds that the various emotions emerge from an original undifferentiated state and branch off from one another in orderly succession, as shown in Figure 7. In all such results the implication is that there is a natural order or rate or process, a developmental law, characteristic of the species or even transcending the species. Thus, both the sigmoid curves illustrated in Figure 6 and the branching diagram of Figure 7 have exceedingly wide application in describing growth tendencies of various kinds in a great variety of organisms and aggregates of organisms.

Freud (1856-1939) was likewise looking for order and law in nature when he tried to sketch out the stages of psychosexual development. He evolved his scheme of development at a time when there was some doubt whether children had a sexual life at all, and it is one of the aspects of his thought which has been severely criticized, especially by those who do not like to acknowledge biological and genetic factors in human life. Imperfect as it may be, this developmental scheme is one which we must know if we are to appreciate Freud's views on the nature of man. It, too, is based on a maturational way of looking at things.

Freud's psychosexual scheme involves both bodily regions and social relations and depends on a broad definition of sex. For Freud, any bodily pleasure is sexual pleasure—at least insofar as it is

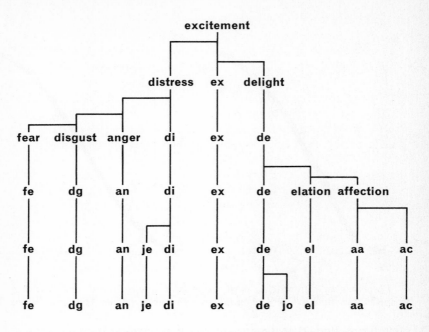

key: aa—affection for adults; ac—affection for children; an—anger; de—delight; dg—disgust; di—distress; el—elation; ex—excitement; fe—fear; je—jealousy; jo—joy

7 *Various kinds of differentiation (in this case, emotional development in childhood) can be represented by a branching diagram. (After Bridges, 1932)*

aroused by stimulation of certain areas which he calls *erogenous zones*. These zones may be stimulated variously but are especially responsive to certain situations and certain objects. In the course of growing up, a child experiences all the kinds of sexual excitation and forms attachments to favorite love-objects. The natural tendency of the little boy is to turn to the mother; of the little girl, to turn to the father. Such heterosexual attachment, of which the relations with mother and father are the first indication, is not perfectly inevitable and may be disturbed in various ways; but it is the biological norm, and in the adult it leads to reproductive union with a suitable member of the opposite sex. Social custom supports this tendency on the whole but does not create it. On the contrary, it is the existence of the sexual tendency, with its numerous vagaries, which gives rise to important aspects of a society's culture, which act back upon the individual with sexual incitements and prohibitions of a most far-reaching kind.[17]

The earliest of the Freudian erogenous zones is the mouth. The whole surface of the infant's body is sensitive, of course; but it is particularly the mouth, in the newborn, which receives and is prepared to receive the maximum sensory pleasure. Sucking provides not only the requisite nourishment but, according to Freud, important amounts of sensual stimulation. There are times when the infant does not suck for nourishment at all, but for sheer pleasure. For both survival and pleasure, then, the mouth of the young infant is a major center of activity. Freud therefore calls this the oral period, the period dominated by the oral erogenous zone. There are two reasons for fitting this oral period into the sexual sequences. In the first place, the quality and the intensity of the pleasure which the infant seems to experience resemble, in Freud's eyes, the quality and intensity of adult sexual pleasure in the act of intercourse itself. In the second place, the oral play of the infant resembles similar activities which are unquestionably a part of the adult sexual pattern—the erotic kissing and sucking and biting of courtship. A continuity exists between the orality of the young child and the erotic orality of the adult.

The dominance of the mouth as the zone of pleasure is gradually yielded to other areas of the body. During the period when control of the bowel is beginning to be established, and for some time thereafter, the child shows intense interest in the anal region and derives unmistakable pleasure from it. Around this region and its functions are developed various activities which are socially directed, and self-consciously so. Anal behavior is not only a source of immediate body pleasure, but it is also a means of pleasing or displeasing, of amusing or gratifying or annoying or injuring others, primarily mother and father. Once again, Freud notes a resemblance between the quality and intensity of anal experiences on the one hand and adult sexual pleasure on the other, and he locates here the origin of many adult sexual practices which are frowned on by our society as abnormal and perverse; for the perversity of the adult is a continuation or sharpening up of normal behavior in the child. This, then, is what Freud calls the anal period of development.

The center of chief excitation then shifts to the urethral zone,

[17] My summary here is a free translation of all my reading of Freud. But the most pertinent reference is his "Three essays on the theory of sexuality," which appeared in 1905.

which comes under full control later than the bowel; and in the act of urination, and in the thoughts and feelings and imaginations which cluster around this act, the child discovers a new source of pleasure similar to the previous ones. The pleasure centering in the urethral zone has social outlets, too. The child takes delight, for instance, in offering to urinate on others, and often does so. There is strong pleasure, with an aggressive tinge, in this act. Excitement full of daring and a sense of power accompany it, and the male is carried by it to the very brink of explicit sexuality. A significant bond between this childhood eroticism and the eroticism of the adult male is found in those common male dreams of urination which end in seminal discharge. Urination and seminal ejaculation are closely linked, anatomically, sensorially, and imaginatively. There is reason, then, for designating a period of urethral eroticism, under the dominance of the urethra and urinary activities.

The step from this to full genital activity is prolonged. There is an early stage, developing directly out of the period of urethral eroticism, which Freud calls the phallic, because, though the child is not yet ready for reproduction, the genitals are frankly involved in his pleasure. The phallic period is marked by much sexual curiosity and by sexual exploration and sexual display. But ordinarily, the sexual knowledge remains incomplete (not simply because information is not given, but also because the child cannot accept it), and the sexual activities fall short of intercourse, or, if intercourse does perchance occur, it does not lead to reproduction. It is because of this incompleteness that Freud calls the period "phallic" rather than "genital," since the latter term is reserved for the mature sexuality of the adult. After the phallic stage is reached, there supervenes a period during which no new developments take place, and during which some of the previous erotic interest of the child may undergo repression and be overlaid by various concealments or denials, particularly in our society. This quiescent, repressive period Freud calls the period of sexual latency. Puberty is a turning point. The upsurge of the sexual endocrines and the maturing of the sexual organs bring a renewed, more urgent interest in sexual matters. Under favorable conditions, the young person then moves on to full adult sexuality leading to reproductive union and the establishment of a family.

This bare outline does scant justice to the complexities and subtleties of sexual development as viewed by Freud. Only a few words of comment will be added here, however, since later chapters will deal with his ideas more extensively.

The child's sexuality is not that of the adult even for Freud. It is preliminary to adult sexuality, but it is diffuse, imperfectly channeled, uncertain of the final sexual object, incapable of true reproductive activity. The budding young man or woman of four or five years may in fact have to renounce his or her sexuality in part, exactly because it is incomplete. The little girl has to put off having a baby of her own, no matter how vividly her imagination may play with the idea of having it at once; the little boy cannot actually take his father's place as master of the house, even though he puts on his father's hat and shoes and clomps about as noisily as possible. The boy cannot marry his mother, and the girl cannot marry her father, after all. In fact, there are many temporary attachments which, precious as they are for the time, have to be surrendered by the child in the interests of growing up. The dolls that are almost babies, the guns that are shining phallic symbols, and many fantastic dreams, also, have to be renounced. Adult sexuality is a goal toward which the growing child moves semiconsciously, by imaginative steps which are both too big and too little, through stages prepared by the shifting physiology of the body and the social attachments necessarily formed in the course of expressing oral, anal, urethral, phallic, and genital impulses, in the context of innumerable interactions with real people, large and small, young and old. The child's sexuality is rooted in the body, shifting from zone to zone but never leaving any zone entirely out; it flowers in the social relations with mother and father, sister and brother, and the relatives and strangers outside the immediate household.

Freud's conception of sex is not the narrowly limited kind which can be adequately expressed in a few anatomical diagrams, a lecture on venereal disease, and some cynical or sentimental remarks on marriage. It is very down-to-earth and does not hesitate to call bodily organs and functions by their right names, but it has a poetic grandeur, too, which has offended some pedantic critics. Freud eventually named the sexual principle Eros, recalling an ancient god, and declared like Empedocles that it was the principle which held the universe together, the creative principle which gives rise to everything positive. Though he dealt with sex as a scientist, he was aware that it is a power such as the poet Lucretius celebrated in his magnificent invocation of Venus in *De Rerum Natura*. The scope of Freud's concept reminds one of the various meanings attached to Venus's name in Roman religion.

In her sway over the productivity of the fields Venus was associated with Priapus; in the springtime with its flowers she was sacrificed to by young maidens; in war she was Victrix; in peace, Concordia and Conciliatrix; on the sea she was Marina; as Libentina (Lubentina) she was the goddess of desires; as Libitina, goddess of death; and as Genetrix, the founder of families.[18]

Sexual maturity and the later years

Biologically speaking, the crest of life is reached on the arrival of sexual maturity. In the human species, this is the time of greatest physical vigor and beauty, the time of rapidly expanding mental horizons, the time of romance and the fulfillment of the reproductive cycle which leads from fertilized egg to fertilized egg in perpetual recurrence. Just as, comparatively, the childhood of man is prolonged, so is the reproductive period. Moreover, its continuity is not interrupted by the seasonal waning typical of most animals.

Many species of animals have only one brief sexual season. Over a river some evening of late spring or early summer you may notice thousands of pale green insects with filmy wings rising and falling in swarms. These are the ephemerids. A type of insect that lives as a worm for many months and then emerges as this delicate creature, the ephemerid exists in the winged form only to reproduce; it does not even have a mouth with which to feed; it lives for a few hours to mate and lay its eggs, and then it dies. Other insects have a sexual period equally brief. The female black widow spider kills her mate and feeds on him immediately after he has accomplished her impregnation. The male bee, which out of the whole swarm of males pursuing the queen female into the upper air succeeds in uniting with her, is destroyed by the sexual act itself. On the whole, the female is more essential for the perpetuation of the species than the male. Even in the human reproductive scheme, though there is ordinarily cooperation between the mates in rearing the young, the woman is still the central and indispensable pivot of the family.

Human civilization, according to some concepts, obscures the sexual roles of the mature man and woman by its conventions. It might

[18] Murray (1875), p. 152.

be more correct to say that human sexuality expresses itself more diffusely than nonhuman sexuality. The various ceremonies and legal codes relating to human sexual intercourse are not so much restraints and disguises as they are manifestations on the intellectual plane of the biological imperative, just as natural courtship, which may take an elaborate form even in birds, is not to be regarded as a delaying action but rather as a vital preliminary to the reproductive union. Social conventions are outworks of the sexual fact; among other things, they secure some protection for the woman, who is more defenceless against male sexual violence than other primate females. Note, however, that rape is not the normal pattern of any primate sexual relations. Usually there is mutuality in the sexual relations of monkeys or apes, a harmonization of sexual readiness in the two sexes, and even a primitive courtesy—as when the male permits the female to take food before himself. In the human case, the arrival of sexual maturity often brings exalted emotions and a flowering of chivalry and imagination. In short, mature human sexuality expands in every direction, shaping and lighting up the body, expressing itself in poetry and music, contributing to the social formalities from the debutante ball to the legal code.

Instead of attempting here a summary of human sexual experience and behavior—an inexhaustible theme—I shall mention a few characteristics of our distant cousins, the chimpanzees, in order to provide a little biological background for the human story.

CHIMPANZEE AND MAN   Robert M. Yerkes has furnished an authoritative, readable account of chimpanzee life as observed in captivity.[19] He tells us that the normal life span of the chimpanzee is probably shorter than man's. The age of puberty in both sexes is earlier. The female's first menstruation occurs at about nine years, with considerable variation around that average. The male's first seminal emission is harder to determine, but at a guess it would be at about the same age. The physiological changes thus initiated require some time for completion. Maturity does not arrive all at once. Neither in chimpanzee nor man is reproductive capacity reached at first ovulation or sperm production. For an indefinite period, sexual unripeness marks adolescence in both species. Yerkes notes that the transition is more unsettling for the female than for the male among the chimpanzees.

[19] Yerkes (1943).

For some months, or even for a year or two, before the onset of puberty, the female chimpanzee who had previously been of good disposition and dependable, friendly, and coöperative, may become mean and unpredictable. She may even seem like a different individual temperamentally, and there may be difficulty in feeding and keeping her in healthy, growing condition because of vagaries of appetite and also a tendency toward depression. Social antagonisms, contrariness, and wilfulness may appear, and the animal may be difficult to get on with either as experimental subject or as pet. Although this transformation of disposition may manifest itself for months or years, ordinarily the original traits reassert themselves after the individual has become sexually mature or has experienced a normal reproductive cycle.[20]

(A similar disturbance has been noted in pubescent girls.[21]) In contrast, the male chimpanzee passes through this period with little alteration of behavior except on the strictly sexual side. Masturbation begins in childhood and becomes more frequent at puberty; it is more common in the male than in the female but in both sexes tends to disappear when opportunities for intercourse are presented.

The sexual life of the female chimpanzee proceeds in regular menstrual cycles, unless interrupted by pregnancy. There is nothing exactly comparable in the male. The outward signs of the female cycle are unmistakable. A notable enlargement of the genital region occurs during the receptive phase. This reaches a maximum about midway of the thirty-five day period from one menstrual flow to the next. Very significant is the fact that the genital swelling coincides with ovulation and that the female is then sexually receptive. The biological design clearly favors intercourse at the moment of fertility.

Courtship in the chimpanzee is usually not elaborate, but there does occur a game of pursuit which becomes more rapid and excited until the female crouches or flattens out on the ground to receive the male. Copulation, accompanied by numerous pelvic thrusts, is brief. Within some ten seconds the male is finished, and the female rushes away. Repeated copulations are common, however, when the female is in heat. As Yerkes remarks, this assures the presence of fresh sperm at the moment of ovulation.

There are many points of similarity between chimpanzee and human menstrual cycles. Indeed, evidence exists that women, in spite of the modifying influences of civilization, are more sexually recep-

[20] *Ibid.*, p. 58. Used by permission of the Yale University Press.
[21] Tryon (1939).

tive around ovulation than at other times, though the desire to avoid pregnancy may interfere with recognition of the fact. Data published by McCance and associates, as summarized in Figure 8, indicate a peak of both sexual feeling and intercourse at that time. In this connection, it may be recalled that ancient Jewish law supported the biological tendency by forbidding intercourse during the menstrual flow and for a week after its cessation. Since this law could hardly have been founded on direct knowledge of the ovulation cycle, it may have been derived from the natural rhythm of desire in women themselves. In the fifteenth chapter of Leviticus, beginning at the nineteenth verse, we read: "And if a woman have an issue, and her issue in her flesh be blood, she shall be put apart seven days: and whosoever toucheth her shall be unclean until the even. . . . And if any man lie with her at all, and her flowers be upon him, he shall be unclean seven days; and all the bed whereon he lieth shall be unclean. . . . But if she be cleansed of her issue, then she shall number to herself seven days, and after that she shall be clean. And on the eighth day she shall take unto her two turtles, or two young pigeons, and bring them unto the priest, to the door of the tabernacle of the congregation. And the priest shall offer the one for a sin offering, and the other

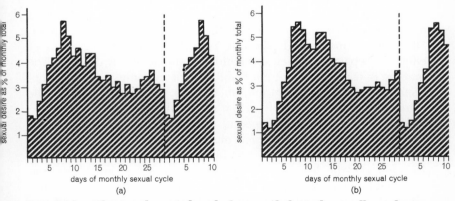

8 a and b   *The female sexual cycle has psychological as well as physiological aspects. These graphs, based upon numerous instances of strong sexual feeling or intercourse as recorded by women keeping sexual diaries, show a monthly pattern much the same for (a) single women (1246 diary entries) as for (b) married women (1618 diary entries). In both samples the peak day (about 5.6% of the diary entries) is the eighth after the onset of menstruation and the percentage stays above average (3.6%) until past the time of ovulation. (After McCance et al., 1937)*

for a burnt offering; and the priest shall make an atonement for her before the Lord for the issue of her uncleanness." Incidentally, we see in this passage how the fundamentals of human biology may be linked through law and ceremony to the highest expressions of a culture.

The maternal behavior of the chimpanzee resembles the human mother's in many respects and seems to gain from experience. "As soon as the infant has emerged from her body," writes Yerkes,

> the experienced mother, unless disturbed or distracted by happenings about her, gives her attention chiefly to it. She places it on her abdomen or breast and lets it cling to her. From time to time she handles it gently and freely and moves it about. Presently she cleans it by the typical grooming procedure. By contrast, the inexperienced mother, isolated from adult companions at the time of parturition, may act as if afraid of her first-born and refuse to touch it or to allow it to cling to her. Curiosity usually prevails in the end, and she either pokes at it exploringly, with fingers, straws, or sticks, or moves it about tentatively, but without letting it hold on to her and with no effort to clean, nurse, or otherwise care for it. Whether in nature a mother ever abandons her first-born and lets it perish from neglect or rough treatment is doubtful.[22]

Normally, the attachment between chimpanzee mother and child becomes intense and continues so for about two years, the mother caring for and training the child, the child clinging to the mother. Some of the most vivid pages in Yerkes' book are descriptions of efforts to separate mother and child. The maneuver is difficult. The mother is usually on the alert and full of cunning, and her emotional reaction to separation, if it does occur, is violent. The chimpanzee father has little or nothing to do with his offspring.

According to Yerkes, the period of chimpanzee life which holds the most charm for the human observer is childhood. The young ape is playful, affectionate, sociable, full of curiosity and tricks. In adulthood he becomes more serious, irritable, slow, less companionable, more self-centered. "These changes are somewhat more obvious in the male than in the female, probably because of her long-continued and intensive preoccupation with the youngsters of the family and the more varied demands for social services which are made on her."[23]

The parallels between man and chimpanzee brought out in this brief résumé are meant to underline the proposition that a bio-

[22] Yerkes (1943), p. 68.   [23] *Ibid.*, p. 60.

logical pattern runs through the human life history. Man and chimpanzee are far from being the same. But as living creatures, as mammals, and as primates, they share in certain qualities and sequences as inevitably as the earth circles around the sun. Human culture does not create these facts; it elaborates on them.

STAGES IN HUMAN LIFE   Apparently, the habit of keeping the whole course of human life in view when considering any psychological topic is not usual in America or elsewhere. At any rate, Pressey and Kuhlen, who favor this attitude, state that in 1939 they believed that their volume, *Life: A Psychological Survey,* was unique in "covering the life span with emphasis on the adult and older years,"[24] and that the texts which have since dealt with the life span have "tended to minimize development and change past 20."[25] In the meantime, a good deal of work has appeared which provides detail on the later years and makes it all the more obvious that development does not cease at about the age of graduation from college. Indeed, it might be said that some of the most significant human experiences belong primarily in the years of maturity and old age, and it is an oddly truncated view of human life which leaves them out. For a consistent life span approach, Pressey and Kuhlen's new volume, *Psychological Development Through the Life Span,* is recommended. It is packed with interesting detail.

Here there is only space to refer to a single study, a project started in Vienna under Charlotte Bühler a number of years ago and left incomplete, probably because of the political disturbances of those years. The investigators employed biographies and interviews to obtain information on three classes of facts: the external events of life, the subjective reactions to these events, and major accomplishments and productions. I rely on Frenkel-Brunswik's article for the following summary.[26]

The Bühler group found that the curve of life could be satisfactorily marked off into five phases: (1) birth to the stage of sexual potency at about 15; (2) the next ten years of continuing growth to the height of mature vigor at about 25; (3) the plateau period of maturity up to about 45; (4) a period of decreasing vigor leading to cessation or near-cessation of reproductive potency at about 55 (in the male); and (5) the terminal decline to death. Incidentally, this is the same scheme that we get from Shakespeare's Jaques if

[24] Pressey and Kuhlen (1957), p. xxi.   [25] *Ibid.*
[26] Frenkel (1936).

we condense the puling infant and whining schoolboy into phase 1, and the age of the slippered pantaloon and the empty husk at the end into phase 5.

The curve of life ascends, levels off, and descends; the ascent is cut across by the critical fact of the attainment of sexual potency, the descent by its loss. This curve is paralleled by corresponding facts of behavior, experience, and accomplishment.

Behaviorally speaking, phase 1 is marked by dependency on the home and the school. Shortly after the beginning of phase 2, the youth turns away from home to occupations and personal attachments of his own choice. During this period the activities have an expansive and preparatory character. Between 26 and 30 years of age, after the beginning of phase 3, a definite occupation is chosen and a home established, and the behavioral period thus begun continues slightly beyond the termination of the plateau of biological maturity: this is the period of greatest variety and fruitfulness of work, and the most wide-ranging social contacts. During biological phase 4 there begins, at around 48 or 49 years of age, a restriction of activities and social contacts (important relatives and friends die), and more taxing occupations are surrendered in favor of quieter ones or even complete retirement from regular work; the unrest of adolescence may return, interests become more diffuse, and work formerly valued may be destroyed or depreciated. The decline beginning in phase 4 becomes more pronounced in phase 5, though critical illnesses and other sharply restrictive events may not be definite in their effects until about age 64. The authors of these studies note that there is a tendency for important turning points in the behavioral history to lag behind the biological turnings, and increasingly so as age advances. Their explanation is that the declining biological attributes of strength and speed and energy are partly compensated for by accumulations of skill and knowledge and wisdom in the later phases.

Subjectively, too, the biological curve and its turning points seem to be important. Biographies of famous people and interviews with common workmen alike revealed that during the period of biological ascent there is a general expansiveness and during the period of descent a general retrenchment. But perhaps the most distinctively *human* phenomenon in the adolescent phase is the self-questioning about the purpose of life in general and one's own life in particular. For some individuals this search for meaning is a temporary ruffling of the biological pattern; for others, it is the consuming passion of a whole lifetime. This adolescent questioning may come back with renewed force at the other sexual turning point, often assuming the form, "What *has* my life been worth?" Concern with religion, which may have occupied the adolescent, can again become prominent.

Frenkel-Brunswik and Weisskopf made a special study of the evaluation of wishes and duties by people of various ages from 15 to 80. They found a tendency for wishes to predominate over duties in the early period, but to yield more and more to dutifulness as age advanced. Furthermore, the wishes of older persons were found to be less restricted to their immediate environment and personal advantage, tending to reach out to society at large or at least to their families. The shift from egotistical need-involvement to a sense of duty to society is illustrated by the contrast between the money-making youth and middle age of Andrew Carnegie and the philanthropy of his later years—a change initiated by a questioning of himself and doubts as to the value of his career.

Tolstoy is another example of values changing as life advances, Frenkel-Brunswik writes:

> We meet him first as an officer, enjoying a licentious existence and making only temporary ties. Whatever work he does during this time is not planned. At one time he is occupied with one thing, at another time with something else. In the third phase of his life he is still vitally interested in life itself, even though his life had already taken a definite course. He is married and lives on his estates, enjoying his bodily prowess in such activities as hunting and other outdoor life. In this period, also, he writes his great novels. However, one day, when he is fifty years old, he is overcome by a fit of depression. He finds life meaningless, it has lost its power to intoxicate him, and it is necessary for him to fight against a strong impulse to commit suicide. He himself stressed the fact that to the same degree that he earlier strove toward life and experience, in that degree he now strove away from life. He first found a meaning in life again through absorption in religion.[27]

As any mature person will feel, or any young person who has read many biographies, this story of Tolstoy and all those others abstractly summed up by the Vienna psychologists have a familiar ring about them. What is borne in upon us is that, in broad outline, any individual's story is every individual's story. Our common human nature unites us all.

[27] *Ibid.*, p. 17.

Commentary

We have been viewing the human individual as a closed biological system undergoing development in time from conception to death. Admittedly, every individual is different in some respects from every other; and, also, the system is by no means impervious to the influence of the environment. Nevertheless, the biological curve does have an ascending and a descending limb, and critical turning points, and sequences of events which occur regularly in individual after individual. The evolving system which the curve abstractly describes has laws of its own, is semi-independent of the universe around it, and terminates as surely as it begins. If we could study the millions of examples of this organismic system with the same dispassionateness that we bring to the study of simple plants and animals or to the study of chemical systems evolving in the laboratory, we should experience the same intellectual pleasure that the discovery of order in nature usually affords.

One consideration, however, must give us pause. We are not in the position of the child who watches one soap bubble after another swell up in the bowl of his little clay pipe, detach itself, and float away as an entrancingly colored sphere, tinily reflecting the world around, to burst eventually from inner causes or from collision with a thorn. Each observer is himself one of these bubbles. The laws of the system are our own personal laws; it is our own evolution that we are talking about, and the end is our end. To the sensitive human being (and what human being is not?) even the cycles of nonhuman life and the seasonal changes which put leaves on the trees and strip them off again in the autumn have a poignancy of self-reference which is inescapable. So Gerard Manley Hopkins, to a child:

> Margaret, are you grieving
> Over Goldengrove unleaving?
> Leaves, like the things of man, you
> With your fresh thoughts care for, can you?
> Ah! as the heart grows older
> It will come to such sights colder
> By and by, nor spare a sigh
> Though worlds of wanwood leafmeal lie;
> And yet you will weep and know why.
> Now no matter, child, the name:
> Sorrow's springs are the same.
> Nor mouth had, no nor mind, expressed,
> What heart heard of, ghost guessed:

It is the blight man was born for,
It is Margaret you mourn for.*

At the particular spot where a real individual finds himself in the universe, its lawfulness presses sometimes all too heavily upon consciousness. The individual does not know how to limit himself to his role, to keep time and measure. Children object to growing up, or they try to hasten the process by cigarette and lipstick; young women run across state lines for marriage licenses and then try to jump out of hospital windows to avoid giving birth; old men draw back from dying and young men hang themselves behind shower curtains. "Gad, she'd better," growled Thomas Carlyle when it was reported to him that a philosophical lady had decided to accept the universe. But even crusty, cross-grained, dyspeptic old Carlyle had his bit of trouble in accepting it.

References for chapter 3

Bridges, K. M. B. (1932) Emotional development in early infancy. *Child Development,* 3, 324-41.

Dennis, W. (1941) Infant development under conditions of restricted practice and of minimum social stimulation. *Genetic Psychology Monographs,* 23, 143-91.

———, and Dennis, M. G. (1937) Behavioral development during the first year as shown by 40 biographies. *Psychological Record,* 1, 349-61.

Driesch, H. (1908) *The science and philosophy of the organism.* London: Black.

Frenkel, E. (1936) Studies in biographical psychology. *Character and Personality,* 5, 1-34.

Freud, S. (1953-) Three essays on the theory of sexuality. In *The standard edition of the complete psychological works of Sigmund Freud.* London: Hogarth. Vol. 7.

Gesell, A. (1930) *Guidance of mental growth in infant and child.* New York: Macmillan.

——— (1954) The ontogenesis of infant behavior. In Carmichael, L. (Ed.) *Manual of child psychology.* 2nd ed. New York: Wiley, pp. 335-373.

———, and Amatruda, C. S. (1945) *The embryology of behavior.* New York: Harper.

McCance, R. A., *et al.* (1937) Physical and emotional periodicity in women. *Journal of Hygiene,* 37, 571-611.

* From *The Poems of Gerard Manley Hopkins,* New York, Oxford Univ. Press, 1948.

McGraw, M. B. (1946) Maturation of behavior. In Carmichael, L. (Ed.) *Manual of child psychology.* New York: Wiley, pp. 332-69.

Murray, A. S. (1875) Aphrodite. In *Encyclopaedia Britannica.* 9th ed. Vol. 2.

Patten, B. M. (1947) *Human embryology.* New York: McGraw-Hill.

Peterson, J. (1925) *Early conceptions and tests of intelligence.* Yonkers-on-Hudson: World Book.

Pressey, S. L., and Kuhlen, R. G. (1957) *Psychological development through the life span.* New York: Harper.

Shirley, M. M. (1931) *The first two years: a study of twenty-five babies.* Minneapolis: Univ. of Minnesota Press. Vol. 1.

Shuttleworth, F. K. (1949) *The adolescent period: a graphic atlas.* Evanston, Ill.: Society for Research in Child Development.

Stockard, C. R. (1921) Developmental rate and structural expression: an experimental study of twins, "double monsters," and single deformities, and the interaction among embryonic organs during their origin and development. *American Journal of Anatomy,* 28, 115-277.

Terman, L. M., and Oden, M. H. (1947) *The gifted child grows up.* Stanford, Calif.: Stanford Univ. Press.

———— (1959) *The gifted group at mid-life; thirty-five year's follow-up of the superior child.* Stanford, Calif.: Stanford Univ. Press.

Thorpe, W. H. (1956) *Learning and instinct in animals.* Cambridge, Mass.: Harvard Univ. Press.

Tryon, C. M. (1939) *Evaluations of adolescent personality by adolescents* (Society for Research in Child Development Monographs, Vol. 4, No. 4). Washington: National Research Council.

Yerkes, R. M. (1943) *Chimpanzees: a laboratory colony.* New Haven: Yale Univ. Press.

4

LEARNING:
THE DEVELOPMENT
OF SENTIMENTS
AND SKILLS

Preview   *Not all aspects of organism-environment relations are prearranged. New objects in the environment are continually being discovered by the organism, and the adjustments of the organism to the environment are continually being refined. Insofar as these changes are guided by the environment we speak of learning. Learning is conveniently divided into object-learning and skill-learning. The concept of sentiment applies especially to object-learning. This concept, which stresses the emotional properties of objects, appears under different names in numerous authors concerned with personality theory. The most significant objects in our experience are other persons. Not only are they the foci of complex sentiments, but many of our skills are significant because of reference to them.*

If it is true that there is orderliness in the system of the individual organism, it is equally true that there is orderliness in the world into which the newborn emerges. It is possible to conceive of the adjustment between these two orderly systems, the organism and the environment, as prearranged, keeping time with each other as do two synchronized watches.

One can point to obvious examples. The child exchanges the uterus which supplied it with oxygen through its umbilical cord for an all-encompassing sea of air which supplies this same oxygen through the child's respiratory passages—on the simple condition that the child will go through the motions of breathing, for which the machinery of the body is already beautifully prepared. The environment is no less prepared for the child's body than the child's body is prepared for the environment. The child's respiration removes oxygen from the air and returns carbon dioxide; carbon dioxide is taken up by the green leaves of plants, and these, in cooperation with the sun, breathe back oxygen. Such reciprocal interchanges between child and environment go on perpetually, without the child or the child's parents having to take any thought about them. In a somewhat less obvious way, and by a looser and less inevitable arrangement, the hunger of the child is met by the turgidity of the milk-filled breast. The need of the mother as well as the need of the child is satisfied in the mutuality of nursing. If the breast is deficient in milk, the child suffers; if the child does not suck enough, the mother suffers. Such adjustments as do take place must be largely unconscious on the child's side; and on the mother's side, at the physiological level of lacteal secretion, they are equally so.

Some of the arrangements between organism and environment, however, are arrived at by progressive adjustments to which the name *learning* is applied. Learning is a broad and somewhat indefinite concept. There is no universally accepted definition. Hilgard defines it as "the process by which an activity originates or is changed through responding to a situation, provided the changes cannot be attributed to growth or to the temporary state of the organism (as in fatigue or under drugs)."[1] This definition certainly takes care of much that we call learning. Interpreted very literally, however, it might seem to confine learning to the development of skills in a static environment, but it is evident from Hilgard's actual treatment of the subject that he does not so restrict the term.

For some psychologists, it seems absolutely necessary to an understanding of learning to regard the organism, certainly the human

[1] Hilgard (1957), p. 232.

organism, as a *perceiver* engaged in the process of discovering *what* the situation is. We cannot assume that the situation as the experimenter perceives it is the situation as the child perceives it. To be more specific, we cannot assume that what the experimenter calls a stimulus or stimulus object exists as such for the child at all. From this point of view, our first task as students of learning is to find out how and in what guise *objects* appear within the organism's experience. This stress on perception has been at times regarded with disfavor by certain theorists, and considered in fact inapplicable even to the human organism, where introspection at least should have guaranteed its applicability; but this is exactly because these theorists have tried to exclude introspective data from science. There is evidence that this state of affairs is changing, and that more and more psychologists are willing to take perception into account, at least as an "intervening variable" between stimulus and response. Such is Hebb's recent opinion.[2] As for Hilgard, whose definition of learning is superficially open to the criticism that it neglects perception, the fact is that he uses the concept of perception freely and pertinently in many contexts. No better introduction to the dominant theme of the present chapter can be found than in Hilgard's words:

> We do not know what the world looks like to the newborn infant. If we hazard a guess, we may choose between the world as a "blooming, buzzing confusion" (as William James put it) or as a relatively undifferentiated background on which simple figures begin to emerge. Whatever the infant may see at first, we know that he soon achieves order in the world. The question is: How?

And he answers this question:

> The child achieves order in his perceptual world when he discovers enduring objects in this world. . . .[3]

The small child's world of objects

Piaget has studied the development of the intellectual life of children for many years, and he has published his observations and reflections in a series of notable books. The one which deals most centrally with our present topic is *The Construction of Reality in the Child*.[4] According to Piaget, the child's progress in the discovery of a world of more or less permanent objects is steplike enough to justify marking off six stages in the first two years after birth. It is

[2] Hebb (1958).   [3] Hilgard (1957), p. 364.
[4] Piaget (1954).

the logic of these stages rather than their exact dating which is important for us. Piaget's observations were made on his own three children, Jacqueline, Lucienne, and Laurent. The chronology may not be representative of children in general, therefore; but we might expect the *succession* of stages to hold true.

DEFINITION OF TERMS In describing and explaining the child's progress, Piaget makes use of three major concepts: the schema (*pl.,* schemata), assimilation, and accommodation.

(1) *Schemata* are special organizations of the organism, involving both sensory and motor aspects, which govern its relations with the world. For example, early in the human child's life the sucking schema exists; that means that an organized readiness for the act of sucking is present, whether at the moment sucking is going on or not. In the same way, there may be a visual schema or an auditory schema or a coordinated visual-auditory schema, and so on—namely, a dynamic organization which operates as a whole toward certain ends and not necessarily in perfect harmony with the opportunities presented by the world around. The schema may be simple or complex, poorly or richly differentiated, and adequately or inadequately attuned to the environmental realities.

(2) *Assimilation* is the process which tends to force prevailing circumstances into the requirements of a schema. The sucking schema might be said, for example, to aim at the nipple of the mother's breast; but, in absence of that, anything whatsoever may be sucked—fingers, corner of a blanket, a toy, the tongue, saliva, and so forth. From the point of view of the sucking schema, everything exists to be sucked. In the same way a particular visual schema demands its appropriate object, bending the visual world to its own ends, even to the point of hallucination.

(3) *Accommodation,* on the other hand, is the process of yielding to current circumstances by which the schema undergoes modifications fitting it more closely to the actual environment. Accommodation takes on more and more importance as time advances, but it does not abolish assimilation. Both processes depend on the existence of a schema or schemata, and both contribute to learning. Learning, from Piaget's point of view, is both receptive and creative.

THE DISCOVERY OF OBJECTS AND THEIR PROPERTIES—*Stages 1 and 2* The predominant schema at first is the schema of sucking.

This is well established by the second week after birth. By this time the schema has advanced from empty sucking or sucking at random to the point where it includes a vague definition of the nipple as something different from the skin surfaces around it. But the infant has no conception yet of itself as a hungry child or of the breast as an object in space. A part of the environment has become assimilated to the sucking schema, that is all. The schema now contains a firm sensory element which was not present at first. The nipple is by no means a distinct object; it is a feeling conveyed through the sucking lips, perhaps it is an odor and a taste, but it is probably not visualized. The breast does not exist apart from the infant, nor the infant apart from the breast; both are enclosed within the spaceless, selfless, and yet thoroughly egocentric sucking schema. Still, a differentiation is beginning to take place—between the schema of empty sucking and the schema which includes some sensory content derived from contact with the breast. This is the first step toward the discovery of objects.

About a month later—approximately the sixth week—schemata involving faces and voices have emerged, but separately. The familiar voice is not yet joined to the familiar face. There are really no objects yet, but only "pictures" without permanence or any location in time or space, though the quality of familiarity give them anchorage in the child's own activity. Toward the end of the second stage there is some coordination of auditory and visual schemata, so that the child acts as if he knew, for example, that a certain voice belonged with a certain face.

The "pictures" of the first two stages are not reacted to as if they continued to exist after disappearing. Although the child may seem disappointed if they do not reappear, he makes no effort to search for them. The baby's failure to search for what has disappeared is interpreted by Piaget to mean that there is for him no space in which to search, no distinct baby to do the searching, and no permanent object to be searched for.

Stage 3   This stage lies between the time when the child begins to grasp what he sees (3 to 6 months) and the time when he uses his hand to remove screening objects from before the object which he wants to see (9 to 10 months). One of the steps along the way is simply noticing where an object has dropped. This seems to occur earlier for objects which have dropped from the child's own hand and come to rest close by than for objects dropped from someone else's hand. In the latter case, the baby may stare with astonishment at the empty hand. When his own hand is the one from which the object has dropped, he may behave as if the activity of the hand might restore the object magically. For example, Laurent at 7 months drops a cigarette box which he has been swinging to and fro.

> He then immediately brings his hand before his eyes and looks at it for a long time with an expression of surprise, disappointment, something like an impression of its disappearance. But far from considering the loss as irremediable, he begins again to swing his hand, although it is empty; after this he looks at it once more! For anyone who has seen this act and the child's expression it is impossible not to interpret such behavior as an attempt to make the object come back.[5]

If a screen is interposed between the child's eyes and the object for which he is reaching, the object simply ceases to exist as a thing to search for. But if the child has as much as a fingertip on the object, he may continue to grope for it though the view has been cut off. The object with which the child has no sensory contact at all is as good as gone altogether. Toward the end of this stage a very small fraction of a familiar object will suffice to initiate search for the whole object. Thus, Lucienne at 8½ months will reach for the protruding head of a celluloid stork partially hidden under a cloth and pull the stork out, though this behavior fails to occur if only the stork's feet are exposed. Total disappearance, however, is still total annihilation. Laurent at 7 months had been on a diet for a week and clung hungrily to his bottle when it was emptied, but he became calm and ceased crying with desire when the bottle disappeared behind his father's back.

Stage 4 Eventually the child begins to look behind screens that hide an interesting object from view. Jacqueline at 9¾ months repeatedly gave up reaching for an object in her lap when her father's hand concealed it, but a few days later her conduct radically changed. She would now grasp his hand and thrust it aside in order to get at the thing hidden. This sort of game is a clear indication to Piaget that the unsensed object continues in some fashion to exist for the child. Yet even at this stage the child's conception of an object seems to have curious limitations; objects seem to be anchored in odd ways to schemata. A child a year old may be baffled if an object previously found under a cover at point *A* is now hidden, before the child's eyes, at point *B;* the

---

[5] *Ibid.,* p. 22. Used by permission of Basic Books.

child will proceed to search for it at *A*, the old hiding place! The same phenomenon happens under natural conditions and in reference to the most important objects. Thus, Lucienne at 1¼ years is in the garden with her mother when her father appears; she sees him coming, smiles at him, clearly recognizes him. But when she is asked by her mother, "Where is papa?" (her father standing four feet away from her in plain sight),

> Lucienne immediately turns toward the window of my office where she is accustomed to seeing me and points in that direction. A moment later we repeat the experiment; she has just seen me 1 meter away from her, yet, when her mother pronounces my name, Lucienne again turns toward my office. Here it may be clearly seen that if I do not represent two archetypes to her, at least I give rise to two distinct behavior patterns not synthesized nor exclusive of one another but merely juxtaposed: "papa at his window" and "papa in the garden."[6]

Stage 5 During the first half of the second year the child comes to be able to pass the test of uncovering an object hidden at point *B* which was previously hidden and found at point *A*. This is a step toward the realization that an object is not static when unobserved, necessarily, but it is still not that realization in full. The child capable of passing the above test may act as if the invisible object must be permanently fixed where it was seen to disappear. Take Jacqueline at 1½ years.

> Jacqueline is sitting on a green rug and playing with a potato which interests her very much (it is a new object for her). She says "po-terre" and amuses herself by putting it into an empty box and taking it out again. For several days she has been enthusiastic about this game. I then take the potato and put it in the box while Jacqueline watches. Then I place the box under the rug and turn it upside down thus leaving the object hidden by the rug without letting the child see my maneuver, and I bring out the empty box. I say to Jacqueline, who has not stopped looking at the rug and who has realized that I was doing something under it: "Give papa the potato." She searches for the object in the box, looks at me, again looks at the box minutely, looks at the rug, etc., but it does not occur to her to raise the rug in order to find the potato underneath. During the five subsequent attempts the reaction is uniformly negative.[7]

Jacqueline is acting as if the potato ought to be in the box because it was there when potato-in-the-box disappeared.

[6] *Ibid.*, pp. 58 f.   [7] *Ibid.*, p. 68.

Stage 6 During the second half of the second year the child makes the revolutionary discovery that an absent object can move or be moved. Jacqueline, only a few days after the experiment described above, makes this discovery. Her father has been amazing her with his magician's power of causing a ring hidden in one hand to appear in the other. Twice she looks in the empty hand and not in the other. On the third trial, however, her behavior changes. "This time I place the ring in the right hand and then pass it into the left one. Jacqueline looks in the right hand, astonished at not finding anything, then grasps the left one and laughs at her success."[8]

This triumph of the intellect over mere appearances is not final and complete, however. Even the adult repeatedly fails to hold this principle in mind—the principle that objects are independent of him in the fullest sense, capable of moving and changing and existing when he is not present to watch them, following their own laws. Think how often people are surprised at the changes in a friend after a few years of separation. It is even more difficult to realize that your friend has an equal right to be amazed at the changes in you! Nevertheless, in spite of frequent regressions to more primitive thinking, arrival at Stage 6 puts at the child's command an understanding of the real independence of objects.

In the meantime, the child has been making discoveries about one special object—his own body—and discriminating it more and more sharply from the other objects with which it was at first confused. By the end of the second year the child moves in a world of interrelated objects, neither schemata nor "pictures." In Piaget's words: "The child ends by completely reversing his initial universe, whose moving images were centered on an activity unconscious of itself, and by transforming it into a solid universe of coordinated objects including the body itself as an element."[9]

THE NATURE OF THE PROCESS OF OBJECT DISCOVERY Development of object perception follows a regular sequence applicable to all children, according to Piaget. Should the sequence be thought of as an unfolding of hereditary potential, a pure maturation? Piaget does not think so. The environment is real, and it is this reality which is revealed by the child's interactions with it. The child comes to know the environment, and in this process changes occur both in his behavior and in his perceptions. This a kind of learning,

[8] *Ibid.*, p. 71.   [9] *Ibid.*, p. 86.

though it does not quite fit the Hilgard definition unless "activity" is interpreted very broadly to include "knowing." To *know* objects involves more than memorizing a list of fixed items in the environment, and more than the linking of a conditioned stimulus to an unconditioned response in classical conditioning terms, and more than the reinforcement of an operant in Skinner's terms, and more than the reinforcement of a response by drive reduction in Hull's terms. To know objects is, first of all, to discover them. Once they are discovered, the terminology of various learning theories (like those above) may begin to fit; but, as far as I can make out, most of the learning theories which have entered into our textbooks presuppose objects rather than account for them. The experimenter who talks of applying a stimulus to an organism does not usually spend much time asking himself about the nature and origin of the stimulus as an experienced object. But this is exactly what Piaget is concerned with, and his account does throw some light on the matter.

Here an important question rises. Must the environment furnish particular sorts of guidance if object learning is to occur? Is there, in fact, any environment capable of sustaining human life which would *not* furnish this guidance? The child normally grows up under the supervision of nurturing parents, and it may be that the child-parent relationship is ordinarily such that the necessary perceptual stimulation is provided as automatically as the air provides oxygen or as the breast provides milk. Such a view could be argued for on the basis of the wide variety of child rearing practices which *appear* to be successful. On the other hand, probably nobody has carefully analyzed the relationship between the early experiences of the child and his subsequent adult views concerning the nature of the environment. Whatever guidance the child may get from parents and nurses in this respect must be almost altogether spontaneous and unreasoned, since it is only an analysis such as Piaget's which begins to put us in a position to give deliberate thought to it. No environment can be absolutely barren for a child who has any freedom of action at all. His own hands and feet and senses in a naked, uninhabited room provide endless entertainment and instruction. Any environment, as scientific research shows us, is inexhaustibly rich in secrets just waiting to be discovered; but of course it may seem barren to anyone who does not bring courage and curiosity to it. It seems reasonable that under certain circumstances the child's initiation into this inexhaustible world can be unfavorable to rapid, progressive development in the discovery of objects and their interrelations. The psychoanalysts at least have speculated that the early mother-child interaction may be so feeble or inharmonious that the child never develops an adequate sense of objects. Melanie Klein, for instance, has devoted a good deal of attention to the problem of the meaning of the breast to the infant and speculates that much depends on the quality of the breast (or bottle) as experienced by the suckling—whether it is satisfying or frustrating, "good" or "bad," comforting or threatening, and the extent to which it appears in both negative and positive aspects.[10] The problem is one which will be considered in later chapters.

THE DEVELOPMENT OF THE IDEA OF CAUSALITY—*Stages 1 and 2* Piaget insists that the child is never simply passive. "Visual and auditory images are less external realities exerting pressure on him than they are nourishment sought in order to maintain a constantly growing activity."[11] From the child's activity emerges his conception of cause-and-effect. In the beginning, there is an indefinite sense of power—indefinite, because the child has not yet made the distinction between object and self which would give the power a point of origin and a point of application. His activity results in a creation, but it is not he who creates. No identifiable cause creates the breast which the child sucks, but the act of sucking is met satisfyingly by the breast which is sucked; and the sucking and the breast constitute one reality. This gratifying reality produces an unbounded sense of well-being and even, to use the strong language of the psychoanalysts, a sense of omnipotence. All this interpretation of the child's state of mind must be inferred, of course, from the child's behavior. The inference, furthermore, is not a mere logical process but involves the observer's empathy with the child—which, after all, cannot be ignored.

Stage 3 At this stage, which Piaget labels the magico-phenomenalistic, the secondary circular reactions (as Piaget calls them) are set up, i.e., combinations of separate schemata. For example, the child not only moves his hands and feels them move, as in the early grasping schema; he also watches them move and so studies the movement as both a visual and a kinesthetic fact. Furthermore, he discovers that he is able to set other things in motion, such as a rattle, by some motion of his own body. He discovers also that

[10] Klein (1946).   [11] Piaget (1954), p. 225.

98   THE PERSONAL WORLD

events not originating in any motion of his may have some mutual relation, as when he realizes that a voice, which is one event, is related to a face, which is a different one. But this realization of a causal connection is at first very obscure.

Adults take their hands and their manual powers for granted. Not so the child at Stage 3. For example, Laurent at 3½ months waves his hands vigorously and then gazes at them intently. This intent gaze is not because he has never seen them before, but apparently because he is just beginning to realize that he can move them. Five months later Laurent is still engaged, at times, in studying their motion.

> Laurent looks at his hands most attentively, as if he did not know them. He is alone in his bassinet, his hands motionless, but he constantly moves his fingers and examines them. After this he moves his hands slowly, looking at them with the same interested expression. Then he joins them and separates them more slowly while continuing to study the phenomenon; he ends by scratching his covers, striking them, etc., but watching his hands the whole time.[12]

Piaget infers that it is not the unfamiliarity of the hands as objects which holds Laurent's attention after all these months, but the unfamiliarity of the fact that they are governed by his intentions.

Discovery of one's hands and their obedience to one's intentions is fully as significant as the fact that they are there. It is an immense step in establishing the boundaries between one's body and other objects; it is a step also in the implementing of conscious purposes. In fact, according to Piaget, it is a step in the acquisition of self-consciousness. For to realize the hand as an object is to become aware of oneself as a subject, to realize the body's submissiveness to one's will is to discover that will.

The complementary emergence of object-consciousness and self-consciousness first enables the child to operate in a thoroughly effective means-end fashion. Yet this opportunity is not consistently seized. At the magico-phenomenalistic stage and for a long time thereafter, much of the child's wishing is expressed in magical gestures rather than in the careful adjustment of means to ends. Magical thinking is, in fact, a common feature of adult life, and very prominently so in some human societies. The most conspicuous examples given by Piaget are occasions when the child puts forth considerable muscular effort and appears to be emotionally excited,

[12] *Ibid.,* p. 232.

producing the impression that he expected the discharge of energy alone to be enough to prolong or begin the events which interest him. Doubtless Skinner would explain the phenomenon just as he explains "superstition" in the pigeon—as a special case of operant conditioning.[13] I take it that Piaget prefers to regard the behavior in question as less under stimulus control than that—as more purposive and conscious.

A striking example of this behavior in an 8-month infant is given by Piaget:

> Jacqueline is lying down looking at a saucer which I swing about 50 centimeters in front of her eyes. She reveals a lively interest and expresses her pleasure by the well-known behavior of arching herself upward, with her weight on her feet and shoulder blades, and then letting herself fall in a heap. I pass the saucer before her again. She watches it smiling, then stares at it seriously and attentively and arches upward a second time. When Jacqueline has fallen back again I pass the object before her once more; the same play three more times. After this I hold the object motionless before her; she arches herself again two or three times, then proceeds to something else. I resume twice; as soon as the saucer is motionless, Jacqueline arches upward again. I then definitely pause in my game; Jacqueline nevertheless draws herself up five or six times more, while looking at the object, then tires of it. Every time the child's gesture has been followed by the saucer's movement, Jacqueline has manifested great satisfaction; otherwise, an expression of disappointment and expectation.[14]

Many times, for more than a month, Piaget plays this sort of game with Jacqueline. Repeatedly she uses arching as if she trusted its magical power. Even after Piaget quits rewarding the gesture by doing the thing that interests her, she uses it again and again, and often, when the gesture is unsuccessful, she expresses surprise, as if the failure were unbelievable.

The child at this stage evidently does not believe that it is always necessary to bring about a mechanical contact in order to move something. Yet he does not always resort to magic either. It appears to depend on circumstances whether he will use magic or the method of direct contact. Thus, Piaget found that Laurent tried to prolong a game of finger-snapping by the sort of energetic magical gesture described, as long as the father was too distant to touch; but he grasped and shook his father's hand when he was near enough, apparently in an effort to get him started again. Of

[13] Skinner (1948).   [14] Piaget (1954), p. 238.

course, in this case too the child shows little appreciation of the independence of the behaving object. He treats his father's hand like a rattle rather than like a hand dependent on someone else's will. Is there not a trace of magic in this, too?

Impersonal objects as well as persons have power of action in themselves, but it appears to be chiefly through the observation of persons that the child comes to realize that objects are autonomous and sometimes beyond his control. Piaget, like the psychoanalysts, lays great stress on the significance of personal interaction in infancy. "We must recognize," he writes,

> that to the child at this stage another person constitutes a more lively center of actions than any object whatever. It is enough to observe the subject's expression to realize this difference. On the one hand, in the presence of a person the child seems to await events rather than to bring them about as he does in the presence of things. When a person appears, the child is reserved for a moment, ready to follow in the direction indicated and thus attributing to the person a certain spontaneity. On the other hand, the child unquestionably smiles and laughs more often in the presence of persons than of things—proof that the former excite him more than the latter and that in his eyes they are invested with greater vitality. It is therefore very probable, as we have glimpsed several times, that contact with persons plays an essential role in the processes of objectification and externalization: the person constitutes the primary object and the most external of the objects in motion through space.[15]

Stage 4   The child now begins to realize the power which exists in objects and often attributes to them a greater or at least a different autonomy than they possess. For example, Jacqueline at one year of age puts down objects on a surface and lets go of them quickly, as if she expected them to move away when released. In this way she sits and waits for a ball to roll.

Stage 5   Later, a more accurate estimate of the independent powers of objects is achieved, and in general the concept of causality is mastered in a preliminary fashion. That is to say, the causal properties of objects which are immediately present are realized.

Stage 6   At last, the transition is made to representative causality, that is, to recognizing causes which are not immediately perceptible. The child's efforts in this direction are often erroneous in detail, but the essential victory is that the child is now able to

[15] *Ibid.*, p. 252.

make inferences about the cause of effects when only the effects are definitely known. In the second half of her second year, Jacqueline, seeing the mist rising from the side of a mountain, says, "Mist smoke papa," and it is clear from other remarks that she means something like "Papa makes the mist with his pipe." As Piaget has noted, the human being is the most vivid object and the most autonomous in the child's experience. The extension of papa's power from the making of smoke to the creation of mists, and later clouds, is easy and natural.

COMPLEMENTARITY   Step by step the child rises to conceptions which seem contrary to his first assumptions. Out of his original egocentrism comes his idea of a real world which does not depend on him for its existence or its powers. Out of his magical operation on objects comes his belief that they are autonomous, able to act without regard to his wishes. The earlier stages leading up to these results do not just vanish, however. They remain side by side with the later stages, continuing to furnish starting points for new progressions from egocentrism to realism on new occasions of bafflement.

The discovery of objects involves the simultaneous discovery of the space in which they exist. Space develops out of an originally subjective matrix which is not even self-conscious. As this undifferentiated subjectivity is sacrificed, self-consciousness is gained. This is Piaget's important concept of *complementarity*. The more definitely space and the objects within it are recognized as independently real, the more definite becomes the awareness of oneself as a center of conscious perceptions and wishes. As shown in Figure 9, Piaget pictures the relationship between organism (X) and environment (Y) as that of one sphere enclosed within another. Consciousness develops at the boundary of interaction (A). This consciousness is directed simultaneously toward the external world and toward the internal. Any advance in object-consciousness is matched by a complementary advance in self-consciousness.

The first engagements between organism and environment are of a practical order, and the concepts are concepts of practice: if you do this, that happens. As the child matures, he becomes more and more interested in what might be called pure theory. Doubtless pure theory has its practical aspects, but the child becomes able to think about the relations between objects, and between himself and objects, without being concerned for the moment about

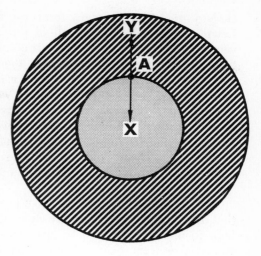

9 *Piaget's complementarity diagram pictures consciousness (the arrows) as developing simultaneously toward the subject (X) and the environment (Y). A is the point of interaction between self and world. (After Piaget, 1954)*

hunger or thirst or other drives and possessive longings. This is the stage of representative thought. It seems probable that animals, although they certainly work out practical schemes of relationship with the environment and have their practical objects, do not reach this level of pure reflection on the nature of things. Most human beings do not go far in that direction either. But the capacity is there, and sometimes in childhood there is a budding of scientific and philosophic modes of thinking as well as artistic accomplishment, usually doomed to be choked out in later years.

Sentiments: objects emotionally charged and enchained

For personality theory, one of the most important things about objects is that for the perceiver they are often, perhaps always, emotionally charged. A second and correlated fact is that the amount of emotional charge varies from object to object. The result is that for every individual his world of objects is organized—not simply spatially into near and far, right and left, above and below, but even more importantly into more and less valuable, more and less exciting, and so on.

For the perceiver this emotional power seems to reside in the object itself, although psychological analysis regularly establishes it on a *relationship* between the subject and the object. Anthropology recognizes this phenomenon in a term like *mana*. In psychology we encounter many terms for it: Freud speaks of *cathexis*, Lewin of *valence*, McDougall of *sentiment*. These theorists give very high place to it in their explanation of human behavior. Even theorists who have not concerned themselves much with personality have admitted it, at least as an afterthought. Thus Hull states that "Lewin's use of the expressions 'valence' and 'field force' corresponds roughly to our use of the expression 'reaction potential.' "[16] It is clear from Hull's discussion, however, that he is mainly interested in the Lewinian concept because of its bearing on animal locomotion in space and not because of its bearing on the subjective valuation of the world of objects.

HOW DO OBJECTS HAPPEN TO HAVE EMOTIONAL CHARGE? The fact that objects may be emotionally charged (cathected, valent) is open both to introspection and to observation of behavior. Most or all animals are prone to establish a home base, for example, to which they repeatedly return, out of positive longing or when fleeing from danger, and which serves them at all times as a point of orientation. Nests and burrows and houses are visible examples. But the home base need not be anything so obvious. I once experimented rather informally with some rats in a large boxlike enclosure, to see what they would do when frightened. According to my experience, a rat alone in such a space will soon establish a home base at a particular spot, in one of the corners in this instance, and explore from there and retreat to it when startled. The favorite corner seemed to have no special features by which it might be identified or which made it more comfortable or safer than some other corner, though no doubt it did acquire after a while the rat's own body odor. I lay no stress on this experiment except as an illustration of the phenomenon of the home base. It is entirely possible that the chosen corner *did* have some original attractiveness for the animal, as compared to other corners.

Other features of the world besides corners may serve as home base. Indeed, we can say with confidence that every species of animal has some preferences in this regard. A given species of bird, for example, can be counted on to build in a certain kind of location a species-typical nest: both the design of the nest and its placement are characteristic of the species. Again, the most powerful attachments between individuals are commonly those between one mem-

[16] Hull (1952), p. 267.

ber of a species and another member of the same species. In particular, the attachment of a child to its mother is likely to be very strong in certain species, and the mother in such cases is the home base *par excellence*. Such preferential attachment, more or less predictable for each species, points to some kind of guiding plan in the original, inherited nature of the organism.

Harlow has recently revived the interest of psychologists in this essential fact of animal life, the fact of strong attachment to certain objects. He has investigated especially the child-mother bond. The latest detailed report of his work available to me is an article in *Science* entitled "Affectional Responses in the Infant Monkey."[17] According to Harlow, the young monkey like the young human being has a vital need for contact with a mother or a mother-substitute, and he emphasizes that it is the contact rather than some other benefit such as nursing at the mother's breast (or bottle substitute) which is decisive. The young monkey will work for this contact and prolong it by vigorous action, and he must be assured of it if he is to display any great confidence in exploring a novel environment. Under normal circumstances, the mother who bore him becomes this highly cathected object; but if there is no real mother, a substitute of some kind will partially or wholly take her place. Harlow has experimented with inanimate mother-substitutes and has measured in various ways the strength of the baby monkey's attachment. There are two results of this experimental work which I would stress. (1) Of the two inanimate mother-substitutes used by Harlow—one made of a cylinder of wire mesh topped by a cubical head, the other made of a cylinder of wood enclosed in soft terry cloth and topped by a round and more lifelike head—it has uniformly been the second which has given the orphaned monkey more comfort. (2) It is the contact, rather than the association of the contact with being nursed, which has proved to be the critical variable. In the article cited Harlow makes the greatest theoretical capital out of this second result. He notes that it is a common theory among psychologists, sociologists, and anthropologists (probably because of the strong influence of Hull) that learning is based on drive reduction.

This theory proposes that the infant's attachment to the mother results from the association of the mother's face and form with the

[17] Harlow and Zimmermann (1959).

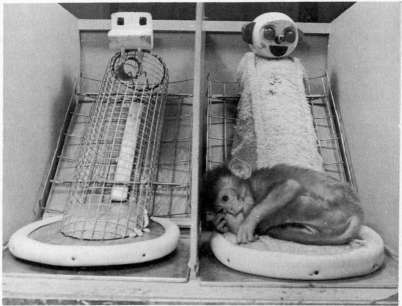

H. F. Harlow, R. R. Zimmermann, *Science*, 1959

10 *A monkey given access to two different artificial mother-substitutes prefers the one which is more like its natural mother.*

alleviation of certain primary drive states, particularly hunger and thirst. Thus, through learning, affection becomes a self-supporting, derived drive.[18]

But Harlow's results contradict this. One of the variables he manipulated was nursing; the mother-substitutes could be equipped with a nursing bottle put in position like a breast; some were so equipped, and others were not. The pertinence of this manipulation to the drive-reduction hypothesis is summed up in these words:

> With increasing age and opportunity to learn, an infant fed from a lactating wire mother does not become more responsive to her, as would be predicted from the derived-drive theory, but instead becomes increasingly more responsive to its nonlactating cloth mother. These findings are at complete variance with the drive-reduction theory of affectional development.[19]

But if the drive-reduction theory does not explain the infant's attachment to the mother, what does? The answer appears to be

[18] *Ibid.*, p. 421.   [19] *Ibid.*, p. 423.

contained in the first of the two results stressed above. The young monkey is immediately drawn to an object resembling its normal mother, and the greater the resemblance the greater the attachment; or, in other words, the emotional charge (cathexis, valence) of the object is greater the more nearly it corresponds to the object expected and required by the infant monkey's inherited constitution. It would be a more exact interpretation of the results of the Harlow experiments to say that the object must have the specific quality of softness of skin, but he himself thinks that other variables may be involved. The reader must understand that I am here interpreting Harlow's results, not reporting his own theory. He rejects the drive-reduction derivation of the affectional attachments; he does not say that the infant monkey has an innate idea of the desired object—it is I who suggest this.

Instinct theory (as developed by McDougall, for example) seems to me to have an advantage over drive theory precisely because of its most unpopular feature, namely, its emphasis on innate ideas. It assumes that the organism is innately equipped and ready to perceive its goal objects, when the time and the circumstances are ripe. Instinct is thus not a blind force, governed simply by pleasure and pain or "drive-reduction," but rather a purposeful groping toward something dimly foreseen or at least recognizable at the moment of encounter. The newborn monkey, McDougall would say, has an untaught, unconscious idea of a mother, perhaps very general and vague at first, which enables him to discover a more or less appropriate object in the environment to cuddle up to.

A currently popular term for an environmental factor serving as the objective correlate of an innate idea is *releaser*. This ethological term is accepted by writers, like Hilgard, who are disinclined to speak of instinct or innate idea although the ethological concept is close to these latter.[20] A releaser may be defined as an object or aspect of an object which sets off complex behavior without prior individual experience with it. The behavior might be the clinging behavior of the young monkey and the releaser might be the mother monkey or a substitute modeled after her. Now, we cannot just assume that an object with certain features, such as a mother monkey, will be the only one capable of releasing the clinging behavior of the baby monkey; it is fairly certain from general observation of the species that a mother monkey usually

[20] See the section entitled "The problem of instinctive behavior," in Ch. 5 of Hilgard (1957), pp. 119-24.

suffices, but exactly what it is about her that is of critical significance can be discovered only by experimental analysis. One of the important aspects of the mother monkey for her baby is the soft skin to which he can and eagerly does cling. For all we know, that softness· may be about all the newborn monkey can perceive; and the clinging to her skin and the sucking at her breast may not be very distinguishable experiences at that early age. In the case of the human infant, as the research of Spitz has shown, social smiling, when it first occurs at around the age of two months, can be released by an extremely generalized "face" which resembles the human face as we adults perceive it only in the grossest manner. By 6 months the baby has become more perceptive and requires a face with more familiar detail. The generalized face has prepared the way for the more specific, individual face.[21] If anything like an innate idea guides the responses of monkey or human baby, it is evident that it is one which would apply to a wide variety of particular mothers—a schematic kind of skin, a schematic kind of face, able to accommodate any individual mother and many inanimate substitutes.

Imprinting is another ethological term which has begun to find favor with psychologists. It refers to a type of learning occurring suddenly at an especially sensitive period of development which results in the emotional and behavioral attachment of a young animal to a place or individual, sometimes quite firmly and specifically. Under natural conditions, the process attaches the individual to its own species and to the normal breeding habitat. Human experimenters, however, may step in and utilize the process to attach the animal to an object different from the normal. The possibilities are well illustrated in an article by Hess.[22] In one experiment he used mallard ducklings hatched in an incubator. Under normal circumstances the ducklings would have been hatched near their mother, and when she moved they would have responded by following her, expressing emotional excitement by typical duckling sounds. The experimenter, however, substituted an artificial mother in the form of a mechanical decoy and put the incubated duckling in the presence of this object at chosen times within a few hours after hatching. In this way he was able to decide what the most sensitive time for imprinting was; this proved to be between 13 and 16 hours after hatching. Furthermore, he was able to test the effects of the imprinting experience.

[21] Spitz (1946).   [22] Hess (1959).

One of the tests was to take these artificially imprinted ducklings down to the duck pond and give them the opportunity to remain close to the mechanical decoy or join a live female mallard. They stuck with their artificial decoy. Other incubated ducklings, not previously exposed to the decoy for imprinting, immediately joined the live mother ducks and ignored the decoy. The significance for the present discussion of this and similar ethological experiments is that a certain kind of object may suddenly acquire an emotional charge, in a single or few exposures, which will continue for a long time, even for years, thereafter. This seems hard to explain unless we assume an innate readiness to respond emotionally and actively to a special class of objects. But this is virtually a definition of instinct, as understood by McDougall.

The notion of instinct is often badly misinterpreted as the proposition that an animal will display a certain kind of behavior rigidly and automatically without reference to the nature of the environment. This is a mere parody of the concept as employed by a psychologist like McDougall or an ethologist like Lorenz or Tinbergen or Thorpe.[23] Instinct, as conceived by such writers as these, is rather an inherited readiness to detect and react to certain objects or classes of objects in the environment, *if* they make their appearance at the appropriate time (which may be confined to a brief critical period or may be spread out over a whole life, depending on the instinct in question). The readiness may be so sharply focused that only an object with very precise characteristics will serve to release the reaction, or so broadly receptive that a wide range of objects will release it. For example, imprinting in some species requires something rather specific like a color; in others, something more general, like motion, will do. No doubt it is ridiculous to "explain" animal behavior by inventing an instinct for every behavior pattern we do not understand; but it is far from ridiculous to look for species-specific readinesses to respond in certain ways to certain kinds of objects, as modern instinct theorists do. It is on this sort of basis that the emotional charge of certain objects may be understood; for the instinctive reaction is typically vigorous, emotional, whole-organism-engaging, and obviously expresses a high positive or negative valuation of the object which elicits it.

The main point which I am making here is that a fruitful instinct theory is one which insists on the role of object-perception.

[23] Cf. McDougall (1923), Lorenz (1952, 1958), Tinbergen (1951), and Thorpe (1956).

In a paper which attempts to discountenance instinct theory, Beach notes that, "Among experimentalists, Lashley suggested that instinctive behavior is unlearned and differs from reflexes in that instincts depend on 'the pattern or organization of the stimulus,' whereas reflexes are elicited by stimulation of localized groups of sensory endings."[24] Unfortunately, in his negative summing up, Beach entirely overlooks this important remark of Lashley's about the dependence of instinctive behavior on object-perception, or, in Lashley's words, "the pattern or organization of the stimulus." In general, this neglect of perception seems to be responsible for the confusion of instinct with simple reflexes like the knee jerk.

At any rate, some concept of instinct, disguised or not, is very much alive in modern psychology. Beach appears to regret it in his article, but he admits that, "Although there are militant opponents of the instinct doctrine among present-day psychologists, it is undoubtedly correct to say that the concept of instincts as complex, unlearned patterns of behavior is generally accepted in clinical, social, and experimental psychology."[25] I would judge also that Beach is correct in alleging that instinct, in the general use of the term, is restricted to "complex, unlearned patterns of behavior" —that is to say, the *perceptual* side of instinct by which the unlearned pattern of behavior is anchored to the environment is often disregarded. Any instinct theory which omits perception of the environment is, I agree, faulty. Beach himself could not condemn so sterile a conception more heartily than does William McDougall (1871-1938), the arch-instinctivist of modern psychology.

SENTIMENT THEORY   Sentiment theory, as developed by McDougall out of an elaborate suggestion by Shand,[26] is primarily an attempt to account for the emotional charge (cathexis, valence) on objects. It depends heavily on the instinct concept. To understand it, therefore, we first have to explore further what McDougall means by instinct, or, as he later calls it without essential modification, *propensity*.

[24] Beach (1955), p. 404.
[25] *Ibid.* For an up-to-date, sympathetic discussion of instinct, see Fletcher (1957).
[26] Shand (1914). McDougall always seemed to feel a little apologetic about having capitalized on Shand's ideas before Shand's book was published, and was very careful to admit his indebtedness. McDougall made use of sentiment theory in his *Introduction to social psychology* (1908).

An instinct, for McDougall, is an inborn, unlearned principle of action. It is goal-directed. It is, in effect, a natural purpose existing in the organism, expressed in three ways: (a) as an *idea,* however vague, of a certain kind of goal-object; (b) as a *felt urge* to a particular kind of action with reference to that object; and (c) as an *emotional state* peculiar to the goal-object and the urge to action. An instinct may be expressed in all three ways at once, or more emphatically in one way than in the other two.

McDougall drew up several lists of instincts at different times, but he always regarded these lists at tentative. They are nothing like as important as the instinct concept itself. This, notice, is not a fixed pattern of behavior, but a tendency, a purpose, a direction of behavior toward an object. In describing any particular proposed instinct, McDougall attempts to bring out the three aspects mentioned above. For example, the food-seeking instinct involves an *idea* of food, the *urge* to eat, and the *emotional excitement* of hunger. He comments in one place:

> We may arrange the instincts in a scale, in the descending order of complexity of bodily adjustments; and we find that the corresponding qualities of emotional excitement then form a scale of diminishing degrees of specificity. Accordingly, common speech has definite names, and indeed a variety of synonyms, for the qualities of the upper end of the scale, and no special names for the qualities of the lower end. For the emotional qualities that accompany the play of instincts of the upper part of the scale are as easily recognizable as are the symptoms or bodily expressions of these instinctive excitements; while the qualities of the lower end of the scale are as little specific as are the bodily expressions: and, if we wish for psychological purposes to refer to the latter, we have to invent names for them.[27]

The list of instincts offered by McDougall on this occasion runs as follows, arranged in order from the most to the least complex in bodily adjustments: escape, combat, repulsion, parental, appeal, pairing, curiosity, submission, assertion, social, food-seeking, acquisition, construction, and laughter. He adds:

> The minor instincts of scratching, sneezing, coughing, urination, and defecation are so simple in their bodily expressions that we cannot recognize as specific qualities the excitements which accompany their exercise; though the impulse of each may on occasion be excited in great strength.[28]

[27] McDougall (1923), pp. 323 f.   [28] *Ibid.,* p. 325.

Once again, let the reader be reminded that it is McDougall's general concept of instinct rather than this or any other particular list which deserves his close attention. McDougall's analysis of behavior never reached the degree of refinement on the motor side now being attained by the ethologists, who have been able to trace elements of complex behavior patterns as genetic traits.[29]

The instincts listed by McDougall play much the same role in the discovery of objects as do the schemata of Piaget. Intellect advances, McDougall says, "from knowledge of a few objects of a very highly general type, towards knowledge of the multitude of concrete individual objects and their peculiar qualities and relations."[30] An animal, he argues (in language which ethological research supports),

> perceives, knows, or recognizes few, if any, individual objects as such; rather, it perceives and reacts to objects of certain kinds, those which it is prepared by native constitution to perceive; and each object is, for the animal, merely a representative of its class, and is marked as such by some relatively simple feature or sensory pattern, corresponding to one of the few cognitive dispositions possessed by the animal.[31]

On the other hand, the knowledge possessed by a highly cultivated human intellect, detailed and far-reaching as it may be, "is not an independent new formation deposited by some sense-impression, but is formed by a gradual growth and differentiation from pre-existing dispositions."[32]

But it must be remembered that emotion is an essential aspect of instinct. Every object of an instinct, therefore, receives an emotional accent. Now, there are certain objects which are especially potent in releasing instinctive reactions, but these as well as others may become the focal point for *other* instincts in the total repertoire, so that a given object in the course of time, as the individual interacts with it, acquires a complex emotional charge. The object becomes the nexus between various instincts, the repository of various emotions; and the sentiment, i.e., the acquired mental disposition focused upon the object, is equally complex. A simple sentiment is the case where a single object receives the emotional charge from a single instinct; a complex sentiment arises from an object which has become the nexus of several instincts. This type of analysis appears in Freudian theory under the head-

[29] Lorenz (1958). [30] McDougall (1923), p. 382.
[31] *Ibid.* [32] *Ibid.*

ing of *ambivalence*. But ambivalence suggests opposition, as between love and hate, while a complex sentiment for McDougall may combine instincts which may just as well be in harmony with one another as in opposition. The closest kindred in psychoanalysis to a McDougallian sentiment is the *complex*, but McDougall's term has the merit of not implying anything pathological as the term "complex" does. It can be applied equally well to healthy and to pathological states.

A sentiment, then, according to McDougall, is derived from an instinct or a variety of instincts by the commerce of the individual with the particular objects of his world, and it functions like an instinct, readying the individual to perceive and react to particular objects with emotion. The emotional power of the sentiment may not, to be sure, be particularly evident when the individual is in close, satisfying relation to the appropriate object; but the reality of the emotional valuation of the object explodes into prominence in expressions of distress or fear or grief when the object is removed. Look back to the picture of Harlow's monkey resting peacefully at the foot of the mother-substitute in Figure 10. The picture would be quite different, it would be full of agitation and insecurity, if the little monkey had this sentiment-object removed from it and it were left without it in a strange environment. One way of assessing the emotional power of sentiment-objects is to withdraw them.

The language that we use about these things is much less important than grasping the central idea that objects are rarely if ever emotionally neutral and that one way in which they acquire their emotional charge appears to be by encounter with certain inherited dispositions in the experiencing organism, whether these dispositions are called instincts or something else. It should be noted, too, that there are contemporary American psychologists who have made vigorous use of the concepts and terms employed by McDougall. Adams has signalized the relationship of sentiments to objects by calling sentiments the organs of perception[33] and has devoted an important monograph to showing their relevance to personality theory.[34] In this monograph, *The Anatomy of Personality*, Adams blends the thinking of McDougall with that of Lewin in a set of formal propositions which deserve the attention of every serious student. For another example, Cattell has made extensive use of McDougall's thought in many of his publi-

[33] Adams (1953).   [34] Adams (1954).

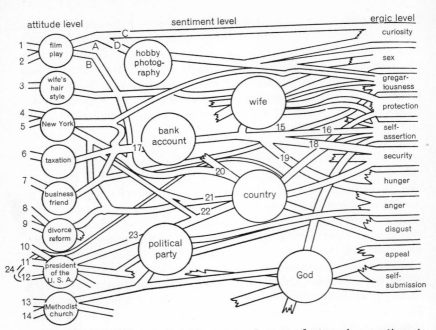

11 *Cattell's "dynamic lattice" suggests the complexity of a sentiment system. (From R. B. Cattell, Personality, copyright 1950 by McGraw-Hill Book Co., Inc. Used by permission of the publisher.)*

cations, paying special regard to the sentiment concept. The illustration from Cattell (Figure 11) puts the sentiments as dominant structural units in the "dynamic lattice" of personality. The diagram is useful for suggesting the complexity of what Cattell calls "a fairly typical citizen."

CONCERNING THE TRANSFER OF EMOTIONAL CHARGE (CATHEXIS, VALENCE) FROM ONE OBJECT TO ANOTHER   If an object exists which is capable of arousing an emotional reaction, then a similar emotional reaction may be elicited by other objects either through *generalization* or through *associative linkage.*

(1) Generalization   Ivan Pavlov (1849-1936) early investigated stimulus generalization. His conditioning procedure is well known. One of his statements on the subject is this:

If you form a conditioned reflex, for example, to the ticking of a metronome, and then try other sounds, you will find that these other sounds at first also produce the salivary flow. . . . If you make a conditioned stimulus from a tone of 1,000 vibrations, and afterwards try other tones of various vibrations, all of them have an effect. If you repeatedly combine mechanical stimulation of the skin (pricking) with feeding, finally this pricking calls out every time a secretion of saliva. Now when you subject other parts of the skin to the same pricking, they all cause the salivary secretion. . . . There is a form of experiment in which we do not connect the activity of the salivary gland with the present stimulus, but with its remains, or *trace,* i.e., we give the stimulus and then allow an interval to elapse after its termination before putting acid into the mouth of the dog, or before feeding it. In the *trace reflexes,* the excitation spreads still further. After forming them to the given stimulus, you will find that saliva flows in response to many different stimuli.[35]

In some cases it is possible to demonstrate a "generalization gradient." That is to say, the effectiveness of the new stimuli depends on their similarity to the original conditioned stimulus. Thus, in a famous experiment by Hovland the subjects were emotionally aroused by mild electric shock delivered to the wrist, and this arousal was accompanied by a tone of a certain vibration frequency; when, as a result of the conditioning procedure, the tone was capable of emotionally rousing the subjects, i.e., when it had become a conditioned stimulus, as indicated by the galvanometer attached to the skin, Hovland tested the effectiveness of other tones of different vibration frequencies which he knew to be distinguishable from each other by the subjects. The amount of the galvanometer deflection proved to be less the larger the difference in vibration rate from the original conditioned stimulus.[36]

In the examples cited, the emotionally charged object was an "object" in only the slimmest sense—a stimulus with a minimum of pattern. But the same sort of phenomenon occurs when there is object-perception in the full sense. There is some evidence that when the stimuli are patterned objects, such as words or pictures or living people, the generalization which occurs may be more steplike than in the sort of experiment described by Hovland, though this is a moot point. There is bountiful evidence in clinical literature of the generalization of emotional effects from some particular traumatic object. That is to say, a very emotional experience with one person often results in a similar reaction to other, superficially very different persons; and this effect may spread

---

[35] Pavlov (1928), p. 157.   [36] Hovland (1937).

very far, so that a traumatized person's whole social life is distorted and crippled by the "stimulus equivalence" of numerous people to the one traumatizing person.

Where generalization appears to be very strong, the question arises whether, as a matter of fact, the supposedly different objects appear different to the person concerned. Our perception of objects is always imperfectly individualized. We may in fact mistake one object for another. An experimenter who found that a subject conditioned to respond emotionally to a red color also responded that way to a green color might consider the possibility that his subject was color-blind. The babies in Spitz's experiments seemed to smile equally at ugly masks and their beautiful mother's face because they did not *see* any difference. At the same time, we do know that persons can distinguish at least visually between two different objects and still react to them emotionally the same way, because of the generalization process.

(2) Associative linkage It is an insight probably as old as reflective thinking that when two objects occur together in our experience and one of them arouses us emotionally, the other object is likely to pick up the emotional charge of the first. The preciousness or repulsiveness of a chair or a garment or a trinket or a scrap of paper or a whole city can be traced back in many instances to association with some one loved or hated person. Persons especially are the originating points of these extensively radiating effects, and one of the great merits of psychoanalysis is that it recognizes and lays stress on this fact. Nevertheless, the principle involved has very wide application. All conditioning experiments are based on it.

But what is the principle? Some theorists seem to think that all that is necessary to bind two things together is that they should appear together. Others speak of the need for "reinforcement." The term comes from Pavlov, but its meaning changes with the theorist and it is sometimes questionable just what is meant. Let us glance at Pavlov's usage. In the well-known salivary conditioning experiments the situation was this: Presentation of food to a hungry dog caused it to salivate, i.e., an unconditioned stimulus (US) produced an unconditioned reflex response (UR); on the other hand, another stimulus like the sound of a buzzer did not have this effect until it was paired a number of times with the US-UR sequence; the buzzer sound was the conditioned stimulus (CS), and it was said to be *reinforced* as a stimulus for salivation when it was accompanied (usually followed) by the US-UR sequence. The importance of reinforcement was demonstrated by the fact that if the CS appeared repeatedly without the US, it ceased to produce the salivary secretion; its effectiveness as a stimulus for that response was *extinguished*. Of course, it tended to recover its effectiveness spontaneously after a period of time, but that is another story. The point here is that the power of the CS to produce salivation was seen as dependent upon its being closely associated with the US. The US is the reinforcer.

A fact which Pavlov was aware of but perhaps did not stress enough is that an unconditioned response to an unconditioned stimulus like food is a good deal more than a small segment of behavior, such as the secretion of the salivary gland which he was accustomed to measure and use as his index of the dog's responsiveness. A hungry dog reacts pretty totally to a piece of food. In fact, he shows all the signs of emotion and urge to action in reference to the object that McDougall would expect to occur on the arousal of the hunger instinct. It is not just the salivary gland that is involved. For that matter, a dog's reaction to the sound of a buzzer in a laboratory is pretty total also. It has all the marks of McDougall's instinct of curiosity, perhaps mingled with the instinct of escape. The dog orients sharply to the buzzer, with ears pricked up and muscles straining. After repeated exposures the dog takes the thing more quietly, but never does he become so indifferent, even in apparent sleep, that he does not give some sign of taking notice. It is typical of the so-called conditioned response in this case that the behavior of the dog is a kind of compromise between attending to the buzzer and attending to the food. He will, for instance, in the test trials when no food is dropped into his pan, glance toward the buzzer and then toward the pan, perhaps repeatedly alternating, salivating like a good dog all the while. The salivation is only one small part of all that is going on. Yet it is true, nevertheless, that the buzzer sound does acquire special properties from its association with the important fact of getting food. Among other things, it seems to pick up some of the emotional significance which the food itself has.[37]

Perhaps it will be clear from this brief discussion that the kind of associative linkage that Pavlov dealt with involves the transfer

[37] For an attempt to bring the whole dog back into the conditioning picture, see Zener and McCurdy (1939).

of some of the emotional charge (cathexis, valence) from one object to another. Not that the buzzer becomes equivalent to the food—any more than the so-called conditioned response is an exact duplicate of the unconditioned response to food. The buzzer sound simply becomes a new sort of thing because of its saturation with the emotion of hunger, and it may in addition (it certainly would, in the case of a human being) come to signify the approach of something more interesting, as the *tap-tap-tap* of heels down a corridor, in a particular rhythm and speed, may not only send a lover's blood pressure up but also evoke a picture of his girl approaching before she is actually in sight.

SENTIMENT HIERARCHIES Since there are for each person tremendous numbers of objects, both concrete and abstract, from a pin to the universe, his sentiments likewise are very numerous, for every experienced object is the core of some sentiment. A lucid discussion of this point is found in Adams's monograph under his Proposition 1, which reads: "There is a sentiment for every discriminated object of a given personality."[38] Some objects, however, are far more important than others for a given personality, being the centers of extensive and rich sentiments based upon multiple experiences and many different, powerful emotions. It is these great sentiments which dominate and tend to organize the whole collection of sentiments. McDougall gives special prominence to the sentiment of self-regard. This very complex sentiment, with the self—especially as the object of emotions derived from assertion against others and submission to them—as its core, has wide ramifications and is continually active because of the continual presence of the self. The quality of the self-regarding sentiment—whether it is marked by contempt or respect, confidence or uncertainty, depression or elation, and so on—saturates the personality system and tends to give it emotional unity. Every sentiment, however, is potentially the leading sentiment; that is, the center of the collection of sentiments *could* be any object whatsoever. A personality could be organized around a passionate greed for pins, but it would probably not strike us as a fine one. McDougall's view is that the strongest and finest personalities are organized around the self, because the self in a sense contains all other objects, is always present, and is inherently worthy of being valued. The reader may disagree with this view, which obviously touches on

[38] See Adams (1954), pp. 17-19.

problems of ethics and religion. Our concern here, however, is not what is the best object to have at the center of the personality, but simply the proposition that personalities do in fact display a hierarchy of sentiments.

Adams enters into an interesting debate with himself on the nature of the hierarchy. He has no doubt about the reality of the hierarchy, but he encounters trouble in trying to conceptualize it. His Proposition 4 states: "A sentiment at a given time, t, has at least the tension of its next superordinate sentiment." He then goes on to explain that "a sentiment may have *more* tension than one of which it is a member, but it cannot have less. You may want a specific food or woman more than you want food or women in general, but not less than that."[39] He then confesses that he is not entirely happy about Proposition 4 and the consequences which flow from it, and proceeds:

> I think this discomfort may be traced to some such considerations as these: although few students of personality (as usual, McDougall is an exception) have recognized the problem, we clearly need a principle of organization of personalities comparable to that provided for plant and animal organisms by the principle of gradients of physiological dominance. It is equally clear that Propositions 2, 3, and 4 provide, jointly, a candidate for this function. But in the physiological gradients the dominant end of the gradient is the region of *highest* energy as measured, for example, by rate of metabolism, while Proposition 4 ascribes at least as great energy to member sentiments as to those that include them, leaving open the possibility that their tension may be *greater* than that of their superordinate ones. Is there something wrong here?[40]

I think that Adams's paradox can be avoided. The trouble comes from assigning a superordinate position in the sentiment system to an abstract *class* of objects. This is customary in logic or in logical structures like the Linnaean classification of animals and plants, where a broad category contains a narrower one and so on down to the concrete individual members, as in the succession *phylum, subphylum, class, order, family, genus, species, particular individual specimen.* But the logic of sentiments, if I may use the phrase, seems to be just the reverse of this. A sentiment tends to be more intense the more concentratedly unique its object is. A truly passionate lover does not care for Woman in the abstract, or the whole collection of individual women, but for one single

[39] *Ibid.*, p. 22.   [40] *Ibid.*, pp. 23 f.

unduplicatable Beatrice. Or, to put the matter conversely, the power of the object of a sentiment is greater the more concretely individual it is, the farther removed it is from abstraction. The core of a sentiment system is a particular rather than a general something, and the power flows out from that center by generalization and associative linkage to other objects. A dominant sentiment-object is indeed highly energetic, and other objects are subordinate to it as the planets are subordinate to the sun. We rightly look for sentiment systems and for a hierarchical arrangement within systems and between systems, but I believe it is an error to conceive of them as logical classes in logical structures of the sort mentioned above. The problem may have arisen for Adams because he was trying to fuse the field-theory concepts of Lewin with the rather different concepts of McDougall, which tend to be monadological. In one important exposition of his personality theory, McDougall in fact adopts outright the term "monad" in place of the word "sentiment" to express his conviction that the elements of personality structure are concrete, living units. It is in this exposition that he discusses the hierarchical question most explicitly, comparing the organized personality not to a field of disembodied energy here and there gathered up into more or less solid foci, but to a social organization like an army or the Roman Catholic Church composed of individual concrete units arranged in grades of power from the Commander-in-Chief or Pope, on down.[41]

It may be well to illustrate here the notion of a sentiment hierarchy with a particular case, since it cannot be too much emphasized that there is no reality to sentiment hierarchies except in particular cases. A sentiment hierarchy is always individual and personal. The case here is a pathological one, chosen exactly because it is dramatic enough to drive home the living power of what is meant by a sentiment system. The story is condensed from Janet.[42]

Irène was the daughter of a poor French couple who had lived in straitened circumstances as long as she could remember. The father drank excessively. The mother was subject to worries which became at times overwhelming, and eventually she developed tuberculosis. Irène, at around 20 years of age, was supporting both of her parents as a seamstress, often working far into the night. Moreover, she had to nurse her tubercular mother and endure

[41] McDougall (1926), p. 546.   [42] Janet (1911), pp. 506-44.

brutal treatment from her father. In the dreadful final weeks of her illness, the mother not only demanded of Irène the usual services of the sickbed but, wanting her daughter to die with her, also insisted that she eat out of the very dishes into which she had coughed up her lungs. On the night that her mother died, her father fell in a drunken sprawl across the corpse and vomited on it. Other circumstances besides these stamped the experiences of those days in bruising, indelible detail into Irène's memory. Between the exhaustion produced by her incessant work and sleepless nights and the horror of the experiences through which she was forced to pass, Irène at the time of her mother's death was on the verge of collapse. She moved about as if in a dream. At the funeral she was overcome by hysterical laughter. A short while later she entered the hospital in a state of confusion, one of the primary symptoms being loss of recollection for the whole period surrounding her mother's death. But this forgetfulness, or amnesia, was only one aspect of Irène's behavior, and it was contradicted in the most curious ways by other aspects. She often fell into trances. When she did, she acted as if the events which had been forgotten were being lived through again: she was again present with her mother, hearing and seeing her vividly and shrinking away from her with fascinated horror when she made some extravagant demand. In short, Irène's personality was organized around experiences which centered on her mother. In the trance state this was unmistakable: the objects which dominated her consciousness then could not have been more livingly present than they were. But in the waking state, too, when she seemed to have forgotten them, these same objects ruled over her. The amnesia from which she suffered was simply the negative side of the trance hallucinations. As one reads Janet's account, one is reminded of an octopus with long strangling arms. At the center of Irène's personality, like the head of an octopus, was the face of her mother carrying an unbearably heavy charge of emotion, and reaching out in every direction from there were chains of memories dating from before and after her death, like an octopus's long arms. Irène could either gaze directly at the octopus and feel it drawing her into death, as she did in the trance states; or she could avert her gaze and, in so doing, surrender extensive tracts of her personality, as it were, thus getting peace of mind by the sacrifice of a part of her life. But so extensive and so powerful was this organization of objects within her personality that even the new experiences which she had were continually being engulfed into it. Her attempt to save herself by discarding the pathological system was only partially successful. Janet's therapeutic efforts were directed toward removing the amnesia and bringing the experiences of the trance states out into the full light of waking consciousness. This he finally accomplished, but slowly and painfully. Those events most distant from the mother and her death were the easiest to manage, those centering upon her face the hardest.

This example illustrates that an interconnected system of psychological objects (mother, father, Irène in her role of servant, etc.) is not a passive thing, like a rock collection. It is living, and it tends to reach out for still other objects. It grows continually. At the periphery it is less powerful than at the center. Such an organization is not necessarily pathological. What made it so in Irène's case was the nature of the central region, which was full of the most distressing emotions. If this region had been pleasant and hopeful the same type of organization would have been a source of strength.

Skills: behavioral traffic with objects

In dividing the topic of learning into sentiment-learning and skill-learning I am doing roughly, but not exactly, what other theorists do when they divide it into "classical" and "instrumental conditioning" (Hilgard and Marquis),[43] "respondent" and "operant conditioning" (Skinner),[44] or "conditioning" and "problem-solving" (Mowrer).[45] Mowrer, who has made a particular issue of the dual nature of learning, has argued that Pavlovian conditioning largely elicits emotional responses whereas the process of problem-solving involves "intellectual" responses. It would be more faithful to Mowrer's language to speak of conditioning as visceral-glandular learning mediated by the autonomic nervous system, and problem-solving as skeletal-muscle learning mediated through the central nervous system.[46] My adoption of language different from Mowrer's for discussing the same general areas is not due to any lack of interest in his work or that of other S-R (stimulus-response) learning theorists, and I should not want to discourage anyone from making the utmost of S-R laboratory ex-

[43] Hilgard and Marquis (1940).   [44] Skinner (1938).
[45] Mowrer (1950).
[46] *Ibid.*, Ch. 9, "On the dual nature of learning," pp. 222-74.

periments in trying to understand personality development; but it is necessary to indicate in some way that my orientation is in fact somewhat different, and I know no better way of doing it than by using terms like "object" and "instinct" and "sentiment," which imply a different emphasis and will do students of personality no harm to know about. The main difference between the S-R way of looking at things and the one which I have adopted is, I think, in the status I assign to perception. In general, S-R theorists tend to reduce perception to a minor role or obscure its distinction from behavioral action on the environment by calling both the behavior and the perception "responses." Hebb has lately referred to this obscurantism in stinging language, while taking note of the increased interest in perception manifested by psychologists of diverse theoretical schools.[47] Sometimes a peacemaker arises among the warring camps and hopefully suggests that everybody would be in agreement if only they would stop using different vocabularies. But it is not quite as simple as that. Science is a cooperative effort, but it is also a struggle and debate is of the essence.

By skill-learning I shall here mean the modification of the organism's locomotion through its environment or its action upon the objects therein, and I shall once again emphasize the importance of native tendencies.

NATIVE TENDENCIES, INDIVIDUAL DIFFERENCES, AND SELECTION   The practical manipulator of plant and animal behavior has to keep in mind the natural trends of the organism. These trends, even when they are quite specific, usually allow some latitude for variations which may be far enough from the average to be surprising. There are two kinds of behavioral variation: the variation of individuals in a group from the average of the group, and the variation of an individual's repertoire from his own average. Both kinds of variation play into the hands of the ambitious trainer.

Consider what can be done with a flowering plant. It has a powerful tendency to grow toward light. We know now that a hormone, auxin, produced in the apex of the stem is essential for this behavior. We may eliminate the tendency by cutting off the auxin-producing tip. This is somewhat comparable to cutting off the head of an animal. The plant is now uncontrolled by light, but it is scarcely good material for the plant-educator to work with. Suppose the plant is left intact, what then? It can be made

[47] Hebb (1958).

to bend in any direction—even twist into loops—by using light as the agent of control. In a sense, it is extremely docile, extremely teachable. It will perform interesting tricks for the sake of the light, and if these are the tricks which the plant-educator wants the educational problem is easily solved. But suppose he wants the plant to disregard the light in its growth? What can he do, short of cutting off its head? He can attach a heavy weight to the tip, and force it downward away from the light. But the weight must indeed be heavy.

The training of animals also has to take account of native tendencies and their particular inherited motor and perceptual abilities. Thorpe sums up recent commentaries thus:

> It might appear that the astonishing performances of circus animals are evidence against the importance of innate behaviour in mammals. That they are evidence of their remarkable powers of learning is true enough, but, as the studies of Hediger (1955) have shown—although many entirely new actions are, with great patience, taught to circus animals—the basic secret of circus training is to utilize, as far as possible, the natural, and in many cases no doubt inborn, abilities of the species. As R. C. Noble (1950) truly said, "The elephants rolling tubs and barrels, the seals balancing and throwing balls with their snouts, the tigers leaping through flaming hoops and the monkeys riding horseback or performing on trapezes, are doing things foreign to their normal experience but not to their natures. The elephants roll pieces of sun-baked clay anthills about in their native forests; seals on a rocky islet pose characteristically with their snouts held high; wild monkeys hang tenaciously to their mothers during the early months of infancy and swing from swinging branches. The trainer who prevails upon a dozen lions and tigers to assume and maintain certain positions in an exhibition cage has undoubtedly studied and exploited the animal's innate reaction to "flight distance."[48]

The animal or plant trainer exploits the natural tendencies of the organism, and a part of his success depends on clever selection. He prefers those individuals that are easily induced to do what he wants them to do. This fact of species and individual differences is important also for the scientific student of learning. If he is not wary he may fall into the trap of supposing that everything has come out the way it has because of his maze arrangements or his schedules of reinforcement. I call attention again to Schmidt's

[48] Thorpe (1956), pp. 407 f. Used by permission of the Harvard University Press, and Methuen & Co. Ltd.

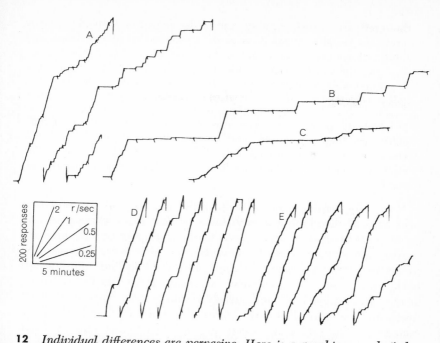

12 *Individual differences are pervasive. Here is a graphic record of the different lever-pressing performances of five children subjected to the same schedule of fixed-interval reinforcement in a Skinner-type conditioning experiment. Each child pressed a lever as frequently as he liked, receiving a trinket (reinforcement) from the machine at fixed-time intervals as determined by the experimenter. Though the experimental conditions were the same for all, each child produced a different pattern and rate of responding. (From Long et al., 1958)*

little paper on the maze behavior of two species of earthworms.[49] The differences between individual children in their lever-pressing performance after at least 10 sessions on a fixed-interval schedule are suggested by the great differences of pattern and rate in the tracings made on the cumulative recorder tape, as obtained in careful experiments by my colleague Eugene Long and shown in Figure 12. Pavlov was acutely aware of the problem of individual differences, as anyone who works long with a motley assortment of dogs must be. He wrote, for example:

In the elaboration of conditioned reflexes, both positive and negative, we observe in dogs enormous differences in the speed of formation of

[49] Schmidt (1955).

these reflexes, in their stability, and in the degree of absoluteness they attain. In certain animals it is easy to produce positive reflexes, and these reflexes are stable under varying conditions; but in these dogs, it is very difficult to elaborate inhibitory reflexes, and in some animals it is impossible to obtain them in pure and exact form, for the reflex will always contain an element of positive activity. This is the characteristic of one group. At the other extreme, however, there are animals in which the positive conditioned reflexes are formed with great difficulty, are highly unstable, and become inhibited by the slightest change in the surroundings, i.e., they lose their effectiveness. The inhibitory reflexes, on the other hand, are quickly formed and remain stable.[50]

Now, one consequence of these reflections is that the educator who aims at developing a high level of skill in everybody in any given performance is very likely to be disappointed; he may, of course, aim at mediocrity for everybody a little more successfully, by urging the less gifted forward and holding the more gifted back; and he may be even more successful if he sets the standard at near the lowest level and merely requires everybody to do that much and no more. But this is more the policeman's role than the educator's. The real educational question is whether and by what means a performance can be improved, given a certain individual, and to what extent.

IMPROVING A PERFORMANCE: BIRD SONG   It may help to tease out some of the complexities of the learning problem if we consider for a moment a skill to which learning undoubtedly contributes something, namely, a bird's singing.

Among the birds, singing is primarily a male occupation. In many species it is associated with changes in the gonads, which in their turn are governed by seasonal changes in the amount of sunlight. Seasonal stimulation of the gonads may be partially replaced by injection of the male hormone. In fact, this treatment is so effective that if given to a female canary she will sing like a male. An article by Herrick and Harris[51] describes the results of injecting testosterone phenylacetate into five young female canaries. Within twelve days after injection they were all singing sporadically, and in a few days more were singing in a sustained and vigorous fashion exactly like males. After a period of time the singing ter-

[50] Pavlov (1928), pp. 373 f.   [51] Herrick and Harris (1957).

minated. Another injection of the hormone set them to singing again, until once more the chemical effects wore off.

We legitimately conclude from this experiment that the *impulse* to sing is provided in some fashion by the male hormone. Is the *pattern* of the song likewise chemically controlled? Unfortunately, the paper cited tells us nothing about the prior experience of these birds, so that we do not know whether latent learning due to hearing male canary song could be brought in to explain the results. We must fill the lacuna by drawing on other studies. Huxley has reported that young canaries exposed only to the song of the nightingale develop a song intermediate between those typical of the two species.[52] This definitely points to modification of the innate pattern by experience.

More detailed information is obtainable in the case of the chaffinch (*Fringilla coelebs*), which has been studied by Thorpe. In considering this information, we must not forget that there are differences between the various species of birds in their susceptibility to outside influence. The mockingbird, for instance, is notoriously imitative, whereas many other species sing only the song of their kind and may be only slightly imitative even within those limits. The chaffinch is a bird whose innate pattern of song is influenced by hearing the song of its own species. Thorpe studied these birds under three experimental conditions: (1) where the young birds were normally reared by their own parents and then separated from them at the end of their first summer, but kept among other birds of different species and within hearing of wild chaffinch song in the ensuing spring; (2) where the young birds, reared by their parents and then separated from them, were kept out of hearing of all bird vocalizations except those of similarly isolated young; and (3) where the young birds were hand-reared from the beginning and kept isolated all along, so that they had the example neither of their parents nor of other mature birds. Birds under the first condition developed a perfectly normal chaffinch song; under the second condition they varied slightly from the normal; but under the third condition they departed significantly from the normal, retaining the basic outlines of chaffinch song but omitting certain details. In this third case the young birds noticeably influenced one another.

[52] Huxley (1942).

Each isolated community of such birds builds up, during the period February to April inclusive, an entirely individual but extremely uniform community pattern, the resemblances throughout the song being so close that it is often very difficult to distinguish the songs of the different members of the group one from another even when subjected to a detailed analysis by the sound spectograph.[53]

Thorpe concludes from his experiments that experience of hearing other birds affects the innate chaffinch song pattern and does so both long before singing has begun and for some time after it has become active. His words are:

It appears, then, that the difference between the hand-reared birds and those which had a normal fledgling and early juvenile life, but which were isolated from September onwards, is explicable only on the assumption that some characteristics of the normal song have been learnt in the earliest youth, before the bird itself is able to produce any kind of full song. It seems that these birds have by their first September learnt that the song "should" be in three phrases, and that the terminal phrase should contain a more or less elaborate flourish. The details of this terminal phrase, with its flourish, are apparently not learnt then, but are worked out by competitive singing with other members of the group in the following spring.[54]

THEORY OF SKILL-LEARNING   A general theory of skill-learning, if based upon Thorpe's results (which I believe could be duplicated in many animals besides birds and with reference to many skills), would emphasize three major points, viz.:

1. An impulse toward a certain kind of activity must arise in the organism.
2. This impulse-driven activity must be guided by models of three kinds: (a) innate patterns, (b) early examples, and (c) contemporary examples.
3. The activity must be practiced for some length of time to reach ultimate refinement.

These principles, I believe, are worth long and serious consideration, but the commentary here will be brief.

The impulse is indispensable. All educators of human beings are aware of the importance of motivation, but perhaps too often motivation is thought of as dependent on some kind of external in-

[53] Thorpe (1956), p. 371.   [54] *Ibid.*, pp. 371 f.

centive like grades or money or other reinforcement at the disposal of the educator. Instead of besieging the young with such external inducements, it might be better strategy to lie in wait for the desired natural impulse to manifest itself and then encourage it by offering not extrinsic rewards like grades, which are frequently merely distracting, but a useful example or model, plus sincere interest by the educator himself. It is very interesting, however, that a strong impulse may arise and carry a young person to considerable achievement in the face of outright discouragement by others. This does not mean that examples can be entirely dispensed with; but the young person who receives no adequate example from his home or school milieu may actively seek it out elsewhere.

After the impulse toward a certain activity has been detected, the educator may usefully furnish contemporary example, and the learner may consciously practice. Fruitful practice, of course, is something more than sheer repetition; it is repetition with intention —the intention to achieve perfection or at least to become better. The educator, by furnishing an appropriate example and monitoring the learner's performance, steers him toward the goal and in many instances of course will have a much clearer idea of that goal than the learner himself. Hence arises a common difficulty: the educator becomes impatient because the learner does not approach the goal as rapidly as would be possible if he clearly perceived it, and the learner becomes discouraged because he does not see that in reality he *is* approaching it. But here we are talking about conscious practice, which can only take place after the impulse has led to activity. We must not overlook item 2(b), the early examples which seem to be effective without benefit of activity.

Latent learning has often been denied, and on the basis of well-designed laboratory experiments. Nevertheless, it seems to occur. In Thorpe's chaffinch experiment it surely does, and it is Thorpe's opinion that the drift of the available evidence is definitely for it. He states:

It is noteworthy that MacCorquodale and Meehl (1954), although starting out with a highly critical attitude, found themselves, after a very detailed study, 'somewhat more impressed by the over-all trend of evidence than we had expected to be'; and when we consider the strong support now available from other and lower animal groups, we seem safe in taking latent learning as remarkably well established.[55]

[55] *Ibid.*, p. 92.

We must, evidently, accept latent learning as a fact, and admit that we do not very well understand the conditions for it. My own hunch is that social attachments are a critical factor. The young, when strongly attached to their parents, may pick up in seeming passivity an enormous amount of knowledge from them by a process like electromagnetic induction—a process which was at least partially covered by McDougall's phrase "primitive passive sympathy." Some such process could result in the young storing up for later use various kinds of models or examples of performance. Perhaps this is essential for high achievement.

Some curious introspections by Titchener may not be out of place here. One of these is the following:

> I have practically no gift of musical composition, and my skill as a performer is below zero. On the other hand, I come of a musical family, and was fortunate enough to hear a great deal of the best piano music in my childhood. My musical endowment . . . consists in a quick and comprehensive understanding of a composition, a sort of logical and aesthetic *Einfühlung*, an immediate (or very rapid) grasp of the sense and fitness of the musical structure.[56]

What he got from his passive childhood experience, then, was an awareness of musical pattern which would have served him well if he had gone on to active performance. But actually there was more to it than this readiness to appreciate. That early experience seems to have left behind some active reverberations, to which the above footnote refers; for Titchener states:

> If I may venture on a very sweeping statement, I should say that I never sit down to read a book, or to write a paragraph, or to think out a problem, without a musical accompaniment. Usually the accompaniment is orchestral, with a preponderance of the wood-wind,—I have a sort of personal affection for the oboe; sometimes it is in the tone-colour of piano or violin; never, I think, is it vocal. Usually, again, it is the reproduction of a known composition; on rare occasions it is wholly unfamiliar.[57]

Whether early learning is a matter of passive induction or conditioning or problem-solving it is becoming increasingly clear that a strong positive sentiment for the teacher is vital, and this applies to later learning also. Mowrer brings out the significance of the strong positive sentiment in his interesting paper on talking birds.[58]

[56] Titchener (1909), p. 205. Used by permission of Mr. John B. Titchener.
[57] *Ibid.*, p. 9.   [58] Mowrer (1950), pp. 688-726.

It is true that he emphasizes reward—the offering of food and drink, but he also says:

> While one has been following the training procedures just described —which are all directed toward getting the bird to talk—one has also been doing something else: one has been training the bird to be tame, affectionate, and dependent. This latter part of the total procedure is no less important than the part which is more specifically directed toward getting the bird to say its first words; for it is only after a very close relationship has been established between bird and trainer that the bird's greatest possibilities as a talker will be realized.[59]

Some of Mowrer's remarks might be interpreted to mean that he thinks the establishment of this positive sentiment is dependent on rewarding the bird by reducing its hunger drive, but we may question such an interpretation in the light of various studies, including that of Harlow and Zimmermann cited earlier.

If the positive sentiment for the trainer or educator or friend is to eventuate in learning anything from him, there must be some superiority on his side, and it must be recognized by the learner. In an old practical handbook for farmers by Magner a good deal of attention is paid to this factor. The horse trainer, he says, must establish his superiority over the horse. Both technique and personal character are involved. As for technique, Magner used a number of simple leverage devices for turning the horse around or throwing him to the ground without injury. As for personal character, he says:

> The least intimation, in action or expression, of weakness or lack of confidence, is simply fatal in the management of horses of a spirited, aggressive character. The tone of voice, the expression of countenance, in fact every action, must imply confidence. It requires in the man the most absolute truthfulness and honesty with a horse, to have him understand without confusion or excitement, as well as establishing his confidence by kindness; and all these, we see, are requisites of the highest character.[60]

Children, too, respond to superiority and are quick to detect fake. Bad as ignorance of a subject is in one who professes to teach it, dishonesty and that cowardly false kindness which ignores faults will also suffice to impair the educational process. Ignorance, dishonesty, and cowardice are no more desirable in a kindergarten teacher than in a horse trainer.

[59] *Ibid.*, p. 692.   [60] Magner (1889), p. 76.

Major Brickwood, another old writer on horse-training, also stresses the character of the trainer, mentioning a natural fondness for animals, patience, and courage as requisites; but he notes, too, the importance of the early formation of a positive sentiment by the animal for man in general. "The colt should be handled from the day of its birth, so that it may grow thoroughly accustomed to man, without ever having experienced the feeling of fear."[61] When Brickwood comes to the technical details, he stresses gradualness and the avoidance of impossible tasks. Since the Ninth Edition of the *Encyclopaedia Britannica*, in which his essay appears, may not be readily available to the reader, I quote at some length:

> When about six months old the colt should receive his first lesson in jumping. Where practicable, there is no better plan than to feed him in one spot, the approach to which is guarded by a stout rail, which should in the first instance lie on the ground, and over which he must step in order to reach his corn. In the course of about a month the rail may be raised 6 inches, and so on from time to time, but the process should be gradual in the extreme; 2 or 3 inches a month is sufficient until it is a couple of feet high, where it should remain for a time, but at three years the colt should jump it at 3 feet. Before he reaches this age the saddle should have been put on and left there for half an hour at a time, the groom letting the girths and stirrups flap about. At three years the pupil should be backed by a light weight; if the rider be the usual attendant, so much the better, for then it is improbable that much resistance will be shown. The riding exercise should be varied by the young horse being led by a rather long rein over roughish ground, such as a common or a ploughed field, when it is not too hard, and over little ditches and very low fences, but they must be small, as it is very undesirable to have a horse refuse at first, or to have him fall down in attempting a jump. He should be subsequently ridden over small places, but should always have a lead given to him by an old horse; and the two should stand in adjoining boxes, so that the colt may be accustomed to his pilot. At four years old he may be ridden to the meet, and suffered to see a fox hound, but should on no account be ridden up to the hounds, nor should he be used as a regular hunter till he is six,—if not till seven it will be all the better for him.[62]

These prescriptions will perhaps remind the reader of the teaching machines advocated by Skinner in the last few years,[63] or the suggestion of Rock that rote subjects like the multiplication table should

[61] Brickwood (1881), p. 192.
[63] Skinner (1958).

[62] *Ibid.*

be taught one unit at a time with long intervals between units to avoid retroactive inhibition.[64]

There are doubtless many practical hints in the experimental literature which have not been utilized in the teaching of skills as fully as might be. There are also some hints which have not been utilized in learning theory as fully as might be. The role of the experimenter himself as the object of positive or negative sentiments is one of these. They affect the outcome of experiments, for one thing. Take this illuminating comment by Maier on experiments designed to produce neurotic stereotyped behavior (i.e., fixated position responses) in rats:

> A further point of interest and possible importance is mentioned here in the hope that it may encourage other experimenters to report similar observations. This is the role of the experimenter in influencing the behavior of animals, particularly under stress. Some years ago two research assistants were working in adjacent rooms on related problems, each with three groups of twelve or more rats from the same colony, over a period of a semester. One of them obtained the usual number of fixated position responses (over 50 per cent) in each of the successive groups with which he worked; the other was unable to obtain a single fixation. Although they compared procedures on preliminary training, methods of testing, and other general routines, they were unable to determine the reason for the differences. Motivational considerations also failed to throw light on the matter. The researcher who was unable to obtain fixations required them for his doctoral dissertation, so that his results did not correspond with his motives. However, it was discovered that he felt sorry for the rats, and this may have caused him to pet the rats between trials somewhat more than other researchers.[65]

If such an attitude in an experimenter can upset the predictions in Maier-type frustration experiments where the rats take a considerable beating from the reinforcement schedule, there is every reason to suppose that a similar factor enters powerfully into human learning situations. And in fact we know that a teacher's sympathy and love can go a long way toward mitigating the rigors of study, making difficult things easy, dull things exciting, virtue more attractive than vice. One of the most charming expositions of this thesis is Roger Ferdinand's "Les 'J 3' "—a modern French play about a gang of roughneck schoolboys transformed into civilized gentlemen and ardent students by a touch of love.

[64] Rock (1958).   [65] Maier (1956), pp. 375 f.

Learning and personality

One brief definition of personality in common use is that it is the way an individual behaves toward his environment. It is commonly believed that learning has a lot to do with this. This chapter by no means contradicts that view, but it attempts to show, on the one hand, that learning has an important hereditary base and, on the other, that the perception of and attachment to objects are aspects of the process which must not be neglected. Among the numerous objects which the growing child comes to discriminate, the most important are those which he identifies as persons. Sometimes the persons identified as such by the child are not human, but it is eminently the human being who qualifies for this role. For his objects, and particularly for his person-objects, the child develops sentiments, and these sentiments become organized in hierarchical fashion within the personality system. At the same time, he develops all manner of skills by which he appeals to, coerces, circumvents, escapes, moves toward, reshapes, destroys, clings to, and in other ways acts upon the objects which surround him. It must be evident to the reader that the discovery of objects and the learning of sentiments and skills constitute an inexhaustible subject which this chapter, long as it may seem, has barely skimmed. The next chapter will continue the discussion by concentrating on the single topic of the decisiveness of critical moments and conditions.

References for chapter 4

Adams, D. K. (1953) The organs of perception: sentiments. *Journal of Personality*, 22, 52-59.
—— (1954) *The anatomy of personality*. Garden City, N.Y.: Doubleday.
Beach, F. A. (1955) The descent of instinct. *Psychological Review*, 62, 401-10.
Brickwood, E. D. (1881) Horse. Part II: history, management, and breeding. In *Encyclopaedia Britannica*. 9th ed. Vol. 12, pp. 184-99.
Cattell, R. B. (1950) *Personality: a systematic theoretical and factual study*. New York: McGraw-Hill.
Fletcher, R. (1957) *Instinct in man in the light of recent work in comparative psychology*. London: Allen & Unwin.
Harlow, H. F., and Zimmermann, R. R. (1959) Affectional responses in the infant monkey. *Science*, 130, 421-32.
Hebb, D. O. (1958) Alice in wonderland or psychology among the bio-

logical sciences. In Harlow, H. F., and Woolsey, C. N. (Eds.) *Biological and chemical bases of behavior.* Madison: Univ. of Wisconsin Press, pp. 451-67.

Herrick, E. H., and Harris, J. O. (1957) Singing female canaries. *Science,* 125, 1299-1300.

Hess, E. H. (1959) Imprinting. *Science,* 130, 133-41.

Hilgard, E. R. (1957) *Introduction to psychology.* 2nd ed. New York: Harcourt, Brace & World.

————, and Marquis, D. G. (1940) *Conditioning and learning.* New York: Appleton-Century.

Hovland, C. I. (1937) The generalization of conditioned responses. I. The sensory generalization of conditioned responses with varying frequencies of tone. *Journal of General Psychology,* 17, 125-48.

Hull, C. L. (1952) *A behavior system: an introduction to behavior theory concerning the individual organism.* New Haven: Yale Univ. Press.

Huxley, J. S. (1942) *Evolution: the modern synthesis.* New York: Harper.

Janet, P. (1911) *L'état mental des hystériques.* Paris: Alcan.

Klein, M. (1946) Notes on some schizoid mechanisms. *International Journal of Psycho-Analysis,* 27, 99-110.

Long, E. R., Hammack, J. T., May, F., and Campbell, B. J. (1958) Intermittent reinforcement of operant behavior in children. *Journal of the Experimental Analysis of Behavior,* 1, 315-39.

Lorenz, K. Z. (1952) *King Solomon's ring.* New York: Crowell.

———— (1958) The evolution of behavior. *Scientific American,* 199 (December), 67-76, 78.

Magner, D. (1889) *The farmer's encyclopedia.* Battle Creek, Mich.: Magner.

Maier, N. R. F. (1956) Frustration theory: restatement and extension. *Psychological Review,* 63, 370-88.

McDougall, W. (1908) *An introduction to social psychology.* London: Methuen.

———— (1923) *Outline of psychology.* New York: Scribner's.

———— (1926) *Outline of abnormal psychology.* New York: Scribner's.

Mowrer, O. H. (1950) *Learning theory and personality dynamics.* New York: Ronald.

Pavlov, I. P. (1928) *Lectures on conditioned reflexes: twenty-five years of objective study of the higher nervous activity (behavior) of animals.* New York: International Publishers. Vol. 1.

Piaget, J. (1954) *The construction of reality in the child.* New York: Basic Books.

Rock, I. (1958) Repetition and learning. *Scientific American,* 199 (August), 68-70, 72.

Schmidt, H., Jr. (1955) Behavior of two species of worms in the same maze. *Science,* 121, 341-42.

Shand, A. F. (1914) *Foundations of character*. London: Macmillan.

Skinner, B. F. (1938) *The behavior of organisms: an experimental analysis*. New York: Appleton-Century.

——— (1948) "Superstition" in the pigeon. *Journal of Experimental Psychology*, 38, 168-72.

——— (1958) Teaching machines. *Science*, 128, 969-77.

Spitz, R. A. (1946) The smiling response: a contribution to the onto-genesis of social relations. *Genetic Psychology Monographs*, 34, 57-125.

Thorpe, W. H. (1956) *Learning and instinct in animals*. Cambridge, Mass.: Harvard Univ. Press.

Tinbergen, N. (1951) *The study of instinct*. Oxford: Clarendon.

Titchener, E. B. (1909) *Lectures on the experimental psychology of the thought-processes*. New York: Macmillan.

Zener, K., and McCurdy, H. G. (1939) Analysis of motivational factors in conditioned behavior: I. The differential effect of changes in hunger upon conditioned, unconditioned, and spontaneous salivary secretion. *Journal of Psychology*, 8, 321-50.

5

LEARNING:
CRITICAL MOMENTS
AND CONDITIONS

Preview   *The effect of environmental influences depends upon the current relations between organism and environment, and also upon the timing and emotional power of events. Children growing up under the care of loving parents appear to have developmental advantages over those from more impersonal environments. Particular deprivations and conditionings may be crucial in the early years. Traumatic experiences are capable of setting in motion important long-term processes. But also seemingly trivial events may have this decisive effect. It is the meaning of events which counts, and this depends greatly on the stage of development at which the individual has arrived.*

It should not surprise us that some conditions of the environment are more critical for personality development than others, and that there are moments when an influence from the environment can be especially powerful. To specify the conditions and the moments is certainly not an easy task. Besides, the study of these matters has just barely begun. So important is the topic, however, that the scrappiest evidence and the most tentative conclusions have extraordinary interest.

Generally favorable and unfavorable conditions

Largely as the result of psychoanalytic investigations, the early period of life has come to be regarded in recent years as enormously significant for the future of the individual. From all sides have come studies bearing on one proposition in particular, namely, that the infant or young child whose relations with a mother or mother-substitute are not close, warm, and continuous is doomed to an impoverished life. Much of this literature makes up in moral fervor for what it lacks in the way of evidence, and we have been swept emotionally into an era of child-care philosophy at marked variance with the tough-minded instructions of government bulletins on child care thirty years ago, when the behavioristic theories of Watson were much in vogue. The reaction against the Watsonian prescriptions is not simply a product of emotionalism, however; and the caliber of scientific work in this field is steadily improving.

A general survey of the pertinent information was made by Bowlby in *Maternal Care and Mental Health,* a monograph published by the World Health Organization in 1951.[1] He finds that, with few exceptions, the empirical studies support the hypothesis of the importance of mother-love. In his opinion it is the first year which is most vital, though older children too may suffer acutely from loss of the mother or diminution of her love. "At what age," he asks, "does the child cease to be vulnerable to a lack of maternal care?" He answers that probably vulnerability diminishes slowly and asymptotically.[2] By this he means that the curve of vulnerability may be like a curve of growth, sloping off to a plateau of relatively great resistance after adolescence.

Workers who have had intimate contact with children undergoing maternal deprivation have been impressed with the apparent contradictions inhering in the child–mother relationship. On the one hand, children who are forced to live with a minimum of

[1] For a simplified version of this report, see Bowlby (1953a).
[2] Bowlby (1951), p. 26.

maternal care seem to be self-contained, quiet, well-behaved, stoical when separated from their mothers. On the other hand, those who are close to their mothers react to deprivation with outspoken grief and thus seem more vulnerable to loss than the others who have never enjoyed much love. Such an expert as Anna Freud, however, cautions us that the surface calm of the unloved child is a more sinister index of fundamental damage than the violent grief of the child who has previously been loved a great deal. For personality development, it seems, as Tennyson says,

> 'Tis better to have loved and lost
> Than never to have loved at all

even at an early and vulnerable age.

According to Bowlby, the older child (5 to 8 years old) tolerates separation from the mother better the more loving the relationship has been. The calmness of the reaction in this case is not to be confused with the stoicism of the love-starved. Both the passionate grief of the young child and the calm of the older on being separated from a loved mother are to be interpreted, Bowlby thinks, as expressions of the reality and vitality of the love relationship. The stoicism of the love-starved is different: it is an apathy which manifests the absence of love and the child's incapacity for forming warm attachments. The sentiment structure, to use our theoretical language, is damaged, and the child is thus incapable of making the moral and intellectual progress which depends on such positive sentiments as are possessed by the well-loved child. The theory is attractive. Let us examine the evidence.

INSTITUTIONAL CHILDREN: FREUD AND BURLINGHAM   A child experiencing complete maternal neglect in the earliest days of infancy would die in a short time, if no substitute were found. In normal communities, however, such an infant is likely to be taken over by someone else. The substitute may be an institution. Now, institutional care differs from ordinary maternal care chiefly in not providing the child with a close personal relationship with an adult. Otherwise, the institution may do a good job. Its dietitians may supply more nourishing food than a mother would, and it may offer the advantages of spacious quarters and prompt medical attention. Nevertheless, many observers believe that children in institutions undergo psychological stunting.

Anna Freud and Dorothy Burlingham, reporting on their experience with British wartime residential nurseries, admit that the child living in an institution may appear to surpass the child living in a family during the first five months of life. They state that their nursery children during this period surpassed, in general physical development, children of comparable age in "the average proletarian household."[3] But after this period the scales begin to turn against the institution child. Family children, because of their interaction with adults (particularly the mother), become livelier and more sociable.

In the period from one to two years, the picture again is mixed and seems at first glance to favor the institution child. In particular, the institution child displays greater muscular activity and calmer, more efficient eating behavior, though noticeably inferior speech development and habits of cleanliness and self-control. On close inspection, even the apparent superiorities look doubtful. The greater muscular activity is, in part, due to bored restlessness and absence of restraint in the bare open spaces of the nursery buildings. The good feeding behavior means that the food is simply food, a queller of hunger, a drive-reducer. For the family child food has special emotional meanings bound up with the mother who provides it. Food is in part a symbol for the mother. As such, it enters into the communication going on between mother and child and shares in their lover's quarrels. As for speech and habit-training, in which the family child is openly superior, these are developments which are expedited by a mother's presence. Little children running around in a room together, as they do in a nursery, have scant need for speech, and if this is their prevailing human contact they do not acquire it very fast. A child with a mother, in contrast, is induced not only by the mother's constant example but also by the personal relationship to explore the intimacies of speech, which may be regarded as a further development and refinement of the total communication going on between them since the first nursing contacts. Cleanliness habits, also, stem from the loving reactions of the child to the parental demands; they are simple bodily skills, charged with emotion, which the little child *can* acquire to please a mother more rapidly than without that inducement.

According to this analysis of the facts, already at the end of the second year the institution child is deficient in two major respects, as compared to the family child: (1) he lags behind in speech,

[3] Freud and Burlingham (1944), p. 12.

habits, and social graces, and (2) he suffers a general emotional impoverishment. It is the latter deficiency which is the more basic.

Freud and Burlingham do not neglect to point out that children living primarily with their age-mates rather than with adults do develop a variety of emotions and social skills appropriate to their primitive horde life. The social bonds thus formed, I should like to suggest, may be a positive cause for some of the developmental lags, since the norms of such groups would tend to alienate the child from the values of the adult world. But the child, it appears, is not really satisfied with gang life. One who has not been too long in a peer group will seize greedily upon a mother or mother-substitute if one is available. With very little encouragement an institution child will build up the fantasy of a loving mother or father. Yet this so eagerly desired relationship, if it exists in reality, necessarily plunges the child into experiences which are painful. As Freud and Burlingham remark, children may be as good as gold in the nursery and exasperatingly difficult at home. "This is not—as many nursery-school teachers seem to think—due to the fact that the mother does not know how to handle the child whereas the teacher does. It is due to the difference in the emotional response to the mother and teacher respectively."[4]

The family and the nursery provide two different environments and lead to different consequences in personality development. They are not to be assessed without reference to values and without reference to the future. Freud and Burlingham say:

> An infant in a residential nursery may acquire the rough-and-ready methods of social adaptation which are induced by the atmosphere of the toddlers' room; methods of attack and defence, of giving in and sharing, "swapping," etc.; it may further acquire conventions and behaviour patterns in obedience to the nursery-routine and in imitation of its elders. But neither of these processes, though adding to the growth of the child's personality, will lead to the embodiment of moral values. . . . Identification of this latter kind takes place under one condition only: as the result and residue of emotional attachment to people who are the real and living personifications of the demands which every civilized society upholds for the restriction and transformation of primitive instinctive tendencies.[5]

According to their view, then, the mother's role goes far beyond the provision of food and protection. In the atmosphere of love which she and the child in conjunction can create, intellect

[4] *Ibid.*, p. 58.   [5] *Ibid.*, p. 125.

and morality flourish as they do not where this atmosphere is lacking. The particular quality of the mother and her ideals clearly matters; it is not simply mother love which is involved, it is also mother-example as made living and powerful through love. As the reader can see, all this is in harmony with the learning principles discussed in the previous chapter, where it was argued that even in the case of horse training the quality of the human guide and the animal's sentiments for him are essential factors.

INSTITUTIONAL CHILDREN: OTHER STUDIES   Firm statistical and experimental data on the theory represented by Freud and Burlingham would be desirable. Perhaps all studies so far are defective in one way or another, but there are several which deserve respectful attention.

Gesell and Amatruda paint a generalized picture of the kind of institution which may produce developmental lag. They have in mind a composite of several institutions known to them. Such an institution is not a place where there is gross neglect or a strikingly abnormal population of children; it is, in their words,

> near average size, moderately well staffed and equipped, and under medical supervision. The children range, shall we say, from a few weeks to a few years of age. The population is ever changing. Some children come on a brief emergency basis, but there is a strong tendency for all to remain longer than was intended. The institution has a good local reputation for the care which it bestows on its charges. Some of them have come from miserable homes. The general level of the education and intelligence of their parents is low average rather than high average, but there are always some exceptions in both directions of the mentality gradient—a few bright, others not so bright.[6]

Children in the care of such an institution, they find, display some typical deficiencies or lags in their developmental schedule. These are outlined in Table 7, where the final item (definite improvement, with improvement in environment) is meant as an index of environmental as opposed to genetic causation of the depression of the developmental quotient (DQ). This item reflects Gesell's usual confidence in the genetically determined maturational resources of the child, for he supposes that the genetic capacity can be restrained but not deracinated by such an environ-

[6] Gesell and Amatruda (1947), p. 320.

Table 7
Symptoms of institutional retardation in young children

symptom	approximate age of appearance	
diminished interest and reactivity	8-12	weeks
reduced integration of total behavior	8-12	"
beginning retardation evidenced by disparity between exploitation in supine and sitting positions	12-16	"
excessive preoccupation with strange persons	12-16	"
general retardation (prone behavior relatively unaffected)	24-28	"
blandness of facial expression	24-28	"
impoverished initiative	24-28	"
channelization and stereotypies of sensori-motor behavior	24-28	"
ineptness in new social situations	44-48	"
exaggerated resistance to new situations	48-52	"
relative retardation in language behavior	12-15	months
definite improvement	whenever improvement in environment occurs	

Adapted from Gesell and Amatruda (1947), p. 327.

ment. Bowlby omits it in his reproduction of the table in his WHO report, as if judging it irrelevant. Yet for this stage of life at least there is confirmation of Gesell's position from Freud and Burlingham. They say that a child taken from a residential nursery may blossom out surprisingly in speech and other social graces after a few days with loving adults in a home. Bowlby and most of those on whom he relies look altogether more pessimistically on the retardations wrought by institutional living.

One of Bowlby's mainstays is a study by Goldfarb which purports to show that permanent intellectual and emotional scars are left by two or three years of institutional care in early childhood.[7] Inasmuch as this is a key document in the history of the question of institutional influence, it will be examined here carefully, although the conclusion we shall be forced to is that it does not prove its thesis, however true the thesis itself may be.

Goldfarb's sample consisted of 15 children 10 to 14 years old who had spent about 3 years in an institution which they had en-

[7] Goldfarb (1943).

tered, on the average, at 4½ months, and who had afterwards lived in foster homes. These children were matched in age and sex with a control set of 15 who had never been in an institution but had been transferred from their original homes into foster homes at an average age of 14 months.

There is an unfortunate flaw in Goldfarb's study. His evidence for the original equality of these two sets of children is indirect and not very satisfactory. It is based upon the argument that the hereditary background was similar, and he even suggests that if there was any inequality it favored the institutional children. What are the facts that he appeals to? He points out that the mothers of the two sets of children came from the same countries in the same proportions (10 in each case from the United States, and 5 from Russia, Poland, or Austria), and that the mothers of the institutional children had a better occupational and educational record—whence he concludes: "It is apparent that hereditary background will be of negligible significance as a means of explaining any observed differences in favor of the foster home group or to the disadvantage of the institution group."[8] Skeptics will not be convinced by so tenuous a line of reasoning. They will ask why mothers so capable, economically and intellectually, as those of the institutional children should have turned them over to an orphanage in the first place. Goldfarb's indirect and incomplete answer to this question is that 73 per cent of the institutional children were born out of wedlock. But this fact (compared with the fact that 33 per cent of the foster home children were born out of wedlock) suggests that the mothers of the institutional set were less foresighted and less sensitive to the welfare of their children than were the mothers of the foster home set. We cannot be quite comfortable about the alleged superiority of the mothers of the institutional children.

Goldfarb believed that he found two sorts of defects attributable to the early childhood experiences of the institutional children—a stunting of intelligence and certain disturbances in the social-emotional sphere. Table 8 presents his comparison of the two sets of children with regard to intelligence test performance (Wechsler-Bellevue) at adolescence. The difference between the compared groups is statistically significant, as indicated. In regard to the social-emotional sphere, he states concerning their behavior in a frustration experiment:

[8] *Ibid.*, pp. 107 f.

Table 8
Institution vs. foster-home children's scores on the Wechsler-Bellevue intelligence test

	institution children (N=15)		foster-home children (N=15)		difference in mean IQ	t	probability
	MEAN IQ	S.D.	MEAN IQ	S.D.			
verbal	74.26	11.26	96.44	10.09	22.18	5.69	less than .01
performance	76.66	13.82	94.97	10.99	18.31	4.02	less than .01
whole scale	72.39	10.45	95.37	9.05	22.98	6.43	less than .01

Adapted from Goldfarb (1943), p. 111.

Both groups seem to approach the problem with equal degree of cooperation, but the institution child is emotionally more apathetic, is less concerned with success and less moved by failure or social competition, and he is more likely to disregard limitations or prohibitons. The institution child is thus adjusting on a more superficial level and is less motivated by ordinary social and human identifications.[9]

Goldfarb's conclusion that the observed differences between the two sets of children are to be explained by their early childhood histories is called into question by Bodman[10] on empirical grounds. Bodman suspects that the intelligence of the two sets was not equal originally, and that the social-emotional differences are correlated with the intelligence differences. In his own study of English children (50 from institutions, 52 from own families), Bodman found that hereditary background was at least as important as nature of residence. He was chiefly concerned with social adjustment, and hence he tried to equate the two sets for intelligence but actually wound up with a difference of several points in favor of the family children (90 IQ vs. 99.5 IQ). On the Vineland Social Maturity Test, the social quotient of the institution children was 92.9 as opposed to 106.5 for the family children. From this Goldfarb might have concluded that the institutional life was having a depressing effect. But Bodman noticed that the institution group had a very high proportion of defective relatives. To be precise, 74.3 per cent of these children had "insane, defective, epileptic and antisocial relatives," whereas this was true of only 11.5 per cent of the family children.[11] When the children were classified by hereditary background rather than by place of resi-

[9] *Ibid.*, p. 121.   [10] Bodman (1950).
[11] *Ibid.*, p. 249.

dence, those with poor backgrounds were found to have a social quotient on the Vineland of 91.6 as compared with 105 for those with good backgrounds. In short, whichever method of classification was used—residence or heredity—the measured difference in social maturity was about the same.

Perhaps the most judicious conclusion from these and similar studies is that hereditary and selective factors cannot be left out of the reckoning when children from institutions are compared with children from families, but that institutional life may indeed have some depressing effect on development. Bowlby himself has conceded that heredity must be allowed for when estimating the seriousness of the removal of love objects, though he has been led to this position more by studies on animals by such workers as Lorenz and Scott than by studies on human beings.[12]

The existing data do not permit us to say confidently that early maternal deprivation has long-term deleterious effects. The hypothesis is clear-cut and subject to testing, it is based on reasonable theory, but the studies which have been adduced in its favor are methodologically or factually weak. The strong assertions of Spitz, for example, rest upon very doubtful evidence.[13] We may only hope that adequate studies will be forthcoming.

EFFECTS OF WARM PARENTAL CARE We have been considering the possible effects of early childhood environments lacking in richness and warmth. What about the opposite condition? Could intensely warm parent-child relations have a stimulating effect?

Much of the literature on child rearing is heavy with foreboding. Even maternal love has been decried. Watson in 1928 traced most of the psychological ills of mankind to too much mothering, and dedicated his book sardonically "To the first mother who brings up a happy child."[14] Like Anna Freud he had noticed how regularly the child who is the object of solicitous mother love resorts to tears, tantrums, and clamoring demandingness. His evaluation of this behavior, however, is very different from hers. For her it is a sign that the child-mother relationship is a live, going affair; for him it is a sign of disease. More recently, too, and under psychoanalytic influence (Watson also was under that influence and feared the Oedipus complex as he feared disease

[12] Bowlby (1953b).
[13] See Spitz (1945, 1946), and Pinneau (1955).
[14] Watson (1928).

germs), some writers have suspected that the loving home breeds psychological disorders.

More than a trace of this attitude is present in Levy's book on maternal "overprotection."[15] Though his selection of cases was meant to isolate the effects of nonoptimal mother love, his data may still be used to answer the question of whether intense parental care stimulates a child's development.

Levy defines maternal overprotection as involving excessive contact ("continuous companionship of mother and child, prolonged nursing care, excessive fondling, or sleeping with the mother long past infancy"[16]), infantilization ("the performance of activities in the care of the child beyond the time when such activities usually occur"[17]), and prevention of social maturity ("active prevention of children's growth in the direction of self-reliance"[18]). Under these conditions in the particular sample of children chosen (19 males, 1 female) there was, according to Levy, a monotonously regular pattern of selfish and uncontrolled behavior—reminiscent of the behavior pointed out by Freud and Burlingham as typical of the child-mother relationship, though perhaps exaggerated.

Of Levy's 20 children, 11 were classified as examples of *indulgent* overprotection.

> Their behavior toward the mother was marked by disobedience, impudence, temper tantrums, excessive demands, and the exercise of varying degrees of tyranny. This type of behavior represented the chief complaint of the mother at the time she referred the child. It is a simple continuity of undisciplined infantile response, each complaint registering the line of maternal surrender.[19]

The 9 children who were classified as examples of *domineering* overprotection were, on the contrary, extremely submissive.

What was the fruit of this unpromising-looking mother love? We may note three aspects of some importance—intelligence, school behavior, and friendships. The IQ's of the 11 overindulged and monstrously undisciplined children were, from lowest to highest: "below average," "average," 109, 110, 113, 117, 128, 133, 140, 141, and 146. Only 3 of them were disciplinary problems at school; the conduct of the other 8 was rated as good or excellent. For example, "an eight-year-old boy (Case 1), though defiant, oppositional, and brutal in his behavior at home, was an excellent student, fond of

[15] Levy (1943).   [16] *Ibid.*, p. 40.   [17] *Ibid.*, p. 53.
[18] *Ibid.*, p. 71.   [19] *Ibid.*, p. 161.

school, anxious to get there on time, and always given a score of A in conduct."[20] As to the 9 children overpowered by domineering mothers, they too, with one exception, were well-behaved at school; but their IQ's were lower than those of the other group, being "average" or "below average" for 5 of the 9. All the overprotected children (possibly there was one exception) had difficulty in making friends or participating in the regular social activities of other children. They were inclined to prefer the company of books.

To sum up, we may say that maternal overprotection seems to interfere with the establishment of satisfactory peer relationships, but that it is not unfavorable to good conduct in the disciplinary setting of the schoolroom, where indeed the child may shine as a model pupil. The *indulgent* mothers had children who averaged superior in intelligence; the children of the *domineering* mothers were less well endowed. It would appear that freedom and intellectual superiority go together. But Levy's data and analysis do not enable us to decide whether the freedom enjoyed by the indulged child is the cause or the consequence of this superiority.

A trace more positive is the evidence presented in a monograph by Baldwin, Kalhorn, and Breese.[21] These authors found that parents whose behavior toward their children could be described as warm, democratic, and indulgent, or simply as warm and democratic, not only had brighter children than did those who were cold, autocratic, and nonindulgent, but had children who during the three years of observation were *increasing* in IQ while the other children were standing still or slightly declining. If there is any disadvantage to what they call the democratic home, it is that the children, like Levy's overprotected sample, hang back a little socially. They say:

> The *democratic* parents seem to surround the child with an atmosphere of freedom, emotional rapport, and intellectual stimulation. This serves to accelerate the child's intellectual development. In the preschool years it would seem that intellectual development is the most accelerated and social development seems to be slowed. The child in nursery school tends to be rather solitary and interested in the intellectual tasks of the nursery school environment. This may be because the home is too nice and cosy. The child leaving such a home, possibly unprepared for the buffets of nursery school social life, has, at the same time, a well developed intellectual interest which

[20] *Ibid.*, p. 166. [21] Baldwin, Kalhorn, and Breese (1945).

guides his nursery school activities into interesting and acceptable channels.[22]

My own interpretation, based on sentiment theory, would be a little different in emphasis: Children with the background described would have formed sentiments which would lead them to gravitate to social relations of a different kind from those usually encountered in a nursery, and they would thus hang back from the peer-relationships offered because they were disappointingly immature, both emotionally and intellectually. There is confirmation for this hypothesis in the statement by Baldwin, Kalhorn, and Breese that such children are likely, as they grow older, to move out into the social current and even to become popular—because of their inner security and basic friendliness, supported by their good relations with their parents.

The types of parental care called *democratic* by Baldwin and his co-workers are not precisely the same as what Levy calls *indulgent,* but there is a core of likeness. We must therefore be impressed by the similar results of these independent studies. Yet, though the drift of the evidence favors the view that association with a devoted adult is intellectually stimulating to a child and socially limiting (in the sense that it restrains peer attachments and horde behavior), one is left in doubt by the preceding two studies as to whether the observed differences are to be attributed to the environmental factors or might be accounted for by heredity alone, since, for example, inherited intelligence might explain both the warm, democratic behavior of the parents and the intellectual superiority of their children in the Baldwin, Kalhorn, Breese study. Fortunately, there are other studies which indicate that the social influence is a real variable. Some of these will be briefly noted here.

McCarthy presents evidence that the language development of a child is accelerated by contact with adults.[23] Her conclusion is reinforced by Davis's study of only children, twins, and singletons with brothers or sisters, in which it was found that: "1. Only children are definitely superior to children with siblings in every phase of linguistic skill. 2. Singletons with siblings are in turn somewhat superior to twins."[24] In regard to social responsiveness, Rheingold found in a carefully designed experiment that eight weeks of intensive "mothering" of 6-months-old orphanage babies by a single

[22] *Ibid.*, p. 69.   [23] McCarthy (1930).
[24] Davis (1937), p. 137.

Table 9
Mean social scores of babies at end of Rheingold experiment*

stimulus person	experimental babies (N=6)	control babies (N=6)
experimenter	37.2	24.2
examiner	28.2	25.0
stranger	28.0	23.2

Adapted from Rheingold (1956), p. 25.
* Analysis of variance yields an F of 7.18 for the difference between the experimental and control groups. That means that the probability is less than .05 that the difference is accidental. (See Rheingold, 1956, p. 26.) As is apparent from the table, most of the difference is due to the babies' reactions to the experimenter herself. Although the experimental babies seem to be slightly more friendly than the controls to unknown persons (i.e., "examiner" and "stranger"), they are most noticeably responsive to the "mothering" experimenter.

adult—Rheingold herself—resulted in significantly higher scores on a specially designed test of sociability than for the control babies, who, though well and tenderly cared for, had no single "mother."[25] Table 9 presents the results in terms of test score at the end of the eight experimental weeks. As will be noted, the experimenter is the person who elicits most response from the experimental babies, but the examiner, who was only slightly in contact with them, and the total stranger elicited more response from these specially treated babies than from the controls. In each case the difference between experimental and control babies is statistically significant, marginally so for examiner and stranger, very definitely so for the experimenter.[26]

More direct evidence of the stimulating effect of adult attention to the child has been obtained in a biographical study of eminent

[25] The social tests consisted of a number of behavioral situations (e.g., adult standing near baby's crib and smiling); the baby's responsiveness was scored in terms of facial expression, etc., the higher scores going to the more definite signs of welcome. The test situations were formalized and the scoring system practiced before the experiment proper was begun. As for Rheingold's "mothering," it is evident that it could hardly have achieved for 6 babies in an orphanage the intensity possible for 1 baby in a home.
[26] How strong were the sentiments developed in the babies and the experimenter? There is some evidence that both parties were affected. Rheingold did not investigate the question formally, but she reports that two of the babies she had "mothered" were definitely upset after her ministrations were terminated—one of them precisely on the day when, according to previous schedule, she should have been present. As for herself, she notes: "Needless to say, the experimenter became deeply attached to the experimental babies." (Rheingold, 1956, p. 20.)

geniuses.[27] Selection of the twenty men investigated was determined by their eminence and the availability of biographical material. The guiding question was whether any consistent pattern of childhood experience could be extracted from the data which might help to explain their remarkable intellectual achievements. It was concluded that two environmental factors were especially noteworthy. (1) Most of the twenty had received in early childhood a very large amount of loving and intellectually stimulating attention from adults —father, mother, or others. (2) Most of them had been limited in their contacts with children outside the family, and many of them had grown up primarily or exclusively in the daily company of adults who were interested in their intellectual progress. In general, we see here the same pattern—stimulation by loving adults, isolation from contemporaries—which seems to play a role in the intellectual development of the children studied by Levy, by Baldwin and his co-workers, and perhaps by McCarthy and by Davis. In the genius study there was, in addition, the suggestion that the combination of adult stimulus and relative isolation from age-mates may have intensified the fantasy life, leading to increased self-consciousness, originality, and independence—qualities needed by innovators in the realm of thought.

No single study in the group we have been reviewing can be taken as *proving* the thesis that the development of the child is favorably influenced by intensive parental care and unfavorably influenced by the lack of it; but in sum, as Bowlby remarks when commenting on the supposed negative effects, the weight of the evidence is impressive. But the evidence is two-sided: it points to contrary effects, or rather it points to a conflict of values. A society which favors intelligence and individuality will approve of the hothouse effects of the loving family; one which favors horde life and group conformity will distrust the family influence, and we shall see efforts—as we do every day, all around us—to replace the influence of the small family devoted to its one or few children with the influence of larger masses of age-equals such as are found in our public schools.

The effect of specific pressures

We have reached the tentative conclusion that general deprivation of parental (especially maternal) love has restrictive effects on

[27] McCurdy (1957).

the developing personality. But there are hypotheses more specific than that. It is said that there are critical periods and critical experiences in the early stages of life which have unusually decisive power.

One of these hypotheses is that the amount of oral gratification which the infant receives from nursing at the breast determines the whole future emotional orientation toward life. If full gratification is obtained, so the hypothesis goes, the infant will become an optimist; if not, a pessimist. A study by Frieda Goldman was designed to test this hypothesis.[28] She assembled a number of adult optimists and pessimists, as defined by their answers to a questionnaire, and then inquired into how long they had been breast-fed. According to the hypothesis, early weaning should go with pessimism, late weaning with optimism. And this is the way the data fell out. That is, the correlation between length of the nursing period and degree of optimism was positive and statistically significant, although not extremely high. The flaw in the study is that the optimism-pessimism differences may have stemmed from *continuous* loving or unloving care over the years; the short or long nursing period may have been no more than a sign of the mother's degree of generosity toward her child.

A more recent study built on the same lines as Goldman's but dealing with a more complex hypothesis—that a character-type marked by the three combined traits of orderliness, stinginess, and obstinacy is derived from early childhood anal eroticism—has been attempted by Beloff.[29] It failed to demonstrate the hypothesized relationship, which was put forward by Freud, but the failure cannot be taken as decisive since it is doubtful whether the study isolates either the character-type or the anal erotic conditions required by the hypothesis in its original form. What it does show is that (1) there is zero correlation between age of completed toilet-training and responses of graduate student subjects to a questionnaire meant to reveal anal erotic character traits, and (2) there is a positive .51 correlation between the questionnaire scores of the graduate students and their mothers. The mother-child correlation could be explained on hereditary grounds (compare the results of Pearson reported in Chapter 2) or on grounds of general educational influence exerted by the mother on the child: the data of the study do not allow us to decide.

[28] Goldman (1948, 1950). [29] Beloff (1957).

ANTHROPOLOGICAL STUDIES   Cross-cultural studies alert us to the fact that what is considered bad and unhealthy in one society may be the ideal in another. Mead describes child-rearing practices in Bali which, she says, would be condemned by most psychiatrists and which do in fact seem to promote schizoid personality traits. This outcome is so exactly fitted to Balinese culture that "visitors from America and Europe go away describing a kind of paradise."[30] Mead's reasons for calling these happy people schizophrenic are as follows: In Bali there is much cultivation of trance states, common resort to the trick of falling asleep in the face of difficulties, and an elaborate development of ritual and fantasy expressed in traditional dramatic forms—all of which typify schizophrenic behavior. Furthermore, "on a test devised for schizophrenics in the West, the Balinese yielded results indistinguishable from the schizophrenics'."[31] As for the child-rearing practices to which Mead attributes the so-called Balinese schizophrenia, she has this to say about the children:

> They look like dolls, and they are treated like playthings, playthings which are more exciting than fighting cocks—over which the men spend many fascinated hours—or the kites and crickets which amuse little boys. Everyone joins in the mild titillating teasing of little babies, flipping their fingers, their toes, their genitals, threatening them, playfully disregarding the sanctity of their heads, and, when the children respond by heightened excitement and mounting tension, the teaser turns away, breaks the thread of interplay, allows no climax. Children learn not to respond, to resist provocation, to skirt the group of elders who would touch or snatch, to refuse the gambit when their mothers borrow babies to make them jealous. They develop an unresponsiveness to the provocative intent of others at the same time that they remain plastic to music and pattern. It is a childhood training which, if followed here, would seem dangerously certain to bring out schizoid trends in the growing child's character.[32]

These are fascinating observations, and very likely there is some linkage between the Balinese child-rearing routines and their cultural emphasis on imagination and the arts, but it is exceedingly doubtful that the schizophrenes in our society are brought up in any such way, and we do not in fact know how much of the Balinese

[30] Mead (1955b), p. 175.   [31] *Ibid.*, p. 177.
[32] Mead (1955a), pp. 43 f.

adult character is attributable to their upbringing and how much to inherited temperament.

Anthropological studies like Mead's are rich in suggestions but usually not sharply focused on particular psychological hypotheses. Whiting and Child, however, have been able to make ingenious use of accumulated anthropological data to check on the possible relationship between several kinds of infant frustration and certain aspects of human culture.[33] Their hypotheses are psychoanalytic. One which yielded positive results concerns orality, and we may well examine their procedure in testing it.

The hypothesis in point is that there is a connection between the tendency of a society to attribute disease to oral causes and its tendency to frustrate oral needs in infancy. The hypothesis involves a number of processes accepted by psychoanalysts which cannot be discussed in detail here. To put the matter quite simply, the argument runs that denial of complete oral satisfaction to the infant by interfering with sucking at the breast or pleasure-sucking before the child is ready to give up this activity produces a heightened sensitivity concerning the mouth and its functions, as if the mouth had been injured, and leads to the feeling that the mouth is a target for hostile forces. Hence Whiting and Child hypothesize that in a society where this occurs there will be some commonly accepted theory to the effect that disease enters the body by way of the mouth or may be emitted from the mouth. Specifically, they look for explanations of disease in terms of (1) the ingestion of food and drink, and (2) orally emitted spells or incantations.

Testing the above hypothesis requires two judgments: (1) a judgment of the degree to which a particular society typically frustrates the oral needs of infancy, and (2) a judgment of the degree to which the society entertains the kinds of explanation of disease just mentioned. Such judgments are subject to error. Whiting and Child, by various precautions, tried to hold judgmental error to a minimum and especially guarded against corruption of the judgments by knowledge of the hypothesis being tested. Results are presented in Table 10. As can be seen at a glance, those societies which explain illness in oral terms are more prone than others to excite oral frustration ("oral socialization anxiety") in the course of child-rearing. The median score for oral socialization anxiety lies between 10 and 11. Three-quarters of those societies having oral theories of disease lie above the median, whereas less than a fifth of

[33] Whiting and Child (1953).

those which lack such theories do. Statistically, the difference is clearly significant, and the hypothesis is confirmed. Confirmation

Table 10
Relation between oral socialization anxiety and oral theories of disease

	oral theories present	anxiety rating*	oral theories absent	anxiety rating
	Marquesans	17		
	Dobuans	16		
	Baiga	15		
	Kwoma	15		
	Thonga	15		
	Alorese	14		
	Chagga	14		
	Navaho	14		
	Dahomeans	13		
	Lesu	13		
	Masai	13		
	Lepcha	12		
	Maori	12		
	Pukapukans	12		
	Trobrianders	12	Lapp	13
	Kwakiutl	11	Chamorro	12
MEDIAN IN ANXIETY	Manus	11	Samoans	12
	Chiricahua	10	Arapesh	10
	Comanche	10	Balinese	10
	Siriono	10	Hopi	10
	Bena	8	Tanala	10
	Slave	8	Paiute	9
	Kurtatchi	6	Chenchu	8
			Teton	8
			Flathead	7
			Papago	7
			Venda	7
			Warrau	7
			Wogeo	7
			Ontong-Javanese	6

Adapted from Whiting and Child (1953), p. 156.
* The numbers refer to the sum of ratings by 3 judges. Since each judge could rate the severity of oral socialization anxiety from 1 (lowest) to 7 (highest), the minimum possible sum would be 3, the maximum 21. Here the range is from 6 to 17.

Those familiar with chi square (χ^2) will see at once that there is a significant association between oral socialization anxiety and oral theory of disease, according to the table. Whiting and Child apply the t test to the difference between the mean ratings for societies with and societies without an oral theory of disease and obtain a probability of less than .0005 that the difference is accidental. (See Whiting and Child, 1953, p. 164.)

does not, however, tell us whether the oral frustration is the cause of the oral theory of disease or the oral theory of disease is the cause of the oral frustration, or whether both must be referred to a third factor. In our own society, for instance, there is some association between the knowledge that diseases may come from getting germs in the mouth and the practice of warning children against thumb-sucking and other kinds of oral gratification, and it seems entirely rational to us to explain the warning in terms of disease theory; but to explain the disease theory as resulting from oral frustration (of, say, Pasteur in particular or all of us in general) would seem the height of absurdity. In science, of course, we cannot afford to be restrained too much by common sense, but it nevertheless remains true that demonstration of a statistical relationship between two variables does not settle the question of causation. The Whiting and Child demonstration, therefore, does not permit us to say whether oral frustration in childhood is critical for the establishment of an oral theory of disease.

In spite of their inevitable limitations, the studies we have been reviewing in this section undoubtedly point the way to future investigations which may be expected to be increasingly fruitful in the years to come.

Early childhood conditioning

Proponents of conditioning theory have sometimes created the impression that the personality traits of infants might be shaped quite readily by standard conditioning procedures. Actual experimental results, however, are scanty and ambiguous. It is certainly not true that infants can be conditioned to just anything at any time. Experimenters have found that it calls for a good deal of patience to catch babies awake enough to attend to the stimuli which they wish to apply; and when a baby is busily engaged in sucking, which is his chief activity when he does happen to be awake, the ordinary experimental procedures seem to make little impression on him. One might say that babies are insulated to a considerable degree from the experimenter's buzzers and bells.

There is something paradoxical in all this. On the one hand, it is evident that the infant in the first few weeks does come to recognize some of the regular features of his environment and does develop emotional attachments, especially to the mother; and on the other hand, experimenters have some trouble in establishing conditioned responses. Perhaps the answer is that the stimuli to which infants are naturally attuned are not those favored by the experimenters. In fact, some versions of conditioning theory have made it appear that any stimuli at all could be associated with any responses at all by a simple pairing of stimulus and response. Sophisticated conditioning theory does not commit this error, but it is doubtful whether any theory is quite abreast of the facts, and certainly experimenters run into plenty of difficulties. The childhood conditioning experiments are, nevertheless, full of interest.

MOTOR RESPONSES Wenger did several experiments with very young infants.[34] In one experiment with three infants which began when they were 2 days old and extended until they were 9 days old, he succeeded in getting eyelid closure as a conditioned response to a tactual vibration on 69 per cent of the presentations, at a maximum. Since in a control series the percentage of eyelid closures occurring without benefit of conditioning was 29, Wenger judged that the conditioning effect might be estimated as the difference between 29 per cent and 69 per cent. It took three days and 124 paired stimulations before any evidence of conditioning appeared. The experiment was continued with one infant for six months. The highest percentage of conditioned responses ever obtained during that period, after numerous stimulus pairings, was 89. Persistence of some degree of responsiveness to the conditioned stimulus could be detected two months after discontinuation of the training. Wenger was disappointed to discover that hundreds of paired stimulations never did raise the conditioned response to the 100 per cent level. (Perhaps the effects were profounder than the index symptom of eyelid-closure led Wenger to think. Note the discussion of Kantrow's results below, pp. 160 f.) Even more disappointing to Wenger was another experiment in which an auditory stimulus was paired with sucking. Eight weeks of stimulation produced no indication of conditioning in the two infant subjects.

Two Russian investigators, Kasatkin and Levikova, have emphasized the following points: (1) conditioned responses obtained in early infancy are very unstable, and (2) the degree of maturity of the infant is an essential variable. In one of their experiments, where an organ tone was used as the conditioned stimulus for the sucking

[34] Wenger (1936).

Table 11
Infant conditioning: organ tone trials

infant	age at outset	number of paired stimulations	age at first appearance of conditioned response
A	1 month 1 day	29	1 month 13 days
B	25 days	74	1 month 9 days
C	11 days	131	1 month 4 days

Adapted from Kasatkin and Levikova (1935a), p. 6.

response, the age at which conditioning appeared was about the same for the three infant subjects although they were started on the conditioning program at different ages and received very different amounts of stimulation.[35] Table 11 presents the facts in condensed form. Very similar were the results reported in another article by the same experimenters. This time the conditioned stimulus was a colored light, and the age at which the quite unstable conditioned responses appeared was more advanced than in the previous case.[36] Table 12 presents the facts. The dependency of conditioning on maturity is clearly brought out by this table. For example, infants D and I first exhibit the conditioned response at 1 month 29 days, although infant D was started on the program much earlier and received five times more paired stimulations than infant I. Taking the table literally, we might conclude that at least 200 pairings were wasted on infant D because given too early in life.

Table 12
Infant conditioning: colored light trials

infant	age at outset	number of paired stimulations	age at first appearance of conditioned response
D	14 days	260	1 month 29 days
E	17 days	233	1 month 29 days
F	17 days	220	1 month 27 days
G	1 month 2 days	126	1 month 28 days
H	1 month 15 days	38	2 months 1 day
I	1 month 17 days	49	1 month 29 days

Adapted from Kasatkin and Levikova (1935b), p. 424.

[35] Kasatkin and Levikova (1935a).
[36] Kasatkin and Levikova (1935b).

EMOTIONAL RESPONSES   In the studies preceding, the conditioned response was a limited segment of behavior. Or rather, it was such limited segments that the experimenters chose to observe. These tiny bits of activity may actually have represented a massive, total state of the organism, and they may not have been the most fortunate choice among the various reactions which might have been observed. Perhaps Watson and Rayner were following a more correct path when they recorded the whole of little Albert's behavior rather than a fraction of it, crude though their methods may have been.[37] They observed how the white rat (CS) became an object of fear for him after the banging of the steel bar (US) and how this fear transferred to other objects. They did not rely on a single small movement, but tried in their fashion to grasp the total cognitive and emotional state of the child. Certainly the emotional aspect of conditioning is fundamental.

Luckily, we have a conditioning experiment by Jones directly aimed at following an infant's change of emotional state in the face of an objective change.[38] (1) In one conditioning series, Jones used an infant 7 months old. With this infant, a girl, he tried the effect of pairing a weak clicking sound with a mild electrical stimulus delivered to the skin. The index of reaction was a fall of the electrical resistance of the skin, as measured by a galvanometer. This is the "PGR," or psychogalvanic reflex (also called the "GSR," or galvanic skin response), one of the most sensitive indices of emotional intensity available.[39] After six pairings, a conditioned PGR began to appear. Upon further conditioning the response occurred frequently and often quite vigorously, though by no means every time. Probably it failed to appear at times because the infant was inattentive to the conditioned stimulus; but also there were phenomena of adaptation and extinction, as well as that interesting reaction of falling asleep which Pavlov noted as a neurotic symptom in his dogs and which Mead says is cultivated by the Balinese as a technique for handling difficulties. In short, the subject gave evidence both direct and indirect of being emotionally affected by the stimulus situation, even though the unconditioned electric stimulus was very mild. (2) More revealing still is what happened in another conditioning series. In this case, a light was paired with an electric stimulus a few times only and during the training period produced no strong

[37] Watson and Rayner (1920).   [38] Jones (1930).
[39] McCurdy (1950).

responses; but when the infant, after several days of rest, was brought back into the situation, the conditioned PGR proved to be quite strong. At this critical moment Jones noticed a significant change in the infant's overt behavior, too: whereas she had previously reached for the light, or smiled and chuckled at it, she now scolded or coughed or spit towards it when it came on. One would say that during the rest interval following the conditioning session a change had come over the infant's way of perceiving the situation, so that the irrelevant pleasing light had been transformed into a sign or perceived cause of the discomfort from the electrical stimulus. Here is an example of a step-function, a sharp change of behavior—perhaps connected with an equally sharp change of cognitive and emotional state.[40]

After this introduction to emotional conditioning, we may be in a position to understand what was happening in Kantrow's study of feeding responses.[41] In her experiment the subjects were 16 infants (10 male, 6 female) ranging in age at the outset from 1 month 14 days to 3 months 27 days—all old enough to be conditionable, according to Kasatkin and Levikova. (We should note, however, that in terms of Piaget's developmental scheme they were still at the stage of disembodied "pictures.") Kantrow's measure of conditioning was the frequency of sucking movements during the five seconds a buzzer sounded before the nipple of a nursing bottle was inserted into the infant subject's mouth. This frequency was checked against the frequency of sucking during the control periods, i.e., the intervals of from 25 to 120 seconds between withdrawal of the bottle and the next sounding of the buzzer. Kantrow inferred that the buzzer was acting as a conditioned stimulus if the number of sucking movements during the five-second buzzer period exceeded the number during any five-second interval of the control period. A conditioned sucking response, so defined, appeared in all the infants after from 16 to 72 pairings of buzzer and bottle in from 3 to 7 feeding sessions. But the truly interesting result is that continuation of the training beyond this point did *not* push the frequency of conditioned responses steadily toward higher values. On the contrary, the 5 infants who were kept on the conditioning schedule for from 19 to 32 consecutive sessions *declined* in conditioned response frequency after reaching a peak between sessions 9 and 15. Now, a literal interpretation of these results would force us to conclude that re-

[40] For an interesting discussion of step-functions, see Ashby (1952).
[41] Kantrow (1937).

peating the pairings beyond a certain stage caused the power of the conditioned stimulus to drop off or weakened the connection between it and the bottle. But if we regard the sucking movements as merely one index of the infant's mental state, then we can conceive of the sucking response waning without its emotional-cognitive basis being removed. There are concrete reasons for taking this line of interpretation. For one, the buzzer continued to have the effect of making the baby quieter; in fact, the decline of the conditioned response might be accepted as a part of this soothing effect. For another, when extinction of the response was undertaken (i.e., the bottle was withheld after the buzzer had sounded), the buzzer's sound did not now merely cause a decline of sucking but positively increased the amount of crying—which says as clearly as an infant can say anything that the failure of the bottle to appear after the buzzer had announced its coming was a painful disappointment. By this interpretation, Kantrow's conditioning procedure had built up something deeper and more pervasive than a sucking response; it had built up an *expectancy*, to use the language of Tolman,[42] or a *sentiment*, to use the richer and more adequate language (it seems to me) of McDougall.

My stress on this point is provoked by the apparent discrepancy between the insignificant-looking results of conditioning experiments on infants and the extreme importance which psychoanalysts and others attach to that period of life. If it is true, however, that the major effect of conditioning procedures (and their real-life counterparts) is to build up sentiments rather than to evoke forced movements or reflexes or motor responses, then the effect could be in the main covert, silent, unobserved, so long as the sequences of events were undisturbed by the extinction process. The important evidence would appear when there was some interruption of the accustomed state of affairs. If the conditioning sequence were such as to lead the infant to anticipate with pleasure, then its interruption would produce an outburst of unpleasant emotion. If it were such as to lead to aversion or paralyzed anticipation of the unpleasant, the result of interruption might be less noticeable, since uncertainty rather than a burst of glee might replace the previous definite expectation of unpleasantness and the behavior remain quiet, unless anxiety about the uncertain future should begin to be expressed in agitation. The deferring of a pleasant expected event is immediately painful, but the deferring of an unpleasant expected event is

[42] Tolman (1932, 1949).

not quite the reverse of that and hence not immediately pleasant. In either case, emotion is likely to be felt and often expressed, though up to the moment of the disturbance there may not have been any striking evidence of sentiment strength.

I cannot forbear citing one more study, one of the oldest but also one of the most interesting, on conditioning and the extinction of conditioning in young children. It makes all my previous points on this topic, and a few more. This is the work reported by Mateer in *Child Behavior.*[43] Mateer's conditioned stimulus was a bandage slipped over the eyes; the unconditioned stimulus was a bit of chocolate candy placed in the mouth. Mouth movements and swallowing which occurred after the bandage was applied and before the candy was placed in the mouth were taken as the conditioned response. The experimental subjects were 50 normal children (24 boys, 26 girls) ranging in age from 12 to 89 months. The purpose was to observe the effect of age on the conditioning process. Mateer found that age did indeed matter. In the first place, the older children acquired the conditioned response more rapidly than the younger ones. In the second place, the nature of this change of behavior varied with age, as was revealed most clearly during the extinction period. Says Mateer:

> It was found impossible to effect this unlearning without severe emotional disturbances in the youngest nine of the children tested. . . . Usually the second, always the third or fourth trial, brought crying and no further attempt was then made. . . . No difficulty was experienced with children over twenty-eight months of age.[44]

Mateer's younger children, then, reacted like Kantrow's babies, but more definitely and too violently to be ignored. The older children, too, in their different way, indicated that the experimenter had aroused a wish and then disappointed it, making it plain that they held the experimenter directly responsible. But their reactions were controlled and in many cases were quite self-consciously aimed at winning the experimenter over. Mateer reports:

> A number of them said "Oh, it's candy," "It's fudge," "It's sweet," when first fed but by far the greater number of these verbal reactions came during the first few trials of the period when I was trying to develop unlearning. Some of them only smiled sheepishly or looked at me shyly when the bandage was taken off without candy having been given. Several asked, "Is the candy all gone?" "Won't I get any

[43] Mateer (1918). [44] *Ibid.,* p. 154.

more to-day?" while one little girl offered to go to the store and buy me some more. Another little fellow broke out into an unusual stutter and said, "You—you—you forgot to give me the candy that time." Another counted, "That's two times I didn't get any, this is three times." Others contented themselves with stating, apparently to the ceiling, that they liked candy. One impudently begged, "Give me just a little bit this time, won't you?" Another stated circumspectly, "I opened my mouth that time," and then on the next trial, "I opened my mouth again," but, when I asked why, she said, "I don't know," although her confusion and shy changing of the conversation indicated that she probably was attempting to give me an indirect intimation of her desire for candy.[45]

The older children have a clear awareness of the role of the experimenter; they do not attribute any magical powers to the conditioned stimulus, which simply functions as a sign that the experimenter is about to give them candy. The situation may be different for the younger children; at any rate, they react to disappointment with greater violence. The older children employ subtle diplomacy. Their relative lack of emotion shows that they attach little importance to the link between blindfold and candy which the conditioning process is supposed to establish. They understand the world better than that. They look to the true cause behind the appearances. Yet here, too, their approach is temperate, because the experimenter, after all, is only playing a game with them and their emotions are nothing like as heavily invested in the game as would be necessary for a strong reaction.

GENERAL REMARKS ON CONDITIONING   The following conclusions appear to be justified. (1) Whether a sequence of events such as conditioning experimenters employ has any important effect on a young child depends on the child's age and his particular state of need at the time. (2) The effective conditioned stimulus becomes the core of a sentiment rather than a trigger for a peripheral automatic reaction. The sentiment may express itself in various ways. In fact, it may exist in silence until an interruption of the expected sequence provokes an emotional outburst, or, in milder cases, instrumental maneuvers like those of Mateer's older children. (3) It is conceivable, though not actually proved by the human experimental studies, that brief conditioning could leave an emotional residue (a sentiment) which would not be dissipated for years.

[45] *Ibid.*, pp. 187 f.

Animal studies which will be cited later in this chapter support the possibility. (4) Important, long-term effects of conditioning do not depend primarily on numerous repetitions but on the critical factor of the state of the organism at the time of the conditioning experience and on subsequent developments, such as sudden reorganization of the meaning of the experience (perhaps illustrated in the second Jones experiment) and the occurrence or nonoccurrence of extinction during a sensitive phase. Doubtless, we do not understand very well the processes occurring in the organism by which the effects of past experience are transformed, but these processes do occur, as demonstrated in the memory experiments of Bartlett[46] and Wulf[47] and others, in research into poetic creation like that of Lowes,[48] and in a major portion of the investigations of psychoanalysis. The organism is dynamic, and even the apparently simple linkages of conditioning are subject to its dynamism.

Skills

If it is necessary to take age into account when dealing with so-called classical conditioning, it is doubly necessary when considering the development of skills. Here again there is a paucity of information. Most skill-learning studies pay little attention to age. Yet there is some evidence of a marginal kind which raises grave doubts as to whether skills originate in practice at all, though it would go against all common sense to deny that practice contributes to the ultimate refinement of a skill. It will help us to focus our problem if we consider two cases in which very respectable art work was produced without benefit of practice. One is the case of people living under such primitive conditions that the activity of drawing was extremely rare or totally absent. Another is the case of a boy born blind and remaining so until the surgical removal of cataracts at the age of seven.

The first case concerns the Orotchens, a small nomadic tribe living in the far east of the U.S.S.R. These people live very simply, moving about a great part of the year with their herds of reindeer, but settling down for a few months during the summer. The reindeer is an extremely important animal for them; it is the pivot of

---

[46] Bartlett (1932).
[47] Wulf (1922). Hebb (1949), p. 13, rejects Wulf's data and conclusions but says nothing about the other lines of evidence here cited.
[48] Lowes (1927).

13 *These drawings of reindeer were made by a fifteen-year-old Orotchen who had reportedly not had prior art experience. Such performances raise questions about the value of practice in a skill as compared to inherited ability and factual knowledge. (From Schubert, 1930)*

their economy, furnishing them with food, shelter, and clothing. One would expect the people to know this domestic animal well. In fact they do, and the evidence comes out very clearly in the drawings they are able to make with little or no instruction. According to Schubert's article on the subject,[49] the young students who produced the kind of work illustrated in Figure 13 had received no art instruction from their teacher and had had slight if any opportunity to handle paper and pencil before. Indeed, the school which they were attending at the time, in the summer of 1927, was the first boarding school in the history of the Orotchens, and the teacher was not only no artist but had no appreciation of the superior quality of the art work of his pupils. At Moscow the drawings aroused interest because they were so reminiscent of the cave art of paleolithic man and because they were done without prior artistic exercise or any example in the Orotchen culture, which seems to be particularly barren of art, either decorative or representational.

More startling is the account given by Meier of Loran Lockhart.[50] This boy, born with congenital cataracts in both eyes and therefore unable to distinguish anything visual except light and darkness, was able, after he had partially recovered his sight through surgery, to paint pictures at or above the level to be expected at his age. The experience of color was something that especially pleased him, and

[49] Schubert (1930).
[50] Meier (1936). This account may seem all the more startling to some readers who have interpreted the remarks of Hebb (1949) on congenital cataract patients as meaning that seeing has to be learned from the ground up. He says in fact (pp. 19 f. and elsewhere) that perception of *Gestalten* is independent of experience, i.e., objects are seen, but without the meanings attached by experience. Cf. Piaget (1954), discussed in the preceding chapter of this book.

he plunged into the making of paintings with delight. He depicted the country things seen in or near his cabin home, such as chickens and wheelbarrows, but, according to Meier (who has made the study of artistic talent his specialty), he used them freely for compositional effects. Here, then, is an example of a skill which owed nothing or next to nothing to practice. We might suppose, it is true, that the performance would have been still better if the boy had enjoyed the advantage of years of prior experience; but we really do not know. It may be that intelligence and the untaught maturation of nerve-muscle coordinations, plus the upsurge of delight in the new visual world, were quite sufficient in themselves.

Do we not have a right to wonder, after hearing of cases like these, whether practice effects may not be overestimated? As Tinbergen has remarked, apropos of certain experiments on animals: "We have seen that the gradual improvement of the swimming movements in tadpoles and of flight in young birds is primarily due to growth and not to learning. However, this seems so utterly improbable to the naive observer that, if experimental proof were lacking, most people would not hesitate to consider them clear examples of learning."[51] Most activities which we speak of as being improved by practice are carried on by people because of their pleasure in them or because of their usefulness as means to other ends. They are consequently repeated over and over again; and, in the course of time, they may come to be performed with increased efficiency or grace or power. It is natural to conclude that the change is a function of the repetition rather than simply of the time elapsed. On the other hand, there are cases like those just described and there are the experiments to which Tinbergen refers—facts which raise a question about the exact contribution made by practice.

WHAT DOES PRACTICE DO? With these thoughts in mind, let us turn to an experiment by Hicks on the acquisition of motor skill in children.[52] Hicks used two sets of children, matched for age and sex, but differing in the fact that one set received a great deal of practice in a certain performance while the other was receiving none. To take a specific instance: he compared a set of 30 children (in 4 age groups) practicing over a period of 8 weeks in 8 sessions of 10 trials each at throwing a ball at a large, slowly moving target, with another set of 30 matched against the former and treated like

[51] Tinbergen (1951), p. 143.   [52] Hicks (1930a).

them in every respect except that they received no target practice (at least in the laboratory) during that period. Both sets of children were used in an initial session in order to establish what their performance level was at that time, and again in a final session at the end of the 8-week period during which one set was practicing and the other was not. Table 13 sets forth the results in terms of score points on the initial and final tests for both groups. The maximum possible score was 25 points for a hit in the exact center of the target, and 1 point was deducted from that for every inch of distance away from the center. All experimental conditions, such as distance of the child from the target, were carefully controlled. As the table shows, the practiced and nonpracticed children performed about equally well at both the beginning *and the end* of the experiment. Both sets as a whole were somewhat better at the end than at the beginning, but the specific practice had not put the practiced children significantly ahead of the others. If we read the table vertically, we see that the greater the age of the children the better their performance. In a second paper reporting another skill study, Hicks reaches the same position as before:

> These results support the conclusions of the former paper that improvement in skill may result from factors other than specific practice, such as the influence of structural maturation and of general practice. Probably no one doubts that specific practice must at times be given

Table 13
Initial and final target scores of Hicks' practiced and unpracticed groups

years of age	treatment	number	initial test		final test	
			AVERAGE	S.D.	AVERAGE	S.D.
3	practice	6	4.3	3.8	8.7	1.4
	control	6	5.4	5.5	8.0	3.5
4	practice	9	11.7	4.7	12.4	2.3
	control	9	11.2	5.2	12.1	2.4
5	practice	9	14.0	5.3	13.6	2.6
	control	9	12.6	2.6	13.3	2.9
6	practice	6	15.6	2.2	16.2	1.7
	control	6	17.2	1.9	17.2	2.2
all	practice	30	11.7	5.7	12.8	3.2
	control	30	11.7	5.6	12.6	4.0

Adapted from Hicks (1930a), pp. 92-97.

to young children, but for what skills and under what conditions is as yet largely undetermined.[53]

What was true in 1930 is still true. We know that practice is necessary for the achievement of high skill, and yet why and under what conditions we do not know.

We might ask whether the chief gain from practice is not simply knowledge. Practice could be viewed as the repetition of opportunities to *observe* what needs doing to reach a certain result—as a continuing analysis of the means-ends relations involved. There is support for this interpretation in the work of Mattson.[54] Mattson, like Hicks, found that children practiced in a certain skill were indistinguishable from others not so practiced, *if* the skill was a simple one. If the skill required more complex manipulations, then a difference did appear in favor of the practiced children, although the unpracticed still showed a considerable gain from maturation alone. It is obvious that the more complex the manipulations are, the more there is to discover about the various possibilities; and this means that there must be more exploration and hence more time for "practice."

Knowledge, however, does not have to be in terms of any particular sense mode, or in terms of language. The typist may know by touch what he cannot repeat in words or put in a visual diagram. We must beware of identifying words with effective knowledge. One of the serious faults of verbal learning—the parrot-talk of the schools—is that the formulae so acquired cannot be translated immediately into appropriate action. But if, on the one hand, there may be empty verbal formulae without application, there may also be application combined with tongue-tied inexpressiveness. So we find theorists of art and music talking about things which seem vague and remote to the practical artist or musician, and the artists and musicians on their side mumbling about what it is they do and value without communicating much of anything. In everyday affairs, likewise, we find people doing things contrary to what they say they are doing or wishing to do, and often enough with total unawareness of the discrepancy between word and act. There are many skills which have never reached the level of words and which perhaps never will. This is generally true of the arts. Even literary art cannot very well be acquired by reading how-to-do-it books. Much depends on sensitivity to the sound values of words, color and con-

[53] Hicks (1930b), p. 296. [54] Mattson (1933).

notation values, flow and stress, and also on the power of organizing ideas—reactions and operations difficult to convey in words even to the professional user of words. That is why treatises on rhetoric are so unsatisfactory and why literary skill is often referred to as a gift. It is not entirely a gift. Much hard work goes into it. But all this work results in knowledge which is not fully expressible except in the act of composition itself. On top of this, one must urge that desires and values from the deepest, most inaccessible regions of personality set the engine of composition into motion and even re-design and reconstruct it in the very process of using it.

Practice, then, as an exploration of the possibilities of action, is no doubt valuable. But as sheer repetition of a familiar pattern it may be worse than useless. At any rate, the periods of idleness be-tween practice sessions are often not wasted. However we explain it—whether by the decay of useless habits, by reminiscence, by consolidation, or otherwise—everybody knows what it is to come back to some performance after a vacation at a higher level of skill than when it was last practiced. Once again let us remind ourselves that the organism is dynamic.

Traumatic and other seminal experiences

As brought out early in this chapter, the general emotional climate in which a child grows up seems to affect his development by pro-moting or retarding it. Specific events also play a role, as the sections on conditioning and the development of skills have stressed; but this role involves more than a penetration and patterning of the organism from the outside. The main function of an event may be to initiate dynamic processes in the organism for the rejection or in-corporation of the event, for new developments in the sentiment systems and skills carrying the organism far beyond the initiating moment.

Language such as I am using here is more congenial as a rule to, say, a psychoanalyst than to a reflexologist, or so it is often imagined. I am therefore especially glad to find very similar language being used by a laboratory worker in the direct line of descent from Pavlov. I refer to Gantt, who, on the basis of years of conditioning experiments with animals, has formulated two dynamic principles to help explain nervous breakdown.[55] These two principles he labels *schizokinesis* and *autokinesis*. The first of Gantt's two principles,

[55] Gantt (1953).

schizokinesis, has to do with organic disharmony, "a basic discrepancy between the more external expressive movements (which, being in our consciousness, appear to us usually as voluntary and purposeful) and the generally hidden visceral responses, which are ordinarily out of consciousness."[56] It refers to a splitting of organic functions and clearly has pathological connotations. The other principle, *autokinesis,* works toward unification of the organic functions and is pathological only under special conditions. Gantt applies the term to two classes of facts: (a) the normal retention of conditioned reflexes and their spontaneous recovery after extinction, and (b) "the development of neurotic symptoms in dogs several or more years after the animal had been removed from the traumatic situation—symptoms, however, definitely related to the original conflict, which had developed its trace in the nervous system."[57]

The general bearing of these principles is brought out by Gantt in the following words:

> Since my studies have been particularly concerned with pathological behavior, the "spontaneous" development or autokinesis that I have seen has to do especially with symptoms of maladjustment. The function of spontaneous restoration, however, could well be a force for therapy. Moreover, if, on the basis of a conflict, it is possible for the individual to elaborate a symptom and a perversion of behavior, it is plausible to believe that from a single interview or from a single event, howsoever brief, there may ensue the most profound developments. This is a common experience in therapy and in life. The stimulation leaves a change in the nervous system and, on the basis of this trace of the excitation and without any repetition of the stimulation, the development proceeds gradually or swiftly through the months or years. We can now see, both from the laboratory and from experience, that the organism is in reality a dynamic, moving structure, carrying within itself some of the forces for its own evolution or dissolution.[58]

CLINICAL EXAMPLES   A psychic trauma, in the strong sense of the word, is an event of such powerful emotional impact that all the resources of the organism have to be utilized to preserve organic integrity. It is an event which calls for an extensive healing or balancing process. The healing may leave permanent scars, the balancing may go on perpetually without resulting in workable stability, or there may be failure and the organism may go to pieces

[56] *Ibid.,* p. 157.   [57] *Ibid.,* p. 158.   [58] *Ibid.,* pp. 161 f.

or lose balance completely. Such an event—or, more properly, complex of events—was experienced by Janet's patient Irene, as described on an earlier page. Her efforts at repair left tremendous and noticeable scars, and the wound opened again and again. A few more examples will be useful here.

In citing the two following cases from Bettelheim I do not wish to imply that traumata produce schizophrenic children. There is plenty of evidence that much more is involved, especially genetic factors. Bender and Grugett have shown that schizophrenic children may have enjoyed average or better than average parental care,[59] and Prout and White in a comparison of schizophrenics and their healthy siblings discovered no evidence that the schizophrenics had been subjected to any severer experiences than their brothers and sisters who had not fallen ill.[60] Bettelheim himself, however, regards traumata like those described below as contributing heavily to schizophrenic pathology, and we can certainly see how they might.

CASE I Prolonged observation of a boy's behavior convinced us that his delusions of persecution and anaclitic depression were the consequence of a severe traumatization, possibly some dark and terrible secret, which may have taken place before his verbal abilities had fully developed, and which he therefore could not easily reproduce in any other form than that of vague but totally destructive images. Despite his parents' cooperation with our effort to establish a detailed early history, they were unable to provide any information about such a secret, nor could the boy himself recollect anything but death anxiety and overwhelming rage, which he had to repress totally.

Following the lead that this child clung frantically to his older brother, we eventually succeeded in having the latter shed light on the "killing secret." He told us that when the younger boy was not yet three years old, the older brother and some of his friends had played a hanging game with the boy as victim. The rope had cut off the child's breathing and he was only revived after artificial respiration had been applied. Dreading that the boy might tell, the older ones established a regime of terror. Repeatedly and severely they beat up this youngster, threatening even worse tortures if he should ever reveal the story. In order to make the threat more effective, they repeatedly locked him up in a dark and inaccessible excavation and kept him there for prolonged periods despite his terrified screaming. (It might be mentioned that, although this boy has been with us for some time, only anxious phantasies of being locked up in dark rooms

[59] Bender and Grugett (1956).   [60] Prout and White (1956).

have spontaneously come to light. The trauma of hanging has not been recovered so far.)[61]

Cruelty is not something that happened far away and long ago, in Hitler's Germany or during the Inquisition. It happens today in America, too, and sometimes (we don't know how often) as monstrously as this. Bettelheim argues that this child's schizophrenia was the consequence of enormous fear, rooted in reality. He may be right. The facts of another case are scarcely more pleasant.

CASE II Before the age of three, chance observations led an adopted boy to guess his mother's adulterous relations. During the year following his discovery, and although he did not fully understand what he had stumbled on at the time, the mother repeatedly threatened to kill him if he should ever tell anyone what she did in her relationship to the other man, or should even so much as mention his name. As the child grew older, he was threatened daily that he would be killed if he told anyone about the mother's affair. Then, before he was five, the mother deserted husband and son without warning. Our observations led us to feel that this boy stood under dreadful fear for his life, that he was hiding a terrifying secret, the nature of which did not seem clear to him. Only through a former servant, who had been sent away from the home after the affair began, was it possible to learn in some detail about the early and repeated traumatization of the child. Subsequently, memories of these threats were spontaneously produced by the boy in play sessions.[62]

EXPERIMENTAL EXAMPLES Events like those described by Bettelheim, occurring at a tender age, are bound to be overwhelming, and it would be strange indeed if they left behind no personality-distorting traces. But events do not need to be so obviously terrifying as these to have traumatic power. Much depends on the circumstances surrounding the focal event. A series of experiments by Liddell and his associates illuminate this point.

In Liddell's experiments, the purpose is to analyze the conditions which produce or prevent neurotic reactions to a particular event. He has found it convenient to use goats as his experimental animals, especially because a goat mother typically bears twins. One of the kids can be treated in one way while the other is being treated in another, and their reactions can then be compared. Thus, in one experiment, a kid is confined alone in a small room while its twin

[61] Bettelheim (1956), p. 513. Used by permission of the *American Journal of Orthopsychiatry.*
[62] *Ibid.,* pp. 514 f.

is confined in a duplicate room but in the company of its mother. The twins are then put through a conditioning program in which they receive electric shocks (very mild) on the foreleg, regularly preceded by a ten-second period of darkness. The period of darkness thus becomes the conditioned stimulus for reaction to shock. It must be emphasized that the shock is so mild that it is just perceptible when applied to the experimenter's finger. Twenty such pairings of darkness and shock are given every day during the conditioning phase. The first notable conclusion is that the two kids act very differently. The kid which is alone (though free to move around in the room as much as it wishes) soon comes to avoid the center of the room and to press up against the walls; later, its movements become more restricted, and finally it cowers against the wall in one corner, apparently afraid to stir, practically immobilized during the two minutes of full illumination between darkness signals.

> But the twin in the other room, with its mother present, behaves quite differently. During the two-minute intervals between the darkness signals it moves freely around the room. Somehow the mother's presence protects the baby goat from the traumatic influence of the monotonously rigid pattern of tensions to which its twin in the adjoining room succumbs.[63]

Now, this is interesting as showing that the traumatic force of a stimulus does not lie necessarily in the energy of the stimulus; but the sequel is more interesting still. Liddell has followed up the effects of this early experience by testing his goats two years later. The mature animals were subjected to stress by bringing them into the laboratory every day for twenty days and keeping them in restraining harness for two hours while shock was administered to the foreleg after a ten-second darkness signal once every six minutes. The results: "The four goats which had had their mothers with them during their early experience showed no evidences of abnormal behavior in response to the severe stress of the two-hour daily session. The other four exhibited the familiar signs of experimental neurosis."[64]

Liddell's results are noteworthy. They tell us that the theory of early traumata has real substance, and that lifelong consequences may flow from events which might easily go unnoticed in a retrospective account. A mere trifle, objectively considered, will suffice.

[63] Liddell (1954), p. 57.   [64] *Ibid.*

On the other hand, Bettelheim's examples show us that events by no means trifling may be repressed or kept secret, so that they too may be hard to discover by later probing. Perhaps in these two facts—the significance of the apparently trivial, and the concealment of the obviously important—we have a clue as to why it is that objective types of investigation of the past history of psychological sufferers have so often yielded inconclusive data on the trauma theory. It is regrettable, too, that the theory in question has been so uniformly phrased in pathological terms; for if a single incident can give rise to pathological results, why should it not, as Gantt suggests, give rise to beneficial results? In fact, we might ask whether Liddell's young goats who faced the early stress conditions in the company of their mothers were not positively strengthened rather than merely protected from fear.

References for chapter 5

Ashby, W. R. (1952) *Design for a brain.* New York: Wiley.

Baldwin, A. L., Kalhorn, J., and Breese, F. H. (1945) Patterns of parent behavior. *Psychological Monographs,* 58, No. 268.

Bartlett, F. C. (1932) *Remembering.* Cambridge: Cambridge Univ. Press.

Beloff, H. (1957) The structure and origin of the anal character. *Genetic Psychology Monographs,* 55, 141-72.

Bender, L., and Grugett, A. E., Jr. (1956) A study of certain epidemiological factors in a group of children with childhood schizophrenia. *American Journal of Orthopsychiatry,* 26, 131-43.

Bettelheim, B. (1956) Schizophrenia as a reaction to extreme situations. *American Journal of Orthopsychiatry,* 26, 507-18.

Bodman, F. (1950) Constitutional factors in institution children. *Journal of Mental Science,* 96, 245-53.

Bowlby, J. (1951) *Maternal care and mental health* (Monograph Series, No. 2). Geneva: World Health Organization.

———— (1953a) *Child care and the growth of love.* Harmondsworth, Eng.: Penguin.

———— (1953b) Some pathological processes set in train by early mother-child separation. *Journal of Mental Science,* 99, 265-72.

Davis, E. A. (1937) *The development of linguistic skill in twins, singletons with siblings, and only children from age five to ten years* (Institute of Child Welfare Monograph Series, No. 14). Minneapolis: Univ. of Minnesota Press.

Freud, A., and Burlingham, D. T. (1944) *Infants without families.* New York: International Universities Press.

Gantt, W. H. (1953) Principles of nervous breakdown—schizokinesis and autokinesis. *Annals of the New York Academy of Science,* 56, 143-63.

Gesell, A., and Amatruda, C. S. (1947) *Developmental diagnosis, normal and abnormal child development.* New York: Hoeber.

Goldfarb, W. (1943) The effects of early institutional care on adolescent personality. *Journal of Experimental Education,* 12, 106-29.

Goldman, F. (1948) Breastfeeding and character formation. Part I. *Journal of Personality,* 17, 83-103.

———— (1950) Breastfeeding and character formation. Part II. *Journal of Personality,* 19, 189-96.

Hebb, D. O. (1949) *The organization of behavior: a neuropsychological theory.* New York: Wiley.

Hicks, J. A. (1930a) The acquisition of motor skill in young children: a study of the effects of practice in throwing at a moving target. *Child Development,* 1, 90-105.

———— (1930b) The acquisition of motor skill in young children. II. The influence of specific and general practice on motor skill. *Child Development,* 1, 292-97.

Jones, H. E. (1930) The retention of conditioned emotional reactions in infancy. *Journal of Genetic Psychology,* 37, 485-98.

Kantrow, R. W. (1937) An investigation of conditioned feeding responses and concomitant adaptive behavior in young infants. *Univ. of Iowa Studies in Child Welfare,* 13, No. 3, 1-64.

Kasatkin, N. I., and Levikova, A. M. (1935a) On the development of early conditioned reflexes and differentiations of auditory stimuli in infants. *Journal of Experimental Psychology,* 18, 1-19.

————, and Levikova, A. M. (1935b) The formation of visual conditioned reflexes and their differentiation in infants. *Journal of General Psychology,* 12, 416-35.

Levy, D. M. (1943) *Maternal overprotection.* New York: Columbia Univ. Press.

Liddell, H. S. (1954) Conditioning and emotions. *Scientific American,* 190 (January), 48-57.

Lowes, J. L. (1927) *The road to Xanadu: a study in the ways of the imagination.* Boston: Houghton Mifflin.

Mateer, F. (1918) *Child behavior.* Boston: Badger.

Mattson, M. L. (1933) The relation between the complexity of the habit to be acquired and the form of the learning curve in young children. *Genetic Psychology Monographs,* 13, 299-398.

McCarthy, D. (1930) *Language development of the preschool child* (Institute of Child Welfare Monograph Series, No. 4). Minneapolis: Univ. of Minnesota Press.

McCurdy, H. G. (1950) Consciousness and the galvanometer. *Psychological Review,* 57, 322-27.

—— (1957) The childhood pattern of genius. *Journal of the Elisha Mitchell Scientific Society*, 73, 448-62.

Mead, M. (1955a) Children and ritual in Bali. In Mead, M., and Wolfenstein, M. (Eds.) *Childhood in contemporary cultures*. Chicago: Univ. of Chicago Press, pp. 40-51.

—— (1955b) Life in Bali. In Soddy, K. (Ed.) *Mental health and infant development*. London: Routledge & Kegan Paul. Vol. 1, pp. 174-79.

Meier, N. C. (1936) Art ability without instruction or environmental background: case study of Loran Lockhart. *Psychological Monographs*, 48, No. 213, 155-63.

Pinneau, S. R. (1955) The infantile disorders of hospitalism and anaclitic depression. *Psychological Bulletin*, 52, 429-52.

Prout, C. T., and White, M. A. (1956) The schizophrenic's siblings. *Journal of Nervous and Mental Disease*, 123, 162-70.

Rheingold, H. L. (1956) The modification of social responsiveness in institutional babies. *Society for Research in Child Development Monographs*, 21, No. 2.

Schubert, A. (1930) Drawings of Orotchen children and young people. *Journal of Genetic Psychology*, 37, 232-44.

Spitz, R. A. (1945) Hospitalism. In Fenichel, O., *et al.* (Eds.) *The psychoanalytic study of the child*. New York: International Universities Press. Vol. 1.

—— (1946) Hospitalism: a follow-up report. In Fenichel, O., *et al.* (Eds.) *The psychoanalytic study of the child*. New York: International Universities Press. Vol. 2.

Tinbergen, N. (1951) *The study of instinct*. Oxford: Clarendon.

Tolman, E. C. (1932) *Purposive behavior in animals and men*. New York: Appleton-Century.

—— (1949) There is more than one kind of learning. *Psychological Review*, 56, 144-55.

Watson, J. B. (1928) *Psychological care of infant and child*. New York: Norton.

——, and Rayner, R. (1920) Conditioned emotional reactions. *Journal of Experimental Psychology*, 3, 1-14.

Wenger, M. A. (1936) An investigation of conditioned responses in human infants. *Univ. of Iowa Studies in Child Welfare*, 12, No. 1, 9-90.

Whiting, J. W. M., and Child, I. L. (1953) *Child training and personality: a cross-cultural study*. New Haven: Yale Univ. Press.

Wulf, F. (1922) Über die Veränderung von Vorstellungen (Gedächtnis und Gestalt). *Psychologische Forschung*, 1, 333-73.

II

PSYCHODYNAMICS

6

CONSCIOUSNESS
AND THE
CONSCIOUS SELF

Preview   *Consciousness is the process of knowing. It includes a great variety of different experiences. One of the most important is the realization of the distinction between the knower and the known. The knower, the "I," has been variously described but in one way or another is commonly recognized as a unique pivot of experience. There seems to be a natural tendency for "I"-consciousness to increase during childhood. Further increase may require deliberate effort or other special conditions. The dialectic of this development has been expounded by Kierkegaard, and it is probably assisted by such conscious discipline as that of the ascetic mystics. The degree of "I"-consciousness is an important personality variable. Furthermore, discussion of it logically precedes any consideration of the Unconscious, which will be the topic of the following three chapters.*

Our theme up to now has been the human being as a biological organism which we could observe from the outside, as an object in space. By careful self-control it would be possible to hold rigidly to that point of view and include nothing in our description of the human being except spatial and kinetic properties. The preceding chapters have not been quite that behavioristic. They have now and then considered the human being as conscious of himself and his surroundings. In the present chapter human consciousness will be made the central theme.

Even if we were only interested in the prediction of bodily movements, we should be interested in consciousness and the conscious self, for, as the physicist Arthur Compton has underlined, a conscious human being can predict his own behavior with far greater certainty than a physicist can predict the behavior of the objects of physical science.[1] Or if we were primarily interested in the Unconscious as viewed by the psychoanalytically oriented, we should still be interested, because without some recognition of the fact of consciousness the very concept of the Unconscious would be impossible. Both historically and logically the study of consciousness precedes the study of the Unconscious. Entirely apart from such excuses as these, however, the topic of this chapter deserves a central place in a book on personality.

It is a curious twist in the history of psychology—and as a reviewer of a recent symposium on the mind-body problem has said in reference to Zener's paper on "The Significance of Experience of the Individual for the Science of Psychology," it is a tragic twist[2] —that any apology should be needed for bringing consciousness into a psychological discussion. Yet we must realize how matters stand. Hilgard has stated it accurately:

> Psychologists are by no means unanimous as to the place of private experience (consciousness) in a science of psychology. Some extremists believe that private experiences have no place in science; they believe that such experiences belong to the province of the artist or poet. But most psychologists hold that these private experiences are just as much a part of the real world as more observable activities, and they accept the *verbal report* of these experiences as data for science.[3]

It is against this background that a discussion of consciousness must take place, and to avoid confusion it must be clearly stated

[1] Compton (1952).   [2] Peters (1959).
[3] Hilgard (1957), p. 4.

that one who is serious about consciousness does not regard "private experiences" as somehow less observable than "public experiences" and does not accept "verbal report" or any other index of conscious processes as a substitute for them. Skinner, who accepts the distinction between public and private events, is firm in rejecting the strategy of identifying verbal report with the event it reports.

> The verbal report is a response to the private event and may be used as a source of information about it. A critical analysis of the validity of this practice is of the first importance. But we may avoid the dubious conclusion that, so far as science is concerned, the verbal report or some other discriminative response *is* the sensation.[4]

I cannot state my own position better than by agreeing with Skinner here.

A word must be said about "public" and "private," however. A person may speak as confidently and truthfully of seeing the objects of a dream as of seeing his face in a mirror or the sun in the sky. All these are equally observable for him. So also are his feelings, his intentions, his decisions, though these cannot be classified as visible or even as "things." On the other hand, it is doubtful whether another person could ever take up exactly the first person's point of view with regard to *any* of these contents of consciousness. In that sense, all that anyone experiences is private to himself—the face in the mirror, the sun in the sky, as well as all the rest. But there is the marvelous fact of communication. By words, by gestures, by postures and facial expressions, by painting, by music, we manage to convey to others some awareness of our awareness and even, in a manner of speaking, give our private contents of consciousness to each other to handle and evaluate. The private thus becomes public; that is to say, it is shared by two or more persons. This communication gives us great pleasure and it is the indispensable foundation of those great public works, the sciences. But there would be no communication if there were nothing to communicate, and every communication originates in the content of someone's consciousness. Now, some of this communication takes the form of pointing. One can point at the sun in the sky or the face in the mirror, and others can follow the pointing finger and discover out there before them something corresponding to what was pointed at. Sometimes there is a little confusion, and one sees a bird instead of the sun or the frame of the mirror rather than the face in it; but, with persistence,

[4] Skinner (1953), p. 282.

we iron out these disagreements. Pointing, however, does not usually suffice for the objects of dreams, or for feelings, intentions, and decisions. The communication problem here is a trifle more difficult, but in principle it is the same problem. Perhaps it is not more difficult—a great deal depends on the state of consciousness of the communicators. To point out the sun to a person who cannot see at all is futile. Other approaches in that case are possible, to be sure; for instance, the sun's heat can be perceived by both the seeing and the blind. The face in the mirror would be a tougher problem. As for dreams and intentions and such, the problem is not really so grave if we happen to be dealing with someone who is conscious of dreams and intentions of his own; he can at least have a general knowledge of what is meant. But if he is a stranger to such contents of consciousness, the communication problem becomes very grave; in fact, as grave as that of sharing the face in the mirror with the blind man. We may then be driven to exclaim, in a burst of sympathy or exasperation, "Oh, I *wish* you knew!" In short, the problem of communication is basically a problem of common experience or the capacity for it.

How many of our disagreements in psychology stem from the dissimilarity of our experience has never been fully explored, but it is a safe bet that most of them do. Take, for example, the matter of visualizing, i.e., the power of calling up a visual image of something formerly seen. Long ago Galton found, to his astonishment, that there were numerous scientists who did not have this power and who, moreover, were inclined to deny that anyone else did. "They had no more notion of its true nature than a colour-blind man, who has not discerned his defect, has of the nature of colour. They had a mental deficiency of which they were unaware, and naturally enough supposed that those who were normally endowed were romancing."[5] Galton himself had the power, or it would have hardly occurred to him to start the investigation. Among modern psychologists the proportion who do not have visual imagery appears to be exceptionally high. Roe in a study of eminent research scientists[6] in America asked biologists, physicists, psychologists, and anthropologists what sort of imagery they used in thinking out their research problems. Of the 9 experimental psychologists and 4 clinical, child, or social psychologists of her sample, only 2 professed to use any visual imagery in their work, and these were both experimentalists. Quite a number of

[5] Galton (1880), p. 302.　　　　　　　　　　[6] Roe (1951).

them did profess to use *verbal* imagery, and this may have something to do with the stress on verbal report or verbalization which is so characteristic of psychological writings on thought and feeling these days. Roe's study, though based on small numbers, may furnish a clue to some of our debates about consciousness. Highly verbal or imageless psychologists may have trouble in realizing what the few with strong visual imagery mean when they refer to imagining something, and the small minority of visualizers may feel crushed under the verbalizing majority. However this may be, Roe found a significant difference between the psychologists and the anthropologists (social scientists) on the one hand and the biologists and physicists (natural scientists) on the other, as Table 14 shows. This must mean that lack of visual imagery is not a prerequisite of *all* high-level scientific work, in spite of Galton's speculation that hard thinking may have reduced the visualizing capacity of the scientists he knew.

I have cited a dissimilarity of experience in a relatively private area of consciousness as a possible cause of scientific quarrels. It would be easy to cite many gross dissimilarities of a more public nature. I will mention only one, however, and this outside the field of psychology. When P. A. Čerenkov, the Russian physicist, first produced the luminescence now known as "Čerenkov radiation" by irradiating pure water with gamma rays, he was unable to convince many physicists who came to see the demonstration that the glow was really there. They were "highly sceptical and hinted at visual hallucinations"[7]—for one thing, it had been an established principle that nothing moved faster than light and Cerenkov's claim appeared to violate this principle. But the skepticism must also have been partly due to nothing more profound than a visual

Table 14
Association between field of science and imagery type

	visual	verbal	imageless	N
biologists	10	4	3	17
physicists	10	4	4	18
psychologists and anthropologists	2	11	6	19
TOTAL NUMBERS	22	19	13	54

Adapted from Roe (1951), p. 465.

[7] Tamm (1959), p. 172.

sensitivity less acute than his. The fact of the matter is that certain particles *can* move faster than light *in certain media* (i.e., not *in vacuo*) and thus radiate light, a phenomenon which had not been recognized before Čerenkov did his experiment. Suppose, however, that Čerenkov's experiment—in the teeth of this skepticism—had not been repeated and expanded, as it has been; the charge of "hallucinations" might have stuck. If this kind of thing can happen in physics, it must surely happen in psychology. We have to beware of denying the reality of other persons' experiences solely because they fall outside our own range of perception and theory.

Condillac's statue

It may help us to appreciate consciousness in its own right if we adopt the device of the French philosopher Étienne de Condillac (1715-80) of imagining a statue of a man endowed with no sensory power but that of smell. "If we give the statue a rose to smell," he writes, "to us it is a statue smelling a rose, to itself it is smell of rose."[8] That is to say, a perceiver so limited would, at the moment of his first sensation, know only that one sensation and be completely filled by it. He would have no conception of a material body, either his own or that of a rose. He would not think of the smell as being caused by a flower or as being mediated by a sense organ or a brain. The smell would be all in all. In order for the statue to connect the fragrance with either his nose or the flower, he would have to be endowed with some other sense— sight or touch—and would have to reason about the comparisons which would then be possible. For that matter, the observers of the statue, if they were restricted to seeing, would not suspect that the statue in holding the flower to his nose was having an experience of a pleasant odor. So the statue would be oblivious of the observers, of his own body, and of the rose; and the observers would be unaware of the fragrance which constituted the statue's whole experience. The observers, seeing the statue as a form in space, would completely miss what the statue was to itself, namely, a delightful, all-sufficient fragrance. And the statue in turn, if capable of understanding the thought of the observers

[8] The quotation is from Condillac's *Treatise on the sensations*, tr. by G. Carr (Los Angeles: Univ. of Southern California School of Philosophy, 1930). The treatise originally appeared in 1754.

(which in Condillac's analysis would be impossible), would be amazed at their misconception of his essence.

Each of us is like the statue. Our own experience is unique and cannot be shared in its concrete, singular reality with any other mortal. But we do communicate to some extent and in a general way share each other's worlds. In fact, the illustration of the statue presupposes that the reader himself has the capacities for experience (and even the concrete experiences) which Condillac in his essay one by one adds to the statue's repertoire. It is precisely because our experience is so wide that we can understand the limited experience attributed to the statue.

One conclusion which Condillac reaches as he reflects on his statue is that a being confined to one sense alone would have numerous experiences transcending that sense or any sense whatsoever. There would be desire and memory and imagination and, most important of all, an awarenesse of selfhood—the conception of something basically unchanging in the midst of the changing experiences.

> Our statue being capable of memory, there is no smell which does not recall to it that it was once another smell. Herein lies its personality. If it is able to say "I" it can say it in all the states of its duration; and at each time its "I" will embrace all the moments of which it might have preserved the recollection. I admit that it could not say "I" at the first smell. What we understand by this word "I" seems to be only possible in a being who notices that in the present moment he is no longer what he has been. So long as there is no change, he exists without any reflexion upon himself; but as soon as he changes, he judges that he is the same as he formerly was in another state, and he says "I."[9]

The "I"

Consciousness precedes self-consciousness! But once it has arrived, the "I" becomes a point of stability in the flux of experience. More than that, it acts as an organizer bringing order into the flux. By merely preferring the fragrance of a rose to the stench of carrion it begins to set up value hierarchies. It may go beyond that and establish conscious principles for such ordering.

Once the "I" begins to operate, it does not readily vanish—even in dreams. Yet it is possible for self-consciousness to yield to a

[9] *Ibid.*, p. 43.

state of consciousness lacking this organizing center. Koffka provides an example. A mountain climber, Professor Eugen Lammer, while descending a treacherous glacier in the Alps, fell through a softened snow bridge into a crevasse; bumping against the icy walls as he fell, he was knocked senseless. His return to consciousness he described in the following words:

> . . . fog . . . darkness . . . fog . . . whirring . . . grey veil with a small lighter spot . . . fog . . . faint dawn . . . a soft humming . . . dull discomfort . . . fog . . . something has happened to somebody . . . gloomy fog, and always that lighter point . . . a shivering shudder: something clammy . . . fog . . . how was it? . . . an effort at thinking . . . ah, still fog; but besides that light point there outside, there emerges a second point inside: right, that is *I*! . . . fog, dull ringing sound, frost . . . a dream? . . . Yes, indeed, a wild, wild, wild dream!— It has dreamed—no, rather *I* have dreamed. . . .[10]

The "I" here enters the stream of consciousness late, and then somewhat waveringly. The stage expressed by "something has happened to somebody" reminds me of a dream once told me by a student. In the dream he saw his roommate writhing in pain. When he woke up he discovered that the pain was his own: he was suffering from an attack of appendicitis.

The origin of self-consciousness in the individual life is hidden in the obscurity of all beginnings. Many of us are able to remember how, as children, we puzzled ourselves with wondering what it would be like to be someone else and concluded that it is impossible to be any "I" but that which one is. But such reflections must come at a relatively late stage in the development of self-consciousness.

Helen Keller, who was permanently blinded and deafened by scarlet fever when she was 19 months old, thinks that in her own case self-consciousness did not become sharply focused until she had acquired finger-language at the age of eight. According to her recollection at twenty-eight, her life before that time was purely sensory and impulsive. For example, when she craved ice cream, she had the taste of it on her tongue and she could feel in her hand the turning of the freezer. The involuntary gestures which accompanied these sensations told her mother what she wanted. After beginning to learn finger-language from her devoted teacher, Anne Sullivan Macy, she was still for a time not much farther ad-

[10] Koffka (1935), pp. 323 f.

vanced. "I merely felt keen delight in obtaining more easily what I wanted by means of the finger motions she taught me. I thought only of objects, and only objects I wanted. It was the turning of the freezer on a larger scale."[11] Only when she learned the meaning of "I" did consciousness fully arrive. After that, "I was eager to know, then to understand, afterward to reflect on what I knew and understood, and the blind impetus, which had before driven me hither and thither at the dictates of my sensations, vanished forever."[12]

One must ask whether the "I" actually fails to appear in some individuals. Certainly, in many cases the "I" seems to be in negligible control. I am sure that I have talked to college students whose self-awareness was scarcely more than Helen Keller's when she was beginning to learn finger-language. I remember one vigorous, personable, dashing young man in particular who drove one of the finest convertibles on campus and whose ambition was to become a big speculator in real estate. He fairly well convinced me that he was telling the truth when he said that he did not know what thinking was. It is possible that for him both he and his automobile were in the same category as glittering unthinking objects moving mindlessly through space.

We find the opposite condition, too. When "I"-consciousness has reached a high level, the words of Rabindranath Tagore apply:

> At one pole of my being I am one with stocks and stones. There I have to acknowledge the rule of universal law. . . . But at the other pole of my being I am separate from all. There I have broken through the cordon of equality and stand alone as an individual. I am absolutely unique, I am I, I am incomparable. The whole weight of the universe cannot crush out this individuality of mine. I maintain it in spite of the tremendous gravitation of all things. It is small in appearance but great in reality. For it holds its own against the forces that would rob it of its distinction and make it one with the dust.[13]

Mystical intensity

The intensity of "I"-consciousness varies through an immense range. At a high, though not the highest level, is the state described by Wordsworth in "Tintern Abbey," where he speaks of

[11] Keller (1909), pp. 116 f.   [12] Ibid., p. 117.
[13] Sādhanā, the realisation of life (New York: Macmillan, 1914), p. 69. Used by permission of Macmillan & Company Ltd. (London).

> *. . . that blessed mood,*
> *In which the burthen of the mystery,*
> *In which the heavy and the weary weight*
> *Of all this unintelligible world,*
> *Is lightened:—that serene and blessed mood,*
> *In which the affections gently lead us on,—*
> *Until, the breath of this corporeal frame*
> *And even the motion of our human blood*
> *Almost suspended, we are laid asleep*
> *In body, and become a living soul. . . .*

It would be a serious mistake to dismiss this as "just poetry." Wordsworth is describing an actual experience, and one which has been known to many other people, not necessarily poets.

Less familiar than Wordsworth's lines, but more pointed, are the words of the English naturalist Richard Jefferies (1848-87) in *The Story of My Heart*:

> Sometimes I have concentrated myself, and driven away by continued will all sense of outward appearances, looking straight with the full power of my mind inwards on myself. I find "I" am there; an "I" I do not wholly understand or know—something is there distinct from earth and timber, from flesh and bones. Recognizing it, I feel on the margin of a life unknown, very near, almost touching it: on the verge of powers which if I could grasp would give me an immense breadth of existence, an ability to execute what I now only conceive; most probably of far more than that. To see that "I" is to know that I am surrounded with immortal things.[14]

Jefferies was a man who allied himself to no religion, but experiences of the quality and intensity which he describes here are often catalogued as mystical. There is no harm in that, provided that the term does not prevent us from acknowledging their reality in the lives of genuine (and not unhealthy) human beings. For all we know, experiences like Jefferies' may be extremely common. True, they are not often mentioned in conversation or textbooks; but then, many perfectly real and common things are not mentioned in ordinary conversation or in textbooks. On the other hand, the fact that such experiences are often regarded as odd and incomprehensible does suggest that the level of consciousness which they represent is not as common as eating and drinking. So far as I know, there has been no thorough statistical inquiry. In a recent book on the psychology of religion the author states that he

[14] Quoted in Butler (1927), p. 334.

has not paid much attention to mystical experience "simply because of the lack of statistical evidence about it."[15]

In the highest mystical experience, the acute consciousness of self is made the launching platform for a flight toward the Eternal. So St. Augustine describes how he entered into the innermost part of himself, and, having entered, "with the eye of my soul (such as it was) saw above the same eye of my soul, above my mind, the Unchangeable Light."[16]

Mystics agree that withdrawal of attention from external sensation is a necessary prelude and that the mystical vision is a very inward reception of a reality which can be expressed only by analogy with, not by means of, sensory experience. They also typically regard their highest moments as imperfect glimpses. So Pope Gregory the Great (590-604) compares the mind of the contemplative to a fortress with a narrow slit-window splaying inwardly, admitting very little of the true light but enough to light up the whole room, and goes on to say:

> He that keeps his heart within, he it is who receives the light of contemplation. For they that still think immoderately of external things, know not what are the chinks of contemplation from the eternal light. For that infusion of incorporeal light is not received along with the images of corporeal things; because while visible things are thought of, the invisible light is not admitted to the mind.[17]

The reader who has had no personal mystical experience or who regards mystical experience as pathological and illusory may nevertheless gain some insight into the mystical state of mind by considering Helen Keller's remarks on her efforts to include color and sound in her conception of reality in spite of her blindness and deafness:

> It strains my mind to separate color and sound from objects. Since my education began I have always had things described to me with their colors and sounds by one with keen senses and a fine feeling for the significant. Therefore I habitually think of things as colored and resonant. Habit accounts for part. The soul sense accounts for another part. The brain with its five-sensed construction asserts its right and accounts for the rest. Inclusive of all, the unity of the world demands that color be kept in it, whether I have cognizance of it or not. Rather

[15] Argyle (1958), p. 66.
[16] *Confessions.* In *The works of St. Augustine* (Edinburgh: Clark, 1876), p. 157.
[17] Quoted in Butler (1927), pp. 102 f.

than be shut out, I take part in it by discussing it, imagining it, happy in the happiness of those near me who gaze at the lovely hues of the sunset or the rainbow.[18]

We who are able to see the colors and hear the sounds denied to Helen Keller recognize that her groping phrases bear some relation to the reality we know, although we are certain that she does not enjoy that reality as we do. Perhaps, in the same way, mystics are right in believing that their "trembling glances" are not merely an acute flare-up of subjectivity but are a true, though imperfect, apprehension of supreme reality.

One thing is clear: mystical experience can happen to the most rational of people. It happened to Blaise Pascal. Now, Pascal (1623-62) was a scientist, one of the greatest, and a man with a practical, even worldly, as well as theoretical turn of mind. It is true that he lived in the seventeenth century, but consider his modernity! Mortimer comments:

> A modern [Englishman], starting out for the office, may glance at his wrist-watch, tap the barometer, slip into the nearest tobacconist's shop for a purchase and receive his change from the cash machine, board an omnibus and presently settle at his desk. How remote might seem the French geometer who got mixed up with Jansenism before Versailles was built! Yet Pascal originated that barometer, invented that calculating machine, was the first man to think of an omnibus and to organize a line of public vehicles, and was perhaps the only man before the twentieth century habitually to wear a wrist-watch.[19]

This Pascal, aged 31, was sitting alone in his room one November night, reading the seventeenth chapter of St. John's Gospel. He was then seized by his mystical experience. It lasted for two hours. We know about it because he scribbled down some broken notes immediately after and sewed them into the lining of his doublet, where they were found after his death eight years later. This famous document, which fairly trembles with emotion, begins:

The year of grace, 1654.
Monday, 23d. November, Feast of S. Clement, Pope and Martyr, and of others in the Martyrology
Vigil of S. Chrysogonus, Martyr, and others,
From about half-past ten in the evening until about half-past twelve

[18] Keller (1909), pp. 108 f.   [19] Mortimer (1959), p. 12.

FIRE

God of Abraham, God of Isaac, God of Jacob, not of the
philosophers and savants
Certitude. Certitude. Feeling. Joy. Peace.
God of Jesus Christ.
My God and Thy God
"Thy God shall be my God"
Forgetfulness of the world and of everything except God
He is to be found only in the ways taught in the Gospel
Grandeur of the human soul
Righteous Father, the world hath not known Thee, but I have
known Thee
Joy, joy, joy, tears of joy. . . .[20]

From that time on Pascal was a changed man; not startlingly
changed, but changed. Some have not liked the change. Eric Bell,
for instance, in a popular work on mathematicians, sees him as
lost to the good cause of science, his talent wasted in fanaticism.[21]
Others have been impressed by the literary and intellectual bril-
liance of the writings which followed—the *Provincial Letters*, the
Pensées—and, perhaps more important, the increased humility,
patience, and love. However the mystical event may be interpreted,
we may be sure that it was intensely real for Pascal, and that it
changed him.

Phenomenology of the "I"

If we take middle ground, between sleep or sensory chaos on
the one hand and intense mystical experience on the other, how
is the "I" to be described?

For myself, it is not a sensation or accumulation of sensations.
It is not the body. It is not the world spread out around the body.
It is not pain or pleasure. It has no weight or extent. It is simply
the pivot of all these things. Inhabiting my body, though without
precise location, it is primarily a center which perceives; but it
also wills some of my acts, and imagines and hopes and fears. It is
deeply entangled with the world, which it sometimes passionately
loves, but it is detachable from it. It does not take pride in itself,
although it suffers from certain vanities about the body and its
acts and other objects to which it is attached. When it is most

[20] *Ibid.*, pp. 123 f.   [21] Bell (1937).

completely absorbed in work (i.e., in perceiving and thinking), the concentration of attention momentarily banishes it from consciousness along with numerous objects in the surrounding world. But it comes back into its own as easily as do those external objects. If there is anything that it regrets about itself, it is that it should have to be burdened by self-consciousness; for it is fully as shy as it is invisible.

Now, I maintain that this brief description is no mere empty verbalization. If it sounds odd to others, it can only be because it does not match their own experience. It is as veracious and accurate (and inadequate) as would be my description of the typewriter at which I am working at this moment. That, too, might sound odd to a reader who had never seen a typewriter, or one exactly like mine. It is true that I cannot touch the "I," or point to it, or draw a picture of it. In this respect it differs from the typewriter. It is nevertheless very much a part of my experience.

To make it perfectly clear that my experience of the "I" has some features in common with that of other men, I will quote a few sentences from the physiologist Sherrington. (Incidentally, he starts out with much greater confidence in the universality of his own experience than perhaps he should.) He writes:

> We, I fancy shall agree that the awareness which is the 'I' or 'self' has its different dominant phases. Sometimes it is dominantly the 'I-doing', sometimes dominantly the 'I-feeling', sometimes dominantly the 'I-perceiving' and so on. In all these situations, perhaps especially the last, the 'I' finds itself surrounded by sensual space, but that space never actually attaches to it or gives it extension. Sensual space never gets grip of the 'I'. It does not reach the 'I'.[22]

A little farther on in the same book he contrasts the "I" with its objects:

> When therefore the self is aware of a thrush on the lawn as 'there' with implicit relation to the self's own self as 'here', besides the difference that the former is projected the latter not, there are larger other spatial differences between the two. The former has spatial extension, contour, magnitude, colour, audibility, etc.—the latter none of these. The former is further a cluster of spatial associations, e.g. that, were I to take it up ever so gently I should feel something ticking far faster than a seconds' clock inside a feathery warm handful. But the latter, this

[22] Sherrington (1941), p. 332. Used by permission of the Cambridge University Press.

'self' within me has no such associations visible, tangible, or sensible. As to space it is an unwittingly inferred 'position' only.[23]

Both Sherrington's description and my own are meant to be nothing but descriptions. A metaphysical conclusion might be drawn from them, but they are not metaphysical statements. That is why I am untroubled by whatever differences there may be between these reports and those of David Hume and William James. One should be prepared for individual differences here as elsewhere. Actually, there is not complete difference, and less with Hume than with James. The difference lies in their greater stress on the sensory content of their introspections.

The Scottish philosopher Hume (1711-76), in a famous passage where he is trying to refute the notion of a simple, nonextended, spiritual substance (which in fact could not be admitted into his system because his presuppositions rule it out), states:

> For my part, when I enter most intimately into what I call *myself*, I always stumble on some particular perception or other, of heat or cold, light or shade, love or hatred, pain or pleasure. I never can catch *myself* at any time without a perception, and never can observe anything but the perception. When my perceptions are removed for any time, as by sound sleep, so long am I insensible of *myself*, and may truly be said not to exist. And were all my perceptions removed by death, and could I neither think, nor feel, nor see, nor love, nor hate, after the dissolution of my body, I should be entirely annihilated, nor do I conceive what is further requisite to make me a perfect nonentity. If any one, upon serious and unprejudiced reflection, thinks he has a different notion of *himself*, I must confess I can reason no longer with him. All I can allow him is, that he may be in the right as well as I, and that we are essentially different in this particular. He may, perhaps, perceive something simple and continued, which he calls *himself;* though I am certain there is no such principle in me. But setting aside some metaphysicians of this kind, I may venture to affirm to the rest of mankind, that they are nothing but a bundle or collection of different perceptions, which succeed each other with an inconceivable rapidity, and are in a perpetual flux and movement.[24]

If we take Hume literally, and without any suspicion of irony, he denies the presence of any such self as Sherrington affirms; but if

[23] *Ibid.*, p. 334.
[24] The quotation is from Hume's *Treatise of human nature,* Everyman's Library edition (London: Dent, 1911), Vol. 1, p. 239. The work first appeared in 1739-40.

we take into account the contrasts in his language, he leaves us undecided, for the phrase "a bundle or collection of different perceptions" seems to connote something different from what is connoted by "could I neither think, nor feel, nor see, nor love, nor hate" where he comes close to Sherrington's language. He speaks there as if the self were an activity or a capacity for activity *toward* objects, but his other expression identifies it with the objects themselves, as the logic of his system relentlessly requires.

James in some respects follows Hume. He begins his discussion of what he calls the "Spiritual Self" by assuming that everyone would agree that there is an *active* conscious something concerned with the qualities and contents of consciousness "which seems to *go out* to meet these qualities and contents, whilst they seem to *come in* to be received by it" and which is "the source of effort and attention, and the place from which appear to emanate the fiats of the will"[25]—an assumption which, as we have just seen, Hume apparently struggled to avoid. But after this introduction James declares that introspection shows him no such thing as a spiritual element, but only muscular sensations, mostly in the head; and he continues:

> In a sense, then, it may be truly said that, in one person at least, the "Self of selves," when carefully examined, is found to consist mainly of the collection of these peculiar motions in the head or between the head and throat. I do not for a moment say that this is all it consists of, for I fully realize how desperately hard is introspection in this field. But I feel quite sure that these cephalic motions are the portions of my innermost activity of which I am most distinctly aware. If the dim portions which I cannot yet define should prove to be like unto these distinct portions in me, and I like other men, it would follow that our entire feeling of spiritual activity, or what commonly passes by that name, is really a feeling of bodily activities whose exact nature is by most men overlooked.[26]

This is a description which differs enough from the others previously cited to justify James' doubt as to whether it would fit everyone. It bears strongly the mark of a particular type of imagery—the kinesthetic—to which he seems to have been especially prone. We know at least that James was not inclined to use visual imagery, for in two footnotes on the studies by Galton and Binet he tells us that he was an extremely poor visualizer.[27] A systematic com-

[25] James (1890), Vol. 1, pp. 297 f.   [26] *Ibid.*, pp. 301 f.
[27] James (1890), Vol. 2, pp. 53, 61.

parison between the imagery of various psychologists and their views on the self might be revealing.

What seems to be clear is that when mature men introspect, their conclusions regarding the self differ in some details. This is no invalidation of introspection. It simply means that "I"-consciousness varies from person to person. Here, too, there is individuality.

Some consequences of "I"-consciousness

LYING   Given the conscious presence of the "I," certain mental phenomena become possible which would otherwise be impossible. An example is lying. A lie is not just behavioral inconsistency, nor is it fully defined in terms of deceiving others. The heart of it is a contradiction between what one thinks or feels and what one chooses to express. It is a cleavage between the innermost and outermost regions of the personality. It is therefore a threat to personal integrity or unity or wholeness, a "schizokinesis" in Gantt's terminology, no matter what the temporary advantage may seem to be. This is what Francis Bacon (1561-1626) had in mind when he wrote,

> And therefore Montaigne saith prettily, when he inquired the reason, why the word of the lie should be such a disgrace and such an odious charge? Saith he, *If it be well weighed, to say that a man lieth, is as much as to say, as that he is brave towards God and a coward towards men.* For a lie faces God, and shrinks from man.[28]

Lying is often regarded as a moral fault. Yet it may be argued that the baby who cannot lie has not reached as high a stage of development as the child who can, just as it may be argued that a man who knows how to lie and does not has reached a higher stage than a man who knows how to do it and does. The ability to lie indicates some measure of self-consciousness. It may also be a step toward the full appreciation of truth.

DISSOCIATION   Another phenomenon, somewhat related to lying, deserves our attention. This is the separation of the "I" as thinker from the thought processes themselves. There are moments when the succession of thoughts seems to escape from control. In lying, the "I" keeps its grip on the expressive mechanism of the body

[28] "Of truth."

but misuses it; in this other condition, it has only so much control over the mechanism of thought (a more private thing than the mechanism of expression) as an automobile driver might have over his machine if he started it down the road and then jumped out to watch it running on without him.

This kind of dissociation sometimes happens when one is both trying to follow out a line of thought and to go to sleep. An interesting question in the thinker's mind may then elude him, and he discovers to his dismay that he does not know what it was he started to think about, though a dusty cloud of imagery may swirl up behind it. As Silberer has noted, the dusty cloud on some occasions is shaped into a dream in which the initial problem is continued in a fashion. He called this the *autosymbolic phenomenon*. Here is one of his examples:

> One afternoon (after lunch) I was lying on my couch. Though extremely sleepy, I forced myself to think through a problem of philosophy, which was to compare the views of Kant and Schopenhauer concerning time. In my drowsiness I was unable to sustain their ideas side by side. After several unsuccessful attempts, I once more fixed Kant's argument in my mind as firmly as I could and turned my attention to Schopenhauer's. But when I tried to reach back to Kant, his argument was gone again, and beyond recovery. The futile effort to find the Kant record which was somehow misplaced in my mind suddenly represented itself to me—as I was lying there with my eyes closed, as in a dream—as a perceptual symbol: I am asking a morose secretary for some information; he is leaning over his desk and disregards me entirely; he straightens up for a moment to give me an unfriendly and rejecting look.[29]

The effect of this vivid imagery was almost frightening. Startled back into fuller self-consciousness, Silberer realized the equivalence of the imagery to the defeated struggle of thought. In such an instance we catch the "I" abandoning control of the thought-machinery, and the machinery turning around and threatening its former master.

Now, these possibilities of lying and dissociation, by which the "I" is separated from its instruments, may become actual in anyone who has reached the level of "I"-consciousness. Though the effects may at first be strictly inward, they typically have reverberations in outer relations. The person who is inwardly confused is

[29] Silberer (1951), pp. 195 f. Used by permission of the Columbia University Press. This paper first appeared in German in 1909.

very likely to produce some turmoil in society, too. We need not be moralistic about lying to see that it is dangerous to society as well as to individuals; nor do we have to be cynical to observe that it is exceedingly common.

Maslow's comments on those creative and healthy people whom he calls *self-actualizing* suggest that honesty is related to a general development of consciousness and self-consciousness. He says:

> Closely related to self-acceptance and to acceptance of others is (a) their lack of defensiveness, protective coloration, or pose, and (b) their distaste for such artificialities in others. Cant, guile, hypocrisy, "front," "face," playing a game, trying to impress in conventional ways: these are all absent in themselves to an unusual degree.[30]

Honesty is wholeness and freedom—freedom from fear.

Development of consciousness as an ascent with critical moments

One of the most significant ways in which personalities may be ranked is in terms of the extent and the intensity of their awareness of themselves and the world around them. At any given age there are individual differences in this respect; but, very broadly speaking, we expect an increase of consciousness with age. This increase, however, appears not to be a perfectly gradual process inevitably associated with advancing years.

A sketchy general outline of the process would be the following. (1) The baby does not at first distinguish even between its body and surrounding objects. When it does begin to make that distinction, it also begins to discover the "I"; and, as Piaget's principle of complementarity holds, every step in the discovery of objects is accompanied by an increase of self-awareness. (2) Next, perhaps, comes the distinction between the sensed and the imagined. The dream is put in a different category from the world as perceived through the bodily sense organs, though the "I" is in contact with both. This increases self-awareness, too, just as foreign travel does. (3) Later, maybe much later, there may come moments of moral or intellectual awakening when the person puts to himself the question about the origin of his own actions, realizes that he can resist or act upon impulses, can enjoy and create as well as others, is in short a responsible agent. (4) Further ascent may require

[30] Maslow (1956), p. 169.

special discipline. By a deliberate turning away from sensory perception and a concentration on the nature of the self one may discover the self in depth and have a glimpse of reality beyond the self as an infinite, eternal order transcending and including both what is sensed and what is dreamed.

This is extremely sketchy and it does not indicate the fine grain of the process, the numerous little steps along the way; nor does it indicate the sense of effort, and the pain and terror, which may accompany even the little steps.

THE EFFORT AND PAIN AND TERROR OF DEVELOPMENT The growing boy or girl often shrinks back from assuming adult independence even while clamoring for it. The prospect of being responsible for one's actions is not altogether pleasant. Sometimes the change is abrupt and radical. Take this example. A college student describes himself as callow and ignorant when he first arrived on the Princeton campus as a freshman. He got drunk the first night he was there, and he repeated this performance time after time in the next three years. During this whole period he was trying, mostly with little success, to fit in, to become one of the boys, to shock others and satisfy his own crude impulses. His life was erratic and compulsive. Then suddenly he became aware of himself and his deficiencies. "For the first time in three years I started to think rationally. What could I do with myself? It was time to face facts and to become a man. By trying to belong I was merely denying my own personality. I spent weeks in thinking."[31] A summer in South America, where he felt no compulsion to be anybody but himself, helped him in making the transition from an uneasy crowd-man to a much more confident individualist. Other events, such as falling in love, also helped him to find himself. But the sheer mental effort to see things as they are was an important factor, as he recognizes in his account.

Another example will be instructive with regard to the hesitations and fear with which one may approach self-realization. The example comes from the history of a young woman graduate student whose problems had become so heavy that she had contemplated suicide. During psychotherapy she discovered that she was continually wishing to have someone else to depend on; it was one of her bitter complaints that her professors did not give her

[31] Butz (1958), p. 100.

enough guidance. At the same time she began to see that she herself did little that was positive; for instance, she did not participate actively in the classes which she condemned as fruitless. It was in this state of mind, hovering between semiconscious dependency and a recognition of her own responsibility, that the following dialogue took place. The quotation is from Rogers. Notice the conflict of feelings as she begins to be conscious of a budding independence.

CLIENT   Well now, I wonder if I've been going around doing that, getting smatterings of things, and not getting hold, not really getting down to things.

THERAPIST   Maybe you've been getting just spoonfuls here and there rather thaan really digging in somewhere rather deeply.

C   M-hm. That's why I say—(*slowly and very thoughtfully*) well, with that sort of a foundation, well, it's really up to *me*. I mean, it seems to be really apparent to me that I *can't depend on someone else* to give me an education. (*Very softly*) I'll really have to get it myself.

T   It really begins to come home—there's only one person that can educate you—a realization that perhaps nobody else *can give* you an education.

C   M-hm (*long pause—while she sits thinking*). I have all the symptoms of fright (*laughs softly*).

T   Fright? That this is a scary thing, is that what you mean?

C   M-hm (*very long pause—obviously struggling with feelings in herself*).

T   Do you want to say any more about what you mean by that? That it really does give you the symptoms of fright?

C   (*laughs*) I, uh—I don't know whether I quite know. I mean—well, it really seems like I'm cut loose (*pause*), and it seems that I am very—I don't know—in a vulnerable position, but I, uh, I brought this up and it, uh, somehow it almost came out without my saying it. It seems to be—it's something I let out.

T   Hardly a part of you.

C   Well, I felt surprised.

T   As though: "Well for goodness sake, did I say that?" (*both chuckle*).

C   Really, I don't think I've had that feeling before. I've—uh, well, this really feels like I'm saying something that, uh, *is* a part of me really (*pause*). Or, uh (*quite perplexed*), it feels like I sort of have, uh, I don't know. I have a feeling of *strength,* and yet, I have a feeling of—realizing it's so sort of fearful, of fright.

T   That is, do you mean that saying something of that sort gives you at the same time a feeling of strength in saying it, and yet at the same time a frightened feeling of what you have said, is that it?

C M-hm. I am feeling that. For instance, I'm feeling it internally now —a sort of surging up, or force. As if that's something really big and strong. And yet, uh, well at first it was almost a physical feeling of just being out alone, and sort of cut off from a—support I had been carrying around.

T You feel that it's something deep and strong, and surging forth, and at the same time, you just feel as though you'd cut yourself loose from any support when you say it.

C M-hm. Maybe that's—I don't know—it's a disturbance of a kind of pattern I've been carrying around, I think.

T It sort of shakes a rather significant pattern, jars it loose.

C M-hm. (*Pause, then cautiously, but with conviction*) I, I think—I don't know, but I have the feeling that then I am going to begin to *do* more things that I know I should do. . . . There are so many things that I need to do. It seems in so many avenues of my living I have to work out new ways of behaving, but—maybe—I can see myself doing a little better in some things.[32]

The special point of this illustration is that, as Rogers remarks, uneasiness attends the discovery of one's uniqueness even though that discovery reveals one's strength. In more intense experiences of change we might expect the uneasiness to mount to the level of terror. As the poet Rilke wrote, "*Jeder Engel ist schrecklich!*" Every illumination, every annunciation of new things, is frightening.

Progress in consciousness and self-consciousness brings some individuals to crises of suffering such as have been described by the mystics as the "dark night of the soul." Underhill writes:

Over and over again, the Christian mystics—always with astonishment and dread—have found themselves led to this position; have fallen from the splendours of illumination to the horrors of Gethsemane, and discovered in the self-naughting which they believed to be a joy, a torture almost beyond their powers of endurance. "It is impossible," says St. Teresa, "to describe the sufferings of the soul in this state." "In this upper school," said his Heavenly Visitor to Suso, "they teach the science of Perfect Self-Abandonment; that is to say, a man is here taught to renounce himself so utterly that in all those circumstances in which God is manifested, either by Himself or in His creatures, the man applies himself only to remaining calm and unmoved, renouncing so far as possible all human frailty."[33]

[32] Rogers (1956), pp. 208 f. Used by permission of Harper & Brothers.
[33] Underhill (1929), pp. 136 f.

Again, in regard to the same experience, Underhill quotes St. John of the Cross, one of the great mystics and the greatest lyric poet of Spain:

"The divine excess . . . so breaks and bruises the soul, swallowing it up in profound darkness, that the soul, at the sight of its own wretchedness, seems to perish and waste away by a cruel spiritual death . . . for it must lie buried in the grave of a gloomy death that it may attain to the spiritual resurrection for which it hopes. David describes this kind of pain and suffering—though it really baffles description—when he says, 'The sorrows of death have compassed me. . . . In my tribulation I have called upon our Lord and have cried to my God.' But the greatest affliction of the sorrowful soul in this state is the thought that God has abandoned it, of which it has no doubt; that He has cast it away into darkness as an abominable thing."[34]

But if the darkness of the dark night is hard to endure, a sudden bright prospect may also be dreaded. When Augustine was praying to be saved from his sins, he appended, "But not yet, O Lord!" The idea of giving up one's familiar bad habits, excuses, crutches, claims on other people's sympathy, vices, crimes, pathologies, in exchange for strength and health and happiness is not altogether attractive in reality. If it could be done very, very gradually, a bit at a time, it might not be so bad, for everyone recognizes that change is a part of life. But some change is and must be radical, violent. If you are a bird on a branch teetering between staying and flying, as Kierkegaard has noted, you cannot effect a gradual transition between being branch-borne and being air-borne; if you are to fly, you must launch out all at once and leave the security of the branch behind.

The dialectic of selfhood

Perhaps no writer has given more attention to the problem of selfhood than the Danish philosopher Søren Kierkegaard (1813-55). Contemporary psychologists who have paid tribute to his work include Mowrer, Rogers, and May. An extensive, but incomplete, summary of his views was given by May in *The Meaning of Anxiety* in 1950. Rogers, in the essay from which the dialogue between therapist and graduate student was taken, exclaims that Kierkegaard wrote as if he had observed such clinical sessions as he, Rogers, was describing. But Kierkegaard published *The Concept of Dread*

[34]*Ibid.*, p. 139.

and *The Sickness Unto Death* a hundred years before the tape-recording of clinical interviews had become accepted practice. Kierkegaard's chief subject of observation was himself.

One of Kierkegaard's claims upon our interest is that he regarded anxiety—or dread, or despair—as the unavoidable accompaniment of any imperfection in one's realization and acceptance of one's unique self. Kierkegaard recognized in anxiety something typically human, extremely common, and acutely present in himself. He did not hold himself above it, looking at it curiously as if it were a strange foreign object, safely locked up behind the bars of an asylum.

His very special interest for us here is that his analysis of the varieties of despair involved him in an analysis of the various states of the self in relation to itself and the rest of reality. These various states may be regarded as developmental stages. The next few pages summarize Kierkegaard's analysis as presented in *The Sickness Unto Death.*

The opening words of this book are these: "Man is spirit. But what is spirit? Spirit is the self. But what is the self? The self is a relation which relates itself to its own self."[35] Kierkegaard explains the last sentence by stating that man is a synthesis of opposites—the infinite and the finite, the eternal and the temporal, freedom and necessity. When this synthesis of opposites turns reflectively upon itself and is related to itself there emerges the positive self which we recognize as "I." The self, then, is a synthesis. But whence the synthesis? One possibility is that it is completely original, self-created. Kierkegaard, however, rejects this answer in favor of the proposition that the self depends for its existence on a higher power. This logically introduces still another relation—that between the self and the power on which it depends. Hence Kierkegaard states: "The self cannot of itself attain and remain in equilibrium and rest by itself, but only by relating itself to that Power which constituted the whole relation."[36]

From these various relationships issue the kinds of despair of which we are capable; for despair, as Kierkegaard defines it, is the effort or tendency to get rid of any of these relationships. The self must will to be what it is and it must will to be dependent on the

[35] Kierkegaard, *The sickness unto death,* tr. by W. Lowrie (Princeton: Princeton Univ. Press, 1941), p. 17. Used by permission of Princeton University Press.
[36] *Ibid.,* p. 18.

Power which created it if it is to escape anxiety in every form. In order to arrive at this state of perfect health, it is necessary to be fully conscious of one's spiritual existence and of the supreme cause of it. The willingness to be what one is and to accept one's dependency is vitally associated with consciousness. In Kierkegaard's words:

> Generally speaking, consciousness, i.e. consciousness of self, is the decisive criterion of the self. The more consciousness, the more self; the more consciousness, the more will, and the more will the more self. A man who has no will at all is no self; the more will he has, the more consciousness of self he has also.[37]

THE SOURCES OF DESPAIR   Despair or spiritual imperfection may result from excess in the direction of finiteness or of infinity, of possibility or of necessity—in short, from a lack of balance in the synthesis of opposites which man is. It may also result from lack of consciousness; or, if there is consciousness, from weakness or defiance in willing to be oneself.

(1) A man may be lost in infinity, by lacking focus or limit in his feeling, knowing, and willing, squandering his resources of emotions on abstractions, piling up knowledge that contributes nothing to knowing himself, failing to bring his unbounded desires to a definite point of application on any real task. Contrariwise, a man may lose himself by turning his back on the infinite and concentrating on the narrowly limited moment or thing.

> . . . while one sort of despair plunges wildly into the infinite and loses itself, a second sort permits itself as it were to be defrauded by "the others." By seeing the multitude of men about it, by getting engaged in all sorts of worldly affairs, by becoming wise about how things go in this world, such a man forgets himself, forgets what his name is (in the divine understanding of it), does not venture to believe in himself, finds it too venturesome a thing to be himself, far easier and safer to be like the others, to become an imitation, a number, a cipher in the crowd.[38]

In other words, the self may be lost either through seeming to be an infinitesimally minute and ineffective particle in the overpowering vastness of the universe, into which it is dissolved; or through being deprived of spiritual kinship with all this boundlessness, by a timid restriction to the practical moment, the everyday routine,

[37] *Ibid.,* pp. 43 f.   [38] *Ibid.,* p. 51.

the trivial. In the first case, the self has no precise, unique center; in the second, it becomes little more than a muscle twitch.

(2) Then there is the despair which grows out of uncurbed possibility. Everything appears possible in the dim future, any wish or fear *might* be realized. Once a man has given himself up to the nonactual possible, he is lost—in wishful dreaming or in nightmares of fear. Kierkegaard compares such a man to a fairytale knight who catches a glimpse of a rare bird, so near that he thinks he might capture it, but when he approaches, "it flies off again, until at last night falls, and he has become separated from his companions, being unable to find his way in the wilderness where he now is."[39] The self is thus lost because it never commits itself to anything actual. In contrast to this is the despair of necessity, when everything is seen as held in iron laws. But no law is above God, and for Him all things are possible. The absence of God is the absence of possibility.

There are two subspecies of the despair of necessity, both of them consisting of the denial of God as an eternal source of possibility: fatalism and Philistinism. "The fatalist is in despair—he has lost God, and therefore himself as well; for if he has no God, neither has he a self. But the fatalist has no God—or, what is the same thing, his god is necessity."[40] Because for the fatalist there is no freedom, he cannot pray. As for the other subspecies:

> Philistinism lacks every determinant of spirit and terminates in probability, within which the possible finds its insignificant place. . . . Devoid of imagination, as the Philistine always is, he lives in a certain trivial province of experience as to how things go, what is possible, what usually occurs. Thus the Philistine has lost his self and God. For in order to be aware of oneself and God imagination must enable a man to soar higher than the misty precinct of the probable.[41]

(3) The intensity with which despair is experienced varies with the degree of consciousness. An individual in an *unconscious* state of despair may appear to be happy, but he is simply not spiritually awake; if a Socrates comes along and questions his foundations of happiness, he becomes furious. Why? Because "he is too sensuous to have the courage to venture to be spirit or to endure it."[42] Unconscious despair is extremely common, in Kierkegaard's opinion. Certainly the attempt to gain or regain this state is common—by alcohol or other means.

[39] *Ibid.*, p. 57. [40] *Ibid.*, p. 62. [41] *Ibid.*, p. 63.
[42] *Ibid.*, p. 67.

A step above unconscious despair in the spiritual scale is the state of conscious despair in which one imagines that one could be, and wishes to be, another self. This is a symptom of the inadequacy of the self-concept. Indeed, the self in this case is confused with externals—one's clothes, or memories, or social position, or title, or picture in the paper. To judge by modern advertisements this conception of personality is widespread; they recommend a new suit or a fine car or a lipstick for "building your personality." Kierkegaard characterizes the attitude in an amusing story:

> It is related of a peasant who came cleanly shaven to the Capital, and had made so much money that he could buy himself a pair of shoes and stockings and still had enough left over to get drunk on—it is related that as he was trying in his drunken state to find his way home he lay down in the middle of the highway and fell asleep. Then along came a wagon, and the driver shouted to him to move or he would run over his legs. Then the drunken peasant awoke, looked at his legs, and since by reason of the shoes and stockings he didn't recognize them, he said to the driver, "Drive on, they are not my legs."[43]

With a further increase of self-consciousness, the effort to lose oneself in externals, though continued, is not quite successful. A man who has reached this level will be aware enough of his self to be ashamed of it. If only in the form of adolescent embarrassment and awkwardness, he will be self-conscious and will have to exert a certain amount of will power to keep the fact hidden. Such a man tends to be introverted, though he fights against it by trying to be extroverted. He may welcome solitude. This, for Kierkegaard, is a sign of his spiritual superiority to those who constantly need society and wallow in sociability. He points out that "in ancient times as well as in the Middle Ages people were aware of the need for solitude and had respect for what it signifies. In the constant sociability of our age people shudder at solitude to such a degree that they know no other use to put it to but (oh, admirable epigram!) as a punishment for criminals."[44] But Kierkegaard warns against the danger of solitude; the result of introversion may be a self-destroying pride.

The ultimate despair is reached by the man who is so conscious of himself and of the eternal, irrevocable nature of self that he accepts himself in a spiteful mood of defiance. He wills to be himself hatefully and viciously. He is like Shakespeare's villainous hero

[43] *Ibid.*, p. 85.   [44] *Ibid.*, p. 103.

in *King Richard III*, or like Milton's Satan. He braces himself on himself to deny God or hurl defiance at Him.

According to Kierkegaard's analysis, then, full selfhood can be achieved only by an expansion and intensification of consciousness; but every increase of consciousness carries with it an increase of realized anxiety—until "by relating itself to its own self and by willing to be itself, the self is grounded transparently in the Power which constituted it."[45] At that level of self-development and not until then, despair is overcome.

From consciousness to the unconscious

Today there are numerous straws in the wind suggesting that psychology is veering once again back to its ancient concern with consciousness. But for a long time it has been in other quarters. Especially has it been preoccupied with the Unconscious.

No full historical treatment of the concept of the Unconscious can be attempted here. It may be noted, however, that it is a concept which both logically and historically follows the concept of consciousness. Consciousness is necessary in order to have something with which to contrast the Unconscious; for unconscious processes are those which are *outside* consciousness, and perhaps in opposition to it. Historically, as Eduard von Hartmann (1842-1906) remarks on the first page of his *Philosophy of the Unconscious,* "Mankind very naturally began its researches in Philosophy with the examination of what was immediately given in Consciousness."[46] Hartmann's extremely influential book first appeared in German in 1868 and rapidly went through numerous editions. It owed something to Leibniz, Herbart, and especially Schopenhauer, but Hartmann is right in regarding his conception of the Unconscious as new—at least, as new as an idea can be after centuries of philosophy. As for empirical evidence, Hartmann lays great emphasis on instinctive behavior; both in man and in the other animals he points to complex patterns of action moving toward dimly foreseen goals under great urgency and without benefit of learning, purposive action unconsciously originating and unconsciously steered. He also stresses the phenomenon of inspiration in all its forms—artistic, philosophical, and religious. Nor does he neglect the phenomena of hypnotism and hysteria which were to be the direct starting points for the Freudian developments at the end of

[45] *Ibid.*, p. 216.   [46] Hartmann (1890), Vol. 1, p. 1.

the century. In fact, one can find in Hartmann some of the most typical of the Freudian ideas—the strong emphasis on sex, the assessment of love and religion as illusions based on sex and the Unconscious, and certain characteristics of the Unconscious itself, such as its conservatism.

It is curious that Freud's references to Hartmann are scanty and not very much to the point, for Margetts, in a historical sketch, states that Hartmann's work had a profound effect on nineteenth-century thought and that most medical men of the time were familiar with it.[47] It is also curious that in Jones's three-volume biography of Freud the name of Hartmann appears only once in the index and the page to which it refers does not mention Hartmann at all.[48] Is this a case of repression at work? Or is it true that Freud based his concept of the Unconscious strictly on his clinical material?

In any case, we know that Freud, whose name is stamped so conspicuously on the Unconscious today, had antecedents. Hartmann was not the only one, and he may not have been the most important. Certainly, the most immediate influences acting on Freud were contemporary scientists like Charcot and Bernheim, who were investigating hysteria and hypnotism, and, of course, Freud's own contacts with his patients and other human beings whom he observed with a vigilant eye and thought about day and night. Nor must we forget that Freud also studied himself. In all this rich material of observation, Freud was continually being reminded that forces outside consciousness seemed to be always intruding on it and sometimes seemed to take full possession, producing unwanted ideas and imperative and irrational desires over which the "I" apparently had no control. This was the empirical fact: The conscious "I" was not master in its own house. How explain this except by appeal to the Unconscious?

References for chapter 6

Argyle, M. (1958) *Religious behaviour*. London: Routledge & Kegan Paul.

Bell, E. T. (1937) *Men of mathematics*. New York: Simon & Schuster.

Butler, C. (1927) *Western mysticism*. London: Constable.

Butz, O. (Ed.) (1958) *The unsilent generation*. New York: Rinehart.

Compton, A. H. (1952) Man's awareness and the limits of physical science. *Science,* 116, 519.

Galton, F. (1880) Statistics of mental imagery. *Mind,* 5, 301-18.

[47] Margetts (1953).   [48] Jones (1953-57).

Hartmann, E. von (1890) *Philosophy of the unconscious.* Tr. by W. C. Coupland. London: Kegan, Paul, Trench, Trübner. 3 vols.

Hilgard, E. R. (1957) *Introduction to psychology.* 2nd ed. New York: Harcourt, Brace & World.

James, W. (1890) *The principles of psychology.* New York: Holt. 2 vols.

Jones, E. (1953-57) *The life and work of Sigmund Freud.* New York: Basic Books. 3 vols.

Keller, H. (1909) *The world I live in.* New York: Century.

Koffka, K. (1935) *Principles of Gestalt psychology.* New York: Harcourt, Brace & World.

Margetts, E. L. (1953) The concept of the unconscious in the history of medical psychology. *Psychiatric Quarterly,* 27, 115-38.

Maslow, A. H. (1956) Self-actualizing people: a study of psychological health. In Moustakas, C. E. (Ed.) *The self: explorations in personal growth.* New York: Harper.

May, R. (1950) *The meaning of anxiety.* New York: Ronald.

Mortimer, E. (1959) *Blaise Pascal: the life and work of a realist.* New York: Harper.

Peters, R. S. (1959) Review of Feigl, H., *et al.* (Eds.) *Concepts, theories and the mind-body problem,* Minneapolis: Univ. of Minnesota Press, 1958. *Contemporary Psychology,* 4, 358-60.

Roe, A. (1951) A study of imagery in research scientists. *Journal of Personality,* 19, 459-70.

Rogers, C. R. (1956) What it means to become a person. In Moustakas, C. E. (Ed.) *The self: explorations in personal growth.* New York: Harper.

Sherrington, C. (1941) *Man on his nature.* New York: Cambridge Univ. Press.

Silberer, H. (1951) Report on a method of eliciting and observing certain symbolic hallucination-phenomena. In Rapaport, D. (Ed.) *Organization and pathology of thought: selected sources.* New York: Columbia Univ. Press.

Skinner, B. F. (1953) *Science and human behavior.* New York: Macmillan.

Tamm, I. E. (1959) Radiation of particles with speeds greater than light. *American Scientist,* 47, 169-77.

Underhill, E. (1929) *The mystic way: a psychological study in Christian origins.* London: Dent.

7

THE UNCONSCIOUS:
PRELIMINARY VIEW

Preview   *The theory of the Unconscious has developed because neither environmental stimulation nor the conscious will seems adequate for explaining behavior. Hypnotism and the study of mental disease have contributed very heavily to the theory, especially as formulated by Freud. This chapter, therefore, presents some of the facts of hypnotism, hysteria, and other phenomena which interested the medical men of Freud's generation, as well as some non-Freudian views on unconscious processes, in order to put the influential Freudian views in perspective.*

René Descartes (1596-1650) defined the human being as a machine endowed with a reasonable soul. He pointed out that, externally considered, a machine might be constructed by men which would look and act like a human being; but he thought that such a machine would never be capable of true language and would

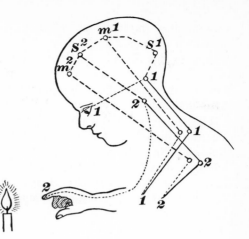

14 *A familiar diagram represents the child as a reflex machine. The picture is taken from James's* Principles of Psychology *(1890), but the concept is at least as old as the speculations of Descartes (1596-1650).*

not have the adaptability conferred by reason.[1] Many of Descartes' successors doubted the necessity of including a reasonable soul or even consciousness in their model of man and devoted themselves to working out a reflex-machine theory of human behavior. Among the earliest of these was Julien Offroy de La Mettrie.[2] Even more tender-minded thinkers, like William James, have paid their respects to the machine model. In the second chapter of his *Principles,* he puts an illustration, tracing back to the Austrian anatomist Theodor Meynert (1833-92), which has been repeated in many a textbook since. In essence, it represents a child as a simple machine activated by environmental stimuli (see Figure 14).

The simple machine concept of a human being has never been quite satisfactory. For one thing, a given stimulus rarely elicits exactly the same response twice; and so it has always been necessary to imagine something capable of change inside the "machine" —at least a residue of past responses (memory) or a complex structure (habit)—to account for "its" variable behavior. In short, unobservable and even mysterious processes have had to be assumed in order to explain the elementary fact that the child who mindlessly reaches out and touches a candle flame does generally not act that way again. Then there is the fact of the "machine's"

[1] The discussion will be found in Descartes' *Discourse on method,* Everyman's Library edition (London: Dent, 1912), pp. 44 f. The work first appeared in 1637.
[2] See J. O. de La Mettrie, *L'homme machine* (1748). For a translation, see *Man a machine,* tr. by G. Bussey and M. W. Calkins (Chicago: Open Court, 1927).

spontaneity—the fact that "it" seems to get going on "its" own without much reference to the immediate environment. Skinner has paid tribute to this aspect of behavior by classifying a large percentage of it as *operant*, i.e., occurring without known environmental cause.[3] Finally, there are those sudden or radical changes, often labeled pathological, not very easy to explain by reflex, or habit, or operants.

Of course, from the point of view of consciousness the simple machine model is radically unsatisfactory, as Descartes realized. But consciousness also, as previously remarked, often seems inadequate to explain what goes on. In particular, conscious *decision* does not seem to take care of everything. Obsessive thoughts may occur—tunes, imagined actions, memories, etc.—and run on and on maddeningly, quite against the will. Or one acts on impulses or is overcome by emotions that do not correspond at all to conscious ideals or aims. And curious physiological changes occur in the body by processes which one is not able to follow or understand.

Neither the concept of the machine controlled by environmental stimuli nor that of the conscious will controlling the machine meets all the problems of psychology. A solution which appealed to many thinkers in the late nineteenth century, especially to those who were privileged to observe some of the odder facts, was to postulate mental processes lying beyond the reach of the conscious mind—processes which acted like a purposive, striving, ingenious mind but which were unrecognized by the person concerned as having anything to do with his own conscious willing, or, for that matter, with the world around him.

The ripeness of the times

It is not possible in a short chapter to survey more than a very limited sample of the facts and ideas which persuaded nineteenth-century thinkers to adopt the Unconscious or some variant of it for explaining human behavior. Nor is it possible in so short a space to untangle the various meanings of the Unconscious which were entertained. For some the Unconscious was purely mental, for others it was the physiological stuff of the brain, for still others it was a confused mixture of both. "Unconscious cerebration" was a phrase often in use. A writer at the turn of the century named A. T. Schofield, an English physician, made the accompanying diagram (Figure 15) the frontispiece of his volume *The Uncon-*

[3] Skinner (1938).

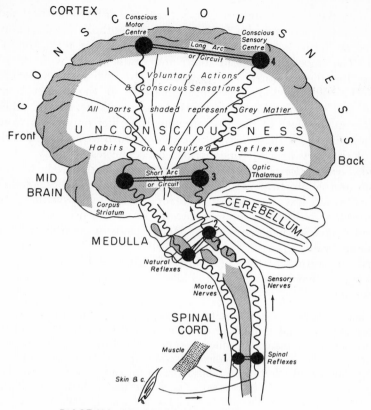

DIAGRAM OF SENSORI - MOTOR ARCS.

15 *Textbooks often show pictures of the human brain labeled with psychological terms. In this old diagram, much of the bold labeling ("Consciousness," etc.) is not justified by known facts, as the author confesses. In spite of this, he explains the numbers, arrows, and pathways as various ways that "sensory nerve currents" may be tranformed into motion, either as unconscious reflexes or voluntary actions. (From Schofield, 1901)*

scious Mind, a work consisting largely of quotations from the leading authorities of the period.[4] The diagram obviously invites the reader to identify both conscious and unconscious processes with the activity of the brain. Yet against the bold lettering of the diagram are set the minute words of warning: "This is purely diagrammatic. No such defined Centres or Arcs have been as yet demon-

---

[4] Schofield (1901).

strated in the Brain"; and, in fact, an entirely different orientation to the subject seems to be indicated by the author's introduction, where the term "mind" is frequently used but the term "brain" never. The uncertainty about mind and brain is still with us, of course. But the situation is now different: In 1898 when Schofield wrote his introduction, apparently unaware of the existence of Freud and very much aware of Hartmann and dozens of other workers in the field of the Unconscious, the chief opponents were psychologists with their insistence on consciousness and their ridicule of the very idea of "unconscious consciousness"; today, when Freud's conceptions have filtered down, albeit debased, to the movies and comic strips and the slang of the street and Schofield's authorities are less than names even for professional psychologists, the problem is how to interest anyone in consciousness, so preoccupied have we become with the Unconscious or possibly the unconscious brain.

One interesting feature of Schofield's attitude toward the Unconscious is that he saw it as a challenge to scientific materialism. He writes:

> It may be asked, why was not an attempt made sooner to give these unconscious faculties their proper place? It *was* made determinedly years ago in Germany, and since then in England by men who, to their honour, undeterred by ridicule and contempt, made noble and partially successful efforts to establish the truth. But it is only now that the pendulum—so long swayed over to the materialistic side of the world's clock, under the pressure of Huxley and Tyndall and others, whose great works on this side led all men for a time to forget almost that there was another—has begun to swing back; and men's ears are now open to hear, and their hearts to believe Spirit truths, especially as they are supported as they now are from the other side by the best physiologists. The psychological moment has, we trust, arrived for establishing the Unconscious on a firm and lasting basis.[5]

One of the facts which had much impressed this English physician was the great frequency of faith cures, whether at the hands of a charlatan, a quack pharmacist, a Salvation Army or Christian Science healer, or an ordinary medical man. He saw that the omnipresence of this fact, everywhere and at all times, was in contradiction to professional medical instruction. It seemed to him to require the concept of an unconscious mind, a power not open to external observation or introspection but inferred from its effects

[5] *Ibid.*, pp. xiv f.

in causing and curing disease at a mere word or the laying on of hands, as if it were something intelligent and purposive and extremely knowing.

I mention this practically unknown author to demonstrate that the current of thought which was to make the fame of Janet, and the greater fame of Freud, was prevalent enough at the end of the nineteenth century (before Freud had made his mark) to have caught the attention of a practicing physician who had a reputation and a place of his own, no doubt, in the London of his day but is not remarkable for any special scientific achievement.

Let us now look at some of the details which gave point at that time to the concept of the Unconscious.

Hypnotism

Interest in hypnotism[6] was especially keen in Freud's student days. The subject had come out from under the cloud of disrepute which had settled around it in France at the time of the Revolution when a committee of learned men (among whom was Benjamin Franklin) examined and rejected certain ideas propounded by Mesmer, and it was once more a topic of serious study, especially in Liébeault's clinic at Nancy and in Paris at the Salpêtrière, the great insane asylum presided over then by Charcot.[7] Freud was for a time a pupil of Charcot's and thought enough of hypnotism to visit Nancy and translate the heavy book of Bernheim on the subject. An associate of Freud's at the Salpêtrière was the psychologist Janet, whose work on hysteria is notable.

Before this time a great deal of valuable work on hypnotism (earlier called "mesmerism") had been done by several courageous British medical men, and in England during the Charcot period there were many persons interested in both the theory and the practice of the art. Among them was J. Milne Bramwell (1852-1925), whose excellent book will be the chief source of the illustrative facts cited here.[8]

Hypnotism is a social phenomenon, involving a hypnotist and one or more subjects. The hypnotist is popularly believed capable

[6] "Hypnotism," derived from the Greek word for "sleep," was a term invented by James Braid, whose work is discussed in the following pages.

[7] For historical background, see Zilboorg (1941), especially Ch. 9, "The discovery of neuroses."

[8] *Hypnotism: its history, practice and theory,* first published in 1903. The quotations are from the 4th edition (1930).

of doing anything he wishes with his subject by his hypnotic power. The belief is far from true. No hypnotist succeeds in hypnotizing everyone who submits to his procedures, and the amount of his control varies widely even with tractable subjects.

Suppose we have a tractable subject. By various techniques he may be brought into a state of trance, which has some kinship to sleep but is not the same. The hypnotist may now induce him to do, say, and imagine things which may appear quite out of the ordinary. Usually this is brought about by words or other signals, but there are reports, made in good faith by reputable scientists, of telepathic influence—whether true or false I do not know. An established fact of great theoretical importance is that the subject in the posthypnotic state may carry out instructions previously given during trance and not know that he is doing so at the command of the hypnotist. The subject may be perfectly conscious of the thought or act; it is the *origin* which he fails to recognize. In those cases, he may succeed in resisting the mysterious impulse to think or act in a certain way and still be unable to trace the impulse to the hypnotist. He is said to suffer amnesia, or forgetfulness, for the trance period even though he acts upon the suggestions made to him then.

Hypnotic suggestion may go so far as to produce physiological changes usually thought of as beyond voluntary control. The following is an example of the control achieved by James Braid (1795-1860), as described by Bramwell:

> He hypnotised a patient who was nursing, and suggested an increased secretion of milk in one breast. On awaking she had no recollection of what had been done, but complained of a feeling of tightness and tension in the breast. Her husband then told her that Braid had been trying to increase the secretion of milk. She was sceptical as to the result, as her child was fourteen months old and the milk had almost disappeared. Her breast, however, almost immediately became distended with milk, and a few days later she complained that her figure was deformed in consequence. Braid again hypnotised her and successfully repeated the experiment with the other breast. The patient suckled her child for six months longer, the supply of milk being more abundant than it had been at any time since her confinement.[9]

Bramwell does not attempt to explain how the hypnotic suggestion could produce such an effect, nor is that our concern here. The point to be remembered is that the effect followed from an

[9] Bramwell (1930), p. 88.

event in trance which the patient could not recall. The hypnotist's words affected her mammary glands without leaving a trace in her consciousness.

General or specific anesthesia may also be achieved hypnotically. Before the period of chemical anesthesia with ether and chloroform, the Scottish surgeon James Esdaile (1808-59) performed hundreds of major operations in India on patients under hypnosis, without discomfort to them. For a year (1846-47) a government hospital was put at his disposal in Bengal, and his work was observed and commended by an official committee of British medical men. After the government facility was withdrawn the enthusiastic Indians supported him in another hospital by voluntary contributions.

Esdaile's method of preparing his patients for an operation was to put them in bed in a darkened room, have them close their eyes and try to go to sleep, and then move his hand over the body and breathe from time to time on the head and eyes. After an hour of this procedure, many were ready for surgery without pain. Esdaile found that mesmerizing, as he called it, exhausted him. He eventually turned over most of the mesmeric preparation to Indian assistants and devoted himself to the surgery. An example of his degree of success is the following astonishing case. A patient, aged 40, came to the hospital suffering from an enormous tumor of the maxillary antrum which had "pushed up the orbit of the eye, filled up the nose, passed into the throat, and caused an enlargement of the glands of the neck." When an assistant failed to mesmerize the man after two weeks of effort, Esdaile himself took the case.

In half an hour he was cataleptic, and a quarter of an hour later I performed one of the most severe and protracted operations in surgery; the man was totally unconscious. I put a long knife in at the corner of his mouth, and brought the point out over the cheek-bone, dividing the parts between; from this I pushed it through the skin at the inner corner of the eye, and dissected the cheek-bone to the nose. The pressure of the tumour had caused absorption of the anterior wall of the antrum, and on pressing my fingers between it and the bone it burst, and a shocking gush of blood and matter followed. The tumour extended as far as my fingers could reach under the orbit and the cheek-bone, and passed into the gullet—having destroyed the bones and partition of the nose. No one touched the man, and I turned his head in any position I desired, without resistance, and there it remained until I wished to move it again; when the blood accumulated, I bent his head forward, and it ran from his mouth as from a spout. The man never moved, nor showed any sign of life, except an occasional indistinct moan; but when I threw back his head, and passed my fingers into his throat to detach the mass in that direction, the stream of blood was directed into his windpipe, and some instinctive effort became necessary for existence; he therefore coughed, and leaned forward to get rid of the blood, and I suppose that he then awoke.

The patient made a good recovery, and informed Esdaile that he knew nothing of the coughing or the operation until it was over.[10]

The preceding illustrations should be enough to impress on the reader the power of hypnotism in favorable cases.

Hypnotic theory: mesmerism vs. suggestion

Two main lines have been followed in hypnotic theory. The first may be represented by Mesmer and disciples like Esdaile; the second, by Braid and by Liébeault and Bernheim. The first line emphasizes the transmission of some kind of power from the hypnotist to his subject; the second stresses the mental state of the person being hypnotized.

Esdaile's hypnotic technique has been described. It consisted in making passes of the hands over the subject's body and occasionally breathing on his face. This procedure goes back to Mesmer and much farther back than that. In fact, Esdaile learned that it had been practiced in India for ages. It has already been noted that Esdaile felt that he was exhausted by the act of mesmerizing; this corresponded to his theory that something vital flowed out of him in the process, quite as Mesmer believed in a magnetic fluid. In Esdaile's words:

> There is good reason to believe that the vital fluid of one person can be poured into the system of another. A merciful God has engrafted a communicable, life-giving, curative power in the human body, in order that when two individuals are found together, deprived of the aids of art, the one in health may often be able to relieve his sick companion, by imparting to him a portion of his vitality.[11]

Esdaile opposed the view that the hypnotic effects could be accounted for by suggestion. He had observed that trance alone might be beneficial to health without any specific suggestions at all. He also made the very important point that many things

[10] *Ibid.*, p. 159.   [11] *Ibid.*, pp. 275 f.

happen during a hypnotic session which neither the hypnotist nor the hypnotized could have anticipated. In common with earlier mesmerists, he believed that the mesmeric power could be transmitted through intermediate objects or even telepathically.

The mesmeric line of theory was eventually revised by Braid, and his ideas have tended to prevail down to the present. He at first, it is interesting to note, was skeptical regarding the phenomena themselves. When, as a highly reputable physician and surgeon of forty-six, he witnessed a mesmeric exhibition in November, 1841, he denounced it as a mere sham. He examined the mesmerized girl, however, and had his skepticism shaken by finding that the pupils of her eyes were contracted to small points and that a pin forced under one of her fingernails seemed to cause no pain. Hardly more than a month later he himself was lecturing on the subject. His theory at first was that the hypnotic trance was brought on by benumbing certain muscles and nerve centers; he therefore labeled the condition "neuro-hypnotism" to indicate that the nerves were put to sleep. Later he dropped the prefix, as he shifted his emphasis from the physiological to the mental side of the formula; and, indeed, he wished to eliminate the word "hypnotism" too, because he had come to realize that the condition was not really one of sleep. By 1847 he believed that the phenomena of hypnotism could be explained strictly in terms of mental concentration, for which he invented the word "mono-ideism"; the deep trance was only a special stage of mono-ideism, a stage in which the mental concentration had reached a maximum. At this stage, dominant ideas could be developed by suggestion to the point where they would act upon the body, as in the case of increased lactation cited above.

Braid ridiculed the notion of a vital power as assumed by Esdaile. He argued that the vital supplies would be depleted in proportion to the number of people influenced. A mesmeric theorist could, of course, meet this argument by contending that the vital power did not originate in the hypnotist but merely flowed through him as a convenient channel. Braid, in fact, did not deny that energy was involved, but he maintained that the energy was chiefly that of the *subject's* nervous system. The role of the hypnotist was to set in motion powerful mind-body processes in the other person, and he could do this with a minimum of effort on his own part.

Suggestion was a key word for Braid. He demonstrated experimentally that objects like Perkins' tractors, magnets, and drugs in sealed glass tubes, to which some workers attributed hypnotic power, did not produce hypnotic effects unless the person being exposed to them believed that they had the power. It was the idea aroused by the object rather than the object itself which was hypnotic, and for this, the word of the hypnotist was enough. Braid did not, however, go as far as Liébeault and Bernheim later did in assigning irresistible force to suggestion. He thought that the hypnotic subject remained conscious and rational and did not respond in a purely automatic way but accepted or rejected suggestions more or less at will.

Braid's mature theory, according to Bramwell, included the following eleven propositions, quoted here in Bramwell's words:

1. Hypnosis could not be induced by physical means alone.
2. Hypnotic and so-called mesmeric phenomena were subjective in origin, and both were excited by direct or indirect suggestion.
3. Hypnosis was characterised by physical as well as psychical changes.
4. The simultaneous appearance of several phenomena was recognised, and much importance was attached to the intelligent action of a secondary consciousness.
5. Volition was unimpaired, moral sense increased and suggested crime impossible.
6. *Rapport*[12] was a purely artificial condition created by suggestion.
7. The importance of direct verbal suggestion was fully recognised, as also the mental influence of physical methods.
8. Suggestion was regarded as the device used for exciting the phenomena, and not considered as sufficient to explain them.
9. Important differences existed between hypnosis and normal sleep.
10. Hypnotic phenomena might be induced without the subject having passed through any condition resembling sleep.
11. The mentally healthy were the easiest, the hysterical the most difficult, to influence.[13]

Bramwell, who is much in sympathy with Braid, is particularly emphatic as to points 4 and 5. For example he was not able to induce a shopkeeper (whom he had repeatedly hypnotized) to act as if he were a dissenting minister preaching a sermon or as if he

[12] *Rapport* refers to a specially close relation between hypnotist and hypnotized, such that suggestions from others are ineffective.
[13] *Ibid.*, p. 294. There is now some experimental evidence that crime (see point 5) *can* be hypnotically induced. For a general review of the present status of hypnotic theory, see Weitzenhoffer (1953).

were a fishmonger, selling his wares, although he quickly fell in with the suggestion that he was the circus man Barnum and that the physicians in the audience were wild beasts. Bramwell's explanation is that the first role was rejected because the subject was himself a Dissenter serious about his religious convictions, and the second because he considered the occupation of fishmonger socially below him; but that neither piety nor feeling for social status or the prestige of physicians interfered with the Barnum role. In short, this subject's hypnotic behavior was in keeping with his character when awake. As for the point that the moral demands of the hypnotic state may be stricter than those of the waking state, Bramwell cites the case of a girl who refused to have her chest medically examined when in a somnambulic trance (sleep-walking state), though she had not previously objected when awake.

Bramwell finds no theory quite adequate to the facts, but he tends to favor the view of F. W. H. Myers (1843-1901) that the hypnotic state is not a weak and narrow state of consciousness but rather the reverse. For Myers, hypnotism was a method of bringing to the fore a subliminal consciousness or self, i.e., one which was kept subliminal (under the threshold) during the waking state. The Myers theory is briefly summarized by Bramwell in these words:

> He held that to the subliminal consciousness and memory a far wider range, both of physiological and of psychical activity, was open than to the supraliminal. The latter was inevitably limited by the need of concentration upon recollections useful in the struggle for existence; while the former included much that was too rudimentary to be retained in the supraliminal memory of an organism so advanced as that of man. The recollection of processes now performed automatically, and needing no supervision, passed out of the supraliminal memory, but might be retained by the subliminal. The subliminal, or hypnotic, self could exercise over the nervous, vasomotor, and circulatory systems a degree of control unparalleled in waking life.[14]

Deferred action of unconscious ideas

The name of Myers ought to be rescued from the obscurity into which it has fallen in psychological circles, if for no other reason than that he was writing a great deal like Freud before Freud was widely known, and without any debt to Freud himself. He wrote an interesting paper on hypnotism in 1887 which has some observa-

[14] *Ibid.*, p. 359. For a fuller discussion, see Myers (1903).

tions on posthypnotic suggestion worth our attention here. As Myers points out (in a passage reminiscent of Freud's *Psychopathology of Everyday Life* of later date), the phenomenon of posthypnotic suggestion resembles more prosaic events which happen daily but usually pass unnoticed:

> Take the most trivial and familiar case. I glance down a list of books to see if a book by *Helmholtz* is in it. It is not, and I remember absolutely nothing of the list. Some time afterwards I see a book by *Herzen* advertised. I at once feel that I knew there was an author of that name. His name, in fact, was on that former list, and I unconsciously received the deferred suggestion—only capable of revival by seeing the word *Herzen* again—that there was a scientific author of that name.[15]

He compares this to what happens in posthypnotic suggestion; he thinks that the final recognition of the name in the above case differs only in oddity from the posthypnotic subject's perceiving his black hat turn blue an hour after the hypnotist has implanted the idea. The same mental operations are involved. Myers goes on to describe these mental operations (in language strongly influenced by the Industrial Revolution), thus:

> In the hypnotic subject's case one loom (so to say) in the vast manufactory within him has been disconnected from the general system of driving-gear, attached to driving-gear of its own, and set to turn out a special pattern, independently of the orders executed by the remaining looms in the factory. And similarly in my case the little bobbin (so to say) with the name *Herzen* inscribed on it, went on spinning by itself without connection with my general scheme of memories. Only it was so small an item that its disconnected action and its subsequent attachment to the main system attracted no notice, or, at least, excited no surprise. *Deferred* hypnotic suggestion, in fact, like the *immediate* hypnotic suggestion of which I have already spoken, is an advantage taken of the increased dissociability of mental elements which results from the inhibition of certain co-ordinative mental centres or activities in the hypnotic trance.[16]

Notice in this quotation the introduction of the notion of *dissociation of ideas*. The roots of this notion go far back into history and are many-branched, but probably it has never been so fully exploited as in the period of Myers and subsequently. It is virtually the keystone of Janet's psychology of hysteria, and it plays an important though subordinate role in Freudian theory.

[15] Myers (1887), p. 163.   [16] *Ibid.*, p. 164.

We must not be lulled into complacency by the simplicity of the above illustration, however. An idea may in some sense become detached from others and sink into the Unconscious to rise again later; some features of behavior can be explained in that way. But the following case of deferred suggestion contains some elements which, as Myers is very ready to admit, are not so easily explained by the dissociation formula. In particular, the powerful action of the idea on the body is, to say the least, noteworthy.

Louis V——, whom Myers calls "one of the most important documents which Nature has ever submitted to the psychologist," was an asylum patient in whom it was possible to produce bleeding at the nose and hemorrhagic stigmata on the skin by hypnotic suggestion. In the first recorded experiment, he was told under hypnosis that he would fall asleep at four o'clock on a certain day, come into the doctor's study, sit down and cross his arms, and then bleed at the nose. All happened as suggested. On another occasion the doctor traced Louis' last name on his forearms (one of which was paralyzed) and told him that he would go to sleep at four and bleed on the lines thus marked out by the blunt-pointed instrument, which had left no visible marks. At the hour named he fell asleep and soon the tracings on one arm stood out distinctly red and a few drops of blood oozed out through the skin, though a moment before the trance there was no sign that the arm had ever been marked. The paralyzed arm showed no such reaction. Later, according to Dr. Mabille, who reported on the case at Grenoble in 1885, there came the startling sequel of autosuggestion. Louis had been suffering from insomnia. Dr. Mabille accordingly hypnotized him one morning (August 5) and told him that in the evening at a certain hour he would begin to feel sleepy and ask the attendant to put him to bed, and he would then sleep, hearing, feeling, and seeing nothing, until five the next morning. These suggestions were quite effective. But Louis had a surprise for the doctor. After going to sleep he started a dialogue with himself which duplicated a scene of two days before when Dr. Mabille had suggested the appearance of a bleeding "V" (not the whole name this time) on his arm. In about a quarter of an hour (the same length of time as before), the patient

was seized with the crisis which we usually observe in him when the stigmata have been suggested to him. At the end of this crisis we examined his arm and we saw a V, and the V was covered with blood. This bloody effusion was produced at a place where a V had been suggested by me on August 3. . . . The same phenomena were twice produced during the same night, in the same place, and by the same procedure. V—— then awoke exactly at 5 a.m., without knowing that he had been asleep, and with the conviction that he had just been picking flowers in the garden of the asylum.[17]

Louis V—— no doubt had a special constitution. We may note, for example, that the arm which exhibited the bleeding was also hyperesthetic, i.e., especially sensitive. Nevertheless, stigmatization is not so rare and not so strictly confined to hospital patients that it must be regarded as simply an "abnormality." For all we know, the capacity may exist in every human being but only come to realization under special conditions. We do not understand the conditions, it is true, but the fact of stigmatization is beyond dispute and it should not be brushed aside as a mere oddity of hypnotism or hysteria. It is by studying hypnotism and hysteria and other special states that we begin to appreciate the mysterious depths of human nature and understand its fundamental laws, just as it is by studying matter under extremes of temperature and pressure and so on that men advance the science of physics. The phenomena observed in a giant cyclotron are "rare" and "abnormal" but physicists respect the minutest details thus revealed, because they regard them as telling them something important about the nature of reality. We may very well adopt that attitude toward stigmatization and phenomena even more dazzling.

A modern case of demon possession

If the Unconscious were limited to the kind of material so far described, we might think of it as a strange but relatively quiet animal, keeping mostly to the dark and easily controlled by fairly simple techniques. We need a more full-bodied case history to correct any such impression. I do not know of a better one for the purpose than Janet's "Un Cas de Possession et l'Exorcisme Moderne," delivered as a lecture at the University of Lyons in 1894.[18] Janet in the nineteenth century could look at the complexities and monstrosities of this case with the cool eye of reason. In an earlier century, as the title implies, the patient would undoubtedly have been regarded as possessed by demons, and ecclesiastical exorcism might very well have been the treatment given.

Achille, as Janet calls his patient, was a man of thirty-three when he entered the Salpêtrière. He was from a somewhat super-

[17] *Ibid.,* p. 169.　　　　　　　　[18] Janet (1898), Vol. 1, pp. 375-406.

stitious peasant family, and his father had been accused of giving himself to the Devil and even collecting a fee from the Enemy of Mankind at an old tree every Saturday—a story at which the father laughed, though he was indeed superstitious. Achille was studious though not brilliant as a youngster and had gone to the local high school. Janet sees premonitions of future trouble in the fact that he tended not to make friends, though he was affectionate, and that he was picked on by the other students at school. Also, he sometimes had headaches. All the same, he settled down in a little business after school, married at twenty-two, and with his devoted wife lived happily and undisturbed by serious illness until a short while before he entered the Salpêtrière. He had one child, a daughter, who was normal.

The change began in Achille after a business trip which kept him away from home for a few weeks. On his return he was gloomy and preoccupied, paid little attention to his wife and child, spoke little. After a few days he was having difficulty in speaking at all. The doctor who was called in hinted at various diseases, including diabetes. Achille recovered speech and began to complain of pain and fatigue and thirst and inability to eat. Yet all the medication did no good, and a month later he consulted another doctor. This one concluded that he was suffering from angina pectoris. Immediately he developed all the appropriate symptoms. He took to bed and sank into utter despair. His sleep was fitful, he muttered incomprehensible words, tears filled his eyes. One day he embraced his wife and child as if to bid them farewell, stretched out on the bed, and became motionless. For two days he seemed to be on the brink of death. Then suddenly he sat up, eyes wide, and broke into a wild laugh. In Janet's words:

> This was a convulsive laugh which shook him all over, an exaggerated laugh which twisted his mouth, a lugubrious laugh which kept up for more than two hours, truly satanic. From that moment everything was changed; Achille leaped out of bed and refused any sort of care. To all their questions he replied: "Don't do anything, it's useless, let's drink some champagne, it's the end of the world!" Then he would cry out horribly, "They're burning me, they're cutting me to pieces!"[19]

His sleep, when he slept at all, was troubled. When he was awake, he kept talking of demons around him and in him, tormenting

[19] *Ibid.*, p. 383. This and subsequent quotations from Janet are my translations.

him and forcing him to blaspheme God and twisting his body convulsively. After some three months of this, during which time he tried more than once to commit suicide, he was brought to the hospital. There the demons plagued him as dreadfully as ever. A striking feature of his behavior, exactly like that reported of demoniacs in the Middle Ages, was that the voice in which he spoke the Devil's words was audibly different from the one in which he spoke his own.

> He muttered blasphemies in a deep bass voice: "Damn God," he said, "damn the Trinity, damn the Virgin," then in a higher-pitched voice and with tears in his eyes: "It's not my fault if my mouth says these horrible things, it's not me, it's not me, I tighten my lips so that the words won't come out, won't make a noise; it doesn't do any good, the Devil says these words just the same inside of me, I really feel that he says them and that he makes my tongue move in spite of me."[20]

He often saw and heard hideous diabolic forms and voices, and his whole body seemed to be dominated by them, so that muscular control and sensation would at times desert him, now in one place, now in another.

Efforts by others to exert some sort of control met with extreme resistance. The hospital chaplain had no success, and Janet's attempts at hypnotism failed. Then Janet discovered that if he put a pencil in Achille's hand he could obtain through automatic writing[21] contact with the rebellious forces which were tormenting him, for the words he wrote proved to be answers to Janet's questions and commands. Janet was now in communication, so to speak, with the Devil; and when the Devil asserted that he was stronger than Janet and would not obey him, Janet took advantage of the Devil's well-known vanity and challenged him to prove his power by raising Achille's left arm. The arm rose, and Achille was astonished when Janet called attention to the fact, and lowered his arm with apparent difficulty. Achille attributed the arm's movement to the Devil's usual mischiefmaking. From this point on, Janet was in control. He succeeded in getting the Devil to put Achille to sleep, and now, with his patient in the somnambulic trance state, Janet was able to communicate freely with him about his feelings and his

[20] *Ibid.*, p. 384.
[21] In hypnotic or mediumistic trance and in hysteria, a hand may write in seeming independence of consciousness. For a recent application of Janet's trick, see Watkins (1949), Part IV.

past; he thus learned facts about him which no one else knew and which Achille himself in the waking state did not recognize. The heart of these facts was that Achille was gripped by remorse because of sexual infidelity to his wife during the business trip which preceded his illness.

THEORETICAL REFLECTIONS   There is the story of Achille! What is the theory which explains it? We have to pay attention not only to Janet's words but also to his actions. Janet *says* that the explanation is simple: Achille was suffering from remorse, and this emotion had been elaborated into a dream of persecution by demons. Nevertheless, Janet *acts* as if the demons were independent forces: he converses with them, tries to circumvent them by various tricks, and finally brings in Achille's wife (not in the flesh, but as an image in Achille's mind) to combat them by pardoning Achille for his fault. Does one converse with a feeling of remorse? Not at all! Are the demons real, then? To Achille they are, and to Janet they almost are. To Achille they are just as real and frightful and external to himself as would be a pack of mad dogs bearing down on you, dear reader, with their tongues hanging out and their eyes glaring. And Janet has to play at believing in them, if no more, in order to deal effectively with his patient.

We may, in fact, distinguish three theories, or levels of theory, in Janet's handling of the case. (1) At one level he treats the experiences of his patient as literally true: he deals with the demons as demons. (2) At another level he regards the demons as dream-figures, symbolizing the emotion of remorse. At this level he speaks of the dream itself as an invading force. For example, after recounting how Achille's premonition of death in the early stage of his illness led on to the dream that he was dead and thence to the dream that the demons had seized him and Satan had entered his head and heart through the wounds made by them in his body, Janet comments:

> The normal personality with its memories, its organization, its character which had hitherto continued in existence as well as could be expected, in the face of the invading dream was completely annihilated. The dream, hitherto subconscious, finding no resistance any longer, grew and overwhelmed his whole mind. It developed enough to form complete hallucinations and to express itself in acts and words.[22]

[22] Janet (1898), Vol. 1, pp. 399 f.

(3) At a third level Janet considers the dream and all its works as a complex and slowly evolving idea, an *idée fixe* which is capable of growth. It is a network of a multitude of different images, visual, auditory, kinesthetic, and so on, which, if necessary, may be teased apart by a clever therapist and *decomposed*. The decomposition of the idea may then be followed by a process of *substitution* by which the idea is rebuilt of *new* images which replace old images that have been removed or are added to old images that prove refractory to removal. Thus, in another case, that of Justine, Janet dealt with morbid hallucinations of naked corpses by adding articles of clothing to them until they were ridiculously costumed and so deprived of some of their terror; and he took the word "cholera," which was at the center of Justine's fears, and decomposed it into separate syllables to which he attached harmless words (like "cotton"), thus rendering it so meaningless that it no longer directly affected her. His treatment of Achille to some extent employed the same method.[23]

Incidentally, Janet found that revising a fixed idea by the method of decomposition and substitution was by no means easy. He felt that he was up against something which actively resisted. His patients, too, felt the strain. Some of them experienced violent head pain in the process.

The unconscious in Janet's theory

In many respects, Janet's thought about unconscious processes resembles Freud's, which we will meet in the next chapter. This ought not to surprise us. The two men were contemporaries, influenced by the same currents of medical psychology and the same sort of observations on hypnosis and hysteria, and both had come under the guidance of Charcot. Janet's theory stayed closer to the descriptive surface than Freud's and did not develop as much specialized terminology, and it gives an impression of lightness, almost of frivolity, when compared with the solid earnestness of Freud. Nevertheless, Janet was dealing with virtually the same problems and often in much the same way. I will try to list some of the ideas which seem to me to be inherent in Janet's various discussions, though I cannot point to any place where he himself states them in exactly these words.

[23] For the case of Justine and details on the decomposition-substitution method, see Janet (1898), Vol. 1, pp. 156-212. Also see Watkins, *loc. cit.*, for examples of contemporary application of Janet's method.

(1) According to Janet, many persons think and do a wide variety of things without realizing the connection of these thoughts and deeds with prior experience. There are thus two psychological levels: what one is aware of and what one is not distinctly aware of although it is equally a part of the total person. The processes of the second level (which Janet often refers to as the "subconscious") influence the behavior of the waking person and may violently disturb him.

(2) The processes at this second, subconscious level tend to be repetitive, and they change, if at all, very slowly. They are nearly immune to outside influence, as if sealed off from the environment and existing as an independent system. Contact can be established with the subconscious level by an observer; but when the subconscious processes are brought as close to consciousness as this, the personality tends to split (as in automatic writing, for example) or to change totally (as in the case of demon possession), at least from the point of view of the observer.

(3) The subconscious processes appear to manifest intelligence and purposeful volition. Though their effect on the first level of personality may be such as to produce the impression of some automatic and senseless interference with normal life, they constitute on their own terms something like a consciously striving personality rather than a jumble of disconnected events or even a purely mechanical system. Thus, when Janet got in touch with the second-level processes of Achille through the trick of automatic writing, he found that he was dealing with something that gave itself a personal name ("the Devil") and otherwise expressed itself as motivated and aware.

(4) There seems to be an especially close relationship between the second-level system and those bodily functions which are not ordinarily under first-level voluntary control. For example, to cite a case already mentioned (though it is not Janet's), the stigmatization of Louis V—— seemed to depend on the hypnotic trance state. Parallels can be found in Janet's own work.

(5) Between the first and second levels a sort of boundary exists, and certain phenomena may be regarded as boundary phenomena. For example, a headache may indicate that a fixed idea is yielding to decomposition or is at least on the point of retiring from the first level of consciousness to the second, or, conversely, is on the point of emerging from the second, subconscious level into the first.

(6) The two levels are often in opposition. One may invade the

other, giving rise to startling symptoms out of keeping with the rest of the dominant personality state, or the two may alternate. The latter solution of the conflict is the origin of multiple personalities, so called, such as Azam's Félida,[24] Prince's Miss Beauchamp,[25] or Thigpen and Cleckley's Eve.[26]

(7) Knowledge of the second level can frequently be obtained through dreams reported at the first level. My impression is that this aspect of Janet's thought is not at all well known, and I should like to draw special attention to it. In one place he remarks that it would be interesting to study the general laws which govern dreaming, and he makes it clear that he thinks of dreaming as an activity which goes on perhaps continuously in everyone. He comments:

> Most often it is monotonous, it remains for long periods ever the same, unmodified by external circumstances. One person dreams of making millions, another commands an army and conquers a barbarian country, another still colonizes a desert island in the manner of Robinson Crusoe or plays the handsomest part in a love story. But each remains faithful to his own story and recites it endlessly. If the story changes, it is most often with astonishing slowness, and I have notes on some observations in which minor new incidents that might have been added to the story at once did not, in reality, come into the dream until after several months. In addition, these modifications hardly depend on whim of ours, and they take place slowly, following the laws of a peculiar logic which presides over our dreams as it presides over the delirious states of the insane. One might note also that these dreams are hardly conscious; we know vaguely that we have them in us, but we cannot always describe them exactly, for we have preserved only a very confused memory of them. Often it happens that we are surprised at hearing our story, as if it had sprung up and developed in us without our knowledge.[27]

(8) To the above statements which stay close to the descriptive level must be added some others which have an explanatory function for Janet. He speaks repeatedly of fixed ideas and dissociation. The fixed ideas, as already pointed out, are conceived of by Janet as complex and persisting clusters of sensory-motor images which have become dissociated from other (less fixed?) ideas which constitute our conscious being. They have taken off on their own, so to speak, and from that fact derive their power to disturb; for in their isolation they not only retain their original power but add

[24] Azam (1887).   [25] Prince (1906).
[26] Thigpen and Cleckley (1957).   [27] Janet (1898), Vol. 1, pp. 393 f.

to it by growing, sometimes monstrously, unchecked as they are by the external environment and other, more pleasant ideas. Fixed ideas often originate in some overwhelming emotional experience, some dreadful calamity. They become isolated and grow pathologically, however, because of the person's inherited psychic weakness or lack of energy. The dissociation, according to Janet, is due to the falling apart of what was all along a loosely and weakly aggregated system.

Janet's use of this simple explanatory apparatus may be illustrated once more by the case of Justine. Her fixed idea had to do with death by cholera. The originating experience was the actual sight of two cholera-spotted corpses when she was a girl of seventeen. According to Janet, her already genetically weak, easily unbalanced nervous system was still further weakened at a later time by attacks of typhoid fever and influenza. At the age of forty, when she arrived at the Salpêtrière, she was subject to frequent convulsions of terror set off by the recollection of those two corpses and by various other ideas which had branched off from this. Suppose that we grant the validity of the account. We may still be troubled by the question, What *is* an idea? I have already given Janet's answer, but his exact words in discussing Justine will not be superfluous:

This patient presents us with an interesting example of a certain class of ideas. What the idea of cholera is when brought, if we may say so, to the last degree of perfection, we now see in her: an assembly, a system of images, derived from all the senses, of which each one is clear enough and complex enough to become effectively real, to become objective in the form of hallucinations and movements. Let us add, too, that, precisely because they form a system, these images are so attached to one another that the presence of one of them suffices to call up the others in a determinate order. Justine's nervous attacks are not new phenomena independent of these hypochondriacal preoccupations: the very idea itself of cholera is thereby displayed to perfection, along with the emotion which is a part of the system and cannot be separated from it. The abnormal aspect which the idea takes on during the attack results simply from its excessive development. The idea appears to be isolated from the rest of life, it blossoms out only at the moment when the patient loses consciousness, and it seems to leave behind it no memory. In reality, a certain amount of consciousness does accompany the idea and it does leave behind a certain memory, but the consciousness and the memory are a special sort and are closely attached to the idea, which seems to constitute an independent psychological entity. The elements stirred up with reference to this idea are so numerous and so complex that they completely fill the sphere of consciousness and suppress every other function and every other thought.[28]

Janet obviously regards ideas as far more than the pale symbols of things. They are active, they develop, they surge up with enormous power. They are, in fact, rather like demons. Of course, Janet does not call them that, except when hard pressed; he calls them ideas, and he assumes some kind of connection between them and the cells of the brain—though without being at all clear as to the nature of the connection.

Communication between the unconscious and consciousness

In all the preceding discussion it should have been apparent that the theory of the coexistence of two or more mental states generally assumes that there is or may be communication between them. Thus, a subordinated mental state is not called "unconscious" or "subconscious" because nothing at all reaches the conscious self from that level, but because the consciousness of what *is* present there is in some way imperfect or misleading.

ANESTHETIC PERCEIVING   Some paradoxical results obtained by Binet in experiments on hysterical subjects with anesthetic skin areas have a direct bearing on the problem.

Binet stimulated these anesthetic areas in various ways and discovered that very often a conscious experience did in fact attend the stimulation, but without tactile sensation and without proper localization. For example, he would stimulate an anesthetic hand three times and then ask the subject what he was thinking of; the reply, without any apparent connection with a sensation from the hand, might contain some reference to the number three. He noticed that in some cases the relationship between the stimulus and the response might be still closer. Sometimes the subject would say, "I am thinking of three in the shape of three points," or, at other times, "I see bars and clubs." At first Binet took these statements for imaginative elaborations with no particular relevance for the conditions of stimulation. Then it struck him that there was a correlation between what he did to the hand and what the subject reported. "Points" were mentioned when the anesthetic hand was

[28] *Ibid.*, p. 162.

pricked. "Bars and clubs" were mentioned when a *finger* was moved by the experimenter several times. Binet concluded that an appropriate *visual* experience might take the place of the expected *tactile* experience. No sensation of contact or pain or movement reached the subject from the anesthetic hand, but the event leaked over, so to speak, into a different sense modality and thus gave the subject (i.e., the conscious self) an informative experience which was misleading in that it was visual rather than tactile, and imperfect in that it did not indicate the hand as the source of it. In other words, the conscious self was receiving a puzzling message from the Unconscious.

Binet writes:

> In the course of time, when the experiments are repeated, ideas suggested by unconscious perception become extremely intense. I have most often seen them take the form of visual images. The visual image becomes, according to the patients, as dazzling as the sensation of an electric light. It objectifies itself and may obliterate external objects like a real hallucination.[29]

In some cases the visual counterpart of the stimulus applied to the anesthetic skin is very much more accurate than would be expected of a normal subject. Binet cites in particular an experiment in which he pressed a steel disk, the surface of which had a design in relief, against an anesthetic area on the back of a young girl's neck.

> The disk, which the patient had never seen, of course, was held in contact with the skin for some moments. The patient became restless and complained of dizziness. She saw luminous spots of circular shape that burned before her eyes. Each time that the pressure on the disk increased the vividness of the sensation increased, and if the pressure became too strong it produced the same effect as a jet of electric light. throwing the patient into catalepsy.[30]

He asked the girl to draw what she saw when he was pressing the disk lightly against her neck. In spite of the disadvantages of total lack of art education and of having to draw with a muscularly atrophied arm, the poor girl's sketch of her visual image is rather strikingly similar to the stimulus disk in both size and design, as shown in Figure 16a. A normal subject under the same conditions was much less accurate. Three years later Binet repeated the experiment with the same hysterical girl, but used a disk with a different

[29] Binet (1896), pp. 212 f. [30] *Ibid.,* p. 213.

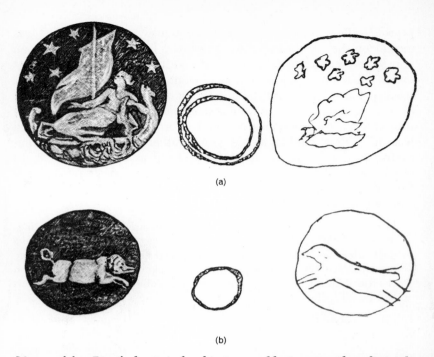

(a)

(b)

16 a and b *Binet's hysterical subject was able to see rather distinctly the design of a metal disc pressed against the back of her neck. Her drawings are at the right; at the left are the test designs. In the middle are the drawings of normal subjects under the same stimulus conditions. (From Binet, 1896)*

design. Once again, as shown in Figure 16b, there was evidence of a remarkable sensitivity.

We have, then, this paradox: A girl who is less sensitive than the normal, in that she has an anesthetic patch of skin, is more sensitive than the normal by virtue of the fact that stimulation of this anesthetic area may give rise to a sharply defined and accurately representational visual image. This sounds astonishing. Yet the phenomenon may be a great deal more common than usually supposed. For example, when we are asleep and dreaming, a tactile or auditory stimulus may be translated into a pretty adequate visual image of the stimulating object.

The phenomenon demonstrated by Binet is important, whether common or rare. It makes intelligible one possible meaning of "communication between the Unconscious and consciousness." It also takes us close to the debatable question of telepathy; for, if a coin pressed against the back of the neck can be vividly seen—through the skin, as it were—though not felt, we are within a step or two of admitting the possibility of clairvoyant and telepathic perceiving. We shall return to this topic in Chapter 14. Here, however, I wish to emphasize only one point bearing on our general scientific orientation to the facts of human experience, namely this: Binet would have been badly mistaken if he had continued to regard the visual experiences of his subjects as "just imagination."

MULTIPLE PERSONALITY   The communication between the Unconscious and consciousness, or between the phases of a personality, or between the distinct systems which appear in cases of multiple personality, may be more roundabout than in Binet's anesthetic subjects. Azam's Félida scribbled herself notes when she felt herself about to shift over from one state to another, in order to keep her affairs straight. Prince's Miss Beauchamp, using a crystal ball, perceived events out of her past without recognizing them as such, and she also left notes to herself—notes that were sometimes highly puzzling to the recipient state, especially when they came from that one of the four states which was named "Sally" to the one named "Miss Beauchamp." Perhaps it would not be inappropriate at this point to summarize Miss Beauchamp's case as observed by Prince so that the reader can appreciate the intricacies and problems involved in a case of multiple personality. For this purpose, I shall use a résumé of my own, written a few years ago:

. . . Miss Beauchamp, a college student, came to Prince for medical attention in 1898, when she was twenty-three years of age and he was forty-four. Her symptoms were "headaches, insomnia, bodily pains, persistent fatigue, and poor nutrition." Failing to relieve these complaints by conventional methods, Prince on April 5 began to employ hypnosis, with good results. Except for an amnesia covering the hypnotic periods, the waking and the hypnotic states appeared to be the same; the same mood of weary depression obtained in both. But one day in April the patient's manner while under hypnosis changed: she suddenly became vivacious, bold and saucy, and stutteringly began to refer to herself in the nonhypnotic state as "she," as if talking about someone else entirely. Prince now believed that he had three distinct personalities on his hands where there had been only one before, and, accordingly, labeled them BI, BII, and BIII. BI was the original Miss Beauchamp, BII the first hypnotic state, and BIII this new hypnotic state, for which the name "Sally" was soon adopted. A little over a year later (June 7, 1899) a fourth personality, as Prince conceived it, emerged from a spontaneous trance, and was labeled BIV. BIV was the exact opposite of BI and knew practically nothing about any of the other three personalities, though known to the two hypnotic states, BII and Sally. Since all these different states represented different moods and different memories, and since they alternated freely with one another, the patient's behavior was often highly discontinuous and contradictory both to herself and to Prince. . . . There was . . . at least one fixed point always present in the distracted firmament of her experiences. Regardless of changes in mood and lapses of memory, regardless of the alternation of presumed distinct personalities, Miss Beauchamp continued to visit and write to Prince. For seven years he was the gravitational center of her world. This is surely a fact of paramount importance, nor is it any less so for being so perfectly obvious. Indeed, her relationship to him is a far better reference point for judging her personality changes than is the "real, original, or normal self" which Prince assumed. When she was submissive to him, she was BI; when flippant and flirtatious, BIII; when rebellious, BIV. Prince reacted with considerable emotion to these various attitudes toward himself. He was gentle with BI, amused with BIII, and severe with BIV. To understand how he felt, one only needs to read the letters to him. Those from BI are respectful, serious, apologetic, frequently confessing to sins and asking for forgiveness, typically thanking him for "all his kindness and patience." Those from BIII are slangy, saucy, and teasingly affectionate, though sometimes bursting out with expressions of mock rage. The following will give some idea of the style, and something more: "Know all men by these presents that I, Sally, being of sound mind and in full possession of all my senses, do hereby most solemnly promise to love, honor, and obey Morton Prince, M.D., situate in the city of Boston, state of Massachusetts, from this time forth, *toujours*. Amen, amen, amen." BIV in general refused to write, but now and then would get off something like this: "Dr. Prince, —Will you be good enough to address my letters properly." It is oversimplifying matters, of course, to characterize any of these states or personalities by a single attitude, as they were all to some extent fluid, particularly the volatile Sally; but the point is that, in so far as they can be so characterized, it is above all with reference to their relations with Prince.[31]

In the case of mediums, the events occurring in the trance state (I speak of those where the genuineness of the personality change seems to be well attested) may remain unknown to the waking state except through dreams or through the accounts given to the

[31] McCurdy (1941).

medium afterwards by observers of the trance. In short, in these extreme cases of multiple personality the division between phases is so great that there is even resort to forms of communication—letter-writing, oral reports by others—commonly employed by separate individuals.

A term often used to refer to the condition in which there is a division between states or levels of the personality is *amnesia*, which means simply "absence of memory." But amnesia covers many degrees and orders of separation between the personality states or systems. There is the slight amnesia where you grope for a name and then have it, there is the profounder amnesia of the hypnotic subject vis-à-vis his trance state, there is the still profounder and more radical amnesia of Irène (see pp. 120 ff.) or such mediums as fall into authentic trances. Moreover, we have to deal with the fact that one state of a personality may have a more extensive memory than another. Thus, a hypnotic subject in a trance state may know about what is going on in the trance state and also a great deal about the waking subject and other things in addition, whereas the waking subject may be amnesic for the trance and those other things remembered in the trance. So it was with Miss Beauchamp: Sally knew about Miss Beauchamp and her past, Miss Beauchamp did not know about her past or about Sally, except by report and inference. The amnesic boundary between states or phases or systems of a personality, then, may be more permeable in one direction than in the other.

"But," someone may ask, "is there nothing more substantial about these so-called phases or states or systems than the mere fact that at one moment a person may remember certain things and at another moment certain others?" That in itself is really a considerable fact, as anyone knows who has had to struggle to remember something that he needs to know and that he knows he does know if only he *could* remember it; and as anyone should be able to imagine when he hears about someone's having strayed away from home without any memory of his name or occupation or relatives. Nevertheless, there is point to the question, and we can answer that the phases or states or systems may be so different from one another and so consistent in their traits that in radical cases it seems only fair to refer to them as separate or quasi-separate "personalities."

We learn, for example, in Prince's *Dissociation of a Personality* that states BI and BIV (as explained in the passage above) were exact contraries in a long list of tastes and behavioral traits. All close observers of such cases seem to have been impressed by the variety and consistency of the amnesically separated states of each individual. Some have gone further and tried to study the characteristics of the separate states by experimental and statistical means. An example, more recent than the period to which this chapter has been devoted but continuing the observations of the earlier period, is Carington's "The Quantitative Study of Trance Personalities."[32] In this study the normal conditions of three mediums—Mrs. Garrett, Rudi Schneider, and Mrs. Leonard—were compared with their supposed "controls," (i.e., other personality states presumed to be taking possession of them) by means of word-association tests and psychogalvanic reactions rigorously handled by the statistical methods of R. A. Fisher. Carington found distinct differences between Mrs. Garrett and her "control" as well as between the several states of Mrs. Leonard, but none between the two presumptive states of Rudi Schneider. These results harmonize with the general impression that the normal and trance states of the two women were honestly different, whereas more than a little suspicion attaches to Rudi Schneider.

Behavioral studies such as Carington's are certainly desirable, but they cannot replace the investigation of consciousness and its boundaries. There is pretty sound evidence of serious memory gaps occurring in persons who may not strike the casual observer as behaviorally very disturbed; and, on the other hand, skilled actors may alter their behavior for different dramatic roles without necessarily forgetting their off-stage connections with the world. It is entirely too superficial to consider only outward behavior in hysteria, multiple personality, mediumship, and so on, attractive though this solution of the mysteries of human nature may at first seem. Carington, of course, was perfectly aware of this but saw the value, too, of quantitative methods applied to even the periphery of behavior. On the basis of this work, Carington raised the question whether the diverse personality states seen in some persons can be adequately explained as phases of one general unconscious root or whether they must be taken to be quite as distinct and independent as any other individuals in the world around us. The same question plagues us at every step, of course, when we study closely such a case as Janet's Achille, the transformations which take place in hypnosis, the dramatic changes of hysteria, and many

[32] Carington (1934).

other phenomena for which the Freudian theory of the Unconscious was devised.

We may now pass to that theory. One of its chief claims on our attention is that it is based, at least in part, on a special method of exploring the Unconscious, of which the interpretation of dreams is the main stratagem. We shall therefore approach it from that angle.

References for chapter 7

Azam, E. (1887) *Hypnotisme, double conscience, et altérations de la personnalité*. Paris: Baillière.

Binet, A. (1896) *Alterations of personality*. Tr. by H. G. Baldwin, notes and preface by J. M. Baldwin. New York: Appleton.

Bramwell, J. M. (1930) *Hypnotism: its history, practice and theory*. Philadelphia: Lippincott.

Carington, W. (1934) The quantitative study of trance personalities. *Proceedings of the Society for Psychical Research*, 42, 173-240.

James, W. (1890) *The principles of psychology*. New York: Holt. 2 vols.

Janet, P. (1898) *Névroses et idées fixes*. Paris: Alcan. 2 vols., Vol. 1.

McCurdy, H. G. (1941) A note on the dissociation of a personality. *Character and Personality*, 10, 35-41.

Myers, F. W. H. (1887) On telepathic hypnotism, and its relation to other forms of hypnotic suggestion. *Proceedings of the Society for Psychical Research*, 4, 127-88.

———(1903) *Human personality and its survival of bodily death*. London: Longmans, Green. 2 vols.

Prince, M. (1906) *The dissociation of a personality*. New York: Longmans, Green.

Schofield, A. T. (1901) *The unconscious mind*. New York: Funk & Wagnalls.

Skinner, B. F. (1938) *The behavior of organisms*. New York: Appleton-Century.

Thigpen, C. H., and Cleckley, H. M. (1957) *The three faces of Eve*. New York: McGraw-Hill.

Watkins, J. G. (1949) *Hypnotherapy of war neuroses: a clinical psychologist's casebook*. New York: Ronald.

Weitzenhoffer, A. M. (1953) *Hypnotism: an objective study of suggestibility*. New York: Wiley.

Zilboorg, G. (1941) *A history of medical psychology*. New York: Norton.

8

THE UNCONSCIOUS: FREUD

Preview *Freud sought for knowledge of the Unconscious in dreams, which he regarded as produced by unconscious forces. Through the study of dreams he arrived at certain notions as to how they are constructed, which are as follows. In most cases the basis is a wish, often a sexual wish. The wish, however, is met by a repressive counterforce. The result is that the manifest dream is usually a distorted symbolization of the wish. Wishes originate in the Unconscious, especially in the region called the Id, and are governed by the pleasure-principle. The opposition to wishes arises in the Ego and the Superego. The Ego is governed by the reality-principle and by the conflicting demands of Id and Super-ego; the latter is mainly acquired from the parents during childhood by the process of introjection. Freud's theory of mental structure attempts to describe the relations between these various parts dynamically, in terms of the distribution of psychic energy,*

238 THE PERSONAL WORLD

which he identifies largely with libido, or sexual energy. Libido flows along instinctive pathways. The Freudian theory, though it originated in the effort to deal therapeutically with neurotics, gradually developed in his hands until he and other psychoanalysts judged that it was capable of explaining all human behavior, both individual and social.

More than anyone else in modern times Freud took the Unconscious as his province. He knew that he was not alone in this area of psychology; he was aware of his predecessors; but he saw himself as more seriously committed to the task than they, and in this he was doubtless right. There was a kind of fierce defiance in his determination to explore the unknown depths. The motto he placed on the title page of his most important book was *Flectere si nequeo superos, Acheronta movebo.* Freely translated, these wrathful words of Juno (from the *Aeneid*) mean, "If Heaven won't help me, I'll raise Hell!" The Unconscious of Freud does indeed have a more hellish look than what was similarly designated by Herbart, Fechner, Helmholtz, James, and others before him. The nearest rival in the infernal regions of the mind was Janet; and Janet, as Freud contemptuously remarked, thought of the Unconscious not as a reality but merely as "a manner of speaking," a *façon de parler.*

The royal road into the unconscious

The Interpretation of Dreams was published late in 1899. Freud considered it his greatest achievement. Not only was it his most sustained intellectual effort, but it dealt with a subject which in his opinion led more directly to a knowledge of the Unconscious than any other. Dreams, he said, constituted the main highway, the royal road, into the depths of the mind. The opening words of the book clearly indicate its scope:

> In the following pages, I shall demonstrate that there is a psychological technique which makes it possible to interpret dreams, and that on the application of this technique, every dream will reveal itself as a psychological structure, full of significance, and one which may be assigned to a specific place in the psychic activities of the waking state. Further, I shall endeavour to elucidate the processes which underlie the strangeness and obscurity of dreams, and to deduce from these proc-

esses the nature of the psychic forces whose conflict or co-operation is responsible for our dreams.[1]

We must first look at Freud's technique and then come to the deductions about the psychic forces.

The basis of the technique is a kind of self-observation on the part of the subject. The attitude required is different from that adopted by a thinker trying to solve a problem or a speaker trying to make a good impression. The thinker brushes aside irrelevant thoughts, the speaker tries to be persuasive and charming and is careful to avoid offending his audience. The self-observer, on the contrary, must relax all his defenses and simply take note of whatever thoughts may come, without regard for morality or logic or sensibleness or any of the usual restraints of rationality or good manners. If one can only succeed in being attentive but noncritical, one will discover that consciousness is invaded by innumerable thoughts, many of them astonishing. If now the self-observer will communicate these thoughts (free-associate), either by writing them down or speaking them, he will provide the kind of material needed for interpreting his dreams. The state of mind which favors such free production of ideas is similar to that of a person on the verge of sleep. Freud recommends lying down and closing the eyes. (Here is part of the explanation for the famous psychoanalytic couch.)

The ideas which emerge in this unbridled condition of the mind are by no means random. Freud discovered that if he took a fragment of a dream and used it as the starting point for the self-observer who had dreamed it, the ideas which rushed up in response would bear some relation to the dream and help to explain it. In fact, it is an essential rule of the Freudian technique of dream interpretation to break the dream up into parts and accumulate ideas around these parts by free association. Freud insists upon this. He writes:

> If I ask a patient who is as yet unpractised: "What occurs to you in connection with this dream?" he is unable, as a rule, to fix upon anything in his psychic field of vision. I must first dissect the dream for him; then, in connection with each fragment, he gives me a number of ideas which may be described as the "thoughts behind" this part of the dream.[2]

[1] Freud (1950), p. 3.
[2] *Ibid.*, pp. 15 f.

No matter how coherent the dream may appear on the surface, Freud does not accept it at face value; he thinks of it as a conglomerate of psychic formations which will not make sense until fragmented and subjected to the free-association procedure. The alert reader will notice a resemblance between this way of going about the matter and the "decomposition" technique which Janet used in the effort to destroy his patient's *idées fixes*. The aim is entirely different, however; Janet was seeking to reduce the meaningfulness of a psychic content by disintegrating it, Freud to increase meaning by expansion of consciousness.

Let us see what happens when Freud applies his method. A portion of the first dream analyzed in *The Interpretation of Dreams* is this: "I take her to the window and look into her throat. She offers some resistance to this, like a woman who has a set of false teeth. I think, surely, she does not need them."[3] When Freud allows himself to think about this fragment (for it is from a dream of his own), he is reminded of a pretty governess who had a denture which she had tried to conceal, and of other patients similarly embarrassed by physical defects. The way the patient in the dream, Irma, stands at the window reminds him of a close woman friend of hers—a woman who had a condition of the throat superficially like Irma's, but possibly diphtheritic rather than hysterical. It occurs to Freud that this woman might be a more satisfactory patient than Irma, because more intelligent and cooperative. Still another woman comes to mind, because of something unfamiliar about Irma's appearance; and this is a woman who would have resisted psychoanalytic treatment. The "thoughts behind" this fragment of the dream seem to yield three women in addition to Irma; or, to put it differently, Irma in the dream seems to represent herself and three other women at the same time. The image in the dream is a *condensation* of four women into one.

Here we encounter one of Freud's principal ideas about how dreams are formed and thus about how the Unconscious works. Condensation is an unconscious process by which memory images (themselves in the Unconscious) are fused together to produce some single item in the dream which is consciously experienced. A single person or scene or activity in the dream may sum up a great number of separable persons or scenes or activities existing in some manner in the Unconscious. The result in the dream as reported, the

[3] *Ibid.*, p. 19.

manifest dream, may be thoroughly mystifying; but the mystery can be dissolved by undoing the dream-work and getting back to the *latent dream thoughts.* The free-association technique, according to Freud, allows us to do this.

The manifest dream is often obscure and apparently meaningless, as Freud freely admits. Condensation accounts for part of the obscurity, by squeezing together many ideas into one. Another unconscious process which has the same obscuring effect is *displacement.* As everyone knows, there is often a lack of proportion between the importance of one's feelings and intentions, on the one hand, and the trivial nature of what they are focused on, on the other. For example, we read in a newspaper story that one man killed another in a quarrel over a nickel. Or we find in Shakespeare's *Othello* that a little handkerchief becomes the pivot of an enormous tragedy. Or we notice day by day how worked up we ourselves may get over very minor things. Of course, we are here talking about appearances. It is very unlikely that the deadly quarrel reported in the newspaper was really simply about a nickel. We know that the handkerchief in Shakespeare's drama was important only because it was used as evidence, false evidence, to arouse gigantic passions. We know, too, if we reflect on it, that the trivialities of our own lives gain their importance by association with important things. So it is in the dream, according to Freud. What stands out as the most vivid point in a dream may have acquired this prominence by carrying a charge of emotion originating somewhere else entirely; or a meaningful element of the dream which deserves to be prominent may have shrunk into the background because the emotion which belonged to it has been withdrawn. In short, a shift of emotional accent may radically distort the dream. This is *displacement.* An example given by Freud is a dream in which he sees the face of a friend surrounded by a yellow beard which stands out with peculiar distinctness. The beard seems to be the main point; the dream seems to be insisting on this by making it vivid. Yet what this dream is all about, in Freud's interpretation, is the desire for greatness. The beard, in itself a minor fact, has been made to carry all the emotional power of this ambition. An amusing picture by Alajálov illustrates the principle. A dowdy maidenly artist is copying a detail from a large painting. The intensity of her preoccupation with the innocent detail is perhaps all the more furious because of the voluptuous drama so nakedly displayed on the original canvas. She confines her brushwork to a decorative detail, a side issue. Yet we suspect that the central theme

17 *The Freudian principle of displacement is comically illustrated in a* New Yorker *cover by Alajálov.*

publicly exhibited on the museum wall is also present to her mind and may in fact be setting her own emotions on the boil and lending to the fraction she is painting a great part of its interest for her.

Both condensation and displacement might be regarded as a kind of symbolization of the latent dream thoughts, since these thoughts are not represented directly but by the substitute formations to which these processes give rise. But Freud reserves the word *symbolization* for a more or less standardized, stereotyped, stylized way of representing certain particular ideas of general importance, such as birth, death, family relations, and especially sex in all its variety. He even draws up a long list of common dream symbols. Very often these symbolicial elements fail to arouse illuminating associations; they baffle dreamer and dream interpreter both. Consequently, interpretation becomes impossible unless the free-association method is supplemented by a special knowledge of symbols. Even so, the interpreter is warned to exercise all caution: "Critical circumspection in the solution of the symbols must coincide with careful study of the symbols in especially transparent examples of dreams in order to silence the reproach of arbitrariness in dream-interpretation."[4] These reservations having been made, Freud proceeds to explain a large number of things as sexual symbols. The male genital organ, he says, may appear in the dream disguised as a stick, umbrella, knife, hammer, gun, plowshare, or other elongated object or tool or weapon; as complicated machinery; as a bird, snake, fish, or other flying or swimming or penetrating animal; and, in general, whatever has any of the properties of the male genitals—length, erectility, cutting or penetrating action, fertilizing power, etc.—will do as a dream symbol. All hollow containers—boxes, chests, cupboards, ovens, caves, ships, pots, etc.—serve equally well to represent the female organ.

> Again, many of the landscapes seen in dreams, especially those that contain bridges or wooded mountains, may be readily recognized as descriptions of the genitals. Marcinowski collected a series of examples in which the dreamer explained his dream by means of drawings, in order to represent the landscapes and places appearing in it. These drawings clearly showed the distinction between the manifest and the latent meaning of the dream. Whereas, naïvely regarded, they seemed to represent plans, maps, and so forth, closer investigation showed that they were representations of the human body, of the genitals, etc., and only after conceiving them thus could the dream be understood.[5]

Strange as all this may sound to the uninitiated, the occurrence of such symbolization is in fact an almost overwhelming feature of many dreams for anyone who approaches them in anything like the Freudian manner. Marcinowski's device of asking for a drawing may bring sudden conviction to the dreamer of the validity of symbolization. I particularly recall what happened when I once asked a dreamer to clarify, by making a simple sketch, her very confusing description of the path she followed in her dream in going from one building to another where there was a grand piano. She drew a most unmistakable phallus. This was more evident to me than to her at the time, because from her side of the desk the drawing was upside down. When I turned the paper around, she blushed in recognition. Still uncertain whether it would strike everybody the same way, she took it with her to show her roommate. The reaction convinced her that there could be little doubt about its graphic realism, and she made haste to destroy it.

[4] *Ibid.*, p. 241.   [5] *Ibid.*, p. 244.

A few experiments have been performed in order to test out Freud's conclusions about symbolization. An early one by Schrötter in 1912 employed hypnotism and suggestion. He told a deeply hypnotized subject, for example, that she would dream of homosexual relations with a woman friend. The result was that she dreamed of the friend "carrying a shabby travelling-bag, upon which there was a label with the printed words: 'For ladies only.' "[6] The subject in this case is supposed to have been totally unacquainted with Freudian dream interpretation. Freud regarded as especially valuable the results obtained by Betlheim and Hartmann in 1924 because they used, instead of hypnotic subjects, patients suffering from the memory confusions of Korsakoff's psychosis. They told crudely sexual stories to these patients and observed the changes introduced in their retelling.

It was shown that the reproduced material contained symbols made familiar by the interpretation of dreams (climbing stairs, stabbing and shooting as symbols of coitus, knives and cigarettes as symbols of the penis). Special value was attached to the appearance of the symbol of climbing stairs, for, as the authors justly observed, "a symbolization of this sort could not be effected by a conscious wish to distort."[7]

Farber and Fisher in 1943 reported experiments on twenty college students presumed to be unacquainted with psychoanalysis. Five of the twenty, when under hypnosis, showed psychoanalytic insight into sexual symbols. One of the five, when told that a girl dreamed that a big snake crawled into the trunk she was packing, so that she ran away in fright, immediately blushed and hesitantly said that the dreamer was afraid of being seduced, the snake being the man's sex organ and the trunk hers. One immediately understood the dream of another as meaning that she had wet the bed. In another phase of the study a young man was told that he would dream of seeing a woman breast-feeding her child; his dream substituted for the breast a mountain of graceful form. In these experiments we encounter two apparently opposite processes: (1) the translation of dream symbols into plain language, and (2) the translation of plain language into dream symbols. Here is a problem which deserves further discussion, but that will have to be deferred to a later page.

We may take it as certain that there are indeed many indirect references to sexual matters in dreams. But in waking life, too, are

[6] *Ibid.*, p. 261.   [7] *Ibid.*, p. 261.

there not many allusions to sex? The general context enables us to understand these allusions, even when they are deeply disguised behind some image or term which only remotely resembles what it refers to. The dream interpreter's practical problem is just exactly where to infer a sexual meaning among all the embarrassingly rich possibilities. The theoretical problem is *why* there should be indirect representation at all, especially in the privacy of dreams. Freud's answer to the theoretical question involves an idea which is probably the most distinguishing mark of psychoanalysis (aside from transference)—the idea of *repression*. Repression is a censoring or criticizing function in the unconscious portion of the Ego which tends to hold out of consciousness those ideas or impulses which in some way offend the principles or wound the pride or threaten the stability of the individual. Symbolization allows this offensive or dangerous psychic content to slip around the censor, to evade the repression, because it is then disguised enough not to be recognized in the waking state. The private mental situation is comparable to that which is common enough in a social gathering in our part of the world, where basic biological matters like urination, defecation, and sexual activity are likely to be spoken of, if at all, in a roundabout way. Especially is the direct reference avoided if it is in the least degree personal. All kinds of euphemisms are summoned up to avoid forthrightness. One is going to the powder room or rest room; one must wash one's hands or freshen up; one has an appointment or must go home to catch a wink of sleep. Freud argues that it is like this internally; moral sensitivity, or even mere prissiness, strikes deep, and the private dream is not private enough for letting down all defenses. Hence the symbols—clever ways of lying to oneself.

We shall examine the problem of symbols from other angles later. For the moment let us accept Freud's insight as sufficient; it is illuminating, and it helps to make sense out of many dreams (and much other human activity) which would otherwise be unintelligible. We may just note here that the occurrence of visual imagery standing for sexual tension in the body of the dreamer has some kinship with the phenomenon of hysterical perception of stimulation of an anesthetic region, as illustrated in the experiment by Binet cited above. For a person dreaming, his body lying in bed has ceased to exist. He does not feel the mounting bodily excitement which ends, perhaps, in a seminal ejaculation; instead, he sees something—it may be a symbolic image that has no recognized connection with his body at all—through which the bodily tension is represented but not understood.

As Freud says, dreaming tends to prolong sleep by protecting us from a too vivid consciousness of our bodily condition or of our relations to the world to which the body belongs. By dreaming that an alarm clock is pointing to five when, in fact, it is ringing like mad because it is really pointing to eight, the somnolent scholar manages to miss that first class and go on sleeping. When a young man dreams that his roommate is writhing with appendicitis some yards away, he does succeed for a few moments in warding off the realization that the pain is his own. It is more satisfactory to dream under these circumstances than to wake. The state of sleep suppresses consciousness of the state of sleep; the sleeping body, for instance, rarely appears as such in the dream: the dreamed body is usually active—walking, running, swimming, even flying. Like Binet's hysteric, we are in the state of sleep anesthetic to our own bodies and the world around, and yet we continue to receive messages from them. To maintain this separation between experience (the dream) and the conditions of that experience (the body asleep), while at the same time remaining in contact through experience with the sleeping body, the experience would have to be in some measure out of the ordinary; symbolization of some kind would seem to be required by the dissociation. By *seeing* the coin pressed against her neck instead of *feeling* it, Binet's hysteric could keep up her hysterical anesthesia without a total severance between her experience and that part of her body. But the seeing in place of feeling in this case is like Freud's kind of symbolization: it is a replacement of a standard experience by a less expected one. It is worth noting again that Binet for some time failed to recognize the nature of the connection between the visual phenomenon and the tactile stimulation. The inexpert dream-interpreter will likewise fail to notice the connection between the symbolic dream image and what it symbolizes.

Besides condensation, displacement, and symbolization, Freud stresses another cause of dream obscurity. The dream undergoes some changes in the course of being remembered and reported. Between the moment of actual dreaming and the moment of recollection, portions of the dream may drop out entirely or be modified; on top of that, we tend to patch up the dream so as to make it less fragmentary and illogical. This process of editing the dream in the course of recalling it is what Freud calls *secondary elaboration*.

To get at the meaning of a dream, the dream-work of condensation, displacement, symbolization, and secondary elaboration has to be undone, according to Freud. By the technique of free association by the subject and with his own knowledge of dream symbols, the Freudian interpreter goes beneath the surface of the manifest dream to the latent dream thoughts. Here, where the meaning of the dream lies, one discovers over and over again, says Freud, the motive force of a wish, often a sexual one. Freud has been accused of sexualizing everything, of explaining everything in terms of sexual wishes. This is a false accusation. He always recognized other kinds of wishes, not to mention counteracting forces, even in the case of dreams. When he states his well-known formula that the dream is fundamentally a wish-fulfillment, he does not necessarily imply that the wish is a sexual one. It is up to the interpreter to discover what the wish is. No doubt sexual wishes are very common, but there is room for others too. Furthermore, Freud admits at least one important exception to his guiding rule that dreams are produced by wishes aiming at the achievement of pleasure, whether sexual or otherwise: the dream which simply repeats some terrible, real experience, a traumatic experience, such as a moment of horror on the battlefield or in a train wreck. Why should the dreamer return to the scenes of pain and violence and terror from which he has mercifully escaped? Freud does not succeed in giving us a very illuminating explanation of this phenomenon, which forced itself on his attention during the First World War. But he does admit that it does not harmonize with the wish-fulfillment theory.

In the main, however, the clue to dreams for Freud is that they are wish-fulfillments, or at least *attempted* wish-fulfillments. It is possible to find dreams which are very clearly such, dreams in which a starving man enjoys a banquet, a poor man gains wealth, an explorer far from home returns, a lonely man or woman quite simply acquires a sexual mate. Dreams so transparent are relatively scarce, however; and the wish-fulfillment theory has to overcome apparent contradictions in most cases. The dream-work, of course, is capable of hiding the true nature both of the wish and of its fulfillment. Yet there are many dreams which seem to defy the theory even when due allowance is made for the distorting effect of these processes. There are, in short, many very *unpleasant* dreams. Freud does not let this fact undermine his confidence in the wish-fulfillment formula. Indeed, the occurrence of dreams marked by fear provides him with material for a deeper exploration of the Unconscious.

Here is an example of a Freudian interpretation of terror dreams:

A boy of thirteen, in delicate health, began to be anxious and dreamy; his sleep became uneasy, and once almost every week it was interrupted by an acute attack of anxiety with hallucinations. The memory of these dreams was always very distinct. Thus he was able to relate that the devil had shouted at him: "Now we have you, now we have you!" and then there was a smell of pitch and brimstone, and the fire burned his skin. From this dream he woke in terror; at first he could not cry out; then his voice came back to him, and he was distinctly heard to say: "No, no, not me; I haven't done anything," or: "Please, don't; I will never do it again!" At other times he said: "Albert has never done that!" Later he avoided undressing, "because the fire attacked him only when he was undressed." In the midst of these evil dreams, which were endangering his health, he was sent into the country, where he recovered in the course of eighteen months. At the age of fifteen he confessed one day: *"Je n'osais pas l'avouer, mais j'éprouvais continuellement des picotements et des surexcitations aux parties; à la fin, cela m'énervait tant que plusieurs fois j'ai pensé me jeter par la fenêtre du dortoir."* [Brill notes: "The emphasis is mine, though the meaning is plain enough without it."]

Freud did not have the advantage of knowing this boy himself, but he drew upon his general experience with other cases of terror dreams and his dream theory to produce the following conclusions:

It is, of course, not difficult to guess: (1) That the boy had practised masturbation in former years, that he had probably denied it, and was threatened with severe punishment for his bad habit. (His confession: *"Je ne le ferai plus"*; his denial: *"Albert n'a jamais fait ça."*) (2) That under the advancing pressure of puberty the temptation to masturbate was reawakened through the titillation of the genitals. (3) That now, however, there arose within him a struggle for repression, which suppressed the libido and transformed it into anxiety, and that this anxiety now gathered up the punishments with which he was originally threatened.[8]

Repression

The above example is introduced here not as evidence in support of Freud's interpretations, but simply to provide a starting-point for an exploration of the strange country of the Unconscious to which the royal road of the dream has led us.

[8] *Ibid.*, pp. 438 f. The French passage translated: "I didn't dare admit it, but I used to feel ticklings and strong sensations in my organs all the time; finally, that wore me out so that I thought several times of jumping out of my dormitory window."

As already mentioned, repression is an unconscious activity which erects and maintains a barrier within the psychic system, a barrier which prevents or makes difficult the passage of the contents of the Unconscious into consciousness. For Freud, there are two major kinds of unconscious material—past experiences which have been forgotten and instincts. These two are always bound together in some way. The instincts are endowed with energy, and an object or activity or memory which has anything to do with an instinct acquires some of its energy; to use the technical term, is *cathected* or acquires a *cathexis*. Just as a nail brought into contact with a magnet becomes magnetic itself, so an object of experience becomes cathected by contact with an instinct. The sexual instinct, for example, endows the loved person with special value. Anything related to this person (a picture, a handkerchief, a memory image, etc.) also becomes valuable; becomes (to return to the technical language) charged with libido, or sexual energy, becomes sexually cathected. When repression occurs, then, it is directed simultaneously against cathected objects and the instinct or instincts from which they have acquired their cathexis.

In the above case, it is a sexual impulse which is being restrained by repression: specifically, the impulse to masturbate, which involves, among other things, the cathected genitals and memories from earlier years. Freud supposes that there was a time in the life of the boy when he masturbated without compunction, receiving in that way a direct satisfaction of the sexual impulse; but that his behavior had been reproved by those responsible for the boy's bringing up and in fact severely reproved. Repression then sets in. That is to say, something in the boy cooperates with the pressure from the environment by an unconscious, automatic exclusion of the sexual impulse and the ideas related to it. Note that the reaction is unconscious and automatic; it is not the result of a deliberate moral choice. In a sense, what has happened is that the reproving figures of the parents (or whoever was concerned) have taken up residence in the boy himself and continue to exercise their authority internally. But though an instinct and cathected ideas can be repressed—excluded from consciousness and from consciously guided action—they cannot be destroyed. They remain in the Unconscious without loss of power. In fact, they may gain power. In the boy's case, simply as a result of his growing older and approaching sexual maturity in the hormonal sense, the sexual impulses become more and more imperative. But the repression is maintained, except for certain breakthroughs in the form of genital sensations and dreams that bring to the surface the old threats of punishment, now further energized by the increasing sexual urge. The boy suffers intense anxiety, partly because the thwarting of an impulse is inherently unpleasant, partly because the old threats of punishment are vividly reactivated in consciousness, and partly because his whole character structure is in danger of being overthrown by the power of both the sexual impulse and the threats against it. He is quite literally in a danger situation, and the anxiety is quite appropriate. From the boy's point of view, Hell and its devils have risen against him. From Freud's point of view, all that is just an expression, a symbolization, of a tremendous psychic conflict in the Unconscious between sex and the repressive forces arrayed against it.

Incidentally, the devils of the boy's dream would have been reduced by Freud, if possible, to concrete recollections from the boy's own past. Freud once had a twelve-year-old boy as a patient who was prevented from falling asleep by visions of terrifying, diabolic green faces with red eyes. His comment is:

> The source of this manifestation was the suppressed, but once conscious, memory of a boy whom he had often seen four years earlier, and who offered a warning example of many bad habits, including masturbation, for which he was now reproaching himself. At that time his mother had noticed that the complexion of this ill-mannered boy was *greenish* and that he had *red* (i.e., red-rimmed) *eyes*. Hence his terrifying vision, which merely determined his recollection of another saying of his mother's, to the effect that such boys become demented, are unable to learn anything at school, and are doomed to an early death. A part of this prediction came true in the case of my little patient; he could not get on at school, and, as appeared from his involuntary associations, he was in terrible dread of the remainder of the prophecy.[9]

Freud has compared repression to moral condemnation but says it is less conscious and more automatic than that. He has also compared it to running away from something dangerous, but adds that anything like actual flight is really impossible because repression deals with instinctual impulses rather than external objects. Yet it is, he says, in a manner of speaking, midway between condemnation and flight. From the side of consciousness, therefore, repression appears as a *rejection*. From the side of the Unconscious, however, repression appears as an *attraction*—an attraction between those

[9] *Ibid.*, p. 400.

things which already lie under repression in the Unconscious and those which are now being rejected from consciousness. "Probably the trend towards repression would fail in its purpose . . . if there were not something previously repressed ready to receive what is repelled by the conscious."[10]

Repression does not depend simply on the will to forget. It is a genuinely unconscious process in which the magnetic pull from the Unconscious is probably more important than the push of conscious rejection. Freud points out that the repressed, emotionally charged idea, far from being extinguished, "develops with less interference and more profusely. . . . It proliferates in the dark, as it were, and takes on extreme forms of expression, which when they are translated and presented to the neurotic are not only bound to seem alien to him, but frighten him by giving him the picture of an extraordinary and dangerous strength of instinct."[11] Freud notes too, as Janet did when discussing the buried memories of Irène, that the repressed ideas are more easily brought back into consciousness the more remote they appear to be from the central repressed idea to which they are connected. Freud never lets us forget that repression involves the expenditure of energy.

> The process of repression is not to be regarded as an event which takes place *once*, the results of which are permanent, as when some living thing has been killed and from that time onward is dead; repression demands a persistent expenditure of force, and if this were to cease the success of the repression would be jeopardized, so that a fresh act of repression would be necessary. We may suppose that the repressed exercises a continuous pressure in the direction of the conscious, so that this pressure must be balanced by an unceasing counter-pressure. Thus the maintenance of a repression involves an uninterrupted expenditure of force, while its removal results in a saving from an economic point of view.[12]

Repression is a protective measure undertaken against the instincts and their representatives, the cathected ideas. But it is also brought into play against the emotions which accompany the working of instincts. These emotions do not necessarily accompany the cathected ideas. The sexual instinct might, therefore, be analyzed into (1) an urge toward sexual activity, (2) ideas of sexual activity

---

[10] Freud (1953-   ), Vol. 14, p. 148, in his 1915 essay "Repression." Used by permission of the Hogarth Press Ltd. (Chatto and Windus).
[11] *Ibid.*, p. 149.   [12] *Ibid.*, p. 151.

and the sexual object, and (3) sexual emotion. Any or all of these may come under repression, together or separately. It could thus happen that a person might be unaware of a sexual impulse or of sexualized ideas and yet be flooded by sexual emotion. If he is unaware of the sexual nature of his impulse or ideas, the emotion also might not be recognized as sexual but as elation or even as anxiety. In the same way, if the repression fell more heavily on the impulse and the emotion, there might occur various ideas with sexual content although the person who experienced them might be unaware of their connection with any strong impulse or significant emotion in himself. It is harder to conceive of a situation in which the naked impulse would appear unaccompanied by either ideas or emotions of appropriate kind. Perhaps we should think of the instinctive urges as irretrievably unconscious.

Writers other than Freud have attempted to deal with the phenomena of personality division by speaking of a primary and secondary consciousness, or even of several co-conscious systems, where Freud would speak of repression and the Unconscious. He thinks that the most weighty argument against such a point of view is that "analytic investigation reveals some of these latent processes as having characteristics and peculiarities which seem alien to us, or even incredible, and which run directly counter to the attributes of consciousness with which we are familiar."[13] Among these "alien" and "incredible" peculiarities of the Unconscious are the following: (1) The different wish impulses which make up the core of the Unconscious exist side by side without discord; they are independent and yet nonconflicting, no matter how opposed their aims may appear to us when they obtrude into consciousness. Thus sexual and destructive urges may exist together and produce some grotesque compromise in conscious action like sadism. (2) Everything in the Unconscious is positive, certain, assertive; denial and doubt occur only in consciousness. (3) Energy flows freely about in the Unconscious, so that the cathexis which belonged originally to one idea may be drained off into another with the result that the second idea acquires more power as the first is weakened, as appears in dreams where displacement and condensation have been at work on the latent dream thoughts. In contrast to this situation, conscious logic makes strenuous efforts to preserve the identity of each idea; note, for example, the concern of all strict sciences for sharp definitions, unambiguous formulae, clear-cut technical terminology.

[13] *Ibid.*, p. 170, in his 1915 essay "The unconscious."

(4) The Unconscious is timeless, not dealing in temporal relationships nor affected by the passage of time. (5) While consciousness is always taking the external world into account, is always trying to be "realistic," the Unconscious ignores the external world except insofar as it imposes pain or provides pleasure; otherwise, it is self-regulated, as if the external world did not exist.

Because he sees the Unconscious as having distinctive properties different from those usually associated with rational, conscious thinking, and because he sees it as having a great deal of independence, Freud recognizes it as constituting a reality, a psychic reality, in opposition to the more usually recognized reality of the external world. Perhaps it would be more accurate to say that he does so at times. Often enough he speaks as if there were only one "reality," the reality of the external world open to the senses. For example, we find him saying in a 1916 essay (and this represents his most customary attitude) that reality is what we can turn away from:

A perception which is made to disappear by an action is recognized as external, as reality; where such an action makes no difference, the perception originates within the subject's own body—it is not real.[14]

In a later essay (1923), however, he acknowledges so much sympathy for medieval demon theory that he seems to be putting the Unconscious on at least as high a plane of reality as the demons were once put.[15]

Ego, id, and superego

Why is anything repressed? Because it is painful to the Ego. But if by Ego we mean simply consciousness, why should anything be painful to it? Consciousness, one might suppose, would simply delight in consciousness. Long ago the Roman poet remarked how pleasant it was to lie on the top of a cliff and watch two navies locked in mortal combat on the sea below. Scientists like Freud or Pasteur surely derive intellectual satisfaction from studying the ugliest, most frightful things. Why should the Ego object to a memory or an impulse? The answer must be, of course, that the Ego is not simply consciousness. Nor is the Unconscious, perhaps,

[14] *Ibid.*, p. 232, in his 1916 essay "Metapsychological supplement to the theory of dreams."
[15] Freud (1959), "A neurosis of demoniacal possession in the seventeenth century." Used by permission of Basic Books, Inc.

composed entirely of instincts and what has been repressed. Perhaps consciousness and unconsciousness are terms which cut across more significant divisions of the human personality. Freud, at any rate, developed another analysis of personality structure which goes beyond the consciousness-unconsciousness distinction. He added the concepts of Ego, Id, and Superego.

The Ego is that which perceives both the external world and the internal. But it also discriminates between what is good for it and what is bad. It is often represented by Freud as caught in a struggle between external reality, the demands of the Superego, and the impulses of the Id. It is thus an arbiter and mediator, and it attempts to govern in the midst of these contending forces. It not only perceives; it struggles to survive so that it may continue to perceive. In this struggle its first advantage is just exactly that it does perceive; it knows its situation more or less, can foresee the consequences of this and that, and so can make fairly intelligent decisions. Ordinarily, it has the second advantage of being in control of the motor apparatus of the body. It can set the body in motion and steer it about in the external world. This is certainly useful when it comes to dealing with the dangers and opportunities offered by the external world; but mobility of the body is only partly useful when dealing with the realities of the inner world—memories, impulses, regrets, guilt, fear. Often, for example, environment and impulse are in conflict. One may develop thirst in a perfectly dry desert; one may experience insistent sexual desire when there is no sexual mate obtainable; and so on. That is to say, the internal requirements develop whether or not the external situation can satisfy them; and if the external situation fails to provide adequate means to satisfaction, in spite of the mobility of the body, the Ego finds itself in the intolerable position of yearning for what it cannot have. Repression is a device which removes the troubling impulse from consciousness. Sometimes an unfulfilled desire, instead of disappearing, compensates for the deficiency in the environment by provoking hallucination. Saint-Exupéry, in *Wind, Sand, and Stars,* tells how insistent were the sight and sound of water in the desert when he and his companion were nearly dead from thirst; they had to learn to ignore these hallucinations to spare their strength. Their desire for rescue also expressed itself in hallucinations; they would see caravans in the distance and run to hail them; these, too, they had to ignore, and finally they almost missed a real caravan because they mistook it for another hallucination. It is this primitive insistence on the fulfillment of desire which Freud, of course, has made the foundation of his dream-theory.

Repression is perhaps never set in motion simply by a deficiency in the environment. The environmental deficiency is already the equivalent of repression, one might say: the impulse in question is already checked almost as much as it can be if the environment deprives it of an appropriate object. True, and yet it is not environmental lack of opportunity which Freud emphasizes in trying to explain repression. What he emphasizes is something more like moral prohibition. Repression operates where some kind of internal rule or value *forbids* the Ego to enjoy what the mere external circumstances would allow. As he admits, the principle which he is thus calling into play is what has been known for ages as conscience. He, however, does not rest content with that much-used word; he wants us to know that what he is referring to is concrete rather than abstract and largely acquired by experience rather than inborn. The "moral law within" which Kant compared with the starry heavens as a manifestation of divine order and grandeur seems to Freud too often disorderly, savage, petty, and stupid to bear the comparison. In general, he thinks of it as built up more or less at random out of childhood experiences with the parents (or their equivalents) in their role as omnipotent, omniscient authorities. These authority figures are *introjected,* and they take up permanent residence in the Unconscious, where they may become even more threatening, gigantic, heroic, ideal, and so on, than they ever were in life, even in the eyes of the little child. This unconscious system of introjected authority-figures is what Freud calls the Superego, thereby distinguishing it from conscience in the usual abstract sense and indicating that it stands *over* (*super*) the Ego.

Freud tells us that he was led to his conception of the Superego by way of some interesting clinical observations which impressed him so much that he thought they must have their root in some kind of important psychic reality. He writes concerning certain psychotics:

> They complain to us that they suffer continually, and in their most intimate actions, from the observation of unknown powers or persons, and they have hallucinations in which they hear these persons announcing the results of their observations: "now he is going to say this, now he is dressing himself to go out," and so on. Such observation is not the same thing as persecution, but it is not far removed from it. It

implies that these persons distrust the patient, and expect to catch him doing something that is forbidden and for which he will be punished. How would it be if these mad people were right, if we all of us had an observing function in our egos threatening us with punishment, which, in their case, had merely become sharply separated from the ego and had been mistakenly projected into external reality?[16]

Pursuing this line of thought, he notes that little children are quite amoral and that their instinctive pleasure-seeking is restrained, if at all, by the external power of parental authority. But this is a different sort of thing, be it observed, from the restraint exercised by a deficient environment; in fact, the denial of instinctual satisfaction by the parents is saturated with the question, "Am I (the child) worthy of their love?" The physical environment, no matter how harsh, scarcely raises the question of personal worth; but the parents do. "The influence of the parents dominates the child by granting proofs of affection and by threats of punishment, which, to the child, mean loss of love, and which must also be feared on their own account."[17] When this question of worthiness has established itself in the child, so that he asks the parents even in their absence whether they approve or disapprove of his behavior, the Superego has begun to form. Or rather, for the child at this age is no philosopher, he cannot escape from the parents at all: they are embedded in him. It is for the sake of the Superego that repression takes place, so that the beloved and powerful parents who are always present may not be offended.

We must notice, however, that the introjected parents are not very realistic duplicates of the originals. Sometimes they are over-idealized; more often, perhaps, they have an accentuated harshness. In these latter cases,

> the super-ego seems to have made a one-sided selection, and to have chosen only the harshness and severity of the parents, their preventive and punitive functions, while their loving care is not taken up and continued by it. If the parents have really ruled with a rod of iron, we can easily understand the child developing a severe super-ego, but, contrary to our expectations, experience shows that the super-ego may reflect the same relentless harshness even when the upbringing has been gentle and kind, and avoided threats and punishments as far as possible.[18]

[16] Freud (1933), p. 85. [17] Ibid., p. 89.
[18] Ibid., pp. 89 f.

But how odd all this is! Here we have been supposing, no doubt, that if parents are only loving and gentle toward their children, the children will grow up to be sweet and happy. It goes against reason to suppose that it could be otherwise. Yet here is Freud telling us (and surely it is an inconvenient fact for him, too) that people may grow up with very severe, punishing Superegos though their parents have shown them the maximum of loving consideration. And this sounds like a complete contradiction, because the Superego is constructed in the image of the parents! We must understand, of course, that the introjection process is continually adding new elements to the parental nucleus—other influential adults and older friends whose love is important or who represent attractive ideals, including people we read about in books and the newspapers and see in movies and so on. Still, the explanation can hardly lie here, especially since the parental nucleus is considered by Freud to be the primary component, outweighing all others.

Frankly, we are up against a major puzzle. In order to understand Freud's solution it is necessary to look further into his theory of the instincts. But hold the puzzle firmly in mind. We shall come back to it in a moment.

The reigning principle in that part of the Unconscious which contains the instincts, and which Freud distinguishes from the rest of the Unconscious by calling it the Id, is the pleasure-principle. The instincts always strive for satisfaction, and their satisfaction *is* pleasure. The Id is chaotic and completely devoid of morality; it is also completely indifferent to reality; and every instinct in it is clamoring for satisfaction greedily, regardless of reality, morality, or apparent contradictions between the several instinctive aims. Freud at first was chiefly aware of the sexual strivings of the Id; but later he took more and more seriously the notion that there were inborn destructive impulses as well as sexual ones. Somewhat grandly he lumped together the sexual strivings under the term Eros (love) and the destructive ones under the term Thanatos (death). Eros and Thanatos have no trouble in dwelling together in the Id, for the Id knows nothing at all of opposition or contradiction, and the instincts are, according to Freud, immortal. It is only when they are directed on the same external object that they seem to clash. When in fact they do this, the Ego may become aware of that appalling conjunction. Speaking quite concretely, a child may find himself hating and attacking the very mother or father whom he so tenderly loves. The intensity of the hatred, the violence of the attack, may have a truly murderous quality; and this may happen in very young children, and in fact it quite commonly does. Thanatos lashes out without regard for Eros.

Davidson and Fay in their fascinating book, *Phantasy in Childhood,* have described in some detail the very mixed display of loving and hostile behavior in young children. There was a period in the life of Dinah, for instance, when she was constantly interfering with her mother's activities; at the same time, she felt that her mother was doing the same to her. She was sometimes furious with her mother. She would express this fury by look and gesture and wishful commands, like

> 'You can go away in an aeroplane if you like.' . . . At times she would attack her without apparent provocation, sometimes in earnest but usually in play, pulling her hair, pinching her, making movements as if to gouge out her eyes, slapping her face, and biting her arms, while when prevented from biting she would often bang her own head in frustration.[19]

Correlated with this aggressive behavior by Dinah were various fantasies of being threatened or injured by her mother; and, beyond that, other fantasies of attack or robbery or destruction involving strangers. Mixed in with all this were moments of great concern for her mother's welfare and tearful reconciliations with her. The significance of Dinah's behavior for our present discussion is that it appears to unroll before our eyes the process by which the Superego may acquire some of its ferocity: Dinah's own aggressiveness against her mother returns upon herself and is added to the mother-image, making her seem more threatening and punishing, on the principle of the talion—"an eye for an eye an a tooth for a tooth." The Superego stores up charges of aggression originating in one's own Id in addition to those which are introjected directly from others.

Now, Dinah's hostile behavior toward her mother was not unmotivated, according to Davidson and Fay. Already by the middle of her third year, and perhaps earlier, she had been involved in the pattern of rivalry and sexual attraction which Freud has labeled the Oedipus complex. Put very simply and crudely (it is only by reading the Davidson and Fay account that the true complexity of the case can be appreciated), Dinah was at war with her mother because she wanted to take her place as her father's only beloved

[19] Davidson and Fay (1952), p. 146.

and have children by him. Her hostility was, in part, the jealous hostility of a sexual rival. But the obstacles to her sexual ambition were so built into the whole situation that she was bound to experience serious frustration. She could not have babies really, she was too young; she could not dispense with her mother—she loved and needed her; she was not entirely satisfied with her father anyhow; and there were all kinds of mysteries and terrors associated with sex to bring her to a standstill, little girl that she was. She was doomed to defeat. What remains for her? Wrath. Wrath against her mother first, and herself second. The Superego grows in severity in consequence.

We thus arrive at Freud's solution of the puzzle. Freud writes:

> When first the super-ego is set up there is no doubt that that function is endowed with that part of the child's aggressiveness against its parents for which it can find no discharge outwards on account of its love-fixation and external difficulties; and, for this reason, the severity of the super-ego need not correspond to the severity of its upbringing.[20]

Though both Ego and Superego owe their development in part to the environment, they are always in contact with the Id; and when Freud speculates upon their evolutionary origin, he concludes that they too are expressions of the Id. The newborn baby is nearly all Id, with only the rudiments of an Ego and no Superego at all. Or perhaps there is some initial trace of a Superego, passed on through the germ plasm from ancient times; for Freud holds to the Lamarckian hypothesis that racial experiences may have been powerful enough to influence the course of evolution biologically. The rudiments of the Ego are found in the sensory and motor equipment with which the infant is born—equipment which began to be developed millions of years ago when the primitive unicellular ancestor of the race first acquired a sensory region, a primitive eyespot, for example, differentiated out of the hitherto undifferentiated Id and serving to protect the instinct-loaded cell by discriminating between environmental conditions more or less favorable for its survival. This speculative history may account for the shape of the accompanying diagram by which Freud tries to picture the relationships between Ego, Id, and Superego; because, as you see, it somewhat resembles an eye, especially at the upper end where the perceptual-conscious aspect of the Ego makes contact with the environment. At the Id end the diagram is open, to suggest that

[20] Freud (1933), p. 150.

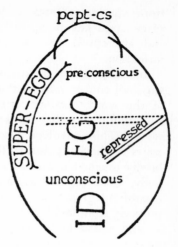

pcpt-cs

pre·conscious

SUPER-EGO

EGO

repressed

unconscious

ID

18 *Freud's diagram of the psychic apparatus suggests a primitive unicellular organism shaped like an eye. (From Freud, 1933)*

the Id is of unlimited extent. Within the diagram Superego and Ego are shown as having commerce with each other and with the Id through breaks in the boundaries, and the position of the dotted horizontal lines indicates that they share in the unconsciousness of the Id. Only a small part of the Ego is fully conscious; most of the region rising above the Unconscious has merely a glimmering of consciousness, as shown by the area labeled "pre-conscious" in which dreams and other manifestations of unconscious activity float about with vague and wavering outlines like fish in murky water.

Id and environment; character

For psychoanalysis as postulated by Freud, personality is considered to be the total organization of Id, Ego, and Superego in relationship to the surrounding world. Personality varies from person to person, however, depending on all the factors named, and it is a major task of theoretical psychoanalysis to explain how the variation happens. In an effort to simplify the task we may say that individual distinctiveness or character is a product of the relations existing between the Id and the environment. Just as the Ego and the Superego may be regarded as modifications of the Id going back into racial history, so other modifications peculiar to each individual may be found. These arise from innate differences in the relative strength of the various instincts making up the Id, from varying accents which experiences with the environment place upon key points in development, and from the repressions and aftereffects of repression, such as projection and reaction-formation.

In order to keep the discussion as simple and concrete as possible, we shall concentrate on the sexual instincts. Notice that the plural of the word "instinct" has been used. It is a cardinal point in Freudian theory that sex is not a single instinct, but a compound of several. Those involved in sex are intimately related to the erogenous zones of the body and to the stages of psychosexual development, briefly touched upon in Chapter 3. Freud believed that the whole body, both on the surface and internally, was erogenous, i.e., capable of giving rise to sexual tension and sexual pleasure when properly stimulated; but he singled out certain regions as especially so and called these "erogenous zones." His views are expounded most succinctly and comprehensively in his "Three Essays on the Theory of Sexuality," a work which stands next to his book on dream interpretation as an influential original production.[21]

Freud tells us that sexuality in humans is present from infancy on, developing, according to an inborn plan, in two great waves separated by a latency period extending from about the age of five years to puberty. Already in the first five years the erogenous zones are manifested by their special yield of sexual excitement; or, to put it in another way, the instincts corresponding to these zones are active. Aside from the fact that reproduction is impossible, the chief difference between the sexual activity of this early period and the adult sexuality which is generally destined to follow is that it has not been organized under the dominance of the genital zone. The mouth, the anus, the urethra, and the penis or clitoris are points of sexual interest, but the sexual aim of intercourse is absent. Stimulation of these regions produces pleasure, and the child seeks out opportunities for such stimulation (that is, he satisfies the unfused instincts), but he does not achieve and cannot completely understand adult sexual union. Freud marks off a succession of periods within this general pregenital period and labels them by the zone of dominant sexual interest—oral, anal, phallic. The final stage, which theoretically should be achieved after puberty, he labels the genital. (See Chapter 3 for a summary of the developmental scheme.)

Now, suppose that one of these pregenital periods were continued into adulthood, either because the environment or the con-

[21] Freud (1953-   ), Vol. 7, pp. 123-245. First published in 1905.

stitution of the individual prevented further development: the result would be a particular character type. Something like this does in fact occur, according to Freud, in the case of those individuals who are classed as sexual perverts. More common are those individuals for whom one of the pregenital instincts has received a heavy accent, has been *fixated* as Freud says, so that the adult sex life takes on a certain oddity. There are people, for example, who are so excited by kissing that nothing further is wanted or needed of the sexual partner. In the Freudian view this is an imperfection in the sexual organization; for the proper role of the pregenital instincts in adult sexuality, according to him, is to prepare the way for sexual intercourse of the normal kind, to serve as a part of the foreplay of lovemaking, but not as the final aim. Various imperfect forms of personality development, then, can be identified according to which pregenital fixation has taken place and to what degree.

Another factor closely related to fixation must be recognized. Sexual development in an individual may have proceeded more or less normally, but difficulty in acquiring a heterosexual mate may have forced him (or her) back on some earlier stage of development and made it permanent. Here we are dealing with *regression*.

Again, we may have the case where a favored kind of sexual behavior has been repressed. Since the repressed urge does not die away, it may be necessary for the individual to reinforce the repression by a *reaction-formation*. For example, he may have a tendency to oral sexuality which is intolerable to the Superego and hence repressed. The individual's defenses may extend far beyond a mere abstinence to a positive opposition to all kinds of oral activities—smoking, drinking from bottles, chewing gum, eating particular kinds of food (e.g., milk because reminiscent of nursing or sausages because reminiscent of the penis), etc.—which become unconscious symbols in some fashion of the repressed activity. Or by the process of *projection* he may charge others with having the forbidden urge which threatens to break through his repression and overwhelm him.

In Freud's eyes a process like the latter, by the time it has passed through the various structures of the personality, may produce some very strange results. It is his thesis, for instance, that paranoia, which is typically marked by delusions of persecution, is based upon repressed homosexuality, in which paranoiac projection leads to regarding the loved person as the persecutor. An uncomplicated projection of repressed homosexuality would result simply in re-

garding the other person as a homosexual; but the repressed homosexual impulse in the paranoiac is so powerful that the attribution
of homosexuality to another person makes that person an object of
fear and the fear makes him (or her) into an enemy and a persecutor
who must be hated. The paranoiac therefore takes on a particular
character: he (or she) is a person stamped with the traits of
suspiciousness, irritability, hostility. Freud's "Psycho-Analytic Notes
on an Autobiographical Account of a Case of Paranoia (Dementia
Paranoides)"[22] gives a full and complex analysis of such a case.

If we follow through these lines of reasoning, we see that we
might base an elaborate taxonomy of "character types" on the
scheme of psychosexual stages. Freud made some suggestions in
that direction, and several other psychoanalysts have followed them
up, particularly Karl Abraham, some of whose views will be briefly
summarized here.[23] I simply expound these views, leaving it to
the reader to criticize them.

Abraham agrees with Freud that three outstanding traits of the
anal character are orderliness, stinginess, and obstinacy. But he
stresses the ambivalence of anal characters and notes that the contrary of these traits may exist alongside of them, so that the total
picture may be quite complex. On the whole, however, a kind of
nonadaptability or rigidity marks the anal character; he may alternate somewhat jerkily between order and disorder, stinginess
and reckless spending, obstinacy and spinelessness. It is the emphasis on order and control which tends to override the other,
opposite traits; and so we find among anal characters a good many
who are fond of statistics and schedules, even though they may not
make effective use of either. Money is likely to play an important
role. Since, according to the Freudian formula, feces equals money
in the language of the Unconscious, the *childhood attitude* toward
the bowel and its product (see Chapter 3) is carried over to financial
matters. Miserly stinginess is the equivalent of constipation; controlling money is like *controlling defecation*. Holding on to things
in general is characteristic. There are people who cannot part with
possessions, no matter how useless: they pile them up until perhaps
the accumulation becomes unbearably great, and then they have a
big housecleaning. This pattern of behavior, which is certainly fairly
common, gratifies the same desires felt in childhood (and later, for
that matter) and expressed by retention and expulsion of the con-

[22] *Ibid.*, Vol. 12, pp. 8-82. First published in 1911.
[23] Abraham (1949), pp. 370-417. First published in 1927.

tents of the lower bowel. The emphasis on retention is illustrated by Abraham's "rich banker who again and again impressed on his children that they should retain the contents of the bowels as long as possible, in order to get the benefit of every bit of the expensive food they ate."[24] Most of the traits mentioned are details which may vary from individual to individual of the anal type. The fundamental fact is that the anal character is one which remains fixed at a level of development which is deficient in altruism. In the technical language of Abraham, a child who has been forced too soon and severely into anal regularity and control will continue to rebel inwardly, though outwardly compliant; and "its libido will continue in a tenacious narcissistic fixation, and a permanent disturbance of the capacity to love will result."[25]

Abraham's treatment of the oral character is shorter. One reason for this is that, in his opinion, character traits are the result of repression of those pregenital elements which cannot be worked into adult sexual life, and since orality is more easily assimilated into adult sexuality than anality, there is less repressed material of an oral kind to be transformed (by sublimation and reaction-formation) into character traits. Besides this, the anal stage of development tends to take over remainders of the oral stage and work them over in anal terms. For example, oral retentiveness (holding food in the mouth) becomes anal retentiveness (holding back feces). In general, there seems to be greater sociability in oral character traits than in anal ones, but this is more apparent than real. Optimism and talkativeness are more characteristic, for instance; but the optimism is that of the spoiled darling rather than that of the benevolent philosopher, and the talkativeness may not be very sensitively adjusted to the needs of others. Furthermore, we must take into account the sucking and the biting stages of the oral period. The pleasanter characteristics are attached to the earlier stage. "People who have been gratified in the earliest stage are bright and sociable; those who are fixated at the oral-sadistic stage are hostile and malicious."[26] Fixation at these stages may result either from overindulgence or from underindulgence, from too much or too little gratification at the breast. A trait like optimism, of course, would point to indulgence rather than deprivation.

The genital character has overcome the *narcissism* and ambivalence which stigmatize the oral and anal traits. Put in positive terms, the genital character has a capacity for affectionate love

[24] *Ibid.*, p. 383. [25] *Ibid.*, p. 374. [26] *Ibid.*, p. 403.

which makes other people valuable to him. "We are led to the conclusion," writes Abraham,

> that the definitive character developed in each individual is dependent upon the history of his Oedipus complex, and particularly on the capacity he has developed for transferring his friendly feelings on to other people or on to his whole environment. If he has failed in this, if he has not succeeded in sufficiently developing his social feelings, a marked disturbance of his character will be the direct consequence.[27]

One of the gravest of these disturbances is mere absence of affection from the sexual impulses. Sexual activity which is marked by indifference (or cruelty) toward the sexual partner is far from the ideal which Abraham has in mind, and it clearly cannot enrich one's other social relations. The genital character is independent without being selfish; he values other people and wishes to help them; he is not moved by strange, irrational impulses, or held in check by crippling inhibitions; in short, he is harmonious, highly conscious, and able to give and receive love freely. He is not to be confused with the man who devotes his life to making and bragging about sexual conquests. This is the phallic type, one who has not successfully lived through the Oedipus complex and whose capacity for love is still imperfect. Abraham's analysis is supposed to apply to women as well as to men, of course.

The expansiveness of Freudian theory

Freud usually denied that he had any interest in constructing a general world view. We cannot, however, take him at his word. It is true that he always preferred to base his thoughts on some particular fact, and that he had a great gift for teasing apart the interweaving strands of ideas and motives leading up to particular events in individual human behavior, but he certainly did not rest content with the clinical study of individuals or with developing special hypotheses about hysterical symptoms. He ranged far and wide, and dealt very boldly with art and literature, the origin of society and social institutions, the history of the Jews, contemporary civilization, war, and religion. He did in fact construct a general world view, extending from the individual to the cosmos—a view which emphasized the power of the irrational forces of the Id and

[27] *Ibid.*, p. 410.

the illusory character of much that human beings have considered most precious and real.

At the individual level, Freud brought into question the status of the conscious self and its perceptions. The Ego in his system is a weak surface phenomenon derived from the Id as the result of its collisions with the external world. The Ego's chief function is to perceive, and secondly to adjust between, the external world and the Id. Primarily it is an instrument of the Id. As such, it is not concerned about reality for its own sake but only for the sake of the Id and its imperious demands. The Ego's perceptions of the world around, therefore, are subject to distortion, and may in fact be no better than hallucinations, i.e., wish-fulfilling dreams produced by instinctual cravings. The Ego's power to act in terms of the little valid perception it may have is extremely limited; it does not have free will. It is dominated by the Id during its existence and wholly disappears at death. Freud's doctrine humbles the self-conscious "I" into a virtual non-entity, the sport of impersonal forces which it can only vaguely know, easily deluded and doomed to suffering and extinction.

At the level of society and its institutions, Freud emphasized the irrationality and confusion of human life. The family is a sexual organization which carries within itself the seeds of every kind of pathology. Love between men and women is an illusion based on the powerful sexual instincts, and friendship between men or between women is a pale form of homosexuality. Religion is a mass neurosis, marked by obsessional ritualism, morbid defense mechanisms, hallucinations and delusions (including an elaborate historical myth with little or no foundation in historical fact), and a prevailing sense of guilt deriving from actual father-murder in the far prehistoric past and fantasied father-murder in the present. War and the peacetime discontents of civilization reveal the essential barbarity of human nature.[28]

[28] I here sum up my general impressions from much reading of Freud, but in this paragraph I have particularly in mind *Totem and Taboo, The Future of an Illusion, Thoughts for the Times on War and Death, Civilization and its Discontents, Moses and Monotheism,* and numerous passages in which love and friendship and affection within the family are rather bluntly treated as etiolated forms of sex. The titles mentioned can be obtained in various editions, some in paperback, and will eventually all appear in the projected 24 volumes of *The Standard Edition of the Complete Psychological Works of Sigmund Freud,* published by the Hogarth Press.

At the level of the cosmos, Freud erected the forces of the Id into universal principles. A continual, never-ending struggle is going on between Eros and Thanatos, the forces of attraction and repulsion, lust and hate, building up and tearing down. The seething conflict within the neurotic or psychotic is a true image of the universe. It is powerful and irrational and eternal, and no God controls it.

I have drawn the outlines of the Freudian *Weltanschauung* in broad, dark, unqualified strokes. It is comprehensive, and it is profoundly pessimistic. In detail, here and there, it may not look so dark, but I do not believe that I have misrepresented it. At the same time, I hasten to add that in many ways Freud himself contradicted his own system. He was never tired of talking about the quiet voice of reason and the value of science and about the necessity of making the Unconscious conscious, and he was endlessly patient in dealing with human misery. That is to say, he acted as if he believed in truth and love, though there was nothing in his system to explain how they could have arisen in such strength and purity.

Science is not quite the impersonal thing that it has sometimes been made out to be, and I believe that it may help the student to understand even some of the technical features of psychoanalysis if we end this chapter on a biographical note. It is the contradiction between Freud and his pessimistic philosophy which I should like to illuminate. His biographer, Ernest Jones, has referred to it in these words:

> In his mature years there was a curious contrast between Freud's personal attitude toward individual people and his impersonal judgment of them in mass. The former was an expression of the optimistic and benevolent qualities in his personality. Unless he had good reasons to the contrary beforehand he would meet a newcomer with the friendly expectation of his being an agreeable and decent person; in this he was of course sometimes disappointed. But when he spoke of people in general he would enunciate much harsher judgments; with rare exceptions they were riff-raff with little good in them.[29]

Jones perhaps finds reasons for this contradiction in Freud's own Oedipus complex and childhood traumata, but it is difficult to leave it at that; for if the ambitious structure of psychoanalysis is in any sense a science, as certainly Freud thought it was, it must

[29] Jones (1953-57), Vol. 3, p. 335. Used by permission of Basic Books, Inc.

have some basis in true perception and true reason, and it cannot be accepted as even approximate scientific truth if it is the pathological extrusion of the author's own sufferings. The contrast which Jones points out is that between Freud vis-à-vis an individual person and Freud vis-à-vis mankind in the mass. Freud's handling of individual clinical problems has the quality of an individual relationship, whereas his *Weltanschauung* has the quality of his attitude toward Man. There is more sensitivity and perhaps more truth in the former than in the latter. Such is my own judgment.

An exchange of letters between Freud and Oskar Pfister may help clarify matters further. Pfister was a Swiss Protestant pastor who cultivated Freud's friendship from an early date and introduced many of the Freudian ideas, though with modifications of his own, into Switzerland and into his own pastoral work. It is a tribute to both men that in spite of fundamental differences in their beliefs and in spite of Pfister's free handling of Freud's ideas, there was never any rift between them. Freud was not always so tolerant of revisionists, as the troubled history of the psychoanalytic movement shows. The bond with Pfister must have been strong and significant. Possibly it was because both men, in their different way, valued the love and truth which the philosophical orientation of one of them seemed to deny. Here are a pair of their letters:

FROM FREUD TO PFISTER, OCTOBER 9, 1918

I have just read your little book and quite believe you when you say that you wrote it gladly. I rejoice in its warmth. It displays all the fine attributes we value in you: your enthusiasm, your love for truth and for humanity, the courageous way in which you profess your opinions, your understanding and also—your optimism. It will without doubt render our cause good service. I mention this practical point, although, as you know, I don't attach much value to it.

Now, praise is always short; strictures have to take longer. I am dissatisfied with one point: your contradicting my sexual theory and my ethics. I grant you the latter; ethics is far from my interest and you are a pastor. I don't cudgel my brains much about good and evil, but I have not found much "good" in the average human being. Most of them are in my experience riff-raff, whether they loudly proclaim this or that ethical doctrine or none at all. That you cannot say out loud, perhaps not even think it, although your experience of life could hardly have been different from mine. If we must speak of ethics I admit to having a high ideal, from which most people I know sadly deviate.

But when it comes to the sexual theory whatever makes you dispute the resolving of the sexual instinct into partial instincts to which our analysis compels us every day? Your contrary arguments are really not strong. Don't you see that the multiplicity of instincts goes back to the multiplicity of erotogenic organs? Fundamentally they all strive to find some expression in the future organism. And has the fact that all organs have combined into a living unity and that they influence, sustain and inhibit one another—even being dependent on one another in their development—prevented anatomy from studying and describing them separately; or prevented therapy from attacking an individual organ which has become the main seat of a pathological process? It is possible that internal therapy often forgets all this correlation of the organs; psychoanalysis is concerned with keeping in mind the inter-relation of instinctual life beyond the distinction between the partial instincts. In science one has first to take things apart and then put them together. It seems to me that you want to make a synthesis without a previous analysis (in psycho-analytic technique there is no need for any special synthetic work; the individual himself sees to that better than we could).

That holds good for all instincts in so far as we can separate them. In your book you have not done full justice to the sexual instincts. You have nowhere said that these really differ from others in having a more intimate connection with, and a greater significance for—*not mental life in general, and this is what matters, the pathogenesis of neuroses*. This comes from their conservative nature, their intimate connection with the unconscious and with the pleasure-principle, and further the peculiarities of their development into a cultural norm.

From a therapeutic point of view I can only envy your opportunity of bringing about sublimation into religion. But the beauty of religion assuredly has no place in psycho-analysis. Naturally our paths in therapy diverge there, and it can stay at that. Quite by the way, how comes it that none of the godly ever devised psychoanalysis and that one had to wait for a godless Jew?

FROM PFISTER TO FREUD, OCTOBER 29, 1918

As to your question why none of the godly discovered psychoanalysis, but only a godless Jew. Well, because piety is not the same as the genius for discovering, and because the godly were for a great part not worthy to bring such an achievement to fruition. Moreover, in the first place you are not a Jew, which my boundless admiration for Amos, Isaiah, the author of Job and the Prophets makes me greatly regret, and in the second place you are not so godless, since he who lives for truth lives in God and he who fights for the freeing of love "dwelleth in God" (First Epistle of John, IV, 16). If you were to become aware of and experience your interpolation in the great universals which for me are as inevitable as the synthesis of the notes of a Beethoven symphony are to a musician I should say of you "There never was a better Christian."[30]

References for chapter 8

Abraham, K. (1949) *Selected papers*. Tr. by D. Bryan and A. Strachey. London: Hogarth.

Davidson, A., and Fay, J. (1952) *Phantasy in childhood*. London: Routledge & Kegan Paul.

Farber, L. H., and Fisher, C. (1943) An experimental approach to dream psychology through the use of hypnosis. *Psychoanalytic Quarterly*, 12, 202-16.

Freud, S. (1933) *New introductory lectures on psychoanalysis*. Tr. by W. J. H. Sprott. New York: Norton.

———— (1950) *The interpretation of dreams*. Tr. by A. A. Brill. New York: Modern Library.

———— (1953-) *The standard edition of the complete psychological works of Sigmund Freud*. London: Hogarth. Vols. 7, 12, 14.

———— (1959) *Collected papers*. New York: Basic Books. 5 vols., Vol. 4.

Jones, E. (1953-57) *The life and work of Sigmund Freud*. New York: Basic Books. 3 vols., Vols. 2, 3.

Saint-Exupéry, A. de (1939) *Wind, sand and stars*. Tr. by L. Galantière. New York: Reynal & Hitchcock.

[30] *Ibid.*, Vol. 2, pp. 457 f.

9

POST-FREUDIAN
DEVELOPMENTS

Preview *Freud's ideas have been examined and modified both outside and within the psychoanalytic tradition. Behaviorists have tried to test some of the Freudian hypotheses experimentally and have tried to encompass his phenomena within the stimulus-response framework, but Freud's concern with consciousness (and mental Unconscious) has always made for difficulties. Within the psychoanalytic tradition Jung enlarged the conception of the Unconscious with his speculations on the archetypes, and Fairbairn has attempted to resolve a contradiction in Freudian theory by laying much greater stress on endopsychic objects and object-relations in general. Boss, an existentialist who passed from Freud through Jung to his present position, has discarded the symbolism of both in favor of a strictly phenomenological evaluation of experience and insists* *that the self is always in a world of real objects and exists by relating to them, whether awake or asleep.*

The impact of Freudian thought is proved as much by the variety of reactions it has inspired as by the international spread of orthodox psychoanalysis. A recent book lists and describes thirty-six different psychotherapeutic systems which owe something vital to Freud.[1] It would be impossible in the space of a chapter to do justice to all these variations on the Freudian theme, plus others that would have to be included if our aim were encyclopedic rather than introductory; nor would it be appropriate to our concern here with general personality theory, since many of the variants focus on therapeutic procedure more than on the intrinsic nature of personality. This chapter will concentrate, instead, on four major developments: (1) the attempt to fuse behaviorism with Freudianism, (2) Jung's expansion of the concept of the Unconscious, (3) Fairbairn's modification of Freud's theory in the direction of greater emphasis on object-relations and endopsychic objects, and (4) Boss's existentialist treatment of dreaming.

Freud and behaviorism

American behaviorists have tended to approach psychoanalysis as basically a theory of learning which might be improved and rendered testable by experimental methods and thus brought into the province of objective science. Freud's mentalistic language and his attention to consciousness naturally strike behaviorists as major flaws.[2] Sears, whose behaviorism is relatively conciliatory, in his "Experimental Analysis of Psychoanalytic Phenomena" begins by lamenting Freud's mistake in basing his system on a conscious-Unconscious dichotomy, though he promptly admits in regard to

[1] Harper (1959).
[2] The following statement about behaviorism is from John B. Watson, founder of the school, in *Behaviorism* (New York: Norton, 1925), p. 3: "Before beginning our study of 'behaviorism' or 'behavioristic' psychology, it will be worth our while to take a few minutes to look at the conventional school of psychology that flourished before the advent of behaviorism in 1912—and that still flourishes. . . . Possibly the easiest way to bring out the contrast between the old psychology and the new is to say that all schools of psychology except that of behaviorism claim that *'consciousness' is the subject matter of psychology.* . . . Behaviorism claims that 'consciousness' is neither a definable nor a usable concept; that it is merely another word for the 'soul' of more ancient times."

such concepts as repression and projection that "descriptions of such processes . . . are clear while embedded in the structure of psychoanalysis but lose their definitive character when removed."[3] The problem for the behaviorist is that he must strip such terms of their connection with the "private events" of consciousness and the still more private events of the Unconscious and somehow translate them into the experimental operations which behaviorism depends on. Faulty as this translation admittedly must be, Sears himself has attempted it on several occasions.

In one of these attempts Sears did an experimental study of projection. His procedure was to get about a hundred fraternity men to rate themselves and their fraternity brothers on a 7-point scale as to stinginess, obstinacy, disorderliness, and bashfulness, and then to work out the correlations between these scores. Two major conclusions stated in the original report in 1936 were these: (1) "Projection was not operative in influencing the judgments of all subjects on any given trait; its occurrence was apparently confined to those who lacked insight." (2) "In the group of subjects who possessed insight a negative correlation was found between amount of trait possessed and amount attributed to others. This suggests the operation of a dynamic process, tentatively entitled *contrast-formation*, which has an effect opposite to that of projection on judgments about others' personality."[4]

In the 1944 study Sears continues to maintain that his 1936 experiment demonstrated projection in the noninsightful, but he makes no further reference to the counter dynamism of "contrast-formation" in insightful subjects. Yet this second principle is more strongly supported by the correlation coefficients in his 1936 paper than is the first. Perhaps Sears did not want to complicate his 1944 summary by bringing in this unexpected difference in result; on the other hand, he was willing to take note of something only a little less odd, namely, that in his experiment there was as much projection of "good" traits as of "bad" by the noninsightful subjects.

The Sears experiment on projection is not easy to follow and I have more than once wandered into error in trying to understand it, but I believe I am right in stating that his results would have been more provocative still if he had included one more set of correlations, to show the relationship between *self*-rating and rating of others. It is possible to infer this relationship by combining Sears's statements about the other relationships, and I have con-

[3] Sears (1944), p. 306. [4] Sears (1936), p. 161.

structed Table 15 in this fashion. Sears had three sets of data—self as rated by self, self as rated by others, and others as rated by self—data which are set forth as pluses and minuses in the three columns of Table 15.

Since Sears tells us that subjects were classified as insightful if their self-ratings agreed with the ratings of them by others, and non-insightful if they did not agree, we know that the pluses and minuses (above and below average ratings) of columns 1 and 2 must be as shown in the table. Furthermore, since he tells us that noninsightful subjects assigned to others the traits that others assigned to them (projection), whereas insightful subjects assigned to others traits opposite to or at least in the other direction from the traits others assigned to them (contrast-formation), we know that the pluses and minuses of column 3 must be as they are shown in the table. From this table there emerges a perfectly simple and uniform relationship between self and others—a negative correlation between self-rated-by-self (column 1) and others-rated-by-self (column 3); regardless of whether the self is classified as insightful or noninsightful, this relationship holds. Such a relationship is not to be explained by either projection or contrast-formation (as defined by Sears). At first, I thought that it might be a statistical artifact, as it could well have been if the method of rating had been the method of ranking; but since, in fact, the subjects used a 7-point-scale for each person rated, the result was not artificially built into the experiment. Yet there the relationship stands, and it seems to mean that people do not usually regard themselves as average in traits like stinginess, obstinacy, disorderliness, and bashfulness—but somewhat better *or* worse than their fellows. Should we erect a dynamic principle here, too? A drive toward personal uniqueness, perhaps?

From a single behavioristic experiment we seem to have arrived

Table 15
Scheme of the various relations in the Sears projection experiment

	self rated by self	self rated by others	others rated by self
lack of insight {	+	−	−
	−	+	+
insight {	+	+	−
	−	−	+

at a superabundance of dynamic principles. Should we accept them all, dismiss them all, or pick and choose as we please? At any rate, the experiment does not seem to be a decisive demonstration of projection as conceived by Freud. The Freudian dynamic concepts, such as projection, are so firmly rooted in his whole manner of thinking about human personality that they cannot really be tested apart from the total Freudian system, which, involving as it does both consciousness and the Unconscious, is beyond the reach of behavioristic experimentation.

Sears has recognized the problem and has stated that it is "doubtful whether the sheer testing of psychoanalytic theory is an appropriate task for experimental psychology."[5] On the other hand, he has recommended raiding psychoanalysis for any experimental leads it may happen to provide and then turning to "the laborious task of constructing a systematic psychology of personality, but a system based on behavioral rather than experiential data."[6] It is clear that Sears is recommending the complete abandonment of Freud's central concerns when he advises that the data of experience should be ignored.

Skinner, another behaviorist, has evaded the Freudian challenge much more cavalierly. He has neither performed experiments to test psychoanalytic theory nor confronted the kinds of problems with which Freud struggled in his Victorian consulting room, merely leveling a few pointed words at the whole mistaken enterprise. In one place he verbalizes the possibility that a whole series of behaviors such as reaction-formation, sublimation, fantasy, dreaming, displacement, etc., might result from a boy's being negatively reinforced for rivalry toward a brother, adding: "Such manifestations are simply the responses of a person who has had a particular history. They are neither symptoms nor the surreptitious expression of repressed wishes or impulses."[7] If human behavior and human suffering are as simple as Skinner makes them sound, then the real problem is why a man like Freud was so desperately wrong about it all. Presumably, Freud should not have been intrigued by the discovery that imagined seduction could play the same role in a hysteric's life as real seduction and should not have wasted hours reflecting on the fact that a man might have a severe and tyrannical conscience though his parents had brought him up most tenderly and lovingly. Perhaps the fundamental mistake was

[5] Sears (1944), p. 329.
[7] Skinner (1953), p. 378.

[6] *Ibid.*

to listen to patients at all, in the old-fashioned way of listening. Verbalizations, yes; meanings, no. Responses, yes; intentions, no. If you get caught up in sympathetic interaction with another human being, as Freud did with his patients, you may lose the cool rationality of a follower of La Mettrie and desert the neat stance of science. In sober truth, that danger is real.

DOLLARD AND MILLER   In a book dedicated to Freud and Pavlov, a determined effort has been made by Dollard and Miller to wed psychoanalysis and behavioristic learning theory.[8] They state that the four indispensable factors in a satisfactory learning theory are *drive, cue, response*, and *reinforcement*. These terms are given considerable latitude of meaning. Thus, they tell us that for *drive* we may, if we like, substitute *motivation* (which does not necessarily imply anything about physiological need, as *drive* usually does); for *cue* we may substitute *stimulus*, which has less the meaning of *sign*; for *response* we may substitute *act* or even *thought*; and for *reinforcement* we may substitute *reward*. Their most radical modification of ordinary S-R language is in the phrase "cue-producing responses," which they trace back to Hull. "Cue-producing responses" are those higher mental processes of thinking and imagining which are usually considered to be outside the behavioristic province, but which must be dealt with in some fashion if one is serious about coming to grips with Freud. The authors comment in a crucial footnote:

> This is a somewhat unorthodox extension of the common usage of the words "response" and "cue." The usefulness of this functional definition depends on the validity of two hypotheses: (1) that the laws governing the learning and performance of the internal processes involved in thought are the same as those governing external responses, such as speaking aloud; and (2) that differential responses can be attached to these internal processes, generalize to and from them, etc., in exactly the same way as they can to external cues.[9]

These are bold hypotheses, as Dollard and Miller well know; and one might wish that the whole book had been devoted to investigating them rather than based on the assumption that they are true. But the truth of these hypotheses is assumed, and the task which the authors set themselves is to show how learning theory can en-

[8] Dollard and Miller (1950). By permission from *Personality and Psychotherapy* by J. Dollard and N. E. Miller. Copyright, 1950. McGraw-Hill Book Company, Inc.
[9] *Ibid.*, p. 99.

compass the problems of neurosis and the Freudian concepts applied to neurosis.

How does learning take place? According to Dollard and Miller, it takes place when (to use the terms they prefer) a *drive* produces *responses* to a *cue* which are *reinforced; reinforcement* is any event which *reduces drive,* as when eating lessens hunger. This drive-reduction learning formula has been subjected to much criticism by learning theorists, but our concern here is not with the correctness of the learning theory but its application.

The neurotic personality, say Dollard and Miller, is the outcome of an unfortunate learning history which renders the victim mysteriously incapable of using and enjoying his or her capacities. "Though physically capable of attaining sex rewards, he is anesthetic; though capable of aggression, he is meek; though capable of affection, he is cold and unresponsive."[10] Dollard and Miller sum up the neurotic as confronted by a therapist as "a person who is miserable, stupid (in some ways), and who has symptoms."[11] The misery, they say, results from conflicting drives, the stupidity from repression and inadequate verbalization, the symptoms from imperfect attempts to deal with the unconscious conflicts. The symptoms, in fact, are habits which have been learned because they partially reduce the misery from which the neurotic suffers. The root of all is a bad education, as they explain in the following passage:

> An intense emotional conflict is the necessary basis for neurotic behavior. The conflict must further be unconscious. As a usual thing, such conflicts are produced only in childhood. How can it be that neurotic conflicts are engendered when there is no deliberate plan to do so? Society must force children to grow up, but it does not idealize neurosis and makes no formal provision in its system of training for the production of neurotic children. Indeed we deplore the neurotic and recognize him as a burden to himself and to others. How then does it happen? Our answer is that neurotic conflicts are taught by parents and learned by children.[12]

According to Dollard and Miller, every child starts life as the helpless victim of tumultuous drives and with thoroughly unhealthy cue-producing responses. They say, in fact, that all human beings begin as psychotics. In their words, the young child

[10] *Ibid.,* p. 12.   [11] *Ibid.*   [12] *Ibid.,* p. 127.

is urgently, hopelessly, planlessly impelled, living by moments in eternal pain and then suddenly finding itself bathed in endless bliss. The young child is necessarily disoriented, confused, deluded, and hallucinated— in short, has just those symptoms that we recognize as a psychosis in the adult. Infancy, indeed, may be viewed as a period of transitory psychosis.[13]

This picture is more terrifyingly chaotic, I believe, than any that Freud ever painted. For Freud the infant is impulsive, it is true, and experiences hallucinations; but the behavior is instinctively patterned and the hallucinations have a meaningful relation to instinctive strivings. The Dollard and Miller picture must be taken as an imaginative projection of the basic thesis of their learning theory, namely, that the origin point of all learning is some powerful, aimless drive. Logically, the infant, having not yet learned anything, is a perfect volcano of undirected, uncontrolled, and wildly seething drive-energy. The normal progress, then, would presumably be from infantile psychosis to childhood neurosis, representing imperfect learning, and then to adult normality, representing perfect learning —a condition in which every drive would be promptly reduced by some appropriate and habitual response. This, however, is not exactly the course of affairs which they sketch out.

Instead, they emphasize four critical learning situations: those concerned with feeding behavior, cleanliness, sex, and conflicts between anger and fear. The personality is built up out of the habits of responding learned particularly in these situations, and if the habits acquired are bad (i.e., not adequately drive-reducing) a neurotic personality is the result. Various particular symptoms (i.e., bad habits) are then reviewed from the angle of learning theory; and phobias, compulsions, hysterical paralysis, regression, displacement, delusions, hallucinations, projection, reaction-formation, alcoholism are all treated as phenomena coming under a few simple learning laws.

In order to handle the Freudian concept of the Unconscious within their framework, Dollard and Miller define it as primarily all that which has not been verbally labeled. In brief, the Unconscious is the unverbalized. Repression, in turn, is the process of removing verbal labels from whatever has previously reached or nearly reached the level of verbalization. They admit that repression is somewhat hard to understand behavioristically, "because we are

[13] *Ibid.*, p. 130.

not used to considering the stopping of thinking as a response. We cannot point to it and study it in the same way that we can examine overt responses."[14] They get around this difficulty by identifying thinking with talking. To stop talking is clearly a response, they state. They then proceed:

> According to our hypothesis, stopping thinking is a somewhat similar response. We do not know to what extent there is any mechanism for producing a generalized response of stopping thinking analogous to the way that clamping the jaws together and keeping the lips closed can stop all talking, but we do know at least that it is possible for a given thought to be crowded out by others.[15]

There is a bit of a *non sequitur* here, I think, but the trend of the argument is that some kind of nerve-muscle arrangement must exist which can stop thinking (i.e., silent verbalization) just as one exists for clamping the jaws shut to stop talking (i.e., audible verbalization). According to Dollard and Miller, punishment for talking (e.g., saying "nasty" words) arouses the drive of fear in the punished child, and keeping the mouth shut is learned because this response reduces the fear. In a similar way, repression (a kind of invisible keeping the mouth shut) is also learned. But the learning in this case is likely to be by way of generalization from the overt learning. In Dollard and Miller's words, they "expect the fears that are attached to saying forbidden words and announcing the intent to perform forbidden acts to generalize to thinking these words and thinking about performing these acts"[16] and thus spread over to the internal verbalization and, by activating the hidden mechanism of repression, eliminate it.

Dollard and Miller offer a diagram (see Figure 19) summing up their theory of neurosis. The arrows indicate the causal relations between the several factors, the heavier lines indicating the more important factors and relations.

Fear is the basic neurosis-producing drive. It may cause symptoms directly or by the roundabout path of repression and conflict leading to stupidity and misery. Misery, it should be noted, is defined parenthetically as "high drive." The symptoms are either direct, unlearned expressions of the fear or the misery, or they are learned responses—in either case serving to lessen the primitive drive of fear or the acquired drive of misery. The task of the therapist is to help the patient discover better ways to deal with his drives.

[14] *Ibid.*, p. 203.   [15] *Ibid.*   [16] *Ibid.*, p. 205.

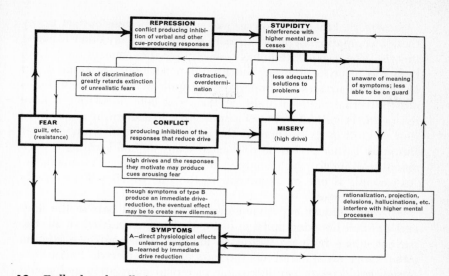

19 *Dollard and Miller's theory of neurosis is exhibited in this diagram. The heavy arrows indicate main causal sequences. (From J. Dollard and N. E. Miller,* Personality and Psychotherapy, *copyright 1950 by McGraw-Hill Book Co., Inc. Used by permission of the publisher.)*

Dollard and Miller recommend the technique of free association during therapy and the technique of suppression ("mental self-control") afterwards. To quote the last two sentences of the book:

> The therapist must be alert to the danger that his patient will continue to practice free association when it is time for action in the real world. He should first teach habits of free association to overcome repression, then later insist upon suppression and that real-world action which alone can reduce misery.[17]

The main contribution of the book is that it brings some of the facets of learning theory into approximate contact with some of the Freudian ideas and exerts a good deal of energy and ingenuity in the effort to make the two alien approaches fit together. But the strain is evident. There is a basic incompatibility between the Freudian attempt to enter into the intimacies of individual experience and to understand behavior as an expression of personal desires and the behavioristic attempt to strip man of private experience as far as possible and to understand his behavior as responses to stimuli under the control of habits.

[17] *Ibid.,* p. 459.

MOWRER   Probably Mowrer has endured the tensions set up by these incompatible approaches more acutely than any other learning theorist. The result for him has been a gradual movement away from both the behavioristic and the Freudian positions. At present, for example, he stresses the importance of guilt in neurotic suffering—not the verbalization of guilt, as the strict behaviorist might have it, nor the feeling of guilt, as a subjective Freudianism might have it—but guilt in its essence, as the awareness of real wrongdoing.[18] But at an earlier period he conducted many animal learning experiments relevant to psychoanalytic concepts, or at least meant to be. An example is one on regression in the rat, which will be briefly summarized here.

Mowrer used an experimental cage with metal bars in the floor and a circuit-breaking pedal at one end. The bars carried an electric current which built up within 2¼ minutes from zero to maximum intensity. A rat standing on the bars after the electric circuit was closed would receive an increasing electrical stimulation and would typically react more and more aversively as the current mounted—jumping, squealing, etc. If the rat pressed the pedal at the end of the cage, the current would be turned off. It would then build up again, and the rat could again turn it off by recourse to the pedal. After a few experiences of this sort, all the rats in a set of five learned to go quickly to the pedal when the electrified floor began to affect them. Mowrer's arrangements were cleverly designed to duplicate in S-R terms the condition of mounting tension which libido in the Freudian scheme is supposed to produce, as well as a device for reducing the tension by appropriate action. The increasing electric current is like increasing sexual desire, and the pedal-pressing is like an orgasm in that it removes the tension temporarily. Now to duplicate regression! Mowrer exposed another group of rats to the same conditions, except that the pedal was covered so that they could not press it and break the circuit. These rats soon developed the habit of standing up on their hind feet when the floor was electrified, so that the area of contact was reduced and the amount of shock minimized. Let us call this Habit A. These rats were now permitted access to the pedal and with a little prodding were encouraged to use it. In a short while they had acquired this second habit, Habit B. They were now behaving like the first group of rats, whose only habit for dealing with mounting tension

[18] Mowrer (1959).

was to press the pedal. How would the two groups of rats react if the pedal itself were made slightly aversive by charging it electrically, too? This might be considered equivalent to putting an impediment in the way of free sexual relations. The answer is that the first group of rats, which had developed only Habit B for dealing with mounting tension, persisted in using the pedal in spite of the discomfort. The second group, however, with a single exception, reverted to Habit A after a few contacts with the electrically charged pedal. Superficially speaking, this is analogous to Freudian regression; it is so in the sense that it is a return to an *earlier* mode of behavior. But there the analogy stops. Regression in the Freudian sense is not simply return to an earlier mode of behavior, but return to a more infantile, poorer, less adequate mode of behavior; and this judgment is not simply in terms of efficiency, but more significantly in terms of values of a personal and social kind which have meaning in the human world but not in the rat world. The experiment does not touch in any real sense the Freudian concept of regression, and Mowrer realized this when he first published the paper in 1940 and even more keenly when he republished it in 1950.[19]

In the face of this imperfection in the experimental analogue, it might be legitimately argued that Sears was right in questioning whether the experimental testing of Freudian hypotheses could be profitable. We remember, however, that he added to this negative remark the positive one that experimentalists should construct personality theories of their own, no doubt with an eye to practical application. Mowrer has done something in this direction, too. In 1938 he published a study of enuresis (bed-wetting) and its treatment by a simple habit-training technique. Now, enuresis is often regarded as a neurotic symptom arising from psychodynamic complexities which are not easy to untangle. Mowrer, regarding it as a mere bad habit, devised an automatic alarm system which would wake up an incontinent sleeper within a second or two after he began to urinate. It was tried on 30 enuretic children of from 3 to 13 years of age and appeared to cure them of their enuresis within two months or less. One question was whether some other symptom would take the place of the enuresis, on the grounds that a neurotic symptom is only a surface manifestation of deeper-lying trouble

[19] Mowrer (1950), "An experimental analogue of 'regression' with incidental observations on 'reaction formation,' " pp. 361-89.

which is likely to find some other vent when it is blocked at its usual outlet. Mowrer notes that he did not apply the method to highly neurotic or psychotic children, but he adds nevertheless:

> Personality changes, when any have occurred as a result of the application of the present method of treating enuresis, have uniformly been in a favorable direction. In no case has there been any evidence of "symptom substitution." Our results, therefore, do not support the assumption, sometimes made, that any attempt to deal directly with the problem of enuresis will necessarily result in the child's developing "something worse."[20]

One might easily draw the inference from these results that personality is indeed, as Dollard and Miller and others have urged, nothing but a bundle of habits—good habits in the "normal," bad habits in the "neurotic."

Yates has severely criticized Mowrer for not accepting this inference and more vigorously advocating the same type of treatment for all neurotic ills. As Yates sees it, the Freudian conception of a particular piece of behavior, like enuresis or a facial twitch, as the expression of psychodynamics is a fundamental error which creates false theoretical problems and impedes efficient therapy. In particular, he holds Mowrer to be wrong in deriving neurotic symptoms from a basic anxiety. Even if we grant that anxiety is present in addition to the overt behavior, neither is any more basic than the other, according to Yates: both are learned responses, and, if there is any relation between them, it is a circular one, the anxiety increasing the probability of the "symptom," the overt "symptom" intensifying the anxiety. He argues that an attack on the overt behavior may remove the anxiety, too; if it does not, there is still gain in removing the bad habit. If simple conditioning techniques are effective, why not use them? Why be dualistic and obscurantist in theory and throw out a good therapeutic technique? He states: "It is clear that, as used by Freud, Mowrer, and other 'dynamic' psychologists, the symptom is regarded as a response to some hidden, basic conflict or anxiety. It will be suggested that this 'vertical,' dualistic approach is unnecessary and should be replaced by a 'horizontal,' monistic approach"[21]—that is to say, by an approach which regards personality as a set of R's, or bundle of habits, all on the same footing and all the product of conditioning.

[20] *Ibid.*, p. 410, in "Enuresis—a method for its study and treatment."
[21] Yates (1958), p. 372.

The debate is a familiar one. On the one side are those who believe that psychic factors precede and cause overt behavior—for whom speech expresses thought, a smile expresses an emotion, a motor act is a means set in motion by a purpose toward an imagined end. On the other side are those who believe either that there are no psychic factors at all or that they can be put on a level with overt acts—for whom speech is verbalization rather than expression of thought, a smile is a facial contortion rather than expression of emotion, and motor acts are in general mechanically determined responses to stimuli from the external world or possibly from the viscera.

But why does Mowrer incline toward the vertical, dualistic, psychic side of the debate which Yates condemns rather than following out the implications of his method for treating enuresis? There is perhaps no single answer to this question. Two facts, however, have impressed Mowrer more than they have impressed Yates, or so it would seem. What Mowrer has called "the neurotic paradox" is one; anxiety is the other. As Freud and many others have noticed, a patient is anything but passive and often gives the impression of warding off therapeutic measures with great energy and with great ingenuity; this apparently self-defeating behavior does not appear to the therapist as something purely automatic but as consisting of highly purposive strategies. This is the neurotic paradox. Says Mowrer: "No clinician with even a modicum of awareness of what transpires in the therapeutic situation has failed to sense these strategies; indeed at times he feels all but overwhelmed by them. As data, as phenomena, they are among our most certain and most important."[22] As for anxiety, Mowrer puts it on a different plane entirely from that of the overt motor symptom. Anxiety strikes at the core of human existence. A facial tic or a habit of bed-wetting are trivial in comparison. Let the facial muscles twitch, let the enuretic wet his bed; these are slight inconveniences, like bruises from playing football, or getting caught in a shower of rain when making a dash for the car. But anxiety—that is massive and terrible and, in Mowrer's opinion, something more than a bad habit.

Jung: the collective unconscious and the archetypes

From inside psychoanalysis have come many modifications of the Freudian ideas. Freud himself was continually rethinking his earlier

[22] Mowrer (1950), p. 489.

statements, and some of the most radical modifications of psychoanalytic theory were Freud's own. Here again, however, it is necessary to limit the discussion to a few points, and I have chosen to consider some lines of thought traceable to Freud but not developed by him. Carl Jung (1875-1961) was once a Freudian whom Freud looked on as his natural successor, but Jung modified some of the Freudian views so radically that a sharp break occurred between the master and the disciple and Jung went on his own independent way.

One of the points of difference was in the conception of psychic energy. Freud preferred to regard this as predominantly sexual; Jung wished to desexualize it and encountered strong opposition from Freud on that account. Less repellent to Freud was Jung's conception of the Collective Unconscious, and he even finds a sort of place for it in his own system. But Jung carefully distinguishes between the most characteristic features of Freud's Unconscious and his own. By the label "Collective Unconscious," Jung indicates that the contents are not derived from individual experience as was the case with repressed material which at first constituted the Unconscious for Freud. More akin are the Collective Unconscious and the Freudian Id, which contains the instincts. In one place Jung in fact compares his "archetypes" of the Collective Unconscious to the Freudian instincts, but it is apparent that this is not the whole story.

Jung defines his principal concepts briefly in the following words:

> In addition to our immediate consciousness, which is of a thoroughly personal nature and which we believe to be the only empirical psyche (even if we tack on the personal unconscious as an appendix), there exists a second psychic system of a collective, universal, and impersonal nature which is identical in all individuals. . . . It consists of pre-existent forms, the archetypes, which can only become conscious secondarily and which give definite form to certain psychic contents.[23]

He brings out the difference between himself and Freud very clearly by discussing Freud's interpretation of Leonardo's famous painting of St. Anne and the Virgin with the Christ child. Freud sees the painting as expressing Leonardo's wish to recover the two mothers of his own childhood—the mother who bore him and the mother who adopted him. The painting thus emerges from a par-

---

[23] Jung (1959), p. 43. This is from the essay "The concept of the collective unconscious," originally published in 1936. Used by permission of the Bollingen Foundation, Inc., and Routledge & Kegan Paul Ltd.

ticular individual's personal experience. Jung objects that the theme of the two mothers is by no means confined to Leonardo or to other individuals who have had two mothers. On the contrary, the theme is widespread in art and myth and individual fantasy. There is, for instance, says Jung, the myth of Heracles, born of a human mother and unwittingly adopted by the goddess Hera; there is the common childhood fantasy that one's own parents are not the true ones; there is the practice of providing a child with godparents to supplement the biological parents. The theme of dual parentage is based, in short, on something universal and profound in the human psyche, an archetype of the Collective Unconscious. The archetype patterns individual imagination and behavior, but it is not derived from personal experience. It is innate. Leonardo's picture arose from this source, according to Jung, rather than from Leonardo's individual history.

Jung, like Freud, has devoted much attention to dreams, for the dream is the royal road into the Collective Unconscious, too. According to Jung, certain archetypes which emerge often in dreams are the Shadow, the Anima, the Animus, and the Old Wise Man. They appear in various guises: the Shadow sometimes takes on the form of the Devil, the Anima may appear as a pixie or a beautiful witch or a fascinating woman out of the past, the Animus as a man or group of men of high intellectual power, the Old Wise Man as a great hero or king or savior. There are also archetypes of individuation which may appear as mandalas, i.e., magic circles or other forms carrying the idea of the union of opposites around a center. But the particular image of an archetype is nothing like as important as the fact that the encounter with one, whether in a dream or waking vision or otherwise, impresses the individual who has the experience as something deeply significant and perhaps overwhelming.

A dream which illustrates this point is one which was repeatedly experienced by a Protestant theologian:

> He stood on a mountain slope with a deep valley below, and in it a dark lake. He knew in the dream that something had always prevented him from approaching the lake. This time he resolved to go to the water. As he approached the shore, everything grew dark and uncanny, and a gust of wind suddenly rushed over the face of the water. He was seized by panic fear, and awoke.[24]

[24] *Ibid.*, p. 17.

Freud might have seen sexual meaning in this dream—the lake among the mountains representing the female genitals or the womb of the mother. But Jung interprets it in a different sense. The dreamer, in his version, approaches the dark, mysterious realm of the Collective Unconscious and there personally realizes the power of Spirit, which is an uncanny thing: "It lives of itself, and a shudder runs through the man who thought that 'spirit' was merely what he believes, what he makes himself, what is said in books, or what people talk about."[25] He has come into direct contact with the same kind of reality which the Elgonyi tribe in Kenya calls "the maker of fear," a god coming in a cold gust of wind or whistling through the grass.

I find in the writings of a British naturalist a reference to the effect of a particular Scottish landscape which would fall in the same category. Says Darling about a place where he went to study the behavior of red deer:

> The cliffs fall steep to the loch and the ground about is as rough as could be with fallen rocks, deep peat hags, and heaped moraines. I have found it a strange place, and the same thought has been murmured to me by some of the few men of the country who have been there. These sensations may be caused through the eye by the dispositions of masses and planes and their relation to the course of the sun, as well as by the huge rock surfaces devoid of vegetation. There are many such places in the Scottish Highlands where seasoned men— myself too—have had to move out at nightfall.[26]

A primitive man would know exactly what to say about such a place; he would say that it was inhabited by a powerful spirit. Jung says that such experiences indicate that one has touched an archetype of the Collective Unconscious.

The sacred dread may be much more intense than in the previous examples. Jung tells us that such was the case with Nikolaus von der Flüe, a mystic of the fifteenth century. Nikolaus had a vision that altered his face so that people were afraid of him:

> All who came to him were filled with terror at the first glance. As to the cause of this, he himself used to say that he had seen a piercing light resembling a human face. At the sight of it he feared that his heart would burst into little pieces. Therefore, overcome with terror, he instantly turned his face away and fell to the ground. And that was the reason why his face was now terrible to others.[27]

[25] *Ibid.*
[26] Darling (1937), p. 19.
[27] Jung (1959), p. 9.

He spent years trying to understand this experience and had it painted or painted it himself as a vision of the Trinity. Jung thinks that the original experience was different from the picture and far more incomprehensible, but that the doctrine of the Trinity enabled the saintly man to handle it in a conventional and socially acceptable way without being driven completely mad.

Religion is rooted in the Collective Unconscious, according to Jung; but the forces it there draws upon are extremely dangerous to the individual, especially if he has discarded the dogmas and symbols by which a flourishing religious system seeks to contain them. In a world stripped bare of these defenses, he says, not only individuals but whole nations are exposed to insanity, as in the case of Hitler's Germany where, according to Jung, the most primitive archetypes thronged to the surface of consciousness and overwhelmed a whole people with a ferocious and archaic paganism.

Most readers of Jung, I suspect, have experienced some difficulty in understanding him. Partly this is due to the nature of his concepts; but it is also due to the frequent ambiguities in Jung himself. One is not quite sure, for instance, about the reality status of the archetypes. We need to consider this problem a little.

For Jung, as for Freud, the dream is a symbolic structure; it is not important in itself, but only in what it points to. But Jung thought that Freud misunderstood the nature of symbolism. A Freudian sexual symbol, for example, is a concrete object standing for another concrete object; but a true symbol, according to Jung, always refers to something which cannot be pictured or otherwise put into perceptual terms. To take a specific case, the myth of the birth of Athena from the brow of Zeus might be interpreted by Freud as cranial birth standing by displacement for genital birth; by Jung it is interpreted as symbolizing in concrete pictorial imagery the origin of Wisdom from the Divine Mind, none of which can be pictured at all in its essence. In the same way Jung treats the archetypal images in dreams as referring beyond themselves to something entirely invisible. Yet—and here is the ambiguity—the images might refer either to intensely real though invisible powers *or* to mere abstractions which are not only invisible but also powerless and nonexistent except as words employed by Jung. It is this sort of uncertainty which we encounter in Jung from time to time.

In his essay "On the Concept of the Archetype," he begins by noting that the concept of the Great Mother embraces various types of mother-goddess and comments that mother-goddesses are obviously derived from the mother archetype.

Freud would not have hesitated to say that all mother-goddesses are symbols of an actual human mother; that the divine figure is the magnified human figure, as seen through the eyes of a child or the persistently childlike in man, with the child's typical overvaluation of the power, wisdom, goodness, and permanence of the mother; and that adults turn to such projected images to compensate for the loss of such an omnipotent, omniscient, immortal mother in their childhood experience.

But Jung hesitates. He recalls that for Plato an archetype or idea was a truly existing reality, in fact, a supreme reality of which the objects on earth were the mere shadows. And so Jung says:

> Were I a philosopher, I should continue in this Platonic strain and say: Somewhere, in "a place beyond the skies," there is a prototype or primordial image of the mother that is pre-existent and supraordinate to all phenomena in which the "maternal," in the broadest sense of the term, is manifest. But I am an empiricist, not a philosopher; I cannot let myself presuppose that my peculiar temperament, my own attitude to intellectual problems, is universally valid.[28]

He goes on to say that, as an empiricist, he can only point out the fact that there are two major temperaments among men—the Aristotelian and the Platonic, the nominalist and the realist, or, as Jung termed them, the extrovert and the introvert. He further points out that the Aristotelian, nominalist, extroverted temperament rules the world today—whence the scientific positivism which rejects any serious belief in Platonic ideas, or spiritual beings, or even human consciousness. One gets the impression that Jung would be a Platonist if he could.

Well, but what about the archetypes? What is his definition, whether Platonic, Aristotelian, or hybrid? Jung replies:

> Again and again I encounter the mistaken notion that an archetype is determined in regard to its content, in other words, that it is a kind of unconscious idea (if such an expression be admissible). It is necessary to point out once more that archetypes are not determined as regards their content, but only as regards their form and then only to a limited degree. A primordial image is determined as to its content only when it has become conscious and is therefore filled out with the

[28] *Ibid.*, p. 75.

material of conscious experience. Its form, however, as I have explained elsewhere, might perhaps be compared to the axial system of a crystal, which, as it were, preforms the crystalline structure in the mother liquid, although it has no material existence of its own.[29]

The Jungian archetype, then, can never be perceived. Plato said of his ideas that they could not be perceived by men in their unpurified condition on earth but might be perceived by those who had been purified in an afterlife; for he held that the ideas had real existence. Jung will not go quite so far. Besides, Jung locates the archetypes in the Collective Unconscious of living humanity rather than in an eternal heavenly realm, and in fact speaks of their being transmitted through the germ plasm.

If Jung's formal definition of the archetype leaves us unsatisfied, we may gain some partial understanding by observing his practical use of the concept. The first thing to notice is that many things can be mother symbols—"the Church, university, city or country, heaven, earth, the woods, the sea or any still waters, matter even, the underworld and the moon,"[30] as well as one's own particular mother. It must be strongly underlined that a particular, living, concrete human individual can function as a symbol of an archetype. We shall return to this after just noting that, according to Jung, the mother archetype and its symbols have a dual aspect:

> The qualities associated with it are maternal solicitude and sympathy; the magic authority of the female; the wisdom and spiritual exaltation that transcend reason; any helpful instinct or impulse; all that is benign, all that cherishes and sustains, that fosters growth and fertility. The place of magic transformation and rebirth, together with the underworld and its inhabitants, are presided over by the mother. On the negative side the mother archetype may connote anything secret, hidden, dark; the abyss, the world of the dead, anything that devours, seduces, and poisons, that is terrifying and inescapable like fate. . . . Perhaps the historical example of the dual nature of the mother most familiar to us is the Virgin Mary, who is not only the Lord's mother, but also, according to the medieval allegories, his cross.[31]

The particular, living, concrete human mother is herself a symbol of the mother archetype. Jung admits that in dealing with patients one may receive the impression that the particular mother in herself alone is the significant factor, but this, he argues, is mostly illusion. Says Jung:

[29] *Ibid.*, p. 79.   [30] *Ibid.*, p. 81.   [31] *Ibid.*, p. 82.

This figure of the personal mother looms so large in all personalistic psychologies that, as we know, they never got beyond it, even in theory, to other important aetiological factors. My own view differs from that of other medico-psychological theories principally in that I attribute to the personal mother only a limited aetiological significance. That is to say, all those influences which the literature describes as being exerted on the children do not come from the mother herself, but rather from the archetype projected upon her, which gives her a mythological background and invests her with authority and numinosity. The aetiological and traumatic effects produced by the mother must be divided into two groups: (1) those corresponding to traits of character or attitudes actually present in the mother, and (2) those referring to traits which the mother only seems to possess, the reality being composed of more or less fantastic (i.e., archetypal) projections on the part of the child.[32]

The therapeutic task is to put the archetypes back where they belong, namely, in the patient: "Our task is not, therefore, to deny the archetype, but to dissolve the projections, in order to restore their contents to the individual who has involuntarily lost them by projecting them outside himself."[33] One gathers that this operation, if thorough, would strip the human mother of her imposing magico-mythic power and in so doing leave her very little power of any kind. Put in the most general terms, the question is whether every element in an individual's experience is simply a part of a vast hallucination projected from the formal, virtually nonexistent archetypes. In practice, Jung does assign properties to the personal mother besides those projected from the mother archetype, but basically, theoretically, what? Here again Jung has a way of sliding away from the questioner.

Yet, in a different context, he does give an answer. It comes where he imagines his audience or a reader asking why he considers it so important to rise to higher and higher levels of consciousness. Jung replies:

This is truly the crucial question, and I do not find the answer easy. Instead of a real answer I can only make a confession of faith: I believe that, after thousands and millions of years, someone had to realize that this wonderful world of mountains and oceans, suns and moons, galaxies and nebulae, plants and animals, *exists*. From a low hill in the Athi plains of East Africa I once watched the vast herds of wild animals grazing in soundless stillness, as they had done from time immemorial,

[32] *Ibid.*, p. 83.   [33] *Ibid.*, p. 84.

touched only by the breath of a primeval world. I felt then as if I were the first man, the first creature, to know that all this *is*. The entire world round me was still in its primeval state; it did not know that it *was*. And then, in that one moment in which I came to know, the world sprang into being; without that moment it would never have been. All Nature seeks this goal and finds it fulfilled in man, but only in the most highly developed and most fully conscious man. Every advance, even the smallest, along this path of conscious realization adds that much to the world.[34]

Now, anyone who has had an experience at all like Jung's moment of realization must agree with him that it is exalting and self-justifying. But is it necessary to draw exactly his conclusions? Note his words: "In that one moment in which I came to know, the world sprang into being; without that moment it would never have been." The addition of the little phrase "for me" would have given the statement a more modest sound. As it stands, it seems to claim for Jung himself the power of *creating* the world. I am not sure that this is what he means, but it may be.

There are some other statements by Jung which have a less egotistic or solipsistic ring. He warns against assuming that the archetypes are abolished by refusing to believe in them. He cites the case of a philosopher who, though he insisted on the absolute unity and indivisibility of the human being, nevertheless was constantly expecting to be invaded by cancer and thus losing his vaunted integrity; and this, too, in spite of the fact that the medical men were constantly assuring him that he had no cancer. In effect, the philosopher, who was a patient of Jung's, was admitting the existence of an alien power (the Shadow, perhaps?) which could rise up against him and even within him whether he would or no, regardless of his state of belief and whether he was conscious of it or not. And Jung says:

> Now whether you believe in a demon of the air or in a factor in the unconscious that plays diabolical tricks on you is all one to me. The fact that man's imagined unity is menaced by alien powers remains the same in either case. Theologians would do better to take account for once of these psychological facts than to go on "demythologizing" them with rationalistic explanations that are a hundred years behind the times[35]

And in another place he says:

[34] *Ibid.*, pp. 95 f.   [35] *Ibid.*, p. 105.

It seems as if it were only through an experience of symbolic reality that man, vainly seeking his own "existence" and making a philosophy out of it, can find his way back to a world in which he is no longer a stranger.[36]

Yet the question remains whether the symbolic reality he refers to is real for Jung.

Jung has opened up some psychological vistas not to be found in Freud, and his great international fame is evidence that he has touched something resonant in the human heart in spite of his obscurities and indecisions. Is it possible that his elusiveness is due to his wishing to be a Platonist in an Aristotelian age? Does his thought oscillate because he wishes to make contact with both positivistic science and religion? Or has he risen above all these categories in which lesser men are caught? He tells the nonreligious that they had better watch out or an archetype will get them. He tells the religious that their historical reference points and revelations are a tissue of myths from the Collective Unconscious. He tells the believer in the existence of concrete things that these are only symbols of archetypes, and he tells the believers in archetypes, himself included, that these are emptier than the symbols which point to them, shapeless shapes, powerless powers, mythical existences without which man could not exist. It is really not strange that no one has tried very hard to square learning theory with Jung!

Fairbairn: endopsychic objects

At first glance W. R. D. Fairbairn may appear to be a very different sort of theorist from Jung; but the two have a certain kinship: both have played down the importance of the Freudian instincts and both have concerned themselves with what Fairbairn calls "endopsychic objects" (i.e., objects within the psyche). Except that both have displayed more awareness of modern physics than most psychoanalysts,[37] the resemblance may stop there, but it is already considerable. The considerable difference is that Fairbairn does not treat endopsychic objects as symbols; for him they have at least as much reality as atoms.

Fairbairn's revisions of Freud stem directly from Freud's own thought and, radical though they are, appear faithful to their origin

[36] *Ibid.*, p. 110.
[37] Jung collaborated with the physicist Pauli at one time. See Jung and Pauli (1955).

instead of either a concession to popular prejudices or an iconoclastic revolt. His theory has developed gradually over a period of years, under the stimulus of Freud's writings and his long practice as a psychoanalyst in Edinburgh.

In an important series of papers, Fairbairn has keenly noted that Freud himself altered his personality theory radically in the course of time without ever abandoning his earlier conceptions or reconciling them with the later ones. Freud's earlier emphasis was on the instincts and pleasure-seeking—largely an Id psychology. Later, it was on the introjection of external objects—a Superego psychology. Fairbairn thinks that Freud was thus moving toward an object-relations theory and away from a purely libidinal one. In Fairbairn's words:

> The progress of Freud's thought is thus seen to lead from his original theory that behaviour is determined by pleasure-seeking to a theory of the personality conceived in terms of relationships between the ego and objects, both external and internal. According to this latter theory, the nature of the personality is determined by the internalization of an external object, and the nature of group relationships is in turn determined by the externalization or projection of an internal object. In such a development then we detect the germ of an "object-relations" theory of the personality—a theory based upon the conception that object-relationships exist within the personality as well as between the personality and external objects.[38]

This trend in Freud was carried further by Melanie Klein. Whereas Freud recognized only one kind of internal object—the parent introjected as the Superego—she recognized several, both part objects and whole objects, both good and bad; she based these on the child's oral relations with the world, but she left it uncertain whether these objects ever had any existence outside the child's imagination. Fairbairn detects a number of inconsistencies in Klein's thinking. (1) She continued to adhere to Freud's hedonistic libido theory; but, according to Fairbairn, "if the introjection of objects and the perpetuation of such objects in the inner world are as important as her views imply, it is difficult to be satisfied with attributing this simply to the presence of oral impulses in the child or to the compulsions of libidinal pleasure-seeking. On the contrary,

[38] Fairbairn (1952), p. 153. Used by permission of the author and of Tavistock Publications (London). (Published in the United States under the title *An Object-Relations Theory of the Personality*, copyright 1952 by W. Ronald D. Fairbairn, by Basic Books, Inc., Publishers, and used with their permission.)

it seems to point inevitably to the conclusion that libido is not primarily pleasure-seeking, but object-seeking."[39] (2) She retained Abraham's theory of libidinal development which states that there is a chronological shifting of emphasis from one erogenous zone of the body to another. Fairbairn points out that this theory dwells on libidinal activities rather than on the objects of these activities. It is not necessarily inconsistent with an object-relations theory, but in its phraseology it ignores objects. Thus, it speaks of an "oral" phase of development instead of a "breast" phase. (3) She also allowed Freud's antiquated instinct-psychology to stand. Fairbairn himself began rejecting it when he saw that libido is object-seeking rather than pleasure-seeking and was confirmed in his view that the instincts were not the only source of energy the more deeply he considered the role which Freud assigned to the Superego in repression; for the Superego, an introjected object, seemed to have a power and activity of its own independent of the instincts.

It is by this course of thought that Fairbairn arrives at his conception of the personality as an organization of independent dynamic structures. This conception does away with the need for an unstructured energy reservoir like the Id. One of the major results of this reorientation in regard to energy is that the Ego emerges as a reality in its own right, and not as a mere surface film on the energy-supplying Id. Fairbairn writes: "Obviously the principle of dynamic structure can only be maintained if the distinction between id and ego is abolished and the ego is regarded as an original structure which is itself the source of impulse-tension."[40] The Ego, furthermore, operates according to the reality principle: it seeks objects rather than pleasure and real interaction with them rather than mere energy discharge.

In Fairbairn's theory, then, a real Ego is seen as engaged in real relationships with real objects, both external and internal. The internal objects are derived both from external objects and from the Ego's relations with these objects; and it is the endopsychic structure resulting from this process and the process itself with which he is chiefly concerned. One way that the Ego deals with "bad" objects (i.e., objects which threaten it or frustrate it) is to internalize them and then repress them; but because the Ego is libidinally bound to the object, it cannot, according to Fairbairn, repress the object without simultaneously splitting off a part of itself. Furthermore, a given object may have both a "bad" and a "good" aspect

[39] *Ibid.*, pp. 154 f.   [40] *Ibid.*, p. 157.

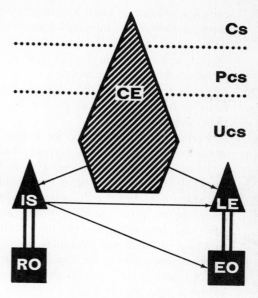

20 *Fairbairn's diagram of the endopsychic situation stresses fragmentation of the Ego by its own aggressive forces. (After Fairbairn, 1952)*

key: CE, central ego; IS, internal saboteur; LE, libidinal ego; RO, rejecting object; EO, exciting object; Cs, conscious; Pcs, preconscious; Ucs, unconscious; →, aggression; =, libido

(ambivalence), and in its internalized (introjected) state it may have to be split up. The result is that the endopsychic structure contains various partial objects to which parts of the Ego are attached.

Figure 20 diagrams the basic endopsychic structure resulting from the activities of the Ego. The Central Ego, partly conscious, partly preconscious, and partly unconscious, is shown with two split-off parts (IS and LE) which have been repressed along with the internalized objects (RO and EO) to which, respectively, IS and LE are libidinally bound. The repression is maintained by the Central Ego's aggression toward its split-off portions. One of these is called the Internal Saboteur—an Ego fragment attached to a Rejecting Object (which may be a mere fragment of a complex object which has been split up). The other is called the Libidinal Ego—an Ego fragment attached to an Exciting Object, i.e., an object or portion of an object which has aroused sexual feelings to a degree intolerable to the Ego. The Rejecting Object and the Exciting Object may both have been derived from a single external object, such as the mother, with whom the Ego has entered into complex relations. That fragment of the Ego which is called the Internal Saboteur (internal destroyer) owes its name to the fact that it acts aggressively toward the Libidinal Ego and its Exciting Object, as indicated in the diagram by the arrows. The diagram thus pictures the dynamic relations between dynamic structural elements called for by Fairbairn's general theory and by his observations on hysteria, multiple personality, and dreams, as well as other phenomena.

Perhaps the reader will be helped to understand Fairbairn by considering a case of this endopsychic structure in action. He cites a dream of a woman patient who, in the dream, sees herself being attacked by an actress; after a moment, the actress resumes playing her stage role, but the dreamer now finds herself gazing at her own bleeding body on the floor, which soon turns into the body of a man and then again into her own body and so on repeatedly. In the first part of the dream, while the actress was attacking, the dreamer's husband appeared to be standing nearby unable to offer protection; as for the male body which alternates with her own in the latter part of the dream, it is wearing a suit like one her husband had recently bought with the assistance of one of his mistresses. This dream, in Fairbairn's eyes, is a particularly transparent example of the endopsychic dynamics diagramed as structure in Figure 20. The Central Ego is present as the dreamer herself who observes all that happens; but the split-off parts of the Ego are also there as the attacking actress (Internal Saboteur) and the attacked and bleeding body of the dreamer (Libidinal Ego). The bleeding body of her husband is the Exciting Object, with which her own body is so libidinally bound that the two are almost one. There remains one other part of the diagram to identify, the Rejecting Object: that is the husband who stands by passively while the actress attacks, corresponding to the husband who in waking life ignores his wife in favor of his mistresses. All three women in the dream—the observer, the attacking woman, the attacked woman—are parts of the dreamer herself; and the ungallant, passive husband (Rejecting Object) and the husband who is so close to her that he shares in her sufferings (Exciting Object) are two aspects of the same man as internalized or introjected into her psychic structure. Let it be added that the three egos in this scheme correspond to the Freudian Ego, Superego, and Id.

Dreams are not regarded by Fairbairn as wish-fulfillments. On the contrary, they are direct views into the endopsychic situation. He does not take the dream quite literally, however; he usually regards the various *dramatis personae* of a dream, in spite of appearances, as parts of the dreamer's Ego. This is dictated by theory rather than by simple observation of the dream. In the actual dream it is often the case that only one figure is clearly Ego, while all the others seem to be as separate from the Ego as are other persons in our waking relationships. To take these apparently independent objects as the Ego in disguise is to concede a theoretical bias which Fairbairn admits and apologizes for and nearly retracts.

Fairbairn's logic and his observations drive him close to the view that the Ego may be plagued by demons. Of course, he is not a demonologist any more than Freud or Jung, who for their part have also acknowledged that the medieval demon theory was not altogether wrong. The point is that certain mental contents which Fairbairn treats theoretically as internalized objects or split-off portions of the Ego do not *appear* that way to the Ego. On the contrary, they appear to have energy and intentions of their own which the Ego cannot control. The fact that these autonomous beings are invisible to others who are not in their power only completes their resemblance to demons. Fairbairn is willing to give his theory a twist in the direction of error rather than to be numbered among the demonologists, and yet. . . . "It remains true that under certain conditions internalized objects may acquire a dynamic independence which cannot be ignored."[41] In much the same spirit of sophisticated compromise, Jung tells us (in a passage already quoted) that it makes no difference to him whether you want to speak of demons of the air or of factors in the Unconscious—the fact is that man is menaced by alien powers. The actual, personal experience of many human beings is on the side of the demonologists. The psychoanalysts have done their utmost to recognize the experiential facts and to incorporate them in their theories without becoming demonologists themselves. At times, as Fairbairn reminds us, the strain on the theorist is great.

The phenomenology of Medard Boss

At the threshold of the modern scientific era, Descartes opened his *Meditations on the First Philosophy* (1641) with the reflection that it is impossible to distinguish dreaming from waking experience: "I perceive so clearly that there exist no certain marks by which the state of waking can ever be distinguished from sleep, that I feel

[41] *Ibid.*, p. 132.

greatly astonished; and in amazement I almost persuade myself that I am now dreaming." Freud, a scientist more than a philosopher, is untroubled by this difficulty and makes a sharp distinction between the two states. When we are awake, according to Freud, we have sensory contact with solid reality; when we are asleep and dreaming, we can only hallucinate the fulfillment of our unsatisfied wishes.

Freud regarded the dream as a piece of mental pathology, as a disease symptom,[42] in spite of the fact that everybody dreams. Yet, as Descartes was so keenly aware, the difference between dreaming and waking experience is anything but obvious. True, we often speak of dreams as odd or grotesque or nonsensical; but how do they compare, factually, with the well-attested happenings of waking life? How does the most horrible and "incredible" dream differ in horror or incredibility from Hitler's extermination camps, or the routine monstrousness of war, or the daily front-page news of murders and rapes and robberies and cruelties without number and fortunes found in decayed houses stacked high with junk and bones and little children chained to bedposts and gangsterism and moonshots and the goodwill journeys of hostile heads of state and so on endlessly, not to mention the steady, unpublicized facts of hospitals, prisons, houses of prostitution, quarrels in the street, emotional storms in quiet gardens, married couples lying back to back in bed consumed with cold hatred? And is the most exalted and lovely dream more exalted and lovely and unlikely than two actual lovers smiling deeply into each other's eyes? Why classify the dreams in which we spend a large part of our lives as peculiar, abnormal, pathological, illusory, and entirely other than our waking experience?

The answer of Medard Boss, a Swiss psychiatrist who began as an orthodox Freudian and then moved by way of Jung to the existentialism of Martin Heidegger,[43] is quite simply that the dream is as real as our waking experience and obedient to the same laws. What the dream reveals, as waking experience does, is that we always exist in

[42] Freud states that in the course of treating neurotic patients he arrived at the view that their dreams should be interpreted like their symptoms, and he quotes with approval the words of Hughlings Jackson which link dreams with insanity. See Freud (1950), pp. 13 and 422. This view of the dream is still prevalent: see Kleitman (1960), p. 88, quoting a psychiatrist: "the dream is the normal psychosis and dreaming permits each and every one of us to be quietly and safely insane every night of our lives."

[43] Contemporary existentialism, originating in the thought of Kierkegaard (see Ch. 6), has many variants. The common feature is a strong emphasis on the individual human being's experience in his unique living and dying.

relation to a world of objects: the objects change and our relations to them change but the fact that we are in relation to them never changes. Boss asserts that there is only *one* reality, and that we are always immersed in it, whether awake or asleep. He does not attempt to explain the dream either as a wish-fulfilling hallucination[44] or as a symbolic manifestation of the archetypes; he does not explain it at all—he simply accepts it. He accepts it as a naturalist accepts the scenes and creatures of jungle or desert, ocean or mountain, the polar ice or his own backyard. And he asks, What is there? What happens there? It is reality, a reality known and acted in by a conscious self, and the study of it tells us about personality; for personality is neither more nor less than the particular relations which a particular self has with reality. Personality change means a change in these relations with the environment, and this means a change in the environment as it appears to the self. A series of dreams may reveal extensive and significant personality change.

Boss is not the first to consider a series of dreams as revealing personality change. This concern is very pronounced in Jung's work, as in books like *Psychology of the Unconscious* and *The Integration of the Personality*. But one of the most striking series to be found anywhere is provided by Boss. It is a set of 823 dreams reported by an engineer in his forties during a three-year psychoanalysis, which was begun because he was deeply depressed and sexually impotent. This engineer had never had a dream before that he could remember. Two days before entering analysis he dreamed that he was in a dungeon which was dimly lighted by one small window too high for him to reach. The bars of the window attracted his attention:

> They consisted of wrought-iron work, the artistry of which was in pronounced contrast to the extreme poverty of the dungeon itself. On closer observation the dreamer noticed that all the bars were mathematical signs and numbers: square roots, integrals, indeed entire mathematical formulae.[45]

This is surely not wish-fulfillment, nor does it call for translation into the archetypes. It requires no devious interpretation. The man is quite literally in a prison, behind the bars wrought by his own preoccupations. He is imprisoned in a lonely, barren cell.

That was the state of his personality at the beginning of psychotherapy. For more than six months he dreamed of machinery, and,

---

[44] Freud admitted exceptions to the wish-fulfillment formula. See p. 248.
[45] Boss (1958), p. 113. Used by permission of Philosophical Library, Inc.

toward the end of this period, of trying to cross broken bridges in his machines and failing. Then for the first time he dreamed of a living thing: a potted plant. There followed dreams of pine trees and roses—sickly, worm-infested roses. Then, for four months, he ceased dreaming. When he resumed dreaming, he began with insects:

Dreams about insects occurred during the subsequent half year 105 times; naturally not without occasional interruptions by old dreams of machines and plants. Then there followed a period of half a year in which he dreamt of toads, frogs and snakes. Originally both animals and machinery had always been of a vague grey colour. One night, however, he was frightened by a bright red snake of tremendous thickness and length. The first mammal he encountered in his dreams was a mouse. He could barely see it disappearing down a mousehole. A little later on, there followed a dream in which a rabbit was being swallowed by a wild pig. From then on pigs began to play a very great role in his dreams and this continued for some weeks; so much so that the patient finally got cross and asked if this piggery would never come to an end. In time however the pigs gave place to lions and horses. The first dream about a human being occurred two years after the beginning of psychoanalysis. It was a dream of an unconscious woman of more than life size in a long blood-red dress, swimming in a large pond far below a vitreous cover of ice. He was terribly frightened at this discovery and ran for help. Half a year later he dreamt that he was dancing at a peasant fete with a woman similarly dressed in blood-red, who was now fully awake and very passionate, and that he fell deeply in love with her. In his waking state, feelings of the complete meaninglessness of life had already begun to disappear at the time he could admit plant-life into his dream world. His sexual potency improved considerably, and finally gave rise to a full love life at the time he dared to begin to dream of lions and horses.[46]

Boss asks the question whether the poverty-stricken dream-life in the early stages did not contradict the waking realities. The dreamer was, after all, a busy and successful engineer who was daily applying his high intelligence to industrial problems and helping to step up his country's manufacturing output; he lived in a world of people, as well as plants and animals and unbroken bridges and machines that successfully crossed these bridges, and he had a wife. As a human object among objects, he had plenty of company, and his stimulus-response collisions were numerous. But this is the surface.

[46] *Ibid.*, p. 114.

A closer examination revealed that he was in fact so asleep during the day, so enmeshed in abstract technical thought, that he was unaware of the full reality of things, plants, animals, people in the street or in business, or even of his wife. . . . In fact, not even the bridge of his waking world was as firm and safe as he persuaded himself and others it was. There had been quite a few occasions when he had a suspicion of the true nature of his daily reality. Whenever he crossed the bridge he suffered from what is clinically known as agoraphobia. More and more frequently he was seized by an inexplicable panicky fear that it might collapse at any moment.[47]

In short, the world of his dreams and the world of his waking experience were akin.

A dream which in some ways exactly complements the series dreamed by the engineer is that of a woman artist in her thirties who was consumed by sensuality. In her dream everything is powerfully and evilly alive. The engineer, at the end of a long series of dreams, is dancing with a woman he loves—a woman who had appeared at an earlier time, one might say, as an unconscious swimmer under ice, and earlier still as a bright red snake, in both cases frightening the dreamer. The artist, in the course of one dream, feels herself change from a woman to a snake and then to a piece of burning wood. Her dream begins by her voluntary disregard of signs warning her against danger. She enters a magic house and encounters a man who combines a suggestion of divinity with more than a suggestion of evil. He drags her off into a dark ravine:

> Because of the weak, pale and iridescent moonlight I can recognize only some of the outlines. I can dimly see that on the floor masses of slimy toads are crawling about with dogs' faces. Horrible creatures with large bats' wings hover in the air. They constantly cuff me and pinch my arms and legs. Even more horrible is the fact that the trees and stones are moving as well. Their forms change as if they were made of gelatine; they flow into each other and reach out towards me as if wanting to suck me in. In doing so they whisper to me incomprehensible magic words. I feel that the mana forces of which the door-plate had warned me are at work not only in the man who had carried me away but even in the stones. The magic spell emanating from all these things forces me to throw myself on the ground. I feel myself turning into a snake and have difficulty in moving without arms and legs. The magician skips behind me, giggling and gloating at the fact that I had become a helpless victim of the forces of his domain. He

[47] *Ibid.*, p. 115.

then starts spitting fire at me from his horrible mouth. Soon I am burning brightly; I have been turned into a stake. This is the most terrible thing of all because now I am completely defenceless. The entire hellish brood now starts yelling gleefully. I can feel it in the very marrow of my bones and am frightened out of my sleep.[48]

Only a psychology which plays down the actualities of human experience can assert that hell is an empty fiction. Here it is. This woman has visited it.

The engineer knew a barren hell, the woman artist knew a densely living one. The mother of a family who had the following dream clearly inhabited a different region, and not a region of hell. She was sitting at her dinner table, enjoying to the full a delicious meal:

> I looked at my husband and my children, and I felt extremely fond of them and very near to all of them, especially to my eldest son. While he had originally been sitting in his usual place at the opposite corner of the table he was suddenly and strangely transported right next to me. In the dream it did not appear strange that he had suddenly changed places without any movement on his or anybody else's part. It was quite reasonable. Nor did it strike me as peculiar that while I was sitting so happily amongst my family, there suddenly appeared colorful bridges, reminiscent of very bright rainbows. They extended across the table between me and my family. A large and golden urn hovered on these bridges between us, and particularly near my favorite son.[49]

Boss makes this dream the text for criticizing various theories which would reduce dreams to something less than what they appear to be. He emphasizes the naturalness, within the dream, of every element and event. He insists that the rainbow bridges and the golden urn do not need to be treated as symbols, any more than any other rainbows or urns. They are elements of richness and delight quite immediately, and they are in harmony with the other elements of the dream—the happiness, the love, the warmth and hope which the woman feels in the presence of her family. Moreover, all these things are in harmony with her life as publicly lived. The fact that urns do not float on rainbows in the ordinary Swiss landscape is no fundamental objection to their doing so in other regions of experience.

Perhaps an even more pertinent text is the dream of a young married woman:

[48] *Ibid.*, pp. 154 f.

[49] *Ibid.*, p. 78.

I saw a dark brown fertile field in which a plough was cutting large furrows. Suddenly I myself became the field and the sharp steel plough went easily through the length of my body and cut me into two halves. Although it hurt, it was indescribably beautiful. I experienced myself as the ploughed-up field, and the furrow as my own flesh, but it was not bleeding.[50]

Now, the nearest tyro of a Freudian dream-interpreter would not hesitate to discover genital symbols here. But there is a difficulty. The dreamer is no prude. She is married, she has often dreamed of undisguised intercourse, and she has no abnormal sexual quirks. Why should this be a dream of sexual relations? According to standard Freudian theory, the dream is a sexual wish-fulfillment which is disguised in this form because the dreamer's Superego cannot tolerate a frank revelation of the wish, complete with human genitals. Boss objects. The dreamer had experienced for the first time in her life only a few days before a completely loving acceptance of the sexual act, and had in fact (though she did not yet know it) become pregnant.

She had often enough dreamt of "very natural" sexual experiences. This occurred while she had known merely the physical stimulation of the sexual act and not as yet love in all its richness. However, once she had experienced this love, the openness and fertility of her whole being became embodied in a freshly ploughed field, the full essence of which corresponded most completely to her new attitude towards heaven and earth.[51]

In other words, it is not because of prudishness that she dreams thus, but because a naked picture of genital contact is not the reality which she is living. Freudian genital symbolism will not do, nor would a Jungian translation into a Mother Earth archetype. It is not a question of symbol or abstraction. Quite simply, the young woman *is* the plowed field. She is the rich and fertile and plow-accepting earth.

Boss's orientation permits him to ask in all seriousness the searching question whether dreams reveal a world with different dimensions and properties from those of the world of waking experience. On the whole, there is much correspondence. Descartes would never have mentioned his doubt otherwise. Boss points to the similarities in the scenes and populations of the two realms. Nevertheless, it is true that in the dream some of the routines of waking-life, at least sophisticated Occidental waking life, are altered. There is more

[50] *Ibid.*, p. 156.   [51] *Ibid.*, p. 158.

magic, there are more sudden transformations and translocations, and the dream environment seems at times to beat more strongly to the rhythm of feeling than a rigid three-dimensional Euclidean world would permit. Of course, nowadays astronomers and physicists do not present us with any such rigid universe anyway. Some of the latest descriptions of our galaxy make the energetic center of it sound astonishingly like a beating heart.

But I am no astronomer, and I feel more certain about the realities of the following dream which Boss presents in illustration of the space-time-heart coordinates of a man who, up to his thirty-fifth year, had seen women as nothing but sex objects and who in general treated other people like tools. This man had fallen in love but still hesitated to burden himself with the expense of another human being. He dreamed:

> My girl-friend and I were in a shabby inn. Like a 3rd class railway waiting-room, it had drab walls and grey, faded furniture. What struck me as most odd was the fact that the whole room was so terribly small, like the room of a doll's house, two yards long, one and a half yards wide, hardly one yard high. We, too, were very small and I very often felt as if I were looking at my girl-friend through the wrong side of opera-glasses, so distant did she appear. Both of us were depressed and bored and seemed to have nothing in common. These feelings were reflected by the atmosphere both of the inn and its surroundings. It was monotonously raining out of a deep grey, cloudy sky, and water was dripping on to the paving in front of the inn. Suddenly the sun broke through. The room became bright. At the same time I felt very attracted to my girl-friend, and found her very pleasant. A wave of warm feelings towards her welled up in me. At that very instant I saw, to my utter astonishment, that the whole room had changed. It had become as gigantically large as the banqueting hall of a magnificent place and its furnishings had become luxurious and tasteful. We two had also resumed our natural size. Unfortunately this did not last for long. The wave of warm feeling in me quickly ebbed away, and simultaneously the room and our own statures contracted. Again we sat in the doll-like inn and again we were terribly bored. Then this whole game began anew and was repeated many times. Corresponding to the rhythmical ebb and flow of my feelings of love towards my girl-friend, the room expanded into magnificence only to contract again to the size of a prison cell.[52]

A technological society may of course ask what practical use can be made of an existential approach like Boss's. Can you harness it

[52] *Ibid.*, pp. 189 f.

to do work? Will it predict and control? Can it be turned into a commercially profitable psychological test? Can it form the basis of a new technical specialty or profession? The proper retort seems to be that such questions indicate that technology has spread like a disease over our profoundest human concerns. Boss's engineer who entered therapy behind the bars of his mathematical formulae is a sample of what can happen. Successful as an engineer, he was depressed, anxious, and nearly dead as a human being. If we need more evidence of the losses and dangers inherent in the prevailing technological outlook, we might heed the words of a University of North Carolina student printed in his college newspaper. Jonathan Yardley in the *Daily Tar Heel* for December 1, 1959, has the following trenchant commentary:

> John Doe is 5' 10" and weighs 170 pounds. He has an I.Q. of 112 and scored reasonably normally on the Rorschach Test. He has taken the Ohio State Aptitude Test and the Michigan Vocabulary Test and the College Board Aptitude Test and Achievement Test and the English Composition Test and a great number of personality tests and creativity tests and perception tests and vocational aptitude tests and interest tests and leisure enjoyment tests.
>
> He belongs to Alpha Beta Chi, which is ranked tenth on the campus in scholastics, twelfth in intramurals, and is considered by the girls to have the eighth best parties, the fourth best looking boys, and the fifth nicest house. John himself is the fraternity's fifteenth ranked scholar, its second best ping pong player, and its fourth ugliest member.
>
> John Doe, his fraternity, and his little world have been channeled, categorized, listed, rated, placed, sub-divided and sub-sub-divided. John Doe and his fraternity brothers and his girl friend and his parents and his automobile and his college and his brain have all been listed in this little world of lists, rankings, and categories.
>
> Because of this categorization, the world of John Doe—our world—has been for the past twenty or thirty years moving rapidly in the direction of de-personalization. In an effort to ease the difficult task of orienting each individual to an increasingly complex culture, man has lost himself in a maze of automation and I.B.M. machines.
>
> Mid-twentieth century America is not only prone to classification by testing; it is highly susceptible to ego inflation through rankings. Thus the pages of every newspaper are filled with the "Top Ten"— tunes, dressers, football teams, hitters, beauty queens, and presidents. Each individual strives to gain status through his own rank or through that of a friend, a university, a team, or even a favorite song.
>
> In colleges and universities tests are given to determine vocational interest and aptitude. They are reportedly very accurate. But what

happens to the boy who always has wanted to be a doctor and is shown by the tests that he would be "happiest" as an ad man? Does he become a doctor who always wonders if he would be happier in Ulcer Gulch, or an advertiser who always wishes he had become a doctor? Do these tests fully account for psychological factors which may have influenced a youth's early choice of profession? The testers say not, but it seems that the effect of these tests could be highly dangerous.

Perhaps the most disturbing element of these tests is that they seem to be trying to eliminate the matter of choice. It has been pointed out that the choice of whether or not to take the tests seriously remains, but this seems a rather small choice. If you believe in the omniscient wisdom of science, you will take them to heart, if not, you will not.

It is not our privilege to question the validity of the vocational tests or of any other tests. It is, however, our right to question the beneficence of their effect on American society. To categorize and catalogue is to rob human beings of emotion and feeling, or to attempt to do so. It is an obvious attempt to make the machine superior to the man, because it has the ultimate power of judgment, and to make man himself into a machine.

George Orwell and Aldous Huxley have written brilliantly and pessimistically of the future lying in wait for mechanistic man. Every student knows all too well the forecasts of *Brave New World* and *1984*. They are not very encouraging. They picture a world dominated by the super-intellect. Huxley's "brave new world" is a sterile society in which individuality, sexuality, and self-respect have been lost to the ever-present god of science. Orwell's immortal "Big Brother" is a personification of all the evils science and intelligence, wrongly used, can bring to mankind.

Science has been one of the greatest factors in human progress. Psychology has probed the depths of man's mind and consciousness with great perception and considerable result. This is a culture based on science, and nothing short of an all-encompassing disaster will change that. Science is the major factor in today's world, but it cannot be the ruling factor. If science, formulas, machines, theories are ever to rule man, man will truly have ceased to be an organism and will have become a machine.[53]

Attitudes have consequences. It is questionable whether the prevailing attitudes of technological science have the consequences we most deeply desire. Boss's existential analysis of dreams tells us that close beneath the surface of an increasingly standardized, mechanized life-space such as our college editorialist describes

[53] Yardley (1959), p. 2. Used by permission of the author.

there throbs a volcanic reality with qualities and dimensions different from those conventionally accepted by the average, educated, civilized John Doe. Both are aspects of the whole truth. But the curious fact is that one cannot be aware of this unless one adopts an attitude like Boss's. From the point of view of technology the world of the dream does not exist. The authentic technological approach to dreaming, if there is any approach at all, is to clamp electrodes to the skull or insert them into the brain and record electroencephalographic tracings. Technology excludes the dream in the very act of approaching it. But Boss's attitude, or something like it, permits us to be aware both of the limitless world of the dream and of the technology which denies that any such world exists.

Boss has done a great service in drawing our attention back to the dream as dreamed. Under the influence of Freud and Jung, one is tempted to become an adept in the esoteric lore of the Unconscious and the art of sometimes tortured interpretations without pausing long enough to discover what the dream itself, the manifest dream, is like. It is a singular fact that in an era which has, in psychological circles, had so much to say about dreaming it is almost impossible to get good answers to the most elementary questions about the content of dreams. For example, do the dreams of women differ significantly from the dreams of men? Here and there one can find scraps of information bearing on such questions, but studies of dream content are notable by their scarcity. If Boss's influence should spread, we might begin to get the kind of serious collection of facts about the dream that has marked the advance of natural science in other departments of knowledge. That is one of Boss's merits—that he encourages us to observe rather than to rest in speculation. Another is that he invites us to consider *all* of an individual's experience as a connected totality operating according to laws which prevail in both waking and sleeping states—just as the laws of physics are supposed to be operative whether it is day or night. Perhaps the nearest that American psychology has come to Boss's general phenomenological position (until the recent existentialist literature) is in the work of Snygg and Combs, whose book *Individual Behavior* made a pleasant stir a few years ago.[54] Any reader who has difficulty in following Boss's line of thought would probably find the Snygg and Combs book useful preparation for it. Finally, Boss's work on the dream is not

[54] See Snygg and Combs (1949), as also Snygg (1941). (A second edition of Snygg and Combs appeared in 1959.)

a mere cranky rejection of theorists he does not understand but a new departure which has profited from their labors, as is usually true of fruitful novelties in science.

A few words of guidance for the perplexed

Encounter with so many different views and arguments in one chapter may have left the reader dizzy. He may recover some of his stability by focusing on one thought—that we have been dealing here with the reactions of different human beings to certain facts of human experience. Let us take dreaming as typical of these facts.

The reaction of behaviorists is to consider dreams as outside science and not susceptible to experimental proof.

Freud's reaction is to treat the dream, the manifest dream, as a jumble of symbols pointing obscurely into the unknown depths of the psychophysical organism. By interpreting the symbols he thinks to arrive at some appreciation of the nature of the Unconscious, which he eventually describes as composed of repressed material, sexual and aggressive instincts (the Id), introjected parental figures (the Superego), and a large portion of the Ego itself. It is because the Unconscious is what it is that the dream is what it is. A brief psychoanalytic interpretation may leave the impression that a dream is a case of the individual's body holding a Caliban conversation with the mind, in the course of which there is much crude and menacing sexual display.

Jung, at any rate, thought that Freud was too fleshly and too personal, and he proposes that beyond the fleshly, personal Unconscious recognized by Freud there lies the Collective Unconscious full of alien powers of a superhuman kind, prior to individual life, independent of human individuals, but often appearing to the Ego in individual shapes of their own—the archetypes. For Jung (as for·Freud) the dream is a symbolic structure, but it symbolizes the archetypes and in doing so confronts the dreamer with something which is not himself—something which not only *seems* alien to the self (as in Freud's theory) but *is*. Such, at least, is one way of reading Jung.

Fairbairn also treats the dream as symbolical, but the distance between the dream symbols and what they symbolize does not appear to be so great. Just as the manifest dream seems to be composed of independent persons and objects in the presence of the observing and acting dreamer, so the Unconscious contains or is composed of independent dynamic units—the Ego and its split-off parts and the internalized objects to which they are attached— acting both libidinally and aggressively. The autonomy of the internalized objects (not to mention the split-off portions of the Ego) is admitted by him to be so striking that he is afraid he will be charged with developing a demon theory. Like Jung, then, Fairbairn stresses that the Ego has to confront, even in the intimate privacy of the dream, things which are not the Ego and did not originate in the Ego (nor in the personal Unconscious) but which have power of their own. It is true that Fairbairn derives this power as far as possible from the Ego in its libidinal capacity— the internalized objects are cathected by the Ego—but he knows how independent a cathected object may act.

Boss shakes off symbolism and treats the dream as personal reality. The living and dying human individual, whether awake or asleep, always finds himself in relation to objects which are not himself; the objects of the dream are quite as much objects as are those of the so-called "real world" of waking experience. One's experience runs from moment to moment, and all these moments are equally real. One lives and dies always in one's own experience, among one's own objects, in one's own unique relation to these objects. The dream is a phase of this continuing experience. As to the Unconscious, that is replaced in Boss's system by the objects themselves and their interrelations and relations with the living and dying subject. Boss is thus a complete phenomenologist, postulating nothing outside the self and its objects as experienced.

We have in this chapter covered a whole spectrum of attitudes toward the dream. For the behaviorists it is scientifically nothing, for the psychoanalysts it is symbol, for Boss it is reality. I myself find Boss's work on the dream refreshing, illuminating, inviting, and I think its implications are full of promise for psychology; but we must wait and see. In particular, I must add that the fate of Boss's dream theory is bound up with the fate of the existentialist philosophy he espouses, and as to that I have neither the competence, nor—if I had the competence—the space, to make an adequate comment.

References for chapter 9

Boss, M. (1958) *The analysis of dreams.* Tr. by A. J. Pomerans. New York: Philosophical Library.

Darling, F. F. (1937) *A herd of red deer: a study of animal behaviour.* London: Oxford Univ. Press.

Dollard, J., and Miller, N. E. (1950) *Personality and psychotherapy: an analysis in terms of learning, thinking, and culture.* New York: McGraw-Hill.

Fairbairn, W. R. D. (1952) *Psychoanalytic studies of the personality.* London: Tavistock.

Freud, S. (1950) *The interpretation of dreams.* Tr. by A. A. Brill. New York: Modern Library.

Harper, R. A. (1959) *Psychoanalysis and psychotherapy: 36 systems.* Englewood Cliffs, N.J.: Prentice-Hall.

Jung, C. G. (1916) *Psychology of the unconscious.* Tr. by B. M. Hinkle. New York: Dodd, Mead.

——— (1939) *The integration of the personality.* Tr. by S. M. Dell. New York: Farrar & Rinehart.

——— (1959) *The archetypes and the collective unconscious.* Tr. by R. F. C. Hull. Vol. 9, Part 1, of *The collected works of C. G. Jung.* Bollingen Series XX, Bollingen Foundation, Inc. New York: Pantheon.

———, and Pauli, W. (1955) *The interpretation of nature and the psyche.* Tr. by R. F. C. Hull and P. Silz. New York: Pantheon.

Kleitman, N. (1960) Patterns of dreaming. *Scientific American,* 203 (November), 82-88.

Mowrer, O. H. (1950) *Learning theory and personality dynamics.* New York: Ronald.

——— (1959) Judgment and suffering: contrasting views. *Faculty Forum,* No. 10 (October).

Sears, R. R. (1936) Experimental studies of projection: I. Attribution of traits. *Journal of Social Psychology,* 7, 151-63.

——— (1944) Experimental analysis of psychoanalytic phenomena. In Hunt, J. McV. (Ed.) *Personality and the behavior disorders,* New York: Ronald. Vol. 1, pp. 306-32.

Skinner, B. F. (1953) *Science and human behavior.* New York: Macmillan.

Snygg, D. (1941) The need for a phenomenological system of psychology. *Psychological Review,* 48, 404-24.

———, and Combs, A. W. (1949) *Individual behavior: a new frame of reference for psychology.* New York: Harper.

Watson, J. B. (1925) *Behaviorism.* New York: Norton.

Yardley, J. (1959) Perspectives by Yardley. *Daily Tar Heel,* 68, No. 58 (December 1), 2.

Yates, A. J. (1958) Symptoms and symptom substitution. *Psychological Review,* 65, 371-74.

III

METHODS OF
DESCRIBING
PERSONALITY

10

TYPOLOGY

Preview   *A typology is a classification scheme meant to reveal significant dimensions of human nature. Major examples are those of (1) Kretschmer (and, later, Sheldon), connecting physique with temperament; (2) Heymans and Wiersma, emphasizing behavior variables; (3) Jung, concerned with mental functioning; (4) Spranger, focusing upon values. All four of these typologies represent theories about personality which are different though not necessarily conflicting, and all four have issued in practical application.*

The first section of this book was concerned with man as a biological species, pursuing a life course determined in its main outlines by the genes but modified in detail by learning. The second section was concerned with man as a conscious being, aware of himself and his environment whether awake or asleep and subject to impulses so seemingly alien and beyond deliberate control that some very influential theorists (followed by perhaps most psychologists) have postulated a dynamic Unconscious to complete the idea of personality as a mental structure. In both sections we have tended to look at the human individual' as dynamic, as an ongoing process or set of processes unfolding in time and undescribable except by a similarly dynamic analysis, ongoing and unfolding. If such an analysis might be likened to a moving picture, we now turn to a mode of analysis which might be likened to a snapshot. For all typological and psychometric approaches try to catch the individual standing still, so to speak; they try to fix and analyze him like a specimen on a slide. The typologist or psychometrician does not necessarily believe that what is thus revealed is unchanging; but the method of approach does yield a static picture, a snapshot, in which all action has been frozen. Of course, it may be urged that if we have enough of these snapshots they can be run off like a movie film, and action will reappear. True enough, and yet the method favors a static view of personality. This strongly appeals to anyone who likes to make accurate measurements, and, on the other hand, repels those who see life as process. The result is tension and quarreling between the two parties, which is clearly evidenced within the psychological profession. In fact, the same tensions and quarrels may break out within one individual, as he inclines first the one way and then the other; and he may be divided against himself. The difficulty, it should be realized, is not confined to psychologists. It is probably the same sort of difficulty as that formulated in the Heisenberg indeterminacy principle, which, as I understand it, states that it is impossible at the same moment to observe *both* the position and the velocity of a particle.

Even within the general field of work which will be examined in this and the next three chapters there is a wide range of possibilities, and we find that psychometricians often do not like typologists, in spite of their essential kinship, regarding them as incomplete scientists who do not know the value of measurement; and there are others still, whom we might call intuitionists or impressionists, who have little patience with either typologists or psychometricians. Clearly, the whole field of personality description is a hornets' nest.

We shall be brave, however, and proceed as if every hornet were a honey bee carrying a valuable drop of nectar which we should like to have. And first, for the typologists.

Some general problems

A typology is a compromise between the view that all people are alike and the view that every person is different. It classifies individuals according to certain key traits, usually few in number. Fragmentary typologies, the remnants of ancient systems surviving as folklore, are in common use. For example, red hair is taken to indicate a fiery temper, a sharp nose to reveal a penetrating mind, a steady gaze to guarantee honesty. It would be economical of time and trouble to know such relationships if they were real, for by noticing a few surface characteristics you could be sure of the emotional tendencies of people, their intellectual capacity, their morality. Most of us apply such rules of thumb now and then. Few of us, however, bother to test these rules. We are not even consistent in our attitude toward them. If a redheaded person is really hot tempered, we note the fact as confirming the rule; if not, we let it pass or smile at our own superstition.

Much more serious about their typologies are the men whose work will be reviewed in this chapter. But, before coming to them, we need to reflect on what is involved in even so simple a variety of typology as that which links hot temper with red hair. There are three things to think about—the red hair, the hot temper, and the connection between them.

To pick out red hair as a classifying term suggests that the trait can be detected and that it deserves the prominence given it. Detection of red hair requires a visual apparatus which distinguishes between that color and another, such as black; it also requires a decision about the cut-off points (where red ceases and another color begins), because there are many shades of red blending gradually into the flaxen on the one side and the brown on the other. These discriminative operations could be built into an instrument which could be used even by a color-blind man, but the instrument might not be any more, and could easily be less, reliable than the inventor himself. At any rate, the development of an instrument to replace a sensitive human observer would not relieve us of the responsibility of deciding whether to use it or not. That decision rests upon more than the detectability of the trait. But if a detectable trait, perhaps insignificant in itself, is connected with hot temper, it gains significance, because a hot temper is something pretty important in social relations.

What, though, *is* a hot temper? We ought to be as clear about this as about the red hair. At first the question seems stupid. Everybody knows what a hot temper is! On further reflection the question seems unanswerable. So much is meant by the phrase, and so much that is vague, intangible, beyond the reach of the senses! It is questions like this which frighten people away from psychology, even including psychologists. Temper is a psychic variable, and such variables have a way of going undefined, or, worse yet, of being ignored as "unscientific." Fortunately, the typologists have not ignored them.

Finally, in regard to the connection between the variables—a concept which may be handled as correlation—we must note that any errors of identification are brought over into the correlation coefficient. For example, if our judgment that someone has a high temper is influenced by the observation that he has red hair, then the asserted relation between the variables will be spurious or partly so. It is spurious because we have been actually treating two variables as if they were one. Genuine correlations depend on making independent judgments of the variables in question. Of course, the degree of correlation cannot be accurately assessed unless the variables are correctly identified. Suppose that there is truly a correlation between red hair and hot temper. We shall miss this truth, or at least we shall lower the true correlation, if we are forever mixing up red hair with black hair and hot temper with general excitability. We must define our variables cleanly.

As to this last point, however, there is a caution which cannot be too emphatically voiced. To define something cleanly is not equivalent to stripping it down to a minute measurable element. Measurement is very important in science, but not measurement for its own sake. We have to consider what we are measuring and why. There are cases where less can be accomplished by measurements than by a sensitive observer. At the same time it must be admitted that science is a cooperative affair and that it flourishes on observations which can be duplicated. For this reason it is desirable that definition of variables should be as precise and understandable as possible. The danger to avoid is triviality. We often need to treat extremely complex wholes as simple wholes, and to do this we may need to use observational methods which may seem primitive and yet be far more effective than all available measurements. One of the most rigorous, most mathematical of American psychometricians selected his own assistants by unstandardized personal observation. How ironical—and how sensible!

To the point here is the attitude of the German psychiatrist Ernst Kretschmer, whose typology we are about to study. In the twenty-second edition of his *Körperbau und Charakter* he has included much more quantitative information than in previous editions (the earliest was in 1921), and yet he nevertheless insists that measurement is an adjunct rather than a basic operation even in research on physique. After remarking that there are weaknesses in any freehand verbal description, he continues:

> Yet it must be emphasized that this method is indispensable as the broad foundation of research on physique and that it supplies much for which neither measurement nor photographic material is a substitute. In the first place there are a multitude of important traits, sufficiently describable in words, such as skin color, vascular condition, hairiness, which cannot be measured and pictured at all or only by intolerably complicated methods. Furthermore, direct optical examination reveals many things much more strikingly and clearly. . . . We put visual description ahead of measurement in our examination schedule. For both should be arrived at independently as far as possible and the eye should not rely foolishly on the statistics. In short, everything depends upon a perfectly artistic, strict discipline of our eyes. A pedantic accumulation of isolated measurements without any idea or intuition of the total structure will get us nowhere. The tape-measure sees nothing. It never on its own leads us to the comprehension of biological types, which is our goal. If, however, we have learned to see, we shall notice that the calipers then furnish us with beautiful, exact confirmations and quantitative formulations and even, in some cases, important corrections of what we have discovered with the eyes.[1]

The typologies of Kretschmer and Sheldon

Kretschmer's basic proposition is that there is a connection between inherited body form and temperament. The latter term refers to general psychic disposition, especially in the emotional area.

Kretschmer distinguishes three major body types, the pyknic (plump), the athletic (muscular), and the leptosomatic (frail), and a minor fourth class, the dysplastic (maldeveloped), which contains exaggerated specimens of the other types as well as disharmonious physiques. A convenient table of characteristics is here reproduced in modified form, though Kretschmer warns us against reliance on a few traits. The table provides merely reference points

[1] Kretschmer (1955), pp. 6 f. Used by permission of Springer-Verlag. My translation of this source throughout.

Table 16
Kretschmer's major physique types

	pyknic	*athletic*	*leptosomatic*
trunk	chest deep, short, vaulted; rib-angle obtuse	shoulders broad, strong; trunk trapezoid; pelvis narrow	chest flat, long; rib-angle acute; pelvis broad
surface	contours soft, rounded out by fat	muscles prominent on solid bone structure	lank or stringy with little surface fat
extremities	limbs short, soft; hands and feet broad, fine-boned	limbs powerful, solid; hands and feet big, sometimes cyanotic	limbs thin, long; hands and feet long, narrow
head and neck	head big, round, flat on top; neck massive, short	head high, solid; neck free, strong; trapezius tense, sloping	head small; neck thin, long
face	face softly molded, broad, flushed; profile weak	face firm, bony, sculptured, high points emphasized; long oval	face pale, narrow, short oval; nose narrow, pointed; profile sometimes sharply angular
hair	head hair fine, tending to baldness; secondary sexual hair medium to pronounced	head hair luxuriant; secondary sexual hair not distinctive	head hair dense, sometimes "fur cap"; secondary sexual hair slight

Adapted from Kretschmer (1955), p. 14.

for morphological judgments which, according to him, are often very uncertain, especially for the unpracticed eye.

Neither doctrinaire nor naïve, Kretschmer fully appreciates the fluid transitions from one body form to another, and he has never maintained that an absolute chasm separates the types, as some critics falsely imply. He has an artist's perceptiveness for the nuances with which he deals. He recognizes the changes which occur with age, and he notes that women are less differentiable than men. He is as acutely aware as his critics that the body is not a static thing like a child's building block but a delicately balanced dynamic organization undergoing both regular and irregular modifications with time and accidents.

What he tries to grasp in this anatomical flux is the fundamental plan of the organism, the architectural idea which it is endeavoring to express. There is a point in time where the expression of this idea is most nearly perfect. Kretschmer has therefore paid attention to the life history of his types. The basic characteristics of extreme leptosomatics (asthenics) appear early and are maintained into old age; even heavy farm work may alter their musculature very little. Other leptosomatics are less easily recognized because they share in certain characteristics of the athletics. As for these latter, their characteristics become clear at about eighteen and more pronounced in later years; even after the involutional changes of old age, the proportions of the head and skeleton identify them. The pyknics are more of a diagnostic problem. Usually not until they are thirty or forty do they show themselves most strikingly for what they basically are, and after sixty they lose some of their distinctiveness. The young pyknic is not necessarily fat and may be confused with the athletic; perhaps the facial proportions and the way the short neck settles into the shoulders are the most distinguishing marks.

The quantitative indices of the types which Kretschmer publishes are not the basis of his typology. As has been explained, these are incidental results. They appeal to workers who do not have much sympathy with the impressionistic visual approach rather than to Kretschmer himself.

The temperamental characteristics which tend to accompany the physique types appear, according to Kretschmer, in exaggerated or distorted form in epilepsy and psychosis. It is not that he thinks of the physique types (with the possible exception of the dysplastic) as signs of mental disease, for the types are as noticeable in the healthy population as among the inmates of hospitals; but it was among psychiatric patients that Kretschmer discovered the purported relationship between physique and temperament, and his most persuasive data bear upon the association of types of mental disease with types of physique. He maintains, as nearly everybody knows, that pyknics, if they fall ill, tend toward manic-depressive (or circular) insanity, leptosomatics toward schizophrenia, and athletics toward schizophrenia and epilepsy.

In his original study Kretschmer focused on manic-depressives and schizophrenics. Table 17 summarizes the results. If the athletics

Table 17
Physique and psychiatric classification: Kretschmer's sample

	manic-depressive	schizophrenic
leptosomatic	4	81
athletic	3	31
mixed athletic-leptosomatic	2	11
pyknic	58	2
pyknic mixed forms	14	3
dysplastic	—	34
undecided and unclassifiable	4	13
TOTAL NUMBERS	85	175

Adapted from Kretschmer (1955), p. 38.

and leptosomatics are lumped together, we find that they make up about 70 per cent of the schizophrenics but only about 11 per cent of the manic-depressives. In contrast, the pyknic and pyknic mixed forms account for about 85 per cent of the manic-depressives and only about 3 per cent of the schizophrenics. None of the manic-depressives are dysplastic, but nearly 20 per cent of the schizo-phrenics are. These figures are striking. Kretschmer concludes from them that body type is lawfully related to psychiatric type.

The above pioneer findings may be compared with those obtained by various investigators in Europe, Asia, and North America from a total of 8099 cases. Table 18, based on a compilation by Westphal, presents the results under three disease categories. The figures, though less emphatic, agree with Kretschmer's early findings, and they supply the further information that epileptics are rarely pyknic.

We must notice, however, that there is less agreement between the

Table 18
Physique and psychiatric classification: Westphal's summary

	manic-depressive (per cent)	schizophrenic (per cent)	epileptic (per cent)
pyknic	64.6	13.7	5.5
leptosomatic	19.2	50.3	25.1
athletic	6.7	16.9	28.9
dysplastic	1.1	10.5	29.5
unclassified	8.4	8.6	11.0
TOTAL NUMBERS	1361	5233	1505

Adapted from Kretschmer (1955), p. 39.

two tables than would be expected if the same methods of classification were being applied. If Table 17 is correct, there should be
a higher percentage of pyknics among the manic-depressives of
Table 18. It is very possible that there were divergencies in classification. But it cannot be decided from the information available
whether Kretschmer was too much swayed by his theory or the
others were less able than he to identify the physique types. As
pointed out before, *if* a real correlation exists between variables,
inaccurate classification will reduce the apparent correlation and accurate classification will increase it. This argument cannot be legitimately used to prove a correlation in the absence of evidence, but
it does indicate the importance of accurate classification and, unless
we want to question the competence and good faith of Kretschmer,
the obviously sensitive originator of the typology, we might infer
from it that the other observers were less accurate. In every field of
science some observers are better than others, and we must take this
into account; and it is surely possible that Kretschmer is more sensitive to the variables that he tries to catch impressionistically than
are other observers or the instruments they use in place of impressionistic observation. I stress this not to defend Kretschmer, but
because of its general relevance to the question of scientific evidence. Of course, the expert observer who cannot communicate some
of his skill to others, or invent an instrument to take his place, will
generally be laughed out of the scientific community no matter how
accurate he is, just as a lone man with good color vision would be
laughed out of a community of the totally color-blind. That is why
sharable methods of investigation and simple tests and instruments
which can be operated by people who are not especially sensitive
observers are so earnestly sought for in science, which is very
much a community enterprise. Even so, instrumentation can be
overstressed.

Let us grant for the moment that Kretschmer is the expert whom
we must take as the criterion of exactness. His figures in Table 17
would then represent the maximum degree of correlation between
physique and psychosis. The correlation is not perfect. Why not?

A possible answer would be that inheritance contributes only a
part to adult physique, while numerous other factors—education,
accidents, the trials of life—also have their important influence,
muting and diverting the hereditary tendencies which Kretschmer
wants to detect. Kretschmer's answer is rather different from this.
For him the morphology of the body and the psychotic breakdown

are only partial manifestations of the underlying constitution, which is complex and may express itself in apparently contradictory ways. A psychosis may be a brief episode in the long history of a temperament and the body changes shape during a lifetime; but that does not mean that the body has lost its inheritance or is less under its influence at one time than another. The genes are dynamic and produce various results in the course of time. Heredity, besides, is not a simple matter. "Let us suppose," writes Kretschmer,

that an individual has received from his parents certain genes, one half of which carry the pyknic-circular tendency while the other half carry the asthenic-schizophrenic. Now both in the body structure and in the psychic picture (e.g., the psychosis) the pyknic-circular potential or the asthenic-schizophrenic potential may alone be dominant. The external picture then shows the usual psychophysical combination. On the other hand, the phenotypical manifestation may be an evenly-weighted alloy, a pyknic-asthenic mixture on the bodily side, a circular-schizophrenic on the psychic.[2]

In illustration, Kretschmer cites the case of a man of 48 who came down with a typical circular depression and after a period in the hospital regained his balance. His body was almost purely leptosomatic, in fact, asthenic; it was contradicted, however, by the pyknic quality of his face. A year later his sister arrived at the hospital with a typical schizophrenia, in harmony with her definitely asthenic physique. The father and mother were different physique types (the father athletic, the mother pyknic) and had the corresponding temperaments. There were two other children, both male: one was like the father, one like the mother. Kretschmer does not attribute the illness of either the son or the daughter to environmental factors, but to the hereditary potential, which happened to be more mixed in the son. He notes that when this patient was mentally healthy he displayed temperament traits as contradictory as his physique, pedantic dryness coexisting with friendly companionableness.

Inharmonious traits may be combined in the same person. A pyknic head may be attached to an asthenic body, a friendly warmth may accompany or alternate with a repellent stiffness. This is the fact. Kretschmer's theory is that the cause is genetic. We should not expect the offspring of diverse parents to be a smoothy blended intermediate type or to resemble one parent exclusively, according to Kretschmer; we may find instead a *mosaic* of opposing qualities. Such inheritance

[2] *Ibid.*, p. 135.

is, in fact, well known. When a white-splashed-with-blue fowl is crossed with a black one and produces a blue Andalusian, the result is plumage with a kind of checkerboard of colors, not white dominantly, nor black dominantly, nor gray. We do not contest the genetic basis of this outcome. Kretschmer argues for a like mosaic effect in human physique and temperament.

It is possible that physique is psychiatrically important even when the diagnosis runs counter to the physique. As is widely recognized, manic-depressives are much more likely to recover from a psychotic episode than are schizophrenes and be able to return to normal life. Suppose, then, that we have a collection of schizophrenes whose physiques range from asthenic to pyknic. According to Kretschmer, the pyknics among them should demonstrate their constitutional tendency toward the temperament found in manic-depressives by recovering more often than the asthenics. Such is actually the case, if we may trust Kretschmer's statistics taken from a study by Enke and Kanthak.[3]

Our discussion so far has dealt chiefly with physique correlated with psychosis. But a physique type does not necessarily prognosticate a psychosis. What Kretschmer maintains is that there is a correlation between physique and temperament; psychoses are correlated with physiques because of the correlation between physique and temperament. A psychosis, he argues, is the pathological blossoming out of an inherited temperament. This contention is supported by studies of the prepsychotic behavior of patients. For example, one investigator concluded from a statistical survey of 351 schizophrenes:

> Schizoid peculiarities appear about twice as often among future schizophrenes as among their parents, about three times as often as among their brothers and sisters, seven to twenty times as often as among the other relatives investigated, and well over fifty times as often as in the general population.[4]

The three major temperaments outlined by Kretschmer are the cyclothymic, the schizothymic, and the collodethymic—respectively correlated with the pyknic, the leptosomatic, and the athletic physiques—designations which do not imply illness any more than the physique designations do. The temperaments differ in three prime respects: mood or sensitivity, tempo, and reactivity to stimuli. In the mood or sensitivity dimension there is an energy range from high to low: cyclothymes include both the quite jolly and the quite

[3] *Ibid.*, pp. 144 f.   [4] *Ibid.*, p. 163.

sad, schizothymes are at one extreme very sensitive and mimosa-like and at the other coldly indifferent, and collodethymes vary from the highly explosive to the thick-skinned and calm. Individuals of each type have a characteristic tempo, the cyclothymes smoothly varying from sparkling liveliness to easy-going quietness, the schizothymes shifting jerkily from listlessness to intense concentration or from one psychic function to another, the collodethymes holding steady to whatever mood or occupation is theirs. Both cyclothymes and collodethymes show by their adequate responses to stimuli that they are in good contact with the surrounding world, though the quality of the reaction is different in the two, the cyclothymes being easier and more natural, the collodethymes more deliberate and volitional; but the schizothymes are often out of touch or out of step with the sequence of events, so that their reactions either occur at the wrong time or seem inappropriate from excess or defect of energy. These temperamental traits are regarded by Kretschmer as permanent in the constitution, manifesting themselves in sickness and health, in occupations and social life, in crimes and in the artistic and scientific productions of geniuses.

Many experimental studies have been stimulated by Kretschmer's work. Correlations have been found between the types and various chemical reactions, perceptual tendencies, and motor performances. There is space here for only a single illustration. One Kretschmerian (Scholl) discovered that perceptual preference for color or for form was related to temperament. He presented colored figures in brief tachistoscopic exposures to 30 subjects whose temperament classification had been determined by their responses to a questionnaire; their task was to identify the figures, and this could be done by noting either the color or the form. Table 19 summarizes the results. Notice that there are intermediate classifications for those who were only moderately schizothymic or cyclothymic, and also for those whose

Table 19
Influence of temperament on color-form perception: Scholl's 30 subjects

	form	form-color	color-form	color
schizothymic	5	1		
schizo-cyclothymic	2	4	1	1
cyclo-schizothymic	1		5	1
cyclothymic		1		8

Adapted from Kretschmer (1955), p. 287.

Table 20

Influence of temperament on color-form perception: Lüth's 156 subjects

	form (per cent)	form-color (per cent)	color-form (per cent)	color (per cent)
schizothymic	80.7	74.6	48.0	27.3
cyclothymic	19.3	25.4	52.0	72.7

Adapted from Kretschmer (1955), p. 287.

reactions in the experiment only slightly favored form or color. If these finer subdivisions of the table are disregarded, one sees that 86 per cent of the schizothymes react primarily to form and a corresponding percentage of the cyclothymes react primarily to color. Another Kretschmerian (Lüth) obtained a similar result in a later study. He used 156 subjects and observed their responses to both tachistoscopic material and Rorschach cards. Table 20 is a summary.

On this side of the Atlantic there has been much less interest in Kretschmer's work than in Europe. This is partly because of the anti-hereditarian trend of American thought and partly because what interest there is has been largely absorbed into the constitutional research of Sheldon (see p. 328 ff.). But there is a further cause: empirical research by American investigators has tended to cast doubt on Kretschmer's conclusions.

An example of negative results is found in an elaborate study by Klineberg, Asch, and Block.[5] Whether this study actually demolishes Kretschmer is doubtful. As in all complex studies, it is possible to overlook important variables while concentrating on others. It may be that some of the discrepancy between the Klineberg, Asch, and Block results and the results obtained by investigators more favorable to Kretschmer can be attributed to the selection of the experimental subjects. Kretschmer bases his typology on the examination of widely varying populations. Klineberg, Asch, and Block, however, deliberately chose individuals who were as much alike as possible in respect to educational, social, and economic backgrounds. The argument for such selection is that it frees the physique-temperament factors (if they exist) from other factors which might be confused with them. On the other hand, such selection may simply limit the quantitative range of the factors under investigation. Suppose, for example, one were testing the assertion

[5] Klineberg, Asch, and Block (1934).

that there were many species of fish in the sea with very different habits of life, and one insisted that this hypothesis could be properly investigated only by looking at the fish caught in a particular kind of net dragged along the bottom of a particular inlet of the sea at a certain hour of the day: it is very probable that this sample would not very well represent the real variety of the fish in the whole sea. The Klineberg, Asch, and Block sample was drawn from a particular locale in a setting where undoubtedly strong selective influences were at work reducing the *temperament* variety; for their sample was made up of college students, and it is certain that colleges select even if they have no very restrictive admissions policy—because those who apply for admission are already selecting themselves, in terms of their ideas as to what is required of college students. For example, in spite of all cynical comments, a college population is likely to include a large proportion of fairly serious, studious people, people who on the whole are not like those found in more random groups. At the same time, while *temperament* selection is somewhat restrictive in colleges, *physique* selection is less so: a college admissions officer is more concerned about whether you are intelligent, stable, industrious intellectually, and socially adjusted than about how tall or fat you are. And according to Kretschmerian theory, it would be entirely possible and genetically understandable for such a process of selection to yield a narrow temperament range within a wide physique range. I do not say that this line of argument does in fact explain away the Klineberg, Asch, and Block results, but it should be kept in mind; and it is at least as credible as the counterargument that Kretschmer and his fellow-workers are incompetent scientists whom we can safely ignore.

The first part of the Klineberg, Asch, and Block study, which gave a negative answer to certain hypotheses about physique and performance, utilized 153 college men whose *temperament* characteristics they did not bother to assess. The second part of the study investigated the relationship between physique and temperament, employing a sample of 79 college women. Temperament in this case was assessed by a questionnaire developed by Kibler, one of Kretschmer's own supporters. The results of this investigation are peculiar on several counts. In the first place, these college women were quite predominantly leptosomatic, although, according to Sheldon's recent *Atlas*, the general female college population inclines definitely toward the pyknic side of the distribution.[6] In

[6] Sheldon, Dupertuis, and McDermott (1954), p. 13.

the second place, the temperament scores of this predominantly leptosomatic sample were predominantly cyclothymic, apparently not merely refuting Kretschmer but proving an exactly opposite physique-temperament linkage. In the third place, the findings of Van der Horst and Kibler, and of Lüth, using the same questionnaire and less restricted samples, present an entirely different pattern, as shown in Table 21. The contrast is clear, but the explanation is not. Though Klineberg, Asch, and Block offer their results as disproof of Kretschmer's typology and evidence against the hereditarian standpoint in general, they fall short of being conclusive.

The strongest support for Kretschmer's typology in America has come from the work of Sheldon, though Sheldon has not directly continued Kretschmer's lines of thought and has made theoretical statements with which Kretschmer disagrees. This work, severely criticized by many psychologists, has continued to gather enough corroboration from others in and out of psychology to deserve respect. As Diamond recently remarked, at the close of a favorable sketch of Sheldon's main ideas: "Sheldon's views have had so poor an audience among psychologists that some moral courage is required to confess to this degree of agreement with them. In honesty, however, they cannot be ignored."[7]

Sheldon has, in effect, replaced the words *pyknic, athletic,* and *leptosomatic* with the words *endomorph, mesomorph,* and *ectomorph;* and he has labeled the corresponding temperaments *viscero-*

Table 21
Temperament (by Kibler's questionnaire) vs. physique: three studies

	cyclothymic (per cent)	mixed (per cent)	schizothymic (per cent)
VAN DER HORST–KIBLER			
pyknic	94.4	2.8	2.8
leptosomatic	12.2	17.1	70.7
LÜTH			
pyknic	93.8	—	6.2
leptosomatic	7.6	—	92.4
KLINEBERG–ASCH–BLOCK			
pyknoid	50.0	25.0	25.0
leptoid	66.2	15.5	18.3

Adapted from Kretschmer (1955), p. 278; Klineberg, Asch, and Block (1934), p. 202.

[7] Diamond (1957), p. 150.

tonia, somatotonia, and *cerebrotonia.* He has concentrated on the task of defining the physiques quantitatively and has done much to bring order into the field of human morphology by publishing photographs and statistics in *Atlas of Men* which give some conception of the frequency, nature, and life history of the various kinds of physiques found in the United States. Sheldon, as most students know, grades the three morphological components of endomorphy, mesomorphy, ectomorphy on a numerical scale running from 1 through 7. The individual is "somatotyped" when he has been correctly assigned the three scale numerals required. The most extreme endomorph would be a person with a 7 in this component, and with 1 in mesomorphy and ectomorphy, yielding the somatotype 711; the most extreme mesomorph would be 171; the most extreme ectomorph 117. Roughly speaking, endomorphy refers to the development of viscera and body fat, mesomorphy to the development of bone and muscle, and ectomorphy to degree of linearity and fragility and amount of skin surface relative to body volume. Somatotyping involves both visual inspection and measurement, usually of standardized photographs of the nude. One simple quantitative index which Sheldon favors is the ratio of height over the cube root of the weight. In an American male sample of 46,000, Sheldon has found 88 different somatotypes. The commonest varieties have component values in the middle range. The 443, for instance, occurs 60 times out of a 1000. Muscle-men with a 171 rating are very rare, and so are 117 walking sticks. Rarer still are 711's and 515's, both of which have an incidence of 1 in 10,000. The distribution of female somatotypes is different from the male: there is less variation from the mean, and endomorphy predominates.

Sheldon's physique work has been fairly generally accepted. Yet Diamond has been impressed by his work on temperament and cites a number of studies confirming Sheldon's views. Of considerable importance is a study by Child which involved applying a 66-item questionnaire to 414 Yale sophomores who had been somatotyped by Sheldon the previous year.[8] To quote from Diamond's summary:

> In advance of the experiment, Child prepared a list of 96 predictions of positive relationships between answers to individual items and standing on morphological components, all in strict accordance with Sheldon's theories. . . . Ten of these predictions were confirmed at the 1 percent level, 10 more at the 5 percent level, while 54 more were confirmed in direction although they did not individually satisfy
> [8] Child (1950).

Table 22
Correlations between temperament and physique for 414 subjects: Child's study

	endomorphy	mesomorphy	ectomorphy
viscerotonia	.13	.13	−.15
somatotonia	.03	.38	−.37
cerebrotonia	−.03	−.38	.27

Adapted from Child (1950), p. 441.

conventional criteria of statistical significance. One prediction was disconfirmed at the 5 percent level, and none at the 1 percent level. The overall result constitutes an overwhelming confirmation of the general validity of Sheldon's theories. Few propositions in the field of personality can claim to have stronger experimental support.[9]

Diamond, like many others, has accused Sheldon of finding abnormally high correlations between his physique and temperament components, but he is impressed by the more moderate correlations found by Child and reproduced here in Table 22. If these and other such correlations support Sheldon, they also indirectly support Kretschmer, for Sheldon's viscerotonic and cerebrotonic temperaments resemble Kretschmer's cyclothymic and schizothymic, and his somatotonic resembles Kretschmer's collodethymic except that Sheldon's emphasis on sheer physical activity is much greater. Both note a tendency to violence in the athletic (mesomorphic) type. One of Kretschmer's followers, Eyrich, found that, according to crime statistics, pyknics were especially disinclined to murder, as compared to athletics and leptosomatics.[10] Not out of harmony with this is the finding of Glueck and Glueck in testing Sheldon's theory that mesomorphs are more frequent among delinquent boys than are endomorphs or ectomorphs, which is not the case among nondelinquents, as shown in Table 23.

The athletic or mesomorphic type is not necessarily criminal, of course. Criminal activity, according to Sheldon and Kretschmer, is just one of the many ways in which the toughness and energy of the type may be expressed. Sheldon has commented shrewdly on the correlations between criminality and mesomorphy as follows:

Delinquency is not, of course, an inevitable expression of mesomorphy. Nevertheless conspicuously persistent criminality—delinquency triumphant—appears to derive from a pattern of personality in which

[9] Diamond (1957), pp. 143 f.   [10] Kretschmer (1955), p. 349.

Table 23
Somatotypes of 500 delinquents and 500 nondelinquents:
Glueck and Glueck's study

	delinquents (per cent)	nondelinquents (per cent)
mesomorphs	60.1	30.7
ectomorphs	14.4	39.6
endomorphs	11.8	15.0
balanced	13.7	14.7

Adapted from Sheldon (1957), p. 126. Misprint corrected.

predominant mesomorphy is an almost necessary ingredient. The same statement could be made for successful football, or successful practical politics, or for success at anything that demands vital energy, love of risk, lust for power, physical courage, ruthless address to a direct objective. These are mesomorphic characteristics.[11]

Elsewhere Sheldon has suggested that the way to eliminate war is to breed mesomorphy out of the race. Kretschmer takes a more favorable view of the athletic collodethyme, whom he considers an unimaginative fellow with a steadying influence on society. Perhaps George Washington would serve as a compromise candidate for Sheldon and Kretschmer—"first in war, first in peace, and first in the hearts of his countrymen."

The characterology of Heymans and Wiersma

A different kind of typology, dealing exclusively with psychological characteristics and ignoring physique, stems from the work of Heymans and Wiersma. Some of its terminology can be traced back through French writers of an earlier day to the ancient doctrines of Hippocrates and Galen, but in method and structure it contains much that is new.

A long article published in 1908 by G. Heymans, a Dutch psychologist, outlines the basic scheme. Heymans explains how he analyzed the personalities of 110 famous individuals by studying their biographies and checking his impressions against a long list of traits. With each individual's traits then in hand, he tried to sum up his personality by assigning high or low marks in three major psychological properties: emotionality, activity, and either primary function or its opposite, secondary function.

[11] Sheldon (1957), p. 126.

The properties emotionality and activity are relatively easy to grasp. The property with the bipolar name, primary or secondary function, requires comment. This property concerns the speed with which one assimilates his experiences. If primary function predominates, one is alertly aware of events in the external world and reacts to them quickly and appropriately; if this function is very strong, the environment provides the stimulus control. If secondary function predominates, one's awareness of the environment leads to delayed rather than immediate reaction; this is muted and perhaps partially disguised by intervening reflection, so that one appears self-governed rather than stimulus-controlled. Actually, everyone functions in both ways—by immediate and by delayed reaction—.to every conscious event. It is the relative prominence of primarity or secondarity which interests the typologist. This concept is so important in the Heymans-Wiersma system that LeSenne's exposition of it may bear quoting here:

> As he is addressing an audience, a professor notices a clock on the wall of the room where he is speaking, pointing to such and such an hour. This perception produces on his body and mind a first group of effects during the whole time that he is conscious of it: mentally he takes note of the hour he reads from the clock, and he reflects more or less clearly on the amount of time remaining. All the effects produced by the idea of the clock *during* its occupancy of clear consciousness comprise the first reverberation, the *primary function* of the idea. But these are not the only effects which the initial perception is to generate. When the perception has sunk from clear consciousness into the subconscious, it continues, perhaps for years, to produce other effects. For example, having read the hour from the clock, the professor will speak more rapidly than he would have done if the hour had been less advanced, but without doing it intentionally; and in the future he will burden himself with fewer lecture notes, because of the long-term effect of an experience retreating farther and farther into his past. All the effects of an idea *after* it has ceased to be present in the field of clear consciousness comprise the second reverberation, the *secondary function* of the idea.[12]

There are eight possible combinations of these properties when marked plus or minus. Table 24 lists these eight combinations, which constitute the eight types of the system. Each of the proper-

---

[12] LeSenne (1945), pp. 88 f. Used by permission of Presses Universitaires de France. My translation of this source throughout. René LeSenne (1882-1954) was a professor at the Sorbonne and a member of the Institut de France.

Table 24
The eight types of Heymans and Wiersma

formula	label	formula	label
EnAP	nervous	EAP	choleric
EnAS	sentimental	EAS	impassioned
nEAP	sanguine	nEnAP	amorphous
nEAS	phlegmatic	nEnAS	apathetic

Adapted from Heymans (1908).

ties is indicated by its initial letter, with an *n* preceding the letter if the property is low or absent; in the case of the third property, Heymans obviously felt that nP would not adequately identify something which he thought was a positive function and therefore labeled S. Users of the system sometimes employ the names to the right for convenience, but these will be misleading if the formulae in terms of three properties are not kept in mind.

Heymans states that correct placement of an individual is not usually difficult, but questions do arise because of certain interaction effects. For example, the appearance of being active may be produced by a strong primarity, and so on. In Heymans' words:

> Strongly emotional natures with predominant primary function, like Byron, easily give the impression of being active, when in fact they are inactive; for, of course, anyone who needs powerful motives to arouse him to activity should be classified as indolent or non-active, and such was the case with these men; yet, because of their more than average emotionality and lack of inhibition, they were usually under the sway of strong motives and hence continually acting; but when the strong emotional motives failed them, they collapsed. In the same way a predominant primary function, because of the extreme power which it lends to events of the moment, may trick us into imagining a higher degree of emotionality than is really present, while, on the other hand, strong emotionality, by permitting emotion-laden ideas to prevail over others, may produce the illusion of a predominant secondary function. One should recognize in general that the person who enjoys and suffers much is not basically emotional unless he reacts thus on slight provocation; not basically active unless, in addition to working often, he requires little prompting to set to work; and not basically endowed with predominant secondary function unless it is trifling impressions which can seize upon him and hold him in their power.[13]

[13] Heymans (1908), pp. 322 f. My translation.

The three interacting properties with which Heymans works are not observable in themselves but can be inferred from certain observable events. These observables are the numerous items of his trait list. Some are fairly obviously related to the basic variables, but many have no such obvious relationship. Heymans admits that in his biographical study he relied on intuition to an unspecified degree. That is, he often found himself pigeonholing individuals into types without following any clear rules of evidence. Still, when he examined the details of his check list, it turned out that the pigeonholing was by no means random: persons assigned to a given type were discovered to have many traits in common and to differ from persons otherwise assigned. For example, the EnAP (nervous) was point by point different from the nEAS (phlegmatic), as theoretically should be the case, in such matters as work habits, persistency, independence, inner harmony, sensitiveness, eroticism, punctuality, and a host of other qualities.

Heymans wished to know if a more objective, rule-controlled study of people from the general population would yield similar results. He wanted especially to guard against any biases such as might have influenced his trait judgments in the biographical study because of the fact that he was testing his own theory.

Material for such an objective analysis was obtained by Heymans later, in collaboration with Wiersma (a Dutch psychiatrist), through a questionnaire which was sent out to some 3000 physicians in the Netherlands. They asked that the physicians pick out families which they were intimately acquainted with and answer 90 questions in regard to the personal characteristics of the individual members. Over 400 physicians replied; information was thus gathered on 2523 individuals. As decided in advance, certain items in the questionnaire were used to type the persons rated— items which had some obvious relationship to the three primary variables. Whether an individual should be called E or nE was decided by the answer to a single question; whether A or nA, by the answers to three; and whether P or S, by the answers to ten. By application of these criteria, 1867 individuals were typed (656 questionnaires were incomplete or otherwise defective), and the types were found to be distributed as follows: 174 nervous (EnAP), 113 sentimental (EnAS), 95 sanguine (nEAP), 439 phlegmatic (nEAS), 257 choleric (EAP), 597 impassioned (EAS), 98 amorphous (nEnAP), and 94 apathetic (nEnAS). If we turn these figures into percentages and rank from most common to least, using the formulae, we have: 32% EAS, 23% nEAS, 14% EAP, 9% EnAP, 6% EnAS, 5% nEnAP, 5% nEAP, 5% nEnAS. We can see then at a glance that not only is EAS the prevailing type, but that its components are also the most common, with activity showing in 74%, secondarity in 66%, and emotionality in 61%.

As just pointed out, 14 items of the 90-item questionnaire were used as defining traits. That leaves 76 other items whose connection with the basic variables has to be determined empirically. In short, we have the materials for a factor analysis. The seven long articles which report the immense research of Heymans and Wiersma[14] contain a mine of data for the statistical student of human nature, especially the last article, which has two elaborate tables of numerical data running for some 21 pages. I have utilized these tables for constructing Table 25. One of the Heymans-Wiersma tables lists all the traits which are above average frequency for each type. By using this information we may extract the six variables (E, nE, A, nA, P, S) in pure form, so to speak. For example, the pure E traits are those which occur with greater than average frequency in every one of the four types containing E (EnAP, EnAS, EAP, EAS). In reading Table 25, please note that the defining traits are starred.

Table 25 should enable the reader to be his own typologist. For instance, if your traits are mainly those under E rather than those under nE, under A than under nA, and under P than under S, then you are an EAP, or choleric type. The table also permits us to construct a picture of each of the eight types free of subsidiary features. The picture based on pure traits, however, will lack those features due to the interaction of variables; and, in any case, no individual need resemble exactly any particular pure type.

We may conclude that Heymans' excursion into mass statistics and objective analysis was fruitful. It enriched and gave firmness to his intuitive conception of the types and led to results beyond his unassisted intuition. At the same time, let us not overlook the fact that the less objective handling of the biographies of famous people was far from empty and vain. The clustering of traits in the 110 individuals of Heymans' biographical study agreed with the clustering in the general population sample at 143 points out of a possible 182. This is definitely satisfactory, especially if we take into account the possibility of real differences between the two samples. It ap-

[14] Heymans and Wiersma (1906, 1907, 1908, 1909).

Table 25

Pure traits for the basic Heymans-Wiersma variables

E (EnAP, EnAS, EAP, EAS) *emotional violent in speech varies between gay and sad talkative ✓ likes animals mentally disordered	*nE (nEnAP, nEnAS, nEAP, nEAS)* calm and composed *not emotional cool and objective in speech uniformly even-tempered uncommunicative about feelings
A (nEAP, nEAS, EAP, EAS) *always industrious *dispatches work promptly quick decisions gift for languages inventive storyteller skillful with hands abstains from alcohol reads a lot always alert and attentive clean and orderly punctual	*nA (nEnAP, nEnAS, EnAP, EnAS)* neglects assigned work *procrastinates indecisive no practical sense narrow intellectually poor observer unskillful with hands forced, uneasy manner reads little distraught not punctual
P (nEnAP, EnAP, nEAP, EAP) lighthearted *quickly consoled over loss *quickly reconciled after quarrel *fickle *likes new scenes, new friends *easily persuaded *craves change *big plans that come to nothing *wants immediate results *contradicts own principles musical talent good at telling anecdotes enjoys eating and drinking self-satisfied likes to exaggerate and embellish entertainment-seeker	*S (nEnAS, EnAS, nEAS, EAS)* actions governed by principles *affected long time by loss *hard to reconcile after quarrel *steadfast *attached to old memories *firm in his opinions *habit-bound *plans for the future *faithful to own principles sexually temperate not self-satisfied allows everyone his freedom politically conservative trustworthy in what he says reliable in money matters speaks with feeling laughs little

Adapted from Heymans and Wiersma (1909), pp. 48-54. My translation.
* Asterisk indicates a defining trait.

pears that a single investigator, operating intuitively, can learn some fairly basic things about human nature from a collection of biographies. Not all the advantage lies with the questionnaire study.

The typological investigations of Heymans and Wiersma have

been almost totally neglected in the United States, in spite of our passion for statistics. The situation is different in France. LeSenne's *Traité de caractérologie*[15] is based on their work and has had some influence. Others who have been interested in LeSenne's approach are André Le Gall, a school official, who addresses his book *Caractérologie des enfants et des adolescents*[16] to parents and educators. Concerned with similar matters was Jean Bourjade, whose posthumous book *Principes de caractérologie,*[17] while favoring the LeSenne system, sympathetically examines a number of other typologies. In general the LeSenne characterologists seem to be interested in developing a broad, supple, practically oriented, psychological taxonomy, with features drawn from various typologies and elsewhere. A few words about LeSenne here may be useful, especially since his work is not available in English.

LeSenne distinguishes between *character* and *personality* and thinks of the Heymans-Wiersma typology as applying to character only. Character is "the totality of congenital dispositions forming the mental skeleton of a human being."[18] Personality, on the other hand, is a changeable product of a character in action under the control of a conscious self. The conscious self is an element of freedom working within the limitations of a character. LeSenne proposes that the Heymans-Wiersma scheme should be supplemented by various other properties, such as amplitude of consciousness, intelligence, and so on, in order to increase the range and flexibility of the characterological foundations laid by them; at the extreme limit of refinement, every individual would be seen as unique, like a distinct species. Among the several additions he recommends, I will mention here a single one which strikes me as especially important. This is the property of egocentricity or allocentricity, which refers to the centering of consciousness on the self or on others. LeSenne writes:

> Human consciousness has two poles. Sometimes it places the "I" at the center of cognition and feeling: it is then egocentric and would be called egotistical if this property were translated into ethical language. For egocentric consciousness, the other person is nothing but an object, viewed by the "I" as mere things are. Sometimes, on the other hand, a man's consciousness unites him with another person, and, as far as possible, he loses himself in that other person, no longer seeing himself except through the eyes of the other, whose ideas, feelings, and intentions are then taken in by the "I" in such a fashion

[15] LeSenne (1945).
[17] Bourjade (1955).
[16] Le Gall (1950).
[18] LeSenne (1945), p. 9.

that they become consciously "mine." In fact, throughout life we oscillate from the one pole to the other. There is not a man so egotistical, so lacking in sympathy, that he does not at moments have to "put himself in the place of the other fellow." Even the cruel do it. And yet there is not a saint, either, who does not at times return to himself, if only to feel the necessity and the reality of parting from himself. Coriolanus was, by turns, the commander and the enemy of the Romans: all of us take our own side against the others and their side against ourselves.[19]

Characterology, in the hands of LeSenne, moves always toward the concrete individual. That is why he is not satisfied with the eight types of Heymans and Wiersma in their simple form, and why he introduces additions. Unmodified, they do not fit the individual closely enough. Nevertheless, even the simple typology, according to LeSenne, enables us to handle some interesting questions better than we could without; in fact, it raises some that would otherwise not occur to us. For example, there is what LeSenne calls "intercharacterology"—the study of how social relations are affected by the types. He says:

> Rudiments of this intercharacterology are detectable everywhere: phlegmatics witnessing the activity of active-emotionals judge them to be "theatrical," the sanguine makes fun of the sentimental's need to retreat to nature and his deficiency of practical sense, and the sentimental in turn reproaches the sanguine for his "cynicism" or lack of appreciation for the needs of the life of feeling.[20]

In view of all the possibilities for research inherent in this typology, and its statistical character from the beginning, it is astonishing that it is practically unknown in the United States where questionnaires and statistics have had an enormous vogue, and where the study of personality and social psychology have always been closely allied. I do not have the faintest idea why this should be.

Jung

Of strictly psychological typologies (as opposed to those which pay some attention to physiology) the most famous is probably Jung's. Two of its principal terms, "introversion" and "extroversion,"

[19] *Ibid.,* pp. 118 f.   [20] *Ibid.,* p. 569.

have become household words. Yet very few of the people who use these words understand Jung's typology or have made any effort to do so.

Jung introduces his book *Psychological Types*[21] with a quotation from Heine on the contrast between Plato and Aristotle: "These are not merely two systems; they are also types of two distinct human natures, which from immemorial time, under every sort of cloak, stand more or less inimically opposed." Plato was an intellectual mystic, conceiving of the material universe and all the men and women in it as a shadow-play of the Divine, recommending an educational system which would lead to an ever-increasing withdrawal from external things into a mystical absorption in the eternal realiites of Goodness, Beauty, and Truth, and urging through his protagonist Socrates that the first duty of man is to obey the Delphic oracle's "Know thyself!" Aristotle, on the other hand, was a physician and scientist, a collector and observer and describer of animals, a tireless classifier of everything from octopuses to the various forms of logical argument, an empiricist who two thousand years before John Locke asserted that there is nothing in the mind except what is brought there through the senses, and in moral questions an advocate of moderation rather than enthusiasm, so fond of the Golden Mean as the rule of life that he declared that even truth itself, in human affairs, can be overdone. Plato was poetic, other-worldly; Aristotle was prosaic, this-worldly. Plato burned to know God face to face; Aristotle was content to trace out the Divine workings in the forms and events of the palpable material world. Even when they dealt with exactly the same topic, the result was different. For example, from Aristotle we learn that dreams are produced by stimulation of the sense organs and by memory of prior sensory experience, helped along by disturbed digestion, and are on the whole quite commonplace and insignificant; whereas, if we look at the matter as Plato did, we regard dreams as revelations of the depths of the personality, visions of the evil and darkness below the surface of things, convulsions of the soul. The contrast represented by these two men, says Heine, runs through all human history.

Jung's book is a working out of this idea. But he is less interested in history than in psychology. The essential point for him is that there are two kinds of mental attitude, and that every person inclines more one way than the other, some slightly, some as decidedly

[21] Jung (1923).

as Plato and Aristotle. It is these attitudes which he names "introverted" and "extroverted."

In order to grasp Jung's meaning it is necessary for a moment to be introverted; for one must recognize as the indispensable element of the Jungian scheme the existence of an immaterial self, an experiencing subject which does not take up space in the world and is not the same thing as the brain. Granted this much, the rest is easy. Over against the subject stands the object. The subject may pay attention either to itself or to the object; it may look within itself, into the inner world, or it may look outside itself, at the external world. To be concrete, you may look through your eyes at the colors and forms and movements of things around you, or you may close your eyes and become aware of your memories and dreams. The turning outward toward the object is extroversion, the turning inward toward the subject is introversion. As you see, this is not a matter of shyness or sociability, though obviously the introverted attitude is less favorable to socializing than is the extroverted.

Everyone is capable of both attitudes. Sometimes we are alertly exploring the world around us with our senses, at other times we are profoundly absorbed in inner contemplation. But one attitude may be dominant in a given person. Hence Jung speaks of an introverted or extroverted type. There are degrees of this dominance. If we could measure introversion and extroversion as we do height, we should expect to find people distributed from one end of the scale to the other in a continuous curve with a single mode at the point of balance between the two attitudes. We should not expect a bimodal distribution, though this is a common mistake about Jung.

Suppose, now, that we have a person from one extreme or other of the distribution, a pronounced introvert or extrovert—is the opposite attitude then a minor factor? Jung's answer is "No!" At this point an extroverted reader may feel like giving up in disgust. But a little reflection will show that the answer is not so unreasonable after all. Consider the behavior of a man walking in his sleep. His eyes are closed, he is mumbling to himself, he is absorbed in a dream; his attitude is one of extreme introversion. Yet he manages somehow to grope about the room, to open a door, to steer his way down a corridor and out into the moonlight. In spite of his self-absorption he demonstrates that he is capable of having dealings with the external world. Apparently, an effective extroverted attitude accompanies his introversion. He is conscious of his dream, of the events of the inner world, and his introverted attitude relates to that; but he moves about in the external world, of which he seems to be only dimly aware, and his extroverted attitude relates to that. As a sleepwalker he is consciously introverted, but unconsciously extroverted. Exactly the opposite happens too. A young woman is sitting with her husband at a table in a public dining room. She notices the entrance of some people she knows and she starts to say something to her husband about them, lifting her hand to shield her mouth as she whispers. At that moment she suddenly recalls a dream in which the same gesture occurred, and she is astonished at the richness and vividness of the memory which instantly unfolds. Her conscious extroverted attitude was occupied by the people and the things around her; but her introverted attitude, we may suppose, was concerned with the dream all along, unconsciously, and seized the opportunity presented by the harmony of the external events with the internal events to make conscious and explicit what it was dealing with in the innermost recesses of her being. So both attitudes are constantly present, keeping the subject in contact with both the internal and the external world, but now the one and now the other is illuminated by consciousness while the opposite is darkened by forgetfulness or inattention.

In one sense, then, everybody is equally introverted and extroverted. But to say this is to disregard the distinction between conscious and unconscious processes. The extrovert is one whose prevailing *conscious* attitude is extroverted; secretly, under cover, an introverted attitude is at work. We reverse the picture to get the introvert. The degree of conscious introversion or extroversion for any given individual, according to Jung, is more or less constant —unless a life crisis upsets and brings about a revolution in the personality system. Dramatic changes may then take place. The dreamy, withdrawn adolescent turns into a vigorous man of affairs; the active soldier becomes a reflective priest.

One more refinement must be added to this description of Jung's typology. He thinks of the personality operating in four functional modes: thinking, feeling, sensing, and intuiting. Thinking and feeling involve value-judgment: thinking does so by bringing separate ideas under general concepts and organizing them systematically, feeling does so by deciding how much things are liked or disliked. These two functions are called *rational,* because they order and organize. The other two, because they lack this organizing effect, are called *irrational*: sensing notes the sheer presence and qualities of things, intuiting leaps beyond sensory notation to recognize the latent or future possibilities in the situation. Intuiting is the hardest of these functions to explain—at least to the nonintuitive—but, at the risk of some misunderstanding, it may be suggested that extrovert intuition is that kind of perception of things which leads to betting on a particular horse, while introvert intuition is the source of mystical visions or sudden intellectual convictions.

Psychological Types is so abstract a book that readers are to be pardoned for seizing on the few concrete pictures all too eagerly. This may explain the common misconception of Jung. For example, near the beginning of a chapter entitled "General Description of the Types," to which a hasty reader might turn for a condensed version of the system, there occur these words:

> The two types are so essentially different, presenting so striking a contrast, that their existence, even to the uninitiated in psychological matters, becomes an obvious fact, when once attention has been drawn to it. Who does not know those taciturn, impenetrable, often shy natures, who form such a vivid contrast to those other open, sociable, serene maybe, or at least friendly and accessible characters, who are on good terms with all the world, or, even when disagreeing with it, still hold a relation to it by which they and it are mutually affected?[22]

Certain types of readers would stop here with the impression that they had nailed it all down: introverts are shy and extroverts are sociable. But actually this is a very preliminary thumbnail sketch, a behavioral picture which completely ignores the all-important distinction between subject and object, the conscious and the unconscious, and the four psychic functions of thinking, feeling, sensing, and intuiting.

By combination of introversion and extroversion with the four functions there arise eight fundamental types. An individual may be predominantly (i.e., consciously) introverted or extroverted, and he may function predominantly in any one of the four ways. If thinking is predominant (i.e., conscious), feeling is suppressed into the unconscious, and vice versa; if sensing is predominant, then intuiting is suppressed, and vice versa. The rational functions make an opposed pair, and so do the irrational functions. If one rational function is dominant, the other is suppressed, being its logical opposite; but the two irrational functions, being on another dimen-

[22] *Ibid.*, pp. 412 f.

sion, are not so much suppressed as put in a subordinate role of *assisting* the dominant rational function. The same holds, with change of terms, if an irrational function is dominant. In short, the pairs of opposite functions are related to one another as the axes of Cartesian coordinates.

On the whole, Jung's typology does not appeal to extroverts. Yet one extroverted investigator (for so he labels himself) has succeeded in being as fair to the system as an extrovert can be, by devising an empirical test based directly on Jung's own words. It will help us to understand Jung, and at the same time acquaint us with the interesting Q-technique of sorting, if we give a little attention here to this work of Stephenson.

Stephenson arranges the eight "components" (as he sees it) of the Jungian scheme somewhat as in Table 26,[23] and then proceeds to outline all the mathematically possible 16 combinations, each one accompanied by descriptive phrases extracted from Jung. Stephenson could be criticized for playing with the combinations in this way, because no real individual would ever be, for example, a conscious thinking introvert (according to Jung) without simultaneously being an unconscious feeling extrovert. I have therefore modified Stephenson's tabulation slightly in order to bring out a relationship which is important to Jung, and have given the combinations, in Table 27 *in pairs* (which Stephenson did not), because, as Jung sees it, unconscious aspects are always combined with conscious ones. For example, a thinking introvert is one who has developed the conscious thinking function to a high degree; but on his unconscious side, the other three functions, especially the polar opposite, feeling, will be comparatively undeveloped and may be expressed in his behavior in odd and disturbing ways. Take in illustration the first pair of entries in Table 27 (which are *samples* of more numerous descriptive phrases in Jung). The sample phrase which describes

Table 26
Jung's eight major components

attitudes	functions		levels
	RATIONAL	IRRATIONAL	
introversion	thinking	sensing	conscious
extroversion	feeling	intuiting	unconscious

Adapted from Jung (1923) and Stephenson (1953).

[23] Stephenson (1953).

the thinking introvert in his *conscious* functioning (TIc) is, "Theories are important to him, facts not." The sample phrase describing him in his *unconscious* functioning (TIu) is "Has a vague dread of the opposite sex," and this refers to the fact that the suppressed *feeling* function is undeveloped and, consequently, distorted and inhibited in its expression. In general, Jung's descriptions of the various types try to bring out how the dominant function is supported by the auxiliary functions and *also* how the suppressed opposite of the dominant function is interwoven into the fabric and produces strange imperfections in the design of the conscious life. Stephenson, by breaking down Jung's complex total descriptions into separate fragments, undoubtedly destroys some of Jung's meaning—in typically thinking extrovert fashion, it might be added. His purpose in doing this—his thinking extrovert purpose—is to prepare Jung's ideas for statistical analysis. For example, he extracts the 80 items from Jung without much concern for their relative importance in the original complex descriptions and treats them as having equivalent weight—in order to have a statistical table with exactly 5 items for each of the 16 combinations, 20 for each of the functions, 40 for each of the levels, and 40 for each of the attitudes, for convenient statistical handling.

Suppose now that we wish to know whether a given individual is introverted or extroverted. By the Stephenson Q-sort technique we proceed as follows. We provide the subject (if we want a self-sort) with a large number of separate statements of traits taken from Jung, each one printed on a card of its own, and we ask the subject to decide for each statement whether it applies to him (1) very definitely, (2) not at all, or (3) somewhere in between. He then places the card in its appropriate pile. When he has finished, we have an indication of what he thinks of himself in terms of these particular statements. If the introvert statements are piled up at one end of the array and the extrovert statements at the other, we should conclude (according to Stephenson) that the subject is introverted or extroverted as the case may be and that we have an estimate of the degree to which this is true. We can have the subject make his choices with reference to the present time, or to the past, or with reference to an ideal rather than his actual self; or we can get an outsider to rate the subject. All such arrays (Q-sorts) may be statistically compared to ascertain the amount of agreement or disagreement between them.

One of Jung's contentions is that differences of type cause mis-

Table 27

The 16 combinations of Jungian components: random selection of descriptive phrases

(c=CONSCIOUS, u=UNCONSCIOUS)

thinking introvert
TIc theories are important to him, facts not
TIu has a vague dread of the opposite sex

feeling introvert
FIc *feels* God, freedom, immortality, or the like
FIu can be mischievously cruel

sensing introvert
SIc is guided by just what *happens* to him
SIu lacks self-judgment

intuiting introvert
IIc scents out new possibilities and pursues them without regard
       for himself or others
IIu can't understand why he is undervalued by public opinion

thinking extrovert
TEc thinking is banal, dull
TEu the end justifies the means for him

feeling extrovert
FEc displays extravagant feelings, which one can't believe
FEu enjoys excellent rapport with others, but hurts by utter tact-
       lessness

sensing extrovert
SEc thoroughly realistic
SEu somewhat captious and pettifogging

intuiting extrovert
IEc seizes new things with enthusiasm
IEu apt to become entangled with unsuitable person. of opposite
       sex

Adapted from Stephenson (1953), pp. 70, 83-85; and Jung (1923).

understanding among people and social conflict. Stephenson has touched on this question in another study. He says:

> I argued that an extrovert's self-appraisal should correlate *specifically* with his assessment of another extrovert well known to him, on the grounds that he would be apt to "seize" on traits peculiar to himself and to the other extrovert; he would give these a "significance" in excess of what they require in order to conform to the general extrovert type to which he himself, and the other person, belongs.[24]

[24] Stephenson (1950), p. 562.

That is to say, whether or not an extrovert appraised another extrovert with complete accuracy, he would particularly notice those traits they had in common.

Stephenson, who calls himself an extrovert, compared his Q-sort self-appraisal with the appraisals made of him by others using the same technique. Five of the judges were introverts, as determined by their self-sorts; their Q-sorts of Stephenson correlated with his own Q-sort .46, .61, .59, .61, .45, for an average of .54. Two of the judges were extroverts, as determined by their self-sorts; their Q-sorts of him correlated with his own .47 and .40, for an average which is 10 points lower than the introvert average. The extroverts were certainly not superior to the introverts in appraising a fellow-extrovert. But— and this is the main point—the extrovert judges were drawing on their *own* personality traits to a much greater degree than the introverts in making their appraisal of Stephenson. Correlations between self-appraisals and their appraisal of Stephenson, for the *introverts*, were .38, .26, .16, .04, and .33, averaging .23; for the *extroverts*, .44 and .55, for an average of nearly .50. Extroverts in describing another extrovert are describing themselves to a considerable extent. Are extroverts, then, emotionally drawn together because of their identification one with another? We do not know from Stephenson's data. It is interesting to note, however, that Stephenson's *wife* is introverted, so much so that her self-appraisal was correlated with his self-appraisal *negatively.*[25]

One would judge from Stephenson's work that Jung's typology is not just empty verbiage and that those test-constructers who in the past have found little confirmation for Jung's analysis may have gone about their task in the wrong way. Two astute psychologists who have recently had something favorable to say about the introversion-extroversion dimension are Eysenck and Adams.[26] On the other hand, little attention has been paid to the four mental functions outside the immediate circle of Jung's disciples.

Spranger's value typology

The typology of Eduard Spranger, described in *Types of Men*,[27] is based on the premise that the values one holds determine the characteristics of personality to a marked degree. He is therefore concerned with distinguishing the major human values and working

[25] *Ibid.,* p. 563.   [26] Eysenck (1953), Adams (1954).
[27] Spranger (1928).

out their mutual relations. In his opinion there are six primary values: theoretic, economic, esthetic, social, political, and religious. These all coexist in every human being, but one is dominant. The relations between them are reminiscent of the relations between the four mental functions in Jung's system; in Spranger as in Jung there is concern with the subordination of some values to others, with the existence of polar opposites, and with the distorting influence of the subordinated values on the dominant one. This will become evident as we go through abbreviated descriptions of the six personality types, or attitudes, corresponding to the six primary values. Let it be carefully noted in advance that Spranger's "types" do not represent any actual human beings but rather what would happen if particular values were lived out to the full by ideally intelligent and thoroughly committed persons. The "types" are abstract "models."

The "theoretic attitude" is the attitude of pure science. Knowledge is the supreme value. The aim is perfect objectivity, stripped of personal considerations. The emotional life tends to sink into the background, and the mind, unconcerned with beauty or utility or prestige or ethics, concentrates on distinguishing truth from error. The economic motive merely embarrasses this intellectualist; he neglects creature comforts, or perhaps becomes miserly as a defense against economic intrusions. Esthetic imagination repels him, because it introduces the subjective and whimsical into a world which he wishes to put into perfect intellectual order; so Plato, though himself poetic, banished poets from his ideal commonwealth. As for social relations, the theoretical man tends to be an individualist, caring neither for relatives nor neighbors nor public meetings. The man who cultivates knowledge intensively is also indifferent to politics where one might suppose that knowledge was power; this indifference may be due to lack of inclination or lack of gift. Religion is often rejected outright; when it is accepted, it is likely to be identified with intellectual progress toward the realization of God as pure Mind, after the fashion of Aristotle.

The "economic attitude" emphasizes what is practically useful, valuing consumable goods and sources of power and the conquest of time and space as an aid in the struggle for existence. Truth is valued as a practical instrument; applied science is cultivated because it seems to promise the elimination of chance and waste. Esthetic values enter as luxuries; the economic man may buy a masterpiece of art to prove that he has outdistanced others in the competition of life, but he does not hesitate to destroy a beautiful landscape for a mine or a factory. His social attitude is egotistical; people are his tools, honor and good will are salable commodities, and if he stresses cooperation it is for the purpose of exploitation. His political motives come out in his effort to dominate other men, reaching through them to a control of natural resources. Religion, too, has its commercial and technological aspects: God is Mammon, a god of wealth, the operator of a complicated lottery who can be influenced by "pull" and by magical practices.

The "esthetic attitude" is one of pure contemplation, a complete surrender to all the variety of real and imagined objects which for the esthetic man have a life of their own. Nature attracts him as living and even conscious in all its aspects; in this respect the esthetic attitude is opposed to modern science with its tendency to discredit animism. Wordsworth was expressing the attitude when he exclaimed,

> It is my faith that every flower
> Enjoys the air it breathes. . . .

and also when he accused science of murdering to dissect. The economic attitude clashes with the esthetic, because the ascription of usefulness to an object destroys its value for esthetic contemplation. Still, there is a sort of economics in the esthetic life—energy is expended in the creation of works of art, and the account books of the inner life have to be balanced between the expansiveness of enthusiasm and the retrenchments of despondency. Socially, individualism is marked; there may be a charming, easygoing sociability like the play of butterflies, but there is no sense of obligation, other people being viewed esthetically rather than sympathetically, though erotic attraction often enters the picture. Through a sense of inner power and through artistic works the esthetic man participates in the political attitude, but he does not engage in the rough-and-tumble of the power struggle; as soon as he detects the encroachments of others, he aristocratically withdraws, saying with Horace, "I hate the common crowd and I shut it out." He is a pantheist, conceiving of the universe as an oceanic harmony of beauty, but the dark shadow of Fate troubles him.

The "social attitude" is essentially the attitude of love. In perfect love the individual disappears in the other person to find himself again there, freed of selfish desire. The attitude may be concentrated on one or a few, as when a mother lives in her children, or it may embrace the universe. For love the objectivity of the theoretic attitude is too soulless, dangerously bordering on pride; love finds positive qualities where truth and justice find flaws or limitations. Economic self-seeking and possessiveness are also contrary to love, which wants to spend, to give away, to put its treasure where its heart is. Love does not demand of its object the properties of beauty which the esthetic eroticist values; need and evil, squalor and sickness are positive challenges to love. Love exerts influence and in this sense is kin to the attitude of power, but it tolerates no power but love and thus, politically speaking, is anarchistic; Christ, who was the embodiment of love, was absolutely nonpolitical. The transition from the social attitude to the religious is easy and natural; it is only when the attachment to other individuals is united with the concept "God is love," however, that the attitude becomes fully religious, and when that happens the individuals whom one loves are seen as children of the Loving Father one loves also. Christianity especially has developed this concept of God and is thoroughly social in spirit.

The "political attitude" is the attitude of power and competition. War is its ultimate expression, and Roman imperialism was its clearest historical embodiment. For the power-seeker it is a congenial maxim that knowledge is power; a Machiavelli sees truth as a political weapon, to be drawn or sheathed as expedient. The political attitude easily joins forces with the economic: not only is money a golden bullet, but many large economic organizations have a distinctly political character. Esthetic trappings are familiar political adjuncts, especially in an aristocracy, and the greatest power-seekers are kin to artists in their creation of grand imaginative schemes. Usually, there is a sharp contrast between the political and the social attitudes, the *Machtmensch* being self-assertive rather than regardful of others; but without some love motive binding him to the community, the power motive would have nothing to build on; or so it was at least with the patriarchs. For the political man, religion is charged with power concepts: God is the omnipotent creator and ruler of the world, the supreme King, under whom the earthly king may hold his power as God's representative, and to whom he may be linked by an ecclesiastical hierarchy that is as fully secular as it is religious.

The "religious attitude" evaluates any particular experiences in terms of their negative or positive meaning for the totality of life, in its full height and breadth and depth. The religious man is steadfastly directed toward the Best, the *summum bonum*. There are three subtypes: the immanent mystic, who affirms life with cosmic enthusiasm, finding traces of the Divine everywhere, even in the humblest things; the transcendental mystic, who flees from the world to become a hermit, absorbed in the contemplation of an experience beyond communication; and the intermediate, who both affirms and denies the world, who recognizes the claims of the other values but still regards them as inadequate, as vessels of clay. Religion does not so much reject the theoretical attitude as transcend it, looking beyond the concerns of science to something deeper; its relations with intellectual activity are very complex, running the whole gamut from outright conflict to profound merging, as with Aquinas, Spinoza, Plato, Pascal. The economic attitude may be enlisted as stewardship to God. Art may be brought into service, but, though there is much religious art, its religious limitations are obvious: it is too finite, too particular, too sensory, to engage the spirit. The social attitude of love meets the requirements of religion in its tendency to self-surrender and in its evaluation of life as sacred; but there is vacillation in it between love of man and love of God, and total surrender to God leads to the apparent social indifference of Christ's imperious "Let the dead bury their dead." The will to power is contained in religion, which believes in the faith that moves mountains and in the intercessory power of prayer. Furthermore, some wars are truly religious wars, and the political organization of a church offers wide scope for the power motive.

Such, briefly, are the six types that Spranger outlines. They are abstract portraits to which mere logic has contributed a great deal: once the values are defined, their relations to the other values almost automatically follow. Spranger's method of arriving at the sketch of the theoretical type, for instance, was not to study the life of Spinoza and other philosophers in the systematic manner of Heymans; when the names of particular individuals are brought in, they serve as illustrations rather than as evidence. Nor does he attempt to justify limiting the major values to just six. He posits these values, and he analyzes their interrelations, as if inductive argument were quite unnecessary. Yet Spranger's book does not actually hang in a vacuum. Indeed, in his preface he insists on the immense psychological resources of literature and points to the advantages of this sort of material for constructing a theory of human nature. He says:

> Some people have objected that this book abandons the concrete ground of experience and reduces psychology to mere speculation. I

cannot admit this objection and beg indulgence finally to indicate the reasons for my stand. Psychological experience is not gained only in the laboratory or the clinic or merely from contemporary human beings but also from the vast number of men of the past whom we know only through literary documents. We need this broadening of our experience all the more since otherwise we should learn only psychological phenomena which correspond to our cultural determinants. What is the value of the most comprehensive mass-statistics compared to the enormous material of different psychic structures which history transmits to us? My psychology aims at an understanding of these historical structures and their transformation even though I can give little space to this aspect.[28]

It is an odd fact that this typology, which has less direct attachment to clinical and experimental data in its origin than any of the other typologies examined in this chapter, is the only one of the four which has been incorporated (in the United States) into a widely used standardized test! Shortly after Spranger's book was published in English, it was made the foundation of a personality test constructed by Allport and Vernon and distributed with a descriptive booklet under the title, "A Study of Values."[29] This test has been popular enough among psychologists to warrant a revised edition.[30] I shall not describe the test in detail; it is sufficient for our purposes here to state that it provides a large number of choices for the subject to make between various situations and occupations representing the six Spranger values. The subject's choices are reflected in scores which, when combined, indicate the relative prominence of each of the values in his personality.

The test works. When various occupational and interest groups take it, their scores fall in line with Spranger's theory. For example, ministers score high in religious value, business administration students score high in economic value, and so on. Certain score patterns regularly emerge for the two sexes: males (851 college men) are predominantly theoretical, political, and economic; females (965 college women) are predominantly religious, esthetic, and social. It is exceedingly interesting that the two sexes should seem to complement each other in this way. The test has even made its entrance into psychological laboratory experiments. For example, studies have shown that tachistoscopically presented words are more easily recognized if they correspond to the perceiver's high

[28] Spranger (1928), p. xii.   [29] Allport and Vernon (1931).
[30] Allport, Vernon, and Lindzey (1951).

values than if they correspond to his low ones.[31] Indeed, the correlation between value rank of words and ease of recognition is on the average quite marked. Spranger, who stressed the unity of the psychic organism, would have been pleased with this result, but probably not surprised.

A few remarks in conclusion

One cannot simply dismiss typological thinking with a wave of the hand as outmoded and unscientific, as is often done. It is the thinking of taxonomists, and taxonomy has proved itself exceedingly important in natural science. Biology without Linnaean classification or chemistry without Mendeleev's table of elements would be badly crippled. It is a similar taxonomical need which the typologists have tried to fill in psychology. Yet it is the fashion in psychology to ignore them or give them short shrift and pass on to other topics. Why? Perhaps there are many reasons Perhaps the central reason has something to do with human freedom. All typologies have a suggestion of fate about them: they set limits, they say that one human individual is not exactly equal to another, they often proclaim or hint at the power of heredity, they indicate that there are different ways of living and that it is impossible to live them all simultaneously, and they inevitably raise the problem of values and the possibility that one mode of life is better than another. The animals and plants do not question Linnaeus, and the chemical substances do not debate with Mendeleev, but we human beings who construct psychology resent being classified and quarrel with our taxonomists. Besides that, any suggestion of limits on our power to do as we please either with ourselves or with other people may disturb us. For example, in this country if nowhere else learning theorists have displayed the greatest reluctance to take any serious cognizance of even the differences between species, much less the differences within a species which have concerned typologists. Yet nothing can be much more obvious than that there *are* differences both between and within species which affect not only the rate but the manner of learning as well. John Thibaut has suggested to me that the status of the nature-nurture controversy has some lawful relation to the social stability of a culture: perhaps the scientists of countries like the United States and Russia, which have rejected hereditary social rank and emphasized individual or group status-

[31] See, for instance, Postman, Bruner, and McGinnies (1948).

seeking, are less favorable to nature (i.e., heredity) as a source of psychological variety than are the scientists of countries like Great Britain and Germany, where individuals are or until recently were somewhat restrained by traditions of hereditary rank. The Russian erasure of the Mendelian laws of inheritance by a political *fiat* some years ago (temporarily, to be sure) is at least an illustration of the influence of cultural values on scientific opinion. The extravagant claim by the father of behaviorism, John B. Watson, in this country a generation ago that he knew enough about conditioning to shape the personalities of babies in any direction he might choose is another expression of the same sort of confidence that the human being is infinitely plastic, and that all are equally so. The question remains: Does heredity count and is it lawful? Or, under another form of words, are there types?

The typologists obviously think that there are types. They do not think that human freedom is therefore necessarily abolished. In fact, LeSenne, who has tried to put the Heymans-Wiersma typology to work in France, regards personality precisely as a product of human freedom operating within the limits imposed by an inherited character, i.e., a type. It cannot be held against typology that it is sheer fatalism. Nor can it be stated that there is no truth in typology because there are different typological systems. The four typologies examined in this chapter differ, it is true; but they do not clash. All four could be used simultaneously in describing a human being, one for his physique and temperament, one for his behavioral tendencies, one for his general intellectual orientation and preferred modes of functioning, and one for his value orientation. If typological thinking could be cleaned up and firmed up and made practical by clear rules of procedure, and if it could be brought into effective contact with the study of learning and social interaction (as LeSenne has proposed), psychology might benefit as much as biology and chemistry do by taxonomy. As for human freedom and the dignity of the individual, there is nothing in these schemes to abrogate either— unless (a danger inherent in all knowledge) they are used for that purpose.

References for chapter 10

Adams, D. K. (1954) *The anatomy of personality*. New York: Doubleday.
Allport, G. W., and Vernon, P. E. (1931) *A study of values*. Boston: Houghton Mifflin.

————, Vernon, P. E., and Lindzey, G. (1951) *A study of values*. Boston: Houghton Mifflin.

Bourjade, J. (1955) *Principes de caractérologie*. Neuchâtel: Editions de la Baconnière.

Child, I. L. (1950) The relation of somatotype to self-ratings on Sheldon's temperamental traits. *Journal of Personality*, 18, 440-53.

Diamond, S. (1957) *Personality and temperament*. New York: Harper.

Eysenck, H. J. (1953) *The structure of human personality*. New York: Wiley.

Heymans, G. (1908) Über einige psychische Korrelationen. *Zeitschrift für angewandte Psychologie*, 1, 313-81.

————, and Wiersma, E. (1906, 1907, 1908, 1909) Beiträge zur speziellen Psychologie auf Grund einer Massenuntersuchung. *Zeitschrift für Psychologie*, 42, 81-127, 258-301; 43, 321-73; 45, 1-42; 46, 321-33; 49, 414-39; 51, 1-72.

Jung, C. G. (1923) *Psychological types*. Tr. by H. G. Baynes. New York: Harcourt, Brace & World.

Klineberg, O., Asch, S. E., and Block, H. (1934) An experimental study of constitutional types. *Genetic Psychology Monographs*, 16, No. 3, 139-221.

Kretschmer, E. (1955) *Körperbau und Charakter: Untersuchungen zum Konstitutionsproblem und zur Lehre von den Temperamenten*. Berlin, Göttingen, Heidelberg: Springer-Verlag.

Le Gall, A. (1950) *Caractérologie des enfants et des adolescents*. Paris: Presses Universitaires de France.

LeSenne, R. (1945) *Traité de caractérologie*. Paris: Presses Universitaires de France.

Postman, L., Bruner, J. S., and McGinnies, E. (1948) Personal values as selective factors in perception. *Journal of Abnormal and Social Psychology*, 43, 142-54.

Sheldon, W. H. (1957) Mesomorphs in mischief. *Contemporary Psychology*, 2, 125-26.

————, Dupertuis, C. W., and McDermott, E. (1954) *Atlas of men*. New York: Harper.

————, and Stevens, S. S. (1942) *The varieties of temperament*. New York: Harper.

————, Stevens, S. S., and Tucker, W. B. (1940) *The varieties of human physique*. New York: Harper.

Spranger, E. (1928) *Types of men: the psychology and ethics of personality*. Tr. by P. J. W. Pigors. Halle: Niemeyer.

Stephenson, W. (1950) The significance of Q-technique for the study of personality. In Reymert, M. L. (Ed.) *Feelings and emotions: the Mooseheart symposium*. New York: McGraw-Hill.

———— (1953) *The study of behavior: Q-technique and its methodology*. Chicago: Univ. of Chicago Press.

11

THE MEASUREMENT
OF TRAITS

Preview   *Many personality tests have been designed for the purpose of measuring traits. They have often been commercially successful and theoretically unsatisfactory. Test construction is becoming increasingly sophisticated, but it is questionable whether the measurement of traits can have the predictive power or the theoretical significance for which psychometricians hope. The problem seems to lie in the nature of personality itself, and only secondarily in the techniques of measurement. This chapter examines the problem with the aid of a few well-known tests, but there is no intention of assessing the relative value of existing tests or offering a survey of the entire test market. Our concern is with some of the elementary questions facing anyone who tries to measure traits and use them predictively.*

Personality tests have been constructed by the hundreds and have had large sales, and many specialists are engaged in administering them to very large numbers of people in schools, factories, businesses, government agencies, and hospitals; and yet their usefulness as instruments of diagnosis and selection is continually being called into question even by those who use them. Not long ago a leading authority in the field of psychological measurement stated that we should be pessimistic about the future of personality testing in general,[1] and more recently still another expert declared that we have probably reached the limits of usefulness of our present orientation and procedures in testing.[2] We do not need to be concerned here with the market phenomenon: we know that people will buy and use all kinds of worthless products, and this seems to be true even of business men.[3] But the doubts of the psychometricians themselves are scientifically important.

Again, our main question here will not be whether objective personality testing is superior to the intuitive clinical approach, though that will have to concern us later. The question is why the psychometricians, in spite of apparent success, should admit at least occasionally to a sense of frustration. And why should this discouragement arise more from the testing of personality traits other than intelligence than from the testing of intelligence itself? The general answer seems to be that personality traits are very elusive. It might not be so hard to measure them if one could catch them and hold them still for a minute, but the best of measuring instruments may not be able to reach them. Yet if the psychometricians have failed to accomplish all that they might have wished, it is certainly not because of laziness or lack of ingenuity in the construction of measuring devices. It is doubtful whether any other group of psychologists can match them for sheer industry and mathematical sophistication.

Let me repeat that this chapter is not concerned with the practical reasons which might be advanced for trait-measuring tests. For one thing, there is money in them. For another, there is an argument which runs as follows and which I quote in the words of a discerning critic:

> Granted that full appreciation (understanding?) of a single human personality is probably impossible. Granted further that even an incomplete understanding can best be achieved only through long and detailed interviews which bring to bear all the psychologist's training and knowledge of human behavior. Nevertheless, psychologists in their professional capacities often find it necessary to make judgments about individual personalities. Tests which attempt to identify and measure

[1] Vernon (1953).   [2] Tyler (1959).   [3] Stagner (1958).

traits, if used with full awareness of their limitations, can often provide useful hints which serve as time-savers by indicating the direction that face-to-face interviews might most fruitfully take.

However sound this argument may be, it has little to do with this chapter, which aims to examine the theoretical foundations of trait-testing and to raise the question whether it might not be wise to shift from a trait theory of personality to a self theory—wise even for those who wish to go on constructing and administering personality tests. What I mean by trait theory and self theory should become gradually clear during the discussion which follows; but I will state here that by "trait" I understand a more or less fixed property of personality and by "self" a conscious, choosing, directing power—in brief, an "I."

The single trait as an object of measurement

There are many aspects of human behavior which can be measured quite as effectively as anything in nature. Reaction times, psychogalvanic responses, energy output, number of words recalled in unit time, loudness of voice, visual acuity, etc. are certainly measurable, as are many physical states of the organism, such as height and basal metabolism. Personality tests, however, usually aim at something rather different from properties such as these— they aim at qualities which affect one's social relations and are subject to ethical or medical or esthetic evaluation. For example, one finds in Cattell's list of surface traits adjectives like honest, loyal, hypochondriacal, self-effacing, debonair, affectionate, secretive, thrifty, frivolous, talkative, enthusiastic, and so on.[4]

Now, the problem of measuring any single one of these traits is basic. If one can be measured, then perhaps the others can; but we cannot very well measure a cluster of them unless we can measure one of them. Let us see if there are any special difficulties in performing this operation. Take an important trait like friendliness. We talk about friendliness in relative terms exactly as we do about height or any other commonly measured attribute. If we have a statistical turn of mind we might conceivably begin to use numbers in referring to a person's friendliness and say, for example, that person X who is very friendly stands at the 99th centile. It is only a step beyond this to begin imagining something like a ruler applied to the friendliness

[4] Cattell (1950), pp. 37-41.

dimension, just as a ruler is applied to height. Here we may hesitate. Friendliness may seem a different kind of dimension. A man's height does not change radically from moment to moment, but friendliness may come and go. Furthermore, it may even co-exist with its opposite: a father clasping his child to him and beating off a kidnapper is friendly to the child and unfriendly to the kidnapper.

Yet, if we think very subtly about the matter, we realize that height does change over time, even in maturity, and also that a man may be simultaneously tall and short—in comparison with two other men. The measurement of friendliness does not appear to be completely different from the measurement of height.

Perhaps we could imitate the inventors of rulers and balances and other common measuring instruments. How did they proceed? Well, apparently by discovering substitutes for themselves. A stick, for example, was used in place of a foot, a balance in place of a person's two hands; the substitutes had the advantage of being constants and also could be refined to measure differences not detectable before. For example, by reading the movement of a pointer against a scale marked off in small units it was possible to distinguish between weights that seemed equal when merely hefted. Can we proceed in like fashion to the invention of a measuring device for friendliness? If so, we must do two things: (1) Consider first how we estimate friendliness without an artificial instrument, and then (2) find or make an instrument which will do the same.

Our real difficulties begin at (1). Some believe that the basis of estimating friendliness is *intuition,* others that it is *inference.* By *intuition* I mean a direct awareness, whether mediated through the senses or not. By *inference* I mean a chain of reasoning.

When I lift two objects, one in each hand, I may be directly aware that one is heavier than the other; I do this without reasoning or without consciously estimating that more units of energy are expended by one arm than by the other to keep the two burdened hands at the same level. Even after I have acquired some knowledge about muscles and energy exchange, I still rely on these intuitive judgments. It is that way with friendliness, too. I apprehend friendliness by an immediate intuition and estimate the degree of it as instantly as I do the loudness of a sound or the brightness of a flash of light. What kind of instrument could substitute? For estimating weights I can use two artificial hands, the pans of the balance, and hang them on an upright support in analogy to my backbone. For estimating sounds and lights I can use mechanical ears and eyes. But what is the natural instrument by which I perceive friendliness? The answer is not obvious. In fact, if I say that friendliness can only be detected through intuition, I must conclude that it can only be detected by a living person, and I confess that I cannot imagine a mechanical substitute for a living person.

If I approach the problem from the other position, however, and say that friendliness can be *inferred* from certain acts, I may conclude that a system of tabulating these indicators will do very well as a substitute measuring instrument. For example, I may regard shaking hands as an indicator of friendliness, and perhaps I may accept the frequency or the vigor of the handshaking as a measure of the amount. If this will satisfy me (it will not satisfy me if I prefer intuition), I can collect the data I need in at least two different ways: I can have a person estimate the frequency and vigor of his own handshaking, or I can have someone else make the observations. It is the second kind of observing which, from a behavioristic point of view, is objective. The other has more questionable status.

Actually, the practice of test construction is a good deal more mixed than the preceding logic might suggest. The indicators most often used are questions which could not possibly be answered validly except in terms of very private experience. For example, Cattell estimates what he calls "Source Trait O" from the answers to questions like the following:

1. Do you have frequent periods of feeling lonely even when with people?
2. Do you often feel just miserable and in low spirits for no sufficient reason?
3. Do you feel not well adjusted to life and that very little works out the way it should?
4. Do you suffer from insomnia and take a long time to fall asleep at night?
5. Do you feel that on several occasions in recent years you have been found fault with more than you deserve?
6. Are you troubled by useless stray thoughts that run through your mind uncalled for?[5]

Only Question 4 seems to be "objective" in the sense of being answerable by an outside observer, and it calls for a kind of observation that is not likely to be made by an outsider. Cattell would say in

[5] Cattell (1950), p. 82.

defense of the "objectivity" of his procedure that the subject answering these questions is not aware that his answers point to "Source Trait O" and so he cannot deliberately falsify his standing on that trait.[6] Nevertheless, it surely makes some difference whether the subject answers honestly or not, and it is certainly clear that the indicators employed do not lend themselves readily to "inter-subjective validation," i.e., agreement by a number of independent observers. There is a loophole, however, for anyone who wants to deny the importance of the private experience to which the questions seem to refer. The questions *can* be regarded merely as "stimuli" and the answers merely as "verbalizations." In that case, one no longer troubles about the presence or absence of the private experience, but simply takes note of the "Yes" or "No" response as a behavioral item. Justification of the test and the particular test items is then based strictly on correlation with other similar elements of behavior: if test scores predict successfully how individuals will behave in other situations, then the test is held to be satisfactory no matter what its inner workings may be. This is "objectivity" in the full behavioristic sense. Many test constructers and test administrators would be completely satisfied with such objectivity; their dissatisfaction arises from the correlations. As Tyler has pointed out, "Seldom do we find a cross-validated multiple correlation with any criterion that exceeds .6. The addition of new dimensions and the increasing refinement in the ways we measure the old ones are not really 'paying off' very well."[7]

There is one further point. All personality tests originate in someone's personal judgment. Some person decides what it is that is to be measured, how it is to be measured, and whether in fact it is measured. A test is an instrument devised by someone to perform a job of assessment. It may perform this job well or ill, but it does not construct itself and it cannot judge itself. This is so obvious as hardly to bear mentioning. I mention it, however, because the mere existence of a measuring instrument and the impersonality of the mathematical procedures which accumulate around it may create the illusion that human minds have entirely vanished from the scene.

Let us now examine objective testing close-up by studying a few notable attempts to construct instrumental substitutes for intuition or personal inference.

[6] See Watson (1959), p. 15.   [7] Tyler (1959), p. 76.

The masculinity-femininity test of Terman and Miles

The assertion that there is a masculinity-femininity dimension in human personality has a strong intuitive appeal. It is not only that we recognize anatomical differences between male and female, but we are aware of a general quality differentiating the sexes. Sexual attractiveness is only one of its manifestations. Of course, if anyone presses us to put this intuition into exact words, we may get tongue-tied. Most people would be equally nonplussed if asked to tell how they know by feel that one weight is heavier than another. We still go on judging weights in that personal way, and we likewise still go on making intuitive judgments regarding the sexual dimension.

Out of this common human intuition, Lewis M. Terman, with the assistance of a distinguished team of co-workers, developed a paper-and-pencil test which surpasses most tests in the usual respects by which tests are judged ready for the market. It is especially admirable in its faithfulness to a criterion. Every item finally retained in the test had to evoke different responses from male and female groups. Consequently, the test as a whole distinguishes sharply between sex groups. The overlap of scores between the male and female subjects is far less than is usually found between the categories which most tests are supposed to distinguish. Knowing the score alone, one can correctly identify the individual subject as male or female far more often than would be possible by mere guessing. And yet a single question, "Are you male?" would separate the sexes far more efficiently than Terman's elaborate instrument. Why, then, did he go to so much trouble? It was because he wanted to measure a personality dimension which he thought of as having various degrees. You cannot measure degrees by a single question answered "Yes" or "No." By the use of numerous questions perhaps you can. As for the fact that some males score more feminine than some females and vice versa, Terman could point out that in many cases intuitive judgment confirmed the score: masculine-scoring women strike the observer as more masculine than their feminine-scoring sisters, and feminine-scoring men not only leave the impression that they should be feminine-scoring but often turn out to be passive homosexuals.

There are two forms of the test, correlating from about .7 to about .9. Each form is divided into seven parts. For administration purposes these parts are identified only by number, but their significance is indicated for the test administrator by the descriptive titles "Word Association," "Ink-Blot Association," "Information," "Emotional and

Table 28
Sample items from the masculinity-femininity test

exercise 1: word association
BAR   drink (M)   prisoner (M)   sand (M)   stop (F)

exercise 2: ink-blot association   brush (M)   centipede (M)
comb (F)   teeth (F)

exercise 3: information
MARIGOLD IS A KIND OF   fabric (M)   flower (F)   grain (F)
                         stone (M)

exercise 4: emotional and ethical attitudes
TELLING A LIE TO AVOID PUNISHMENT IS   extremely wicked (F)
    decidedly bad (M)   somewhat bad (M)   not really bad (M)

exercise 5: interests
WOULD YOU LIKE TO VISIT MANY FAMOUS BATTLEGROUNDS?
    like (M)   dislike (F)   neither like nor dislike (F)

exercise 6: opinions
GREEN-EYED PEOPLE ARE NOT TO BE TRUSTED   true (M)   false (F)

exercise 7: introvertive responses
HAVE YOU EVER KEPT A DIARY?   yes (F)   no (M)

Adapted from Terman and Miles (1936), pp. 485-506.

Ethical Attitudes," "Interests," "Opinions," and "Introvertive Responses." As these titles make clear and as further illustrated in Table 28, the test samples the masculinity-femininity dimension in several ways. Table 28 gives one item from each part, showing the stimulus word or picture or question, the several answers from which the respondent must select one, and the score assigned to each answer.

To get a little insight into how the test was constructed and how much labor went into it, we may follow the course of events for that part labeled "Word Association." Terman refers to the prior work of Wyman in this direction and then describes what his own research team did. He writes:

In devising the M-F association test the procedure followed was in all essential respects that used by Dr. Wyman. First a short English dictionary was scanned in the search for words which looked as though they might bring sex differences in responses if used as stimulus words in an association test. A tentative list of about 500 such words was selected by the senior author, with the assistance of Edith M. Sprague. The selection was based in part on investigational data in the field of sex differences, but to a greater extent on subjective "hunches." Each word in this list was next rated by three judges for probable merit in bringing out sex differences, with the result that the list was reduced from 500 to 220 (110 in each of two forms). The 220 stimulus words were printed in large type on cards like those used by Dr. Wyman and were administered to 400 high-school and university subjects, equally divided between the sexes.[8]

Table 29, which presents only a few from a wide variety of responses, shows the kind of results they got. Their next step was to abandon this method of administration: instead of allowing the subjects to respond with whatever word came to mind, they required them to select from among four supplied on the answer sheet for the "Word Association" exercise. They found this change completely justified:

> The multiple-response form of the association test is better adapted to group testing, requires less time for its administration, and can be scored with far greater rapidity. . . . Our data show that by every criterion the multiple-response method is as good for the present purpose as the older method. It is fully as reliable, gives as wide separation of sex groups, and in fact correlates with scores obtained by the standard method almost as highly as the latter correlate with themselves.[9]

The final step was to select the best items, a process thus described:

> The experimental form of the multiple-response association test was composed of 171 items, 120 from the 220 of the original list and 51

Table 29
Typical responses to certain stimulus words in masculinity-femininity test

	males	*females*		*males*	*females*
BLUE	spectrum	dress	ARM	leg	limb
FLESH	meat	pink	FAIR	weather	blonde
CLOSET	door	clothes	RELIGION	God	church
GARDEN	weeds	flower	WAR	soldiers	hate
HOME	house	happy	STOUT	strong	fat
POWDER	bullet	rouge	GENTLE	horse	mother
CHARM	snake	beauty	HUNT	shoot	find

Adapted from Terman and Miles (1936), p. 23.

[8] Terman and Miles (1936), p. 22.   [9] *Ibid.*, pp. 24 f.

items artificially constructed. It was given to 600 subjects: 100 of each sex in the seventh grade, the junior year of high school, and the university. . . . For the final M-F test 120 words were selected from the 171 used in the experiment just described. . . . The words retained include only those from the original list which showed sex differences in the same direction for at least three out of the four multiple responses in all the groups tested.[10]

Both the role of intuition and the role of the criterion are illustrated in the above excerpts. To what extent was the external criterion of the sex of the test populations decisive? Complete separation of the male and female groups was not achieved. In the language of Terman and Miles, the sex overlap between subjects for the "Word Association" part of the test was 22% for the seventh graders, 14% for the high school juniors, and 12% for the university students. The seventh-grade percentage of overlap, to take a specific example, means that 22 of the 100 boys had scores more feminine or no less feminine than the 22 most masculine-scoring girls. (A given response is classified as "male" if it is more often given by males than by females and vice versa. The total score for the whole test or a section of it is the sum of "male" responses minus the sum of "female" responses.) As *groups* the boys and girls are well separated, but as *individuals* they are not; that is to say, there are very few with scores so definitely masculine or feminine that there would be no possibility of assigning them to the wrong sex. One part of the M-F test separates a standardizing group into male and female so well that there is only an 8.2% overlap. Yet in this case the scores of 71 of the 164 males fall within the female range and the scores of 103 of the 141 females fall within the male range. In other words, in this case of only 8.2% overlap there are actually only 27% of the females with scores so feminine and 57% of the males with scores so masculine that they would not be confused with members of the opposite sex. It must be repeated that Terman's aim was obviously not to produce a test which would separate the sexes as well as the single question, "Are you male?" would do it. But it is well to add right here that the separation actually achieved is enormously greater than is usual in most tests that *do* aim at sharp separation of categories for diagnostic purposes. Many students do not realize that a test may discriminate between *groups* of patients, for instance, at a highly significant statistical level, and still be worthless for detecting individual cases.

The authors of the M-F test were trying to construct a measuring

[10] *Ibid.*, p. 25.

instrument for a dimension which they thought of as associated with anatomical maleness and femaleness enough to justify using the anatomical dichotomy as an external criterion of their success, but not so much that they had to be completely governed by it. As for the meaning of the score points, they had even less external guidance. They clearly assume that there is *some* correspondence between size of score and amount of masculinity or femininity, but they do not go so far as to say that each score point represents an equivalent amount or degree of the sex quality no matter where it occurs in the range of scores; nor do they otherwise assign a particular value to score points. Since the scores obtainable on the test range from more than +400, to more than −400, the degrees of masculinity-femininity which *appear* to be distinguishable are very numerous. In fact, however, the relation between score points and amount of the sex quality is extremely vague. What evidence is there that there is any relationship at all? The authors appeal to two major facts, both of which have cogency for the question because of their intuitive content.

(1) If special groups are rated intuitively on the masculine-feminine dimension, we find that their M-F test scores run in the proper direction. Male college athletes, for example, would be intuitively judged more masculine than a group of male music students. M-F scores agree with this judgment: 46 male college athletes averaged 92.45, 50 male college music students averaged 15.7. If we take the female sex and make a similar comparison, we arrive at the same result: 37 female college athletes averaged −13.7, 50 female college music students averaged −71.1. Some intuitive judges are surprised to learn that 23 firemen and policemen scored less masculine (27.9) than 132 teachers (44.6) or 17 lawyers (62.3), but reflection sometimes brings them around to agree with the test, since it can be argued that firemen and policemen play more of a motherly and protective role than do teachers and lawyers.

(2) If the test's disguise is dropped and a subject is informed what it is intended to measure, he has no difficulty in reversing his score on the basis of his own intuition about the sexes. Kelly, Miles, and Terman performed an interesting experiment on this effect. They first administered the test in its disguised form (under the label "Attitude-Interest Analysis Test") to 52 college sophomores. None of the subjects suspected its true nature. A week later the purpose of the test was explained to them and they were asked to swing the score deliberately to the masculine or feminine side—half

of the men to masculinize, the other half to feminize, and likewise for the women. At a third session, a week later, they were given the same task, but with roles reversed. The striking results are presented in Table 30. It is clear that either sex can perform on the test in three different ways, depending on set. The experimenters exclaim: "In other words, a typical group of males at the most masculine age are able to earn a mean score more feminine by far than the mean of any female group we have tested; a typical female group can make itself appear far more masculine than any male group we have tested!"[11]

The M-F test appears to have high face validity, i.e., it is supported by the intuition of those who take the test as well as by the intuition of those who constructed it. But this very fact makes it highly vulnerable to faking—as Table 30 makes clear. If the test does measure any personality trait by its indicators, it does so on the condition that the subject honestly reports his own real preferences between the alternative responses allowed him. With that proviso, it may be said that the test scores roughly correspond to degrees of masculinity-femininity; but that is not to admit that every score point marks off precisely one degree.

Honesty

The subject who knows what a personality test is designed to show can usually fake his score to show it. Of course, one *could* say that a score is a score and represents a trait no matter what the subject thought he was doing. Test constructers, however, are not always that trusting. They want honest scores. The Minnesota Multiphasic Personality Inventory (MMPI), for example, tries to

Table 30
Effect of intention on masculinity-femininity test scores: college sophomores

	males (N=19)		females (N=33)	
	MEAN	SD	MEAN	SD
naïve scores	66.8	39.2	−56.2	48.1
masculinized scores	208.8	68.9	189.1	93.9
feminized scores	−140.5	51.8	−147.6	62.6

Adapted from Terman and Miles (1936), p. 78.

[11] *Ibid.*, p. 78.

lay a trap for the dishonest. Presumably, if honesty were a trait, a clever test could measure it as well as detect it. But *is* honesty a trait?

The answer given by Hartshorne and May in their justly famed "Character Education Inquiry" is that honesty is not a trait. Their argument is somewhat difficult to follow, but the gist of it seems to be that few or no individuals possess honesty in "some amount" as they might be said to possess "some amount" of masculinity-femininity but that they react to situations opportunistically—sometimes honestly, sometimes dishonestly, depending on what their aims and abilities are at the time. Hartshorne and May define honesty behavioristically: it is a particular way of behaving in a particular situation and no more a trait than any acquired skill:

> Some men, it may be, can learn to be honest more easily than others because of real mental differences of the nature of which we are not as yet aware; but whatever honesty a man possesses resides not in a secret reservoir of honest virtue nor in the ideal of honesty which he may hold before himself as worthy of his best effort, but in the quality of the particular acts he performs.[12]

In one phase of their work, Hartshorne and May studied the behavior of school children of various ages in ten test situations where the children could peep at answers to problems, fake scores, and otherwise cheat. The results were expressed in a cheating ratio, i.e., the number of opportunities to cheat divided into the number of times cheating occurred. The distribution of the children in these terms is shown in Table 31.

Table 31
Distribution of cheating among school children

ratio	number	per cent*	ratio	number	per cent*
1.00	78	3.2	.40	310	12.7
.90	105	4.3	.30	439	17.9
.80	178	7.3	.20	231	9.4
.70	231	9.4	.10	140	5.7
.60	252	10.3	.00	171	7.0
.50	308	12.6	TOTAL	2443	

Adapted from Hartshorne and May (1928-30), Vol. 1, Bk. 2, p. 200.
* The sum of per cents falls short of 100 because the decimal fractions are rounded off to the nearest tenth.

[12] Hartshorne and May (1928-30), Vol. 1, Bk. 1, p. 379. Used by permission of the authors.

About 7% of the children refrained from cheating in all ten situations, as indicated by the cheating ratio of zero; 3.2% cheated every time, as indicated by the ratio of 1.00; the remaining nearly 90% fell at various points in between. Hartshorne and May admit that these figures might be read as measures of an honesty-dishonesty dimension, but they reject such an interpretation. While acknowledging that a given child may be consistent in his cheating ratio, they deny that honesty is a trait with degrees which get expressed in a certain per cent of honest acts. Instead, they stress the nature of the situation confronting the child. That the issue between them and trait theorists is not absolutely clear is proved by the fact that Allport reinterprets their results in favor of trait theory.[13]

One of the Hartshorne and May studies demonstrates the dependence of cheating on the situation. They devised seven tests which differed in the obstacles opposed to cheating. The tests, arranged in order from hardest to cheat on to easiest, were as follows:

INFORMATION TEST, where cheating required erasure of an ink circle and replacement by another.

DISARRANGED SENTENCE TEST, where it was necessary to erase a penciled sentence and replace by another.

READING TEST, where a penciled phrase had to be erased or more words added.

SENTENCE COMPLETION TEST, where the erasure or addition of a single penciled word was sufficient.

SPELLING TEST, where only a penciled check mark had to be added.

WORD KNOWLEDGE TEST, where (after some urging from the examiner to do as well as possible) only a penciled digit had to be erased or added.

ARITHMETIC TEST, where (after strong urging to do as well as possible) a penciled answer could be erased or added.

In summarizing their results the authors combined the spelling test and the arithmetic test and put this combination in last place. Of the 295 children tested, all but 48 cheated at least once. The per cent of cheating increased with increase of opportunity, in step with the test order as described, thus: 2, 17, 43, 51, 59, and 80. Hartshorne and May write: "What we measure by our techniques is not conduct but tendency or attitude, for we remove the external barriers which ordinarily prevent the full expression of the tendency

[13] Allport (1937).

and permit the individual to go as far as he wishes to in the direction of dishonest performance."[14] Their reference to "tendency or attitude" here would mean "trait" to some trait theorists, but it would not mean that to Allport; for he distinguishes as they do between trait and attitude.

Hartshorne and May confess their inability to explain honest or dishonest behavior or to predict it. To be sure, they found some correlations between such behavior and scores on knowledge-of-honesty tests and several kinds of background factors, but the correlations are low and in their opinion throw very little light on the observed behavior in test situations. The individual case baffles them:

> Here, for example, is a girl from an exceedingly poor home. The father is dishonest and of a rather vicious personality. The parental relations are unhappy. The parents' attitude toward the child is unsympathetic or hostile, and their discipline does everything to her except spoil her. They live in the worst part of the community, and the general level of the home background is almost as low as there is. One parent is German and the other Italian, and they report themselves as Catholic. The child herself is of less than average intelligence but is somewhat ahead in her school grade, and her teachers evidently regard her as a nuisance, for her deportment [was graded low]. Furthermore, 60% or more of her classmates cheated on the test taken in school. The child's neurotic index, however is only a point higher than the average. This would seem to be an almost perfect picture of a child who has the handicaps leading most frequently to deception. Yet this child did not cheat at all. We are tempted to resort to the expression, "She's not that kind of girl," which illustrates the case method type of conclusion.[15]

If Hartshorne and May are right—if it is impossible to predict dishonesty or measure it as a consistent trait—how is the measurement of other traits to proceed with confidence if trait measurement depends on accurate reporting by the person being measured? Two general safeguards have been proposed or adopted: one, the most common, to disguise the purpose of the test either by the label or by the nature of the test items; another, to work into the test some kind of "lie-detector." Neither subterfuge appears to be wholly satisfactory. One reason is that even if the subject does not understand the exact purpose of a test he may be generally suspicious of it or react to the purpose which he *imagines* it to be

[14] Hartshorne and May (1928-30), Vol. 1, Bk. 1, p. 387.
[15] *Ibid.*, pp. 309 f.

expressing. Conscious human beings place interpretations on tests and react to these interpretations. Furthermore, many test subjects suspect the psychologist of trying to deceive them (which all too often is true), and they may consequently refuse to accept the purported object of a test—which is particularly embarrassing when the test has been honestly presented. All these complications disturb the accurate functioning of even the best psychometric instrument.

Reliability, validity, and other puzzles

It is an article of faith among test constructers that what a single item or test will not do, a dozen may. That is, they distrust single observations and trust averages. Thus Symonds, in one of the standard textbooks on personality testing, writes:

> A key-note of this book, a point of emphasis to crop out again and again in the discussion of various techniques of investigation, is the emphasis on *adequacy of sampling*. A single observation is unreliable, a single rating is unreliable, a single answer to a question is unreliable. Reliability is achieved by heaping up observations, ratings, tests, questions, measures.[16]

Surely this doctrine is open to question. If a single observation is false and misleading, how can lumping several such observations result in truth? On the other hand, single observations are not necessarily *untrue*. One glance is usually sufficient to distinguish a man from a gorilla, a turquoise sock from a crimson one, a hawk from a handsaw. We do not have to hear an explosion twice to be sure that it occurred once. One taste of a bad egg quite positively condemns the whole egg. Under what conditions, then, is it necessary to make repeated observations? And what is the meaning of reliability?

CONDITIONS REQUIRING REPEATED OBSERVATIONS (1) When an event occurs rarely and the time of occurrence is not known, repeated observations may enable the observer to catch it. I do not happen to know of any psychometric test based on this principle.

(2) When you are not quite sure what you are looking for, repeated observations may yield you something that appears to take a more or less satisfactory form. For example, the masculinity-femininity dimension which was the object of the M-F test was

---

[16] Symonds (1931), p. 5.

nothing defined in advance, nothing that could be perceived by the senses or that the authors were willing to formulate abstractly. Beyond saying that it was something that should correlate positively with anatomical maleness and femaleness they were not willing to go. They accordingly groped around for test items that might fit these vague requirements. Secondly, since they were bent on having a test which would measure and not simply detect, they thought it necessary to multiply observations (i.e., test items) in order to discriminate quantities, on a sort of analogy with the inches of rulers or the degrees of a thermometer. Now, they might have tried for items which were virtually equivalent, as one inch is equivalent to another. For example, they might have drawn up a questionnaire like this: 1. Are you male? 2. Are you somebody's son? 3. Do you have a penis? 4. Were you considered a boy when you were born? 5. When you stretch out your arms in front of you with the palms up and touching on the inner edge, do your elbows remain separated by a noticeable distance? The answers to such questions would probably split the population neatly into two parts, the males receiving a score of $+5$, the females -5. But where would be the dimension with grades of difference? In order to get varying scores it is necessary to ask questions which do not have any such tight connection as these. On the other hand, the questions for a masculinity-femininity test cannot be a purely random hodgepodge, for the answers must correlate to some extent, not exactly defined by Terman and his associates, with the male-female dichotomy. The M-F test was achieved in fact by a sort of rational muddling through. We do not know why there should have been some 450 items (i.e., observations) in the test rather than 150 or 961, or what the score units mean. It is far from clear that each answer scored "M" is equivalent to a rise of one degree in masculinity. The test seems to deal in probabilities rather than in units of measurement; the more frequently an individual responds like the majority of the standardizing male population, the safer it is to guess that he is male. No single response is exclusively a male response (it is unreliable, in Symonds' meaning of the word), but the accumulation of these uncertain responses increases the probability that the respondent is male. The really daring leap which the M-F test constructers make is to assume that increase of probability that the respondent is male is simultaneously an increase in his masculinity.

(3) When you do know what you are looking for and it is

something which varies in quantity from time to time, repeated observations are necessary to establish the average value. It is presumably this that Symonds had in mind when he insisted on the necessity for repetition. It would be an extraordinary piece of luck if a single observation happened to coincide with the average value of a varying quantity. Take cheating, for example. One observation yields the score of either 1 (did cheat) or 0 (did not cheat). Either of these scores might be the true average for a total of, say, 1000 observations, but it is impossible to know. Let us assume that our subject cheats on one occasion and gets a score of 1. On the next occasion he does not cheat, making his average score ½. But the next observation will change this, whatever happens, and it will become either ⅓ or ⅔. The fourth observation may bring the average back to ½, but it may also change it to ¼ or ¾. However, as we go on adding observations, we reach a point where the next observation changes the average almost imperceptibly. If a person has cheated 500 times in 1000 observed occasions, his average of ½ will be changed scarcely at all by another observation. We have arrived at a fairly stable figure no matter how irregular the behavior is. In a sense, we have achieved reliability. We can even predict with great confidence that the addition of 100 observations will not change this figure more than $\frac{1}{10}$ either way. This is not a large error. We begin to feel that we have a grasp on fundamental law. And we do—but it is mathematical law, not a law of human nature! At just the point in the individual's history that we are considering, at observation No. 1000 where we predict his future with confidence (within a small margin of error), he may adopt honesty as an absolute principle of conduct and never cheat again. This moral revolution in himself might pass totally unnoticed by us as, after a hundred more observations, we congratulated ourselves on our successful prediction and the (approximate) stability of his personality at a value of ½ honest. The averaging of observations does indeed lead to "reliability" but, psychologically speaking, this may be a perfectly hollow victory.

INSTRUMENT RELIABILITY   Reliability of a measuring instrument is very desirable, as is reliability in use of the measuring instrument. The human user of even so simple an instrument as a ruler may apply it carelessly; and even when he is as careful as he knows how to be his control may be imperfect so that he does not get precisely the same result every time he measures the same thing. All conscientious measurement has to take into account the errors which result from variations in the instrument and in the user of the instrument. Now if the object of measurement is itself varying, the differences in measurements taken at different times are a compound of variations in the object and the variations of measurement—the latter being what we designate as "error." It is necessary to distinguish between these two sources of variation. The ratio between the one and the other is important: successful measurement depends on having error of measurement small in comparison with the variations which one wishes to measure. If your error of measurement is one inch, you cannot measure variations of one millimeter; you may in fact describe the object as unchanging because your measuring technique is too crude to detect the variation. On the other hand, you will not ignore variations of one foot where your error of measurement is one inch, and it would be incorrect to attribute such variations to your measurement technique rather than to the object.

Separation of error of measurement from variation in the object being measured appears to have been handled successfully enough in the physical sciences. There is more than a little question, however, about the success of psychometricians in making a comparable separation in the area of personality measurement. How is reliability of a physical measuring technique determined? By applying the technique repeatedly to a constant object. Any variation in the measurements obtained is then attributed to the technique (either the instrument, or its application, or both) and the limits of usefulness of the technique are thereby set. The same operation for determining error of measurement can be imitated with psychological tests, but the question is whether the imitation is justified. First of all, is the standardizing object really constant? Perhaps this question is no more answerable in physics than in psychology, fundamentally, but on the surface the situations seem to be different. For one thing, applying a psychological test to a human object changes him: the human object becomes "test-wise"—is changed by the very act of being measured as a physical object is not. In the second place, other changes not due to testing are likely to occur between tests, changes to which the test is sensitive. Is it safe to assume that variations in test score from one application of the test to another are errors of measurement rather than variations in the person taking the test? Is the test being checked against a constant object? It would seem to be more reasonable to say that the test itself—the printed form—is even more constant than any ruler, contributing virtually nothing to error of measurement, and that whatever variation there is comes from the person being measured.

Test constructers, however, do not ordinarily look at the matter in this way. They commonly make the assumption that their human standardizing object is constant and, consequently, that score variations are errors in measurement. Two procedures for establishing test reliability are traditional: correlation of scores on one half of the test with those on the other half, the halves usually consisting of the odd and even items; and correlation of scores on the whole test administered to the same group of subjects at two different times. The first procedure yields what is called *split-half reliability*; the second, *test-retest reliability*. Though to some of us it may appear that these procedures can only tell us about the consistency of the subjects who take the test (and not about the dependability of the test as a measuring instrument), this is not the usual professional opinion. On the contrary, reliability coefficients obtained as above are regarded as showing how dependable a measuring instrument the test is.[17] This way of regarding reliability coefficients gets its full expression in the statement that an unreliable test cannot be valid, i.e., cannot measure what it is meant to measure at all; and this statement, far from being whimsical, is anchored in a mathematical formula of high repute.[18] My own opinion, never-

[17] For an elementary statement, take Hilgard (1957), p. 424: "By *reliability* we mean that the scores are dependable and reproducible, that they measure *consistently* whatever it is they measure. . . . Well-constructed psychological tests of ability commonly have *reliability* coefficients above $r = .90$."

[18] An elementary statement about validity is this from Hilgard, *loc. cit.*: "By *validity* we mean that the test scores represent what they are supposed to represent. . . . To measure *validity*, we must also have two scores for each person. One of these is the test score, the reliability of which we have just been discussing. But the other is some measure of what it is that the test is supposed to be measuring. This measure is called a *criterion*. Suppose that a test is designed to predict success in learning to receive telegraphic code. To determine whether or not the test is valid, it is given to a group of men beginning to study code. Later on, the number of words per minute each man can receive is tested. This later measure furnishes an additional set of scores to serve as a criterion. Now we can obtain a coefficient of correlation between the early test scores and the scores on the criterion. This correlation coefficient is known as a *validity coefficient*."

We are now in a position to understand the import of the statement that an unreliable test cannot be valid. The idea is more precisely expressed in the formula $r_{xy} = \sqrt{r_{xx}r_{yy}}$, where r_{xy} is the validity correlation between the criterion and the test, and where r_{xx} is the reliability coefficient of the

theless, is that this treatment of reliability coefficients is confusing and misleading, as I shall try to explain further. I shall state my points somewhat dogmatically, but I beg the student to examine the reasoning carefully and not let me bully him into agreement.

Split-half correlation tells us mainly about the homogeneity of the test. At one extreme would be a test in which the same item was repeated throughout, the answers to which might be expected to be the same for any one subject taking the test. The split-half reliability ought to be perfect, with a correlation coefficient of 1.00.

At the other extreme would be so random a collection of items that no concept could link any two of them together, and we might then expect the split-half correlation to be zero. In between are the tests actually in use, like the M-F, with split-half correlations of around .8 or .9, indicating that some thread of continuity is recognized by the subjects in the test items.

Test-retest reliability is somewhat different. It tells us, if the subjects are honest, how much they have changed from one time

Table 32
Test-retest correlations for MMPI subscales: college students*

| interval between test and retest | N | \multicolumn{9}{c}{subscales} |
		1	2	3	4	5	6	7	8	9
1 week (F)	26	.73	.84	.71	.84	—	.81	.92	.82	.79
1-2 weeks (M and F)	55	.71	.71	.52	.63	.83	.54	.75	.61	.62
3 months (M and F)	119	.48	.66	.57	.63	.77	.59	.53	.57	.63
2 years (F)	140	.52	.52	.49	.45	.59	.38	.44	.37	.47
2 years (M)	99	.26	.49	.33	.51	.48	.61	.36	.46	.61
4 years (F)	45	.51	.26	.48	.40	.58	.41	.40	.46	.32
4 years (M)	28	.24	.39	.16	.60	.62	.52	.42	.39	.73

Adapted from Dahlstrom and Welsh (1960), Appendix K.
* Each correlation coefficient in this table shows the amount of resemblance between the performance of a certain number of subjects on a first and a second trial with the same MMPI sub-scale. For example, to take the first line, 26 female subjects were given sub-scales 1, 2, etc., *twice*, at an interval of a week; the scores obtained on the first trial (*test*) correlated with those obtained on the second trial (*retest*) .73 for sub-scale 1, .84 for sub-scale 2, etc.

test and r_{yy} is the reliability coefficient of the criterion. It will be obvious, as Adkins (1947) states, p. 169: "This shows that the obtained validity coefficient cannot exceed the square root of the product of the reliability coefficients of the test and the criterion." Assume that we have no question about the reliability of the criterion but that the reliability coefficient of the test is zero; then the validity coefficient r_{xy} will have to be zero. Hence the statement that an unreliable test cannot be valid. The formula is perfectly clear; the only question is whether (or in what way) it bears upon the problem of test construction and test administration.

to the next. Some change is the general rule. Often the change is large. A fairly dependable rule is that the change is greater the greater the lapse of time. Table 32 illustrates this tendency with correlation coefficients drawn from research studies on the MMPI, which is widely used. The smaller the correlation coefficient the greater the change, of course; and it will be observed that, roughly speaking, the coefficients are smaller the greater the length of time from test to retest. Score change over time is not confined to personality tests like the MMPI. Intelligence tests, which have sometimes been regarded as something apart (solidly based on "constancy of the IQ"), also reflect change. Test-retest coefficients for the Goodenough Draw-a-Man Test, for example, are about .9 for intervals of a day but sink to lower values for longer intervals, such as .5 or .6 for an interval of two months; and though the Stanford-Binet is steadier, it is by no means immune to change.[19]

No necessary connection exists between split-half and test-retest correlations. It is conceivable that the first could be low and the second high, indicating that the test was heterogeneous and the subjects consistent over time; or the reverse could be true, indicating that the test was homogeneous and the subjects variable over time. Cronbach has recognized the difference between these two kinds of "reliability" coefficients and has suggested that they be distinguished by calling split-half coefficients *equivalence* coefficients and test-retest coefficients *stability* coefficients.[20] Even if these terms were in daily use, as they are not, we should still have to keep reminding ourselves that the stability referred to in the latter expression belongs to the subjects taking the test rather than to the test.

We ought not to leave this perplexing topic without noting that it is intimately bound up with one of the most fundamental psychological debates. The test is a "stimulus" to which the subject "responds." Efforts to determine the reliability of the test are, from one point of view, efforts to determine the degree of variability of the stimulus. Some psychologists define the stimulus in terms of the response: if the response is weak the stimulus is weak, if the response is strong the stimulus is strong, if the response varies the stimulus varies. This seems to be about the line of thought of those test constructers who judge the reliability of the test by the steadiness of the subject's response. Other psychologists, however, define the stimulus as an object or event with characteristics of its own

[19] See McCurdy (1947).   [20] Cronbach (1949).

independent of the response to it: weak or strong or varying responses from the subject do not necessarily indicate corresponding weakness or strength or variation in the stimulus. This is the line of thought which I believe I have been following in the present discussion. I might add that I think the other point of view with regard to the stimulus comes about partly from refusing to admit perception as an intervening variable between it and the response, not to mention memory and impulse and will.

VALIDITY   Doubtless one of the reasons for aiming at that elusive phantom "test reliability" is that psychometricians fear that some of the test items may be ambiguous and some of the subjects may be careless or dishonest, resulting in a certain proportion of random answers. High reliability correlations are reassuring because they are not likely to occur if any large proportion of the answers are random, i.e., produced as if decided by the toss of a coin. True enough, and yet it is also true that a changing subject can give honest and careful answers on two occasions and legitimately get different scores on a personality questionnaire. If similar variations occur in a whole group of subjects, but in different directions, the result will be a low test-retest correlation and hence low test reliability; and this can lead to the rejection of the test as invalid, in consequence of the fallacy contained in the familiar dictum, "A test which is unreliable cannot be valid." If a test were in fact being administered to people who were changing in different directions in the very traits the test purported to measure, and if it held up through thick and thin, constantly yielding high test-retest coefficients, it would thoroughly disqualify itself. Stability of that sort would only mean that the test was not measuring what it purported to measure at all, but something else which was scarcely changing. It must, of course, be granted that it is a highly legitimate enterprise to try to detect stable elements in personality and measure these as well as changing ones. The point here is simply that neither the reliability nor the validity of a test as a measuring instrument can be estimated by score stability alone.

A measuring instrument is valid if it is appropriate to the thing to be measured and if it is sensitive enough for the purposes for which it is needed. A thermometer is not the appropriate instrument for measuring humidity, and a thermometer designed for the ordinary living room is not sensitive enough to register the heat changes occurring in a germinating maple seed. The question, "Are you male?" is not the appropriate one to ask if you are trying to locate a mathematician, and it is not sensitive enough to distinguish between Benvenuto Cellini and Uriah Heep. One might think that the right way to begin constructing a valid personality-testing questionnaire would be first to consider profoundly exactly what the questions were about and second to study the art of questioning for the purpose of making the questions as appropriate and discriminating as possible. Apparently this has not been the major line of approach. Yet there are signs that it may become so. Cattell has argued eloquently that measurement must follow structure. I do not pretend to fathom the complexities of factor analysis which he advocates, and I do not know what particular quarrels are reflected by the following words, but I applaud the general direction of his remarks and the psychometric trend which they seem to imply. He says:

> I am aware that this reiteration of "no testing without structure" makes me as popular among certain kinds of test constructors in educational and clinical psychology as a Baptist minister reminding people of the Ten Commandments in an establishment for organized vice. But I would repeat that you may use the most impressive scaling procedures, refining Guttman, Coombs, and others to the nth power, and still be merely engaged in a sort of psychometric chess game, as far as any psychological understanding of psychological problems is concerned. If your scale is *not* guaranteed to deal with something psychologically meaningful and organic, it cannot help in psychological procedures.[21]

As for the delicate art of questioning, it is evident that some test constructers are now considering it seriously, at least to the extent of simplifying their questions to the educational level of those likely to be taking the test, with the aid of a word frequency list or something of that sort; but there is probably much more that could be done. Certainly, psychometricians have not always been sensitive to the social and ethical implications of some of their instruments, and sometimes the situation explodes; it did down in Texas not long ago,[22] where a major program of research was damaged by the seizure and destruction of a great batch of tests which had offended a number of citizens by the indelicacy of the questions. Clearly, the emotional repercussions of words and sentences have to be taken into account, too, when the aim is a valid questionnaire test.

[21] Cattell (1959), pp. 45 f.   [22] Nettler (1959).

We may gain some further understanding of the problems of test construction by examining one which tries to measure numerous traits or syndromes of traits all at once. The Minnesota Multiphasic Personality Inventory (MMPI) is such a test. It has attracted a good deal of attention. In 1956, sixteen years after the test was first described, no fewer than 689 publications concerning it had appeared and translations were being made into several foreign languages.[23] The M-F test of Terman and Miles was based in part on the obvious distinction between the two sexes; the MMPI relies heavily on the less obvious distinctions of psychiatric taxonomy.

The MMPI was originated by Hathaway and McKinley, who described the construction process in a 1940 article thus:

> The individual items were formulated partly on the basis of previous clinical experience. Mainly, however, the items were supplied from several psychiatric direction forms, from various textbooks of psychiatry, from certain of the directions for case taking in medicine and neurology, and from the earlier published scales of personal and social attitudes. The original list consisted of more than one thousand items. By deletion of duplicates and of those items which seemed to have relatively little significance for the purposes of this study, the inventory finally contracted to its present form of 504 items.[24]

In 1960, according to Dahlstrom and Welsh, there were 550 items, which they classified as in Table 33. To continue with the Hathaway-McKinley description:

> The separate items were formulated as declarative sentences in the first person singular. The majority were placed in the positive, the remainder in the negative. Interrogative sentences were not used. Simplified wording constituted the language of the items, the words used being selected as far as possible from those in most frequent use according to standard word frequency tables. Also, the statements were restricted to matters of "common knowledge". . . . Each item was printed with its number in large type (16-point boldface) on a 3- x 5-inch card.[25]

It is simple to take the test. One reads a statement, decides whether it is true or false or uncertain as applied to oneself, and then places the card in the appropriate box or stack. Many of

[23] Welsh and Dahlstrom (1956).
[24] Hathaway and McKinley (1956), p. 60.   [25] *Ibid.*

Table 33
Distribution of items in MMPI by general topics

general health	9	political attitudes—	
general neurologic	19	law and order	46
cranial nerves	11	social attitudes	72
motility and coordination	6	affect, depressive	32
sensibility	5	affect, manic	24
		obsessive and compul-	
vasomotor, trophic,		sive states	15
speech, secretory	10	delusions, hallucina-	
cardiorespiratory	5	tions, illusions, ideas	
gastrointestinal system	11	of reference	31
genitourinary system	5	phobias	29
habits	19	sadistic, masochistic	
		trends	7
family and marital	26	morale	33
occupational	18	masculinity-femininity	55
educational	12		
sexual attitudes	16	items for checking on	
religious attitudes	19	honesty	15

Adapted from Dahlstrom and Welsh (1960), p. 44.

the statements refer to private events, as for example, "I seldom worry about my health." Many require the subject to compare himself to others, as for example, "I believe I am no more nervous than most others" (which would have different meanings in different social settings), and many allow for a wide latitude of feeling, as for example, "I love my mother." Nevertheless, most of them can be answered without much hesitation by most persons. In clinical settings the card-sorting method is recommended, and in that case the cards are shuffled before each administration—a procedure which indicates, let it be noted, that the authors and users of the test regard it as a mosaic of independent items in which the important thing is the individual item, not the sequence. Their attitude on this point is not consistent, however, as otherwise they would not provide as they do an alternative questionnaire form in which the items necessarily have an invariable sequence.

The chief original aim of the MMPI was to furnish a simple objective method for discriminating between psychiatric syndromes (i.e., patterns of symptoms), a method which when ultimately perfected would take the task of diagnosis away from fallible psychiatrists. To this end the authors had the cards sorted by patients who had been diagnosed by psychiatrists as belonging to one of the various psychiatric categories, and also by nonpatients with the same general social background as the patients; and those items were then judged discriminating which were responded to differently by a majority of the patients and nonpatients. This procedure is basically the same as that adopted by Terman and Miles for the construction of the M-F test. The major MMPI subscales thus arrived at are the following: (1) hypochondriasis (33 items), (2) depression (60 items), (3) hysteria (60 items), (4) psychopathic deviate (50 items), (5) masculinity-femininity (60 items), (6) paranoia (40 items), (7) psychasthenia (48 items), (8) schizophrenia (78 items), (9) hypomania (46 items), and (10) social introversion (70 items).

A test can hardly be better than the criterion which guided its construction. As psychiatric classifications are rather broad and vague, a test built upon them must share in their indefiniteness. So it is that MMPI subscales (1) and (3), for example—hypochondriasis and hysteria—have 20 items identical in content and scoring for the two psychiatric classes. The test does not draw sharp boundaries between psychiatric syndromes. Neither does it sharply distinguish between the "sick" and the "well." It can be soundly argued, of course, that life is no more discriminating than the test: the inmates of mental hospitals are not vastly different from the people outside. Should we, however, prefer the test diagnosis (since it is "objective") to the diagnosis of a psychiatrist or panel of psychiatrists who might disagree with it? This is a delicate question. It is especially so because there is no universal agreement on what the proper diagnostic categories are. The MMPI is based on one scheme of categories (Kraepelin's), but it might have been based on some other. Perhaps we need not worry about that problem here, but we should realize fully the limited discriminating power of the test. As I have tried to make clear, this discriminative weakness is probably inherent in the realities with which the test is dealing. Every human condition shades into some other. Let us take a concrete example. Table 34 shows how 690 "normals" and 60 "hysterics" stand on the MMPI hysteria subscale. The distributions are in terms of T-scores.[26] Notice that only 5% of the diagnosed hysterics have MMPI scores above the highest-scoring normals. About 64% of the normals fall within the range of scores made by the hysterics. In other words, about two-

[26] T is an artificial score which in this case takes 50 as the mean score of normals and lets 10 points represent the SD of scores. For example, a T-score of 60 would be a score 1 SD above the mean, and so on.

Table 34
MMPI hysteria scores for normals and hysterics

T-scores	normals N=690	hysterics N=60	T-scores	normals N=690	hysterics N=60
97–99		1	58–60	63	1
94–96		1	55–57	76	2
91–93		1	52–54	89	5
88–90		0	49–51	95	3
85–87	2	4	46–48	73	
82–84	1	8	43–45	61	
79–81	2	7	40–42	42	
76–78	2	9	37–39	33	
73–75	3	8	34–36	18	
70–72	11	4	31–33	11	
67–69	14	2	28–30	4	
64–66	34	2	25–27	7	
61–63	48	2	22–24	1	

Adapted from McKinley and Hathaway (1956), p. 91.

thirds of the so-called normal population would have to be classified as hysterical—or, conversely, 95% of the hysterics would have to be classified as normal—on the basis of their MMPI similarity to the medically diagnosed hysterics. By the same line of argument we should have to conclude from the published data that about two-thirds of the so-called normals are hypochondriacal, about 40% psychasthenic, over 50% depressed, about 75% hypomanic, nearly 90% psychopathic deviates. By this logic a large part of the population of the United States are neurotic and psychotic, sometimes in opposite ways at the same time—for instance, both hypomanic and depressed. Is this picture false? If so, why? One reason might be that a complete psychiatric diagnosis will probably involve facts not sampled by the MMPI. For example, the patient who says, "I love my mother" (an MMPI item), may be answering sincerely, and yet may have to add, to complete the psychiatric picture, "I killed my mother." At the best, the MMPI gives us a trait picture; but a person is more than a collection of traits, and his totality is not containable in a trait list.

Whatever the correct position on the theoretical adequacy of the MMPI the practical users of the test have been concerned with trying to make it more discriminating. One proposal is that the items be treated as constituting a pattern. Just as a jumbled list of words is less informative than a grammatically organized sentence, so the items of a test may take on meaning from being properly combined. Meehl has argued that two true-false items might be entirely non-discriminating when taken singly and 100% discriminating when taken together. Such would be the case if all healthy people answered the paired items identically (i.e., either T-T or F-F) whereas all sick people answered one item differently from the other (i.e., either T-F or F-T). Details of this indisputable argument are given by P. E. Meehl in "Configural Scoring," in the Welsh and Dahlstrom book of readings on the MMPI. The research possibilities opened up by his argument are virtually infinite. Consider only the present 550 items of the MMPI (more could be added). Subjects answering in two ways (true or false) could produce 550^2 different patterns of answers, i.e., 302,500; if they answered in three ways (true, false, or uncertain), they could produce 550^3, or 166,375,000, different patterns. Examining these various patterns and their correlation with other variables could occupy research workers a long time. But then, why not? Human personality is certainly complex.

The MMPI has been increasingly used in experimental work. For example, Schiele and Brozek have studied the score changes of men undergoing experimental starvation. They started out with 36 conscientious objectors who were kept on a low-calorie diet for many weeks, losing about a fourth of their original body weight in the process. Schiele and Brozek report:

> All subjects developed emotional and personality symptoms of "semi-starvation neurosis" varying in intensity from mild to severe. In the majority of cases these symptoms receded during the following twelve weeks of controlled rehabilitation. On follow up, after an additional period of twenty-one weeks of unrestricted rehabilitation, the men were back to their prestarvation normal. Thus the psychologic disturbances, induced by the semistarvation regimen and relieved on refeeding can be considered as an experimental psychoneurosis.[27]

In Table 35, 32 subjects' T-scores on the various subscales of the MMPI are shown at four different periods—at the beginning of the experiment (control), after 24 weeks of semistarvation, after 12 weeks of rehabilitation, and after 33 weeks of rehabilitation. A glance shows that the principal changes were in (1) hypochondriasis, (2) depression, and (3) hysteria. These scores rose and fell definitely with the nutritional state. The other subscale scores changed little.

[27] Schiele and Brozek (1956), p. 482.

Table 35

Effect of starvation on MMPI scores: 32 conscientious objectors

conditions	N	T-scores on subscales*								
		1	2	3	4	5	6	7	8	9
control	32	46	54	59	52	70	54	46	48	51
starvation (24 weeks)	32	63	74	70	53	68	54	52	56	51
recovery (12 weeks)	32	54	66	65	53	68	53	49	49	50
recovery (33 weeks)	20	44	51	60	50	67	52	42	44	49

Adapted from Schiele and Brozek (1956), p. 463.
* The tenth subscale, introversion, is not used here.

We know from the comments of Schiele and Brozek that the main effect was depression and that the complaints about bodily symptoms (hypochondriacal and hysterical) were subsidiary. What contribution did the MMPI make in this study? I judge that it provided the experimenters with no information which was not available to them from direct observation, and it was not designed to detect the most impressive phenomena—such as the tremendous and sometimes irresistible craving for food, the loss of sexual desire, and the moral strains produced by the conflict between the pledge to keep to the strict diet and the temptation to yield to hunger. As far as Schiele and Brozek were concerned, they could have done without the test; it did not, I should say, enrich their conclusions. MMPI specialists, however, are happy to note that the test is not insensitive to the psychic effects of partial starvation; this is further evidence for them that the test works. They can argue, furthermore, that one of the main purposes of the test is to put certain information (however limited it may be) in standardized form suitable for mathematical manipulation. MMPI specialists are at least as interested in the possibilities of correlational analysis afforded by the test as they are in its diagnostic or information-getting powers.

Interpretation of MMPI scores for diagnostic purposes is largely predetermined by the way the test was constructed. The possibility of novel interpretations is not ruled out, but inevitably the eight psychiatric categories (two of the ten subscales are not psychiatric) which form its core enter into the assessment. Some interpreters have noted a tendency for the categories to cluster. Thus hypochondriasis, depression, and hysteria are referred to as "the neurotic triad." It is this triad which is affected in the starvation experiment rather than the psychotic cluster of paranoia, schizophrenia, and hypomania. Diamond has tried to go beyond the limits imposed by these psychiatric terms and relate the MMPI dimensions to more general categories not necessarily implying neurotic or psychotic deviation. His discussion[28] has been schematized in a diagram by Dahlstrom and Welsh[29] which I slightly modify and present in Figure 21. The interesting thing about Diamond's analysis is that he sees the trait syndromes as expressions of the relations between selves: depression, paranoia, and so on, are seen as derived from the attitude of a self to itself and to society. This goes beyond the logic of the MMPI and embeds it in a theory which needs to speak of traits either not at all or only in a very secondary fashion.

Some reflections on trait theory

Often trait theory is set up in opposition to type theory. I wonder if this is not misleading. Some typologies consist of trait syndromes, for example the typology of Heymans and Wiersma; and some tests which deal with trait syndromes verge on typologies, for example the MMPI. Typing and trait-testing belong on a continuum; at any rate, they are both concerned with taxonomy. The true opposition, it seems, is that between a trait theory which looks on the traits as elements of personality and a self theory which either refuses to deal with the trait language at all or relegates traits to second place as more or less momentary expressions of a self in relation to other selves.

As persuasive a trait theorist as can be found is Allport, but he has become more and more pronouncedly a self theorist and in doing so has, I think, found less and less use for traits.

Allport defines a trait as "a generalized and focalized neuropsychic system (peculiar to the individual), with the capacity to render many stimuli functionally equivalent, and to initiate and guide consistent (equivalent) forms of adaptive and expressive behavior."[30] He distinguishes trait from attitude by saying that a trait *lacks* but an attitude *possesses* (1) a definite object of reference, (2) the possibility of being specific as well as general, and (3) positive or negative directedness. He writes:

Both *attitude* and *trait* are indispensable concepts. Between them they cover virtually every type of disposition with which the psychology of

[28] Diamond (1957), pp. 175 f.
[29] Dahlstrom and Welsh (1960), p. 80.
[30] Allport (1937), p. 295. Used by permission of Holt, Rinehart and Winston.

self-blame {	depression	← low ← activity → high →	hypomania	} self-gain
	psychasthenia	← high ← conscience → low →	psychopathic	
self-pity {	hysteria	← high ← compliance → low →	paranoia	} self-insulation
	hypochondria	← high ← attachment → low →	schizophrenia	

21 *Diamond's analysis of eight MMPI trait-syndromes puts them into personal and social terms. (After Dahlstrom and Welsh, 1960)*

personality concerns itself. Ordinarily *attitude* should be employed when the disposition is bound to an object or value, that is to say, when it is aroused by a well-defined class of stimuli, and when the individual feels toward these stimuli a definite attraction or repulsion. In some cases either of the two terms (trait or attitude) is correct, as in the case of extroversion or patriotism . . . or conservatism or radicalism. If in the last two cases the object or value against which the person is rebelling, or which he is intent on conserving, can be specified, the term attitude is preferable. If, on the other hand, the radicalism or conservatism is chronic and "temperamental," expressed in almost any sphere of the person's behavior, then the term *trait* fits the situation better. Narrow or specific attitudes are never traits. A man is fond of his dog: he has a kindly attitude toward it. But if in general he is thoughtful of, and sympathetic toward men and beasts, he has a trait of kindliness. The more generalized an attitude (the more difficult it is to specify its object or its polarity of affect), the more does it resemble a trait.[31]

The breadth of the trait concept for Allport is indicated by the list of terms which he considers equivalent, included, or overlapping. These are: *Charakterzug,* complex, directional tendency, ego-system (Koffka), *Eigenschaft* (Baumgarten, Stern), foci of development, general attitude, generalized habit (Dewey), ideal, inner-personal region (Lewin), interest, lineament (Boven), mode of adaptation, mode of adjustment, motor-perceptual region (Lewin), need integrate (Murray), *Neigung* (Lazurski), phobia, *Richtungsdisposition* (Stern), *Rüstungsdisposition* (Stern), sentiment (McDougall), style of life (Adler), subjective value (Spranger), taste, *Triebfeder* (Klages), trend. What all these terms have in common is the notion of a semipermanent structure. They differ widely in other respects. For example, McDougall's "sentiment" is derived from the activity of instincts (a concept which Allport does not like), and it has a

[31] *Ibid.,* p. 294.

386   THE PERSONAL WORLD

definite cognitive object at its core, in contrast to what Allport says about traits though corresponding to what he says about attitudes.

Like many other trait theorists, Allport regards types as dubious fictions. "A man can be said to *have* a trait; but he cannot be said to *have* a type. Rather he *fits* a type. This bit of usage betrays the important fact that types exist not in people or in nature, but rather in the eye of the observer."[32] Traits, he insists, are unique neuro-psychic dispositions in each individual; they are not classes or dimensions. Yet, so difficult is it to remain consistent that this central argument is weakened in both theory and practice. Allport writes:

> Somewhere between the extremes of exaggerated domination and complete passivity, there lies for each normal individual a level of adaptation that fits his intimate requirements. The psychologist does well to recognize all these possible gradations and to postulate a common variable (in this case, ascendance-submission) which, though rough and approximate, permits quantitative scaling. He does not measure directly the full-bodied individul trait that alone exists as a neuro-psychic disposition and as the one irreducible unit of personality. What he does is to measure a common *aspect* of this trait, such a portion thereof as takes common cultural forms of expression and signifies essentially the same manner of adjusting within the social group.[33]

So much for theory. As for practice, Allport is the author of a questionnaire test of ascendence-submission which enables all who will to locate a fellow man with a score on a trait continuum.

At the same time, Allport the trait theorist is one of the most severe critics of trait-testing. He has some very telling remarks to make regarding the error of assuming that every trait in a given list must exist to some degree in everyone. He charges that this assumption is the cause of blurred trait-portraits. For example, when one psychologist required teachers to rate their pupils on each of 231 traits in an arbitrary list, the agreement between the teachers as indicated by correlation coefficients ranged from .14 to .78, with a median of .48. But when the same teachers were allowed to make a selection from among the traits, starring those which seemed to them of capital importance in each child, the agreement rose to values of .93 to .96. The point of this example of Allport's is that the accuracy of individual personality description is spoiled by a compulsory inclusion of traits which, whether common or rare, are not actually found in the personality under scrutiny. In Allport's opinion

[32] *Ibid.*, p. 295.   [33] *Ibid.*, p. 298.

some extremely rare traits, which because of their rarity would be unlikely to appear in a trait list designed for general use, may be almost indispensable for identifying a particular real individual. Such, he says, would be Goethe's trait of listening to everyone without contradicting him, or Beau Brummel's fastidious exhibitionism. Allport is so convinced of this principle that he says flatly: "No investigator . . . would undertake to scale *paranoia* in the general population; yet paranoia *may* on occasion be the very core of personality."[34] Alas, paranoia *has* been scaled for the general population —in the MMPI!

How many traits are there? If each trait is truly unique as Allport argues, and if each individual has numerous traits, there must be billions on billions on billions of them. Language cannot cope with such variety. Yet even within the English language there are more trait names than any test constructer has dared to tackle. According to Allport and Odbert's special lexicon, the number comes to at least 17,953, or more than 4% of the total English vocabulary. After surveying their long list, the authors conclude:

> A trait-name is a range-name. Although traits are real enough entities, trait-names are essentially blankets, covering one trait in one person and other (similar) traits in other people. Though perceived as similar and labeled identically, the trait is never, strictly speaking, in two different human beings exactly the same.[35]

How have trait testers dealt with these facts, if facts they are? I should say that they have, in the first place, simply closed their eyes to those billions on billions on billions of unique individual traits which are valued by Allport, and have, in the second place, refused to deal with the 17,953 trait names in the English language. Their practice has been to limit themselves to as few traits as possible. The most opportunistic way of doing this is to pick up a random handful from some more or less reputable source. A more conscientious way is to start with a long and "comprehensive" list (usually much shorter than 17,953) and then squeeze this down by a combination of armchair meditation and correlational analysis to a much shorter one. The outcome is that, as the list grows shorter, the coverage of the surviving trait names becomes wider. Cattell finds that sixteen great blanket-words, arrived at by factor analysis, will probably do to cover the whole human family. Others are satisfied with fewer and wider blankets. In brief, trait testers

[34] *Ibid.*, p. 302.　　　　　　　　[35] Allport and Odbert (1936), p. 21.

try to find a few summary terms for expressing the perhaps infinite number of varied traits. It is not quite certain that this process of abstraction is the true path of science. At any rate, there is restiveness among the trait testers themselves, and perhaps the yeasty ferment of new and more profitable ideas.

A concise statement of the present state of affairs, mixing pessimism with optimism, is the address of Leona Tyler, speaking as president of the Western Psychological Association. In regard to current testing theory she says:

> We have worked out techniques for measuring hundreds of traits. We have attempted to match particular individuals with particular situations, in schools, in industry, and in military settings. We have developed skills that enable us to help individuals make their decisions, solve their problems. Out of this activity has come a sort of model that we use in thinking about the general phenomena of individuality. The basic concept is that of dimension. Each of the traits that have been identified can be thought of as an axis along which any one person's position can be located. In this system the *uniqueness* of the individual is defined by his *combination* of measurements along all possible dimensions. A person is represented by a point in *n*-dimensional space. No one else occupies exactly the same position.[36]

The practice of measurement, notice, does not end in practice: the practice has a powerful effect on the way in which personality itself is conceived—namely, in this instance, as a point in mathematical space. Something protests, in the language of feeling and the language of reason both:

> Useful as this approach has been, I have found myself questioning more and more whether it is really adequate at this stage in the development of our science. For one thing, it does not *feel* quite right. Most people find it hard to think of themselves as points in *n*-dimensional space. . . . For another thing, the system shows signs of becoming completely unworkable . . . because of the proliferation of dimensions. . . . But the most important reason I see for questioning the adequacy of this way of looking at things is that we are no longer making the progress with it that we have a right to expect. Correlations with criteria significant for theory or for practice are not going up very much. Seldom do we find a cross-validated multiple correlation with any criterion that exceeds .6. The addition of new dimensions and the increasing refinement in the ways we measure the old ones are not

[36] Tyler (1959), pp. 75 f. Used by permission of the American Psychological Association.

really "paying off" very well. The possibility is at least worth considering that we are approaching the limit of what can be done with this particular system.[37]

She concludes that an entirely different orientation is needed, and she confesses:

> What I have been coming to believe is that individuality will continue to elude us as long as we restrict our thinking to models based on dimensions or trait continua. Little by little, evidence has been accumulating that some of the crucial defining features of psychological individuality are to be found in two aspects of experience and behavior that are not easily expressed as dimensions and that can best be thought of as *dis*continuous. I call these two aspects of individuality *choice* and *organization,* though I am by no means certain that these are the best labels.[38]

If we turn again to Allport and take him at a later stage in his thinking about personality, we find that he has subtly modified his earlier views in the direction of a greater emphasis on the self as a forward-looking, choice-making entity. He does not actually discard his earlier views, but the term "characteristic" which he employs instead of "trait" has less the sound of an independent unit of structure, and his emphasis on the term "intention" has the effect of referring us back to a self which has the power to choose and thus to display or even create traits. It is possible that I am reading a little more into Allport's language than he would approve, for I notice that the following words seem to cling to traits as quasi-permanent units and even bring intentions under that conception:

> [1] For present purposes let us use the venerable Greek term *characteristic* to denote any distinctive mark or engraving of personality. Characteristics can be of many orders, ranging from peripheral mannerisms and opportunistic habits to the most central value-orientations of a life. . . . [2] Intentions, as I shall use the term, are complex propriate characteristics of a personality.[39]

It is this second definition which makes me doubt the advisability of equating Allport's "intention" with "choice," which in my understanding is not a structure or engraving but a pure psychic act. Nevertheless, Allport's discussion is infused with the sense of a self in action, in such words as these: "Intentional characteristics repre-

[37] *Ibid.,* p. 76.   [38] *Ibid.,* pp. 76 f.
[39] Allport (1955), p. 89.

sent above all else the individual's primary modes of addressing himself to the future. As such they select stimuli, guide inhibitions and choices, and have much to do with the process of adult becoming."[40] Or again in these words: "Even industrial psychology is learning that long-range intentions guide learning, productivity, and the satisfaction of the worker on the job. A vocational counselor has told me that the most revealing question he asks in his interviews is 'Where do you want to be five years from now?' "[41] I think I detect in Allport's modified language a tendency to subordinate traits, even intentional characteristics, to a freely choosing self, though this tendency is certainly far from actualized in the following passage:

> To summarize: the most comprehensive units in personality are broad intentional dispositions, future-pointed. These characteristics are unique for each person, and tend to attract, guide, inhibit the more elementary units to accord with the major intentions themselves. This proposition is valid in spite of the large amount of unordered, impulsive, and conflictful behavior in every life. Finally, these cardinal characteristics are not infinite in number but for any given life in adult years are relatively few and ascertainable.[42]

This passage can easily be read as harmonizing with Allport's much-reprinted diagram of 1937 (here reproduced as Figure 22) in which there is no self but only "selves," defined as "systems of traits that are coherent among themselves, but are likely to vary in different situations."[43] And yet I believe that there is an underlying difference between the position of 1955 and that of 1937 in some such direction as I have indicated.

If I am wrong in my interpretation of the later Allport, I may at least say for myself that I believe many of the disadvantages of trait theory stem from the assumption that traits are quantitative units of personality structure. It is by no means utterly revolutionary but it does make a difference to regard traits as *expressions* of a self in action, relating itself to itself and to other selves. Trait-measurement may still have its uses under self theory, just as measurement of heat has its uses under molecule and atom theory, but the purpose and the application will have to be different.

---

[40] *Ibid.*, p. 89.   [41] *Ibid.*, p. 90.   [42] *Ibid.*, p. 92.
[43] Allport (1937), p. 140.

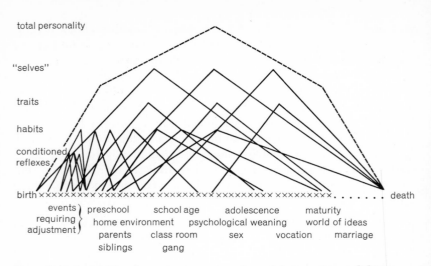

total personality

"selves"

traits

habits

conditioned reflexes

birth ×××××××××× ×××××××××× ×××××××××× ×××××××××× ×××××××××. . . . . . . death

events requiring adjustment	preschool	school age	adolescence	maturity
home environment	psychological weaning	world of ideas
parents	class room	sex	vocation	marriage
siblings	gang

22 *Allport's 1937 schematic representation of integration exhibits personality as an organized bundle of traits (and lower-order units) expanding and contracting from birth to death. (From Allport, 1937)*

References for chapter 11

Adkins, D. C. (1947) *Construction and analysis of achievement tests.* Washington: U.S. Government Printing Office.

Allport, G. W. (1937) *Personality: a psychological interpretation.* New York: Holt.

——— (1955) *Becoming: basic considerations for a psychology of personality.* New Haven: Yale Univ. Press.

———, and Odbert, H. S. (1936) Trait-names: a psycho-lexical study. *Psychological Monographs*, No. 211.

Cattell, R. B. (1950) *Personality: a systematic theoretical and factual study.* New York: McGraw-Hill.

——— (1959) Foundations of personality measurement in multivariate experiment. In Bass, B. M., and Berg, I. A. (Eds.) *Objective approaches to personality assessment.* Princeton: Van Nostrand, pp. 42-65.

Cronbach, L. J. (1949) *Essentials of psychological testing.* New York: Harper.

Dahlstrom, W. G., and Welsh, G. S. (1960) *An MMPI handbook: a guide to use in clinical practice and research.* Minneapolis: Univ. of Minnesota Press.

Diamond, S. (1957) *Personality and temperament.* New York: Harper.

Hartshorne, H., and May, M. A. (1928-30) *Studies in the nature of character.* New York: Macmillan. 3 vols., Vol. 1.

Hathaway, S. R., and McKinley, J. C. (1956) Construction of the schedule. In Welsh, G. S., and Dahlstrom, W. G: (Eds.) *Basic readings on the MMPI in psychology and medicine.* Minneapolis: Univ. of Minnesota Press, pp. 60-63.

Hilgard, E. R. (1957) *Introduction to psychology.* 2nd ed. New York: Harcourt, Brace & World.

McCurdy, H. G. (1947) Group and individual variability on the Goodenough Draw-a-Man test. *Journal of Educational Psychology,* 38, 428-36.

McKinley, J. C., and Hathaway, S. R. (1956) Scales 3 (hysteria), 9 (hypomania), and 4 (psychopathic deviate). In Welsh, G. S., and Dahlstrom, W. G. (Eds.) *Basic readings on the MMPI in psychology and medicine.* Minneapolis: Univ. of Minnesota Press, pp. 87-103.

Nettler, G. (1959) Test burning in Texas. *American Psychologist,* 14, 682-83.

Schiele, B. C., and Brozek, J. (1956) "Experimental neurosis" resulting from semistarvation in man. In Welsh, G. S., and Dahlstrom, W. G. (Eds.) *Basic readings on the MMPI in psychology and medicine.* Minneapolis: Univ. of Minnesota Press, pp. 461-83.

Stagner, R. (1958) The gullibility of personnel managers. *Personnel Psychology,* 11, 347-52.

Symonds, P. M. (1931) *Diagnosing personality and conduct.* New York: Century.

Terman, L. M., and Miles, C. C. (1936) *Sex and personality.* New York: McGraw-Hill.

Tyler, L. E. (1959) Toward a workable psychology of individuality. *American Psychologist,* 14, 75-81.

Vernon, P. E. (1953) *Personality tests and assessments.* New York: Holt.

Watson, R. I. (1959) Historical review of objective personality testing: the search for objectivity. In Bass, B. M., and Berg., I. A. (Eds.) *Objective approaches to personality assessment.* Princeton: Van Nostrand, pp. 1-23.

Welsh, G. S., and Dahlstrom, W. G. (Eds.) (1956) *Basic readings on the MMPI in psychology and medicine.* Minneapolis: Univ. of Minnesota Press.

12

THE ANATOMY
OF IMAGINATION

Preview *Freud's work with dreams has directed the attention of those concerned with personality assessment to the formal analysis of imaginative products. Two clinical devices developed under this influence are the Rorschach test and the Thematic Apperception Test (TAT). An approach more purely theoretical is the analysis of imaginative literature. All such approaches are difficult to evaluate and often strike critics as too dependent on intuition. Nevertheless, workers in this area of so-called projective techniques have made attempts at objective procedure and predictive validation and very often are no more intuitive than those who favor so-called objective testing.*

One of the consequences of Freud's emphasis on dream analysis is the proliferation of so-called projective techniques of personality assessment. The aim of these approaches is to examine personality in depth or at least some way below the surface. The aim is thus similar to Freud's, but the procedure may have little relationship to his. Often, though not always, the focus of interest is on patterns of organization, and the terms of the analysis (i.e., the units which are seen as organized) are usually rather different from the behavioral and experiential items of the trait testers.

I objected in the last chapter to drawing a sharp line between trait-testing and typology. Here I must object equally to contrasting the *methods* of so-called objective trait-testing with those of so-called projective testing. Doubtless the aims are different, and users of projective techniques are manifesting a greater interest in human imagination, but the anatomy of imagination may be, and often is, as objective, quantitative, and dry as the analysis of responses to a trait questionnaire. As for the relative merits of the two approaches, there is more room for debate. Neither approach can claim consistently high predictive power, but it is sometimes asserted by those who regard trait-testing as good, tough-minded positivism that the predictive power of projective techniques is peculiarly low; and this criticism is often joined with the charge that projective testers are unusually sloppy and intuitive in their thinking, "intuitive" being equated with "nonscientific."

Projective tests may be as bad as their worst critics say (though I personally believe that they are not a whit worse than trait questionnaires), but it is unnecessarily confusing to mix up criticism of the Rorschach test and the Thematic Apperception Test (TAT), which will be discussed in this chapter, with criticism of intuition, which will be discussed in the next. Users of these two techniques, even though they are tapping the vital regions of the imagination, are not necessarily given to intuition. Some may be, but there are numerous others who cultivate statistics with ardor and who go out of their way to suppress whatever glimmerings of intuition they may enjoy. Let it be added that intuition is not necessarily a bad thing, even for science, and that it should certainly not be equated with sloppy thinking—any more than statistics should be equated with straight thinking. But more on this anon. Our present task is to describe the Rorschach, the TAT, and the analysis of imaginative literature.

The Rorschach test

The materials for the Rorschach test consist of cards on which are printed bilaterally symmetrical ink-blots, some black-and-white, some in color. The subject is asked to look at these irregular splotches at not more than arm's length away and report what he sees. In a way, it is an application of the age-old game of seeing pictures in the flames of an open fire, in shadows cast on a wall, in clouds, in all sorts of chance patterns. What seems to have attracted the Swiss psychologist Hermann Rorschach to ink-blots especially was the great variety of responses to such material. He saw in this an opportunity to study individual differences. It was around 1910-12 that a friend of his employed such blots to stimulate schoolchildren in their imaginative writing and shared the results with Rorschach. Impressed by the obvious differences in their reactions, Rorschach pondered seriously over the possible link between blot responses and personality traits. Later he took up the subject more systematically. In 1921 he published in Switzerland his *Psychodiagnostics*, in which he explained his use of a standard set of ink-blots and reported certain results. The book did not attract much attention at the time and in 1922 Rorschach died, at the age of 38, leaving his research and his theory in an unfinished state. The test which he proposed, however, is now with slight modifications in world-wide use, and a huge literature has grown up around it.

Though it seems common sense to say that the Rorschach ink-blots stimulate the imagination, and this is the position Piotrowski takes in his book *Perceptanalysis,* Rorschach himself tried to distinguish between imaginative activity and the responses to his blots. He asserts: "The interpretation of the chance forms falls in the field of perception and apperception rather than imagination."[1] In his opinion, the ink-blots excite sensations and arouse memory images; the subject's task is to connect the perceived pattern before him with a suitable memory image. If the condition of the subject is such that he is unaware of exerting any effort to achieve this junction (as in senile dements, epileptics, schizophrenics, some manics, and the feeble-minded), he may think that he is having a straight-forward perception and is astonished that anyone else should see anything different. But in the normal case there is a sense of striving to get a good fit, and the subject realizes that he is interpreting rather than perceiving. So says Rorschach. Piotrowski on the other hand, though generally faithful to Rorschach, writes:

> Some creative imagination is needed to interpret the blots meaningfully and nearly all persons enjoy being creative even when the creative

[1] Rorschach (1951), p. 16. Used by permission of Verlag Hans Huber.

imagination is modest and limited. . . . Rorschach noted that nearly all subjects consider the test to be one of imagination. It is proper and wise to corroborate this belief when the subject voices it because it is a true belief.[2]

Piotrowski in fact lays considerable stress on how easy and natural the responses normally are.

One reason why Rorschach denied that the test had much to do with imagination is that he was not particularly interested in the *content* of the responses. It is exactly in this respect, he says, that his method differs from the method of his predecessor Szymon Hens, who

> addressed himself to the problem of the content of the interpretations exclusively and did not go beyond the concept of imagination, in a case where only perception can be considered basic. His conclusions, therefore, concern the content rather than the pattern of perceptive process which has been my principal concern.[3]

Rorschach concentrated on *form* analysis. He was interested in the general features of the responses rather than in their specific content. He singled out for special attention the *form, color,* and *movement* indicated by the responses, and whether the ink-blot was interpreted as a *whole* or in *detail.* I italicize these words because they are technical terms in Rorschach's vocabulary.

A *form* (or F) response is one which is clearly governed by the shape of the blot. The decision whether the F is a good one and should be called F+ depends upon the frequency with which that response is given by a standardizing group of normal persons. If it is frequently given, it is labeled thus even though for the test administrator it has little to commend it. F responses are supposed to indicate an active intelligence, but not that alone; a state of depression, for instance, "improves the sharpness of form visualization, while elation dulls it."[4]

Color (or C) responses, which refer to the color rather than the shape of the blots in the case of the colored cards, indicate the strength of emotional and impulsive elements in the personality, according to Rorschach. Subjects who tend to keep their emotions in check may react to color with "color shock," i.e., rejection of the card or some hesitation in interpreting it.

[2] Piotrowski (1957), p. 49. Used by permission of The Macmillan Company.
[3] Rorschach (1951), pp. 102 f.   [4] *Ibid.*, p. 23.

The response is a *movement* (or M) response if the tester judges that kinesthetic factors enter into the subject's interpretation:

> The subject imagines the object interpreted to be in motion. For instance, in Plate I he sees two angels with fluttering wings. . . . Frequently the gestures of the subject during the test will indicate whether or not kinaesthetic influences are in play. He makes the movements which he is interpreting or indicates them by involuntary innervations.[5]

This judgment is a somewhat ticklish one to make, because the mere statement that a thing is in motion is not enough; there must be evidence that it is *felt* by the subject himself to be in motion. Rorschach placed special emphasis on M responses. Occurrence of many M responses is supposed to signify an active inner life, good productive intelligence, and so on. It even makes a difference whether the perceived movement is flexor or extensor in type:

> Subjects who usually see extension movements are fundamentally different from those who see only bent, burdened or twisted figures. In Plate V, held vertically, one of the first type saw a danseuse stretching herself upwards and backwards, making passionate movements, while one of the second type saw a bent old woman carrying two umbrellas under her arm. Subjects who see extension movements are active individuals with strong drive toward self-assertion, though they often show neurotic inhibitions. Those who see flexion movements are passive, resigned, neurasthenic individuals.[6]

The interpretation of a blot as a *whole* or in *details* of it taken separately, and also the order (whether from *whole* to *detail* or vice versa), is considered significant. Normal subjects usually begin with a *whole* interpretation and then descend to *details*. Theoretically, this is the normal order on every card, but Rorschach never had a subject who acted in this way consistently. Nevertheless, he guesses at the characteristics of so abnormally normal a person:

> He would be a know all, have a large store of available associations, and would show a logic far beyond the range of anything that might be called healthy common sense. He would constantly impress one as tyrannical, grumbling, impatient and pedantic. He would also be very proud of his power and stamina of thinking, especially of his logical reasoning ability, but he would show no originality of reasoning nor sense for practical things. He would be original only in his desire to know and do everything. He would have almost no capacity to form

[5] *Ibid.,* p. 25.   [6] *Ibid.,* p. 29.

rapport, would be empty of any temperament, but full of self-righteousness and pride. In fine, he would be a proud but sterile technician of logic and memory.[7]

Rorschach's fictitious portrait is not baseless: it is founded on the observed characteristics of those subjects who most strongly follow the logical order of interpretation—from *whole* to *detail* to *fine detail*.

Rorschach did not absolutely ignore the content of the responses, but he did not treat them symbolically as a psychoanalyst might have; instead, he noted the commonness or rarity of the response. For example, he compared the frequency of an individual's animal responses (i.e., seeing animals in the blot) with the frequencies in the standardizing population. We may illustrate with the *original* responses—those which occur not more than once in a hundred times. Table 36 gives some insight into Rorschach's procedure. This table, which shows the percentage of original responses in various categories of normal and abnormal subjects, constitutes a nearly mechanical guide to interpretation. In fact, it is just such a table which Meehl, in his incisive discussion of statistical versus clinical prediction, recommends as the ideal statistical instrument for diagnostic and predictive purposes,[8] and it would not be hard to devise a thoroughly mechanical substitute for such a table. This is a long way from intuition. The logic is very much that of the MMPI: the significance of the categories of response is determined by the kinds of people who give the response, and the classification of people is primarily psychiatric. Thus, we learn from the table that original responses occur more frequently among average epileptics than among average normals, and that in general the more deteriorated the psychiatric cases are the more frequent are their original responses. Even among the normals, frequency of original responses is related to how "normal" the person is: it is the flighty, the artists, those "not of this world" who yield the high percentages. The statistically rare responses seem to increase in frequency, then, with departure of the person from what the psychiatric mind considers normal functioning.

A complete Rorschach psychogram consists of a statement of the frequency of the various kinds of responses, the ratio of M to F responses, and so on. Since it is related at every point to psychiatric classifications, just as the MMPI is, it can obviously be used as a

---

[7] *Ibid.*, p. 37.   [8] Meehl (1954).

Table 36

Rorschach original response percentages as related to psychiatric categories

per cent original	normal	feeble-minded	schizo-phrenic	manic-depressive	epileptic	organic
0–10	average intelligent	—	simple dement	depressed	—	—
10–20	moder-ately intelligent	—	stereo-typed; catatonic in remis-sion	manic	—	arterio-sclerotic
20–30	intelli-gent; normal in a manic mood	moron	hebe-phrene; preserved paranoid	manic	some with slow de-mentia	Korsakoff
30–40	imagina-tive, high spirits; flighty	moron	scattered	—	average	Korsakoff
40–50	artists	imbecile	scattered	—	early dementia	paretic; senile
50–70	those "not of this world"	imbecile	very scat-tered	—	feeble-minded	senile dementia
over 70	—	—	rare neg-ativistic cases	—	—	—

Adapted from Rorschach (1951), p. 48.

diagnostic instrument in much the same sense as the MMPI. But Rorschach himself seems to have been more interested in the correlation of the test responses to certain basic functions of the psyche. That is to say, he was more interested in the natural structure of the mind than in psychiatric schemes for classifying patients. For example, he pointed out, as we have noted, that the occurrence of numerous M responses signified an intense inner life. He invented or applied terms like "introversion," "extratension," and "coartation" to describe the psychic qualities which he thought were revealed by the test. He was really working toward an analysis of the human psyche and thus a psychological system for describing the individual, rather than simply the refinement of a tool for perpetuating the

Table 37
Contrasting traits of M and C respondents

predominantly M	predominantly C
more individualized intelligence	stereotyped intelligence
greater creative ability	more reproductive ability
more "inner" life	more "outward" life
stable affective reactions	labile affective reactions
less adaptable to reality	more adaptable to reality
more intensive than extensive rapport	more extensive than intensive rapport
measured, stable motility	restless, labile motility
awkwardness, clumsiness	skill and adroitness

Adapted from Rorschach (1951), p. 78.

old psychiatric habits of thought. A sample of what he was trying to do is seen in Table 37, where personal qualities are related by him to preference for M or for C responses.

Note once again that Rorschach was primarily concerned with *form* analysis; he wanted to know how the perceptual activity was patterned rather than what the subject perceived. Piotrowski states that there is now a tendency among Rorschach followers to drift away from this fundamental position and he deplores it. Many users of the test now rely chiefly on content analysis, in imitation of psychoanalysis, and they may not go to the trouble to tabulate responses and score them. In Piotrowski's opinion this trend indicates a lack of skill in classic Rorschach procedure, and he blames desertion of the fundamental principle of the Rorschach technique for the devaluating conclusion that it yields no different result from those accessible to other techniques. There can be no doubt that Rorschach did place his hopes in a strictly quantitative procedure. He went so far as to say: "I consider it quite impossible to obtain a definite and reliable interpretation from the records, even after a great deal of experience and practice, unless the calculations are made."[9]

Perhaps the dissatisfaction of the statistically minded with the Rorschach test is explainable in part by the drift away from Rorschach's personal position on the test. Some of it, however, is due to the nature of the test material itself and the freedom allowed the respondent. Recall how Terman and Miles dealt with freedom to respond to stimulus words in the word association part of their test: they restricted the subjects' freedom by providing a limited

[9] Rorschach (1951), p. 192.

number of responses from which to choose. This was largely for the purpose of assigning a score mechanically to the response without requiring any judgment by the test administrator. The Rorschach method, however, leaves the test administrator some scope for judgment in assigning the responses to categories of M, C, F, and so on. The more rigorous test constructers distrust the test administrators too much to feel comfortable about this. Here, in their opinion, is a leaky place in the method. In addition, they are not likely to be happy about the personal freedom exercised by the test administrator or interpreter of the test when he evaluates the tabulated scores by a sort of intuitive pattern analysis, as one might analyze a complex piece of music by merely listening to it without counting the notes. In sum, proponents of standardized and easily scorable questionnaires object to the ink-blot stimulus, to the freedom of the respondent, and to the freedom of the interpreter of the test responses. All these things seem to them to be full of uncertainty and therefore "unscientific."

Rorschach specialists, on the defensive before this kind of criticism, have tried to meet it in various ways. For example, they have carefully examined the stimulus properties of the Rorschach inkblots themselves. Baughman, for example, in one experimental study systematically varied the color and shading of the blots while retaining their outline. He was pleased to find that these alterations changed the nature of the responses very little and concluded:

> The fact that perceptual behavior is so minimally affected by major changes in stimulus characteristics should make us feel more secure in our use of such techniques for personality evaluation. The fact that we affect behavior so little by such changes in external conditions points up the extent to which such behavior is determined by personal characteristics of the individual, a not unhappy finding. Our need now is to pursue more clearly the formulation of these internal or personal determinants.[10]

The same discovery which makes Baughman happy, however, probably makes a good many others who believe in the determining power of the stimulus unhappy and would alone discredit the Rorschach test.

Another way of meeting the criticisms is to try to demonstrate the predictive power of the test. Since it is often charged that the Rorschacher depends largely on the impressions gathered from the

[10] Baughman (1954), p. 163.

subject while the test is being administered rather than exclusively from the scored responses, much emphasis has been placed on the effectiveness of blind analysis, i.e., the interpretation of test responses without contact with the subject himself. If the congruence between the personality description thus achieved and the personality as known to persons well acquainted with the subject is satisfactory, the blind analysis is considered to have been successful. Piotrowski reports good results:

> The claim is made here that blind analyses can be of a very high degree of validity when they are limited to the description of personality traits. It is more difficult to make satisfactory blind neuropsychiatric diagnoses for a variety of reasons, chief among which is the poor reliability of clinical neuropsychiatric diagnoses against which the perceptanalytic diagnostic impressions are checked. As far as personality description is concerned, more than 80 per cent of the conclusions can be valid.[11]

Unfortunately, Piotrowski gives no details of the hundreds of blind analyses in different settings on which he bases this claim.

This neglect of evidential detail is one of the exasperating features of much of the Rorschach literature. We have many enthusiastic claims, but few strong facts. Yet it may be that the method could be used as effectively for predictive purposes as most tests. Such would appear to be the proper inference from the results obtained in one study, somewhat exceptional, which was designed to check Rorschach scores against definite criteria.

Ruth Munroe has reported that Rorschach scores can be validated both by the method of personal identification and by the method of prediction of adjustment. In one early experiment at Sarah Lawrence College she found that teachers familiar with the students were able to identify them from the Rorschach personality sketches with perfect accuracy. She describes this experiment in the following words:

> We thought it desirable to check the validity of the test for ourselves, however, especially since it had never been used intensively for educational purposes. Accordingly we tested all of the students in 3 representative freshman courses (35 girls), had interpretations written "blind" (that is without any information about the student except her response to the test-blots), and subjected the interpretations to careful study. The interpretations were presented, in groups of five, to the

[11] Piotrowski (1957), p. 25.

teachers; the teachers were asked to match the interpretations with a corresponding list of students' names. This task the teachers were able to perform without error.[12]

Encouraged by this outcome, she then attempted much more extensive investigations. In this connection she developed her inspection technique, aimed at a rapid and efficient evaluation of the Rorschach records; the essence of the technique is a check list of Rorschach diagnostic signs on which can be easily noted any departures from "normal" response. She also worked out a systematic scheme for translating Rorschach records into an adjustment rating. This latter amounts to a prediction of degree of adjustment to college life, and in particular to life at Sarah Lawrence College where Munroe was at that time working. The success of the prediction is displayed in Table 38. The 348 girls involved were from different entering classes, so that their record of actual adjustment covers different lengths of time, i.e., two, three, or four years. The criteria

Table 38
Rorschach adjustment rating vs. external criteria: Sarah Lawrence College students

external criteria	adjustment rating from Inspection Rorschach								
	A ADEQUATELY ADJUSTED		B SLIGHT PROBLEM		C MODERATE PROBLEM		D SEVERE PROBLEM		TOTALS
	N	per cent	N	per cent	N	per cent	N	per cent	N
seen by psychiatrist	5	6.5	6	5.5	8	9.5	24	30.4	43
much faculty consultation	4	5.1	19	17.6	29	34.5	37	46.9	89
committee rating "p"	3	3.9	1	.9	8	9.5	5	6.3	17
adequately adjusted	65	84.5	82	76.0	39	46.5	13	16.4	199
TOTALS	77	100.0	108	100.0	84	100.0	79	100.0	348

Adapted from Munroe (1945), p. 40.

[12] Munroe (1945), pp. 13 f.

of maladjustment were, in order of seriousness, (1) referral to a psychiatrist, (2) faculty concern as evidenced in frequent consultation on the girl's problems, and (3) a rating of "p" ("personality problem") by a committee charged with the task of general academic evaluation; if the girl escaped all of these tags, she was listed as adequately adjusted. The table shows that the Inspection Rorschach ratings were to some extent confirmed by the external criteria. (For example, 30.4 per cent of those rated by the Rorschach as "severe problems" were seen by a psychiatrist as compared with only 6.5 per cent of those rated "adequately adjusted.") The correlation coefficient is, in fact, .55. This is about the level of prediction which we have come to expect from the best psychometric instruments. We may judge that in the Munroe experiment the Rorschach proved to be as efficient predictively as, for example, an intelligence test used to predict college grades.

The Thematic Apperception Test

The Thematic Apperception Test (TAT), first described in 1935, was developed by Henry Murray and Christiana Morgan as a method for investigating fantasy. It consists of a set of pictures, most of which involve one or more human figures. The subject is asked to make up a dramatic story to fit the picture. The story or interpretation thus obtained provides the material for analysis.

According to its inventors, the significance of the TAT is based on the fact that when people interpret ambiguous social situations in real life they expose their own personalities. The TAT pictures are substitutes for such real-life situations. Absorbed in the objective occurrence or the picture, people let down their defenses as they forget themselves. To one with "double hearing" they disclose "certain inner tendencies and cathexes: wishes, fears, and traces of past experiences."[13] Morgan and Murray also had in mind the fact (or supposition) that imaginative literature reveals something about the author.

Choice of the TAT pictures was governed by theoretical considerations and by experimentation. One thought was that in most of the pictures there should be a person with whom the viewer could identify, and this suggested that there ought to be separate

[13] Morgan and Murray (1938), p. 531. From *Explorations in Personality* by H. A. Murray. Copyright 1938 by Oxford University Press, Inc. Reprinted by permission.

sets for male and female subjects and for people of different ages. The twenty pictures used by Morgan and Murray in their early experiments were drawn from several hundred which had been tried out previously with varying success. Most of the pictures finally chosen contain an "evocative object," i.e., an identification figure. The experimenters were well satisfied with the readiness of subjects to superimpose their own experiences and tendencies on these figures:

> That every subject almost immediately projects his own circumstances, experiences or preoccupations into the evocative object was only too obvious. For instance, in one of the early experiments six of the eleven college men who took the test said that the youth in one picture was a student; whereas none of the twelve non-college men who acted as subjects described him as such. To take another case, one of our subjects, whose father had been a ship's carpenter, wanted to go to sea himself, to travel and see the world. This was his dominant fantasy. In his stories three of the scenes were laid on board ship, two in the Orient.[14]

Interesting as it is that subjects project their remembered experiences and conscious aims into the pictures, it is much more so if, as Morgan and Murray believe, they also expose patterns and trends of which they are unaware. The method recommended for discovering such unconscious material is to examine the stories for persistent dramatic configurations. Morgan and Murray put it succinctly thus:

> The following mode of analysis and summary was used: each of the subject's stories was read and diagnosed separately and then the attempt was made to find a unifying thema. If such was evident, each story, if necessary, was re-interpreted and with some elimination and curtailment the series was re-arranged in such a way as to emphasize the important trends, and demonstrate their inter-relations.[15]

Morgan and Murray illustrate their method vividly with the case of a young Russian immigrant to this country who had experienced much danger and suffering at the time of the First World War when he and his mother lived through various trials, including the horrors of bloody religious persecution. His mother risked her life to smuggle in food for her child and her friends, and probably the most pressing fear which the boy had to endure in childhood was that he and his mother might be forever separated. His father

[14] *Ibid.*, p. 533. [15] *Ibid.*, p. 534.

had emigrated to the United States when the boy was only six months old, and not until the boy was eleven did he send for him and his mother to join him. Arrival in this country exposed him to more trouble. The father proved to be extremely unpleasant; he was often drunk, and quarrels between him and the mother were frequent. The boy sided with his mother in these combats. At the time of the TAT the young man, then in his twenties, was working toward a Ph.D. in science, had recently had a disturbed love affair, and was anxious about his mother's health. Against this background he produced TAT stories which were woven together around some basic tensions. For example, his stories in reaction to five of the pictures may easily be subsumed under the one head of "tragic love," an important variant of which was the son-lover thema "interrupted by an accident or stroke of fate which separates the boy from his mother."[16]

To render this thema more concrete, his story about one picture (shown in Figure 23) will be quoted here along with some of the comments by Murray. Virt, the subject's fictitious name, has this to say:

> Mother and boy were living happily. She had no husband. Her son was her only support. Then the boy got into bad company and participated in a gang robbery, playing a minor part. He was found out and sentenced to five years in prison. Picture represents him parting with his mother. Mother is sad, feeling ashamed of him. Boy is very much ashamed. He cares more about the harm he did his mother than about going to prison. He gets out for good behaviour but the mother dies. He repents for what he has done but he finds that his reputation is lost in the city. No one will employ him. He again meets bad companions and in despair he joins them in crime. However, he meets a girl with whom he falls in love. She suggests that he quit the gang. He decides to quit after one more hold-up. He is caught and sent to prison. In the meantime, the girl has met someone else. When he comes out he is quite old and spends the rest of his life repenting in misery.[17]

One is struck by the tone of depression and the sense of guilt present in this story, and when it is taken in conjunction with several others of like tone and guiltiness one is convinced that the story corresponds to something real in Virt. But there is more than emotional tone in the story. There is dramatic action. The gist of the action is that a man by his criminal acts first separates himself from his beloved mother and then from his sweetheart. Twice a single

16 *Ibid.*, p. 544.   17 *Ibid.*, pp. 537-39.

23 *This picture from Murray's TAT series is sometimes interpreted as showing a distressed mother and a guilty son. (From Murray et al., 1938)*

pattern occurs in one brief story. This pattern seems to point to rebellious and hostile motives in the storyteller. But the reaction to the action, too, is important. The hero suffers guilt and is punished for his actions. So much it is easy to extract from Virt's story. Is the application to Virt himself justified? Morgan and Murray comment:

> The conflict of the hero with the mother brings to mind some incidents mentioned by the subject when giving his childhood memories. He said that he had occasionally quarreled with his mother because she nagged him. Once when he was thirteen he ran away and got a job in Pittsburgh. Another time he ran away to Newport News on account of a romantic longing he had for adventure. In regard to the repentance theme in the last story the subject said in his introspections: "That's the way I would feel. If I took my car and stayed out all night I would be ashamed for having hurt my mother, not for anything I might have done. We are really close to each other. She confides everything to me. She doesn't get on well with my father." The subject's conscience is a personal one. It prohibits him from hurting the woman he loves. He is not guided by an impersonal ethical standard.[18]

Such is the kind of evidence on which Morgan and Murray base their confidence in the method. It is intuitive evidence. A reasonably

[18] *Ibid.,* p. 539.

sensitive human being can see, on comparing Virt's TAT stories with his life, that there is a correspondence, a harmonious fit. That is not to say that the details of the stories are exactly repeated in the life of the storyteller. Virt is not revealing that he has actually committed crimes for which he has been sent to prison. He is obviously not an aged man in the last stages of repentance over an ill-spent life. But the feeling of a sort of criminality in connection with his relationship to women—a mother, a sweetheart—is significant. The mother-son tension is certainly real for Virt. It is one of the axes around which his psychology revolves. To understand Virt in his day-to-day living, his attitudes toward people and situations, his moods, and so on, it is illuminating to be aware of the tragic love thema with its hard core of tension between mother and son.

Was Virt aware of this thema? In a way doubtless he was. He was aware of the quarrels with his mother and his fears about her health. In another way perhaps he was not. The central nature of the tension may have escaped him. In fact, the experimenters themselves are not quite sure how to interpret it. One possibility is that the long years of fear about the mother's safety, going far back into childhood, are expressed in the thema. Another is that the Oedipus complex is the cause: exclusive possession of the mother (or any other woman) for himself may be seen by Virt as wrong, leading to a tendency to produce stories in which the possessive craving is frustrated. In this context, the particular childhood through which he passed would be merely incidental. Other young men similarly attached to their mothers but without the traumatic experiences of Virt's early life might be expected to produce such TAT stories when the tension of the Oedipus complex had reached the point of the adolescent rebellion which is so extremely common in our society. In fact, Stein reports that according to his clinical experience:

> The elderly woman and the young man in this picture are usually seen as mother and son. The son may be seen as asking his mother's permission to do something that he had planned for a long time. He may want to leave home to undertake a job in another city, to get married, or to enlist in the armed forces. His desires usually conflict with his mother's.[19]

From this statement it appears that Virt's story is the common one, though with a peculiarly strong depressive twist.

[19] Stein (1955), p. 10.

One might argue negatively that such a story is built into the picture and almost unavoidable. A subject for whom the theme of mother-son conflict was minor or absent might produce a story of the standard pattern, it could be urged, not because of his own needs but because of the picture itself. It is certainly true that the stimulus picture does set some limits: only an insensitive viewer or a very defensive one would fail to remark some kind of painful emotion in the posture and facial lines of the young man. Even so, many different stories *can* be made up—apparently because of the different psychology of each storyteller. Take the following, reported by Stein:

> This is a picture about a son who's just told his mother—oh, let's have him enlist in the Air Force—he's going to enlist in the Air Force. She's very sad about this because she feels that it's too dangerous. But he goes ahead, downs 10 German planes, gets his decorations, and comes home safe and sound.[20]

The bouncy optimism of this story contrasts markedly with Virt's melancholy production. However, it accords well with other TAT stories by this same subject—a successful professional man who had come up through college from a fa:m by dint of intelligence and hard work. No trace of guilt or fear or despair is in the story, nor in the storyteller himself as far as one can judge.

Is it possible to go beyond intuitive appraisal of the TAT and validate it predictively? An article by Gardner Lindzey is both pessimistic and optimistic on this point. If we look at the history of the TAT, he says, we find that the thousands of studies which it has inspired have not resulted in "a high degree of empirical control over this instrument,"[21] and he states the opinion that no advance has been made over Murray's 1943 manual as an introduction to its use. One might draw the pessimistic conclusion that the instrument has little solid value. Lindzey, however, maintains that the fault is not with the instrument but with the users of it, and that it can be as predictively powerful as any other. He illustrates with an empirical study of diagnostic signs of homosexuality. His procedure was to have stories collected from 20 homosexual and 20 heterosexual college men and examined for the presence or absence of 20 indices of homosexuality presumed to be obtainable from TAT records. Sixteen out of the 20 proposed indices did in fact dif-

[20] *Ibid.,* pp. 91 f.   [21] Lindzey (1958), p. 173.

ferentiate between the homosexual and heterosexual subjects in the expected direction, and for 9 of the indices the differentiation was statistically significant at the 5% level or better.[22] It is evident from this experiment that the possibility exists of establishing routine "objective" diagnoses by means of the TAT which might not be in the least inferior to those achieved by the so-called objective tests. But Lindzey calls attention to the fact that the use of these diagnostic signs for the differentiation of homosexual and heterosexual in this experiment is apparently less efficient than the less mechanical procedure of reading the records intuitively. He himself read through the 40 records (which had been collected by others) and separated the homosexual from the heterosexual with 95% accuracy, making only one reversal! "The unhampered clinician functions better than any one of the objective indices and indeed he functions better than any reasonable combination of these indices."[23] Furthermore, he calls into question the value of this sort of diagnostic enterprise in general by pointing out that homosexuals bent on disguising their homosexuality might have succeeded with the TAT (as they certainly might with the M-F test, too), and that asking would be just as effective and a lot simpler.

Predictive power, since it is the kind of thing which can be assessed rather simply by actuarial methods, has often been made the criterion of test usefulness. Lindzey is striking at the roots of this criterion by his remarks. He is furthermore raising once again the issue which Meehl tried to settle in his 1954 discussion of clinical and statistical prediction, where he argued on the basis of empirical evidence as well as on theoretical grounds that objective tests and statistical manipulations were superior to the clinical approach.[24]

Some experimental work has been done with the TAT not aimed at diagnostic evaluation but at the theoretical question as to how the mind works. Such a study is that of Gordon in which a series of TAT stories were compared with a series of dreams from the same persons in order to determine their degree of similarity and thus to answer the question whether the two kinds of imaginative material represented the same psychic layer. I will briefly summarize here.

Gordon's 29 adult psychiatric (nonpsychotic) patients produced 327 dreams and 580 TAT stories. Both dreams and stories were

[22] See Lindzey, Tejessy, and Zamansky (1958) for details.
[23] Lindzey (1958), p. 175. [24] Meehl (1954).

analyzed according to the rules set up by Aron for scoring TAT records in terms of Murray's need-press theory.[25] Forty-two correlations were worked out between the dreams and the stories with respect to the variables employed, such as need for aggression, dependence, sex, etc. All but 10 of these correlations were positive; the total range was from −.20 to .57, and 11 of them were high enough to exceed the 5% level of confidence. Twenty-nine *intraindividual* correlations were also worked out; of these, 18 were above the 5% level. The general conclusions are that the two kinds of material have some kinship but that they do not closely coincide.

Gordon notes certain characteristic differences between the TAT stories and the dreams. He writes:

> Subjects' dreams, as compared with their TAT stories, usually expressed with greater frequency and intensity socially unacceptable material, aggression, tension, and fear, as well as less depression and self-blame. They also showed a greater desire for close companionship, and tended to portray the central character of the projection as passive and inadequate. The central character of dreams was more typically the recipient rather than the originator of the action.[26]

To some extent a complementary relationship existed between the stories and the dreams; for instance, a striving for superiority and independence in the TAT stories was countered by the opposite, namely, a desire for dependence, in the dreams. In the TAT stories there was more concern with keeping up appearances than in the dreams:

> It appears that in his TAT stories the subject attempts, consciously or unconsciously, to keep the central character of his projections from expressing any material that is clearly inconsistent with his concept of self, or that violates cultural sanctions. In the dream, where there is presumably less concern with defending this idealized role and less intellectual control, freer expression is given to the customarily suppressed material. In order to maintain his idealized self-concept, the subject in his TAT stories tends to meet aggression with aggression of his own. In his dreams the subject seems to manifest less initiative and confidence and is overwhelmed by situations that he may have coped with in his TAT stories. It would appear that in dreams the subject is less concerned with maintaining his idealized self-concept of adequacy and maturity and more concerned with escaping threat to his safety.[27]

25 For details of this theory, see Murray *et al.* (1938).
26 Gordon (1953), p. 252.   27 *Ibid.*, p. 253.

Thus Gordon's study teaches us once again that waking consciousness and sleeping consciousness operate at different levels of experience, though without effecting an outright break in our lives.

The analysis of literature

If the little stories made up in response to TAT pictures have some value in personality assessment, why should this not be true of the great stories which constitute imaginative literature—novels, dramas, poems? It is a natural conclusion from general Freudian theory that such material should reveal the personality of the author, in much the same way as dreams are supposed to do. Freud himself followed this line of thought in a number of studies—a note on *Hamlet* in his book on dreams, an extended essay on a novel by the German writer Wilhelm Jensen, a shorter essay on Dostoevsky —and in scattered passages elsewhere. Many other psychoanalytic studies of literature have followed Freud's example. The best known of these is the study of *Hamlet* by Ernest Jones.

Various objections to this way of looking at literature have been raised. One objection is that imaginative literature belongs to an entirely different class from dreams, being a consciously undertaken work always under the control of the author and often composed by borrowing plot, character, and other details from books written by other authors, so that (according to the argument) the published piece of fiction may have no closer relation to the personality of the man who signs his name to it, one might say, than a public library has to the personality of the librarian. Clearly this is not the viewpoint of Freud or of those who take imaginative literature as he does. Another objection applies to the manner in which the psychoanalysts have gone about the analysis of such material. They have very frequently treated the piece of literature as if it were a dream in the most literal sense and have accordingly subjected it to the kind of analysis which Freud recommends for dreams; and this means that they have (1) approached the literary work as a puzzle that had to be explained in terms of the Unconscious, (2) thought it necessary to set it in the context of free-associations—a difficult thing to do in the absence of the author himself, and (3) resorted all too freely to the most extravagant symbolic interpretations.

In order to show what can be done without adopting the traditional psychoanalytic method, while still regarding the literary work as an expression of the author's personality in somewhat the same way as a dream, I will here review some of my own studies. The principal aim of these studies was to develop a sharable scientific method for exploring human personality through the medium of literature—obviously not for the sake of clinical diagnosis or prediction, since the authors I selected were beyond the reach of clinics, but simply in the hope of coming to a deeper appreciation of the nature of personality in particular individuals and in general. In short, the aim was not practical but purely theoretical. Since no one else to my knowledge has thought it worthwhile to adopt my methods or to utilize my results, I conclude that I have not succeeded in making an acceptable scientific contribution. This unsuccessful work may, however, be all the more useful to the student because it is unsuccessful, illustrating as it does how little the progress of science depends on either the inherent interest of the thing observed or the methods adopted for observing it; for I would certainly contend that imaginative literature is inherently of great interest, even from a strictly psychological point of view, and that the methods I have adopted or suggested are clear and sharable. I leave it to the student to decide why nothing has come of this work, one of those minor fossils in the long history of science which is so full of fossils both minor and major, and pass on to describe what I have done.

I began with the thirteen major fictional works of D. H. Lawrence, which he wrote between the ages of 20 and 44. I arranged these in chronological order of writing and analyzed them in terms of the dramatic characters and their interrelationships. Behind this procedure were two theoretical reflections: (1) Personality appears to be something which changes in the course of time, and the time dimension should be considered in studying material which supposedly is a projection of the personality of the author. (2) Much personality theory points to a conception of the personality as a true or quasi-social system, made up of persons in interrelation; and so it should be extremely relevant to study the persons and the relations between them described in a fictional work which is, by hypothesis, a projection of the author's personality.

In Lawrence's novels it turns out that the main characters easily fall into three categories, and it is tempting to regard these categories as representing some substantial components of the Lawrence personality. In the first place, there is always a character (sometimes there may be two within the same novel) whom we might call the ego or center of consciousness, because all the other characters and their actions are, as it were, seen through this character's eyes. This type of character is more than pure consciousness; he has bodily characteristics, too, is usually but not always male, and must be conceived of as a whole person rather than just the function of consciousness; but he is particularly distinguished by consciousness, subjectivity. In the second place, there is usually a "dark" character, marked by physical darkness, by devotion to primitive values and their closeness to the earth and animals, and by their impulsiveness and strong sexuality. In the third place, there are "light" characters opposed to the "dark" ones; these are blond, intellectual, civilized to the point of mechanization in some cases, governed by conscious aims and idealistic values, and sexually deficient. The dramatic relations between these three types of characters change in the course of time. One of the notable changes is that the balance of power shifts from the light characters to the dark, and closely related to this is the fact that the ego characters side with or become identical with the dark characters. The accompanying table-diagram (Table 39) indicates the main lines of succession through the whole series of novels and the shift of power.

If we examine the novels for the relative success of the two antagonistic types in their love affairs with women, we find that in the first novel the victory goes to the light side, if to any; in the third novel the contest is not entirely in favor of the light character; and thereafter, in all the novels where the issue is clearly drawn, the victorious male belongs in the dark category, at first different from the ego character (who is sometimes female), later often the same as the ego character. These changes within the novels appear to correspond to changes in Lawrence which any biographer would detect in outward behavior, quite apart from the novels. But the changes, please note, are not changes in mere abstract principles; for the principles are *carried by persons*, both inside and outside the novels. The historical source of the dark characters seems to have been especially Lawrence's father, an emotional, passionate, uneducated coal miner. The prototype of the light characters may have been Lawrence's brother, William, the shining but defeated hope of his mother. The novels, then, among other things, reflect a family drama, involving mother, father, brother, and sister, in which there are continuing developments as far as Lawrence himself is concerned, although brother, mother, and father are all dead before the fictional dealing with them is completed. One of the clear trends

Table 39
Shift of power from light to dark males in Lawrence's novels: main sexual triangles

novel	author's age	sexual triangles		
		"dark" male	woman	"light" male*
THE WHITE PEACOCK	20-24	George	Lettie	Leslie
		Annable	Lady Christabel	poet?
THE TRESPASSER	25			
SONS AND LOVERS	25-27	Morel	Mrs. Morel	William Paul
		Dawes	Clara	Paul
THE RAINBOW	28-31	Birkin	Ursula	Skrebensky
WOMEN IN LOVE		Loerke	Gudrun	Gerald
THE LOST GIRL	28-35	Ciccio	Alvina	Dr. Mitchell et al.
AARON'S ROD	36			
KANGAROO	37			
THE PLUMED SERPENT	38-40	Cipriano	Kate	Ramon (Joachim)
ST. MAWR	39	St. Mawr**	Lou	Carrington
THE VIRGIN AND THE GYPSY	40-41	Gypsy	Yvette	Eastwood
LADY CHATTERLEY'S LOVER	41-42	Mellors	Connie	Chatterley
THE MAN WHO DIED	42-44	Jesus	Priestess	Anthony

Adapted from McCurdy (1940b), p. 199.
* Except Paul.
** St. Mawr is a horse, but Lou's devotion to him and her desertion of her husband on his account justify his inclusion here.
NOTE: The *unbroken* line indicates success. The *broken* line indicates failure. Three novels are shown by title only, because there is no important male-female-male triangle in them.

is this: Lawrence was at first bitterly opposed to his father, but later he began to see his merits and turned against his mother and her ideals. In the terminology of Freud, these important characters are introjected components of Lawrence's personality with dynamic properties of their own in relation to Lawrence's ego.

I followed up the study of Lawrence with a study of Charlotte and Emily Brontë. I was attracted to this task because I thought it would be interesting to compare two individuals who had grown up in the same family and been exposed to some of the same influences. Furthermore, I thought it might be possible to improve on the Lawrence study in two respects, by being somewhat less impressionistic in the classification of the fictional characters and by developing specific hypotheses about the two authors from the literary analysis alone which might be checked against the biographical data. (1) In the service of the first aim, I objectified my estimate of the relative importance of the fictional characters by counting the number of pages on which each was present and ranked them from highest to lowest in this regard, and I objectified my description of the principal characters (as thus determined) by ticking off their traits from a long list of trait names borrowed from Cattell. Having done this, I could ascertain the amounts of trait overlap between characters and arrive at a quantitative statement of the degree of likeness between them. This operation might be regarded as a kind of free-hand factor analysis, with the peculiar merit that the factors thus derived definitely lie within the personality sphere of an individual, namely the author; that is, it is an *intra-individual* factor analysis (of components within the author) rather than the customary *inter-individual* type. Table 40 gives the amount of trait overlap in percentages for the leading characters of the four novels of Charlotte Brontë and the one novel of Emily. One sees, for example, that William Crimsworth of *The Professor* and Jane Eyre of *Jane Eyre,* in spite of the fact that one is male and the other female, have a high degree of resemblance, with a 70 per cent trait overlap. On the other hand, William Crimsworth overlaps only 5 per cent with Hunsden in *The Professor,* and the overlap between Hunsden and Jane Eyre is 15 per cent, not much greater. But Hunsden has his own kindred. For example, his trait overlap with Rochester of *Jane Eyre* is 45 per cent. These two characters form a cluster opposed to the cluster of William and Jane. By going through the table of trait overlap one comes to the conclusion that here, too, as in the novels of Lawrence, there are three major types of characters in Charlotte Brontë's four novels, and that these are linked with the characters in Emily's *Wuthering Heights.* Figure 24 is a pictorial representation of the facts in Table 40. This figure merely

Table 40
The relatedness of various important characters in five Brontë novels in terms of trait overlap

Column groups: **THE PROFESSOR** (William, Frances, Hunsden, Zoraïde, Pelet, Edward); **JANE EYRE** (Jane, Rochester, St. John, Mrs. Fairfax, Adèle, Diana); **SHIRLEY** (Caroline, Shirley, Robert, Helstone, Mrs. Pryor, Louis); **VILLETTE** (Lucy, Dr. John, Mme Beck, Paul, Paulina, Mrs. Bretton); **WUTHERING HEIGHTS** (Heathcliff, Edgar, Cathy E., Catherine L.)

	number of traits	William	Frances	Hunsden	Zoraïde	Pelet	Edward	Jane	Rochester	St. John	Mrs. Fairfax	Adèle	Diana	Caroline	Shirley	Robert	Helstone	Mrs. Pryor	Louis	Lucy	Dr. John	Mme Beck	Paul	Paulina	Mrs. Bretton	Heathcliff	Edgar	Cathy E.	Catherine L.
THE PROFESSOR																													
William	(41)	..	50	05	30	15	10	70	15	45	30	00	15	55	25	45	30	30	55	60	25	30	30	30	40	15	30	10	20
Frances	(52)	50	..	20	25	10	10	70	30	45	30	15	40	55	50	40	35	35	50	55	40	30	50	55	40	25	40	25	50
Hunsden	(50)	05	20	..	20	25	30	15	45	25	00	25	10	10	35	30	45	10	20	15	40	20	45	35	20	40	05	45	35
Zoraïde	(44)	30	25	20	..	50	30	35	25	30	25	10	05	20	30	55	30	15	40	25	35	75	25	25	45	25	20	20	20
Pelet	(33)	15	10	25	50	..	40	15	30	15	10	15	20	15	25	40	30	10	15	15	30	45	30	20	25	25	15	25	20
Edward	(45)	10	10	30	30	40	..	10	35	25	05	05	10	10	20	45	50	05	15	05	30	30	35	20	25	50	00	30	20
JANE EYRE																													
Jane	(48)	70	70	15	35	15	10	..	25	50	35	05	30	55	30	40	30	35	60	65	35	30	35	35	40	20	40	15	35
Rochester	(62)	15	30	45	25	30	35	25	..	45	10	15	20	20	45	40	55	10	30	20	40	35	55	40	40	55	15	55	50
St. John	(74)	45	45	25	30	15	25	50	45	..	20	10	15	40	35	55	50	25	50	50	50	45	40	45	50	25	35	40	
Mrs. Fairfax	(35)	30	30	00	25	10	05	35	10	20	..	10	30	40	20	15	15	45	40	30	20	25	20	45	05	50	00	20	
Adèle	(32)	00	15	25	10	15	05	05	15	10	10	..	15	15	35	05	10	05	10	05	15	25	40	10	10	20	35	40	
Diana	(21)	15	40	10	05	20	10	30	20	15	30	15	..	25	40	15	20	20	15	30	20	30	35	30	10	45	15	40	
SHIRLEY																													
Caroline	(58)	55	55	10	20	15	10	55	20	40	40	15	25	..	30	20	20	60	40	65	25	15	25	35	25	15	45	15	25
Shirley	(78)	25	50	35	30	25	20	30	45	35	20	35	40	30	..	35	40	25	35	25	55	45	65	60	40	30	35	45	70
Robert	(62)	45	40	30	55	40	45	40	40	55	15	05	15	20	35	..	55	20	30	50	55	45	40	30	50	45	25	25	30
Helstone	(67)	30	35	45	30	30	50	30	55	50	15	10	15	20	40	55	..	15	35	25	45	40	60	25	50	55	15	35	35
Mrs. Pryor	(51)	30	35	10	15	10	05	35	10	25	45	05	20	60	25	20	15	..	40	50	20	15	30	20	15	45	10	20	
Louis	(52)	55	50	20	40	15	15	60	30	50	40	10	20	40	35	50	35	40	..	50	40	45	45	40	50	30	40	20	35
VILLETTE																													
Lucy	(71)	60	55	15	25	15	05	65	20	50	30	05	15	65	25	30	25	50	50	..	25	30	35	30	25	35	10	30	
Dr. John	(70)	25	40	40	35	30	30	35	40	50	20	15	30	25	25	35	45	20	40	25	..	40	55	60	40	25	30	35	
Mme Beck	(69)	30	30	20	75	45	30	30	35	45	25	15	20	15	45	65	40	15	45	25	55	..	40	30	55	30	25	30	35
Paul	(95)	30	50	45	25	30	35	35	55	45	40	35	35	25	55	45	60	55	50	30	55	40	..	60	45	45	30	55	60
Paulina	(68)	30	55	35	25	20	20	35	40	40	25	40	35	35	60	30	25	30	60	35	60	30	60	..	30	35	50	50	65
Mrs. Bretton	(51)	40	40	20	45	25	25	40	40	45	40	10	30	25	40	50	50	20	50	30	45	55	45	30	..	25	40	25	40
WUTHERING HEIGHTS																													
Heathcliff	(87)	15	25	40	25	25	50	20	55	50	05	10	10	15	30	45	55	15	30	25	35	30	45	35	25	..	05	55	30
Edgar	(44)	30	40	05	20	15	00	40	15	25	00	35	15	15	45	25	35	10	20	10	45	30	55	50	25	05	..	10	35
Cathy E.	(63)	10	25	45	20	25	30	15	55	35	00	35	15	15	45	25	35	10	20	10	45	30	55	50	25	55	10	..	55
Catherine L.	(67)	20	50	35	20	20	20	35	50	40	20	40	40	25	70	30	35	20	35	30	50	35	60	65	40	30	35	55	..

Adapted from McCurdy (1947), p. 114.

NOTE: The figures are rounded percentages, derived by dividing one half of the total number of traits possessed by a pair of characters into the number of traits which the pair have in common.

shows the kinship ties of the characters. (2) The second aim mentioned above was to check against the biographical data any hypotheses which might emerge from the analysis of the novels, an analysis which included a search for themes, in the Murray fashion. I was not completely ignorant of Brontë biography at the outset of my study, but I kept this knowledge at its original minimum until after analysis of the novels (which included more than the study of trait overlap, of course) had led to the following hypotheses: (a) Charlotte and Emily furnished a considerable, perhaps a major, influence on the development of each other's personalities; (b) Emily was more like her father or a father-substitute than was Charlotte, and Charlotte more like her mother or a mother-substitute; (c) in their love choices Emily tended more toward a brother or brother-substitute, and Charlotte toward her father or father-substitute; (d) both were exposed to violent emotions emanating from some male, but Emily felt more equal to the demands made on her courage than did Charlotte; (e) Charlotte was more involved than Emily in the Oedipus situation. These hypotheses were satisfactorily confirmed by the biographical data, though some fine points in them (not given here) could not be checked because of the absence of data. Some other inferences made during analysis were also confirmed.

After these results I felt justified in extending the method to an author about whom I could not expect to learn much from biographical sources. In taking up the plays of Shakespeare, I was assuming, rather than trying to test the hypothesis, that an author's fictional productions reflect his personality and the circumstances of his life.[28] What I wished to do was simply to discover what results would issue from an analysis of a richer, more extended series of fictional works than I had dealt with before. Nevertheless, in this case, too, some contact could be established between the literary material and the biographical facts.

Thirty-two Shakespeare plays were chosen for analysis—plays considered by most authorities to be entirely or mostly Shakespeare's work. These were arranged in the probable chronological order, and a count was made of the number of lines spoken by each character. The purpose of this procedure was to provide a quantitative estimate of the dramatic weight of the different characters. I realized that the rank order thus obtained might not correspond in every instance with the estimate based on intuitive impressions; but, on the whole, the quantitative procedure did not seem to violate my own intuitive estimates very seriously. Take the quantitative character weights of the twelve highest ranking characters in *Othello*.

[28] Calvin Hall's review of my book, misunderstanding its aim, quite properly states that Shakespeare is not a suitable author for *testing* the basic hypothesis. See Hall (1954).

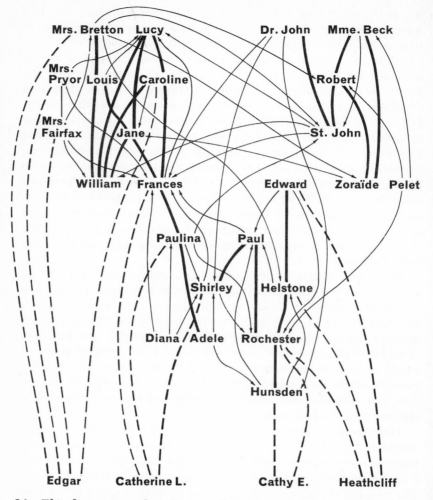

Mrs. Bretton   Lucy   Dr. John   Mme. Beck

Mrs. Pryor Louis   Caroline   Robert

Mrs. Fairfax   Jane   St. John

William / Frances   Edward   Zoraïde Pelet

Paulina   Paul

Shirley   Helstone

Diana / Adele   Rochester

Hunsden

Edgar   Catherine L.   Cathy E.   Heathcliff

24 *This diagram translates into graphic form the data of Table 40. The dark lines (broken and unbroken) show maximum trait-overlap in both directions between characters in different Brontë novels; the light arrow-pointed lines show maximum overlap in one direction. Judging from the degree of trait-overlap, one would say that the characters of Charlotte's four novels fall into three distinct clusters. (After McCurdy, 1947)*

Iago stands in first place, with a count of 1061 lines. Let us assign to him the arbitrary weight of 100, and then state the position of the other characters by figuring their line-counts as a percentage of his. The rank order in *Othello* and the corresponding character weights are then: Iago 100, Othello 80, Desdemona 36, Emilia 24, Cassio 23, Brabantio 13, Roderigo 9, Ludovico 7, Duke of Venice 6, Montano 5, Bianca 3, Clown 2. The same treatment was accorded all thirty-two plays.

One interesting outcome of this method of assigning character weights is that one discovers an underlying mathematical harmony in the ordering of the characters. If the thirty-two Shakespeare plays are taken together and the character weights averaged (i.e., all first-ranking characters being averaged, all second-ranking characters being averaged, etc.), the average weights for first, second, third, etc., characters fall into a series which can be expressed in a simple mathematical formula. In Table 41 the actual average character weights are shown under *Shakespeare;* the figures to the left are derived from the simple exponential formula $T_i = K^i$ where $K = .84$. Except for the interesting gaps at T_1 and T_2, the empirical values are close to the formula values.

What does this result mean? Well, it suggests that the components of a personality tend to fall into a harmonious power relation. We are prepared for this finding by the general personality theory of McDougall, who repeatedly speaks of an orderly hierarchy of power in the collection of sentiments or monads (living units) making up the personality system. It is pertinent that a very similar order is found in other authors. Figure 25 displays in graphic form the results for Shakespeare, Marlowe, Sophocles, and Charlotte Brontë. The figure also shows curves for the comparative frequency of nouns in the writings of Bunyan and Macaulay; and we can bring these

Table 41
Orderliness of character weights in Shakespeare's plays

formula ($T_i = K^i$, where $K = .84$)		Shakespeare (average of 32 plays)	formula ($T_i = K^i$, where $K = .84$)		Shakespeare (average of 32 plays)
T_0	100	100	T_7	30	30
T_1	84	—	T_8	25	25
T_2	71	—	T_9	21	21
T_3	60	63	T_{10}	18	18
T_4	50	52	T_{11}	15	15
T_5	42	40	T_{12}	13	12
T_6	35	35	T_{13}	11	10

Adapted from McCurdy (1953), p. 62.

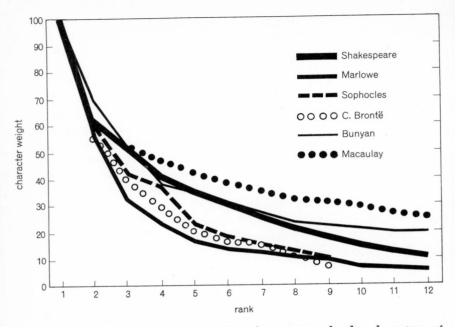

25 *When character-weight is plotted against rank, the characters of Shakespeare's plays fall into a curve generically like many others plotted in the same way. (After McCurdy, 1953)*

curves into relation with the others if we think of the nouns in a piece of discourse as actors, like the characters in a play. Whatever theoretical interpretations suggest themselves, it remains gratifying to find a simple rule of order manifested in the human organism. That the rule is a very general one indeed is clear from a variety of studies made by Zipf, who shows, among other things, that the sizes of cities and towns in a political-economic unit fall into an order resembling that for the Shakespeare characters.[29] The point is that in organic systems (individual or social) the interrelated components have different grades of power, expressible by simple exponential curves like those in Figure 25. Neither in a drama (the projection of a personality) nor in an organic nation are the components (characters, cities) equal; nor do they fall in any kind of order whatsoever, but in a harmonic order.

One out of several lines of analysis followed in my Shakespeare study was to compare the top-ranking characters in the various

[29] See Zipf (1949).

plays. The quantitatively highest character is a man in twenty-seven and a woman in five of the thirty-two plays.

Ignoring exceptions and simplifying to the utmost, with whatever exaggeration that may entail, we may think of the top-ranking Shakespearean characters as one-sixth gentle loyal women and five-sixths proud undependable aggressive men. What can we make of this? If we accept the statement as fact and contemplate it for the moment without wavering from the position that the dramas reflect Shakespeare's personality, and without making any concession to the possibility of there being various angles of reflection, plus refractive distortions, we should conclude that while Shakespeare was usually masculine in his outlook there were times at which feminine elements rose to dominance. Such a conclusion would harmonize with the homosexual trends detected in the *Sonnets* and with the views of biologists and psychoanalysts on the bisexuality of human nature in general. I might add that there is confirming evidence in the work of Charlotte Brontë and D. H. Lawrence. In one of the four novels of Charlotte Brontë the top-ranking character is male; this is William Crimsworth of *The Professor*, the earliest of the four. Back of this fact is a history of several years of definite masculine striving by Charlotte during childhood and adolescence, when in the imaginative play with her brother and sisters she constantly assumed the role of a male hero, especially that of the Duke of Wellington. In the novels of D. H. Lawrence, several times the principal character is a woman, notably Alvina of *The Lost Girl*, and in Lawrence's case there is strong evidence for a corresponding latent homosexuality of more than ordinary amount. A similar inference in regard to Shakespeare would be plausible.[30]

As for the contrast between Shakespeare's leading male and female characters in their personal qualities, it is noticeable enough to have attracted the attention of numerous scholars. We may infer that this dramatic contrast stems from a conflict of impulses in Shakespeare himself:

Like Gloucester in *Richard III*, the male characters are "deformed, unfinished, scarce half made up." The result of their action is generally some disturbance of the peace, some kind of tumult and destruction. It is not out of keeping with this state of affairs that Shakespeare was continually litigating, pertinaciously demanding his rights in the courts even when the monetary sum at issue was small and the debtor supposedly a friend. . . . The nature of the dominant male characters is also easy to reconcile with the traditions about Shakespeare's con-

[30] McCurdy (1953), pp. 89 f. Used by permission of the Yale University Press.

flicts with the local authorities in his youth (whether or not these traditions are true) and with his probable domestic difficulties.[31]

One further word about the top-ranking male characters. Taken chronologically they display certain changes which harmonize with their being produced by a man of increasing years:

> Like the dramatist, the top-ranking male characters are older in the later plays than in the earlier. In the early plays they are young lovers or adventurers; in the later they are fathers and powerful rulers. In the early plays they are fiery and witty; in the later, irascible and severely grave. In the earliest plays they are without a past, so to speak, discovering themselves and plunging precipitously into life; farther along they are in the midst of life, entangled in their past and often longing for the release of death, heavy with grave concerns; and in the very last plays they are almost over the boundary into death, standing remote from life, estranged from it, in a magical illusory world, a visionary baseless fabric ready to fade away into nothingness.[32]

Study of certain patterns of relation between characters was also part of the analytic task. Prominent among the themes investigated were: betrayal, both sexual and political; the Ariel-Caliban contrast; and the mother-son, father-daughter, and father-son relationships. I will briefly illustrate the results by some remarks on the father-child theme. Noticeable attention is given to the father-son relationship in fifteen of the plays. Before *Henry IV* the theme is rather incidentally handled in six plays, in four or five of which some kind of reproach is implicitly or explicitly directed against the sons for failing to live up to the paternal hopes or wishes. The father-son relationship rises to prominence in the first part of *Henry IV*.

> From then on, from the first part of *Henry IV* through *Macbeth* and not even excluding the school-lesson incident in *Merry Wives* (interlude though it is), very serious reproaches and difficult demands are laid upon the sons by the fathers or by reason of their relations with their fathers, and the sons are in general under strong compulsion to justify their existence—to prove to their fathers or on behalf of their fathers that they are worthy of their love and their hopes.[33]

In the last three of the fifteen plays there is again a change: it is the fathers in these plays who are under reproach, and the concern is with the recovery of sons who have been lost. The heightened interest in father-son relations beginning with *Henry IV* is actually quantitatively noticeable, because the line-count weights of fathers

[31] *Ibid.,* pp. 97 f.   [32] *Ibid.,* p. 98.   [33] *Ibid.,* p. 157.

Table 42

Theme: father-son relationship in Shakespeare's plays

date	play	father	son
1592-93	COMEDY OF ERRORS	Aegeon 53*	Antipholus S. 100
			Antipholus E. 78
1593-94	TAMING OF THE SHREW	Vincentio 6	Lucentio 31
1594-95	TWO GENTLEMEN OF VERONA	Antonio 9	Proteus 94
1594-95	ROMEO AND JULIET	Montague 7	Romeo 100
1595-96	RICHARD II	York 38	Aumerle 11
1596-97	JOHN	K. Philip 38	Lewis 29
1597-98	I HENRY IV	King 61	Prince 94
			Lancaster 0
1597-98	2 HENRY IV	King 54	Prince 50
			Lancaster 19
			Clarence 0
			Gloucester 0
1600-01	HAMLET	Polonius 23	Laertes 15
		Ghost 7	Hamlet 100
1600-01	MERRY WIVES OF WINDSOR	Page 37	William 0
1605-06	LEAR	Gloucester 47	Edgar 56
			Edmund 44
1605-06	MACBETH	Duncan 9	Malcolm 30
			Donalbain 0
		Banquo 19	Fleance 0
		Macduff 29	son 0
1609-10	CYMBELINE	Cymbeline 47	Guiderius 26
			Arviragus 21
1610-11	WINTER'S TALE	Leontes 100	Mamillius 0
		Polixenes 41	Florizel 31
1611-12	TEMPEST	Alonso 17	Ferdinand 23

Adapted from McCurdy (1953), p. 148.
* The number beside each name is the character weight; where the number is zero, all that is meant is that the character fell lower in weight than the twelfth character of the particular play.

after this point are distinctly greater than in the preceding period. We find a similar sharp turning-point in the plays dealing with the father-daughter relationship, where the pivot is *Lear*. The weights of fathers of daughters in the first eight of the thirteen plays in which the relationship figures are decidedly less than in the five plays beginning with *Lear*:

> The general conclusion seems to be well justified that in the latter part of Shakespeare's career the father component in his personality, and the accompanying relations, come to a greater prominence. But there

Table 43
Theme: father-daughter relationship in Shakespeare's plays

date	play	father	daughter
1593-94	TAMING OF THE SHREW	Baptista 29*	Katharina 37
1594-95	TWO GENTLEMEN OF VERONA	Duke 52	Silvia 41
1594-95	ROMEO AND JULIET	Capulet 46	Juliet 88
1595-96	MIDSUMMER NIGHT'S DREAM	Egeus 0 (17)	Hermia 62
1596-97	MERCHANT OF VENICE	Shylock 60	Jessica 15
1598-99	MUCH ADO ABOUT NOTHING	Leonato 83	Hero 31
1600-01	HAMLET	Polonius 23	Ophelia 12
1600-01	MERRY WIVES OF WINDSOR	Page 37	Anne 0 (7)
1604-05	OTHELLO	Brabantio 13	Desdemona 36
1605-06	LEAR	Lear 100	Cordelia 15
1608-09	PERICLES	Pericles 100 Simonides 26 (Antiochus	Marina 29 Thaisa 13 Daughter)
1609-10	CYMBELINE	Cymbeline 47	Imogen 100
1610-11	WINTER'S TALE	Leontes 100	Perdita 21
1611-12	TEMPEST	Prospero 100	Miranda 20

Adapted from McCurdy (1953), p. 120.
* The number beside each name is the character weight, where the number is zero, however, all that is meant is that this character fell lower in weight than the twelfth character of the particular play.

are two fairly distinct steps, rather than a gradual change: first, the elevation of the father-son theme to prominence in *Henry IV*, about 1597-98; and second, the elevation of the father-daughter theme in *King Lear*, about 1605-6. The psychological meaning of this alteration would presumably be that certain properties of fatherhood (such as authority and moral severity, for instance) rose to greater importance and affected his behavior or at least mood.[34]

Such relationships as those mentioned above suggest that Shakespeare may have been reacting to definite events in his own life. In spite of the limitations of the biographical material, there is enough to indicate that this is not a mere fancy. For example, the rise to prominence of the father-son theme in *Henry IV* and its supreme place in *Hamlet* do not seem to be accidental, but connected with Shakespeare's relations with his own father. His father,

[34] *Ibid.*, p. 158.

once the chief municipal officer of Stratford, had fallen from economic and social respectability during Shakespeare's adolescence, and he died in 1601. Perhaps he was in declining health in the years preceding his death. At any rate, in *Henry IV* one of the significant facts is the concern of Prince Hal over the illness of his father, the king. Moreover, we know that Shakespeare at the time of that play was pressing hard for a grant of a coat-of-arms to his father, as a compensation (shall we say?) for his father's loss of prestige in Stratford; and that he was joining forces with his father in a legal suit against his cousin, John Lambert, for the recovery of a piece of property lost much earlier through his father's mismanagement and the rapacious greed of relatives. In short, we have evidence that Shakespeare was taking to heart his filial duties at a time when his dramatic works appear to have reached a corresponding critical turn. As for *Hamlet*, the evidence is that it was written either just before or just after the death of Shakespeare's father. It is a mourning piece, and the central issue in it is whether a son should risk everything to carry out a father's wish for vengeance on those who have wronged him. The play thus seems appropriate to Shakespeare's personal circumstances.

I have extracted a few details from my analyses of literature to illustrate the possibilities of such work in personality study.[35] It may be that large comparative studies of this sort would yield some new insights into personality development in general. But, as I have already mentioned, no one has seen fit to push this line of inquiry any further, so far as I know; and this fact may indicate a serious flaw in the method. Allport, in his evaluation of personal documents as a resource for psychology,[36] argues that informal documents like letters and diaries may reveal the writer's personality but that formal literature is too artificial and audience-directed to constitute suitable material. Many literary scholars distrust any psychological approach to literary masterpieces as blundering and dangerous to humanistic values.

Value of projective methods

I have already remarked that the type of personality probe examined in this chapter is not essentially different from the so-called objective test, except in its aim. If we try to compare the two ap-

[35] For full accounts, see McCurdy (1939, 1940a, 1940b, 1944, 1947, 1948, 1949, 1953).
[36] Allport (1942).

proaches in terms of predictive power we discover that the yield from both is low. Vernon was referring to both when he wrote pessimistically of personality testing.[37] Both types were used in an ambitious program of assessment attempted several years ago on clinical psychologists beginning graduate training, and the latest follow-up report makes it painfully clear that neither provided high or even moderately high predictions in regard to a number of important issues.[38] For a prediction-and-control psychology this is bad news. But the question may be honestly raised whether prediction is the only function of tests and other such techniques.

To be able to predict we must have dependable laws. If our tests fail to yield good predictions, it could either be because human beings do not behave lawfully or because we do not understand these laws and have not utilized them in our testing. The assumption behind test prediction seems to be that people will go on behaving in the future as they are behaving at the time of the test. This assumption of constancy does not have much to commend it. People are not necessarily random in their behavior, but they *do* change. The change is often gradual, and logical with a logic of its own; sometimes it is quite abrupt and radical; in either case the constancy hypothesis does not apply.

But tests may have a nonpredictive function. They may be regarded as convenient techniques for arriving at some kind of description of the personality at the moment. The kind of description wanted will dictate the choice of test. We are not quite sure that the so-called projective tests and their kindred (such as analysis of literature) tap a deeper region of personality than do the trait questionnaires, but it seems evident that the region is at least different. Those who still prefer "objective" tests to "projective" tests may argue that we are surer that what we get from them applies to the person taking them, because in an objective test the examiner *asks* him to respond truthfully to certain questions while in a projective test he does not; but at this point we find ourselves in the debate about consciousness and unconsciousness, the ego and S-R behavior, and so on, and that is a debate which we have already had.

References for chapter 12

Allport, G. W. (1942) *The use of personal documents in psychological science.* New York: Social Science Research Council.

[37] Vernon (1953).   [38] Kelly and Goldberg (1959).

Baughman, E. E. (1954) A comparative analysis of Rorschach forms with altered stimulus characteristics. *Journal of Projective Techniques*, 18, 151-64.

Gordon, H. L. (1953) A comparative study of dreams and responses to the Thematic Apperception Test: I. A need-press analysis. *Journal of Personality*, 22, 234-53.

Hall, C. S. (1954) Review of McCurdy's *The Personality of Shakespeare*. *Psychological Bulletin*, 51, 524.

Kelly, E. L., and Goldberg, L. R. (1959) Correlates of later performance and specialization in psychology: a follow-up study of the trainees assessed in the VA selection research project. *Psychological Monographs*, 73, No. 12.

Lindzey, G. (1958) Thematic Apperception Test: the strategy of research. *Journal of Projective Techniques*, 22, 173-80.

———, Tejessy, C., and Zamansky, H. S. (1958) Thematic Apperception Test: an empirical examination of some indices of homosexuality. *Journal of Abnormal and Social Psychology*, 57, 67-75.

McCurdy, H. G. (1939) Literature and personality. *Character and Personality*, 7, 300-08.

——— (1940a) Literature and personality: analysis of the novels of D. H. Lawrence, Part I. *Character and Personality*, 8, 181-203.

——— (1940b) Literature and personality: analysis of the novels of D. H. Lawrence, Part II. *Character and Personality*, 8, 311-22.

——— (1944) La belle dame sans merci. *Character and Personality*, 13, 166-77.

——— (1947) A study of the novels of Charlotte and Emily Brontë as an expression of their personalities. *Journal of Personality*, 16, 109-52.

——— (1948) A mathematical aspect of fictional literature pertinent to McDougall's theory of a hierarchy of sentiments. *Journal of Personality*, 17, 75-82.

——— (1949) Literature as a resource in personality study: theory and methods. *Journal of Aesthetics and Art Criticism*, 8, 42-46.

——— (1953) *The personality of Shakespeare: a venture in psychological method*. New Haven: Yale Univ. Press.

Meehl, P. E. (1954) *Clinical versus statistical prediction: a theoretical analysis and review of the evidence*. Minneapolis: Univ. of Minnesota Press.

Morgan, C. D., and Murray, H. A. (1938) Thematic Apperception Test. In Murray, H. A., *et al.*, *Explorations in personality*. New York: Oxford Univ. Press, pp. 530-45.

Munroe, R. L. (1945) Prediction of the adjustment and academic performance of college students by a modification of the Rorschach method. *Applied Psychology Monographs*, No. 7.

Murray, H. A., *et al.* (1938) *Explorations in personality*. New York: Oxford Univ. Press.

Piotrowski, Z. A. (1957) *Perceptanalysis.* New York: Macmillan.

Rorschach, H. (1951) *Psychodiagnostics.* Tr. by P. Lemkau and B. Kronenberg. 5th ed. Berne: Huber.

Stein, M. I. (1955) *The Thematic Apperception Test.* Reading, Mass.: Addison-Wesley.

Vernon, P. E. (1953) *Personality tests and assessments.* New York: Holt.

Zipf, G. K. (1949) *Human behavior and the principle of least effort.* Cambridge, Mass.: Addison-Wesley.

13

THE INTUITIVE
APPROACH
TO PERSONALITY

Preview   *The natural way to approach other people is to regard them as conscious beings like ourselves trying to express their intentions through their behavior. Such an approach inevitably involves the perceiver with the perceived—a fact recognized by Freud under the heading of transference. Because of this mutual involvement, and for other reasons, the intuitive assessment of personality is often distrusted or at least contrasted with methods of observation like those previously discussed. Does intuition lie outside science? Is it nothing but a crude first approximation to scientific measurement? Can it be cultivated? Should it be cultivated? These are broad strategic questions of the greatest importance for psychology.*

Intuition is often contrasted with inferential reasoning, and science is identified with the latter. Perhaps this is to make the contrast too sharp, but it is evident that our approach to the world in general and human beings in particular may be primarily in terms of our immediate, unreasoned impressions or primarily in terms of abstract principles arrived at by a chain of explicit evidence and logical argument. Paul Meehl has dealt with the contrast as the opposition between "clinical" and "statistical" prediction.[1] After a studious examination of the available data he concludes that statistical prediction making use of objective tests is superior to clinical prediction relying on unformulated impressions. I have already raised the question whether prediction is a sufficient criterion of the usefulness of objective tests themselves, and I raise the question now in a more general form: Is prediction the sole business of science? It seems to me that prediction is nothing but a bonus paid to science for having made many good observations. If this is true, we may benefit by focusing on the nature of observation rather than on the question of prediction. But let us first admit that Meehl, by his use of the term "prediction," was not concerned simply with foretelling the future, but also and perhaps primarily with observational validity, with the fit between observation and fact.

One place where this turn might be given to Meehl's problem is in the passage which discusses a remarkable event described by the psychoanalyst Theodor Reik. After listening to a woman patient ramble on inconsequentially about this and that and remark incidentally that a book was upside down in the bookcase, Reik asked her to tell him about her abortion, and did so apparently with the greatest confidence that he was asking about a fact (as proved to be the case) although nothing the woman had said had come any closer to a confession than the remark about the book upside down. Meehl takes this as an extraordinary case of clinical prediction, and discusses the possibility of devising a table of thought connections which would enable a nonintuitive clerk to come to Reik's conclusion by actuarial procedures. Meehl regards Reik's response to his patient as a matter of an inference obscurely arrived at from vague laws and supposes that it could in principle have been drawn from an actuarial table, though in practice a usable table might be too small to contain anything so rare and strange. He states:

> With Sarbin and Lundberg, I argue that every skilled clinician must be making use of some laws, however vague, which may be of considerable generality, but which nevertheless make it possible for him

[1] Meehl (1954).

to order his material with respect to a given patient in terms of some general nomothetic basic psychodynamics. The problem is, however, to make these highly general laws available to the clerical worker, and to build into her nervous system the appropriate reaction tendencies so that she can use them in the formulation of the individual case, many if not most of whose evidential behaviors will have occurred too rarely to be in any actuarial table.[2]

The reasoning here depends on the validity of the first statement; but one may doubt whether Reik was using laws, however vague, i.e., *formulations* about behavior; he may have been simply *listening* with the "third ear," as he himself would describe it.[3] Laws may in fact impede us in making some observations. If a thing happens, it can be observed—but if you're attending too rigidly to an actuarial table or your little kit of laws, you may fail to observe it. This is not to deny laws or to doubt the usefulness of actuarial tables, but it is to assert that preoccupation with them may interfere with observation—observation which may lead directly into the heart of another person.

In laying stress on observation I am repeating the main theme of the first chapter of this book. We must look, we must listen, we must attend, to have any science at all. After our initial observations have given us a few tentative laws, we must still look, listen, attend. It is foolish to suppose that we caught all the first time. It is also foolish to suppose that there is only one sort of observation. If it were not for the fact that the term "perceiving" implies only certain kinds of direct knowledge, I might prefer to use it in this discussion rather than the term "intuition"; but I need a broader term, and I use this one which is defined in the first dictionary that comes to hand as "direct perception of truths, facts, etc., independently of any reasoning process,"[4] without implying anything more or anything less. If it is necessary to admit clairvoyance or something like that, I will not shrink from doing so; but when I speak of an intuitive approach to personality I do not mean a clairvoyant approach.

The present chapter argues in behalf of intuition and tries to open up the subject a little. It will even say that preoccupation with some of the traditional equipment and methods of psychology may suppress the intuitive mode. But I hope that this will not be misinterpreted to mean that I consider everything else a total loss. My much more modest intention is to point out what everyone knows

[2] *Ibid.*, p. 53.   [3] See Reik (1949).
[4] *The American College Dictionary* (New York: Random House, 1951).

anyhow, namely, that as persons in our nonprofessional roles we continually depend on intuition in our relations with one another, and to ask whether as psychological scientists we are not neglecting our chief resource when we neglect this.

The ordinary uses of intuition

As I sit before the typewriter this morning, looking at words written on a previous day, I notice that my intention to take up my writing task again is expressed in a bodily attitude which another person could certainly observe. I am leaning slightly forward, my hands resting on and gripping my thighs, elbows jutting out, hands pointing inward, and I am conscious of a tightening of muscles from head to toe. I look fixedly at the page before me, or now and again lift my eyes to stare off unseeingly into the distance of the room, as I try to recollect my theme and anticipate its further development. In short, I am reflecting. An observer would not be far wrong if he described my posture as a kind of crouching, like an animal ready to leap on its prey. But my prey is not another animal which I wish to devour, but a thought, something quite immaterial and invisible; and I do not wish to devour it, but capture it and give it a local habitation in words on paper. I doubt whether any observer would come to a different conclusion, given some knowledge of typewriters and some experience of the tension involved in thought. If he described my posture as aggressive, concentrated, eager, I should not disagree with him: such would be my own judgment, and it is strongly supported in my case by being able to know directly the state of mind which gives rise to the public state of my body.

Now if someone catching me at such a moment should congratulate me on my state of calm relaxation, or accuse me of being angry at him, or criticize me for doing nothing, I should think that I had been very badly misunderstood; and if he constantly missed the mark like that, I should say that he was a poor judge of human nature—at least of *my* human nature.

In fact, such gross misunderstanding is probably rare. We can usually do far better. At times we seem to be able to penetrate straight into another person's thought. Perhaps it is not too much to say that the capacity for estimating the emotions and intentions of others is a universal human gift. But emotions and intentions, being essentially invisible, may be denied; and if we deny them, and deny the invisible in general, we put them beyond the reach of our understanding.

An ancient writer, who at the same time seems one of the most modern of men, wrote about our problem in this way:

> Whoever you are who will not believe what you cannot see, consider this: You see bodies with the eyes of the body, you see the thoughts and intentions of your own mind with the mind itself. Tell me, please, with what eyes you see your friend's friendly intention toward you? For no intention can be seen with the eyes of the body. What? do you claim to see in your own mind what is going on in his? But if you cannot see the friendly intention of your friend, how do you manage to reciprocate without believing what you cannot see? Perhaps you will say that you see the intention of another in his behavior. In that case, you may indeed see actions and hear words, but, as concerns the intention itself, you will have to believe it without seeing or hearing it. For an intention is not a color or a shape flung at your eyes, or a sound or melody gliding into your ears; and your friend's intention is not your own, so as to be perceived within your own heart. You must believe what can be neither seen nor heard nor inwardly perceived, if you are to enjoy any friendship at all and be able to repay the affection bestowed upon you.[5]

Augustine tells us that our intuitive relations with one another rest on a continuing act of faith. He goes on to exclaim: "If this faith be taken away from human affairs, the consequence must be great disorder and terrible confusion, surely. For where will there be any mutual affection (since affection itself is invisible), if men are not allowed to believe in what they cannot see?"[6] There cannot be sensitive intuition where there is lack of faith in this sense (belief in invisibles like wishes, emotions, etc.) and without such intuition there cannot be the vital interchange of love. It may even be doubted whether there can be psychological knowledge in the fullest degree.

In order to have an intuitive psychology we must first accept our own subjective processes. Zener, in a recent penetrating analysis of the presuppositions and consequences of behaviorism, has pointed out that this step must be taken if psychology is ever to be a flourishing science.[7] The second prerequisite is the leap of faith which, assuring us that others too think and feel, carries us over to their subjective processes.

[5] Slightly paraphrased from St. Augustine of Hippo, "Concerning faith of things not seen."
[6] *Ibid.*   [7] Zener (1958).

Though the words quoted from Augustine were written about 399 A.D., and in the context of a treatise on religion, they are not out of date or irrelevant here. Heider's recent book, *The Psychology of Interpersonal Relations*, testifies to that. Heider admits that the "mentalistic concepts" he chooses to employ "cannot be measured by a ruler, weighed by a scale, nor examined by a light meter," but argues that they are essential for understanding the relations between persons:

> Social perception in general can best be described as a process between the center of one person and the center of another person, from life space to life space. When *A* observes *B*'s behavior, he "reads" it in terms of psychological entities (and his reactions, being guided by his own sentiments, expectations, and wishes, can again be understood only in terms of psychological concepts). *A*, through psychological processes in himself, perceives psychological processes in *B*.[8]

If Augustine had been publishing in 1958 and had been content to express himself in coolly logical terminology, the result might well have been like Heider's statement:

> One might say psychological processes such as motives, intentions, sentiments, etc., are the core processes which manifest themselves in overt behavior and expression in many variable ways. The manifestations are then directly grasped by *p*, the observer, in terms of these psychological core processes; they would otherwise remain undecipherable. By looking through the mediation, *p* perceives the distal object, the psychological entities that bring consistency and meaning to the behavior; *p*'s reaction is then to this meaning, not to the overt behavior directly, and this reaction is then carried back by the mediation to *o*, etc.[9]

As Heider suggests in this quotation and elaborates fully elsewhere in his book, the central processes, the invisible subjective realities, are mediated and communicated through the body in a great variety of ways. The connection between inner mental state and external bodily manifestation is by no means a simple, rigid, one-to-one affair. Take my previous illustration. It is not necessary for me to be sitting in front of my typewriter, crouched for the spring and with my eyes fixed on the paper, for me to be thinking about what I am to write next. I may in fact be apparently asleep in bed and still be hard at work on my book. It would be an unusual ob-

---

[8] Heider (1958), p. 33. Used by permission of John Wiley & Sons, Inc.
[9] *Ibid.*, p. 34.

server who would be clear about my intentions in a case like that. He would have to be telepathic. Yet we are in general marvelously sensitive to slight expressions, provided we give full play to our natural ability. A gleam in the eye, a quiver of the corner of the mouth, a small change of intonation may communicate volumes. But a great deal depends on the observer: some people notice these things, others do not.

If we are to "read" others as we might a text, we must regard their behavior as the language in which the text is written—as symbols which express the meaning of the text. Only then are we ready to wrestle with the difficulties the text presents. If we fail to see behavior as a language into which a meaning is translated and not as the meaning itself, the text will be unintelligible, or even invisible. Suppose that a man dying of thirst scrawls in pencil on a dirty piece of paper, "I WANT A GLASS OF WATER." We have truly understood him if we bring him water, even if it is in a tin can; indeed, we have understood him if we try or only wish to bring him water when it is impossible to do so. We have not understood him if we pay attention simply to the shape of words and the paper. Suppose that he is so far gone that the words came out, "I WNAT A GLSAS FO WATRE." We can still understand him and prove it by bringing what he needs. It is not the form of a message which is so likely to baffle us as it is the content. When men set their minds to deciphering strange tongues, they are astonishingly successful. But we may hesitate to break the code in our interpersonal dealings for fear the message may unsettle or inconvenience us.

In difficult human encounters things are sometimes complicated by fear and greed and other strong motives, and it may require high courage and benevolence to deal with the humblest needs. In his story "Amy Foster" Joseph Conrad has sketched a scene which makes the point as no words of mine could do. It concerns a shipwrecked foreigner, cast ashore on the coast of England as the lone survivor of a terrible accident on a night of storm. Smith, a householder in the seaside village nearby, unacquainted with the circumstances of the wreck and believing that he is about to confront a vagrant menacing the peace of his home, meets the unhappy castaway among his haystacks the following day. Conrad proceeds:

> Smith is notoriously hot-tempered, but the sight of some nondescript and miry creature sitting cross-legged amongst a lot of loose straw, and swinging itself to and fro like a bear in a cage, made him pause.

Then this tramp stood up silently before him, one mass of mud and filth from head to foot. Smith, alone amongst his stacks with this apparition, in the stormy twilight ringing with the infuriated barking of the dog, felt the dread of an inexplicable strangeness. But when that being, parting with his black hands the long matted locks that hung before his face, as you part the two halves of a curtain, looked out at him with glistening, wild, black-and-white eyes, the weirdness of this silent encounter fairly staggered him. He has admitted since (for the story has been a legitimate subject of conversation about here for years) that he made more than one step backwards. Then a sudden burst of rapid, senseless speech persuaded him at once that he had to do with an escaped lunatic. In fact, that impression never wore off completely. Smith has not in his heart given up his secret conviction of the man's essential insanity to this very day.

As the creature approached him, jabbering in a most discomposing manner, Smith (unaware that he was being addressed as "gracious lord," and adjured in God's name to afford food and shelter) kept on speaking firmly but gently to it, and retreating all the time into the other yard. At last, watching his chance, by a sudden charge he bundled him headlong into the wood-lodge and instantly shot the bolt. Thereupon he wiped his brow, though the day was cold. He had done his duty to the community by shutting up a wandering and probably dangerous maniac. Smith isn't a hard man at all, but he had room in his brain only for that one idea of lunacy. He was not imaginative enough to ask himself whether the man might not be perishing with cold and hunger.*

A reader resolved to misunderstand me or unable to understand me because of a different context of experiences may object to the above illustration that the difficulty was simply that the shipwrecked foreigner did not speak English. This is not the significance of the Conrad parable as I use it. The shipwrecked foreigner of the story is no more cut off from Smith than I am cut off from the English-using reader who does not catch the point of my illustration. Smith fails to understand the poor castaway not only because of the man's language handicap but also because of his own fear and general lack of intuition. Smith is in no condition to meet the vagrant even halfway: he is afraid of him before he meets him and even more afraid when he does, and he cannot read his strange appearance and agitated behavior except in terms of his own readiness to defend himself against this imagined threat to his life. Though it is not often that most of us encounter so dramatic a challenge to our under-

* Used by permission of J. M. Dent & Sons Ltd.

standing as Smith did, we do in fact misunderstand other people very frequently in less conspicuous ways; and it is perhaps because of this steady, day-by-day misunderstanding—this opaqueness in our relations with one another—that so many people (and there are many indeed) carry around a perpetual sense of hurt loneliness.

Defensiveness, receptivity, and Freud

In view of the naturalness of looking and listening, it is something of a shock to learn that Freud made a great advance in psychology by looking at and listening to people. And yet this is what he did, and it was an advance. Above everything, he listened. He listened in order to get the message, in order to understand.

Often we observe others for a defensive or an aggressive purpose. We are all keyed up to action—to sell the prospect, to win at the bridge game, to get out from under the red light faster than the man in the car beside us, to "treat" the patient. The attitude of action puts definite limits on our perceptiveness. We tend to ignore whatever there may be about the other person which is not related to our particular aim. For example, if we are looking around for something to prop up one end of a broken-legged table, we may light on a more or less cooperative human being and use him in place of a stick; and under the circumstances we may fail to note that he loves us or has a divinely beautiful smile. We depersonalize people for the sake of practical aims. We may develop a knack for picking out suitable human tools, or may value instruments like the intelligence tests because we have found that they help us to "fit the man to the job" —low IQ's for one factory, high ones for another. Or, again, a man may cultivate a flair for distinguishing between women who will readily go to bed with him and those who won't and in the service of his strictly sexual aim overlook the other qualities in either category of women. This too is depersonalization. That is to say, it overlooks the full humanity of the other person.

It is Freud's distinction that he did not narrow down his perceptions to any such degree. He tried to understand his patients in their totality. He asked them to let down their defenses, and he in turn did the same, receptively. For Freud asked as much of himself as he asked of his patient. He asked the patient to observe his thoughts and communicate them unrestrainedly (the free-association method), and at the same time he put himself in the same uncritical attitude as a listener. He became, as far as possible, a superconsciousness hovering over and assisting the patient's own consciousness. His task was to submit himself, uncritically, undefensively, purely receptively, to whatever poured out of the patient into his ear.

The art of listening as Freud practiced it may not have been an absolutely new thing in the world, but it was in such contrast with the listening behavior of people in general, not excepting physicians, that every word he says about it is like a revelation.

In *The Interpretation of Dreams* Freud describes the method of listening to oneself which is the foundation of psychoanalysis. I quote at length:

> I have noticed in the course of my psychoanalytical work that the psychological state of a man in an attitude of reflection is entirely different from that of a man who is observing his psychic processes. In reflection there is a greater play of psychic activity than in the most attentive self-observation; this is shown even by the tense attitude and the wrinkled brow of the man in a state of reflection, as opposed to the mimic tranquillity of the man observing himself. In both cases there must be concentrated attention, but the reflective man makes use of his critical faculties, with the result that he rejects some of the thoughts which rise into consciousness after he has become aware of them, and abruptly interrupts others, so that he does not follow the lines of thought which they would otherwise open up for him; while in respect of yet other thoughts he is able to behave in such a manner that they do not become conscious at all—that is to say, they are suppressed before they are perceived. In self-observation, on the other hand, he has but one task—that of suppressing criticism; if he succeeds in doing this, an unlimited number of thoughts enter his consciousness which would otherwise have eluded his grasp. With the aid of the material thus obtained—material which is new to the self-observer—it is possible to achieve the interpretation of pathological ideas, and also that of dream-formations. As will be seen, the point is to induce a psychic state which is in some degree analogous, as regards the distribution of psychic energy (mobile attention), to the state of the mind before falling asleep—and also, of course, to the hypnotic state. On falling asleep the "undesired ideas" emerge, owing to the slackening of a certain arbitrary (and, of course, also critical) action, which is allowed to influence the trend of our ideas; we are accustomed to speak of fatigue as the reason of this slackening; the emerging undesired ideas are changed into visual and auditory images. In the condition which is utilized for the analysis of dreams and pathological ideas, this activity is purposely and deliberately renounced, and the psychic energy thus saved (or some part of it) is employed in attentively tracking the undesired thoughts which now come to the surface

—thoughts which retain their identity as ideas (in which the condition differs from the state of falling asleep). *"Undesired ideas"* *are thus changed into "desired" ones.*

There are many people who do not seem to find it easy to adopt the required attitude toward the apparently "freely rising" ideas, and to renounce the criticism which is otherwise applied to them. The "undesired ideas" habitually evoke the most violent resistance, which seeks to prevent them from coming to the surface. But if we may credit our great poet-philosopher Friedrich Schiller, the essential condition of poetical creation includes a very similar attitude. In a certain passage in his correspondence with Körner (for the tracing of which we are indebted to Otto Rank), Schiller replies in the following words to a friend who complains of his lack of creative power: "The reason for your complaint lies, it seems to me, in the constraint which your intellect imposes upon your imagination. Here I will make an observation, and illustrate it by an allegory. Apparently it is not good—and indeed it hinders the creative work of the mind—if the intellect examines too closely the ideas already pouring in, as it were, at the gates. Regarded in isolation, an idea may be quite insignificant, and venturesome in the extreme, but it may acquire importance from an idea which follows it; perhaps, in a certain collocation with other ideas, which may seem equally absurd, it may be capable of furnishing a very serviceable link. . . . In the case of a creative mind, it seems to me, the intellect has withdrawn its watchers from the gates, and the ideas rush in pell-mell, and only then does it review and inspect the multitude. You worthy critics, or whatever you may call yourselves, are ashamed or afraid of the momentary and passing madness which is found in all real creators, the longer or shorter duration of which distinguishes the thinking artist from the dreamer. Hence your complaints of unfruitfulness, for you reject too soon and discriminate too severely" (letter of December 1, 1788).

And yet, such a withdrawal of the watchers from the gates of the intellect, as Schiller puts it, such a translation into the condition of uncritical self-observation, is by no means difficult.

Most of my patients accomplish it after my first instructions. I myself can do so very completely, if I assist the process by writing down the ideas that flash through my mind.[10]

The preceding words explain what Freud means by "self-observation" and provide all the directions needed. Nothing could seem to be simpler, yet, as Freud's comments and Schiller's imply, such self-observation is anything but common. Perhaps even less common is the seemingly equally simple process of observing others, which is directly modeled on the process of self-observation. Here again the

[10] Freud (1950), pp. 13-15.

chief effort of the observer has to be directed against critical bias. Freud describes the technique in his 1912 paper, "Recommendations to Physicians Practicing Psycho-Analysis." One memorable passage is this:

> The technique, however, is a very simple one. As we shall see, it rejects the use of any special expedient (even that of taking notes). It consists simply in not directing one's notice to anything in particular and in maintaining the same "evenly-suspended attention" (as I have called it) in the face of all one hears. In this way we spare ourselves a strain on our attention which could not in any case be kept up for several hours daily, and we avoid a danger which is inseparable from the exercise of deliberate attention. For as soon as anyone deliberately concentrates his attention to a certain degree, he begins to select from the material before him; one point will be fixed in his mind with particular clearness and some other will be correspondingly disregarded, and in making this selection he will be following his expectations or inclinations. This, however, is precisely what must not be done. In making the selection, if he follows his expectations he is in danger of never finding anything but what he already knows; and if he follows his inclinations he will certainly falsify what he may perceive. It must not be forgotten that the things one hears are for the most part things whose meaning is only recognized later on.
>
> It will be seen that the rule of giving equal notice to everything is the necessary counterpart to the demand made on the patient that he should communicate everything that occurs to him without criticism or selection. If the doctor behaves otherwise, he is throwing away most of the advantage which results from the patient's obeying the "fundamental rule of psycho-analysis." The rule for the doctor may be expressed: "He should withhold all conscious influences from his capacity to attend, and give himself over completely to his 'unconscious memory.'" Or, to put it purely in terms of technique: "He should simply listen, and not bother about whether he is keeping anything in mind."[11]

The simplest things are often the most difficult to believe and practice. I therefore add another quotation from the same paper, to drive home the point that Freudian psychoanalysis is above all the art of open, passive listening:

> It is easy to see upon what aim the different rules I have brought forward converge. They are all intended to create for the doctor a counterpart to the "fundamental rule of psycho-analysis" which is laid down for the patient. Just as the patient must relate everything that his

[11] Freud (1953-), Vol. 12, pp. 111 f.

self-observation can detect, and keep back all the logical and affective objections that seek to induce him to make a selection from among them, so the doctor must put himself in a position to make use of everything he is told for the purposes of interpretation and of recognizing the concealed unconscious material without substituting a censorship of his own for the selection that the patient has forgone. To put it in a formula: he must turn his own unconscious like a receptive organ towards the transmitting unconscious of the patient. He must adjust himself to the patient as a telephone receiver is adjusted to the transmitting microphone. Just as the receiver converts back into sound-waves the electric oscillations in the telephone line which were set up by sound waves, so the doctor's unconscious is able, from the derivatives of the unconscious which are communicated to him, to reconstruct that unconscious, which has determined the patient's free associations.

But if the doctor is to be in a position to use his unconscious in this way as an instrument in the analysis, he must himself fulfil one psy-·chological condition to a high degree. He may not tolerate any resistances in himself which hold back from his consciousness what has been perceived by his unconscious; otherwise he would introduce into the analysis a new species of selection and distortion which would be far more detrimental than that resulting from concentration of conscious attention.[12]

Freud recommends in the above passages (1) a general readiness to perceive and notice, a free-floating unbiased attentiveness, an alertness to the whole being of the other person, and (2) a lack of secret reservations or selfish aims in oneself which might hinder or distort the perceptive activity. It is for the sake of the latter that he prescribes for his followers a training analysis, to help them discover their blind spots. But certainly the path followed to achieving openness and lack of bias is not so important as arriving there, however that is done; for without the inner freedom Freud encourages it is obvious that comprehensive perceptiveness must be impossible.

Freud also recommends in these passages (3) reliance on the unconscious. He tells us that full conscious perception requires that the unconscious of the observer be tuned to the unconscious of the person observed. That is to say, the observer must be set not only for the conscious intentions and moods of the other person and for externals like facial expression, gesture, posture, tone of voice, content of verbal message, etc., but also for those massive, vague, or hidden and unformulated tendencies which are pregnant with the future, potential rather than actual, in the sense that they are not

[12] *Ibid.*, pp. 115 f.

being carried out at the moment in any definite act, even in any definite expressive act, though prepared for expression if the right circumstances happen along. The relationship between conscious and unconscious is something like that between the surface meaning of an ironical statement and its undermeaning. The subsurface meaning is there only for the sensitive listener who is attuned to the mental state of the speaker and who is aware of the environment to which he is reacting. The listener may be aware of it even when the speaker is not, if the listener is keen and the speaker has his reasons for not being aware.

Can intuitive sensitivity be cultivated? According to Freud, yes. It cannot be cultivated by memorizing a set of rules, however. The essence of it is an attitude. One drops all pretense about oneself and others, one ceases to press for personal recognition, and one becomes an innocent eye, an innocent ear, an innocent receptive organ in general. It is the attitude of great naturalists who step out into their backyards (like the French entomologist Fabre) or into the jungle (like the English evolutionist Wallace) prepared for anything—not armed with sophisticated hypotheses out of which they are going to construct imaginary plants and animals, but curious and openminded before whatever may be there in reality, whether ugly or beautiful. We psychologists have typically surrounded ourselves with paraphernalia—brass instruments, electronic recorders, standardized tests, actuarial tables, in short, with scientific equipment—for the observation of others. Freud's practice amounts to the advice that all these things are no better than complicated defense mechanisms.

Transference

We experimental psychologists in our scientific armor, and Freud after he threw away his, have in different ways taken account of the fact that two human beings in contact influence each other. The fact is usually regarded as a nuisance for objective science. If a patient is influenced by the physician's prestige, if an experimental subject reacts to the experimenter, what becomes of science? How can we ever know anything worth knowing about the person we are trying to observe? Much effort has gone into attempts to minimize this source of "error." One of the appeals of the so-called objective test is that it is supposed to be relatively free of the variable of personal interaction. Isolation rooms with one-way screens and heavy soundproofing, plus long-distance recording devices with concealed microphones, enable the experimentalist to treat his human subject as a pure preparation, like a frog's leg separated from its body and trussed up to a kymograph lever. But Freud abandoned the pretense of impersonality along with the equipment, and, instead of being annoyed by the inescapable fact of personal interactions, attended to it and found that it was one of the central variables in therapy. Under the rubric of *transference* he brought a wide range of phenomena having to do with the continuous, reciprocal communication of thought and feeling and impulse between the observer and the observed.

Transference concerns us here because of its bearing on the validity of intuitive observing. We note at once that Freud recognized that the observer could not be immune from the emotional disturbances affecting the person observed, and that he called the observer's emotional reaction "countertransference." Both observing and being observed arouse emotions, and the observed observes and the observer is observed, so that the relationship can become a very lively compound of multiple factors. Freud regarded the transference phenomena as mainly derived from past experience working irrationally in the current situation; but this was not his only conclusion, since emotions affected the current relationship whether or not they originated in the past.

The following remarks, necessarily somewhat complex, are based mainly upon two papers by Freud—"The Dynamics of the Transference" (1912) and "Further Recommendations in the Technique of Psycho-Analysis: Observations on Transference-Love" (1915).

In the earlier of the two papers Freud stresses the condition of the patient before arriving in the psychoanalytic situation. Like every human being, the patient has already acquired a pattern of loving, a stereotype which tends to be repeated in every similar setting. The neurotic patient will probably differ from other human beings in the rigidity of the pattern and in certain distortions of it which interfere with normal satisfactions (otherwise therapy would not have been sought), but neurotic malfunctioning may only throw into sharper relief some of our common human features, revealed by the ebb and flow of passion. According to Freud, when the patient encounters the analyst and the interviews begin,

the cathexis will introduce the doctor into one of the psychical "series" which the patient has already formed. If the "father-imago," to use the apt term introduced by Jung (1911), is the decisive factor in bringing this about, the outcome will tally with the real relations of the subject to his doctor. But the transference is not tied to this particular prototype: it may also come about on the lines of the mother-imago or brother-imago. The peculiarities of the transference to the doctor, thanks to which it exceeds, both in amount and nature, anything that could be justified on sensible or rational grounds, are made intelligible if we bear in mind that this transference has precisely been set up not only by the *conscious* anticipatory ideas but also by those that have been held back or are unconscious.[13]

One consequence of the close observing which goes on in psychoanalysis, then, should be to bring about an apparent change in the patient—a reorientation to the observing physician, by which the physician becomes a focus of already established interests and the patient gains emotional release along old, unconscious channels. The emotions that come to the surface may be both erotic and hostile. In either case, they erupt into the smooth progress of the analysis and even threaten to break it off; that is to say, the patient becomes less inclined to observe himself and report his observations and more inclined to act out the impulses now arising as the repression is lifted. It is the physician's task to keep these reactions within limits and continue to promote self-observation. In Freud's words:

> In the process of seeking out the libido which has escaped from the patient's conscious, we have penetrated into the realm of the unconscious. The reactions which we bring about reveal at the same time some of the characteristics which we have come to know from the study of dreams. The unconscious impulses do not want to be remembered in the way the treatment desires them to be, but endeavour to reproduce themselves in accordance with the timelessness of the unconscious and its capacity for hallucination. Just as happens in dreams, the patient regards the products of the awakening of his unconscious impulses as contemporaneous and real; he seeks to put his passions into action without taking any account of the real situation.[14]

The development Freud is describing is full of dynamite. Sometimes it explodes in violent verbal assault or unmistakable love-making. The quietly observing physician now needs all his *savoir faire*. Even if the patient is meek and restrained, the uncovering of the unconscious impulses is capable of producing as much excitement as was experienced by Conrad's frightened Mr. Smith, "when

[13] *Ibid.*, p. 100.　　　　　　　　　　　　　[14] *Ibid.*, pp. 107 f.

that being, parting with his black hands the long matted locks that hung before his face, as you part the two halves of a curtain, looked out at him with glistening, wild, black-and-white eyes."

The observer in the psychoanalytic situation acts as a kind of superconsciousness hovering attentively over the consciousness of the patient as the patient engages in self-observation. When the patient's consciousness is overwhelmed by impulses rising from the unconscious, released in part by the self-observing attitude he has adopted and in part by the near presence of a fellow human being who may serve as target for these impulses, the superconsciousness of the physician-observer continues to provide what the patient has momentarily lost: the patient's self-observation goes on, as it were, through the medium of the physician. While the patient threatens to become all Id, the physician remains functioning steadily as Ego. With luck, intellectual calm returns to the patient, too.

Now, no matter how desirable it may be for the physician-observer to retain his composure, there are times when it fails him. His own instincts can be aroused in answer to the patient's. This is the countertransference. Freud makes it perfectly clear in the 1915 paper that a hysterical woman's transference-love for her physician may affect him so strongly that he will begin considering whether he should marry her, have an illicit affair with her, or terminate the treatment in sheer self-defense. Freud's advice, of course, is that the harassed physician should do none of these things but proceed by analysis to show the derivative nature of the transference-love and deal with it as a pathological resistance to the treatment. In offering this advice, however, he discusses the physician's predicament sympathetically and admits that the transference-love he has to contend with may be as genuine and honorable as any love:

We have no right to dispute that the state of being in love which makes its appearance in the course of analytic treatment has the character of a "genuine" love. If it seems so lacking in normality, this is sufficiently explained by the fact that being in love in ordinary life, outside analysis, is also more similar to abnormal than to normal mental phenomena. Nevertheless, transference-love is characterized by certain features which ensure it a special position. In the first place, it is provoked by the analytic situation; secondly, it is greatly intensified by the resistance, which dominates the situation; and thirdly, it is lacking to a high degree in a regard for reality, is less sensible, less concerned about consequences and more blind in its valuation of the loved person than we are prepared to admit in the case of normal love. We should not forget, however, that these departures from the norm constitute precisely what is essential about being in love.[15]

Furthermore, this upsurge of love (which Freud defensively calls "abnormal" along with all being in love!) sweeps away the crippling symptoms which brought the patient into analysis. It is not only real, it is curative. And the physician, catching fire in the same blaze, also experiences the pangs of reality. Freud warns the physician against yielding to the patient's demands and his own impulse, but he adds:

> I do not mean to say that it is always easy for the doctor to keep within the limits prescribed by ethics and technique. Those who are still youngish and not yet bound by strong ties may in particular find it a hard task. Sexual love is undoubtedly one of the chief things in life, and the union of mental and bodily satisfaction in the enjoyment of love is one of its culminating peaks. Apart from a few queer fanatics, all the world knows this and conducts its life accordingly; science alone is too delicate to admit it. Again, when a woman sues for love, to reject and refuse is a distressing part for a man to play; and, in spite of neurosis and resistance, there is an incomparable fascination in a woman of high principles who confesses her passion. It is not a patient's crudely sensual desires which constitute the temptation. These are more likely to repel, and it will call for all the doctor's tolerance if he is to regard them as a natural phenomenon. It is rather, perhaps, a woman's subtler and aim-inhibited wishes which bring with them the danger of making a man forget his technique and his medical task for the sake of a fine experience.[16]

Freud makes it plain that some of the emotion in the interview situation of psychoanalysis is a direct result of the observer's activity. The observer keeps the observed aware of being under observation, and the nature of the observation (attention to unconscious impulses) has the effect of altering the observed person's behavior and state of mind. In turn, the observer himself is affected. It is really not possible for a sensitive observer to be the object of passionate love or passionate anger without experiencing some answering reaction in himself. Though by various devices (having the patient lie on a couch with back to the analyst, etc.) a partial insulation of the physician from his patient is achieved, and though the authority of the physician affords some protection, a true interaction takes place such as occurs every day between people who

[15] *Ibid.*, pp. 168 f.   [16] *Ibid.*, pp. 169 f.

allow themselves any freedom in their personal relations. The analytic situation is not an exotic laboratory affair. It brings to intense focus what is present everywhere in human life.

Two aspects of Freud's essays deserve to be thought about hard. There is, for one thing, the fact that a radical personality change may occur suddenly, wiping away the symptoms of a neurosis as if by magic. Secondly, it seems that the nature of the change owes a lot to the nature of the social situation at the time. The first of these observations throws doubt on any doctrine of stable traits, in that it reveals personal qualities as flaming up or dying down, appearing or disappearing, all at once. The second points to the creativity of personal relations.

Reciprocity

Not long ago I was talking to a man who likes to take pictures of flowers in color. He is fonder of flowers than he is of people. I remarked that flowers are very generous—they make no demands on you and hide nothing from you. He agreed eagerly. The trouble with people, in his opinion, is that when you look at them they act very peculiarly: they shrink up or close their faces or turn their backs, become haughty or angry, or do something else unpleasant.

People *are* affected by being looked at, and in some fashion they repay the looker for the way he looks at *them* by the way they look at *him*. The relationship is two-sided. If I assume in advance that the other person is agreeable, the chances are increased that he will be agreeable; and his agreeableness in turn increases my own.[17] This reciprocity prevents me from saying that the world would be all right if only the disagreeable people could be got out of it. Some of the world's disagreeableness is due to one's own assumption about it—not in the sense that one imagines it to be disagreeable though it is not, but in the sense that one's assumption that it or some part of it is disagreeable contributes actively to making it so. Thus, it is possible that Freud's exploration of sexuality vis-à-vis his patients aroused sexual feelings which might not otherwise have appeared, and that even his silent recognition of the importance of sex in human life may have helped to set the stage for this arousal.

Certain it is (to pursue this line of thought further) that many or all sexual affairs depend upon *someone's* initial assumption that there can be a sexual affair. These things do not happen without

[17] See Homans (1950).

preliminaries or accidentally. Intercourse which has not been preceded by some kind of courtship, high or low, long or brief, and involving both partners, is relatively rare. But the courtship may be subtle, almost hidden, and not fully conscious. Even by adopting the clothes fashionable at a given time one may be committed to sexual provocation, although the intention may be more in the mind of the stylist than in that of the wearer. I lay stress on *intention*. Exposure or accentuation of a part of the body is not in itself an invitation; it is the body used as sexual language that counts. There may be more sexual invitation in the way a girl flips her dress as she sits down or in the way she lifts her eyes than in nakedness. If her manner provokes a sexual thought in the male, the thought is in some degree justified; or her manner may itself have been stimulated by a sexual thought already present in the male whom she now appears to solicit; and, in general, we may say that very minute communications from male to female to male prepare the way for deeper involvement. The level of awareness of this process of mutual stimulation may not be very high; and, furthermore, third and fourth parties sometimes enter into it, like Pandarus, the uncle in the story of Troilus and Cressida; so that the culmination may come as a surprise to the lovers, apparently fate-determined. A famous passage of Dante's *Divine Comedy* delicately outlines the process. Francesca with her lover Paolo is encountered among the damned; questioned by Dante about her adultery, she replies reluctantly:

> *A truth in your great teacher's verse is this:*
> *There is no sharper pain than to recall*
> *In time of agony a time of bliss.*
>
> *But, since you wish and I was one to fall*
> *Under the spell of wishes, I now weep*
> *And tell you what you wish, the root of all.*
>
> *Being alone one day where none could creep*
> *Unseen upon us, reading of Lancelot*
> *And Guinevere his Queen, we sank so deep*
>
> *In their delight, our faces would grow hot*
> *If, glancing from the page, our eyes should meet;*
> *And then we came to one more passionate spot.*
>
> *It was where Guinevere, all soft and sweet,*
> *Quenched on her tender lips his lips of fire.*
> *There we were overcome by too much heat*

Ever to part; for, quivering with desire,
My lover kissed me, too. That book, that book!
It traded in flesh, in lust, in love for hire!

We did not pay it, that day, another look.[18]

Here a book, or rather the author of a book, is the mediating third party.

To the degree that I look at another person as tool or customer or enemy or sexual object, etc., to that degree that person becomes for me tool or customer or enemy or sexual object, etc. To be sure, the other person can respond in different ways. Our way of looking at and perceiving the other person defines him for ourselves; but he may break through our definition even though he feels the constraint of it. Sartre, the proponent of one variety of existentialism, laid considerable stress—perhaps too much—on the power of the look. Heider's commentary is this:

> Sartre's theory of the "look" can be interpreted as an emphasis on the power aspect of perception to the exclusion of everything else—though one should be aware of the danger of reading a too concrete psychological meaning into a philosophical discussion. The following quotation is from Schuetz's description of Sartre's ideas: "If another looks at me, a basic change occurs in my way of being. . . . He, by merely looking at me, becomes the limit of my freedom. Formerly, the world was open to my possibilities; now it is he, the other, who defines me and my situation within the world from his point of view, thus transforming my relations to objects into factors of *his* possibilities. . . . My own possibilities are turned into probabilities beyond my control. I am no longer the master of the situation, or at least the situation has gained a dimension which escapes me. I have become a utensil with which and upon which the other may act. I realize this experience not by way of cognition, but by a sentiment of uneasiness or discomfort, which, according to Sartre, is one of the outstanding features of the human condition." Schuetz criticizes this extreme point of view and argues against Sartre's alternatives, "Either the Other looks at me and alienates my liberty, or I assimilate and seize the liberty of the Other." People can perceive each other in the freedom of their actions. If *o* looks at *p*, it is true that *p* becomes an "object" of *o*'s perception; but this does not mean that he necessarily becomes an "object" in the sense that he becomes a thing, an entity at the mercy of outside forces. Though perception can help produce a relationship of mastery and dependence, it does not necessarily do so.[19]

[18] *Inferno*, Canto 5. My translation.
[19] Heider (1958), pp. 71 f.

One reason why a particular look does not necessarily produce mastery is that the other person must in some degree consent or submit: he has his freedom, too. D. H. Lawrence makes the strong statement that if a man is murdered it must be because he has issued an invitation to the murderer by indicating his willingness to be murdered. The power of the look (or, more correctly, the intention behind the look) has to be reinforced by the consent of the one looked at before the little push it gives results in actual motion.

Sartre opens his discussion of "The Existence of Others" in *Being and Nothingness* with the example of shame:

> I have just made an awkward or vulgar gesture. This gesture clings to me; I neither judge it nor blame it. I simply live it. I realize it in the mode of for-itself. But now suddenly I raise my head. Somebody was there and has seen me. Suddenly I realize the vulgarity of my gesture, and I am ashamed.[20]

This is surely a common experience, and very properly Sartre infers from it the importance of the "other"; but it is too much to imply, as he seems to do, that the shame originates in the sole fact of having been made the object of the other's perception. The *nature* of the other's perception matters. An uncouth gesture may become shameful because the other's perception is contemptuous. If the other's perception has a different quality, if it is loving, tender, compassionate, then shame may not be the emotion I have. This is on the assumption that I detect the nature of the other's perception. I may fail to do so, of course. Before a coldly critical audience a pianist may become all fumbling thumbs or become unusually deft before a warmly appreciative one. At the same time, it must be admitted that the audience cannot affect the pianist except to the degree that he is sensitive to it.

Freud stresses perception as sensitivity, as receptivity. Sartre stresses it as power, as limiting power. Neither one has pursued his line of investigation as far as possible. A sensitivity far beyond that practiced by Freud probably lies within human capacity. A power— not the mere limiting power of an "Evil Eye"—may be exercised in the human look: a look may also enhance, elevate, set free. But always there are action and reaction, in a world where every conscious being is both perceiver and perceived, both a source and a receiver of power; each individual finds himself in the midst of a

[20] Sartre (1956), p. 221.

reality which would be there if he were not, but which, once he is in it, he partly helps to make.

Relational symbols and transformations

Henry de Montherlant in *Les Bestiaires* describes a bullfight building up from the first tentative approaches of the torero and the bull to the point when they are so closely harmonized in their lethal dance that for the torero, at any rate, there exists a furious and solemn union between them, broken only by his finally sinking his weapon into the animal's heart. Other sorts of intimate relations with dangerous animals are also possible. A very readable little book, at times no doubt too fanciful for the resolutely skeptical, has been written by J. Allen Boone on this subject.[21] In a fascinating chapter on how to make friends with a rattlesnake, he describes the approach of a slight little woman by the name of Grace Wiley to a furiously angry six-foot diamondback. Standing in a bare room close to the far end of a heavy table on which the snake is coiled up, she faces him as he rattles warningly and darts his head in every direction. She has no equipment but two thin sticks, one with a net at the end, the other with a pad of soft cloth. She remains perfectly still, calmly and lovingly looking at the rattler a few feet away. Soon the big snake is looking straight at her, and then she begins to talk to him in a soothing voice. The rattling ceases, the snake uncoils and glides forward along the table toward her until his head is at rest a few inches from her; then she strokes his back, first with the padded stick and afterwards with both bare hands! And now the snake, which not many minutes before was ready to kill, arches his back like a cat to get the full benefit of the caresses. Must we then regard the stories of Androcles and the lion, of St. Francis and the wolf, as wholly legendary?

I mention these things because they illustrate a principle of unknown scope. We have to recognize that the qualities which we attribute to living creatures are to some extent a function of our relations to them. Are diamondback rattlers and ravenous wolves really friendly? Well, that depends. As for the human species, there are doubtful cases there, too. It takes more than a petting stick to win some of them over! How wide are the possibilities? What are the laws of relationship in detail? We do not know. We do know,

[21] Boone (1954).

however, that human beings are affected by other human beings, that there are numerous unexplored possibilities, that we cannot dismiss any individual as hopelessly beyond the reach of beneficent influences; it may even be that the most powerful influences are the least visible.[22]

No more than a hint can be given here of the subtlety of human relations in action. Let us suppose that Smith sees Jones as malicious and as aiming his malice at him. Smith is affected by this presumption: he shrinks away, or gets up his guard, or fires back with equal malice, or tries to appease Jones. But Jones too is affected: he notices the fear or defensiveness or hostility or kindness of Smith and reacts differentially. Perhaps he takes advantage of the fear to increase it by a more positive show of malice, or strikes down the guard, or fights with more malice against Smith's reactive malice; or perhaps, because he is not really malicious or because having been perceived as malicious he becomes conscious of unconscious malice and regrets it, he counters by working to allay Smith's fear, tempering it by showing openly that he is not malicious or only regretfully so. Or, finally, the kindness of Smith may abate the malice of Jones, or, in reverse, stimulate it by suggesting to the malicious mind of Jones that Smith is weak since kindness may look like weakness to a malicious person. This analysis is at the superficial level of abstract speech where Smith can say to himself, "Jones appears to be malicious," and where Jones can say to himself, "Smith appears to think that I am malicious," and so on. At a deeper level, which may co-exist with this, the contact takes place in terms of nonverbal symbols and sheer unsymbolized emotion. That is the level of anxiety and "hair standing on end" and the "heart melting within you"; it is the level where the man before you is translated into something nonhuman—machine or snake or dog—as in dreams, a translation which may lead to the conclusion that one may be run over by the machine, poisoned by the snake, devoured by the dog. To hold steady before a threatening "other" and to continue to see him as a real human being capable of greatness and goodness, never to lose confidence in his possibilities—that is quite another achievement, but likewise one which has to be founded on something more solid than words.

It is extremely common, of course, for one to picture humans as nonhuman. We have records from the most ancient times bearing witness to this tendency. Paleolithic carvings and paintings, the art

[22] For striking examples, see Standal and Corsini (1959).

of Assyria, Babylon, Egypt, the totemism of primitive tribes all over the world, the totemism of American athletic teams, the totemism of great modern nations, as well as the popular art of Disney, Walt Kelly, and other cartoonists—all testify to the human practice of seeing the animal in the human. Students of the human face have seriously or half-seriously compared animal and human faces and looked for deeper resemblances. For example, Figure 26 is one out of a large number of such designs, executed by the seventeenth-century French painter Le Brun and presented to Louis XIV. This is theriomorphism, seeing man as an animal.

Since the coming of the machine age, we have a new tendency—mechanomorphism. The mechanical conception of man, adumbrated 300 years ago by Descartes, is very much with us today—in cartoons, toys, advertisements, horror movies, World Fair robots, IBM "brains," and the publications of scientists. If I were to make a summary statement of the prevailing tendency toward mechanomorphism I might be accused of irresponsible exaggeration. I must therefore resort once again to quoting. The whole of Norbert Wiener's influential book *Cybernetics* is devoted to the analogy between man and machine. He states:

> It has long been clear to me that the modern ultra-rapid computing machine was in principle an ideal central nervous system to an apparatus for automatic control; and that its input and output need not be in the form of numbers or diagrams, but might very well be, respectively, the readings of artificial sense-organs such as photo-electric cells or thermometers, and the performance of motors or solenoids. With the aid of strain-gauges or similar agencies to read the performance of these motor organs and to report, to 'feed back', to the central control system as an artificial kinaesthetic sense, we are already in a position to construct artificial machines of almost any degree of elaborateness of performance.[23]

When he uses the adjective "artificial" as applied to these machines, he is simply marking them off from the "natural" machines which they resemble, i.e., human beings. He tells us on the next page that the new rapid advance toward full automation "makes the metaphorical dominance of the machines, as imagined by Samuel Butler, a most immediate and non-metaphorical problem"[24]—a development which, he predicts, will devalue the human brain at least as much as the first industrial revolution devalued the human arm. Wiener's most crushing conclusion, however, is simply that man is in principle

[23] Wiener (1948), p. 36.   [24] *Ibid.*, p. 37.

Figure humaine comparée avec celle de l'âne.

26 In the time of Louis XIV, the French painter Charles Le Brun produced many drawings which half-seriously compared the physiognomy of man and animal. In our own day, mechanomorphism (seeing man as a machine) begins to compete with theriomorphism (seeing man as an animal). (From G. Lavater, L'art de connaître les hommes par la physionomie, Vol. 9 [1835], opp. p. 116.)

identical with the machines he is making. The popularity of this point of view is evidenced by numerous advertisements in magazines of large circulation which picture man as a machine or as closely coupled with machines.

Psychology also has shared in the mechanomorphic trend. A relatively mild example is the cover illustration of a leading introductory text, showing a cadaverous puppet hung up on strings; the puppet reappears, looking less cadaverous and more mechanical, on an inside page where it reinforces the statement: "To some extent, we hold the strings by means of which our own behavior can be influenced and fitted to the world about us."[25] A much more serious example is Clark Hull's espousal of mechanomorphism as an aid to scientific objectivity and theory-building. He laments his own tendency to think anthropomorphically about man (i.e., to think of man as man), explains that he has struggled for years against this subjectivism and has sometimes failed to conquer it even when thinking of the behavior of man in terms of the behavior of "subhuman organisms, such as chimpanzees, monkeys, dogs, cats, and albino rats,"[26] and recommends going beyond theriomorphism to mechanomorphism in order to avoid the taint of subjectivity. He states:

> A device much employed by the author has proved itself to be . . . effective prophylaxis. This is to regard, from time to time, the behaving organism as a completely self-maintaining robot, constructed of materials as unlike ourselves as may be. In doing this it is not necessary to attempt the solution of the detailed engineering problems connected with the design of such a creature. It is a wholesome and revealing exercise, however, to consider the various general problems in behavior dynamics which must be solved in the design of a truly self-maintaining robot.[27]

A much fuller treatment of the mechanomorphic theme can be found in an article by Boring, delivered as the presidential address before the Eastern Psychological Association in 1946. He recalls the past difficulties of mechanomorphism and notes how much smoother the path is now:

> While it is hopeless to attempt to make an actual potato into Socrates, it is not at all hopeless to ask what properties a conscious human being must have in order for him to appear with great certainty to be a conscious human being. Psychologists have been asking this question ever since Descartes in the seventeenth century described animals as automata and La Mettrie a century later in his *L'homme machine* argued that the same logic could be applied to man. The French objectivists had, however, to fight not merely formal theological dogma, but mostly a culture permeated by the conception of freedom of the will and all

[25] Smith and Smith (1958), p. 53.
[26] Hull (1943), p. 27.   [27] *Ibid.*, p. 27.

the related infusions from theological thought. Nowadays we are much freer to do without freedom. Instead of theologists we have to fight merely those mystical psychologists who prefer to use language, trusting blindly its communicating power, and rejecting the demand for operational definitions even when communication falters or proves to be bifurcated. After all that is not much to fight about.[28]

He then goes into detail about the revisions needed to achieve a purely objective psychology, stating in his summary that the proper way to describe the functional capacities of man is to work out his input-output characteristics as if he were an electric motor:

> A further step is to reformulate these functions as properties of a *hypothetical robot.* . . . The advantage of playing this kind of game lies solely in the fact that, if you talk about machines, you are more certain to leave out the subjective, anthropomorphic hocus pocus of mentalism. . . . There is still a further step possible along this same road: the design and construction of *actual robots* who perform different human functions as well or better than a man can do. The electronic calculators and computers that the war has brought forth meet the specifications for some psychological functions, and doubtless more human electronic boxes could be built if the result were worth the thought and expense. . . . The only use in actually constructing the robot when he has been designed is to make sure that the design will really do what reason has already asserted it will do. Certainly a robot whom you could not distinguish from another student would be an extremely convincing demonstration of the mechanical nature of man and of the unity of the sciences.[29]

Perhaps these quotations from prominent American scientists will convince the reader that the mechanical image of man is real and powerful in modern thought. It is not the only image, of course, but it is a pervasive one, and it has incalculable consequences for science and for all those who are affected by science. I happen to think that the image is unprofitable for science and damaging to man. The reader may not agree with me (as clearly the authors I have quoted would not), but perhaps all would admit that other images are possible which might affect our human relations differently. A few might even concede that physical science could exist if its mechanical models were taken away from it. As for psychology, would it be entirely wrong to view *man* anthropomorphically?

It may be that science is ineluctably committed to a program of depersonalization. The history of science rather suggests this. If so,

---

[28] Boring (1946), p. 174.   [29] *Ibid.*, p. 191.

then it is idle for me or anybody else to make a plea for the sort of intuitive approach discussed in this chapter, which involves us in anthropomorphism and the most radical personalism. Nevertheless, I think it is possible for us, whether as scientists or not, to conceive of and participate in relations with the universe, and certainly with our fellow human beings, according to a fully personal "I-thou" scheme. That is very different from thinking of other people as animals or machines or things; and it has its own consequences, different from those which come from thinking of them (and ourselves) as animals or machines or things. Stern remarks:

> The relationship of *I* and *Thou* is mysterious. In the world of the natural sciences no two objects can be in the same place at the same time. In the relationship of *I* and *Thou* there is an interpenetration of being. . . . Contrary to the "*I* and *it*" or "*I* and *they*" the relationship of "*I* and *Thou*" is, on the natural plane, related to love—either positively or negatively. It cannot be neutral. Objects in mathematical space are not only separate; they are also opaque. The "*I* and *Thou*" is an illuminating insight. Here the light of reason and the light of charity belong together.[30]

If science can remain faithful to itself only by dealing in "it-it" relations, then it cannot touch the realm of human experience of which I am writing. Regardless of that, it remains true that one of the most significant questions which can be asked about human relations is whether they are occurring at the level of "I-thou" or whether they are depersonalized and proceeding in some degree mechanically.

Does intuitive psychology have a future?

Please notice that I have not said we should discard objective science. I have merely asked whether we can have an intuitive science. I have done so because I think some major human phenomena cannot be observed by objective methods—both because the methods are unsuitable and because they interfere with the occurrence of the phenomena.

As I have tried to indicate, Freud was a pioneer in the exploration of certain areas of human experience by intuitive methods. I think he omitted others. There is not the same authenticity of personal encounter in his remarks about love as in his discussions of

[30] Stern (1954), p. 297.

transference and countertransference. He wrote much on death and mourning, but he did not reveal to us directly the full meaning of his statement that the most important event in a man's life is the death of his father; he does not confront his own experience of his father's death and examine it as he did the transference and countertransference phenomena. We happen to know that the death of Freud's father was indeed important for him and that it influenced his *Interpretation of Dreams*, where we may read much of himself between the lines of the section on "Dreams of the Death of Beloved Persons," in which he outlined the theory of the Oedipus complex, stressed the egotism of children, interpreted dreams of the death of relatives as expressions of the wish for their death, and bluntly stated that "it is only a deceptive appearance if interest in another person is believed to have evoked a dream."[31] This may be Freud's personal confession in a way, but it is not as closely engaged with the experience and as revealing as his writings sometimes are. As to religion, we have some challenging works—*Totem and Taboo, The Future of an Illusion, Moses and Monotheism*—dealing with religious institutions and the conception of religion as a "mass neurosis," but we do not have any discussion by Freud of religious experience of his own and, in the nature of the case, could not, since Freud professed to be irreligious. In short, the range of Freud's intuitive psychology is limited. I mean this not as a criticism but as a simple statement of fact.

Will there be further convincing developments of intuitive psychology? I think there will be. Perhaps the strongest indication at present is the existentialist movement in psychiatry.[32]

References for chapter 13

Boone, J. A. (1954) *Kinship with all life*. New York: Harper.
Boring, E. G. (1946) Mind and mechanism. *American Journal of Psychology*, 59, 173-92.
Freud, S. (1950) *The interpretation of dreams*. Tr. by A. A. Brill. New York: Modern Library.
———(1953-) *The standard edition of the complete psychological works of Sigmund Freud*. London: Hogarth. Vol. 12.

[31] Freud (1933), p. 260.
[32] See, for example, Van den Berg (1955) for a succinct exposition of the phenomenological attitude of existentialism in practice, as well as a very useful historical survey; and the collection of papers edited by May, Angel, and Ellenberger (1958).

Heider, F. (1958) *The psychology of interpersonal relations*. New York: Wiley.

Homans, G. C. (1950) *The human group*. New York: Harcourt, Brace & World.

Hull, C. L. (1943) *Principles of behavior: an introduction to behavior theory*. New York: Holt.

May, R., Angel, E., and Ellenberger, H. F. (Eds.) (1958) *Existence: a new dimension in psychiatry and psychology*. New York: Basic Books.

Meehl, P. E. (1954) *Clinical versus statistical prediction: a theoretical analysis and a review of the evidence*. Minneapolis: Univ. of Minnesota Press.

Reik, T. (1949) *Listening with the third ear*. New York: Harcourt, Brace & World.

Sartre, J.-P. (1956) *Being and nothingness*. Tr. with an introduction by H. E. Barnes. New York: Philosophical Library.

Smith, K. U., and Smith, W. M. (1958) *The behavior of man: an introduction to psychology*. New York: Holt.

Standal, S. W., and Corsini, R. J. (Eds.) (1959) *Critical incidents in psychotherapy*. Englewood Cliffs, N.J.: Prentice-Hall.

Stern, K. (1954) *The third revolution*. New York: Harcourt, Brace & World.

Van den Berg, J. H. (1955) *The phenomenological approach to psychiatry*. Springfield, Ill.: Thomas.

Wiener, N. (1948) *Cybernetics: or control and communication in the machine*. New York: Wiley.

Zener, K. (1958) The significance of experience of the individual for the science of psychology. In Feigl, H., et al., *Minnesota studies in the philosophy of science*. Minneapolis: Univ. of Minnesota Press. Vol. 2.

IV
PROBLEMS

14

AT THE BORDERS
OF SCIENCE

Preview   *To appreciate personality we must recognize the great scope of human experience. It includes, along with the sensory perceptions which are the empirical base of physical science, a variety of other events like dreams and hallucinations and emotions for which physical science has little use. As for psychology, the tendency is to classify such events as purely subjective, i.e., as not referring, as perception does, to an external reality. Now and then, however, we have experiences or hear of experiences which challenge this conception of the matter. Hysterical hyperesthesia, veridical hallucinations, autoscopy, telepathy, mystical visions raise fundamental questions about personality—questions which are often excluded from our textbooks because the facts are doubted or because they do not fit conveniently into psychological theory. To label such facts, if facts they are, as "occult" or "pathological" or "parapsychological" solves no problems and, indeed,* *interferes with scientific advance. It seems better strategy to treat the phenomena openly and see where they lead us.*

The history of science teaches us at least this much: that across the boundaries marking off the "official" science of the day there lie dark regions of old discarded facts and new undiscovered facts into which adventurous researchers are always plunging, sometimes getting lost themselves, sometimes extending the scientific frontiers. So it is in the study of personality. In previous chapters a number of topics have been discussed which a few decades ago would have been thought inappropriate in a college textbook or, in fact, in a scientific convention. For example, hypnotism, which in the past few years has received the stamp of approval of the American Medical Association as a legitimate medical specialty, was once considered unfit for discussion in learned societies; and the theories and practice of psychoanalysis, so dominant now in psychiatry and so influential in the psychology of personality, were met at first with the bitterest contempt in many quarters of the scientific world.

In the present chapter and the two following I shall discuss some topics which lie on or just over the boundaries usually accepted in psychology today. I realize that in doing so I shall expose myself to the charge of being unscientific. This risk is not one which bothers me very much. There is another danger, however, about which I am really concerned. I am afraid that some readers, accustomed perhaps to taking textbook authors as authorities rather than as adventurers in the world of ideas, will not understand that in these chapters I am playing with ideas and inviting the reader to do the same. When I say "playing with ideas" I do not mean that I am being frivolous; I mean that, having stepped into territory which is a little foreign to academic psychology, I find myself up against facts and possibilities which I don't quite know how to handle. I therefore beg the reader to watch me carefully, even suspiciously; it may be that, though I try to be honest and serious, I shall make bad mistakes, treating lies as truth, illusions as facts, and impossibilities as possibilities, and I may at times become rather impassioned about things which the reader may think I should treat more calmly. I shall follow up this general warning from time to time with others more specific.

Telepathy?

Let us begin by recalling the experiment of Binet described toward the end of Chapter 7. His hysterical subject had a distinct *visual* experience of the shape, size, and design of the metal disc which he pressed against the tactually anesthetic skin of the back of her neck. She was seeing the disc through the back of her neck. Before this was verified by her drawing, Binet could easily have maintained that she was suffering from an inexplicable hallucination—that is to say, a sensory experience not corresponding to an external object. Afterwards, if it were any longer to be called hallucination, it would have to be called a veridical (i.e., truth-telling) hallucination. Notice that the girl, too, was put in a disquieting position by her experience. What she saw seemed to be in front of her eyes. If she had reached out her hand to touch the disc, however, it would not have been there and she would probably have concluded that she was hallucinating—unveridically. Yet this would have been an incorrect conclusion. Her visual experience corresponded quite closely with the object and coincided with its being pressed against the back of her neck. Why not call her experience a perception, on a footing with other visual perceptions? I can see only two possible objections to this, one superficial, and the other purely defensive. The superficial objection is that she did not use the proper receptors. The defensive objection is that if this is admitted as a case of perceiving we may be tempted into more extravagant admissions.

It was my good fortune not long ago to be able to test out this problem on a leading American psychologist, a specialist in perception who deserves his wide prestige. The occasion was a party, and it may be that he would not agree with my memory of the conversation; but, as I remember it, our discussion ran as follows. I asked him if he would call the phenomenon reported by Binet a perception. He said that he would. That is, as long as a correspondence was found between a subject's experience and a stimulus manipulated by an experimenter, even though the experience was visual and the stimulus was applied to the skin, he thought it proper to refer to the experience as perception rather than as hallucination. He said that he was not bothered by the fact that the stimulus was not located where the subject herself, guided by the visual image, might have reached for it. The oddity of the connection did not disturb him. When I asked him, however, to imagine the stimulus located on the other side of the earth rather than on the back of the girl's neck, he seemed to think that the oddity was entirely too great. He would in that case have been inclined to speak of hallucination rather than perception. If I followed his reasoning (a difficult thing to do at a noisy party), I judge that he would not have permitted himself the luxury of starting with the *experience* side of the stimulus-experience relationship at all. He might grant (though this was not entirely clear either) that a stimulus presented to a subject under laboratory conditions would give rise to a corresponding subjective experience, but he would not, in his professional role as a psychologist, care to start with any experience and inquire what possible external object there could be to which it might be related. To show how misleading it might be to start with an experience and search for a corresponding object, he cited the case of a friend of his who began to see halos around people's heads and then developed other symptoms which resulted in his being classified as a schizophrene. That psychiatric label satisfied him that his friend's experience was hallucinatory. To my inquiry whether it was theoretically possible that the schizophrenic condition was in part a heightened sensitivity to certain aspects of reality, so that it might be profitable to investigate the halo phenomenon as falling within the category of perceptions not open to normal perceivers, he violently objected. Another member of our little conversational cluster, approaching the matter from a different angle, introduced some questions about the role of the experimenter in a perception experiment. How does the experimenter himself, for instance, decide whether he is perceiving or hallucinating the stimulus which he is presenting to his subject? The perception specialist began by replying that such questions were metaphysical and outside his province. At just this interesting point other obligations required me to leave the party.

Obviously it makes some difference for our theories where we draw the line between perception and hallucination. As long as our friend or our patient reports experiences which we classify as perceptions we admit that he and we share in the same reality, even though we have not had perceptions like his; but when we classify his experiences as hallucinations, we shut the door on him, we say that he is autistic or out of his head, we judge that he has lost his grip on reality and need not be taken seriously any longer. This judgment is a judgment on both the nature of personality and the nature of reality at large. It affects our dealings with our friend or patient, and it also affects our willingness to follow his suggestions as to the nature of the world in which we all live.

Some theorists may find the Binet phenomenon merely inconvenient, like a clinical friend of mine who said that he would rather not think about it. Others may find it merely amusing. Others, whose theories are cast in a harder, more brittle mold, may find it shattering and either reject it as a lie or undergo a mental revolution. Cesare Lombroso, the famous criminologist and neuropathologist, confessed that it made his mind reel when he personally ran into such phenomena. He was forty-six at the time, a mature and distinguished man with strong scientific opinions who thought himself immune to the current spiritualistic nonsense. As he wrote of himself at a later date:

> If ever there was anyone in this world who by his scientific training and by a sort of instinct was resolutely opposed to Spiritism, I was that man; for out of the principle that all force was merely a property of matter, and that the soul was an emanation of the brain, I had created for myself the line of study which was to be my life's work. To think that I, of all men, who for so many years had laughed at the very idea of spirits, and table-turning and séances, should come to believe what I now believe![1]

However, he declares that he had one passion stronger than devotion to the scientific principles with which he was familiar, namely, "a veneration for truth, a resolve to be content with nothing short of the evidence of ascertained facts."[2] It happened in 1882 that he was called upon to examine a girl of fourteen, the daughter of a prominent and capable Italian. She had developed various hysterical symptoms—vomiting, convulsions, hyperesthesias, attacks of paralysis, enormous increments of muscular energy, blindness:

> And at this point extraordinary phenomena began to present themselves. First there was a somnambulistic condition in which she showed an amazing activity in work about the house, a very affectionate disposition towards the whole family and a conspicuous musical talent; at a later stage there was a change of character; she developed a masculine boldness and a lack of moral principle. But the most remarkable fact was this, that while she lost the power of seeing with her eyes, she saw, as clearly as before, with the tip of her nose and the lobe of her left ear. By these improvised organs, though I had bandaged her eyes, she read a letter which had just then come to me by post and she was able to distinguish the figures on the dial of a dynamometer.[3]

[1] Thurston (1952), pp. 334 f.   [2] Ibid., p. 335.
[3] Ibid., p. 336.

It was this experience which turned Lombroso's theories upside down.

Now, observations of this sort are not easily accepted by those who have never made them, especially by those who are aware, as good scientists must be, of the numerous pitfalls in the way of truth and accuracy. At this very moment I am a little uneasy about the Lombroso quotations because they are from a secondary source. I do not have this uneasiness about the Binet experiment, though I still wish that I might have been present. But might I not have doubted my own experience if I had witnessed what Binet and Lombroso report?[4] I think that it is very natural for us to react to things which lie outside the routine of our own experience with fear or protective doubt, and especially when we know that liars abound and that our memories are faulty. On the other hand, we do not want to exclude facts, no matter how queer they may be.

If I knew of any infallible rule for distinguishing between true and false reports, I should certainly bring it in here for the protection of all of us; and if I knew the one right way for estimating the theoretical significance of a true report, I would also state that; but, unfortunately, I do not know these things, and the best I can do is to expose the reader to some of the reports which have struck me as having significance and let him struggle with the consequences as I myself do. Perhaps I ought also to indicate the limits of my own personal experience, aside from reading, as they relate to the subject matter of this chapter. I have never attended a mediumistic or spiritualistic séance. I have performed ESP card experiments with psychology classes in a very skeptical spirit, mainly for the purpose of exercising them in elementary statistics. I used to have long arguments with parapsychologist friends when I was a graduate student, in which I was eternally urging them to specify the *conditions* supposed to be favorable for the production of telepathic or clairvoyant phenomena. From them, as well as on my own, I have learned something about the mixture of credulity and fraud which imperils ESP experimentation. I have, however, been made more sympathetic to

[4] *Any* experience which does not fit into one's preconceptions may be disturbing. A graduate student of my acquaintance who knows more about the subways of New York than celestial phenomena was thrown into some doubt of his own normality by happening to observe one night a colored halo around the moon. He was alone at the time and feared that he might be "seeing things." To reassure himself he called another person out of the house to check up on him. Fortunately for his peace of mind, the witness he called out agreed that the halo was there.

the so-called paranormal phenomena by certain experiences in counseling students, by oral accounts of premonitions confirmed, and by close personal involvement with a case of hysteria which ended in death and which moved me very deeply.

As for self-observations, I can report nothing startling. I have never been hypnotized, I have never had a vision, I have never had a neurosis or psychosis or even been psychoanalyzed. I am not "psychic." In short, I am a very underprivileged psychologist. Still, I can report one little incident in which I seemed to play the role of a telepathic agent and which I took care to note down the same day. The incident was this. I was discussing hallucinations with my graduate assistant, Ronald Fox, one morning (February 23, 1959) and urging him to try to think of such things as the demons of Janet's patient Achille as not entirely unreal—as having reality at least within the patient's world. He was arguing with strong common sense against a viewpoint that seemed rash to him, and I was mentally preparing further arguments of my own. In particular, I was thinking of Auckland Geddes' story about his remarkable Aunt Margaret and how her two dead sisters had appeared to her shortly after her brother's funeral to announce her own imminent death and had again appeared, as they foretold, on the evening that she was to die: she had asked her nephew to arrange two chairs for them beside her bed, and the phantoms sat in these when they arrived. I was visualizing this scene when Fox said, to illustrate his own point, that if someone began to talk to two old ladies sitting in what appeared to him to be empty chairs he would listen sympathetically but would refuse to be taken in. I was not startled by this coincidence, but I was definitely interested. I stopped him and asked him to take special note of what he had just said, and I asked him to complete the imagined scene by describing the hallucinator. He said that he had not imagined anyone in particular, but, on further urging, confessed that he might have been thinking of a middle-aged man. I then told him what I had been thinking, underlining the agreement but pointing out that there was failure of agreement, too, since it was an old lady rather than a middle-aged man who had been the hallucinator in the scene I had been reflecting on. Afterwards, it occurred to me that Mr. Fox had cleverly combined my thoughts with myself so as to make *me* the imagined hallucinator! His argument against my argument was both telepathic and *ad hominem*, a perfectly fabulous combination. I should add that this incident occurred (along with a few others of similar quality, but not so clear-cut) during a period of several months when I was in an emotional state of marked ebullience, sensitivity, and tenderness.

My own telepathic experience is very similar to one reported by the British psychologist William Brown, in an address before the Society for Psychical Research in 1932. It hinges on a Greek word, but it is not necessary to know Greek to understand the point. Brown said:

A few days ago I had an interesting example of telepathy, or at least so it seems to me. I was talking to a man of high classical attainments, and we were discussing the "Prometheus Vinctus" of Aeschylus, especially that phrase in the first speech of Prometheus after he has been bound to his rock, the phrase, badly translated in English as "many-twinkling smile of ocean," but more literally and more elegantly "the innumerable laughter of the waves of the sea." As I thought of the English translation there came to my mind the (imaginary) Greek word πολυγελασμα—a reminiscence of a schoolboy howler I made many years ago. The actual Greek phrase is

$$\pi o \nu \tau \iota \omega \nu \ \tau \epsilon \ \kappa \upsilon \mu \acute{\alpha} \tau \omega \nu$$
$$\dot{\alpha} \nu \acute{\eta} \rho \iota \vartheta \mu o \nu \ \gamma \acute{\epsilon} \lambda \alpha \sigma \mu \alpha \ (11.\ 89\text{-}90)$$

But the first expression came to my mind, I did not articulate it, I just thought it, and, a moment later, like an echo, there came from this classical scholar the word πολυγελασμα. Immediately afterwards he said, "I do not know why I said that. Of course it is wrong. There is no such word." He is inclined to agree with me that it was an example of telepathy. The alternative explanations would be either coincidence, that we both thought of πολυγελασμα, which is improbable; or that he made a mistake, as I made when a boy, but then you must remember that he was a classic who would certainly not make that blunder; and there is the further alternative possibility that I whispered it, and he heard the involuntary whisper, but I think that can be ruled out.[5]

Let us note a few points which may have significance for such experiences. (1) The experiences carry immediate conviction to the one who has them; they are felt to be telepathic, and they do not seem meaningless or nonsensical. It is quite impossible to test them statistically, and yet they have a fitness, a rightness, like an apt phrase in a sentence or an intelligent reply to a remark made in a conversation. It is this suitableness which makes the coincidence hypothesis appear strained—to those who have had the experience. (2) Some warmth or fervor or mutual involvement between the persons concerned seems to be a prerequisite or at least accompani-

---

[5] Brown (1932), pp. 81 f.

ment for these or similar experiences. (3) Strong emotional events may have some bearing on the development of telepathic capacity or at least on the willingness to tolerate the idea of such communications. Severe illness may be one of the conditions. Perhaps bereavement is. I will be frank to say that bereavement has certainly affected my own attitude.

William Brown relates an event from his own life which seems to point in this direction, and which at the same time illustrates my preceding remarks. Brown makes it clear elsewhere that the story is his own:

> I would quote here a case that I can guarantee in all its details, a case which any one who did not know it inwardly might be tempted to dismiss as mere coincidence, but which to the person who experienced it seemed to be more. The little son, aged two and a quarter years, of a scientist lay dying of a serious illness. He was in a nursing-home, in order that he might have the best of care, and his parents had been spending all their time with him, sitting up at night by his bedside. At last he reached a stage where he seemed a little better, and it was necessary for them to get rest, as the nurse felt that the child could be safely left to her. Early the next morning, as the father happened to be looking in the direction of the clock on the mantelpiece in a house some distance away, he heard a loud noise behind him, a sudden bang, and the thought flashed through his mind: "That is my little boy's photograph which has shot off the edge of the piano." He noticed the time—it was twenty to eight—turned round, and saw that it *was* the photograph which had fallen. Shortly afterwards the telephone-bell rang, and the message came through that the little boy had died. The parents hurried round to the nursing-home, and, as they entered the door, the father saw the nurse coming down the stairs. The first question he asked was: "When did he die?" and before she had said anything he *knew* that she would say, "At twenty to eight." He had already communicated the fact to his wife, and she too knew that that was the time. The incident carried with it a strong emotional feeling—curiously enough a feeling of intense relief and peace.[6]

A bit of speculation

Two kinds of so-called paranormal experiences have been illustrated in the preceding examples—veridical hallucination and telepathy. Both kinds of experience exceed the limits usually accepted in current psychological theory, especially in America. Veridical

[6] Brown (1929), pp. 192 f. Used by permission of the Yale University Press.

hallucination (in the cases cited, the term "hyperesthesia" might be preferred) does not fit into the doctrine that visual perception is by the eye, auditory perception by the ear, and so on, without exception. Telepathy does not fit into the doctrine that communication from one person to another is exclusively by sensory cues. Both phenomena suggest that sensory perception and sense-guided communication are specialized modes of obtaining and transmitting knowledge which exist within a more general mode of which we have only momentary glimpses.

Let us be freely speculative here in order to try to accommodate the phenomena mentioned, while continuing to realize that for many psychologists such phenomena do not constitute legitimate scientific evidence of anything.

(1) We might think of telepathy (communication without sensory cues) as simply the most direct form of communication between persons. Ordinarily we depend largely on words and gestures to communicate our ideas, but we notice that the elaborateness of these modes of communication varies widely. Krech and Crutchfield illuminatingly compare the formality and difficulty of verbal communication in different contexts, from talking to oneself or talking to a close friend up through the formal lecture before a largely unknown audience and the written book, and they comment: "In general, the more common the sympathies and context shared by the listener and speaker, the more elliptical, abrupt, unfinished, and grammatically unrestrained speech can be."[7] Reik's surprising success in understanding his patient's very obscure references to abortion, by the method of "listening with the third ear"—a method which, as we have seen, constituted a severe problem for Meehl—comes very close to pure telepathy. A step beyond that carries us to telepathy proper.

(2) Veridical hallucination might in the same way be thought of as the end term in a series going from careful sensory exploration of an object through recognition by minimal cues to the point where all sensory cues have dropped out. The kind of veridical hallucination represented by the accounts of Binet and Lombroso is not quite the end term, since bodily contact was established between the stimulus object and the perceiver or hallucinator. We shall come to purer cases in a moment. In fact, as we have seen, a leading American psychologist specializing in perception was willing to include the unorthodox performance of Binet's hysteric under the heading of

[7] Krech and Crutchfield (1958), p. 475.

perception rather than hallucination. More difficult is the decision about veridical hallucinations where there is no experimenter manipulating a stimulus object in the immediate neighborhood of the subject. We have to deal with a vast array of vivid experiences—dreams, waking hallucinations, visions, apparitions—where the sensory quality is strong though the sense organs seem not to be involved, and where it is uncertain whether we ought to suppose that there is some corresponding reality outside the experience itself. That is to say, from the experience side, there may be no distinction between a visual perception and a visual dream (cf. Descartes, Boss); but the perception is called such because it is believed to refer beyond itself to an object which exists whether perceived or not, whereas the dream or hallucination is called such because it is believed *not* to refer beyond itself to an existing object. Now, the problem, perhaps the insoluble problem, is that once we have left the ordinary space-time framework of sensory perception with which the laboratory worker likes to deal (and we have begun to leave that framework with Binet's phenomenon) we do not know how to locate the stimulus object. One proposed solution, especially popular in the East, is to regard *all* experience of definite objects, including the experience of the eye and ear and so on, as a misleading illusion, the veil of Maya. Another proposed solution, popular in the West, is to make the familiar dichotomy between "real" perception (i.e., sense-organ perception in the recognized space-time framework of experimental science) and "false" or "unreal" perception (i.e., dreams, hallucinations, etc.). A third proposed solution, apparently not very popular anywhere, is the standpoint of naïve phenomenology (which may be the standpoint of the young child) that *all* experience of definite objects, including dreams and waking hallucinations, is perfectly valid, either within the space-time framework or out of it. In this third solution, the subject is taken to be simply a perceiver and not at all a creator of the world of his experience, and hence capable not of producing but only of receiving the images of objects. For such an experiencer, the presence of a definite image is evidence of the existence of a reality apart from himself. Figure 27 diagrams this conception of experience of objects as always referential. The unbroken line stands for the kind of experience which our Western dichotomy classifies as true perception; the broken lines, for that kind of experience which it classifies as hallucinatory or false or "unreal." The broken line which curves around to "Objects near in space-time" refers to ambiguous experiences of the Binet and

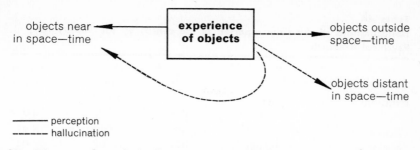

objects near
in space—time

**experience
of objects**

objects outside
space—time

objects distant
in space—time

——— perception
—————— hallucination

27 *We may hypothetically conceive of all experience of objects as referential.*

Lombroso type; the other two broken lines refer to kinds of experience which will be taken up in the remainder of this chapter.

I have invited the reader to be freely speculative. I offer the diagram of Figure 27 in this freely speculative spirit. I will also confess that it attracts me; but it attracts me as hypothesis, not as a confirmed belief. It attracts me because it lets me make room for the behavior of some very interesting human beings without having to pass the judgment "pathological" on them and thus exclude their testimony from the total sum of human observations on the nature of reality. At the same time, I am aware of the immense difficulties presented by any such hypothesis and aware also of the initial difficulty of separating truth from falsehood in the basic data. I hope that the reader will be equally aware of these difficulties, and more aware than I if he can.

Veridical hallucinations?

When hallucinatory experiences coincide appropriately with independently confirmed events, they may be called veridical. It would be interesting to know how frequent hallucinations are in human experience, and how frequently they coincide veridically with significant events. A major, though no doubt faulty, attempt to answer these two questions was the British Census of Hallucinations, conducted by the Society for Psychical Research (SPR) in England, France, the United States, and Germany, with the cooperation of leading psychologists (William James, for one), and reported fully in the Society's *Proceedings* for 1894. Table 44 presents some of the data. As it shows, at least one person in ten among those investigated could answer affirmatively the following question: "Have you ever,

Table 44

Hallucinations of the sane reported in the census by the Society for Psychical Research

		yes	*no*	*per cent* *"yes"*
ENGLAND	men	655	7,717	7.8
	women	1,029	7,599	12.0
FRANCE	men	352	1,952	15.27
	women	327	762	30.02
UNITED STATES	men	411	3,334	10.97
	women	441	2,125	17.14
GERMANY	men	20	316	5.95
	women	31	258	10.72
TOTAL		3,266	24,063	11.95

Adapted from MacRobert (1950).

when believing yourself to be completely awake, had a vivid impression of seeing or being touched by a living being or inanimate object, or of hearing a voice; which impression, so far as you could discover, was not due to an external physical cause?" In all four countries the percentage was distinctly higher for women than for men, reaching 30% in France. It would appear from this study (in which subjects were more or less randomly chosen) that a considerable proportion of the normal population in civilized countries of the Western world is subject to definite hallucination in the waking state. It is possible that the proportion is higher than these figures would indicate, since waking hallucinations like vivid dreams may be forgotten. A certain number of the hallucinations reported were of persons whom the hallucinator recognized. By calculations which need not be gone into here, it was estimated that in the English sample 1 in 43 of these cases coincided with the death of the person hallucinated, whereas chance coincidence should have been in the proportion 1 to 19,000. Actual coincidences were thus 440 times more common than should have happened by mathematical chance. In the German, French, and American samples the excess over chance appears to have been greater.

The problems of sampling and interviewing are better understood now than at the time of the British Census of Hallucinations, and it may be that a new survey with modern refinements would yield more accurate results. Yet it may be questioned whether statistical proof of above-chance coincidence between hallucinations and corresponding events such as offered in the SPR study, or statistical disproof such as might be imagined in a modern survey, can ever be quite satisfactory to anyone. On the other hand, personal experience of such coincidences may be so overpowering as to leave very little room for personal doubt regardless of the statistics. It is true that a science cannot be built on mere personal conviction, but I think we do well to listen to the accounts of people who have some reason for their convictions. It is only by listening to these reports that we can make any progress toward discovering laws. Astronomy is interested in meteors, which are only statistically predictable even now and were less so not many years ago, and psychology might take a similar interest in such sporadic events as veridical hallucinations. We might also reflect that these events are undoubtedly more frequent than the reports. It would not be surprising to find the situation to be comparable in this respect to that for meteors. As for meteors, Payne-Gaposchkin writes:

> One observer's range is very limited, and half a dozen an hour seen by him represents over ten million a day falling somewhere on earth. If allowance is made for the fact that the visual observer sees only the brightest, it is calculated that four thousand million meteors brighter than the tenth magnitude strike the earth daily.[8]

As for veridical hallucinations and related experiences, I should say further that people tend to keep quiet about them unless in congenial company.

Sometimes the experiences lie on the border between imageless telepathy and veridical hallucination. I am thinking of experiences chiefly marked by anxiety: for example, the terrible anxiety which gripped a dear friend of mine at the moment that her son was drowning in a lake miles away. A little further along toward the hallucinatory is what Mildred White Greear relates concerning the Georgia poet Byron Herbert Reece:

> It may come as a surprise to some of his followers that he was extremely gifted in extra-sensory perception. In one poem he calls it "that whisper in my marrow bone." In one of the Steve Hall poems, he tells of knowing of Steve's death before the news reached him by mail. "By sorrow foretortured, I know not how," he writes. His poetry was often autobiographical, and the details honest. The preceding quoted line was not hindsight poetically made foresight, but an actual account of the

[8] Payne-Gaposchkin (1954), p. 244.

communication as it happened. In another line he says, "His spirit wavered from out my trance." When a brother-in-law was killed in Africa, he told of "hearing the plane crash, and awakening." This was three days before his sister was officially notified of her husband's death. But the poet had "heard" at the approximate time of the aircraft accident that took her husband's life.[9]

Let me insert an explanatory remark here. I have no reason to doubt Greear's account of Reece's experiences. She reports these incidents in a biographical sketch of a man whom she, along with others in the same issue of the magazine, was trying to commemorate in a simple, honest way for people who knew his work, and she was not trying to "prove" or "sell" ESP. Yet I know something about the complexities of testimony in such matters, and I do not offer these incidents as irrefutable evidence of telepathy or the like. I do offer them as illustrations of the kind of experiences which many human beings say they have from time to time. They illuminate the kind of world which at least some people live in, and they do, of course, raise a question about the assumption (common in psychology) that all our information about events in the world must came through the ordinary sensory channels. At minimum, we must realize that such experiences affect the behavior and outlook of those people who have them, and we must be prepared to include them in any assessment of their personalities. But we really have some difficulty in leaving it at that; for these experiences seem to require us to construct a theory about the way we exist in the world which would differ from a theory which ignored them. Let me say once again, however, that neither Greear's account of Reece nor any other similar account in the following pages is meant to be taken as weighty, final evidence.

Various collections of hallucinatory incidents have been published. A recent one is a series of articles by Louisa Rhine (Mrs. J. B. Rhine) based upon a large file of letters in the Duke Parapsychology Laboratory. One naïvely written letter runs as follows:

This occurred in the first school I taught. I was then just 18 and doing my practice teaching. There was a young lad (he was 14) who insisted on knowing where I was going to teach. I didn't know at the time. He made it very emphatic on several occasions that no matter where I taught he was going to go to my school and no other. I was seated at my desk shortly after our afternoon studies began when a

[9] Greear (1958), p. 371.

voice said, "Hello, Miss Long." Glancing up, there he stood, smiling at me, hat in hand, holding on to the door. "I told you that no matter where you taught I was going to your school and here I am." Pleased as well as startled, I smiled back, exclaiming, "Truman, how did you get here?" He replied, "Oh, I just came. Where can I sit?" I was aware of the dead silence in the room and every pupil seemed frozen in their places, mingled emotions stamped on their faces, all eyes watching me. Ready to reply I noticed that instead of a solid substance, as he had first appeared the figure was fading out and I could see the details of the room through him. Shaken, I, who hadn't thought of him before, couldn't get this out of my mind. A few days later a letter from my mother telling of Truman's sudden death really made me have the creeps. He had been only slightly ill for a few days and his mother was planning on sending him to school the next day. He had been downstairs eating his noon lunch. At 1:30, the time I saw his apparition, as he started to go back upstairs he collapsed and died, hanging on to the stair post.[10]

An old collection of considerable interest is Camille Flammarion's *L'Inconnu (The Unknown)*. Flammarion (1842-1925), a French astronomer of some note, discusses in this book the general problem of credulity and incredulity and presents a mass of documents bearing on our topic. These documents are mostly letters received in answer to his public request for personal experiences. He examined the hundreds of replies for internal evidence of sincerity, in many cases checked on the reliability of the writers by weighing their official status and reputation, and in some cases made close inquiries. He believed that those he included in his book were honest. From a thoroughly skeptical standpoint these precautions are certainly not enough; one could argue that the uncertainty of memory, the possibility of self-deception, the human pleasure in lying, and so on, could invalidate every item. Nevertheless, we should not too hastily discount Flammarion's winnowing process. One of the letters reads thus:

Allow me to call your attention to a circumstance which seems to me very curious. In the first place, it decided my future life, and, besides that, its circumstances were not ordinary ones. In 1867 (I was then twenty-five) on December 17th, I went to bed. It was nearly eleven o'clock, and as I undressed I sat down and began thinking. My thoughts were fixed on a young girl I had met during my last vacation at the sea-bath of Trouville. My family knew hers quite intimately, and

[10] Rhine (1956), p. 244, paragraphing ignored. Used by permission of the author.

Martha and I became very fond of each other. Our marriage was on the eve of being arranged when our two families quarrelled, and it had to be given up. Martha went to Toulouse, and I returned to Grenoble. But we continued to love each other so sincerely that the young girl refused other offers for her hand. That evening, December 17, 1867, I was thinking about all this, when the door of my room opened softly, and, almost noiselessly, Martha entered. She was dressed in white, with her hair streaming over her shoulders. Eleven o'clock struck—this I can confidently assert, for I was not sleeping. The vision drew near me, leaned lightly over me, and I tried to seize the young girl's hand. It was icy cold. I uttered a cry, the phantom disappeared, and I found myself holding a glass of cold water in my hand. This may have given me the sensation of cold. But, observe, I was not asleep, and the glass of water had been standing on the *table de nuit* at my side. I could not sleep that night. On the *evening of the next day I heard of the death of Martha, at Toulouse, the night before, at eleven.* Her last word had been, "Jacques!" This is my story. I may add that I have never married. I am an old bachelor, but I think constantly of my vision. It haunts my sleep.[11]

Is the story true? If it is, then we must conclude that the writer was in effect *seeing* his sweetheart come to bid him farewell as she lay dying and calling his name more than two hundred miles away. And if the story is true, we can be sure that the man who told it would have been impervious to statistics and arguments designed to prove that his hallucination's connection with his sweetheart's death was a meaningless accident.

I select one other example from Flammarion, the more complex story of a mother who wrote him not many years after the events she describes.

I had a daughter of the age of fifteen; she was my joy and pride. I left her with my mother, while I made a little journey. On May 17, 1894, I was to be at home again. Now on the 16th I dreamed that my daughter was very ill, that she was sobbing and calling for me with all her strength. I woke up much agitated, but I said to myself dreams are all nonsense. In the course of the day I had a letter from my daughter, who made no complaint about her health, only telling what had happened at home. The next day I got back; my daughter did not run to meet me as she always used to do; a maid told me she had been suddenly taken ill. She had a terrible pain in her head. I made her go to bed. Alas! she never again left it. Diphtheria declared itself two days after, and, in spite of all our care, my dear child died on the

[11] Flammarion (1900), pp. 135 f., paragraphing ignored.

29th of May. Now two days before her death I had thrown myself upon my bed, [in] a little sick chamber separated from her only by a door; I closed my eyes, but I did not sleep. My daughter was in a doze, but the nurse was awake. Suddenly a bright light shone in the dark chamber, with a swiftness and a brilliancy like that of a flash of sunlight in August at mid-day. I called to the nurse. She did not answer me for a moment; before she did so I was beside my daughter's bed. The night-lamp had gone out, the flash of light was gone. The nurse seemed paralyzed with fear. In vain I questioned her, but next day she told the servants (and she says the same thing still) that she saw my husband, who died six months before, standing at the foot of my daughter's bed.[12]

Unconscious inference and the superstitious fancies of servants! one might say. But it is clear that the mother could scarcely dismiss the experiences of those two weeks so lightly. Skeptical arguments would seem very flimsy against the experiences themselves—*if* the story is true. "*If* the story is true!"—that doubt is a fortress which no second-hand evidence can shake, statistical or anecdotal.

Flammarion's correspondents usually report only one incident; and they do not take credit for special powers or describe practices intended to produce extraordinary phenomena. They seem, on the whole, to be normal individuals with no tendency to brag about psychic gifts. The events reported seem to have happened to them in much the same way as a fireball or bolide might suddenly streak across the sky or explode. In many cases, of course, there is evidence of strong affection and deep concern as sensitizing factors. Quite apart from our present topic, it is probable that deep stirrings of love heighten consciousness and perceptual powers in general. In the two stories taken from Flammarion it will be noticed that the young man, Jacques, was profoundly in love with the girl of his vision, and that the mother was not only attached to her daughter but had recently lost her husband and was doubtless still under the sensitizing effect of that bereavement.

Now and then we hear of individuals who are credited with more than single flashes of clairvoyance. Often the clairvoyant status is ushered in by severe headaches and convulsions. Perhaps brain disturbance is a key point. Brown, referring to observations made during the First World War, comments:

While working as neurologist to the Fourth Army on the Somme I noticed that the strain of exposure to shell-fire produced apparently

[12] *Ibid.*, p. 393 f.

mediumistic or clairvoyant powers in a large number of soldiers; indeed, quite 15 per cent. of soldiers suffering from shell-shock were found, immediately after the shock, to be easily hypnotizable, and, in a large proportion of these cases, they were found to exhibit powers—characteristics—extremely similar to, if not identical with, the characteristics that one reads about or hears of as belonging to mediums; that is to say, not only could they be easily put to sleep, put into a second mental state which appeared to be quite different from their normal waking state, but, when they were in this state, they appeared to have telepathic powers, they appeared to have clairvoyant powers.[13]

The strange clairvoyant behavior of the Reverend Thomas Hanna began with a fall on his head, and the clairvoyant phenomena so awed the members of his family that they sought to conceal them from the investigators Sidis and Goodhart,[14] who in their turn unfortunately did not think it worth their while to test the patient. A recent study by Schmeidler was aimed at discovering whether brain concussion improved ESP scores. Her results, as summarized in Table 45, show a statistically significant association between concussion and ESP and, if they were on almost any other subject, would be considered acceptable data supporting the hypothesis; but skepticism in this regard is strongly entrenched and is not likely to be budged by statistics.[15] There are other cases pointing to some connection between brain disturbance and the clairvoyant status; perhaps there are many, but I have found no summary devoted to the question. I will cite only one more and give enough detail to indicate the complexity often present.

The case is that of the Reverend Constantine Blackman Sanders, a Presbyterian minister. An account of him was published by a fel-

Table 45
ESP scores of hospital patients: brain concussion vs. others

	above chance	at chance	below chance
suffering brain concussion	13	3	2
with noncranial fractures or recovered from concussion	2	2	7

$(\chi^2$ probability about 1%)

Adapted from Schmeidler and McConnell (1958), p. 78.

[13] Brown (1929), pp. 183 f.
[14] Sidis and Goodhart (1919), p. 173
[15] On invincible skepticism, see Schmeidler and McConnell (1958), pp. 23 f., and Tyrrell (1951), pp. 38-41.

low-minister, the Reverend G. W. Mitchell, in 1876. The little book, though bearing the queer title $X + Y = Z$; or *The Sleeping Preacher of North Alabama*, is a very sober, matter-of-fact, pedestrian composition, presenting the testimony of many named witnesses. Besides the internal evidence of sobriety and probity in Mitchell and his witnesses, we have the word of William James that a letter from a personal friend in 1886 assured him Chief Justice Brickell of Alabama had knowledge of many of the incidents and vouched for the reliability of the witnesses.[16] This external verification is too roundabout to be satisfactory, but we should perhaps be hardly more satisfied if William James himself had written Mitchell's book. Sanders was born in 1831. From early childhood he aspired to the ministry. I infer that it was after his father's death, when he was six or so, that he began preaching funeral sermons over dead chickens, pigs, and other animals, and played at baptizing other children, both white and colored. After formally joining the Presbyterian church in 1851, he became an active religious worker—a candidate for the ministry in 1852, licensed to preach in 1855, and ordained in 1862. It was in 1854 while he was studying for the ministry (at the beginning of his candidacy he could scarcely read and write) that his seemingly robust health was interrupted by illnesses which left him the victim of violent headaches accompanied by intracranial pressure sufficient to open the frontal sutures of the skull at times to the width of a finger. He also began to suffer from convulsions. In this new condition, which the physicians were unable to relieve, unusual psychic powers emerged. He would often fall into a somnambulistic state; he would then converse or preach or sing with extraordinary fervor and ability, and at times he would exhibit hyperesthesia and outright clairvoyance. For example, he described in detail a fire taking place in Salisbury, North Carolina, hundreds of miles away; he often found lost articles; and more than once, apparently with deep emotion, he became aware of the death of some person at a distance. Fully as astonishing as any of his manifestations was his perception of a severe cramp in visible form leaving him, with the assurance that it would never return. Attacks of such cramps had afflicted him for several years—cramps which twisted his body into abnormal positions and brought on a gasping respiration that seemed always on the verge of stopping. On the occasion mentioned, in 1859, he declared to a close friend that he would never again suffer in that way, and the prediction proved true. He often mentioned the

[16] Quoted by Myers (1903), Vol. 2., p. 562.

experience, saying, "I saw it go away. It went up through the top of the house. It was the *ugliest* thing I ever saw."[17] Somnambulistic periods continued until 1876 and were frequent; headaches accompanied these, and at times there was bleeding from the eyes; but the torturing cramps did not return.

Sanders' prophetic vision of cramp leaving his body forever has parallels in other cases of self-diagnosis, some visionary, some not. A neurologist friend of mine, not a fanciful man, sometimes asks his uneducated patients (the educated, he says, would fling the question back at him) what the source of their trouble is. On one occasion he followed this naïve manner of inquiry with an old woman whose symptoms had been baffling the hospital staff for several days and was rewarded with the matter-of-fact reply (which was correct) that she was suffering from a clot on the brain in a particular place. Sidis, no friend of psychical research, recites as fine an example of prophecy as one is likely to see anywhere. A female relative of his had a daylight vision of her recently dead parents coming to announce to her that she would bear twins, a boy and a girl, to be named after them. She was not conscious of any signs of pregnancy at the time; nevertheless, faithful to her vision, she began getting clothes and other things ready for the expected pair, while the neighbors sniggered. Presumably they quit sniggering after the twins, a boy and a girl, actually arrived. Sidis tries to explain the vision as the consequence of obscure internal sensations correctly interpreted by the woman, who had previously borne fourteen children and thus might be considered an expert in such matters.[18]

Autoscopy

A special form of hallucination, surely related to the obscure bodily sensations which Sidis invokes to explain *all* hallucinations, is what is called autoscopy, or the phenomenon of the double. The poet Alfred de Musset describes a series of autoscopic encounters in "La Nuit de Décembre." The opening lines, so simple and touching that it is impossible to bring them over undamaged into English, are these (as I translate them):

> *A child, I kept one evening late*
> *My studious vigil in our great*
> *Cavernous parlor, quiet and dim.*

[17] Mitchell (1876), p. 41.

[18] Sidis (1904b).

Up to my table came and sat
A poor schoolboy in sober black
Who resembled me like my twin.

He had a sad and handsome face.
By the blear candle's wavering blaze
He read my open book with me.
He leaned his forehead on his hand
And till next morning so remained,
Pensive, and smiling tenderly.

Others have had the same kind of experience. Goethe met himself mounted on horseback when he was taking his departure from his sweetheart Friederike. The figure which he saw and recognized as himself was dressed in a gray suit trimmed with gold such as he had never worn before. Oddly enough, eight years later he was astonished to discover that he was wearing just such a costume as he rode back along the same path to visit Friederike once again. Maupassant was disturbed one day while at work in his study by the entrance of a stranger: it was his double, who proceeded to sit down and dictate the remainder of Maupassant's composition before vanishing.

The experience is not fictional and is not confined to writers. Often the image is seen directly facing the observer like a mirror reflection, and sometimes it exactly repeats the observer's actions with appropriate mirror reversal. For example, Lukianowicz tells of a woman who on returning from the funeral of her husband encounters in the dusk of her rooms another woman resembling her in every detail who does whatever she does: when she reaches for the light switch with her right hand the apparition opposite reaches with her left and their hands meet; when she undresses for bed, so does the other; when she lies down, the other lies down beside her. This woman, who had never had the experience before and who seems to have been normal in other respects, knew enough about spiritualistic language to refer to the double as her "astral body." She hoped that the psychiatrist might rid her of it. Lukianowicz describes various other cases of autoscopy in the same report.[19]

The autoscopic hallucination has a definite objective referent, namely, the observer's own body and thus might be thought of as fitting into the backward-curving broken line of Figure 27. Only in certain cases, however, does it simply mirror the body. It may begin that way and then develop more independence; or on the very first

[19] Lukianowicz (1958).

occasion, as in Goethe's case, it may have certain differentiating characteristics. Of course, it always occupies a different locus in space. In a case like Goethe's it also seems to occupy a different moment in time.

Another example of the sort, but where it is the past returning rather than the future approaching, is related by the eminent French neuropsychiatrist, Lhermitte. A woman in perfect health of body and mind was staying up late one evening working at her sewing machine. She thought she heard one of her children stirring about in the bed. She took up the lamp and drew back the door curtain to go to where the child was sleeping:

> What did I see just two steps away? My own image bent over the foot of the bed, enveloped in garments of my own which I had not worn since a particular time; nearly the whole face was turned toward me and the whole attitude of the figure suggested an emotion of deep distress.[20]

As Lhermitte points out, this scene becomes more intelligible when the woman adds that it was precisely there that the dead body of one of her children lay three months before.

Lhermitte believes that it is possible to explain such experiences in terms of lesions of the brain. A case which particularly impressed him was that of his patient Sibylle, a young woman whose double or "astral body," as she called it, was often snatched away into another plane of existence where it had to fight with a very cruel and perverse devil and underwent much suffering. For Sibylle, her double was both body and soul, capable of suffering as a soul and making its presence known as a body. Sometimes she could see it with the eyes of the flesh. "I have seen my astral body as in a mirror," she wrote. "I was a little afraid, for I had enormous eyes, the left blacker than the right, and also I had very slender ankles and long hair."[21] Lhermitte's neurological explanation runs as follows:

> If I have reviewed the case of Sibylle in this chapter, it is because this unfortunate girl, who every night believed herself to be struggling with the most perverse and the most cruel demoniacal powers, was the bearer of a very special cerebral lesion, the result of an attack of epidemic encephalitis at the age of eleven. The illness, serious though it had been, seemed to be completely cured up until the sixteenth year, when there supervened the strange phenomena to which we have just

[20] Lhermitte (1951), p. 134. My translation. Used by permission of Gaston Doin et Cie.   [21] *Ibid.*, pp. 153 f.

alluded. But experience shows us precisely this: that not only is lethargic or epidemic encephalitis characterized by specific cerebral lesions but that these lesions focus upon certain parts of the structure regulating the course of sleep and waking. I can add that it is because of this localization of the lesion that so many patients, either in the course of the acute attack or during the period of convalescence or even long years after apparent cure, become subject to hallucinations, and notably to visual hallucinations and disturbances of sleep.[22]

He goes on to propose that Goethe, Maupassant, Musset, Dostoevsky, and various others who have written from their own experience about autoscopy were likewise suffering from a disease of the nervous system.

Lhermitte's theory brings us back to the problem of perception with which we started. How illuminating is it to say that brain lesions are associated with hallucinations? From a philosophical standpoint, neurological theory of perception in general is open to serious criticism.[23] But suppose we accept neurological theory. Does it help us with our problem? A cerebral tumor or wound or inflammation or circulatory disorder might indeed be expected to yield some kind of nerve activity and thus generate experience. Ordinary perceptions, however, have a similar basis, according to neurological theory. They too occur because of a disturbance of brain tissue. Of course, in the latter case, the disturbance is channeled through the afferent nerves of eye, ear, skin, mucous membrane, etc., rather than through a tumor or wound or inflamed tissue. A neurologist *qua* neurologist might be willing to stay with the neural disturbances and ask no questions about remoter causes, such as objects in space, but this is not our ordinary human attitude in its full innocence; on the contrary, when we experience a definite object it is our immediate, untaught conviction that it is *there*—a thing independent of ourselves the perceivers. Should we as theorists drop into a different attitude as soon as a lesion of the brain is mentioned? Is that the end of the quest? *Can* we, in fact, if we are ourselves the experiencers, brush aside a compelling experience, whether sensory or hallucinatory, by referring it to a neurologist to explain? Should we not dare to ask whether Sibylle's experience of seeing her "astral body" torn away from her and tormented by demons might not be, in a deep under-

[22] *Ibid.*, p. 154.
[23] Hall (1959), p. 78, sums up his criticism in a sentence: "The neurological theory of perception is inadequate in that it omits not some set of mental events standing in relations of cause and effect to neurological ones but the intentionality or referential character of all perception."

standing of it, as realistic a perception as any she could have? It was true, was it not, that her life was being attacked by a cruel and perverse enemy? The doctor's cool observation that she had a brain lesion perhaps expresses the fact less adequately than her hallucinatory vision. Perhaps the filterable virus of encephalitis looks more like a devil than an ultramicroscopic particle when you are personally involved with it. Brain lesion to Lhermitte, demon to Sibylle: Which is the truer picture of reality?

The type of question which I am raising here is perfectly familiar in the literature of existentialism, strange as it may sound to a reader who has never examined the foundations of his belief that there is one "right" way of conceiving the world (either his own way when he is being "objective" or the way of some scientific specialty which he perhaps only half understands) and that every other way must be regarded as somehow abnormal—"subjective," "unscientific," "crazy," "a projection from the Unconscious," etc. It is easy to classify Sibylle as abnormal, but it is not so easy to get away from the practical and theoretical problems she presents. The practical problem is how to rid her of her demons. The brain lesion theory sounds practical; it seems to call for a skilled surgeon—though it turns out that probably such a lesion as Lhermitte indicates is beyond the reach of effective surgery. As for the theoretical problem, it is not clear exactly *how* a lesion in the brain could be experienced by Sibylle in the form of vicious demons tearing at her body. Furthermore, there is a rival theory which might be applied to her case—a theory which says nothing about brain lesions. That is Freud's theory. Freud has argued in "A Neurosis of Demoniacal Possession in the Seventeenth Century" that, in the case he was studying, the Devil was a father-substitute. Now, of course, it could be said that Lhermitte's theory and Freud's are reconcilable. A lesion of the brain might be held responsible for the vivid perception of a devil, whether he were a father-substitute (complete with serpentine penis *and* great pendulous breasts) or no. But how far are we willing to carry this logic of reconciliation? Should we dare to say that the poor neurotic's perception of his true father (before he substituted a bisexual demon for him) was also due to a lesion of the brain? And shall we go on to say that *all* our perceptions are due to lesions of the brain? We seem to have to draw a line somewhere. But where?

The questions pile up, and they are rendered acute by Lhermitte himself. He tells us that there is a type of hallucination—*visual* hallucination—which occurs in those who have lost that part of the brain which is supposed to be responsible for vision. These people are blind in the most absolute neurological sense. The peripherally blind have only lost the use of their eyes; but these, the centrally or cortically blind, have lost the visual projection areas of the brain. The peripherally blind, according to Lhermitte, see darkness, with spatial properties; the centrally blind see nothing at all, neither darkness nor space. The peripherally blind know they are blind, but the others may occasionally be totally unaware of their affliction—because of their hallucinations. Lhermitte mentions a patient suffering from deep lesions of the visual area of the cortex who was convinced that he saw his wife at her customary work and birds and barnyard fowl playing around him, so much so that he would stretch out his hand to caress and feed them. One old man remained aware of his total blindness (due to softening of both occipital lobes) until the day when there surged up before him visions of the sea and mountains, and people so real that he spoke to them though they made no reply. The question has been raised whether this visual experience is not merely the revival of memory images from some other quarter of the brain. Lhermitte answers: "The cortically blind distinguish perfectly between the memory-image which you suggest to them and the hallucinatory image; the first is seen by the mind, the second rises up outside the bodily person and presents itself externalized and objectified."[24]

It appears from Lhermitte's observations that hallucinatory activity no more uses the normal channels of the brain than it uses the normal channels of the sense organs. The hysterics studied by Binet and Lombroso saw things without using their eyes to see them; Lhermitte's centrally blind seem to dispense with the cortical projection areas. From an ordinary neurological view, these are odd and inadmissible reports. The history of science, however, is littered with normal theories slain by abnormal facts, and it may be that eventually such reports as these will be judged factual enough to compel certain theoretical revisions.

The revision is already under way in existentialist psychiatry. It is one of the great points of this contemporary movement that every person, regardless of his psychiatric classification, deserves to be heard as the one authentic authority on the kind of world *he* lives in. That world is not necessarily like our own. This proposition is immediately obvious if we compare the world of an African Pygmy to that of an Eskimo. If we forget some of our assumptions and too-ready

[24] Lhermitte (1951), p. 66.

explanations, according to the existentialists, it is equally obvious that a doctor and his patient, or two friends walking together down the same street, are also not living in the same world, or at least not in the same quarter of it: all we need to do to be convinced is just to listen to them attentively. A second great point is that when a person tells us about his world he is telling us about his personality, because personality is simply a way of being-in-a-world. I am not quite willing to label myself an existentialist, but I accept these two points; and I mention them here to reassure the reader that we have not wandered from our subject.

Professor Flournoy and the medium

The phenomena so far reviewed in this chapter are anchored to some extent, no matter how freakishly, in the common-sense everyday world. Now we turn to experiences which are held by some to transcend all common-sensical bounds, to touch on the supernatural, to put us in direct contact with realities beyond the reach of scientific verification. I refer to mediumistic trance and mystical ecstasy. Though these may prove to be subjects too bizarre, too doubtful, too elusive, too impossible and absurd to come into the mainstream of psychology, I beg the student to keep in mind one thing at least: mediums and ecstatics *do* exist. Here are real people passing through intense experiences. Their behavior may puzzle and astound us, but we cannot always turn the questions aside by ridicule or the charge of fraud or the little swear-words of psychopathology.

Fake mediums and mystics whose aim is to gull the public no doubt abound, but I am not referring to these, no matter how interesting they may be. I am referring to sincere individuals whose experiences convince them (and may also convince scientists of the caliber of William James, Sir Oliver Lodge, and William McDougall, to name a few) that they at times come under the sway of powers not very easy to explain in common-sense or scientific terms. Mediums believe that they have contact with spirits—sometimes with spirits of the dead—through whom they temporarily acquire special knowledge or special abilities. Mystics are in a different class: though mediumistic types of knowledge and ability may appear or seem to appear in them, their whole aim is to adore and serve God with their entire being. Both mediums and mystics, including many of the Catholic saints and Jesus Christ himself, have been classified by modern psychiatrists as hysterical or schizophrenic. The psychiatric diagnosis, however, amounts to little more than a recognition of a resemblance between certain psychiatric patients and these remarkable individuals; it does not tell us much about their experience and behavior and their being-in-the-world, even if we happen to know what terms like "hysterical" and "schizophrenic" mean. It is necessary to examine individual cases and think about the phenomena themselves if we wish to evaluate such personalities and the powers which are claimed for them. Fortunately, a few psychological studies of mediumship do exist. One of the most interesting is a colorfully titled book, *From India to the Planet Mars*, by Théodore Flournoy (1854-1920), a distinguished Swiss psychologist.

Flournoy addresses himself to the task of examining and demolishing the supernatural claims of a charming young medium to whom he gives the fictitious name "Mlle. Hélène Smith." He is not able to reach his negative conclusions, however, without invoking psychological principles (of unconscious mental activity) which, as F. W. H. Myers remarks, were intolerable to official science twenty years before; and Myers presses home the point that the acceptability of these principles is increased for Flournoy and others by the inacceptability of the rival principle of spirit possession.[25] In short, Flournoy's explanations of his charming young woman protect him against belief in discarnate spirits; and they also protect him, if I am not mistaken, against the charming young woman herself.

Flournoy, a professor of psychology at the University of Geneva, describes Mlle. Smith as a beautiful, vigorous woman, about thirty years old. She held a responsible position in a commercial establishment. She also kept house for her mother and still had energy and time left over for long spiritualistic séances on Sundays and sometimes on weekday nights. Her mediumship, strictly amateur, had begun about three years before Flournoy met her in 1894. He speaks highly of her character.

In the trance state Mlle. Smith was extraordinarily impressible. Flournoy happened to fan himself with his straw hat toward the end of one session when her eyes were beginning to flutter open. The result was that for the next several days she claimed that the hat repeatedly appeared as a sharp hallucinatory image a few feet before her eyes—without seeming support and unidentified except for the vague feeling that it had something to do with him. The

[25] Myers (1903), Vol. 2, pp. 130 f.

autonomy of the hat, appearing thus out of context, naturally gave it a supernormal quality for Mlle. Smith. This kind of revivification of the past is used by Flournoy to explain many of her even more remarkable experiences.

For example, Flournoy believes (though he cannot prove) that her subconscious impressibility and her capacity for turning memories into hallucinations are all that are needed to explain an incident which, to Mlle. Smith herself and her spiritualistic friends, seemed a convincing demonstration that her familiar spirit, Leopold, truly existed. Flournoy does not doubt the incident, which concerned a lost breast pin. The pin was only a trinket, but Mlle. Smith valued it enough to look high and low for it and finally insert an advertisement in the "Lost" column of a newspaper. One evening, after some mysterious rappings on her bed, she saw a hand shaking the breast pin before her eyes. At a séance afterwards her spirit, Leopold, by means of table-tilting gave elaborate directions for locating the missing pin and ordered the party of friends to go out immediately with a lantern to search for it. To their amazement they found the pin at the designated spot. "For the psychologist," writes Flournoy,

> this constitutes a very beautiful and interesting example of cryptomnesia, well worthy to figure among the very instructive cases collected by Mr. [F. W. H.] Myers, in which the memory of a subliminal perception (i.e., registered immediately without striking the normal personality) appears as a revelation in a dream of ordinary sleep, or under some equivalent form of automatism. Here is "Leopold"—the subconsciousness of Hélène—who, having felt the pin fall and noticed where it rolled, first manifested himself in a passing nocturnal vision, and then took advantage of the next spiritistic gathering to restore completely her latent memories. It is not necessary to see anything intentional in this restitution, the simple play of association of ideas sufficing to explain that the memory of the pin stored up in a subliminal stratum and stimulated by a desire to recover the lost object might have mechanically reappeared at the moment of the seance, thanks to mediumistic autohypnotization, and gushed forth under the dramatic form, naturally appropriate to the environment, of an apparently supernormal piece of information furnished by Leopold.[26]

It is according to these principles that Flournoy deals with Mlle. Smith's most bizarre performances. He goes farther. He does not admit that the subconscious play of ideas necessitates any con-

[26] Flournoy (1900), pp. 405 f.

ception of a secondary personality. He thinks that Leopold and the other *soi-disant* spirits are purely illusory.

A single fundamental personality, putting the questions and giving the answers, quarreling with itself in its own interior—in a word, enacting all the various roles of Mlle. Smith—is a fitting interpretation, which accords verÿ well with the facts as I have observed them in Hélène, and very much better than the theory of a plurality of separate consciousnesses, of a psychological polyzoism, so to speak. This last theory is doubtless more convenient for a clear and superficial description of the facts, but I am not at all convinced that it conforms to the actual state of affairs.[27]

The professor and the medium appear to entertain rival theories about her personality. Flournoy preserves its unity by invoking subliminal perception, the mechanical association of ideas, and role-playing. She, it seems, follows a different line of reasoning. She too regards herself as a unity, a single self, but she does so by taking her hallucinations and her possessing spirits as independent realities not created or managed by her. From her point of view the halluci-nated straw hat, the hand shaking the breast pin before her eyes, the message delivered by the tilting table are thrust upon her from outside her unitary self; her familiar spirit, Leopold, is an invader from another world, a real independent person who in a previous life (for she believes in reincarnation) was Cagliostro when she herself was Marie Antoinette. None of this can Flournoy admit. He will not charge Mlle. Smith with lying, but he insists that she subconsciously works over information acquired through the sense organs and then brings it into consciousness as an hallucination or as a certain im-pulse to action—like a dramatic impersonator on the stage, but more automatically.

These are rival theories—the professor's and the young lady's—and the partisans are deeply involved emotionally with one another as well as with their theories. We must forget that one is a mature and distinguished professor of psychology and the other younger and unlearned. It would be possible for their roles in the argument to be reversed while the isues remained the same. Mlle. Smith has her own direct experience on her side (Flournoy does not deny it), and she is borne along on powerful feelings. Professor Flournoy has his reputation and the current theories on his side, and he also wishes

[27] *Ibid.*, pp. 118 f.

(I think) to defend himself against spirit-doctrine and the lady who opposes him; and so he applies the opposite of feeling and direct experience, i.e., rationality and inference. He tries to undercut her beliefs with evidence—not her belief in direct experience as such, but her belief that she learns the truth about things in a supernatural way. I will illustrate his procedure in a moment. It consists, in part, of matching her supernatural communications against the knowledge of experts. Obviously, if she makes a statement about history or geography, one can check into it. If one finds nothing to support her, then her statement is left hanging in doubt; on the other hand—and this is the maddening thing—if the evidence, written or spoken, does support her, then the possibility exists that she obtained it by the usual means from that or a similar source. Flournoy does not regard his opponent, however, as a fraudulent trickster; he believes her honest, and he is impressed by the knowledge she communicates and the manner in which she communicates it. He is in a difficult position. He is like the loving parent of a child with mathematical genius who, let us imagine, gives the answer to a problem which the parent cannot solve and does so more rapidly than any expert mathematician in the world could do it; and the child tells the parent that the answer came to him directly, and the parent, though loving and trusting the child, cannot believe it, and besides does not know whether the answer is right; and so he searches through books for the answer, and finds it and finds that the child's answer is right—but at the same moment suffers from the doubt whether the child himself might have found the answer in the very same book, and then lied about it.

The paradox of Flournoy's position comes out clearly in what he calls the "Hindoo cycle." Early in 1895 Mlle. Smith began to have visions (during séances attended by Flournoy) testifying to her prior incarnation as a princess of ancient India. Her familiar spirit, Leopold, who guided her through her trances and communicated with the sitters, was able to inform those around as to what was going on during the trance state. One dramatic somnambulistic pantomime of smiles and tears in April apparently had the following significance:

> Hélène is in India, in her palace of Tchandraguiri, in Kanara, *in 1401*, and she receives a declaration of love from the personage with the curly hair, who is the Prince Sivrouka Nayaka, to whom she has been married for about a year. The prince has flung himself upon his knees, but he inspires in her a certain fright, and she still regrets having left

her native country in order to follow him. Leopold affirms that she will remember, on awaking, in French, all that the prince has said to her in Sanscrit, and that she will repeat to us a part of it, but not all, because it is too private. After awaking she seems in reality to recall clearly her entire dream, and tells us that she found herself on a hill, where they were building; that it was not exactly a city, nor even a village, since there were no streets; that it was rather an isolated place in the country, and that which was being built was not in the form of a house; it had holes rather than windows (a fortress and loop-holes).[28]

To this fragment of a very elaborate story must be added the important fact that in Mlle. Smith's eyes Professor Flournoy himself was the present incarnation of the Prince Sivrouka to whom she, as the Princess Simandini, was married in that remote time in India. Now, Mlle. Smith was an attractive woman, and the professor would have had to be a callous man indeed not to be thrilled a little when his name was tenderly linked with that of the Indian prince of yore; for Mlle. Smith carried some of the amorous passion of her former life over into this, and Flournoy must have known it.

It is not an enviable task to have to question one's own romantic identity in a woman's mind and the authenticity of her love by doing scholarly detective work. But Flournoy was thorough. He consulted dictionaries and encyclopedias: he did not find himself or the princess in them. He consulted Oriental specialists: they shook their heads, and one replied that the very name "Sivrouka" seemed highly unlikely in a Hindoo prince. He still did not give up. In the end he was rewarded. Or was it reward? In an old history by De Marles he found some relevant passages. One was this:

Kanara and the neighboring provinces on the side towards Delhi may be regarded as the Georgia of Hindustan; it is there, it is said, that the most beautiful women are to be found; the natives, however, are very jealous in guarding them, and do not often allow them to be seen by strangers.

And another:

Tchandraguiri, which signifies *Mountain of the Moon,* is a vast fortress constructed, in 1401, by the rajah Sivrouka Nayaka. This prince, as also his successors, belonged to the sect of the Djaïns.[29]

Was this evidence on the side of Mlle. Smith? Not for Flournoy. It only showed that her delusions about a past life in India could have

[28] *Ibid.,* p. 287.   [29] *Ibid.,* p. 299.

been built up by cryptomnesia out of these literary morsels, though in all of Geneva he could find only two copies of De Marles' history, and both of these very dusty. Besides, it seems that the experts did not have much respect for De Marles, and these particular items of information were not given by other sources. It was almost as if De Marles existed solely for the purpose of gulling the spirits and the spiritualists with dubious intelligence!

It is puzzling why Flournoy went to so much trouble to try to prove that Mlle. Smith was a fraud in the face of his denial that she was anything but that. A part of the answer must be that he felt her great charm and, like a psychoanalyst dealing with transference-love, was compelled to protect himself against it where it was most vulnerable, namely on the intellectual side. Reincarnation or no reincarnation, the Hindoo cycle was a very lovely poem, composed out of strong emotions and presented in the most dramatic fashion, and very clearly concerned with the relationship between Mlle. Smith and Flournoy. Their contact ceased not long after the publication of Flournoy's book. The break must have been due as much to Mlle. Smith's having her beliefs about spirits doubted and her emotions treated with indifference as to the fact that a wealthy American lady came along to endow her in her capacity as a medium.[30] I mention these things because I think the investigation of mediumship cannot ever be divorced from the emotional interaction set up between the investigator and the person under investigation. This interaction is both favorable and unfavorable to the investigation—favorable in that it encourages the phenomena to appear (e.g., the Hindoo cycle), and unfavorable in that it puts the investigator in an emotional situation and interferes with an impartial attitude toward what happens. If we add to this difficulty the fact that many psychologists do not care to get mixed up with the "occult," we can see why firsthand studies of mediumship are rare.

Professor Janet and the ecstatic

What is real? That central question, for which the method of external verification adopted by Flournoy was so unsatisfactory, is even more baffling in the case of a religious ecstatic than in the case of a medium. The very fact that ecstatic experiences are religious types them as illusions for some; and since they are often accompanied by alarming bodily conditions, many psychologists dispose

[30] See Schiller (1902).

of them as part of the symptom-complex of some disease, particularly hysteria. This conclusion implies that religion itself is a disease, since mystical ecstasy is one of the important sources of religion. There is no denying that the relationship between hysteria, ecstasy, and religion is close. But should we therefore discard religion? It might be said, and in fact it has been said again and again, that these are not scientific questions and that science should pass them by; but whatever science may have done, scientists at least have not passed them by.

Pierre Janet's masterpiece, *De l'Angoisse à l'Extase*, is a detailed physiological and psychological study of a religious ecstatic confined to a mental hospital and classified as mentally ill. In the first of the two volumes, Janet confesses:

> I have often been surprised to see how religious writers, analyzing ecstasy from the writings of consecrated ecstatics, were accustomed to give as a distinguishing mark of ecstasy the sentiment of the divine, the feeling of being in God, of being a part of God. I used to think they were wrong to define a psychological state by the object imagined by the subject in that state; that a delirium might be psychologically the same no matter what the object, whether loss of fortune or loss of child; that ecstasy ought to be defined by the modification of psychological processes which constitutes it independently of the thought which occupies the mind during this period. I wanted in this connection to avoid the difficulties which religious problems always raise and to study lay ecstasies, in which the ecstasy would have its fundamental psychological characteristics but in which the mind would be thinking about something besides the religious life. I realize today that I was mistaken and those authors were right. Religious thought is intimately entwined with ecstatic thought; the true ecstasies are religious ecstasies.[31]

Several different conclusions might be drawn from this statement, but, lest there be any misunderstanding, it must be pointed out at once that Professor Janet puts no higher estimate on his ecstatic, Madeleine, than Professor Flournoy put on his medium, Hélène. When Janet first encountered Madeleine she was a patient in the Salpêtrière, the famous Paris mental hospital at which Janet did much of his research, particularly on hysteria. Becoming interested in her case, which he believed to be hysteria, he encouraged her to write down her ecstatic experiences and thoughts, on which huge

[31] Janet (1926, 1928), Vol. 1, pp. 127 f. My translation. Used by permission of the Presses Universitaires de France.

manuscript he based much of his study of her. Madeleine writes concerning herself: "I find that after every painful sacrifice my soul is for several days more separated from things and more united to God. The things of earth which wounded me touch me less and less, nothing distracts me from my intimate Union, and I experience ineffable joy."[32] Janet will not let these words stand; if Madeleine had told the truth, he says, she would have written the following instead: "After a great effort to adapt myself to a real situation, I am exhausted, I renounce all adaptation to external things, and I take refuge completely in dreams."[33] And if we in turn translate Janet's words we find him saying that the professor's psychologically trained senses are more to be trusted than all the ecstatic's blissful visions and that the one real thing in her case is not the God or Christ on the Cross which *she* sees but the exhausted body which *he* sees twisting in convulsions or stretched out in rigid immobility on the hospital bed. Could the issue possibly be more sharply joined?

Madeleine sometimes uttered prophecies. Janet, of course, regarded these as nonsense, and so his account furnishes no historical background for evaluating them: they are presented simply as expressions of her pathological state of mind. In 1900, like a modern Cassandra, she was writing:

I should like to be mistaken, but I see that we are going to wade deep in blood and mud. France is very guilty, but she will be terribly punished. The god of today is the golden calf, everything is bought and sold, but the Heavenly Father will reinstate His laws and will purify His children in chastening them. O proud and insane France, thou wilt bow thy head, but the baptism to which thou wilt have to submit will be a baptism of blood since thou no longer believest in that of water. For the moment a veil conceals our wickedness, but it will soon be lifted and our gangrenous wounds, uncovered, will exhale an odor of rottenness. The enemies of France have undertaken to spread among us everywhere dissension, impiety, immorality, and death; they send forth emissaries under orders to corrupt souls and sow the germs of disease. Associations exist for diminishing the population, for leading people into licentiousness and moral ruin. They will make war break out in our midst, then our enemies will crush us. We shall all be chastised by the rod of iron, by fire, and by flood. A horrible scandal will break out in France, serious in quite a different way from that of Panama, and it will first bring in its train a civil and religious war. Then we shall have to do battle with all the nations united by their indignation against us, and they will want to dismem-

[32] *Ibid.*, Vol. 2, p. 567.   [33] *Ibid.*

ber a shrunken and divided France. Russia will bring France under subjection and will render her schismatic. . . . The web of the spider is stretched out everywhere and the poor flies let themselves get caught in it.[34]

No doubt we have here an expression of Madeleine's state of mind, but is that all? She does not foretell the future very precisely, it is true. But should a psychologist entirely ignore the objective reference of her words? They paint a general picture which has some resemblance to the subsequent history of France in the twentieth century. Janet, as he prepared his manuscript for the press in 1926, on reading over these lines by his former patient might have looked back to 1914 and shuddered and looked forward and trembled; but he probably merely shrugged his shoulders and went on with his checking.

Madeleine's ecstatic states were very frequent. During them her major experience was one of love between herself and God. She has an overwhelming awareness of infinite power and infinite submission, of agony and sweetness, of immensely expanding desire; she feels capable of enduring anything for the love of God and incapable of satisfying her own infinite longings:

I should like to seize all the creatures, to embrace them all while speaking to them of God, for they all speak to me of God; I embrace the birds, I embrace the flowers in the garden. I feel my heart filling up more and more with a mad love which calculates no longer, which no longer sees, no longer reasons; my transports are such that I make extravagant gestures. It is worse than ever, I can no longer bear this torrent of impressions at once delicious and agonizing, I am mad and I am becoming mad with loving, it is very true that I am mad, that I have the madness of love and I do not want to be cured of it. I want to love still more, I want to see love embracing everything, transforming everything, deifying everything. I feel that it will require not less than an eternity to satisfy my thirst for loving God and all the souls in Him, my love wants to embrace heaven and earth, waves of love swell the universe to the bursting point. I no longer have any thoughts, any words, I have nothing more than a cry: I love, I love, I love, I am loved, I am loved, I am loved!!![35]

Janet, sighing wearily, remarks that the psychologist, unable to share in this beautiful emotion, must endeavor to discriminate between the real and the imaginary in it. In his opinion it is a case of

[34] *Ibid.*, Vol. 1, pp. 169 f.
[35] *Ibid.*, pp. 80 f.

28 *Janet's patient, Madeleine, though not a trained artist, often produced creditable drawings and paintings. Here is a Nativity. (From Janet, 1926, 1928)*

mortal flesh being wasted on an empty concept. He admits that she has her hallucinations and that in fact her hallucinations are numerous and vivid, ranging through the whole life of Christ, from birth to crucifixion. (Madeleine was, incidentally, an untrained artist and produced with meticulous brushwork some creditable pictures which indicate her powers of visualization. The charming nativity scene of Figure 28 is an example.) Of her visual imagination in a nonecstatic state, Madeleine writes:

> I can contemplate internally a host of things as if it were a matter of pictures projected by a magic lantern. This faculty of imagining persons in a vivid manner is greater the more I advance in the love of God: the divine love is like a telephone which makes distances vanish. Portraits of people are no longer useful to me, I see them better in my heart than when I look at their photographs.[36]

It is not on her visual experiences, however, either in or out of ecstasy, that Madeleine lays stress. It is rather on the experience of divine love. Her thoughts were continually directed toward God, and she often was acutely aware of God's love at work in her sur-

[36] *Ibid.*, p. 87.

roundings as well as in herself. When she was imprisoned as a vagrant at Saint-Lazare she caught sight of a little flower growing out of a crack in the stone wall, and it was for her like a bouquet sent from God. Her general attitude is well expressed in the following words:

I often take pleasure in contemplating little insects. For example, to save the lives of little flies that fall into the milk, I pick them out, wash them, and see them complete their toilet on my finger. They then seem tame, and I can examine them at leisure; afterwards I stimulate them to fly away. One of these flies seemed to recognize me and be grateful; I soon became passionately attached to it, I was happy that it did not want to leave me, and I felt a great solicitude for it. While contemplating it I thought how God also takes pleasure in disengaging my soul from the glue of worldly things and how, when it is entirely detached and purified, it will at last take its flight. Then an interior voice said to me: "Will you go on being amazed that God deeply loves man although he is but an atom before Him? What you have wanted to do for this fly, God has really done for you. He has given you an immortal soul. He has sacrificed His life to save you. He gives you His body and His blood for nourishment in the sacrament of the Eucharist. Your love toward Him is quite powerless, but He is God. He can do everything. Is it then surprising that He places His omnipotence at the service of His love?"[37]

Janet has little patience with this manner of interpreting the world. He says that it is too easy a way of getting the answers you want. He even accuses Madeleine at times of playing a game; and her ecstatic state is *"cette comédie,"* even when it is a case of agonized participation in the crucifixion. It is clear that he rejects the beliefs which are fundamental for her, and he objects to the theory and practice of a boundless divine love. As Janet says, Madeleine was not a psychologist like himself and so she did not know that her beautiful experiences were nothing but the reflection of bodily processes. Madeleine on her side could have retorted (though she did not) that Janet was not a mystic and did not know that the human body is the temple of the Holy Spirit.

Though Janet regarded Madeleine as a pathological case, a poor woman afflicted with a strange disease, he did not deny her a certain respect, tinged with amusement. Her life was consistent. It was more or less consciously modeled on the life of Saint Francis of Assisi. She had in fact devoted herself to poverty, humility, and charitable works for many years before she arrived at the hospital. Even there

[37] *Ibid.,* pp. 85 f.

she caused no trouble, and when her strength permitted she proved very good at nursing the other patients. After leaving the hospital she returned home, where she continued her life of austere self-denial and mystical contemplation and seized any opportunity to be practically helpful to others. It is important to recognize that she did not seek notoriety. It was by accident that she came to Janet's attention in the hospital, and it was at his request and under his urging that she wrote the two thousand pages of manuscript upon which his book is based. Janet judges her prose style to be well above the average, her verse not quite so good, and her pictures remarkable. He says that she was a good woman. She was forty-two at the time she entered the Salpêtrière, and she stayed there several years —how many is not clear. During her residence she experienced stigmatization of hands and feet and breast some twenty-two times, occasionally under as strict controls as Janet could devise. She seems to have looked on Janet as a kind of agnostic father confessor, and she continued to write to him after her return home. A heart condition which also afflicted her gradually became worse, and she finally died of a heart attack in April 1918, at the age of sixty-four. To the end she remained faithful to her life of prayer though the ecstasies were rarer, and her death was peaceful.

A simple theory of ecstasy

True ecstatics are rare. That is why documents like the writings of Madeleine are unusually precious to the psychologically inquisitive. Even more precious are the writings of world-famous ecstatics like Saint Teresa of Avila and Saint John of the Cross. For the religious, of course, they have a higher value still, but because of the content which to a rationalist like Janet is unimportant. Yet for all the rarity of ecstasy and its special value (at least as a medical curiosity), it cannot be completely dissociated from one of the commonest of human phenomena, dreams. Ecstasy is certainly kin to dreaming, and we all dream. Any theory of the one is, at least in part, a theory of the other.

We have already been over several theories of dreaming. I do not intend to lengthen this chapter by any further theorizing on that topic, but there is an experimental study which I should like to mention, and a theoretical viewpoint latent in Freud which I should like to emphasize.

Several years ago some investigators at McGill University began a study on the practical question of why it is that people who have to give prolonged attention to a monotonous object such as a radar screen often fail to respond when the event they have been waiting for occurs. In the course of this study they stumbled on the fact (they were genuinely surprised) that people who are cut off from a varying sensory input often have hallucinations. The McGill subjects, healthy male college students, were paid to lie on a comfortable bed in a lighted cubicle for continuous long periods of time (two or three days or more), wearing gloves and long cuffs to limit tactual perception, goggles that transmitted only diffused light, and with hearing limited by the soundproofing of the room, masking noises, and a U-shaped foam-rubber pillow (containing earphones) in which they had to bury their heads. They were allowed to break the monotony by eating and going to the toilet occasionally. The subjects, though they were being well paid, soon found these conditions of ease disagreeable. Hallucinations were partly responsible for their dissatisfaction. The experimenters were unaware at first of what was going on. As they report,

> Among our early subjects there were several references, rather puzzling at first, to what one of them called "having a dream while awake." Then one of us, while serving as a subject, observed the phenomenon and realized its peculiarity and extent.[38]

They had already run eight subjects. They had not questioned them on the phenomenon systematically because of their unpreparedness for it; but they did question the remaining fourteen. All those questioned reported hallucinatory imagery, which they said was a new experience for them. The hallucinations were varied and included visual, auditory, tactual, kinesthetic, and somesthetic elements. One subject reported getting an electric shock when he reached out to touch a doorknob, visually hallucinated. Two experienced the phenomenon of the double, at least to the extent of finding themselves with two overlapping bodies. Figure 29 is a drawing made by one subject to illustrate what he meant. There were numerous other odd experiences. The subjects reacted in different ways, some with amused interest, some with annoyance, some complaining that the hallucinations were so vivid as to interfere with sleep.

The general theory suggested by Bexton, Heron, and Scott's study is that hallucinatory activity is held in check by sensory

[38] Bexton, Heron, and Scott (1954), p. 73.

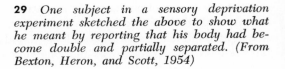

29 *One subject in a sensory deprivation experiment sketched the above to show what he meant by reporting that his body had become double and partially separated. (From Bexton, Heron, and Scott, 1954)*

bombardment and that it emerges when this bombardment is sufficiently reduced. Hallucinatory experience, according to this theory, would have to be regarded as not only a normal but a universal human capacity. Its association with so-called abnormal states may mean nothing more than that these states—whether by brain injury, chemical changes, drug ingestion, intense concentration, or other conditions—releases the normal hallucinatory function by reducing sensory input. The importance of closing the sensory channels is demonstrated by the dreaming of ordinary sleep. It is also noteworthy that all those who deliberately cultivate hallucinatory experience or who experience hallucinations as an incident in their religious exercises typically insist on the need for reducing sensory input—by retiring to a solitary place, closing the eyes in prayer, ceasing to be concerned about the environment, and rendering the body immobile and insensitive. Even self-flagellation, practiced by some ascetics, may contribute to the same end by drowning out other sensations, though at first sight it may look like sensory bombardment. If we think about ascetic practices from this angle—as a technique for replacing sensory perception with hallucinatory perception and even passing beyond to a pure state of consciousness free of all imagery—we shall probably have to surrender the limited notion that all ascetics are masochists chiefly interested in self-punishment. On the contrary, they may be deliberate seekers after a special kind of illumination which can be obtained, according to certain views which are by no means naïve, only by a special kind of discipline.

Mystics of this stripe, far from being vague sentimentalists or victims of disease, are rather the equivalent of experimental scientists, taking their own consciousness instead of the external world as the focus of their experimental operations. The greatest mystics, however, like the greatest experimental scientists, know that technique is not everything. Mystical illumination also depends—perhaps, chiefly depends—on what in theological language is called the grace of God.[39] The Freudian viewpoint which I wish to emphasize is that the activity giving rise to dreaming is prior to sensory perceiving of the external world; it is, in his terminology, the *primary* process, to which sensory perceiving of the external world is *secondary*. On this view ordinary waking perception is simply a special modification of unconscious activities adjusted to space-time operations.[40] This well-known Freudian position is completely in line with the experimental results of Bexton, Heron, and Scott, and the world-wide, age-old doctrine and practice of ascetic mysticism.

A simple theory of ecstasy, prompted by the foregoing reflections,

[39] For a serious introduction to mysticism, see Hügel (1927), Underhill (1929), Butler (1927), Zaehner (1957).

[40] I am prepared to admit that the above statement about Freud's primary and secondary processes may be wrong. I have read the section entitled "The Primary and Secondary Processes" in *The Interpretation of Dreams* many times, but I confess that it is full of obscurities for me. As well as I can make out, Freud postulates two psychic systems with opposed characteristics: the first system can only seek motor discharge, can only wish; the second can inhibit the first and steer it by means of a roundabout process of thought (and attention to the external world through the sense-organs?) to "real" gratification. This second system develops out of the first. The activity of the first system is the "primary process," that of the second the "secondary process." I will now quote what looks like a key passage, though it may not help the reader of this book any more than it has helped me: "When I termed one of the psychic processes in the psychic apparatus the *primary* process, I did so not only in consideration of its status and function, but was also able to take account of the temporal relationship actually involved. So far as we know, a psychic apparatus possessing only the primary process does not exist, and is to that extent a theoretical fiction; but this at least is a fact: that the primary processes are present in the apparatus from the beginning, while the secondary processes only take shape gradually during the course of life, inhibiting and overlaying the primary, whilst gaining complete control over them perhaps only in the prime of life. Owing to this belated arrival of the secondary processes, the essence of our being, consisting of unconscious wish-impulses, remains something which cannot be grasped or inhibited by the preconscious; and its part is once and for all restricted to indicating the most appropriate paths for the wish-impulses originating in the unconscious." (Freud, 1950, pp. 454 f.)

would be that it is a condition arrived at by withdrawing from the world of sense-organ perception and standing at the far end of the continuum of intense experiences provided for by the primary process (Freud). It should be added, however, that arrival at that point depends not only on contemplative technique but on a special constitution also—a constitution more often found in women than in men and frequently but misleadingly (because pejoratively) labeled "hysterical." This constitution includes a great capacity for becoming identified with, possessed by, united to one's loved objects.

To make it plain that the ecstatic state is not restricted to people in hospitals, like Janet's Madeleine, I will conclude this discussion with a few excerpts from the autobiography of Saint Teresa of Avila (1515-1582), the great Spanish mystic, who in Janet's era might have been inhabiting the Salpêtrière instead of reforming the Carmelites. This autobiography, written at the bidding of her confessor, is largely an account of her prayer experiences. She distinguishes four levels or degrees of prayer: meditation, quietude, sleep of the mental faculties, and union. I will refer here only to the last two.

Teresa describes the prayer of the sleep of the faculties thus:

. . . This state is a sleep of the faculties, which are neither wholly lost nor yet can understand how they work. The pleasure and sweetness and delight are incomparably greater than in the previous state, for the water of grace rises to the very neck of the soul, so that it is unable to go forward, and has no idea how to do so, yet neither can it turn back: it would fain have the fruition of exceeding great glory. It is like a person holding the candle in his hand, who is soon to die a death that he longs for; and in that agony it is rejoicing with ineffable joy. This seems to me to be nothing less than an all but complete death to everything in the world and a fruition of God. I know no other terms in which to describe it or to explain it, nor does the soul, at such a time, know what to do: it knows not whether to speak or to be silent, whether to laugh or to weep. This state is a glorious folly, a heavenly madness, in which true wisdom is acquired, and a mode of fruition in which the soul finds the greatest delight.[41]

And she says, further on, in words reminiscent of Janet's patient, but reminiscent also of the Psalmist and Beethoven:

[41] From *The Complete Works of Saint Teresa of Jesus, Vol. I,* in the translation of E. Allison Peers, from the critical edition of P. Silverio de Santa Teresa, C.D., published by Sheed & Ward, Inc., New York, 1944. Vol. 1, p. 96.

O God, what must that soul be like when it is in this state! It would fain be all tongue, so that it might praise the Lord. It utters a thousand holy follies, striving ever to please Him Who thus possesses it. I know a person who, though no poet, composed some verses in a very short time, which were full of feeling and admirably descriptive of her pain: they did not come from her understanding, but, in order the better to enjoy the bliss which came to her from such delectable pain, she complained of it to her God. She would have been glad if she could have been cut to pieces, body and soul, to show what joy this pain caused her. . . .[42]

She goes on to remark that this experience illuminates the conduct of the martyrs: they received their strength from God and scarcely felt the tortures to which they submitted. Still, this is not the highest state of prayer; for a residue of images and recollections may continue to flit around, like moths, slightly annoying though not really harmful.

In the prayer of union with God, the highest degree, the last restraints disappear. The faculties are abolished. The body becomes powerless, and the soul is unable to communicate the happiness which it experiences. In fact, it is a prime characteristic of the prayer of union that no communication with the external world takes place. The soul is completely absorbed in God as in a great fire; and, being absorbed, it is transfigured, as a piece of black iron thrown into fire becomes incandescent. Or, in Teresa's favorite metaphor of the garden, it is as if the soul were inundated by a storm of rain and every flower in it opened and shed abroad its perfume. The great gift comes when least expected, though nearly always after long mental prayer. There are marked bodily effects:

While seeking God in this way, the soul becomes conscious that it is fainting almost completely away, in a kind of swoon, with an exceeding great and sweet delight. It gradually ceases to breathe and all its bodily strength begins to fail it: it cannot even move its hands without great pain; its eyes involuntarily close, or, if they remain open, they can hardly see. If a person in this state attempts to read, he is unable to spell out a single letter: it is as much as he can do to recognize one. He sees that letters are there, but, as the understanding gives him no help, he cannot read them even if he so wishes. He can hear, but he cannot understand what he hears. He can apprehend nothing with the senses, which only hinder his soul's joy and thus harm rather than help him. It is futile for him to attempt to speak:

[42] *Ibid.*, pp. 97 f.

his mind cannot manage to form a single word, nor, if it could, would he have the strength to pronounce it. For in this condition all outward strength vanishes, while the strength of the soul increases so that it may the better have fruition of its bliss. . . .[43]

And the soul may be completely ravished away:

> In these raptures the soul seems no longer to animate the body, and thus the natural heat of the body is felt to be very sensibly diminished: it gradually becomes colder, though conscious of the greatest sweetness and delight. No means of resistance is possible, whereas in union, where we are on our own ground, such a means exists: resistance may be painful and violent but it can almost always be effected. But with rapture, as a rule, there is no such possibility: often it comes like a strong, swift impulse, before your thought can forewarn you of it or you can do anything to help yourself; you see and feel this cloud, or this powerful eagle, rising and bearing you up with it on its wings.[44]

Whether this statement is taken literally or not (and she means it literally), it is perfectly clear that rapture or ecstasy is an extraordinary experience. The cataleptic or nearly dead body is attended by intense consciousness, a consciousness of such power and delight that everything else shrinks into insignificance beside it; and this consciousness, so sharply alive in contrast to the body, is for Teresa irresistible proof of Divine Love.

It would be interesting to know what the consensus of modern psychological opinion on Teresa would be. I can only guess. I think it would be very similar to Janet's opinion, so fully expressed in his study of Madeleine. The reason I cannot be more definite is that the topic of mysticism is usually avoided. One of the most recent psychological studies of religion, though avoiding extensive treatment of the subject on the grounds of lack of statistical evidence, does not hesitate to summarize a series of psychopathological diagnoses, in which Teresa is included, in the following uncompromising style:

> *Summary.* Some minor religious leaders have clearly been suffering from paranoia, hysteria, schizophrenia or other mental disorders. Many well-known religious leaders and mystics have had symptoms resembling those of the same disorders, but have also lived more organized and productive lives than would be possible had they been genuinely mad.[45]

[43] *Ibid.*, pp. 108 f.   [44] *Ibid.*, pp. 119 f.
[45] Argyle (1958), pp. 111 f.

30 *Bernini's famous sculpture of St. Teresa in ecstasy is, of course, not based upon observation of Teresa herself, but it does realistically portray the appropriate facial expression.*

It is the last sentence which applies to Teresa. I hope that my own presentation, which I suppose would express a minority opinion among psychologists, has made it clear that I see a good deal more in Teresa—and in Madeleine—than hysteria.

Commentary

In this chapter I have been trying to expand the reader's conception of human experience (hence, human personality) by bringing forward examples of reported telepathy, veridical hallucination, autoscopy, mediumship, and mystical ecstasy. Such material raises questions about one's theory of perception. I hope that the reader will agree with me that it makes some difference what theory one adopts. If one's theory rules out the possibility that experiences of telepathy, conversation with spirits, union with God, etc., might be referential (i.e., pointed toward realities beyond the perceiver himself), then reports of such events will have to be treated as erroneous, deluded, or crazy. If one's theory, on the other hand, admits the possibility that such experiences might be referential, then the reports may be treated with more respect. Please notice, however, that to frame hypotheses like that diagramed in Figure 27 is *not* equivalent to stating a belief.

On grounds of personal experience and trust in the reported experiences of others, I myself accept telepathy and think there may be some rules governing it. It may be that my own usual skeptical attitude toward such experiences in myself interferes with their occurrence; in fact, I believe this. As to mediumship and ecstasy, my state of mind is more confused. I am deeply moved by accounts of these conditions and I regard mystical experience as a profound source of valuable insights into the meaning of life; but I am perplexed by many of the details.

Some readers may wonder why I have not presented and examined the parapsychological work of J. B. Rhine and his associates. It is not because I have a low opinion of that work, which I believe has been honestly and scientifically done. My main reason is that I have wished to concentrate here on questions of experience and not on questions of experimental verification and control of psi faculties. A secondary reason is that I thought I could not handle the many complex logical, experimental, and statistical questions connected with that work as briefly as would have been necessary in this chapter.[46]

References for chapter 14

Argyle, M. (1958) *Religious behaviour*. London: Routledge & Kegan Paul.

[46] A good introduction to the aims and methods of the Rhine group is Rhine and Pratt (1957).

Bexton, W. H., Heron, W., and Scott, T. H. (1954) Effects of decreased variation in the sensory environment. *Canadian Journal of Psychology,* 8, 70-76.

Brown, W. (1929) *Science and personality.* New Haven: Yale Univ. Press.

———— (1932), Psychology and psychical research. *Proceedings of the Society for Psychical Research,* 41, 75-88.

Butler, Dom C. (1927) *Western mysticism.* London: Constable.

Flammarion, C. (1900) *L'inconnu.* New York: Harper.

Flournoy, T. (1900) *From India to the planet Mars.* Tr. by D. B. Vermilye. New York: Harper.

Freud, S. (1950) *The interpretation of dreams.* Tr. by A. A. Brill. New York: Modern Library.

Greear, M. W. (1958) In memoriam, III. *Georgia Review,* 12, 365-71.

Hall, E. W. (1959) The adequacy of a neurological theory of perception. *Philosophy and Phenomenological Research,* 20, 75-84.

Hügel, F. von (1927) *The mystical elements in religion.* New York: Dutton. 2 vols.

Janet, P. (1926, 1928) *De l'angoisse à l'extase.* Paris: Alcan. 2 vols.

Krech, D., and Crutchfield, R. S. (1958) *Elements of psychology.* New York: Knopf.

Lhermitte, J. (1951) *Les hallucinations.* Paris: Doin.

Lukianowicz, N. (1958) Autoscopic phenomena. *American Medical Association Archives of Neurology and Psychiatry,* 80, 199-220.

MacRobert, R. G. (1950) Hallucinations of the sane. *Journal of Insurance Medicine,* 5, No. 3 (July), 3-12.

Mitchell, G. W. (1876) $X + Y = Z$; *or the sleeping preacher of north Alabama.* New York: W. C. Smith.

Myers, F. W. H. (1903) *Human personality and its survival of bodily death.* London: Longmans, Green. 2 vols., Vol. 2.

Payne-Gaposchkin, C. (1954) *Introduction to astronomy.* Englewood Cliffs, N.J.: Prentice-Hall.

Rhine, J. B., and Pratt, J. G. (1957) *Parapsychology: frontier science of the mind.* Springfield, Ill.: Thomas.

Rhine, L. E. (1956) Hallucinatory psi experiences. I. An introductory survey. *Journal of Parapsychology,* 20, 233-56.

Schiller, F. C. S. (1902) Review of Flournoy's *Nouvelles observations sur un cas de somnambulisme avec glossolalie. Proceedings of the Society for Psychical Research,* 17, 245-51.

Schmeidler, G. R., and McConnell, R. A. (1958) *ESP and personality patterns.* New Haven: Yale Univ. Press.

Sidis, B. (1904a) An inquiry into the nature of hallucinations. I. *Psychological Review,* 11, 15-29.

———— (1904b) An inquiry into the nature of hallucinations. II. *Psychological Review,* 11, 104-37.

————, and Goodhart, S. P. (1919) *Multiple personality*. New York: Appleton.

Thurston, H., S.J. (1952) *The physical phenomena of mysticism*. Chicago: Regnery.

Tyrrell, G. N. M. (1951) *Homo faber: a study of man's mental evolution*. London: Methuen.

Underhill, E. (1929) *The mystic way: a psychological study in Christian origins*. London: Dent.

Zaehner, R. C. (1957) *Mysticism, sacred and profane*. Oxford: Oxford Univ. Press.

15

PSYCHOSOMATICS

Preview   *The psychosomatic approach in medicine is a recognition that the human being is more than a visible body. Disease and death affect a psychophysical whole: the sick and the dying are not simply bodily machines out of fix, but conscious persons in the midst of their experiences which are sometimes very strange and terrifying. Furthermore, there are many cases where a "purely subjective" experience seems to precipitate the bodily changes of disease. Concern with such interrelations has led to various attempts to establish lawful connections between mental states and bodily states; and this is a challenging field of work, even though the suggested laws are thus far extremely tentative.*

The term "psychosomatic" appears more and more frequently in medical literature. At the clinical level, as Laín Entralgo points out and documents,[1] doctors from time immemorial have treated the patient as a whole human being, with thoughts and wishes and emotions and hopes and fears as well as a body. But at the level of theoretical explanation of disease, they have often and in some eras prevailingly emphasized physical causation—brain lesions, microbic infection, vitamin deficiency, etc.—to the virtual exclusion of those other aspects of the whole psychophysical being which it is convenient to designate by the term "mind." There are indications that the coldness which patients (justly or unjustly) sometimes complain of when speaking of doctors and hospitals can be traced back to this kind of theoretical orientation. We might expect a psychosomatic outlook to lead to fuller doctor-patient interaction and also to novel ideas on the treatment of disease.

In fact, Freud had a psychosomatic outlook, and it led to both the above-mentioned results. Much that goes under the heading of psychosomatics today is directly traceable to him. Yet it is clear that Freud's thought has not, at the theoretical level, persuaded even some of his followers that the *psychic* factors deserve quite the stress he gave them. In a recent volume edited by Felix Deutsch and titled *On the Mysterious Leap from the Mind to the Body,* after a phrase of the master's and in honor of the hundredth anniversary of his birth, all the ten M.D. discussants of the question whether the phrase was warranted expressed the conviction, with varying degrees of firmness, that the phrase was misleading: they objected both to the "mysterious leap" and to the mind-body dualism.[2]

One often detects signs of uneasiness in the psychosomatic literature. Hamilton deplores the mind-body implications of the title of his own book, *Psychosomatics.*[3] In the collection of medical essays edited by Desmond O'Neill under the title *Modern Trends in Psychosomatic Medicine,* there are many warnings against being too psychosomatic.[4] One of the leaders of psychoanalysis in this country, Franz Alexander, is at pains to assure his medical colleagues that he is anything but a psychophysical dualist, again and again recurring to the theme that their suspicions are unfounded. He writes at one point:

[1] Laín Entralgo (1956). This book (see References for this chapter) is a brief but learned history of the mind-body problem in medicine, written by the Rector of the University of Madrid Medical School.
[2] Deutsch (1959), pp. 11-26.
[3] Hamilton (1955), p. 3 f.   [4] O'Neill (1955).

The term "psychosomatic" has been subjected to much criticism, chiefly because it seems to imply a dichotomy between mind and body. This dichotomy is precisely what the psychosomatic point of view tries to avoid. And if we understand psychic phenomena as the subjective aspect of certain physiological (brain) processes, this dichotomy disappears.[5]

Undoubtedly the dichotomy disappears, but so also does the stress on the psychic—since mind is thus made into an epiphenomenon of the brain. At another point Alexander writes:

> The recognition of psychological forces, a psychological approach to the problems of life and disease, appears to some as a relapse to the ignorance of the dark ages when disease was considered as the work of an evil spirit and therapy was exorcism, the expelling of the demon from the diseased body.[6]

He naturally rejects any such interpretation of the theory and practice of psychoanalysis, but it is obvious that he would not have mentioned this criticism or the one above if he had not been aware that many of his associates in medicine had suspicions about this attempt to bind psyche (soul, mind) and soma (body) together.

Freud was perfectly conscious of his break with the somatic orientation of the medical theory of his day and evidently took delight in challenging it. Perhaps Alexander would have had an easier time with critics if the master had not been so brash. But there can be little doubt that Freud meant seriously what he wrote in a 1923 essay:

> Despite the somatic ideology of the era of "exact" science, the demonological theory of these dark ages has in the long run justified itself. Cases of demoniacal possession correspond to the neuroses of the present day; in order to understand these latter we have once more had recourse to the conception of psychic forces. What in those days were thought to be evil spirits to us are base and evil wishes, the derivatives of impulses which have been rejected and repressed. In one respect only do we not subscribe to the explanation of these phenomena current in mediaeval times; we have abandoned the projection of them into the outer world, attributing their origin instead to the inner life of the patient in whom they manifest themselves.[7]

[5] Alexander (1950), p. 49.　　　　　　　　　　[6] *Ibid.*, p. 18.
[7] Freud (1925), Vol. 4, pp. 436 f., "A neurosis of demoniacal possession in the seventeenth century."

These are strong words, but they are not too strong to indicate Freud's true position on the psychosomatic question.

I wish to make it plain to the reader that I myself incline toward a psychophysical dualism and that, for theoretical purposes, the sharp distinction between mind and body which Descartes made seems to me useful. This view may be wrong, of course; but I state it definitely here because it affects my analysis, whether right or wrong, of psychosomatic problems, and the reader should be aware of it. I wish to add, however, that I share with existentialist writers the view that "mind" is probably never in actuality a pure subjectivity, i.e., never thought or wish or emotion or feeling or the like quite separated from some appropriate object. When we think, we think about something; and our wishes and emotions and feelings always (are there ever exceptions?) refer beyond themselves to something. I believe that I have maintained this position through all the preceding chapters, but it needs special emphasis here and further clarification.

We exist within a world, a world of objects peculiarly our own and never quite the same for any two people. To know a person we have to know about this world of his. We can, of course, detect fear or some other emotion in him without knowing what he is being emotional about. But emotion so perceived is too general, almost abstract; in order to know *his* emotion we have to discover the nature of the world of objects within which the emotion operates. As Spinoza said long ago, our happiness (and likewise other states of mind) depends on the nature of the object to which we are attached. When we inquire into the nature of an individual personal world, however, we are often tempted to ignore or twist to our own liking those features of the description which to us "make no sense" or seem to defy the "laws of science." In the case of a sick person, for instance, we are ready to notice an alteration in his body and give credence to his statement that he is in pain—i.e., we pay some attention to both sides of the psychophysical whole (the visible body and the invisible pain)—but we may not ask about or give full value to his experience of the world around him. Yet it is a significant part of his illness, as Van den Berg says, if the wallpaper looks different to him, if the telephone has a different sound, if in general his world has a new, sick physiognomy.[8] Those whom we call neurotic or psychotic (as if the terms mattered!), and the dying, often tell us about worlds that

[8] Van den Berg (1955), pp. 34 f.

516 THE PERSONAL WORLD

are amazingly different from that good, common-sense world of our own to which we would like to restore them. To the extent that we shrink away from them in unbelief or try vigorously to correct their "distorted" view of things with cheerful admonitions or "scientific" explanations, we cut ourselves off from them, we fail to understand them; and, on the theoretical level, we develop conceptions of personality which are not in touch with all the pertinent facts.

It is because I share in the existentialist emphasis on the importance—both practical and theoretical—of the personal world that I have dared to mention demonic experiences, and will do so again in this chapter. I think these experiences are important for any theory of personality, and I think furthermore that they are pedagogically useful because they bring out so strongly the fact that personal worlds *are* different. To return to Lhermitte's patient, Sibylle—we surely cannot understand her, perhaps it would never have occurred to anybody that she was a medical case, unless those dreadful tormentors who tore at her body and soul were taken into account: it is not just the wallpaper which had changed in her sickroom—her world had been *invaded*, by monsters who were no less monstrous to her because they happen to seem improbable to us. May I assure the reader that I have no special fondness for demons? I have, however, met people and read about people who would no more have been satisfied with the explanation that their demons were a hallucinatory projection of their own invisible repressed wishes than you would be with the explanation that the book in your hand is a hallucinatory projection of your repressed childhood sexual curiosity. It is out of mere respect for raw human experience (inadequately communicated, no doubt) that I claim a place for demons, along with automobiles and "rocks and stones and trees," as real objects in some personal worlds.

To sum up these prefatory remarks, I may say that I approach the psychosomatics of health and disease and dying from the angle of a psychophysical dualist who admits the validity of the existentialist stress on being-in-a-world, a world of varied objects pointed to and permeated by our thoughts and feelings and emotions and wishes and hopes and intentions even while apparently (and I should say, really) existing and acting independently of ourselves. That is to say, I assert that the "I" is really different from its objects, though a constant strong and subtle interaction binds them together into a whole which we call "personality" or "being-in-the-world."

Mind and body

Let us start our psychosomatic analysis with the body, and, first, with the bodies of others. We recognize at once that there is an important distinction between a living body and a dead one, though it may be hard to say just what that distinction is. In fact, it is not a distinction which many of us have had the opportunity (much less the wish) to study very carefully. Hebb writes:

> I took a poll of an undergraduate class of 198 persons, including some nurses and veterans, to see how many had encountered a dead body. Thirty-seven had never seen a dead body in any circumstances, and 91 had seen one only after an undertaker had prepared it for burial; making a total of 65 per cent who had never seen a dead body in, so to speak, its natural state.[9]

In practice as well as in theory the distinction between living and dead presents difficulties. There are states of a living body in which it is so still and so lacking in the vital signs of breathing and pulse that expert observers are amazed that it can resume normal activity. I translate here from Gilles de la Tourette's *Traité clinique et thérapeutique de l'hystérie* an account by Pfendler of his personal experience with a fifteen-year-old girl—who fell into a lethargy after three weeks of repeated convulsive attacks:

> The most famous doctors of the time were called into consultation and declared that she had only two or three days to live. In fact, the following day when I was at the foot of the bed she made a movement, rose up, threw herself on me as if to embrace me, and then fell back as if smitten by death. For four hours I was unable to detect a single trace of life, and with MM. Frank and Schoeffer I tried every possible thing to discover a spark of life in her—neither mirror, nor burnt feather, nor ammonia, nor pin pricks would give us any sign of sensibility; galvanism was employed without the patient showing any contractility. M. Frank even thought she was dead but advised me to leave her in bed still. For twenty-eight hours, no change; already it seemed that one could faintly smell the odor of decay; the death bell had rung, her friends had just finished dressing her in white and crowning her with flowers, everything was in readiness for the burial. To convince myself that decay was in progress, I again approached Mlle de M. . . . but it was no further along than before; and what was my astonishment when I thought I noticed a slight respiratory movement! I examined her again, and I saw that I was not mistaken. Thereupon I applied massage and irritants, and, after an hour and a half,

[9] Hebb (1958), p. 341.

respiration increased, the patient opened her eyes, and amazed at the trappings of death regained consciousness and said to me with a laugh, "I am too young to die!" She was carried then into another apartment where she was soon overcome by a sleep which lasted for ten hours. Convalescence proceeded quite rapidly with the aid of aromatic baths and tonics, and the patient, her nervous system entirely clear of its morbid state, appeared as fresh and healthy as before.[10]

I regret that my example of apparent death is not more up-to-date. The literature on such topics is hard to come by. Possibly the routine of hospitals, the accuracy of modern methods of examination, our smooth professional handling of illness and preparations for burial, and a relative absence of the old-style family physician who tried to make up for his lack of knowledge and technical equipment by lingering at the bedside, have rendered such accounts obsolete. No doubt there are many devoted doctors and nurses who exhaust themselves in watching over and trying to revive the nearly dead, and it may be that some of them have in recent times observed cases like Pfendler's but have not written on them; but, at any rate, my efforts to find modern descriptions have been unavailing. My guess is that similar cases still occur, but that the modern attitude toward death and these ambiguous states of apparent death is less favorable to the kind of clinical description which can be found in the nineteenth-century literature and earlier. I believe it is true (and in saying so I do not mean to be expressing an unfavorable opinion of doctors, who as far as my observations go constitute a very select class of fine human beings) that the philosophical orientation of our times, with its stress on scientific objectivity, its confidence in technology, and a predominantly somatic conception of disease, is such as to discourage serious professional interest in the mental state of the dying or the comatose. By premedical and medical training our doctors are strongly inclined toward the somatic side of the psychosomatic being-in-the-world of their patients, in spite of the influence of Freud and in spite, too, of their own personal capacity for sympathy. Perhaps the diminished religiousness of our times is also to be reckoned with: one is not so likely to pay attention to the last gasps of a mortal as of an immortal soul. In short, for some cause or other, the medical literature on the final or death-like moments is scant.

Sleep itself has some of the ambiguity of death. Elizabeth Madox

[10] Gilles de la Tourette (1895), Vol. 2.1, pp. 222 f. My translation. Used by permission of the Librairie Plon.

Roberts catches this in a poem about a little child searching for her playmate and finding him asleep. Or was he asleep?

> I looked for him everywhere
> Because I wanted him to play;
> And then I found him on his bed
> Asleep, but it was day.
>
> His eyes were shut behind the lids—
> He couldn't lift them up to see.
> And I looked at him very long,
> And something in him looked at me.
>
> And he was something like a cat
> That is asleep, or like a dog;
> Or like a thing that's in the woods
> All day behind a log.
>
> And then I was afraid of it,
> Of something that was sleeping there.
> I didn't even say his name,
> But I came down the stair.[11]

The nearly dead or profoundly sleeping body is like Condillac's imagined statue—capable of experience though deprived of expression. Pfendler says of his case:

> During her lethargic state, when all functions appeared to be suspended, *her energies were concentrated in the sense of hearing, for she understood and was aware of everything that took place around her* and quoted to me afterwards some Latin words of M. Frank's. The most frightful experience for her was to hear the funeral preparations without being able to come out of her state.[12]

The body revealed nothing of the activity of her mind.

The living body in a waking state is generally distinguished from the dead or sleeping body by certain kinds of activity visible to an observer. It might be possible to study these activities in a purely objective spirit. The ordinary observer, however, finds himself interpreting the motions of a human body as expressions of purposeful mind. In fact, he may scarcely notice the body as a space-occupying object at all. Just as an experienced reader concentrates on the mean-

---

[11] From *Under the Tree* by Elizabeth Madox Roberts. Copyright 1922 by B. W. Huebsch, Inc., 1950 by Ivor S. Roberts. Reprinted by permission of The Viking Press, Inc.

[12] Gilles de la Tourette, *ibid.*, p. 223.

ing of a book rather than on the letters and words, so most of us concentrate on what message a human body is conveying rather than on anatomical details.

This is a psychosomatic attitude toward the other person. A purely somatic attitude would leave out the aspect of subjectivity accompanying the body's activities. From such a point of view, a human body, even the body of one's patient or friend, would be regarded as mindless. It would then appear as a three-dimensional object having a certain volume and weight and heat, curiously colored and patterned externally, giving off certain odors and noises because of the working of complicated internal organs, which are so many chemical machines for the transformation of energy, derived from the sun but mediated through ingested fuels (such as meat, potatoes, and vitamin pills), fanned into a quiet blaze by the regular inspiration of air. Broken down by fire, this voluminous body reduces to water and gas and a very small quantity of solid matter. Sliced up into thin sheets for microscopic analysis, it turns out to be composed of billions on billions of cells, each with its glassy essence of protoplasm in knots and strands—so that it can be conceived of in the living state as a vast society of closely packed units throbbing together in incomprehensible unity, every single unit breathing and carrying on the fundamental transactions of life, many of them circulating rapidly in the lymph and blood and being replaced by others as they wear out, many holding fairly steadily to fixed stations in liver or bowel or heart or brain, the whole constituting an enormous perishing universe destined one day to collapse, grow suddenly cold and dark, and dissolve into the primal elements. Such is the mindless body. Huge volumes of anatomy and embryology and physiology do not begin to exhaust its infinite detail. Of the many types of cells in the brain, only a few are slightly known; it is still a matter of speculation how those familiar organs, the muscles, contract; the throbbing of the heart, a hundred thousand beats a day, is a miracle. The body is enough and more than enough. Must we complicate things by adding mind?

We must, because without mind somewhere no body could be known. Mind—as the act of knowing—is necessary in an observer who knows the bodies of others, even if he stops short of attributing minds to these others (as I myself stop short of attributing minds to machines). But the observer who knows these other and possibly mindless bodies knows his own body and, if he admits mind in himself, he must admit that it is closely associated with a body very similar externally to the bodies of those others and hence that it is very likely that those bodies too possess or are possessed by mind. That is one way of reasoning about it. Actually, I think our awareness of the minds of others—their knowing, their willing, their feeling—is ordinarily quite direct and without need of argument; it is only when we become sophisticated and scientific that we feel any need of arguing about it.[13]

Observation of one's own body yields a different set of experiences from those obtained by the observation of another's body. True, we may see our bodies as if they were not our own by means of mirrors and photographs, and by tape recording we may hear our voices as if they were not our own; but the usual visual and auditory experience without these aids is different. Because of the placement of our eyes we see our own bodies from a different angle and in a more limited way than we see the bodies of others, and we see them as no one else can see them. Our voices too are peculiarly our own because of the associated vibrations in the skull and throat. And notice how it is with touch. The experience from sliding one's hand over other surfaces of one's body is distinct from that which follows from sliding it over the surfaces of another's body, because in self-touching sensations arise not only from the exploring hand but also from the explored surface; and this double touch is both united and distinguished within the same consciousness. When I press the palm of my right hand against the palm of my left hand, I feel the warmth and pressure in *both* contacting surfaces, and the muscular and joint strains in *both* arms; but when I press my right hand in exactly the same way against the left hand of someone else, I experience these sensations in only one hand and arm—the one I call mine. When I lie down on a bed in a dark room with my eyes closed, and lie silently without moving, my body becomes for me a vague cloud of organic sensations, pierced here and there by points of itch or tickle, or stabbed at times by pains little or big. One of the things curiously absent or only slightly present in one's own body is the experience of weight: to move someone else is hard work, to move oneself (in a rested, healthy state) is hardly any effort at all. What *is* the body, as experienced from the inside? Well, it is something pretty vague and fluid, something full of possibilities, sharply visible at one moment, invisible at the next, constituted chiefly of pressures and strains at the next, a shifting phantasmagoria. Still, we have an

[13] On the inference of mind in others, see Adams (1928).

idea of its relative permanence. When we go to sleep at night, we expect to find it there again in the morning. Furthermore, it seems to be extremely useful in communicating with others: it flashes pictures to their eyes, sounds to their ears, which tell them pretty well how we feel and what we want. Finally, it is a flexible instrument enabling us to carry out our will on the surrounding world by pushing, pulling, hauling, lifting, lugging, and so on.

The psychosomatic relationship is always prominent in self-observation. If we define mind as the power and act of knowing, the power and act of willing, and the power and act of feeling (or emotion), we can give a precise and empirically useful meaning to mind-body (psychosomatic) questions. In a state of health we are aware of a close psychosomatic harmony; we know our bodies as instruments responsive to our will and suffused with calm power. In a state of disease we know our bodies as disordered instruments rebellious against our will and shot through with pain. Externally considered, from a purely somatic point of view, the body in disease presents some abnormality of appearance, some deviation of temperature or blood chemistry, some unusual activity or inactivity, etc.; but internally considered, from the inevitable psychosomatic point of view of the sick person himself, the body is an instrument turned into an obstacle, a rebellious and unreliable servant, an intimate friend become a vicious enemy, a source of distress and shame and terror, of chills and fevers, of torment by fire and ice and internal tearings and alienation from the surrounding world. Alienation from others is one of the most terrible aspects of disease. Other people shun my disfigured and disordered body, to spare their own feelings or to avoid infection—even relatives and friends do so; and the professional man, the doctor, when he comes, for all his kindness, adds to the tortures by his probings and his treatments, and above all by his failure to communicate with that in me which is not the piece of meat he is inspecting and preparing to lay on the chopping-block but a conscious, frustrated, suffering fellow human being. The alienation, of course, is not simply one-sided. The sick man himself may be unwilling to communicate; loathing his body and the world, he may fight his helpers, turn his face to the wall, and die. Even at the verge of death, even when the observers are saying all is over, there is good empirical reason for believing that mental activity has not ceased. I have mentioned one case where the person was close to death and yet mentally active; I will now bring forward a few others. If they strike the reader as bizarre, as "unscientific," I can only say that I have taken them from sources as unimpeachable as one is likely to find anywhere.

Sir Benjamin Brodie, an eminent medical man of the last century, sergeant-surgeon to Queen Victoria, and once president of the Royal Society, wrote these restrained words:

> I have purposely avoided using the word unconsciousness, for as to that it is plain that we know nothing. The mind may be in operation, although the suspension of the sensibility of the nervous system, and of the influence of volition over the muscles, destroys its connection with the external world, and prevents all communication with the minds of others. It is indeed difficult to say even when the external senses are completely and absolutely closed. I might refer to numerous facts which have fallen under my observation as illustrating this subject; but the following will be sufficient. An elderly lady had a stroke of apoplexy; she lay motionless, and in what is called a state of stupor, and no one doubted that she was dying. But after the lapse of three or four days, there were signs of amendment, and she ultimately recovered. After her recovery she explained that she did not believe that she had been unconscious, or even insensible, during any part of the attack. She knew her situation, and heard much of what was said to those around her. Especially she recollected observations intimating that she would very soon be no more, but that at the same time she had felt satisfied that she would recover; that she had no power of expressing what she felt, but that nevertheless her feelings, instead of being painful or in any way distressing, had been agreeable rather than otherwise. She described them as very peculiar; as if she were constantly mounting upwards, and as something very different from what she had ever before experienced. Another lady, who had met with a severe injury of the head, which caused her to be for some days in a state of insensibility, described herself as having been in the enjoyment of some beatific visions, at the same time that she had no knowledge of what had actually happened, or of what was passing around her. I have been curious to watch the state of dying persons in this respect, and I am satisfied that, where an ordinary observer would not for an instant doubt that the individual is in a state of complete stupor, the mind is often active even at the very moment of death.[14]

After this sober, secondhand account of what it is like to be near death, it may be illuminating to consider a firsthand account from another British physician. Baron Geddes (1879-1954), whose dis-

[14] Brodie (1859), pp. 131-33.

tinguished career included medical practice, a professorship of anatomy, numerous high posts in the British government, service as British ambassador to Washington, private business, further government service in World War II, records in his family biography three separate "thanatoid" (i.e., deathlike) experiences of his own. The first, occurring in 1935 after a severe attack of gastro-enteritis which caused his heart to stop (it was restored to action after a few minutes by an injection of camphor), was reported by him to an expert stenographer while he was in the process of coming back to—what? Not to consciousness; he had never lost consciousness. Not to life; he had not been extinguished. Is there any correct way of putting it, except in terms of the mind coming back to the body? Geddes later included these notes in a bicentenary address to the Royal Medical Society (published in the *Edinburgh Medical Journal,* n.s. IV, vol. XLIV, 1937). A portion, as given in the biography, is this:

. . . at no time did my consciousness appear to me to be in any way dimmed, but I suddenly realized that *my* consciousness was separating from another consciousness, which was also me. These for purposes of description we could call the A and B consciousnesses, and throughout what follows the ego attached itself to the A consciousness. The B personality I recognized as belonging to the body, and, as my physical condition grew worse and the heart was fibrillating rather than beating, I realized that the B consciousness belonging to the body was beginning to show signs of being composite—that is, built up of "consciousnesses" from the head, the heart, the viscera, etc. . . . These components became more individual and the B consciousness began to disintegrate, while the A consciousness which was now me, seemed to be altogether outside my body, which it could see. Gradually I realized that I could see not only my body and the bed in which it was, but everything in the whole house and garden—and then I realized that I was seeing not only "things" at home, but in London and in Scotland, in fact, wherever my attention was directed it seemed to me; and the explanation I received, from what source I do not know, but which I found myself calling to myself my Mentor, was that I was free in a time dimension of space, wherein "now" was in some way equivalent to "here" in the ordinary three-dimensional space of everyday life. I next realized that my vision included not only "things" in the ordinary three-dimensional world, but also "things" in these four or more dimensional places that I was in. From now on the description is and must be entirely metaphorical, because there are no words which really describe what I saw, or rather, appreciated. Although I had no body I had what appeared to be perfect two-eyed vision (one of the eyes had in fact been blind for twelve years) and what I saw can only be described in this way—that I was conscious of a psychic stream flowing with life through time; and this gave me the impression of being visible, and it seemed to me to have a particularly intense iridescence.[15]

He goes on to say that he seemed to himself to be a local area of condensation in the psychic stream, a sort of cloud that was not actually a cloud, and that this condensation was, as it were, colored blue.[16] He recognized several other people as thicker or thinner condensations of different colors—in this inadequate, metaphorical way of putting it. Simultaneously he was aware of the fuss being made over his body and was annoyed that they were trying to resuscitate him: "I came back into the body really angry at being pulled back, and once I was back all the clarity of vision of anything and everything disappeared, and I was just possessed of a glimmer of consciousness which was suffused with pain."[17]

The mind-body relation is anything but fixed. The study of psychosomatics is necessarily concerned with varying relations between dynamic entities.

Emotion, and disease as emotional expression

One aspect of mind is emotion. Emotion generally has noticeable bodily expression. When the emotion is extraordinarily intense, the changes in the body both externally and internally may be so great and so disabling that we classify them under disease. Psychosomatic medicine is often presented as the view that emotions cause disease.

Everyone interested in this particular approach should, of course, be acquainted with Charles Darwin's book on the expression of the emotions, written in 1872. I will quote a few passages here to illustrate his treatment of the subject. Two contrasting emotional states are grief and joy. Of the expression of grief Darwin writes:

[15] Geddes (1952), pp. 351 f. Used by permission of Faber & Faber Ltd.
[16] Cf. Tertullian's quotation from a Montanist sister, in his treatise on the soul: "Amongst other things, there has been shown to me a soul in bodily shape, and a spirit has been in the habit of appearing to me; not, however, a void and empty illusion, but such as would offer itself to be even grasped by the hand, soft and transparent and of an etherial colour." In A. Roberts and J. Donaldson, *The Ante-Nicene Fathers* (New York, Scribners, 1908), Vol. 3, p. 188.
[17] Geddes (1952), p. 352.

After the mind has suffered from an acute paroxysm of grief, and the cause still continues, we fall into a state of low spirits; or we may be utterly cast down and dejected. Prolonged bodily pain, if not amounting to an agony, generally leads to the same state of mind. . . . Persons suffering from excessive grief often seek relief by violent and almost frantic movements . . . but when their suffering is somewhat mitigated, yet prolonged, they no longer wish for action, but remain motionless and passive, or may occasionally rock themselves to and fro. The circulation becomes languid; the face pale; the muscles flaccid; the eyelids droop; the head hangs on the contracted chest; the lips, cheeks, and lower jaw all sink downwards from their own weight. Hence all the features are lengthened; and the face of a person who hears bad news is said to fall. . . . After prolonged suffering the eyes become dull and lack expression, and are often slightly suffused with tears. The eyebrows not rarely are rendered oblique, which is due to their inner ends being raised. This produces peculiarly-formed wrinkles on the forehead, which are very different from those of a simple frown; though in some cases a frown alone may be present. The corners of the mouth are drawn downwards, which is so universally recognized as a sign of being out of spirits, that it is almost proverbial. The breathing becomes slow and feeble, and is often interrupted by deep sighs. As Gratiolet remarks, whenever our attention is long concentrated on any subject, we forget to breathe, and then relieve ourselves by a deep inspiration; but the sighs of a sorrowful person, owing to his slow respiration and languid circulation, are eminently characteristic.[18]

Is this already disease?

Joy is expressed very differently:

Joy, when intense, leads to various purposeless movements—to dancing about, clapping the hands, stamping, &c., and to loud laughter. Laughter seems primarily to be the expression of mere joy or happiness. We clearly see this in children at play, who are almost incessantly laughing. . . . Laura Bridgman, from her blindness and deafness, could not have acquired any expression through imitation, yet when a letter from a beloved friend was communicated to her by gesture-language, she "laughed and clapped her hands, and the colour mounted to her cheeks." On other occasions she has been seen to stamp for joy.[19]

Darwin gives minute descriptions of the characteristic expressions of various other emotions, all of which affect the external appearance of the body, the circulation, respiration, etc., in discriminable ways.

[18] Darwin (1910), pp. 176 f.
[19] Ibid., pp. 196 f.

As far as he can, he tries to relate emotion to his theory of the struggle for existence, but the theory is too narrow to encompass all the facts unless the conception of nature red in tooth and claw is replaced or supplemented by a generous recognition of the cooperative aspects of social existence. Darwin notes:

> The movements of expression in the face and body, whatever their origin may have been, are in themselves of much importance for our welfare. They serve as the first means of communication between the mother and her infant; she smiles approval, and thus encourages her child on the right path, or frowns disapproval. We readily perceive sympathy in others by their expression; our sufferings are thus mitigated and our pleasures increased; and mutual good feeling is thus strengthened. The movements of expression give vividness and energy to our spoken words. They reveal the thoughts and intentions of others more truly than do words, which may be falsified.[20]

Fine as Darwin's descriptions are, they lack the vividness which can only be achieved by a writer's describing a particular person at a particular time. In the following instance we see various emotions in a particular person occurring in rapid succession and affecting the body very powerfully, like a spring day of alternating sunshine and rain moving over a wide landscape. John Wesley, the English theologian, was summoned to a house where a girl of fifteen had fallen into a trance during an afternoon religious service:

> I went down immediately . . . and found her sitting on a stool and leaning against the wall, with her eyes open and fixed upward. I made a motion as if going to strike, but they continued immovable. Her face showed an unspeakable mixture of reverence and love, while silent tears stole down her cheek. Her lips were a little open, and sometimes moved, but not enough to cause any sound. I do not know whether I ever saw a human face look so beautiful. Sometimes it was covered with a smile, as from joy, mixing with love and reverence; but the tears fell still, though not so fast. Her pulse was quite regular. In about half an hour I observed her countenance change into the form of fear, pity, and distress; then she burst into a flood of tears, and cried out, 'Dear Lord; they will be damned! They will all be damned!' But in about five minutes her smiles returned, and only love and joy appeared in her face. About half an hour after six I observed distress take place again; and soon after she wept bitterly, and cried out, 'Dear Lord, they will go to hell! The world will go to hell!' Soon after, she said, 'Cry aloud! Spare not!' and in a few moments her look

[20] *Ibid.*, p. 364.

was composed again, and spoke a mixture of reverence, joy, and love. Then she said aloud, 'Give God the glory.' About seven her senses returned. I asked, 'Where have you been?' 'I have been with my Saviour.' 'In heaven, or on earth?' 'I cannot tell; but I was in glory.' 'Why, then, did you cry?' 'Not for myself, but for the world; for I saw they were on the brink of hell.' 'Whom did you desire to give the glory to God?' 'Ministers, that cry aloud to the world; else they will be proud; and then God will leave them, and they will lose their own souls.'[21]

One is reminded of the girl John Donne celebrated in "Of the Progress of the Soul," on the second anniversary of the death of Mistress Elizabeth Drury:

> . . . *we understood*
> *Her by her sight; her pure and eloquent blood*
> *Spoke in her cheeks, and so distinctly wrought*
> *That one might almost say her body thought.*

How far can the body go in expressing a thought emotionally? It can go as far as stigmatization. From St. Francis of Assisi on down the true stigmatics appear to have acquired the symbolic lesions in their hands, feet, side, and elsewhere, by intensely emotional meditation on the sufferings of Christ. Though the most famous stigmatics are Roman Catholic saints, we must apparently lay stress on the emotional factor rather than on religion in any restricted sense. Says Obermayer, a leading American dermatologist: "I think there is sufficient evidence that stigmatization does occur through the mechanism of hysterical identification. . . . Its rarity suggests that a tremendously strong emotional force is indispensable to its creation."[22] Obermayer publishes photographs of a contemporary Catholic priest with very noticeable lesions in his hands, and comments:

> Padre Pio, a Capuchin priest born in 1887, lives a saintly life in Pietrelcina, a mountain town near Foggia, Italy, and has been continuously stigmatized since 1918, the longest known period of stigmatization.[23]

But to make it plain that he does not regard stigmatization as confined to religious experience, dogmatically or ecclesiastically speaking, Obermayer also cites cases where it was emotional participation primarily rather than strictly religious meditation which seemed to

---

[21] *The Journal of the Rev. John Wesley, A.M.*, ed. by N. Curnock (London: Epworth Press, 1938), Vol. 4, p. 347.
[22] Obermayer (1955), p. 172.   [23] *Ibid.*, p. 167.

be determinative. For example, there is the case of the sister of a soldier condemned to run the gantlet, i.e., to run stripped to the waist between lines of soldiers under orders to strike him on the back as he ran:

> At the hour assigned for the punishment she felt, when at home with her family, the sensation of the wounds her brother was receiving. In an ecstatic state, moaning and groaning, she fainted and was placed in bed. It was discovered that she bled from woundlike lesions on her back.[24]

Obermayer speaks of emotional stigmatization as rare. Just how rare it is we cannot be sure. A medical examination which was confined to studying the lesions and did not inquire into the history of their origin might overlook many cases where the process was like that in the case just cited. If we refer only to religious stigmatics of the type of St. Francis, the number recorded is more than 300. This is the place to call attention to a very important fact. The capacity for emotional expression as strong as this is far more often found in women than in men. Of the 300 stigmatics listed by Jacobi, according to Obermayer, 41 are men, giving a ratio of about 6 women to 1 man. This ratio corresponds closely with that found in a recent study of conversion reaction (hysteria) at North Carolina Memorial Hospital, where of 589 patients so diagnosed 489 were female.[25] I do not think this ratio should be interpreted as pointing to a special weakness in the female sex. I think that it points first of all to a greater capacity or greater frequency of the capacity for sympathetic involvement with others; on top of that, it may be that emotion flows over more readily into intense bodily expression in women. But the main conclusion that I should draw is that more women than men fully participate in the lives of those around them by emotional identification. This is seen at its height in hysterical identification, by which Obermayer explains stigmatization.

We might put emotional bodily effects in a series, beginning with the diffuse instinctive expressions which Darwin describes and ending with precise effects such as occur in religious stigmatization where strong emotion is guided by a particular idea to a particular local manifestation. In between we could put hysterical reactions which are not understood by the person himself as either common expression of emotion or as the manifestation of a meaningful idea,

[24] *Ibid.*, p. 170.   [25] Sowers and Huff (1959).

such as that of the crucifixion of Christ. An example of this middle category is a strikingly simple case described by Abse. A British soldier stationed in India developed a localized area of excessive sweating on the underside of his left wrist which, during acute attacks, would discharge drops of perspiration in a regular stream. After dermatological examination he was referred to the psychiatrist, Abse, who probed into the patient's sexual life and discovered that he had made a firm decision when he came to India, out of fidelity to his wife in England, to have no sexual relations with Indian women. Nevertheless, he had been instinctively attracted to a woman who worked next to him in his office and occasionally, in leaning over to point out something in the work on her desk, he had rested his left wrist lightly on her shoulder. One may suppose that the Indian heat in conjunction with the emotional heat thus aroused started the wrist sweating where it came in contact with the woman's shoulder. At any rate, the pathological sweating which later developed was apparently energized by sexual emotion and guided in its location by the history of physical contact with this woman. Within a week after the beginning of the psychiatric consultations the wrist area had become normal.[26]

In order to understand and deal with cases like Abse's, it seems to be necessary to help the patient bring his emotions and ideas to a more conscious level. Psychoanalytic technique was devised exactly for this purpose. Yet, without being psychoanalysts, we can appreciate after a fashion the impact of emotion on the body whether accompanied by a particular idea or not; and, on the other hand, even psychoanalysts do not profess to understand completely how the transition is made from thought and impulse to some particular bodily symptom serious enough to engage the interest of a medical specialist.

Regardless of special theories, it is clear that the expression of emotion goes deep into the organism. Changes of circulation at the surface which show up in the rosiness of a blush or the pallor of fear are accompanied by circulatory changes elsewhere in the body. Emotion reverberates through the whole system. Dunbar notes that Cannon wrote, as early as 1909:

There is no doubt that just as the secretory activity of the stomach is affected in similar fashion in man and in lower animals, so likewise

[26] Abse (1950), pp. 19-23.

gastric and intestinal peristalsis are stopped in man as they are stopped in the lower animals, by worry and anxiety and the major affective states.[27]

So responsive are the internal organs to interpersonal reactions that the very process of examination in a clinic may have marked effects on a patient. For example, Ruggles reports, according to Dunbar:

A patient with a rather atonic stomach was returned to her dressing room for a few minutes to permit another examination to be completed. She became enraged at this procedure and when she again appeared behind the screen her stomach had lifted, contracted to half its former size and showed rapid, vigorous peristalsis. The stomach subsided with her anger and soon returned to its normal state.[28]

As every honest introspectionist knows, the emotional disturbances of the interior are much less easy to control than the external expressions. Modern tools of examination merely confirm this old knowledge. For instance, Dunbar reports that Fleiner writes:

Diagnostically these X-ray pictures of the colon are often of more value than the patient's facial expression, which can be controlled voluntarily, or distorted conventionally, the result being an expression which is harmless and well balanced. The expressive movements of the colon as they appear in the picture, on the other hand, do not deceive, they are unfalsifiable and unmistakable. Questioning many patients as to their attitudes and experiences and moods, only after having looked at their intestinal pictures, I then obtained unrestricted information.[29]

Moral struggles may be reflected in the viscera. An example is furnished by Ruggles:

An apparently normal business man developed an obstruction in his sigmoid during an emotional crisis where he had to sacrifice either his principles or his position. Opaque enema showed a complete block and the patient only escaped laparotomy because his physician was wise enough to repeat the examination several times.[30]

Operation on this man would have been equivalent to resorting to surgery to wipe out an emotional expression on the face; one could do that and still leave the grief or anger untouched and free to ex-

[27] Dunbar (1947), p. 294. Used by permission of the Columbia University Press.
[28] *Ibid.*, pp. 299 f.   [29] *Ibid.*, p. 300.   [30] *Ibid.*, p. 299.

press itself in other ways. Everyone agrees that much surgery is unnecessary, as well as other forms of symptomatic treatment, but where the medical orientation is primarily somatic the psychic aspect of the psychosomatic organism is bound to be overlooked.

The doctors are no more at fault, however, than the patients themselves and the whole of our (relatively) somatically oriented society. Even necessary surgery can be a sardonic exclamation point at the end of a long chain of emotional effects. Walker outlines such a course of events in his book, *Patients and Doctors*.[31] In the beginning a man suffers from chronic indigestion traceable to worry and a tendency to bolt his food. Psychological treatment, or self-reflection on his part, might resolve the emotional difficulties and lead to a more reasonable mode of life. This being omitted, the indigestion grows worse and the man consults his doctor but insists that he is too busy to follow the doctor's advice. Later, the worsening of his condition forces him into a hospital; he is X-rayed, and discovers that now he has a duodenal ulcer. Prolonged rest, a light diet, and alkaline medication are prescribed; but he rushes back to work and the old emotional strains. After a period of time, the ulcer becomes so bad that a surgeon recommends removal of a portion of the stomach; and so, at great expense of money and time, the gastrectomy is performed, and the man is cured, rather absurdly, of his indigestion. By tracing back a bodily disorder to the emotional fountainhead, as Walker does here, we discover one of the meanings of disease: it is an incarnation, unduly prolonged, of an emotional state.

Walker believes that the public has some understanding of the psychosomatic principle, in this form. But Walker admits that the understanding has curious limitations. Patients who accept the principle as applied to others may not apply it to themselves. When the doctor speaks of their pain as psychogenic, these patients expostulate, "But this is real!" Which amounts to saying that the mind is not real.

Syndrome shift

All emotion has a double aspect. Great fear, for example, is both paralysis of the body and terror of the mind. The same duality appears in disease. But the accent may lie more one way than the other. The accent may also shift back and forth from one side to

[31] Walker (1957).

the other of the psychosomatic composite and shift around within either the bodily or the mental field. In other words, the symptoms may vary.

As an example of syndrome shift within the bodily field, Groen, Bastiaans, and Van der Valk mention a patient of theirs who suffered from very high blood pressure and attacks of cardiac asthma coming nearly every night: "The attacks of cardiac asthma abruptly disappeared when this man developed an embolism of the left medial cerebral artery, followed by hemiplegia and aphasia."[32] Here one bodily disease condition is suddenly replaced by another.

Closely related to the above is the temporary suppression of a bodily ailment by a psychic tension—which these authors call the Van Loghem phenomenon, in reference to the following experience. The patient in the case was Van Loghem himself, a physician. On a day when he was scheduled to make an important address he was suffering from a cold. As Van Loghem tells the story:

> The cold had become very severe in the course of the day. When I was dressing after dinner, the rhinorrhea was so copious and I felt so unpresentable that I considered cancelling my appointment by telephone. At about 7.45, while in the taxi and not far from home, I suddenly realized that I no longer had a cold. I had no need to use even one of the pile of handkerchiefs with which I had armed myself, either during the address or during the interval or on the way home. I did not feel I had a cold and enjoyed my unexpected and sudden cure. At about 11 o'clock, soon after my return home, the symptoms recurred. They were associated with peculiar sensations of tightness, swelling and tension in the nose such as I have never experienced, either before that time or since. The sensations lasted throughout the night, interfering with my sleep.[33]

Presumably, the cold germs did not vanish for Van Loghem's benefit, but simply were not able to produce the inflammation and other cold symptoms while strong concern in carrying out the task was present. The psychic element of strong purpose was enough to afford a temporary cure. When this had faded, the bodily affliction returned.

Sometimes the shift is from somatic symptoms to psychic, sometimes the reverse. Groen, Bastiaans, and Van der Valk have summed up their collection of 21 such cases in a table, of which Table 46 here is a slightly modified version. One fact emphasized in this table

[32] Groen, Bastiaans, and Van der Valk (1957), p. 34. Used by permission of the Elsevier Publishing Company. [33] *Ibid.*, p. 43.

is that therapeutic measures, instead of causing a shift from disease to health, may simply cause a change in the form of the disease.

The tabular presentation is too condensed to do more than suggest how varied syndrome shift may be. We gain a little more insight from the case histories. Here is one referring to the second case in the upper part of Table 46:

> A 50-year-old man who had marked compulsive-neurotic characteristics but was quite capable of dealing with his work as the head of a fairly large firm, entered a depression on the occasion of his son's suicide. As a result he was admitted to a mental hospital and given electroconvulsive therapy. Little attention was initially paid to his mild gastric symptoms, but the ECT course had to be discontinued when he suddenly had a major gastric haemorrhage which, according to X-ray findings, was based on a duodenal ulcer. He was transferred to a clinic for internal diseases where his depression proved to have disappeared, although he had only had three sessions of ECT. The gastric pain showed considerable aggravation, however, and pyloric stenosis developed. In this case, therefore, there was a shift from a depression to a duodenal ulcer.[34]

There are a number of problems here—why the father's grief over his son's death led to a depression requiring hospitalization, why the doctors resorted to shock treatment, why they paid no attention to his gastric symptoms; but, above all, why a deep depression disappeared when a duodenal ulcer developed.

If we study the table we find no regular connection between duodenal ulcer and any particular psychiatric condition either before or after. Depression is a feature of every case, however, with the possible exception of the one listed as "asocial." Do we dare say that depression is a specific cause of duodenal ulcer, or that duodenal ulcer is a specific cure for depression? The hypothesis sounds extravagant and superficial. It is easy enough to see a general connection between a depressed emotional state and an ulcer in one direction, but why should the depression be relieved by the ulcerous lesion? Looking at the matter very naïvely and letting our primitive animistic tendencies take over, we discover that there was good sense in the demon theory of disease after all, as Freud says. A malevolent Something, a cunning and treacherous Enemy, often seems to prowl through the organism, attacking first here and then there, appearing to retreat from one quarter only to descend with

[34] *Ibid.*, p. 38.

Table 46
Syndrome shift: cases of Groen, Bastiaans, and Van der Valk

	first disease	*second disease*	*cause of displacement*
FROM PSYCHE TO SOMA	melancholia agitata	rheumatoid arthritis	psychotherapy
	compulsion neurosis; depression	duodenal ulcer	electroshock, psychotherapy
	hysterical depression	duodenal ulcer	psychotherapy
	hysterical pains	duodenal ulcer	prohibition against making display of her troubles
	asocial behavior, i.e., burglary	duodenal ulcer	stay in mental hospital
	hysterical fits	ulcerative colitis	stay in mental hospital plus humiliation
	anorexia nervosa	habitual constipation and abdominal pains	hormone treatment and psychotherapy
	hysterical hemicrania	neurovascular asthenia	psychotherapy
	hysteria; self-mutilation	essential hypertension	stay in mental hospital
FROM SOMA TO PSYCHE	ulcerative colitis	depression; suicide	psychotherapy
	ulcerative colitis	hallucinatory psychosis	admission to hospital
	ulcerative colitis	hysterical depression	husband's changed attitude
	duodenal ulcer	neurasthenia; hypochondria	partial gastrectomy
	Graves' disease*	depressive psychosis	treatment with radioactive iodine
	Graves' disease	conversion hysteria	treatment with radioactive iodine

Adapted from Groen, Bastiaans, and Van der Valk (1957), p. 41.
* Exophthalmic goiter.

	first disease	second disease	cause of displacement
FROM SOMA TO PSYCHE (cont.)	bronchial asthma	psychopathia	change of environment
	bronchial asthma	hysterical psychosis	misconceptions in the environment
	bronchial asthma	morphinism	morphine prescribed by physician
	bronchial asthma	low back pain and headache	ACTH-therapy
	psoriasis	depression (hypo-chondriasis)	X-ray treatment
	generalized eczema	acute psychosis	electroshock

violence on another. A modern way of putting it is to say that the problem is not the symptoms but the disease.

Syndrome shift is by no means a new conception. For example, Mitchell, reporting on the case of a woman of thirty-six, comments very pointedly on the "mutual interchangeableness of somatic and mental affections," and this in fact is the theme of many a case history long before that time. But Mitchell's report has the special merit of experimentally demonstrating this interchangeableness. He writes:

When the obsessions of the early stage of the last illness disappeared, the physical manifestations began. When cessation of the muscular twitching and ability to walk were obtained, there occurred a series of dreadful dreams, which affected the patient very strongly. When the most persistent of all the bodily symptoms—the right hemianalgesia —was removed by suggestion, she passed almost immediately from a state of comparatively normal health into a state of profound depression, accompanied by phobias and obsessions. In the middle of the night, some hours after the disappearance of the hemianalgesia, she wrote a most pitiful letter to her sister, in which she expressed the fear that she was going out of her mind, and begged her sister not to send her to an asylum. I received a letter from her next day, in which she said "the awful thing in her head" kept shouting at her and telling her to do dreadful things. So great was her distress, and so evident seemed the connection between the disappearance of the hemianalgesia and the appearance of the morbid mental symptoms, that I decided to bring back the bodily defect by suggestion, in the hope that by so doing the mental troubles might be ameliorated. I was careful not to give any indication to the patient why I wished the loss of sensibility to return, yet with the recurrence of the hemianalgesia she soon returned to her ordinary state and became free from all mental distress.[35]

In Mitchell's case there is more than a mere temporal succession of events—there is a cohesion so strong that we have a right to speak of a causal link between them, though it is not clear what this link is. The patient herself has no etiological theory, but her behavior and certain information that she provides do leave her physician with a vivid impression of dealing with active purposive forces, or rather with *one* active purposive force, "a very obstinate and capricious person, who seemed to have some unusual kind of control over her own bodily organism."[36] One morning the patient's father heard her crying out and went into her bedroom, where he saw her struggling in apparent terror, though asleep. Later she called in her sister, and now blood was streaming from her right eye and oozing from her right ear. She was by this time fully awake, and in this state, Mitchell says, she could explain nothing about the bleeding. He hypnotized her. Under hypnosis she told him that during the night "a nasty man had attacked her, and hit her on the head with a hammer."[37] When Mitchell referred to this episode as a dream, she insisted that, on the contrary, it was completely real.

It is fortunate for our science if not for our peace of mind that there are doctors who are willing to report observations which puzzle them. Let us look carefully at Mitchell's patient. She suffers from a visible haemorrhage for which there seems to be no explanation. But we know that prior to that she was observed to have been struggling in her sleep, as if oppressed by a nightmare. When Mitchell puts her into the hypnotic state she recalls the nightmare experience—from the inside. This experience is directly related to the haemorrhage. But how can a *dream* of hammer blows produce bleeding? The patient's own answer (under hypnosis) is that the man with the hammer was not an empty phantom but solid reality. Before getting this explanation our problem was to find any at all. After getting it, our problem is how to become reconciled to it.

[35] Mitchell (1912), p. 303.
[37] *Ibid.*, p. 304.

[36] *Ibid.*, p. 304.

Let me remind the reader that I claim the privilege of playing with ideas—a game which has to be played now and then if science is not to come to a standstill—and I hope that the reader, too, will be able to join in. Mitchell's case, when I look at it in the round rather than piecemeal, baffles me. Naturally, there would be no problem if I could just reject the report; but Mitchell (1869-1944) was a competent enough medical man to belong to various British scientific societies and to serve as editor of the *British Journal of Medical Psychology* (1920-1935) as well as to write many quite acceptable books and papers, and I cannot in good conscience dispose of the report in that way. On examining my own thoughts, I find that the moment of bafflement comes when Mitchell introduces into his account the words of the patient herself about the happenings in her own personal world. Actually, I am also somewhat puzzled by the syndrome shift between psyche and soma which he has described, but this sort of thing is so commonly reported nowadays and so much in line with the study by Groen, Bastiaans, and Van der Valk discussed a few pages back, that I may accept it almost unthinkingly. Again, if Mitchell had stopped with a simple, objective account of the contortions of terror and the subsequent bleeding from ear and eye, I might have contented myself with some speculations about a violent circulatory disturbance which ended in the bursting of blood vessels. In short, I tolerate very well a somatic account, or even a psychosomatic account involving that "mysterious leap from the mind to the body" which Freud puzzled over; but I am disturbed when I am brought into the interior of the patient's world, so to speak, and see there a nasty man with a hammer hitting her on the head, and then step back into Mitchell's world where there is no such man and observe the blood streaming from his patient's eye and oozing from her ear. How do we correlate these two worlds, the world of the sufferer and the world of the observer? The blunt, direct way to do it is to take the patient at her word. But this, in effect, is to accept demon theory. We thus find the phenomenological approach of existentialist psychiatry leading us into a quandary; for, if we accept demon theory, we are plunged back into the dark ages and numbered with the superstitious by people whose good opinion we should like to keep, and if we do not, the correlation between the patient's world and the physician's world seems to break down at a crucial point.

We have become used to explaining bodily symptoms in psychic terms, at least if we have been influenced by Freud, but we have not become used to his statement that, in the long run, demonological theory has justified itself. Practically speaking, as patients ourselves, we may not even accept the prevailing psychoanalytic theory. Walker, formerly Hunterian Professor of the Royal College of Surgeons, tells us:

> Whilst laymen can now appreciate the fact that emotional conflicts have repercussions on the body which may end in physical illness, few are yet able to listen with any sympathy to attempts on the part of their doctors to explain to them the nature of psychogenic pain.[38]

He goes on to advise doctors that on a first visit to a patient it is better to label a pain "neuritis" or "neuralgia" rather than "psychogenic." The former labels have the proper somatic tone. On later visits, says Walker, the doctor may find that the patient has, without any prompting, begun to talk about himself in language more psychological, undergoing a syndrome shift, so to speak, from somatic to psychic complaints. The shifting about of the symptoms reminds Walker of a living, purposive organism so much that he thinks "we can readily understand why, in pre-scientific times, a sick man was said to be possessed of a demon."[39] He continues:

> Possession by a devil is an excellent simile for illness, but it does not lend itself to consulting-room use. If a patient were to inquire of me what had gone wrong with him and I were to reply, "You are possessed of a devil", my answer might easily terminate our doctor-patient relationship. But if in order to avoid affronting him I were to frame my answer more tactfully, and, omitting all mention of a devil, were to reply in my most scientific manner: "Something has disturbed the harmony of that complex of mind and body you call 'yourself', and this has set going within you a chain of living events which causes you distress", my patient would still not be satisfied. His dissatisfaction with me would be deepened were I to add, what was quite likely to be true, that his illness was *purposive* in nature and that actually he had no *desire* to get well.[40]

What is it that demon theory and Freudian theory have in common? The emphasis on the power of psychic, purposeful, and essentially invisible forces. How do they differ? In the degree of independence of the human body assigned to these forces. Freud, in an extremely vague way, locates the elements of the Unconscious —the repressed memories and wishes, and the instinctive purposes

[38] Walker (1957), p. 151.   [39] *Ibid.*, p. 152.
[40] *Ibid.*, pp. 152 f.

of the Id—somewhere in the soma, perhaps in the brain or autonomic nervous system or glands, or perhaps indefinitely diffused; from which bodily locus the invisible psychic forces work, sometimes even creating by "projection" visible and tangible forms having all the malevolence and ugliness of a medieval demon. Demonological theory, on the other hand, does not permanently anchor its psychic forces in a particular human body; instead, it conceives of them as free purposeful beings capable of shifting from place to place, though sometimes they "materialize" before human eyes and obsess the mind or, worst of all, invade and possess the body of some poor wretch.

Charcot, Freud's teacher at the Salpêtrière, was quite aware of demonology, which of course he rejected. Nevertheless, he included in his concept of hysteria the "demoniacal attack" as illustrated in the accompanying sketches (Figure 31). These are not pretty pictures, though prettier than some others from his clinic, and the verbal descriptions of such attacks may be uglier still. It is quite understandable why earlier theorists, having witnessed such attacks singly and in epidemic form, should have spoken of demon possession: it was not only because of the ugly violence of the attack, but also because of what the patients said about their experience—they saw, they felt, they heard, they smelled their attackers—attackers which the physicians and exorcizing priests and other spectators did not see but did believe in.

If we reflect now on Mitchell's case, we can perhaps understand that the invader of her personal world might satisfactorily be classed as a demon, given just the facts and definitions we have been considering. But there are other facts. The chief among these is the decay of religion. The free-thinking French psychiatrists of the nineteenth century who swept demoniacal attacks, religious ecstasy, and stigmatic saints into the category of hysteria had small respect for disembodied spirits or other traces of religious supernaturalism. A battle-line was drawn between the Charcot school and pious medical men like Antoine Imbert-Gourbeyre, whose two-volume work *La Stigmatisation* (1894) was published in opposition to their views. It is not the battle itself which interests us here, but the effect on our current theories. That effect is marked, I believe, and subtle. A perfect illustration of what I mean is an episode described by Ernest Jones in his biography of Freud. Jones relates that Freud liked to talk, especially after midnight, about uncanny experiences with his patients—telepathy, wishes and predictions coming true, and the

31 *Whether called demon-possession or* grande hystérie, *the kind of attack illustrated in these pictures from Charcot's clinic is terrifying to witness. It is possible that such attacks are rarer in our day than in Charcot's, but they still occur. (From Gilles de la Tourette, 1891, 1895)*

like. Jones himself (whose relation to Freud was something like that of Wagner to Faust in Goethe's poem) disapproved of his master's flirting with superstition. Referring to these stories on a particular occasion, he writes:

> When they were concerned with clairvoyant visions of episodes at a distance, or visitations from departed spirits, I ventured to reprove him for his inclination to accept occult beliefs on flimsy evidence. His reply was: "I don't like it at all myself, but there is some truth in it," both sides of his nature coming to expression in a short sentence. I then asked him where such beliefs could halt: if one could believe in mental processes floating in the air, one could go on to a belief in angels. He closed the discussion at this point (about three in the

morning!) with the remark: "Quite so, even *der liebe Gott*." This was said in a jocular tone as if agreeing with my *reductio ad absurdum* and with a quizzical look as if he were pleased at shocking me. But there was something searching also in the glance, and I went away not entirely happy lest there be some more serious undertone as well.[41]

Here we see two courageous modern scientists shrinking from certain facts and theories because they might lead on to religious beliefs to which they were antipathetic. A similar consideration makes demon theory unattractive to many. My point, of course, is not that I accept demon theory myself, but that the current rejection of this theory is *partially* due to antipathy to religion. In general, scientific theories seem to rest on something more than facts of observation and pure reason.

Fashions in disease

Though certain aspects of disease are constantly appearing (such as pain, anxiety, convulsions, fever, and so on), it is noticeable that the prevalent disease syndromes vary from region to region and from age to age. Great epidemics like the Black Death of the fourteenth century may sweep over the world with prodigious power and then recede and be almost forgotten. No medical intervention accounts for the decline of this disease, though medical theory can explain it, and no therapeutic measures are known which could be counted on to stem it if it should flare up again.[42] Yet *Bacillus pestis* is still with us and continues to breed in men and rodents in various parts of the earth, including the United States (see Figure 32). In the same way the epidemics of demon possession, dancing mania,

[41] Jones (1953-57), Vol. 3, p. 381.
[42] For a discussion, see Smith (1941). India suffered from a severe epidemic of plague which began in 1896 and mounted by 1904 to a million deaths and more in a year. The British Plague Commission established the fact that plague was transmitted by rats and efforts at control were made—in a land where the living conditions and abundance of rats pointed to the need. Yet, according to Smith, the eventual decline of the epidemic cannot be attributed to the control measures: "In 1935, when plague deaths in British India were but 32,000, the public health commissioner reported that 'the decrease cannot be attributed, at least in rural areas, to permanent improvement in sanitary conditions. Housing and other conditions inherently favourable to the rat populations are to a large extent essentially the same as when plague first made its appearance in Bombay forty years ago.'" (*Ibid.*, p. 321) Camus' famous novel, *The Plague*, which is obviously based on serious research into the history and characteristics of plague, uses the mysterious qualities and effects of the disease to enforce his pessimistic philosophy.

and religious convulsions, which are mentioned in the history books as colorful evidence of human instability in the centuries following the Black Death, have also apparently receded. Yet they have not absolutely disappeared, and it is doubtful whether we know any more about controlling them than we do about the plague. Presumably whatever gave rise to these epidemics is still around, whether demons or the Unconscious or something else. At any rate we find isolated cases of these things too, and not necessarily among the superstitious.

Disease in some form, under some name, is always with us. As one variety declines in ferocity, another gains. We may speak of syndrome shifts for the whole population of the globe. To take a minor example, consider the status of respiratory diseases among white males in the United States from 1900 to 1955. The death rate for pneumonia-influenza and tuberculosis has declined. But the rate for lung cancer has gone up. These trends can be correlated with facts about medical practice and the tobacco industry, etc., so that we may get the impression that a further extension of good medical practice and the elimination of tobacco smoking, along with some other things, might rid us of these diseases. So they might. But it would be a mistake to assume that further advance would eliminate

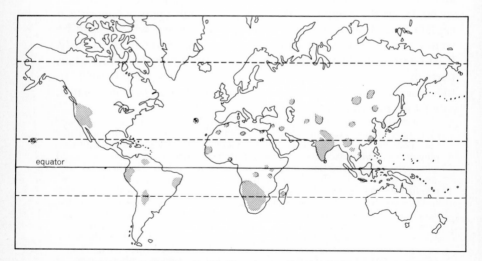

32 *Plague (the Black Death) has not vanished from the world. The shaded areas of the map roughly indicate active or latent centers of infection in the twentieth century. (After Smith, 1941)*

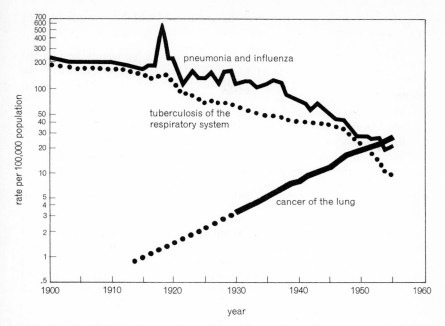

33 *As one kind of disease is suppressed, another rises to prominence. The graph shows contrary trends in the lethality of three types of respiratory disease in the United States, 1900-1955. Death rates are standardized for age on the 1940 population. (U.S. Bureau of the Census)*

all disease. Death stands unchanged, and all the ways to death may as well be called disease.

Disease is the approach of death, the disordering of the psychophysical unity which may lead to its dissolution. We take many illnesses lightly. It may seem ridiculous to speak of a common cold as the approach of death. Yet people sometimes die of colds. They die of many ailments that are not taken seriously. They even die of the advance of science.

Radiation sickness is one of the new kinds of disease, and we know that our military technology based upon pure science is a major cause of it. The immediate and the lingering effects of the single bomb on Hiroshima might be called a man-made plague.[43] The enormous plague of radiation sickness which would result from an all-out atomic war is a commonplace modern fear. But other types of man-made plague are in preparation. I extract the follow-

[43] For a full medical report, see Hachiya (1955).

ing from a widely distributed encyclopedia which any schoolchild can read:

> BIOLOGICAL WARFARE, the use of disease-producing agents against the personnel or food supply of an enemy. It has been stated that German agents in World War I injected disease-producing germs into American cattle which were being shipped to Europe. But not until World War II did biological warfare become an organized science of destruction. During this war more than $50,000,000 was spent in the U.S. for biological-warfare experiments. More than 3000 scientists were employed in the development of new offensive and defensive weapons, none of which were put to actual military use.[44]

Anyone who takes comfort from that last clause should go on to the next paragraph:

> The chief offensive biological weapon developed during World War II was a poison, the toxin of the disease called botulism. This toxin was isolated in pure, crystalline form, and methods were developed for producing it on a large scale. One seventh of a microgram of the pure toxin, taken internally, is a fatal dose, so that one ounce could kill 180,000,000 people, more than the combined populations of the U.S. and Canada. Military officials suggested that this poison might be introduced into the food or water supplies of an enemy either by fifth columnists or by spraying from aircraft.[45]

And this delightful thought is added: "Toxins such as that of botulism do not suffer from the disadvantage of endangering the attackers."[46] In this time of rapid scientific and military progress, I apologize for using so dated a source, but its language is clear and sufficient for the present discussion.

War itself may be fruitfully regarded as a disease, the most persistent of the diseases, repeatedly breaking out in epidemics. Richardson, a physicist-psychologist-mathematician, has so treated it in some very sophisticated studies. Some of the main points in one of his books, as stated in a chapter entitled "Analogies With Disease" and headed by the words of McDougall (a medical man as well as a psychologist) "The world is sick with a terrible intermittent fever," are these:

> First, fighting is infectious; the infection is borne by sights and sounds, by rumor, by newspapers, by cinema shows, and by radio. Second, some people are naturally immune. Third, there is something in war

[44] *New Funk & Wagnalls encyclopedia* (1950), Vol. 4, p. 1335.
[45] *Ibid.*   [46] *Ibid.*

analogous to the rise of temperature in fever. Fourth, a long and severe bout of fighting confers immunity on most of those who have experienced it; so that they no longer readily join in fights. Fifth, this acquired immunity is not permanent but fades out after a decade or two. Also there arises a new generation, not rendered immune by experience.[47]

Richardson does not stop with analogies, of course, but goes on to analyze the disease scientifically and mathematically.

The curious thing about many diseases, such as radiation sickness and the epidemics of botulism which biological-warfare experts seem to be preparing and war itself, is that they seem obviously the result of human purposes and therefore within the control of human beings. From another point of view, since they are *not* controlled and few people seem willing to admit that they are in favor of them, such diseases can be made to appear no more the fault of any human being than the Black Death. We usually picture ourselves as the innocent victims of disease and death rather than as the causal agents. Perhaps only a few very sensitive schizophrenes locked up in our asylums *really* feel that they are causing or might cause a worldwide holocaust.

Freud located death (Thanatos) inside of us. Most of us probably feel that death is an enemy located outside of us. We are ambiguous about the matter, perhaps. Sometimes, for example, we feel guilty about being sick, even when it is something as apparently unwilled as pneumonia or a heart attack. A person may apologize for dying.[48] At other times, we feel purely victimized. This ambiguity in our personal attitudes is reflected in our theories of disease. At the risk of seeming to be obsessed by one particular problem, I will illustrate what I mean by drawing on Aldous Huxley's account of the famous demon epidemic at Loudun in the seventeenth century. Though I do not regard Huxley's book as a scientific treatise, I think it does contain a great deal of carefully garnered fact; and it is certainly adequate for illustrating the point that we may be of two minds regarding the internal or external origin of a psychosomatic disease state. At the same time, it illustrates the point that fashions in disease change, that (to use other terminology) society as a whole experiences syndrome shifts; for epidemics of the kind described by

[47] Richardson (1960), p. 232.
[48] According to the newspapers, Clark Gable reacted to the heart attack which preceded his death (November 16, 1960) by saying to his pregnant wife: "I feel terrible doing this to you and the baby."

Huxley no longer seem to occur in the Western World, or not so conspicuously as they once did.

As Huxley tells the story, the outbreak of demon possession at the Ursuline convent in Loudun, which combined with other events to bring the priest Urbain Grandier to execution on the charge of sorcery, can be explained by the lusts of Grandier, the vengefulness of his fellow-citizens, the erotic fantasies of the prioress of the convent, and the fanaticism of the Roman Catholic exorcists. In short, Huxley provides a sociological-psychological explanation, tracing the disease back to human motives. To those actually involved, of course, the explanation was different: they had been invaded by alien powers, malevolent spirits, demons. Demons or not, the disease was clearly infectious and sometimes fatal. For convenience of exposition, I will consider separately (1) the fate of Grandier's opponents, (2) the condition of the possessed nuns, and (3) the experience of Father Surin, who devoted himself to curing the prioress, Soeur Jeanne des Anges.

After the accused priest, Grandier, had been burned at the stake, disease and death descended on his accusers. Father Lactance, who had helped to torture Grandier and had sought diabolic information from the possessed nuns about his torments in hell, began to suffer pangs of conscience, developed a fever, cried out that God was punishing him, was beset by devils, and a month after the execution "knocked the crucifix out of the hand of the priest who had administered Extreme Unction, and died."[49] The next to go was Mannoury, a surgeon who had willingly assumed the task of plunging a long needle into Grandier's body to discover whether the devil had marked him with anesthetic patches.

> One night, shortly after the death of Father Lactance, he was sent for to bleed a sick man, who lived near the Porte du Martrai. On the way home, his servant with a lantern walking ahead of him, he saw Urbain Grandier. Naked, as when he had been pricked for the devil's marks, the parson was standing in the Rue du Grand-Pavé, between the counterscarps of the castle and the Cordeliers' garden. Mannoury halted, and his servant saw him staring into the vacant blackness, heard him asking someone, who wasn't there, what he wanted. There was no answer. Then the surgeon began to tremble all over. A moment

[49] Huxley, *The Devils of Loudun* (New York: Harper, 1952), p. 224. Copyright 1952 by Aldous Huxley. Used by permission of Harper & Brothers, and Chatto and Windus Ltd.

later, he fell to the ground, screaming for pardon. Within the week he, too, was dead.[50]

Then it was the turn of one of the judges, who went mad and died after being accused of magic by some of the demoniacs. At last, one of the toughest of Grandier's foes, Father Tranquille, was infected by the demons he was trying to exorcize from the nuns, suffered horrible torments for a year, and succumbed in 1638, less than four years after Grandier's death.

> The devils left the dying man and forthwith entered the body of another friar, who was kneeling by the bed. The new demoniac became so frantic, that he had to be held by half a dozen of his colleagues, who had the greatest difficulty in preventing him from kicking the hardly lifeless corpse.[51]

Meantime, the demon possession at the Ursuline convent continued. Its character can be glimpsed from the eyewitness account of Thomas Killigrew, an Englishman, later to become a playwright, in November 1635. Killigrew describes the quiet preparations for exorcism, the modesty of the nuns as they lay down on couches before the altar, the apparent sleep. Then follow the demoniacal agitations of Soeur Jeanne, as painted by Huxley on the basis of Killigrew's account:

> Surin now set to work on the Prioress. In a few minutes Balaam made his appearance. There were writhings and convulsions, abominable blasphemies, frightful grimaces. Soeur Jeanne's belly suddenly swelled, until it looked like that of a woman far gone in pregnancy; then the breasts puffed themselves up to the size of the belly. The exorcist applied relics to each part as it was affected, and the swellings subsided. Killigrew now stepped forward and touched her hand—it was cool; felt her pulse—it was calm and slow. The Prioress pushed him aside and began to claw at her coif. A moment later the bald, close-shaven head was bare. She rolled up her eyes, she stuck out her tongue. It was prodigiously swollen, black in color and had the pimply texture of morocco leather. Surin now untied her, ordering Balaam to adore the Sacrament. Soeur Jeanne slid backward off the seat and landed on the floor. For a long time Balaam stubbornly resisted; but at last he was bullied into performing the act of worship demanded of him. "Then," writes Killigrew, "as she lay on her back, she bent her waist like a tumbler and went so, shoving herself with her heels, on her bare shaven head, all about the chapel after the friar. And many

[50] *Ibid.*, pp. 224 f.   [51] *Ibid.*, p. 226.

other strange, unnatural postures, beyond anything that ever I saw, or could believe possible for any man or woman to do. Nor was this a sudden motion, and away; but a continuous thing, which she did for above an hour together; and yet not out of breath nor hot with all the motions she used." All this time the tongue hung out, "swollen to an incredible bigness, and never within her mouth from the first falling into her fit; I never saw her for a moment contract it. Then I heard her, after she had given a start and a shriek that you would have thought had torn her to pieces, speak one word and that was 'Joseph. At which all the priests started up and cried, 'That is the sign, look for the mark!' On which one, seeing her hold out her arm, looked for it. Mr. Montague and myself did the same very earnestly; and on her hand I saw a color rise, a little ruddy, and run for the length of an inch along her vein, and in that a great many red specks, which made a distinct word; and it was the same she spake, 'Joseph.' This mark the Jesuit said the devil promised, when he went out, he would make."[52]

The best we can do for all this by way of nondemonic explanation is to say that it was a case of suggestion and autosuggestion acting on a naturally hysterical constitution.

But what is a hysterical constitution? As applied to Soeur Jeanne, it means a young woman with vivid and not altogether creditable emotions, a hankering after notoriety, and unsettled aims in regard to her religious life. Father Surin seems different, an intense, reserved, clear-headed ascetic, with an aversion for self-display. Was he, too, hysterical? If so, his was not the extroverted hysteria of Soeur Jeanne. In fact, compassion seems to have been the foundation of his twenty years of suffering. Father Surin saw the prioress not as an amusing spectacle or as a "case" but as an individual soul in dreadful straits. He offered her more than the mechanical ritual of exorcism—he offered sympathy, spiritual instruction, unremitting patience, Christian love, and finally himself.

One day, after a peculiarly horrible display of diabolic beastliness, Surin prayed that he might be permitted to suffer on behalf of the Prioress and in her stead. He wanted to feel all that the devils had caused Soeur Jeanne to feel; he was ready himself to be possessed, "provided that it should please the divine Goodness to cure her and lead her into the practice of virtue." He further asked that he might be allowed to undergo the ultimate humiliation of being regarded as a lunatic.[53]

[52] *Ibid.*, pp. 251 f. [53] *Ibid.*, p. 236.

The remarkable thing is not that his prayer was answered: the theory of autosuggestion is equal to explaining the good father's demon possession, if it can explain Soeur Jeanne's; the remarkable thing is that the compassion existed and could generate such a prayer. Surin got what he asked for. The demons began to assault him. He continued his ministrations to Soeur Jeanne in spite of them. He wrote to a friend, advising him to love God and let Him do as He likes:

"Love's work is to ravage, to destroy, to abolish, and then to make new, to set up again, to resuscitate. It is marvelously terrible and marvelously sweet; and the more terrible, the more desirable, the more attractive. To this Love we must resolutely give ourselves."[54]

The demon assaults were only the first phase. Soeur Jeanne was cured, but Surin's agony lasted for years. He passed into the depths of despair, he became unable to walk or talk, he had enormous bodily pains and frightful visions, he believed that he was damned, he tried to commit suicide by flinging himself out a window down a cliff, and yet after all this terror and humiliation, lasting for twenty years, he recovered his speech and the power to write and walk and once again visited the sick, preached, heard confessions, and directed souls. In the final months before his death in 1665 (thirty years after his prayer of self-sacrifice at Loudun) he wrote about the torrential peace of God, undoubtedly from his own experience:

"Only the peace of God can march in such equipage, like the noise of the rising tide as it comes, not to ravage the land, but to fill the bed prepared for it by God. It comes as though fiercely, it comes with a roaring, even though the sea be calm. This roaring is caused only by the abundance of the waters, and not by their fury; for the moving of the waters is not by a tempest, but by the waters themselves, in all their native calm, when there is not a breath of wind. The sea in its fullness comes to visit the earth and to kiss the shores assigned for its limits. It comes in majesty and in magnificence. Even so it is in the soul when, after long suffering, the immensity of peace comes to visit her."[55]

The demon possession of those dark times (which Charcot labeled "hysteria" or "hystero-epilepsy," thus driving away the demons from his theory without driving out the disease) seems to have struck down all sorts of different people—physicians, judges, priests, nuns,

[54] *Ibid.*, p. 283. [55] *Ibid.*, p. 310.

the cruel and the kind, the virtuous and the unvirtuous, extroverts and introverts. It had the infectiousness and impartiality of any epidemic disease. Was it, then, an obscure virus infection causing a lesion of the brain? Or mass suggestion and autosuggestion? Or repressed wishes arising from the Unconscious of a whole community? For those who experienced it, it was demonic. But is the demonic somatic, psychic, or psychosomatic? Or is the demonic something for which we no longer have a name?

The search for specific causation

It has often been stated that certain diseases can be explained by the beliefs current at a given time. Thus the belief in supernatural agencies has been held responsible for disease episodes like that at Loudun. By extension, we might have a comprehensive theory of disease relating it to the total conditions of life. One author who has sketched out such a theory is Guirdham, his thesis being that the pattern of disease largely depends on the religious and philosophic outlook of a community.[56] Another is Bion, who has developed his ideas from studying the behavior of individuals in groups by a modified psychoanalysis: he postulates a protomental level (shared by individual and group) where diseases start and get their direction toward particular psychic or somatic symptoms.[57] Neither of these theorists discards the prevailing theory of infection by micro-organisms, but they both de-emphasize it by putting it in a larger context. Their views are representative of an emerging trend which has not been worked out in full detail and which cannot be, without a thorough analysis of the individual-in-society, and even metaphysics.

More traditional psychosomatic medicine, as presented by Alexander, likewise regards disease as multicausal. The factors which he thinks must be included in the functional equation for disease are not less than nine, i.e., hereditary constitution, birth injuries, organic diseases of infancy which increase the vulnerability of certain organs, nature of infant care (weaning habits, toilet training, sleeping arrangements, etc.), accidental physical traumatic experiences of infancy and childhood, accidental emotional traumatic experiences of infancy and childhood, emotional climate of the family and spe-

[56] Guirdham (1957).
[57] Bion (1950). The specific reference is to one article, but this cannot be fully understood without reading the others in the series of which it is the fifth.

cific personality traits of parents and siblings, later physical injuries, and later emotional experiences in intimate personal and occupational relations.[58] The "psychic" elements in this list are the emotions resulting from interpersonal relations. As far as possible, Alexander translates emotions into nervous system terms (i.e., he translates the psychic into the somatic) and attempts to connect specific psychosomatic diseases with the activity of the sympathetic and parasympathetic branches of the autonomic nervous system. It is his hypothesis that certain bodily dysfunctions are caused by specific kinds of emotional stress, so that it should be possible to predict from knowledge of the kind of stress endured what the bodily symptom would be. According to Hamilton, however, Alexander himself in 1934 and 1947 "clearly rejected this hypothesis because of the evidence from his investigations, and concluded that the problem of specificity is one which would not be solved from the psychological approach."[59] In his 1950 publication Alexander insists that a prediction formula would have to include a fairly large number of non-psychic factors—at least five—in his tentative list of nine. One might conclude that Alexander's stress on the "psychic" in "psychosomatic" is not very heavy.

The search for specific psychic causation nevertheless remains on the psychosomatic agenda. One form the search has taken has been to look for correlations between particular disease syndromes and particular psychological types or traits. There are bright spots here and there in the literature, but, according to Hamilton, they do not add up to high total illumination. For example, while praising a study of asthmatics by Brown and Goitein, he shows that the asthmatics do not differ from the controls in quite the way the authors thought they did, his own conclusion from their data being that "the asthmatics show conative secondary function more frequently than the controls, and vivacity, repression of passion and personal ardour much less."[60] Again, the effect of stress situations is interesting but surprising. A Hungarian doctor, for instance, reports that, contrary to what psychoanalytic theory might suggest, asthmatics appear to benefit from conditions of anxiety and persecution such as occurred in postwar Hungary. In Hamilton's words:

> While undergoing deportation, confinement to the ghetto or labour camps, 57 of his patients lost their asthma, while only one developed his under such circumstances. During the siege of Budapest, while

[58] Alexander (1950), p. 52.   [59] Hamilton (1955), p. 6.
[60] Ibid., p. 34.

they were confined to their cellars, 27 of his patients lost their symptoms, while only 3 became worse.[61]

Hamilton's review of these and many other empirical studies inclines him to the judgment that trait theory has little to offer ("Empirically it is found that the traits discovered in each disorder are in fact very much the same") and that psychoanalysis is likewise disappointingly nondiscriminating ("Empirically, we find that the dynamics are always the same, and the interaction of libido, aggression, dependence and so on, are much alike from one condition to another"), and he concludes that we must wait for a more adequate theory of personality.[62] It is clear that Hamilton thinks this more adequate theory will have to include the fact that the individual is always in dynamic interaction with other people, as well as the fact that one's *conscious* attitude toward the world is highly important.

Obviously, psychosomatic theorists cannot be satisfied with the general proposition that connections exist between disease syndromes and psychological factors. It ought to be possible, if the general proposition is true, to specify these connections. Hamilton's call for a more adequate theory of personality simply recognizes that the search thus far has not been very successful and that a new line of search is probably required.

References for chapter 15

Abse, D. W. (1950) *The diagnosis of hysteria.* Bristol: Wright.
Adams, D. K. (1928) The inference of mind. *Psychological Review,* 35, 235-52.
Alexander, F. (1950) *Psychosomatic medicine, its principles and applications.* New York: Norton.
Bion, W. R. (1950) Experiences in groups, V. *Human Relations,* 3, 3-14.
Brodie, Sir B. C. (1859) *Mind and matter, or psychological inquiries.* New York: Wood.
Darwin, C. (1910) *Expression of the emotions in man and animals.* New York: Appleton.
Deutsch, F. (Ed.) (1959) *On the mysterious leap from the mind to the body.* New York: International Universities Press.
Dunbar, F. (1947) *Emotions and bodily changes.* New York: Columbia Univ. Press.
Freud, S. (1925) *Collected papers.* London: Hogarth. Vol. 4.

[61] *Ibid.,* p. 37.   [62] *Ibid.,* p. 210.

Geddes, Sir A. C. (1952) *The forging of a family*. London: Faber & Faber.

Gilles de la Tourette, G. A. E. B. (1891, 1895) *Traité clinique et thérapeutique de l'hystérie*. Paris: Plon, Nourrit. 3 vols., Vol. 2.1.

Groen, J., Bastiaans, J., and Van der Valk, J. M. (1957) Psychosomatic aspects of syndrome shift and syndrome suppression. In Booij, J. (Ed.) *Psychosomatics, a series of five lectures*. Amsterdam: Elsevier, pp. 33-59.

Guirdham, A. (1957) *A theory of disease*. London: Allen & Unwin.

Hachiya, M. (1955) *Hiroshima diary: the journal of a Japanese physician, August 6–September 30, 1945*. Tr. and ed. by W. Wells. Chapel Hill: Univ. of North Carolina Press.

Hamilton, M. (1955) *Psychosomatics*. New York: Wiley.

Hammond, E. C. (1958) Smoking and death rates—a riddle in cause and effect. *American Scientist*, 46, 331-54.

Hebb, D. O. (1958) The mammal and his environment. In Maccoby, E. E., Newcomb, T. M., and Hartley, E. L. (Eds.) *Readings in social psychology*. 3rd ed. New York: Holt, pp. 335-41.

Jones, E. (1953-57) *The life and work of Sigmund Freud*. New York: Basic Books. 3 vols., Vol. 3.

Laín Entralgo, P. (1956) *Mind and body*. Tr. by A. M. Espinosa, Jr. New York: Kenedy.

Mitchell, T. W. (1912) A study in hysteria and multiple personality, with report of a case. *Proceedings of the Society for Psychical Research*, 26, 286-311.

Obermayer, M. E. (1955) *Psychocutaneous medicine*. Springfield, Ill.: Thomas.

O'Neill, D. (1955) *Modern trends in psychosomatic medicine*. London: Butterworth.

Richardson, L. F. (1960) *Arms and insecurity*. Chicago: Quadrangle Books.

Smith, G. (1941) *Plague on us*. New York: Commonwealth Fund.

Sowers, E., and Huff, W. (1959) 600 patients with diagnosis of conversion reaction. Unpublished paper, University of North Carolina.

Van den Berg, J. H. (1955) *The phenomenological approach to psychiatry*. Springfield, Ill.: Thomas.

Walker, K. (1957) *Patients and doctors*. Harmondsworth, Eng.: Penguin.

16

PREFERENCES, CREATIVITY, AND LOVE

Preview   *Every person tends to arrange the things of his world in order of preference. Strong emotions sweeping over this orderly personal world may radically change it and produce a new order with new elements: such personal revolutions appear to be one of the conditions favoring artistic creation, which is one expression of creativity in general. Both gradual and abrupt changes in the ordering of the personal world are often felt to be progress in the discovery of the highest good, either in a limited or an absolute sense. This feeling hints at the existence of laws of relationship between the person and his world which, if discovered and adhered to, would make for fullness of being and authentic joy. Ethical rules may be regarded as attempts to delineate these laws, but many people have found, if only for moments, that the laws are summed up and transcended in love.*

In this chapter more than in any other I shall be making statements which may seem to go beyond the business of science and which will have little routine scientific support. Besides that, they may seem to lack coherence, being more in the nature of scattered glimpses than a fully developed system. I beg the reader's indulgence: the statements do at least bear upon human personality, and, if read sympathetically, will appear to be what they are—namely, tentative and groping efforts to understand what I do not yet understand, though others may.

I take my departure from the well-established fact that most people who have ever been asked to arrange a collection of things in order of preference have usually had no great trouble in doing so. I infer from this fact that people do in general establish preference orders for the things of their world. Indeed, I believe that from the lowliest "I like this better than that" up to the most comprehensive philosophy we have to do with an ordering process which is personally significant. Championing a scientific system, or constructing one, is a major expression of this human tendency. To say that science is concerned with reality rather than personal whim is no objection; for each of us is concerned with reality, and it is only from the point of view of others that we may appear whimsical; though, of course, if any two of us agree that there is such a thing as ultimate reality we shall necessarily be engaged in trying to reconcile our personal differences about it.

Some empirical studies of preferences

As to simple preference orders, we have a good deal of information from laboratory experiments. I will pick out a few of these to illustrate the subject.

LINES AND ODORS   Martin many years ago studied the preferences of ten young college women with regard to some very unexciting linear diagrams. There were 41 of these: 16 straight lines, 6 circles, 8 semicircles, 8 small arcs of circles, Hogarth's undulating "line of beauty" and its reverse, and 1 ellipse. Figures of the same shape differed in size, thickness of line, and position. The subjects were asked to compare each figure with each of the others and to state a preference at each comparison. Five of them went through the set once (820 comparisons), the other five twice (1640 comparisons). Clear-cut preference orders emerged for all but one of the subjects.

Each order was different. For example, one subject placed the lightly drawn and fragmentary figures high in her list. Another placed them low. For the latter subject the darkly outlined circle took second place, for the former it was down at the very bottom. The correlation coefficient between these two orders was −.025, according to my calculations.[1]

Taking the Martin experiment as representative, we may say that persons typically exhibit bias in making their choices and that, secondly, they do not exhibit the same bias. It is true that when individual preference orders are combined, they do not usually cancel one another: a group order arises from the individual orders. Still, it would be misleading to speak of consensus governing the choices in such an experiment, nor is it usually easy to discover a single principle running through all the orders. The principle of choice, when one can safely point to any, is an individual matter.

Martin did not study how enduring such preference orders may be. Others have done so, however. The uniform result is that there is appreciable stability. Beebe-Center, for example, had 8 subjects rank 14 odors in order of preference, then retested them after 2 weeks and again after 5 to 7½ months. The individual orders remained fairly steady over the 2-week period—the test-retest correlation being .83 on the average, with the range from .69 to .96. The amount of change was not much greater over a period of several months—the average test-retest correlation being .75, with the range from .50 to .94. Preference orders, even in small matters, appear to have as much stability as other personality traits which are not so obviously related to acts of choice.[2]

Our laboratory studies tell us that individual preference orders exist and persist. We need not go into any further detail on these points, but it may be useful to examine more closely the nature of *group* preference orders. For this purpose I select a study on colors by von Allesch.

COLORS   Von Allesch explored the reactions of 10 persons to 12 colors, or rather to 3 shades of 4 colors—red, yellow, blue, and green. He started with the expectation that, if he could make his color stimuli pure and uncomplicated enough, he would get uniform re-

[1] For details and further discussion, see Martin (1906) and McCurdy (1954).
[2] For the odor experiment and others, see Beebe-Center (1932). Pratt (1956) has specifically discussed the stability of esthetic judgments.

actions from his subjects. This sort of expectation has frequently, if mistakenly, guided experimental designs in psychology. To von Allesch's surprise, the reactions were extremely varied. According to introspective reports, the colors elicited a great array of experiences, and the preferences expressed by the subjects were so different that von Allesch concluded that the old doctrine of inherently beautiful or ugly colors was disproved.[3]

Nevertheless, I find on averaging the 10 individuals that a group preference order does exist in the von Allesch results—though it lacks the steepness of gradient of an individual preference order. This group order puts the cool colors (blue and green) above the warm colors (red and yellow). Nine of the 10 subjects express this order of preference, and the one exception is neutral. But if the cool-warm dichotomy is expanded into the four basic colors, the group order (blue, green, red, yellow) agrees with only *one* of the ten individual orders, and this lone agreement also disappears when the series is expanded to its full length of twelve items. The group preference order has, then, a very shadowy sort of existence, unsustained in detail by *any* of the individuals who make up the group.

Suppose that these persons had to live in the same house and agree on the color scheme! Persuasion and pressure might eventually lead to a practical outcome, but it is clear that no actual color scheme could please them all equally well. Certainly their average or group order would not reconcile the differences. It takes little imagination to see that social problems in their widest range are epitomized here. Neither a dictatorship nor a majority vote can ever produce basic agreement.

There is another point, a little more subtle. It would be a mistake to assume that individual preference orders were reflections of a group mind even if all the individuals should happen to agree (and I know of no such case in the experimental literature). Individuality of choice is not a matter of simply disagreeing with others. One may agree with other people without for an instant giving up one's independence. The danger of loss of independence comes there where one *pretends* to agree. It is delightful to have a group of people who really do agree on something, and anything but delightful to have a group who cannot get beyond merely pretending.

MUSIC   The facts already mentioned hold up in every sort of preference order study. Whether the material consists of trivial lines

[3] Allesch (1925).

Table 47

Ranking of composers by musicologists

	1938	*1944*	*1951*
1	Bach	Bach	Beethoven
2	Beethoven	Beethoven	Bach
3	Wagner	Mozart	Brahms
4	Mozart	Wagner	Haydn
5	Palestrina	Haydn	Mozart
6	Haydn	{Brahms (6.5)*	{Schubert (6.5)*
7	Brahms	{Palestrina (6.5)	{Debussy (6.5)
8	Monteverdi	Schubert	Handel
9	Debussy	Handel	Wagner

Adapted from Farnsworth (1957), p. 126.
* Because the bracketed composers received equal votes, they are tied for ranks 6 and 7; hence they should be given equal rank, i.e., 6.5.

or grand philosophical statements, one finds individual preference orders persisting through time, one finds great diversity in these individual orders, and one finds that a group order emerges from the combining of the individual orders.[4] I bring in Farnsworth's study of musical taste here, not because it adds anything to these positive conclusions, but because it sharpens up a question which is inherent in all preference order studies.

Farnsworth asked members of the American Musicological Society to rank 92 composers in order of preference on three occasions—in 1938, 1944, and 1951. Table 47 shows the top nine of these composers for the three samplings. There was fairly steady group agreement over this period of time. The correlation for the whole list of 92 composers was .95 as between the ranks given in 1944 and 1951, and .85 for the longer time span between 1938 and 1951. Similar results were obtained in a poll of college students in 1938, 1945, and 1953.[5]

Musical taste is clearly not random. But what keeps it from being random? Farnsworth favors a social pressure theory. Our tastes are undoubtedly influenced by others; music teachers, musical performers, and the composers themselves surely exert social influence upon our musical preferences. Individuals outside the musical field may also have an effect. For example, there may be a trace of Hitler's influence in Table 47. Hitler was known to be fond of Wagner's music. Could Wagner's decline in rank from third in 1938 to ninth in 1951

[4] For philosophy, see Morris (1956).   [5] Farnsworth (1957).

be explained by the repugnance of American musicologists to Hitler?

But is fashion everything? Let us note again that the very existence of a group preference order depends upon the existence of individual preference orders. No fashion could get started unless there were at least *one* person in the group with a distinct bias toward it. Then let us note the fact that the individual expressing a preference for one piece of music as compared to another is saying something about his relationship with an object—the piece of music—outside himself. Now, in regard to this second fact, it is significant that when music lovers move from preferring one piece of music to preferring another they often feel that they have made progress in their understanding of music. Composers too are conscious, like other artists, of striving toward perfection and of advancing in their art. They sometimes outrun their public and leave the applause behind. I doubt whether a majority vote is the way to discover the direction in which perfection lies, but it may nevertheless represent the striving of individuals to state what is best.

The unshakable facts are that individuals do arrange all sorts of things, including music, along a value continuum and that individual arrangements differ. Must we conclude that each person's best is exclusively his own and that there is no absolute best to which the varying personal orders are pointed? Even if so, we should have to suppose that each individual may move from a better to a best in his own personal system, in view of the tendency to self-improvement just mentioned. But it is clear that a mere reshuffling of the items at hand is not the last word. A person may put one item of a limited collection at the top as the best in that collection, and still be far from satisfied with it. Outside any limited collection there lie other possibilities, among which are some which come much nearer to the true best. Suppose that in the Martin experiment the girls had been offered a Fra Angelico painting along with the circles and fragments of circles and so on with which they were dealing. There might very well have been total agreement that the Fra Angelico was the best item, almost infinitely preferable as a piece of graphic art to anything else in the collection.

In general, I think, the value order an individual adopts is a function of (1) the limits imposed by the collection with which he is dealing and (2) his awareness of what lies outside that collection. The latter affects him although it is vague and dim, and known to him only under the nearly empty label "the best." If this best, or some approximation to it, should actually enter the confines of his limited system, it might be expected to have a powerful and revolutionary effect on the preference order—some such effect as that produced by the entry of a Fra Angelico into a collection of scribbles. I believe that such a point of view on the value question may reconcile the apparent contradiction between the fact that individual preference orders differ and the fact that each individual tries, or at least seems to try, to order his limited collections along a dimension headed by best.

Passion and creativity

The careful student will have noticed that my last remarks had a barely tiptoe contact with the experiments cited. The remarks in this section will have even less contact with experimental work. It is true that within the last few years creativity has become a popular theme of investigation,[6] and that psychologists as well as others have been trying to learn more about it, but I have the impression that just the most important aspects of creativity are those which are scientifically the least manageable. To judge from the (largely anecdotal) information which we have, creativity involves emotions and inspirations and total personal involvement which lie beyond the reach of experimentation.

By "creativity" in this context I mean something which resembles but is not confined to original production in the arts and sciences: I mean the power to see the world in new ways, to utilize fruitfully the abilities which one has, to expand and reorganize one's life, to transcend one's previous limitations.

THE ROLE OF EMOTION   The philosopher Leone Vivante, appealing to the evidence of English poetry, contends that emotional states in general reveal the presence of "an original, self-active principle, which characterizes life and spontaneity as contrasted with mechanism."[7] This "self-active principle," whatever its particular emotional quality, has this feature constantly: that it tends to break down barriers, transcend the present moment, threaten the very existence of the external world and the self as distinctly bounded objects. Using

---

[6] The whole September 1958 issue of *Scientific American* was devoted to this subject; see especially the article by Barron (1958). Anderson (1959) has provided another symposium which includes stimulating discussions by thirteen contributors, more than half of whom are well-known psychologists.
[7] Vivante (1950), p. 1.

Shakespeare as an example, he quotes one of the characters in *Pericles* (V.i.192 ff.):

> O Helicanus, strike me, honoured sir;
> Give me a gash, put me to present pain;
> Lest this great sea of joys rushing upon me
> O'erbear the shores of my mortality,
> And drown me with their sweetness.

Such joy even has a negative aspect—it seems destructive; but, in destroying, it creates—sweetness, newness. Vivante, still basing his remarks on lines from Shakespeare, notes that the freshness of joy has certain natural or inherent modes of expression: "The creative *novelty* . . . is naturally expressed in and through the image, both externally and internally conceived, of *budding*, and that of *morning*, and gives to them their poetical and their ontological significance."[8]

It is my good fortune to be able to illustrate Vivante's words with some spontaneous lines written by a high school girl on receiving a totally unexpected but meaningful gift:

> Often the bud opens slowly,
> Gently rippling and uncurling
> Its silky petals.
> You can watch its happy blooming
> Till the flower turns shining
> To your face.
>
> But sometimes, it's caught unaware.
> The tight green case, holding its prize,
> Bursts wide open—
> Right in your eyes the brilliant bloom
> Reflects the sun. Your heart is caught
> In its glow.
>
> You thank yourself and curtsy low
> To the slow-blooming flower
> In peace.
> But you and the other rise
> As one, and sing to the world
> For joy.

Joy needs no external justification. It is self-sufficient. It is more than that—it is generous, overflowing, creative. It is an uprushing original power which produces out of itself something which may release the same upsurging energy in another person. Habits, cus-

[8] *Ibid.*, p. 18.

toms, practical considerations crumble before it, and the stereotyped and petrified come alive.

There is power also in joy's apparent opposite, sorrow, a power which likewise overrides barriers and creates an open space in which life may expand. Joy aspires and rises, sorrow despairs and sinks; but both the upward and the downward motions carry a person out of himself into unsuspected regions. Sorrow too is creative. Without dwelling on the multifarious evidence of the arts, let us just note that strong sorrowful emotion confers eloquence. Bosanquet, for example, calls attention to

> the dignity of utterance which a great passion or a great sorrow will sometimes confer upon a common man, raising him for the moment to the level of words and actions which no one who has witnessed them can forget, and from which all that is trivial has been refined away as by a fire.[9]

The poet Keats believed that physical pain and other forms of suffering were necessary for spiritual development. Walker, commenting on this belief from the point of view of a medical man, doubts whether one can generalize about pain. He thinks that pain in some cases is totally unprofitable. Nevertheless he adds:

> By nothing less than the intervention of severe pain can this unthinking and headlong career of ours through life be momentarily interrupted, so that we are forced to face the issues from which we are always escaping. A merciless stab of cardiac pain, a fierce struggle for breath, and the flimsy world in which we have hitherto been dwelling first sways, then breaks in two, and finally falls apart, revealing behind it the othernesses we have always preferred to run away from. Measured by the clock, this glimpse of the momentary darkness fringed with light has lasted only a moment or two, and then the pain recedes, so that we find ourselves back again where we were before, staring at the old and familiar things—the pattern on the bedspread, the shaded light in the bedroom, the picture hanging opposite us. But somehow they have lost for us some of their former solidity. They are much less convincing than they formerly were, having become transitory, tawdry, and unsubstantial things, resembling stage properties. During those agonizing minutes through which we have just passed, life and death flowed together, and although it was death that eventually withdrew, in withdrawing it took with it some of our illusions and some of our complacency. Yes, life's play-acting has started again, and here we are

[9] Bosanquet (1913), p. 42.

strutting about and talking much as we did before, but perhaps with a little less assurance and belief in the truth of what we are saying.[10]

That is one kind of suffering and, as Walker sees it, it has, or can have, a creative function within the personal world, in that it reveals novelty and reorganizes one's facts and values.

The deep spiritual pain of bereavement may also be creative, opening up new possibilities, revealing unimaginable dimensions of experience, producing a divine intoxication. C. S. Lewis writes that the effect of the unexpected news of the death of his friend the English writer Charles Williams (1886-1945) was to make the surrounding world seem *strange*. He continues:

> That sense of strangeness continued with a force which sorrow itself has never quite swallowed up. This experience of loss (the greatest I have yet known) was wholly unlike what I should have expected. We now verified for ourselves what so many bereaved people have reported; the ubiquitous presence of a dead man, as if he had ceased to meet us in particular places in order to meet us everywhere. It is not in the least like a haunting. It is not in the least like the bittersweet experiences of memory. It is vital and bracing; it is even, however the word may be misunderstood and derided, exciting. A lady, writing to me after his death, used the word *stupor* (in its Latin sense) to describe the feeling which Williams had produced on a certain circle in London; it would almost describe the feeling he produced on us after he had died. There is, I dare say, no empirical proof that such an experience is more than subjective. But for those who accept on other grounds the Christian faith, I suggest that it is best understood in the light of some words that one of his friends said to me as we sat in Addison's Walk just after the funeral. "Our Lord told the disciples it was expedient for them that He should go away for otherwise the Comforter would not come to them. I do not think it blasphemous to suppose that what was true archetypally, and in eminence, of His death may, in the appropriate degree, be true of the deaths of all His followers."[11]

Vital, bracing, exciting, and intoxicating was the experience of the disciples after the death of their Master, and they entered a new mode of being and action, no longer cramped by fear or inhibited by self-centeredness. In the appropriate degree, as Lewis's fellow-mourner said, the same outpouring of life has followed other deaths.

[10] Walker (1957), p. 182.
[11] In Preface to *Essays presented to Charles Williams* (London: Oxford, 1947), p. xiv.

Such experiences as these cannot be brought within the scope of experimental science. They cannot be arranged for beforehand or anticipated. They cannot be wished for. They simply happen. To know about them we have to ask those to whom they have happened and listen to them. To know them intimately we must ourselves undergo them. Yet, if we are to understand anything important about creativity, I think, we cannot avoid these regions of deep emotion which no one can enter except by special invitation—an invitation which everyone shrinks from receiving.

THE TENSION OF SELF-TRANSCENDENCE It must be admitted that the condition of self-transcendence when emotion rides high may be, and often is, brief. In the subsequent descent, the high flight may seem to have been unbelievable, even worthless and silly. Exactly this happened to Shelley in connection with his poem *Epipsychidion.* The poet vividly imagines a perfect union between kindred spirits—his own and Emilia Viviani's—satisfying aspirations which have haunted him from childhood:

> *We shall become the same, we shall be one*
> *Spirit within two frames, oh! wherefore two?*
> *One passion in twin-hearts, which grows and grew,*
> *Till like two meteors of expanding flame,*
> *Those spheres instinct with it become the same,*
> *Touch, mingle, are transfigured; ever still*
> *Burning, yet ever inconsumable . . .*
> *One hope within two wills, one will beneath*
> *Two overshadowing minds, one life, one death,*
> *One Heaven, one Hell, one immortality,*
> *And one annihilation.*

The epithets he uses strain to express a feeling of adoration which utterly deifies the young woman:

> *Seraph of Heaven! too gentle to be human,*
> *Veiling beneath that radiant form of Woman*
> *All that is insupportable in thee*
> *Of light, and love, and immortality!*
> *Sweet Benediction in the eternal Curse!*
> *Veiled Glory of this lampless Universe!*
> *Thou Moon beyond the clouds! Thou living Form*
> *Among the Dead! Thou Star above the Storm!*
> *Thou Wonder, and thou Beauty, and thou Terror!*

The impact of Emilia Viviani on Shelley had been extraordinary. The English critic Edward Dowden writes:

> Her youth, her charm, her sorrows awoke in Shelley all the idealizing power of his imagination; she became to him, as it were, a symbol of all that is radiant and divine, all that is to be pursued and never attained—the absolute of beauty, truth, and love. While for the man she was a living and breathing woman, fascinating, and an object of tenderest solicitude, for the poet she rose into the avatar of the ideal.[12]

Yet after the poem was in print the poet recoiled from his own experience. He wrote to a friend: "The Epipsychidion I cannot look at; the person whom it celebrates was a cloud instead of a Juno; and poor Ixion starts from the centaur that was the offspring of his own embrace." Shelley's recoil is so typically human that it may seem inevitable. But was it inevitable? Or was it inevitable only because there was some falsehood or lack of proportion or egotistic demandingness in his adoration?

If the context has not made clear what is meant by "self-transcendence," this brief definition may help: Self-transcendence is a condition of human experience in which one's apparent limitations are overcome and one has a sense of boundless possibilities. Some thinkers base their conception of the human person on this condition. Mure writes:

> A finite person is *as such* self-transcending: he *is*, in Bosanquet's phrase, "a *nisus* towards totality." His individuality is half-possessed, an ideal not fully realized, but so far as he does attain it he is neither diluted nor merely enlarged: he is intensified and heightened, and so far no longer merely finite.[13]

Among contemporary psychologists, it is especially Maslow who has recognized and discussed self-transcendence. His language is slightly different, but the meaning is the same. In the "peak experiences," as he calls them, which come now and then to many people, and more frequently and persistently to those whom he calls "self-actualizing," the self as a pinched and demanding Ego is lost in fascinated contemplation of the intrinsic worth of some part or all of the world. He connects this experience with a type of love which has

---

[12] *Poetical works of Percy Bysshe Shelley,* ed. by E. Dowden (New York: Crowell, 1893), p. 15.
[13] Mure (1958), p. 199.

to be distinguished from the possessive craving which ordinarily passes for love. To differentiate them, he speaks of the latter as "deficiency-love" and the former as "Being-love" (since it concentrates on the unique essence of the love-object rather than on one's own narcissistic cravings). Maslow thinks that psychologists and psychoanalysts have studied "deficiency-love" almost exclusively and so have not allowed for "self-actualizing" people and "peak experiences" in their theories of personality. His own investigation of such people and such experiences has convinced him that many of the laws of psychology with which he was previously familiar and in which he believed, are inadequate, because scaled too low:

> Often these have turned out to be no laws at all but only rules for living in a state of mild and chronic psychopathology, and fearfulness, of stunting and crippling, and immaturity which we don't notice because most others have this same disease that we have.[14]

Maslow has emphasized, as well he might, the positive healthiness of self-transcendence. He has paid less attention to the kind of conflict produced by the encounter of self-transcendent and selfish experiences in the same person—which I have tried to illustrate here by the case of Shelley. That, too, deserves note.

CREATION IN THE ARTS AND SCIENCES   Self-transcendence appears to be one of the conditions, perhaps the really essential condition, for artistic and scientific creation. At a minimum, there must be absorption in one's work; and this absorption means a turning away from oneself to what is not oneself—an object, a problem, a possibility. Anything which contributes to this absorption increases the chance of discovery, invention, realization. That is why harsh treatment and bad luck may paradoxically be blessings to the creative person: they detach him from the world of utilitarian aims and urge him into a contemplative solitude, perhaps with the energy of despair, where he can become undistractedly engaged with his objects or problems or possibilities.

Relevant here are some remarks on Anne Frank by Dr. Rosey Pool, an Amsterdam educator. Dr. Pool knew Anne as a school girl before she went into hiding from the Nazis and wrote that diary which is one of the most touching and courageous documents of the war. Her remarks, as reported by a newspaper writer, are these:

[14] Maslow (1959), p. 43. This article is based on Maslow's presidential address, Division of Personality and Social Psychology, American Psychological Association, September 1, 1956.

Anne, she said, had never shown any outstanding talent. She had an ordinary intelligence, though she was a perceptive, imaginative little girl with a good sense of humor and an excellent observer. "She was —cute, I think you would say here." The pressures, the tensions, the fears, Dr. Pool continued, very often brought out in people the best— or the worst. "You didn't live on your normal level. And in her case it worked like a pressure cooker. It gave her maturity, wisdom—far beyond her age and experience."[15]

With the same courage, the sick, blind, politically discredited Milton composed *Paradise Lost,* and his words in Book VII might apply to both of them:

> Standing on Earth, not rapt above the pole,
> More safe I sing with mortal voice, unchanged
> To hoarse or mute, though fallen on evil days,
> On evil days though fallen, and evil tongues,
> In darkness, and with dangers compassed round,
> And solitude.

It is not hard to find instances of great creative work being done under unfavorable-looking circumstances. Mozart, for example, though petted and caressed as a child prodigy, was in his adult life roughly treated by the world, was often in financial difficulties, and was ill and dying when he produced one of his greatest compositions. Whether the hardship contributes directly to the achievement in such cases I certainly do not know, though I see that it might—by wounding the self and stirring up tragic emotion. What seems clearer is that the indirect effect already mentioned—the increase of solitude —may be beneficial. As to solitude, the American poet Richard Wilbur has said: "I think the situation of the creative person should be either one of solitary grandeur—with the door always open, of course, into the world—or one of solitary confinement."[16] As to hardship, the American painter John Ferren has said:

Personal danger, fear, illness, marital explosion and real sorrow can often run parallel to a pregnant "now." The romantic conception is to place them in a cause and effect ratio. A truer interpretation is that *any* strong emotion necessarily pinpoints the mind by freeing it from its habitual distractions, thus permitting the concentration necessary to perceive new structure.[17]

[15] From an interview in the Salisbury, North Carolina, *Evening Post,* January 24, 1960.
[16] Wilbur (1957), p. 60.   [17] Ferren (1957), p. 49.

There is an often-quoted letter which purports to tell how Mozart went about composing, and, though it is now considered not authentically from Mozart's hand,[18] it corresponds so well with the testimony of other artistic and scientific creators that it continues to be used in discussions of creativity. The letter refers to two stages of work—the period of inspiration and the period of writing. The second stage, according to the letter, does not require solitude, but the first does. Of the first stage the letter says:

> When I am, as it were, completely myself, entirely alone, and of good cheer—say travelling in a carriage, or walking after a good meal, or during the night when I cannot sleep—it is on such occasions that my ideas flow best and most abundantly. *Whence* and *how* they come, I know not, nor can I force them.[19]

The last sentence points us to another theme which is constantly coming up: the sense of receiving rather than of making. The "creator" often seems to be passive rather than active.

A writer on mathematical innovation, W. C. Kneale, protests against the use of the word "creation" in general as applied to artistic and mathematical productions. Of artists he writes: "An artist can do no more than select an interesting possibility. Fertility of invention in this sphere is just the fortunate gift of imagining spontaneously many possibilities that prove interesting."[20] Of mathematicians, the same: "Mathematicians can show originality in their work, but only as artists can, that is by selecting interesting possibilities."[21] The sense of receiving is often very strong. Milton in Book IX of *Paradise Lost* speaks of his celestial Patroness, his Muse,

> . . . *who deigns*
> *Her nightly visitation unimplored,*
> *And dictates to me slumbering, or inspires*
> *Easy my unpremeditated verse.*

John Masefield has a poem, "The Woman Speaks," which, according to an interesting footnote, appeared to him in a dream engraven on an oblong metal plate. More pointed still is the testimony of William Blake, according to Yeats:

> "On the day of his death," writes a friend who had his account from Mrs. Blake, "he composed songs to his Maker, so sweetly to the ear

18 Anderson (1938), p. xvii.
19 Holmes (1845), p. 329. The letter is used without mistrust in Hadamard (1954).
20 Kneale (1955), p. 101.   21 *Ibid.*, p. 106.

of his Catherine, that, when she stood to hear him, he, looking upon her most affectionately, said, 'My beloved! they are *not mine. No! They are not mine.*' "[22]

Solitude and receptivity—these are important. Doubtless other things are, too, such as arduous discipline and varied knowledge. One of the finest analyses of the conscious and unconscious preparation for a work of art is John Livingston Lowes' book on Coleridge, *The Road to Xanadu.* But preparation is not enough, just as solitude is not enough. Among the necessities I think we must include the excitement and power of emotion and the leap of faith by which the self is transcended.

Love

The ultimate concern of science is reality. The ultimate concern of ethics, according to Aristotle and many after him, is human happiness.[23] Can the two meet? Is the human desire for happiness in conformity with reality, on certain conditions—such conditions as writers on ethics attempt to set forth in principles of right conduct? Can we conceive of ethical principles which might be as solidly grounded in reality as the most accurate laws of physics? Sometimes reality is pictured as a vast, impersonal system from which the human desire for happiness is excluded. Sometimes it is pictured more personally, but still grimly inflexible—as Fate or Necessity. Either picture forbids us to hope that we may discover modes of living which, because grounded in reality, issue in lasting joy. Reality, so conceived, is a standing rebuke to the eudaemonistic ethics of Aristotle or the even more aspiring ethics of Christianity.

Even if we do not concern ourselves much with such matters, we may have noticed that the literature of science does not seem to deal with the same things as the literature of ethics and religion. Love, for example, does not usually appear in the index of a book on physics, chemistry, geology, astronomy, botany, or zoology. "Of

[22] W. B. Yeats, *Poems of William Blake* (New York: Modern Library), p. xxxix.
[23] Cf. Aristotle, *Ethics,* Book I, Section IX: "For to constitute Happiness, there must be . . . complete virtue and a complete life." Spinoza, *Ethics,* Part V, Prop. XLII: "Blessedness is not the reward of virtue, but virtue itself." Jonathan Edwards, *The nature of true virtue,* where it is proposed that true virtue is benevolent love: "A benevolent propensity of heart is exercised not only in seeking to promote the happiness of the Being towards whom it is exercised but also in *rejoicing in* his happiness."

course!" one might exclaim, "it would be perfectly ridiculous to expect it!" But neither does the term appear regularly in books of psychology, where one might expect it. I have just picked up five at random—two introductory texts, two advanced books on principles of behavior, and a summary of psychoanalytic theories—and have found that the only reference to love under "L" in any index was "Loss of love, fear over," which was in the psychoanalytic book. "Virtue," of course, was not to be found in any, and "happiness" was indexed in only one—and barely mentioned on the two pages listed.

I believe that this shyness of psychologists about love and virtue and happiness is related to their restraint in dealing with religion. Allport has noted that religion and sex seem to have reversed their positions in psychological writing. When William James wrote his *Varieties of Religious Experience,* as Allport remarks, he expressed himself freely and brilliantly, but could hardly bring himself to mention sex:

> Today, by contrast, psychologists write with the frankness of Freud or Kinsey on the sexual passions of mankind, but blush and grow silent when the religious passions come into view. Scarcely any modern textbook writers in psychology devote as much as two shamefaced pages to the subject—even though religion, like sex, is an almost universal interest of the human race.[24]

There is an almost equal timidity about love, which has very close ties with religion—so close, indeed, that in the New Testament God is defined as love, where John writes (I John 4:7-8): "Beloved, let us love one another; for love is of God, and he who loves is born of God and knows God. He who does not love does not know God; for God is love." In fact, Allport puts his finger on this connection between religion and love as the possible cause for the "flight from tenderness" which marks science in general and psychology in particular today.

Yet why the flight—from either religion or love, or the two combined? It is a long story, too long to be told here, even supposing that I could tell it. Partly it is a matter of the demands of scientific method, partly a matter of defending intellectual freedom against the sometimes brutal assaults of conservative forces wearing the name of religion, partly a matter of the decay of religious faith among the scientists themselves. Allport, basing his estimate on

[24] Allport (1950), pp. 1 f.

studies reported in 1948, writes: "Fully two-thirds of the adults in our country regard themselves as religious people, and at least nine-tenths, by their own report, believe in God."[25] It is doubtful, however, that the percentages are so high for scientists. A generation ago they certainly were not. In 1916 Leuba, then professor of psychology at Bryn Mawr, published the results of an investigation which showed that most American scientists at that time were not believers in God, the "greater men" (i.e., the more influential) being less often believers than the "lesser men." Table 48 reproduces a portion of his results. Whatever may be the ratio of belief to disbelief today (I know of no comparable study), it seems likely from these figures that science in this country, and especially psychology, would not for several decades have favored a "tender" approach to religion or, insofar as they are related, to love.

Love, in its higher reaches, cannot be dissociated from religion. Sexual love itself, Eros, tends toward religion, as demonstrated by the ancient worship of Aphrodite, to cite one example; but the love celebrated in the thirteenth chapter of Paul's first letter to the Corinthians and elsewhere in the New Testament, and designated by the Greek word *agape*, is eminently religious. The distinction be-

Table 48
Per cent of American scientists believing in God, as of 1916

	"lesser men"	"greater men"
physical scientists	49.7	34.8
biological scientists	39.1	16.9
sociologists	29.2	19.4
psychologists	32.1	13.2

Adapted from Leuba (1921). Leuba's sample is not of equal size for the various scientific groups, and his reporting leaves it a little unclear what the numbers were; but it appears (*ibid.*, pp. 250 ff.) that his questionnaire elicited responses from about 303 physical-mathematical scientists, 163 biologists, 197 sociologists, and 95 psychologists. His questionnaire, which dealt with various religious questions, went out in two forms. In the first form, the respondent was asked to agree or disagree with the following statement about his belief in God: "I believe in a God in intellectual and affective communication with man, I mean a God to whom one may pray in the expectation of receiving an answer. By 'answer,' I do not mean the subjective, psychological effect of prayer." (p. 223). In the second form, the statement was simplified by omission of the words "in intellectual and affective communication with man, I mean a God." The figures in the table must be interpreted in the light of this definition of God.

[25] *Ibid.*, p. 2.

tween Eros and Agape is similar to that which Maslow makes between D-love (deficiency-love) and B-love (love for the Being of another person). Concerning B-love, he states that it is nonpossessive, does not diminish from being gratified, is not tainted with anxiety-hostility, is generous, mystical, and therapeutic, and makes possible "the truest, most penetrating perception of the other."[26] Regarding the last-mentioned characteristic of B-love, he comments that B-love

> is as much a cognitive as an emotional-conative reaction. . . . So impressive is this, and so often validated by other people's later experience, that, far from accepting the common platitude that love makes people blind, I become more and more inclined to think of the *opposite* as true, namely that non-love makes us blind.[27]

But the perceptiveness of B-love is indissolubly bound up with its creativeness: B-love partly makes what it sees. In Maslow's words:

> B-love, in a profound but testable sense, creates the partner. It gives him a self-image, it gives him self-acceptance, a feeling of love-worthiness and respect-worthiness, all of which permit him to grow.[28]

It is at once evident that the kind of perceptiveness which partly makes what it sees must land us in a scientific predicament. How can the perceptions of B-lovers be verified by the objective methods of a science which is not operating from B-love? As the reader will remember, this is a special form of the question which has appeared several times in the present book, especially in Chapters 13 and 14. Maslow is thoroughly aware of the problem. He is troubled by "lurking doubts" as to the validity of the inspired perceptions of love:

> Frequently enough, love for another brings illusions, the perceptions of qualities and potentialities that don't exist, that are not therefore truly perceived but created in the mind of the beholder and which then rest on a system of needs, repressions, denials, projections, and rationalizations. If love can be more perceptive than non-love, it can also be blinder. And the research problem remains to nag us, when is which?[29]

He is inclined to think, however, that people of superior psychological health, those he calls "self-actualizing," may be trusted, or that at any rate it is a risk worth taking:

[26] Maslow (1955), p. 27 f. [27] *Ibid.*, p. 28.
[28] *Ibid.* [29] Maslow (1959), p. 64.

All peak experiences feel like Being-experience but not all are truly so. And yet, we dare not neglect the clear hints that, sometimes at least, greater perspicuity and greater efficiency of cognition can be found in healthier people and in healthier moments, i.e., some peak-experiences *are* B-experiences. I once suggested the principle that if self-actualizing people can and do perceive reality more efficiently, fully and with less motivational contamination than we others do, then we may possibly use them as biological assays. Through *their* greater sensitivity and perception, we may get a better report of what reality is like, than through our own eyes, just as canaries can be used to detect gas in mines before less sensitive creatures can.[30]

Now, one of the great difficulties with Maslow's reasonable proposal is that precisely those characteristics and acts which mark off a person as especially sensitive and loving may be used as evidence that he or she is mentally unbalanced. The human being who laments the evils that others do not see, who kisses the leper that everybody else avoids, who has incommunicable visions of Divine Goodness while normal people are driving hard bargains and gossiping about their neighbors, who preaches love in time of war, who cures the sick without a license and by unorthodox means, who blesses the scum of the earth and offends the cream of society, who has a sense of mission, who talks with God—such a person may arouse distrust and antagonism and be diagnosed as psychotic. Nevertheless, as students of personality, we have to acknowledge that such persons do exist or have existed, and that the most elevated pronouncements about love have come from them.

One of these pronouncements is that God is love, i.e., that the universe was created by and is preserved and governed by love. One must suppose that a personality difference exists between one who makes or accepts this pronouncement and one who does not; for, if we define personality as a self in relation to its objects, it is evident that a self in loving relation to a loving God and hence to God's creation must be a different sort of personality from a self in no such relation to such a God or such a creation. The difference as stated may sound abstract and formal. It can be practically tested, however, according to the best authorities. One test is whether there is active love (Maslow's B-love) toward other human beings. Thus we read (I John 4:20):

[30] *Ibid.*, p. 64. For Maslow's thinking at an earlier stage, see Maslow (1954).

If any one says, "I love God," and hates his brother, he is a liar; for he who does not love his brother whom he has seen, cannot love God whom he has not seen.

Another test is the absence of fear. Thus we read (I John 4:18):

There is no fear in love, but perfect love casts out fear. For fear has to do with punishment, and he who fears is not perfected in love.

The New Testament writers, of course, derive qualities like these —absence of hate and fear—from a reciprocal relationship of love between the self and God. Their ethics and their psychotherapy (the two are joined) are completely theocentric. Disbelief in God is tantamount to bad behavior and bad health, i.e., hatred and anxiety.[31] But these consequences, in appropriate degree, follow any imperfection of belief—"little faith," God conceived as hostile, God conceived as distant. Not only atheists, then, but also those who deny that God is love and present in all the workings of the universe, according to this view, must suffer ethical and psychological defects.

What does it mean to say that a God of love is present in the workings of the universe? It means, as it meant for Dante, that there is not a particle of matter which is not as fully involved in the Kingdom of God as the most spiritual of aspirations, that indeed it is "Love that moves the sun and the other stars." It means, as it did to Newton, that

This most beautiful System of the Sun, Planets and Comets could only proceed from the counsel and dominion of an intelligent and powerful Being . . . Who being in all Places, is more able by his Will to move the Bodies within his boundless uniform Sensorium, and thereby to form and reform the Parts of the Universe, than we are by our Will to move the Parts of our own Bodies.[32]

It is a meaning which was beginning to disappear from the scientific view of reality when Newton's French disciples, Voltaire, Laplace, and others, taught, before and after the French Revolution, "that the Newtonian system indicated reality as a great machine, in all essentials already known, so that man, body and soul, became part of an invincible and mechanical necessity."[33] One should expect to find consequences of this change of view both in the practical work of science and in the individual personalities of those who reject the Dantean-Newtonian view.

[31] See, for example, Beach and Niebuhr (1955), Ch. 1.
[32] Dampier (1942), p. 188, quoting from Newton's *Opticks*.
[33] *Ibid.*, p. 214.

The post-Newtonian view described by Dampier in the above quotation is one which permits us to handle the universe as a tool, or at least to turn in it as a cog, but scarcely permits us to love it. The other view permits us to love it, and even to enter into an "I-thou" relation with it.

I have touched on these questions of ethics, religion, and science here, briefly and no doubt very inadequately, because, as I see it, they bear significantly upon the structure and quality of individual personalities. Despair and confidence, gloom and cheerfulness, altruistic or criminal acts, and the whole array of "traits," in my opinion, are so many signs of the relationship existing between ourselves and our world; and it is a matter of no small consequence for that relationship exactly how that world appears—an appearance which is partly determined by the socially shared, available ideas.

References for chapter 16

Allesch, G. J. von (1925) Die aesthetische Erscheinungsweise der Farbe. *Psychologische Forschung*, 6, 1-91, 215-81.
Allport, G. W. (1950) *The individual and his religion: a psychological interpretation*. New York: Macmillan.
Anderson, E. (1938) *The letters of Mozart and his family*. London: Macmillan.
Anderson, H. H. (Ed.) (1959) *Creativity and its cultivation*. New York: Harper.
Barron, F. (1958) The psychology of imagination. *Scientific American*, 199, 150-56, 159-60, 162-64, 166.
Beach, W., and Niebuhr, H. R. (Eds.) (1955) *Christian ethics: sources of the living tradition*. New York: Ronald.
Beebe-Center, J. G. (1932) *The psychology of pleasantness and unpleasantness*. New York: Van Nostrand.
Bosanquet, B. (1913) *The value and destiny of the individual*. London: Macmillan.
Dampier, Sir W. C. (1942) *A history of science and its relations with philosophy and religion*. 3rd ed. New York: Macmillan.
Farnsworth, P. R. (1957) *The social psychology of music*. New York: Dryden.
Ferren, J. (1957) The problem of creative thinking in painting. In Industrial Research Institute, *The nature of creative thinking*. New York: New York Univ. Press.
Hadamard, J. (1954) *The psychology of invention in the mathematical field*. New York: Dover.
Holmes, E. (1845) *The life of Mozart*. New York: Harper.

Kneale, W. C. (1955) The idea of invention. *Proceedings of the British Academy*, 1955, 85-108.

Leuba, J. H. (1921) *The belief in God and immortality: a psychological, anthropological and statistical study.* Chicago: Open Court.

Martin, L. J. (1906) An experimental study of Fechner's principles of aesthetics. *Psychological Review*, 13, 142-219.

Maslow, A. H. (1954) *Motivation and personality.* New York: Harper.

———— (1955) Deficiency motivation and growth motivation. In Jones, M. R. (Ed.) *Nebraska Symposium on Motivation.* Lincoln: Univ. of Nebraska Press, pp. 1-30.

———— (1959) Cognition of being in the peak experiences. *Journal of Genetic Psychology*, 94, 43-66.

McCurdy, H. G. (1954) Aesthetic choice as a personality function. *Journal of Aesthetics and Art Criticism*, 12, 373-77.

Morris, C. (1956) *Varieties of human value.* Chicago: Univ. of Chicago Press.

Mure, G. R. G. (1958) *Retreat from truth.* Oxford: Blackwell.

Pratt, C. C. (1956) The stability of aesthetic judgments. *Journal of Aesthetics and Art Criticism*, 15, 1-11.

Vivante, L. (1950) *English poetry and its contribution to the knowledge of the creative principle.* London: Faber & Faber.

Walker, K. (1957) *Patients and doctors.* Harmondsworth, Eng.: Penguin.

Wilbur, R. (1957) The problem of creative thinking in poetry. In Industrial Research Institute, *The nature of creative thinking.* New York: New York Univ. Press.

17

CODA

In conclusion, what is personality? All the chapters preceding have had this as their topic, and yet I should not be surprised to hear that they had not answered the question. We can exhibit some of the details of personality and talk about their relations with one another, but we cannot exhaust the subject, we cannot be finally and unalterably right about it. There is another difficulty—individuality. There is no such thing as personality in the abstract, though there may be abstract discussions of it; there are only personalities. And yet much of the little we know is in the form of generalizations about man rather than in the form of precise descriptions, such as astronomers attempt, of one concrete real world.

Dr. Harley C. Shands in a public discussion a few years ago at the University of North Carolina provided me with the words I had been blundering around all evening to find. He said that I conceived of personality as "the whole universe from the point of view of one individual." I think that nothing less than this will do, and I am extremely grateful to him for having made it clear.

I find it convenient to separate "person" from "personality." A human person is that psychophysical compound which is capable of establishing emotional relations with objects, sensed, imagined, and conceived. Personality is the actual existence of these relations. At every moment a person exists in a reality which supplies him with objects or potential objects in infinite number. For example, he stands in an open field. The landscape stretches out around him in organized fashion, full of familiar and unfamiliar objects ordered before his eyes according to the laws of perspective and terminating at the horizon line, a great circle sweeping the whole way round, part of it immediately visible, the rest conceived as potentially visible. Overhead, similarly seen and conceived, is the arched fine high roof of the sky, with, let us say, the edge of the sun just appearing at the horizon and the morning light delicately altering the sky color and brilliantly lighting up some streaks of cloud. He is aware of the night behind him in time and of his fading dreams, and of the day before him. He is also aware, acutely or dimly, of certain persons who are not visibly present except in imagination. He stands in relations to them as definite as those he has with the land and the sky. He is aware too, acutely or dimly, of birth and death, of galaxies beyond sight, of idols or gods or a God, of the darkness and brightness of human history. And in the midst of all this, there is himself—the person who sees and imagines and conceives and has emotions about so many things—and he is aware of himself. If he moves from where he is standing, he alters his relations with the landscape; even if he does not move, the relations are altered, because the rising sun changes everything. If his mind is altered by an impulse of attraction or repulsion, an emotion of despair or joy, the network of all his relations with objects is changed, both in the landscape and out of it. This change the external observer cannot so easily detect as that produced by a motion of his body. But his bodily attitude, his facial expression, what he says and his tone of voice, as well as communications more subtle still, may indicate to the external observer that a change has occurred. And all these changing relations constitute his personality.

It is evident that no two persons can have the same personality. They cannot occupy the same point in space-time. They cannot exchange persons. They differ both because of their difference as persons and because of their different relations with the universe. But persons can stand in powerful relations to one another. Two human persons in an emotional confrontation may reduce the remainder of the universe—the landscape, the sky, history, the galaxies, the idols or gods or God—to a faint background. It may also happen that the human relationship is a simultaneous apprehension of those things, in which case the rest of the universe takes on a sharper outline, an intenser glow, a more convincing reality.

One's relations with the universe, and hence one's personality, both are and are not within one's control. They are—in the sense that one can make an effort by which the body is moved in space or the mind is altered in its emotions and evaluations. They are not—in the sense that reality is not one's own creation and therefore contains objects and events that can never be fully anticipated or fully understood. *What* one is related to is only in a limited degree a matter of personal choice. *How* one is related to it is also only slightly within one's control. Nevertheless, it is possible to adopt an attitude—call it acceptance or gratitude or faith or what you will—by which all that is and all that happens are occasions for an increase of love, which is for personality exactly what energy is for the physical universe. The opposite attitude is also possible, and that is the way of impoverishment, shrinkage, and destruction.

If such a conception of personality seems to give us few handles by which to manipulate others, I do not think that is an argument against it. Under any conception of personality, other persons are anything but easy to manipulate. I nevertheless think that we can be helpful to one another. When our friend is in despair, we can ask him what it is that he hates. When he is happy, we can ask him what it is that he loves. These questions, or others like them, may enable him to unfold his personal universe in reasonable discourse for his enlightenment and our own.

INDEX

Abraham, K., 264–66, 271 (ref.), 296
Abse, D. W., 531, 554 (ref.)
accommodation (Piaget), 92
Achille, 222–27, 236
activity (Heymans-Wiersma), 331–36
Adams, D. K., ix, 113, 118–20, 134 (ref.), 346, 353 (ref.), 521, 554 (ref.)
adaptation, 42–43, 46–49, 49 (fig.)
Adkins, D., 375, 392 (ref.)
Adler, A., 386
Alajálov, 242, 243 (fig.)
Alexander, F., 514–15, 552–53, 554 (ref.)
Allesch, G. J. von, 558–59, 577 (ref.)
allocentricity (LeSenne), 337–38
Allport, G. W., 5, 19 (ref.), 351, 353 (ref.), 354 (ref.), 368–69, 385–88, 390–92, 392 (ref.), 427, 428 (ref.), 572–73, 577 (ref.)
Allport-Vernon "Study of Values," 351–52
Amatruda, C. S., 61, 87 (ref.), 142–43, 175 (ref.)
ambivalence, 113, 264
amnesia: in Irène, 121–22; in Janet's theory, 222–30; in multiple personality, 233–37
anal character, 152, 264–65; stage, 75, 262
analysis of literature, 413–27
Anastasi, A., 35, 51 (ref.)
Anderson, E., 570, 577 (ref.)
Anderson, H. H., 562, 577 (ref.)
Androcles, 453
anesthesia, hypnotic, 215–16
Angel, E., 460, 461 (ref.)
Anima, 287
Animus, 287
anthropomorphism, 457–59
anxiety: and neurosis, 285; and repressed sexuality, 249–53; and self-development, 197–205. See also despair, dread, fear
Aquinas, St. Thomas, 350
archetype, 285–94
Argyle, M., 188, 206 (ref.), 508, 510 (ref.)
Aristotle, 59, 72, 290, 339–40, 347, 571

Aron, B., 412
Asch, S. E., 326–28, 354 (ref.)
Ashby, W. R., 160, 174 (ref.)
assimilation (Piaget), 92
associative linkage, 116–18
asthma, 553–54
attitude, 385–86. See also sentiment, traits
Augustine of Hippo, St., 188, 200, 435–36
autokinesis (Gantt), 169–70
automatic writing, 224
autonomic nervous system, 553
autoscopy, 484–89
autosymbolic phenomenon (Silberer), 195
Azam, E., 228, 233, 237 (ref.)

Bacon, F., 194
Baggally, W. W., 11, 19 (ref.)
Baldwin, A. L., 148–49, 151, 174 (ref.)
Balinese, and schizophrenia, 153–54
Barron, F., 562, 577 (ref.)
Bartlett, Sir F. C., 164, 174 (ref.)
Bass, B. M., 392 (ref.), 393 (ref.)
Bastiaans, J., 534–37, 539, 555 (ref.)
Baughman, E. E., 402, 429 (ref.)
Baumgarten, F., 386
Beach, F. A., 110, 134 (ref.)
Beach, W., 576, 577 (ref.)
Beauchamp case, 228, 233–34, 235–36
Beebe-Center, J. G., 558, 577 (ref.)
behaviorism: and consciousness, 179–80, 272–74, 435–36; and Freud, 272–85; in personality testing, 359–60; Watsonian, 138, 273
Bell, E. T., 190, 206 (ref.)
Beloff, H., 152, 174 (ref.)
Bender, L., 171, 174 (ref.)
bereavement: and creativity, 565–66; and ESP, 472
Berg, I. A., 392 (ref.), 393 (ref.)
Bernheim, H., 206, 213, 216, 218
Bessel, F. W., 9

Cronbach, L. J., 44, 51 (ref.), 376, 392 (ref.)
Crutchfield, R. S., 473, 511 (ref.)
cryptomnesia, 492–93
cue (Dollard and Miller), 277–81
Curie, M., 10
Curnock, N., 529 fn. (ref.)
cyclothymia, 319–31
Dahlstrom, W. G., 375, 379–80, 385, 392 (ref.), 393 (ref.)
Dampier, Sir W. C., 576–77, 577 (ref.)
Dante, 450–51, 576
Darling, F. F., 288, 312 (ref.)
Darwin, C., 40–42, 47, 51 (ref.), 526–28, 530, 554 (ref.)
Davidson, A., 259–60, 271 (ref.)
Davis, E. A., 149, 151, 174 (ref.)
death: and disease, 543–52; and life cycle, 54, 83, 86–87; and psychosomatic phenomena, 518–26
De la Mare, W., 59
delinquency, 330–31
demons: and brain pathology, 486–88; cases of possession by, Achille, 222–25, Sibylle, 486–87; and demoniacal attack, 541, 542 (fig.), 549–50; and epidemics, 543, 547–52; as objects in personal world, 517, 537–39, 548–51; and theory, Fairbairn, 299; Freud, 249–51, 254, 299, 539–41, Janet, 225–30, Jung, 293, 299
Dennis, M. G., 66, 87 (ref.)
Dennis, W., 66, 68, 70, 87 (ref.)
depersonalization, 306–09, 454–59
Descartes, R., 208–10, 299–300, 305, 455, 457, 474, 516
despair, in Kierkegaard's analysis, 200–05
Deutsch, F., 514, 554 (ref.)
Dewey, J., 386
Diamond, S., 328–30, 354 (ref.), 384–86, 392 (ref.)
Dinah, 259–60
disease: and demons, 222–25, 535–43, 547–52; and hypnotism, 215–16, 221–22; and hysteria, 120–22, 229–30; and *idées fixes*, 222–30; and syndrome shift, 533–52; theories of, 154–56, 513–54; and war, 545–47
Disney, W., 455
displacement, 242–43
dissociation: and autosymbolic phenomenon, 194–95; of ideas, 220; in Janet's theory, 227–30
Dollard, J., 277–81, 312 (ref.)
Donaldson, J., 526 fn. (ref.)
Donne, J., 529
Dostoevsky, F. M., 413, 487
Dowden, E., 567
dread: and collective unconscious, 288; and "dark night of the soul," 199; and Kierkegaard, 200–01. *See also* anxiety, despair, fear
dreams: Boss on, 300–11; compared to literature, 413; compared to TAT, 411–13; Descartes on, 299–300; Fairbairn on, 298–99; Freud on, 238–49, 310; Janet on, 225–30; Jung on, 287–88, 310
Driesch, H., 59, 87 (ref.)
drive (Dollard and Miller), 277–81

Drury, Mistress E., 529
Dunbar, F., 531–32, 554 (ref.)
Dupertuis, C. W., 327, 354 (ref.)

ecstasy: and emotion, 528–29; Janet's case (Madeleine), 496–502; St. Teresa, 506–09, 509 (fig.); theory of, 502–06
ectomorphy, 328–30
Edwards, J., 571 fn.
Ego: in Fairbairn's theory, 296–99; in Freud's theory, 238, 254–67. *See also* "I," person
egocentrism: and allocentricity, 337–38; and realism, 102–03
Eliot, T. S., 54
Ellenberger, H. F., 460, 461 (ref.)
embryonic development, 56–60
emotion: and autonomic nervous system, 553; and creativity, 562–71; and disease, 526–33; maturation of, 70, 73–74; and object cathexis, 103–22; and stigmatization, 529–30
emotionality (Heymans-Wiersma), 331–36
Empedocles, 77
endomorphy, 328–30
endopsychic objects (Fairbairn), 273, 294–99, 297 (fig.)
Enke, W., 324
entelechy, 59, 61
enuresis, 283–85
epidemics: biological warfare, 546; demon possession, 547–52; plague, 543–44; radiation sickness, 545; war, 546–47
epilepsy, and physique, 320–21
equivalence coefficients, 376
erogenous zones, 74–77; and sexual instincts, 262; and character, 262–66
Eros, 77, 258–59, 268, 573–74
ethics, 571, 576
Esdaile, J., 215–17
ethology, 44, 107–09, 112
existentialism: and Boss, 272–73, 299–311; and personal world, 489–90
expectancy (Tolman), 161
experiments and statistical studies: asthma, 553; belief in God, 573; bird song, 126–28; causality learning, 98–102; child-mother bond, 105–07; clairvoyance, 16; conditioning, 117, 157–63; dream symbols, 245; embryonic development, 60; enuresis, 283–84; ESP and concussion, 482; facial asymmetry, 22–24; hallucinations, 475–76; Heymans-Wiersma types, 334–35; honesty, 366–69; hypnotic control, 14, 214–16; imprinting, 108–09; inheritance of traits, 33–38; Jung's types, 343–46; Kretschmer's types, 321–22, 325–28; maternal deprivation, 142–46; object learning, 91–96; occult powers, 10–11; parental warmth, 146–51; personality components in literary works, 418–20, 421–22; plant growth and behavior, 39–42; practice of skills, 164–68; preferences, 557–60; projection, 274–76; psychoanalytic hypotheses, 152–56; reaction-time, 9; regression, 282–83; Rorschach test, 403–05;

sensory deprivation, 503–04; Sheldon's types, 329–30; smiling in infancy, 108; species differences, 17; Spranger's types, 351–52; starvation effects, 383–84; stigmatization, 221–22; stimulus generalization, 114–15; TAT, 410–12; test-faking, 365–66; trance states, 236; traumatization in early life, 172–74; twin dentition, 24; twins reared apart, 27–32; vacuum, 8; variability on tests, 375; visual imagery of scientists, 181–82

explanation, 7–12

expression: and ecstasy, 509 (fig.); of emotion, 526–33; and intuition, 434–39, 449–53

extinction of CR, as done by Pavlov, 117; and sentiment, 161–64

extrasensory perception (ESP): Rhine on, 510; telepathy and clairvoyance, 469–75, 477–78; veridical hallucination, 473–84

extroversion-introversion, 290, 338–46

Eyrich, M., 300

Eysenck, H. J., 346, 354 (ref.)

Fabre, J. H., 444

face: and adaptation to cold, 48–49, 49 (fig.); and facial asymmetry, 22–24, 23 (fig.); and expression of emotion, 150 fn., 288, 526–29; as stimulus to smiling, 108, 116

factor analysis, intra-individual, 417–18, 420

facts and explanation, 7–12

Fairbairn, W. R. D., 272–73, 294–99, 310, 312 (ref.)

fantasy, at Oedipal period, 77, 259. See also imagination, imaginative literature

Farber, L. H., 245, 271 (ref.)

Farnsworth, P. R., 560, 577 (ref.)

Fay, J., 259–60, 271 (ref.)

fear: and collective unconscious, 287–89; in dreams, 248–49, 250–51; in Kierkegaard's analysis, 200–05; in neurosis, 280–81; of self-realization, 197–200

Fechner, G. T., 239

Feigl, H., 207 (ref.), 461 (ref.)

Feilding, E., 11, 19 (ref.)

Félida, 228, 233

Fenichel, O., 176 (ref.)

Fenton, J. C., 68–69

Ferdinand, R., 133

Ferren, J., 569, 577 (ref.)

Fisher, C., 245, 271 (ref.)

Fisher, R. A., 236

fixation, 263

Flammarion, C., 479–81, 511 (ref.)

Fleiner, W., 532

Fletcher, R., 110, 134 (ref.)

Flournoy, T., 490–97, 511 (ref.)

Foley, J. P., Jr., 35, 51 (ref.)

Fox, R., ix, 470

Francis of Assisi, St., 453, 501, 529–30

Frank, A., 568–69

Franklin, B., 213

free association, 240–41, 281

freedom: and conscious self, 337, 390–91; and honesty, 196; and prediction-and-control science, 5; and the Sartrean "look," 451–52; and self-development, 196–205; and technology, 307–08; and typology, 352–53

Freeman, F. N., 27–32, 52 (ref.)

Frenkel-Brunswik, E., 83–85, 87 (ref.)

Freud, A., 139–43, 146–47, 174 (ref.)

Freud, S.: on cathexis, 104, 112–13, 252–53, 271 (ref.); on demonology, 488, 515, 535, 539–43, 554 (ref.); on dream interpretation, 239–49, 394–95, 413, 460 (ref.); on Ego, Id, and Super-ego, 255–62, 271 (ref.); historical background of, 3, 13, 212–13, 219–20, 226; on intuitive psychology, 439–49, 452, 459–60, 460 (ref.); philosophy, 266–71; on primary process, 502, 505, 511 (ref.); on psychodynamics, 18, 238–71, 271 (ref.), 547; on psychosomatics, 514–16, 535, 539–43, 554 (ref.), reaction to, 272–311, 312 (ref.); on repression, 249–54, 271 (ref.); on sex, 53, 73–78, 87 (ref.), 152, 262–66, 271 (ref.), 572; on Unconscious, 205–06, 208, 226, 237, 238–71 (ref.)

Gable, C., 547 fn.

Galen, 331

Galton, Sir F., 43–44, 50, 181–82, 193, 206 (ref.)

Gantt, W. H., 169–70, 174, 174 (ref.), 194

Garn, S. M., 47–49, 51 (ref.)

Garrett, Mrs., 236

Geddes, A. C., 470, 524–26, 555 (ref.)

generalization, 114–16

genetics: and behavior, 25–27, 38–44, 50–51, 53–87; and biological kinship, 24–51; and Mendelian laws, 22; and race, 44–50

genital: stage, 76–77; character, 265–66

genius, childhood of, 150–51

Gesell, A., 53, 61–63, 67–68, 70, 87 (ref.), 142–43, 175 (ref.)

Gilles de la Tourette, G. A. E. B., 518–20, 542, 555 (ref.)

Glueck, E., 330–31

Glueck, S., 330–31

God, 190, 194, 199–200, 203, 205, 216, 224, 268, 270, 339, 347–50, 490, 497–501, 505–07, 510, 529, 543, 551, 572–73, 575–76, 580, 581

Goethe, J. W. von, 388, 485–87, 542

Goitein, P. L., 553

Goldberg, L. R., 428, 429 (ref.)

Goldfarb, W., 143–45, 175 (ref.)

Goldman, F., 152, 175 (ref.)

Goldschmidt, R. B., 22, 51 (ref.)

Goldsmith, G. W., 41, 51 (ref.)

Goodenough, F. L., 376

Goodhart, S. P., 482, 512 (ref.)

Gordon, H. L., 411–13, 429 (ref.)

Gordon, K., 35

Grandier, U., 548–49

Great Mother, 289–92

Greear, M. W., 477–78, 511 (ref.)

Gregory the Great, Pope, 188

introversion-extroversion, 290, 338–46
intuition: in Freudian observation, 439–44; and
future of psychology, 459–60; and inference,
431–34; in ordinary social perception, 434–39;
and reciprocity, 449–53; and relational symbols, 453–59; and transference, 444–49
Irène, 120–22, 171, 235, 252
irrational functions (Jung), 341–45

Jackson, H., 300 fn.
Jacobi, W., 530
James, W., 3–6, 19 (ref.), 91, 192–93, 207 (ref.),
209, 237 (ref.), 239, 475, 483, 490, 572
Janet, P.: on ecstasy, 496–502, 506, 508, 511 (ref.);
on hysteria and dissociation of ideas, 3, 120–22,
135 (ref.), 171, 213, 220, 222–30, 236, 237 (ref.),
239, 241, 252
Jeanne des Anges, Soeur, 548–51
Jefferies, R., 187
Jensen, W., 413
John, St., 572, 575–76
John of the Cross, St., 200, 502
Jones, E., 206, 207 (ref.), 268–71, 271 (ref.), 413,
541–43, 555 (ref.)
Jones, H. E., 159, 175 (ref.)
Jones, M. R., 578 (ref.)
joy, 527–29, 563–64
Jung, C. G.: on collective unconscious, 272–73,
285–94, 299–301, 305, 310, 312 (ref.); on
imago, 446; on types, 314, 338–46, 354 (ref.)
Justine, 229

Kalhorn, J., 148–49, 151, 174 (ref.)
Kallmann, F. J., 26–27, 51 (ref.)
Kant, I., 256
Kanthak, M., 324
Kantrow, R. W., 157, 160–62, 175 (ref.)
Kasatkin, N. I., 157–58, 160, 175 (ref.)
Keats, J., 564
Keller, H., 185–86, 188–89, 207 (ref.)
Kelly, E. L., 365, 428, 429 (ref.)
Kelly, W., 455
Kibler, M., 327–28
Kierkegaard, S., 178, 200–05, 300 fn.
Killigrew, T., 549–50
Kinnebrook, D., 8–9
Kinsey, A. C., 572
Klages, L., 386
Klein, M., 98, 135 (ref.), 295
Kleitman, N., 300 fn., 312 (ref.)
Klineberg, O., 326–28, 354 (ref.)
Kneale, W. C., 570, 578 (ref.)
Koffka, K., 185, 207 (ref.), 386
Kraepelin, E., 381
Krech, D., 473, 511 (ref.)
Kretschmer, E., 314, 318–28, 330–31, 354
(ref.)
Kuhlen, R. G., 83, 88 (ref.)

Ladd, G. T., 3, 6
Laín Entralgo, P., 513–14, 555 (ref.)

Lamarck, J. B. P. A. M. de, 260
La Mettrie, J. O. de, 209, 277, 457
Lammer, E., 185
Laplace, M. S. de, 576
Lashley, K. S., 110
latency period, 76–77
latent dream thoughts, 242
Lavater, G., 456 (fig.)
Lawrence, D. H., 414–17, 423, 452
laws: and observation, 433; and prediction, 428;
and theories, 15–18
Lazurski, A., 386
learning: and critical conditions, 138–56; defini-
tion of, 89–91; and early conditioning, 156–64;
of objects and causality, 91–103; of sentiments,
103–22; of skills, 122–33, 164–69; and trau-
mata, 169–74
Le Brun, C., 455, 456 (fig.)
Le Gall, A., 337, 354 (ref.)
Leibniz, G. W. von, 205
Leonard, Mrs., 236
Leonardo da Vinci, 286–87
Léonie, 14
LeSenne, R., 332–38, 353, 354 (ref.)
Leuba, J. H., 573, 578 (ref.)
Levikova, A. M., 157–58, 160, 175 (ref.)
Levy, D. M., 147–49, 151, 175 (ref.)
Lewin, K., 104, 113, 386
Lewis, C. S., 565
Lhermitte, J., 486–89, 511 (ref.), 517
Libido: in Fairbairn's theory, 295–98; in Freud's
theory, 238, 250–54; in transference, 446
Liddell, H. S., 172–74, 175 (ref.)
Liébeault, A. A., 213, 216, 218
life cycle, 53–87; from conception to birth, 55–
63; from infancy to maturity, 63–78; from sex-
ual maturity to death, 78–87
Lindzey, G., 24, 51 (ref.), 351, 354 (ref.), 410–11,
429 (ref.)
Linnaeus, C., 119, 352
Locke, J., 339
Lodge, Sir O., 490
Lombroso, C., 468–69, 473, 475, 489
Long, E. R., ix, 125, 135 (ref.)
Lorenz, K. Z., 109, 112, 135 (ref.), 146
Louis V——, 221–22, 227
love: in child care, 133, 138–51; in dreams, 304–
06; between Flournoy and medium, 494–96; in
genital character, 265–66; and happiness, 571–
77, 581; and intuition, 435, 459; in mystics,
496–502, 506–09, 550–51; in Pfister's comment
on Freud, 270; sexual, 445–51; in Spranger's so-
cial and religious types, 348–49, 350; and trans-
ference, 445–48
Lowes, J. L., 164, 175 (ref.), 571
Lucretius, 77
Lukianowicz, N., 485, 511 (ref.)
Lundberg, G. A., 432
Lundholm, H., ix
Lüth, K. F., 326
lying, 194–96

on, 103–22; endopsychic, 294–99; of personal world, 517, 580–81; and phenomenology, 299–309, 311
Odbert, H. S., 388, 392 (ref.)
Oden, M. H., 66, 88 (ref.)
Oedipus complex, 146, 259–60, 266, 409, 419, 460
Old Wise Man, 287
O'Neill, D., 514, 555 (ref.)
operant, 97, 100, 210
oral: character, 152, 265; disease theories, 154–56; stage, 75
Orotchens, untutored drawing by, 164–65, 165 (fig.)
Orwell, G., 308

Pain, in self-development, 197–200, 564–65
Palladino, E., 10–12
paranoia, in Freud's theory, 263–64
Pascal, B., 8, 189–90, 350
Pasteur, L., 156, 254
Patten, B. M., 58, 60, 64–65, 88 (ref.)
Paul, St., 573
Pauli, W., 294, 312 (ref.)
Pavlov, I. P., 114–17, 122, 125–26, 135 (ref.), 159, 169, 277
Payne-Gaposchkin, C., 477, 511 (ref.)
Pearson, K., 33–38, 43, 52 (ref.), 152
perception: and archetypes, 290–94; and hallucination, 254–56, 466–89, 475 (fig.); vs. imagination in Rorschach test, 396–97; interpersonal, 431–60; in instincts and sentiments, 107–10, 113; and learning, 90–98; and neurological theory, 486–89; and schemata, 92–98; and S-R theory, 122–23; subliminal, 491–93; and telepathy, 466–75; and Unconscious-conscious relations, 230–33
person, distinguished from personality, 580–81
Peters, R. S., 179, 207 (ref.)
Peterson, J., 71, 88 (ref.)
Pfendler, G.-F., 518–20
Pfister, O., 269–71
PGR (psychogalvanic reflex), 159–60, 236
phallic: character, 266; stage, 76
phenomenology, 299–311, 474
physique: in Kretschmer's typology, 318–31; in Sheldon's typology, 328–33
Piaget, J., 91–103, 112, 135 (ref.), 160, 196
"pictures," 93, 96, 160
Piltdown fraud, 7
Pinneau, S. R., 176 (ref.)
Pio, Padre, 529
Piotrowski, Z. A., 396–97, 401, 403, 430 (ref.)
Plato, 290, 339–40, 347, 350
pleasure principle, 238, 258–62, 266–67, 270
Pluzek, Z., ix
Pool, R., 568–69
Postman, L., 352, 354 (ref.)
postnatal development of child, 64–78
Pratt, C. C., 558, 578 (ref.)
Pratt, J. G., 510 fn., 511 (ref.)
prayer, St. Teresa on, 506–08

prediction: clinical vs. statistical, 432–33; and consciousness, 179; as mark of science, 4–6; by tests, 402–05, 410–11, 428
preference orders, 557–62
premature infants, 61–63
prenatal development, 55–60
Pressey, S. L., 83, 88 (ref.)
Price, G. R., 11
primary-secondary function (Heymans-Wiersma), 331–36
Prince, B., 24, 51 (ref.)
Prince, M., 228, 233–34, 235–36, 237 (ref.)
projection, 263–64, 274–76, 292, 295
projective tests, 394–413
Prout, C. T., 171, 176 (ref.)
psychic energy, 286
psychic phenomena, 466–96
psychophysical dualism, 514–16
psychosexual development, 73–82
psychosomatics: and emotion, 526–33; and fashions in disease, 543–52; and mind-body problem, 513–26; and search for specific causation of disease, 552–54; and syndrome shift, 533–43
"public" vs. "private" experience, 179–81, 183–84
Puységur, Marquis de, 14

Q-technique, 343–46

races, 44–50
Rank, O., 441
Rapaport, D., 207 (ref.)
rapport, 218
rational functions (Jung), 341–45
Rayner, R., 159, 176 (ref.)
reaction formation, 263
reaction potential, 104
reaction time, 9
reality principle, 238, 255, 267
Reece, B. H., 477–78
regression, 263, 282–83
Reik, T., 432–33, 461 (ref.), 473
reinforcement of CR, 116–17, 277–81
relational symbols, 454–59
releaser, 107
reliability, 370–78
religion: and ecstasy, 496–509, 528–29; in Freud's view, 267, 270, 460, 542–43; in Jung's view, 286–94; and science, 572–77; and stigmatization, 529–30, 541
Renner, M., 38, 52 (ref.)
repression: and dreams, 246; as function of Superego, 254–62; as nonverbalization, 279–80; as unconscious process, 249–54
response (Dollard and Miller), 277–81
Reymert, M. L., 354 (ref.)
Rheingold, H. L., 149–50, 176 (ref.)
Rhine, J. B., 11, 510, 511 (ref.)
Rhine, L., 478–79, 511 (ref.)
Richardson, L. F., 546–47, 555 (ref.)
Richet, C., 14, 16, 20 (ref.)

Teresa of Avila, St., 199, 502, 506–09
Terman, L. M., 66–67, 71, 88 (ref.), 361–66, 371, 379, 381, 393 (ref.), 401
Tertullian, 526 fn.
tests: construction of, 357–66, 370–83, 388–90, 396–402, 405–06; of intelligence, 28–31, 34–36, 70–72, 144–45, 307–08; of personality, 31–32, 35–36, 145–46, 307–08, 327–28, 336, 343, 351
Thanatos, 258–59, 268, 547
thematic apperception test (TAT), 405–13
theriomorphism, 454–56, 456 (fig.)
Thibaut, J., ix, 352
Thigpen, C. H., 228, 237 (ref.)
Thorpe, W. H., 72, 88 (ref.), 109, 124, 127–29, 136 (ref.)
Thrasher, J. H., ix
Thurston, H., S.J., 468, 512 (ref.)
Tinbergen, N., 109, 136 (ref.), 166, 176 (ref.)
Titchener, E. B., 130, 136 (ref.)
Tolman, E. C., 161, 176 (ref.)
Tolstoy, L., 85
Torricelli, E., 8
traits: Allport's theory of, 385–88, 390–92; inheritance of, 33–38; measurement of, 355–92; vs. self, 357, 385–86, 390–92
transference, 444–49
traumatic experiences: cases of, 120–22, 170–72; and experiments on goats, 172–73
Tryon, C. M., 80, 88 (ref.)
Tucker, W. B., 354 (ref.)
twins, 24–32
Tyler, L. E., 356, 360, 389–90, 393 (ref.)
Tyndall, J., 212
typology, 314–53; Heymans and Wiersma's, 331–38; Jung's, 338–46; Kretschmer's, 318–28; Sheldon's, 328–31; Spranger's, 346–52
Tyrrell, G. N. M., 482 fn., 512 (ref.)

Unconscious: Freudian, 238–71; post-Freudian, 272–311; pre-Freudian, 205–37
Underhill, E., 199–200, 207 (ref.), 505 fn., 512 (ref.)

valence, 104
validity of tests, 374–75, 377–78
value types (Spranger), 347–52
Van den Berg, J. H., 460 fn., 461 (ref.), 516, 555 (ref.)
Van der Horst, L., 328
Van der Valk, J. M., 534–37, 539, 555 (ref.)
Van Loghem, J. J., 534
verbalization: vs. action, 168–69; vs. consciousness, 179–80, 279–80; in psychology, 179–82; in test responses, 360
Vernon, P. E., 351, 353 (ref.), 354 (ref.), 356, 393 (ref.), 428, 430 (ref.)

virtue, 571–72
viscerotonia, 328–31
Vivante, L., 562–63, 578 (ref.)
Viviani, E., 566–68
Voltaire (F. M. Arouet), 576

Walker, K., 533, 540, 555 (ref.), 564–65, 578 (ref.)
Wallace, A. R., 444
war, as disease, 545–47
Washington, G., 331
Watkins, J. G., 224 fn., 226 fn., 237 (ref.)
Watson, J. B., 138, 146, 159, 176 (ref.), 273 fn., 312 (ref.), 353
Watson, R. I., 360, 393 (ref.)
Weisskopf, E., 85
Weitzenhoffer, A. M., 13–15, 20 (ref.), 218, 237 (ref.)
Wells, W., 555 (ref.)
Welsh, G. S., 375, 379–80, 385, 392 (ref.), 393 (ref.)
Wenger, M. A., 157, 176 (ref.)
Went, F. W., 39, 52 (ref.)
Wesley, J., 528–29
Westphal, K., 321
White, M. A., 171, 176 (ref.)
Whiting, J. W. M., 154–56, 176 (ref.)
Wiener, N., 455–56, 461 (ref.)
Wiersma, E., 314, 331–38, 353, 354 (ref.), 385
Wilbur, R., 569, 578 (ref.)
Wiley, G., 453
Williams, C., 565
Williams, R. J., 22, 52 (ref.)
wish, as basis of dreams, 238, 248–49
Wolfenstein, M., 176 (ref.)
Wolff, W., 22–23, 52 (ref.)
Wolfle, D., 11
Woodworth, R. S., 28–32, 52 (ref.)
Woolsey, C. N., 135 (ref.)
Wordsworth, W., 186–87, 348
Wright, H. K., 24, 51 (ref.)
Wulf, F., 164, 176 (ref.)
Wyman, J. B., 362–63

Yardley, J., 307–08, 312 (ref.)
Yates, A. J., 284–85, 312 (ref.)
Yeats, W. B., 570–71
Yerkes, R. M., 79–80, 82, 88 (ref.)

Zaehner, R. C., 505 fn., 512 (ref.)
Zamansky, H. S., 411, 429 (ref.)
Zener, K. E., ix, 117 fn., 136 (ref.), 179, 435, 461 (ref.)
Zilboorg, G., 213, 237 (ref.)
Zimmermann, R. R., 105, 131, 134 (ref.)
Zipf, G. K., 422, 430 (ref.)

21316